THE BOOK OF TALES

For comments or questions about this book, visit our website:
The Lost Stories Channel, at loststorieschannel.com.

© 2024 by W. Kent Smith – All Rights Reserved
Published in the United States by
Lodestar Cinema Creations,
in association with Staten House
West Covina, California
Smith, W. Kent (1959-)

It should be noted that this book contains much of the same material from a larger work entitled *Tales of Forever: The Unfolding Drama of God's Hidden Hand in History*, published in 2016, and as such differs in that this version presents edited excerpts from Act One, Two, and Three.

Also, this is the companion text to *The Book of Days: In Search of the 5,500-year Prophecy Given to Adam About the Coming of Christ*.

Front Cover and Title Page Painting: *Descent into Limbo*, Andrea Mantegna, 1492

Book Exterior and Interior Designed and Executed by W. Kent Smith

ISBN: 979-8-89379-513-4

Manufactured in the U.S.A.
July 2024

THE BOOK OF TALES

*Stories That Confirm the 5,500-year Prophecy
Given to Adam About the Coming of Christ*

by

W. Kent Smith

Lodestar
Cinema
Creations

in association with

$$\boxed{S}$$

Staten House

Books by W. Kent Smith

*Lies My Professor Told Me About American Politics: Questions
Concerning the Original Vision of the Founding Fathers*

*Conquering Cynicism in a Modern Age: How The Bible in Nature
Provides an Antidote to Doubt and Despair*

*On Earth as It is On Heaven: The Promise of America, Technology,
and the New Earth, Book One, The Promise of America*

*The Book of Days: In Search of the 5,500-year Prophecy
Given to Adam About the Coming of Christ*

*The Book of Tales: Stories That Confirm the 5,500-year Prophecy
Given to Adam About the Coming of Christ*

*Fish Tales (From the Belly of the Whale): Fifty of the
Greatest Misconceptions Ever Blamed on The Bible,
Reel One, The Hook #50-34*

*Fish Tales (From the Belly of the Whale): Fifty of the
Greatest Misconceptions Ever Blamed on The Bible,
Reel Two, The Line #33-18*

*Fish Tales (From the Belly of the Whale): Fifty of the
Greatest Misconceptions Ever Blamed on The Bible,
Reel Three, The Sinker #17-1*

*Fish Tales (From the Belly of the Whale): Fifty of the Greatest
Misconceptions Ever Blamed on The Bible, The Complete Edition,
Hook, Line, and Sinker #50-1*

*Tales of Forever: The Unfolding Drama of God's Hidden
Hand in History, Book One, The Analyses – Part One*

*Tales of Forever: The Unfolding Drama of God's Hidden
Hand in History, Book Two, The Tales – Part One*

*Tales of Forever: The Unfolding Drama of God's Hidden
Hand in History, Book Three, The Tales – Part Two*

*Tales of Forever: The Unfolding Drama of God's Hidden
Hand in History, Book Four, The Analyses – Part Two*

*Tales of Forever: The Unfolding Drama of God's Hidden
Hand in History, The Complete Edition*

For Ted,

Best Friend and Dad

CONTENTS

A CASE FOR THE TALES

I HAVE STUDIED in four seminaries and before that, a leading Christian college, yet never was I introduced to any of the material W. Kent Smith has brought forth here in *The Book of Tales*, a work that sheds light on long-lost truths that the majority of modern Christians know nothing about. God has preserved many things concerning His purposes as well as His indelible fingerprints on history. This book sets out to tell the story of those purposes and of those fingerprints.

My initial interest in *The Tales* was due to my research into a 5,500-year messianic prophecy that I became aware of while studying the Early Church and *The Septuagint*, the Greek translation of *The Old Testament* used by 2nd Temple Judaism and the Early Church. Known as "the prophecy of the Great Five and a Half Days," this messianic prophecy is certainly the greatest promise that God ever gave to mankind. According to this prophecy, given to Adam and Eve when they were expelled from Eden, the Messiah would come to Earth to rescue humanity after 5,500 years.

In addition to my interest concerning this prophecy, I was struck by several questions about 2nd Temple Judaism: What motivated the rabbis in the late first and early second century when they "canonized" *The Hebrew Bible*? Why did *The Septuagint* version of *The Old Testament* have different books from the *Masoretic* Text? And why were so many previously accepted texts, such as *The First Book of Enoch*, completely ignored and excluded? I knew that earlier Jews had had a broader canon of Scripture than the one that the rabbis settled upon at Jamnia, but in many cases, I didn't realize how important these "excluded" books were to understanding so many of our best-known *Bible* stories. Kent's book picks up these themes and digs even deeper, with particular focus upon the 5,500-year prophecy.

According to the 5,500-year chronology of *The Septuagint*, the coming of Jesus perfectly fit the timing of this prophecy and was one of the reasons so many Jews came to believe He was the Messiah. At which time the rabbis proceeded to "tamper" with *The Hebrew Bible* at the end of the first century AD, rejecting *The Septuagint*, and then translating their "doctored" *Old Testament* into three new Greek versions for future Jewish use. Why? One of the main reasons was to obscure the 5,500-year prophecy in order to stop Jews from coming to Jesus as their Messiah.

Worse still, because of the ongoing influence of Rabbinic Talmudic Judaism and the unfortunate influence of the likes of Jerome, many Christians not only remain in the dark about this 5,500-year prophecy but also end up dismissing the best extant sources of evidence for its veracity. When one removes such blinders and trusts the testimony of Early Church writers like Justin Martyr and Tertullian, we see, as *The Book of Tales* shows, that God Himself protected arguably the most significant messianic prophecy of all time. You may not agree with all of the author's conclusions, but I assure you that your "traditions" will be challenged if you allow the evidence he presents through the narratives he tells to inspire you and your faith in the God of *The Bible*.

Just as *First Enoch* serves as an extensive commentary on *Genesis* 6, so too other so-called "apocryphal/pseudepigraphal" books shed much-needed light on aspects of the narratives of Adam and Eve, Abraham and Isaac, and other *Old Testament* patriarchs. Additionally, Kent introduces us to writings from *The New Testament* era that, while well known to the Medieval Church, have been ignored by modern-day Christians due to these works being deemed "non-canonical." Most importantly, these works not only provide greater context to both *Old* and *New Testament* characters and events, but they also further testify to the critical importance of the 5,500-year prophecy.

To inspire millions, movies need to be made about *The Tales*. Following Kent's lead as he depicts events in various works throughout this volume, I propose Enoch as the main character and narrator of one of the greatest stories that has yet to be filmed. Step aside *Lord of the Rings!*

As I told the author when we met, I believe that new evidence is forthcoming that will shed even more light on these issues and convince countless people that the things he contends are in fact true. Of course, only time will tell. But, until then, read *The Book of Tales* for yourself, and your fascination with God will grow, as will your trust in His promises.

For such a time as this...

Rev. David J. Hess
Rock OC Church
Dana Point, California

THE PRELUDE

Although the contents of the following work are instructive, their sole purpose is not simply to instruct. Instead, they are offered as a catalyst to fuel one's God-given imagination so that the infinite mind of the Word might shed some small part of Himself upon all who dare to embrace a knowledge of the sublime as a child seeks to embrace the ineffable mystery of a clear blue sky.

W.K.S. 4.10.16

BOOK ONE

We speak a message of wisdom, but not the wisdom of this age or of the rulers of this age who are coming to nothing. We speak of God's secret wisdom, a wisdom that God has hidden and destined for our glory before time began.

The Apostle Paul, *Letter to the Corinthians*

Roll Call of the Intrepid

FIRST, I HAVE to express my gratitude to the intrepid pioneers who provided the core narratives for this work. Just in case anyone thinks that I have concocted the following storyline entirely on my own, I would like to offer this list of discoverers, translators, and scholars whose monumental contributions have provided the biblical texts that form its backbone. For a more in-depth look at their lives and accomplishments, please refer to the Selected *Biographies* section in *The Credits*.

Among the discoverers who have restored to the world such an unexpected array of lost manuscripts, there are: Johann Grynaeus (1540-1617), a Swiss Protestant divine, professor of *The New Testament*, and collector of biblical manuscripts; Giuseppe Assemani (1687-1768), a Lebanese Orientalist and Vatican librarian; James Bruce (1730-1794), a Scottish explorer and travel writer; and E.A. Wallis Budge (1857-1934), a British Egyptologist, Orientalist, philologist, and author.

Among the translators who have turned many of these manuscripts into works that could be understood by an English-speaking world, there are: William Wake (1657-1737), a British clergyman, dean at Exeter, bishop at Lincoln, and archbishop of Canterbury; Richard Laurence (1760-1838), a British Hebraist, Anglican churchman, and regius professor of Hebrew at Oxford; Moses Samuel (1795-1860), a British author and translator of Hebrew works; S.C. Malan (1812-1894), a British biblical scholar and linguist of Oriental languages; William Wright (1830-1889), a British Orientalist and professor of Arabic at Cambridge; B. Harris Cowper (1822-1904), a British archeologist, historian, and translator; W.R. Morfill (1834-1909), a British professor of Slavonic languages at Oxford; and R.H. Charles (1855-1931), an Irish biblical scholar and theologian.

Among the scholars who invested their considerable skill and effort into making the various manuscripts accessible to the general population, there are: Theophilus of Antioch (c. 120-181), a Syrian theologian, apologist, author, and chronologist; Julius Africanus (c. 160-240), a Libyan historian, traveler, and chronologist; Hippolytus of Rome (c. 170-235), a Greek theologian, apologist, and chronologist; Ephrem the Syrian (c. 306-373), a theologian, deacon, and hymn writer; Giambattista Vico (1668-1744), an Italian historian, political philosopher, and apologist of classical antiquity; George Smith (1800-1868), a British historian, theologian, and author; Joseph A. Seiss (1823-1904), an American theologian, Lutheran minister, and author; E.W. Bullinger (1837-1913), a British clergyman and theologian; Louis Ginzberg (1873-1953), a Lithuanian professor of Judaism and Talmudist; Edgar J.

Goodspeed (1871-1962), an American theologian and scholar of Greek and *The New Testament*; and Cyrus H. Gordon (1908-2001), an American biblical scholar and professor of ancient Near East culture and languages.

Thanks to the visionary efforts of "so great a cloud of witnesses," then, I hereby present the following work; I now present *The Book of Tales: Stories That Confirm the 5,500-year Prophecy Given to Adam About the Coming of Christ.*

Arguments for Authenticity

The Seed of Truth

WHAT IS TRUTH? asked Pontius Pilate of his supplicant prisoner; and in doing so, he was essentially asking this question on behalf of all humanity. But according to the canonical record, Jesus offered no reply to Pilate. So why did He not answer him? If God is no respecter of persons, as the Scriptures assure us, then the One Who was to give His life as a ransom for mankind would certainly have answered such an important question. After all, Jesus stated that this was the very reason He came into the world: "To testify to the truth."[1] Yet based on the Apostle John's account, Jesus was inexplicably silent as to the exact nature of this truth.

Fortunately, for us, though, John was not the only person who recorded the events surrounding this pivotal moment in history. As it turns out, there is another take on this same conversation, which can be found in the apocryphal record known as *The Gospel of Nicodemus*, formerly called *The Acts of Pontius Pilate*. According to this version of the story, Jesus did answer the question.

> So Pilate asked, "What is truth?"
>
> And Jesus replied, "Truth is from Heaven."
>
> To which the somewhat disappointed Pilate replied, "Then truth is not of this Earth; is that it?"
>
> But Jesus looked the governor squarely in the eye and replied, "Don't be too sure, my friend, because truth does exist on this Earth, but it does so among those who, having the power of judgment, are governed by the truth and who form proper judgment because of that truth."[2]

Confronted by such an alternate version, one must then ask the obvious question. Which version of this story should be accepted as the truth? To which I would reply: Maybe they are both true. After all, when one considers that there are different accounts in Scripture of Noah's animals and Judas' death, why would we expect there to be only one version of this event in the life of Jesus? It seems to me that one should look to their own conscience in such matters, because in the final analysis this is all any of us can do in our all-too-human pursuit of historical truth. In other words, one

---

1 *John* 19:37
2 *Nicodemus* 3:11-13

must honestly ask themselves: Do the words of Jesus in this particular story sound like those that would have been spoken by the One Who is the very embodiment of truth? Or do they contradict what one might expect Jesus to have said? The words ring true in both versions, do they not? If so, then why not simply accept the fact that we are dealing with two complimentary versions of the same event.

This, in turn, brings us face to face with the central issue encountered by anyone who reads a work like *The Book of Tales*, because it incorporates, at its core, stories that have all been stitched together from the so-called "apocryphal" record—in particular, *The First Book of Adam and Eve*, *The Secrets of Enoch*, *The Book of Jasher*, *The Letters of Herod and Pilate*, and *The Gospel of Nicodemus*. Naturally, in my own defense, only those stories that could be corroborated by the canonical record were drawn from, while any that contradicted it were summarily rejected. But far from expecting anyone to accept it all at face value, I am attempting, by way of these opening remarks, to provide a framework to make one's own judgment as to whether the apocryphal record can be trusted as a valid source of truth. Notwithstanding the centuries-old debate surrounding this literature, there are ways that one can approach the issue, and I can assure you that the process I am offering will originate from the teachings and principles that are firmly grounded in the Biblical Canon.

What is truth, then? If one is a staunch believer in the traditional view of only the so-called "received texts," then I would quickly remind them that even Jesus taught that truth was not the same thing to each and every person. According to Him, the whole world can be divided into four distinct groups. Each group, when confronted by "truth," will interpret this information based on their own personal frame of reference, and by virtue of these four different perspectives, what constitutes truth will inevitably end up producing four different results. Truth, then, no matter how obvious it seems can never be received in the same way by all people. Consequently, when Jesus spoke of the dispensing and receiving of truth, He compared it to a farmer who went about scattering seeds in a field, and as can be expected, He predicted four very different outcomes. Some seeds were gobbled up by the birds before they even got planted into the ground. Some seeds fell on rocky ground and sprouted, but, because they lacked depth of soil, withered in the heat of the Sun. Some seeds fell among thorns so that when the plants grew up they choked and died before too long. And finally, there were some seeds that fell among good soil; these proved to be the only ones that were able to produce a healthy crop.[3]

By the Middle Ages, this idea of the four-fold nature of assimilating the seed of truth became the impetus of a tradition of biblical interpretation that

---

3 *Matthew* 13:3-9

had its origins in the commentaries of the early Christian Era. Said Stephen A. Barney, professor emeritus of English at the University of California, Irvine, the four levels of interpretation involved: One, a "literal" interpretation of the events of the biblical story for historical purposes, with no underlying meaning. Two, a "typological" interpretation that connected the events of *The Old Testament* with *The New Testament*, particularly in the way that events of Christ's life related to the lives of earlier messianic figures who preceded Him. Three, a "moral" interpretation, which involved how one should act in the present, that is to say, a meaning derived from the "moral of the story." And four, an "analogical" interpretation, which had to do with an understanding of prophetic, or future, events of Christian history, that is to say, Heaven, Hell, and Judgment Day. In this way, the four types of interpretation correspond to all three modes of existence — past, present, and future; literal, with our past; typological, connecting the past with our present; moral, with our present; and analogical, with our future.[4]

To illustrate how this four-fold approach applies to Scripture, Dante, called "one of the greatest literary icons of the Western world,"[5] offered this example:

> To clarify this method of treatment, consider this verse: "When Israel went out of Egypt, the House of Jacob from a barbarous people, Judah was made His sanctuary, and Israel His dominion." (*Psalm* 113:1-2) Now, if we examine the letters alone (literally), the Exodus of the Children of Israel in the time of Moses is signified; in the allegory (typologically), our redemption accomplished through Christ; in the moral sense, the conversion of the soul from the struggle and misery of sin to the status of grace; in the analogical sense, the exodus of the human soul from the slavery of this corruption to the freedom of eternal glory.[6]

Furthermore, this same idea of the four-fold nature of truth was no stranger to either Jewish or Islamic theology. In Judaism it is known as *Pardes*, which refers to four different approaches to interpreting the biblical text. *Peshat* pertains to the "surface," or literal, meaning; *remez*, the "deep," or symbolic, meaning; *derash*, the "comparative," or similar, meaning; and *sod*, the "secret," or mystical, meaning.[7] And in Islam this idea was expressed by Jafar al-Sadiq, the Muslim scholar and Imam, who stated that *The Koran*

---

4 *Dictionary of the Middle Ages, Volume 1: Aachen to Augustinism—Allegory*, Stephen A. Barney (Contributor), p. 180

5 *Icons of the Middle Ages: Rulers, Writers, Rebels, and Saints: Volume 1*—Dante Alighieri, Elizabeth K. Haller (Contributor), p. 244

6 *The Epistle to Can Grande*, Dante Alighieri, pp. 5-6

7 *The Jewish Encyclopedia: Biblical Exegesis—Pardes*

has four similar levels of interpretation: "*The Book of God* has four things—literal expression (*ibara*), allusion (*ishara*), subtleties (*lataif*), and the deepest realities (*haqaiq*). The literal expression is for the common folk, the allusion is for the elite, the subtleties are for the friends of God, and the deepest realities are for the prophets."[8]

No wonder that when Jesus spoke about understanding the things of God, He referred to this four-fold principle of awareness. Therefore, with this multifaceted aspect of knowledge in mind, I would now like to address why I am convinced of the authenticity of the books that all but the ancient world—while in the case of *The Gospel of Nicodemus*, the pre-Reformation world—have deemed apocryphal.

The End of Secrecy

TO BEGIN WITH—IN A truly ironic twist—there is the simple fact that this word *apocryphal* contains an obvious clue as to the mystery of why these books were deemed unacceptable and lost to humanity for so many centuries, because, over time, the word has come to signify something very different from its original etymological meaning. To the modern mind, something deemed apocryphal is anything that is considered "doubtful," "spurious," or "untrustworthy." In actuality, its true meaning, based on its root word, is something that is "secret" or "hidden," as in, anything considered apocryphal is merely a hidden thing to outsiders. In other words, the secret only remains a mystery to those who do not possess the tools of interpretation, but to those "on the inside," as it were, the otherwise hidden meaning of the thing is fully comprehensible.

When understood in this fashion, the nature of the message contained in books like *Adam and Eve*, *Enoch*, *Jasher*, and *Nicodemus* have been exactly that—a body of divinely-inspired wisdom literature, which has precisely fulfilled this desired intention. In this, it is just as the Scripture declares: "No eye has seen, no ear has heard, no mind has conceived, all the things that the Lord has prepared for those who love Him."[9] Continuing in this same vein, Paul then said, "The man without the Spirit does not accept the things that come from the Spirit of God, for they are foolishness to him and he cannot understand them because they are spiritually discerned."[10]

Truth seen from this view, then, is never something that is as straightforward as one would hope for. From a biblical perspective, truth is always something that is veiled, hidden, obscure—the very essence of which is perfectly conveyed via the word *apocryphal*. Consider Matthew's words when he said, "Jesus spoke all these things to the crowd in parables. He did not say

---

8 *Spiritual Gems: The Mystical Koran Commentary*, Jafar al-Sadiq, p. 1
9 *First Corinthians* 2:9
10 Ibid. 2:14

anything to them without using one. In this way, what was spoken through the prophet was fulfilled: 'I'll open My mouth in parables; I'll utter *secret* things which have been *hidden* since the creation of the world.'"[11]

The word being used here for "secret" is the Greek word *krupto*, which means, "to conceal (that it may not become known)." Notice that this word *krupto*, from which we get our English word *cryptic*, is the central component for the word *apocryphal*. According to *Webster's Dictionary*, the word apocryphal comes to us from the Greek word *apokryphos*. What Webster does not mention, however, is that the prefix *apo* denotes the cessation, or reversal, of the word that it precedes; as in, if the root word means "secret" or "hidden," then when it is preceded by the prefix *apo*, the meaning of the word changes to that of "the end of secrecy" or "the reversal of being hidden." Clearly, this means that the real definition of the word *apocryphal* is the "unveiling" of a secret that was previously hidden from view.

Imagine that: The very people who were trying to discredit this so-called "forbidden wisdom" inadvertently chose a word that actually conveyed a latent truth about its destiny. No matter how many centuries of doubt and skepticism obscured its true meaning, the knowledge in these books would one day become "uncovered truth," and finally be seen for what it truly was—the wisdom of God that had been hidden away until it was time to be revealed. In this, it is exactly as predicted in one of the most ancient texts known to mankind—*First Enoch*:

> The word of the blessing of Enoch, how he blessed the elect and the righteous who would exist in the time of trouble, rejecting all the wicked and ungodly. Enoch, a righteous man, who was with God, answered and spoke while his eyes were open and while he saw a holy vision in the Heavens. This the angels showed me. From them I heard all things and understood what I saw; that which will not take place in this generation but in a generation which is to succeed at a distant period, on account of the elect.[12]

Search for Hidden Treasure

APART FROM THE CLUES that the etymological root meaning of the word provide, the prophetic nature of Scripture also supports the idea of the existence of a body of wisdom which—even though it proceeded directly from God—would be lost for an intended duration. Then, at some preordained "set time," this hidden wisdom would, for the sake of a future generation, be hurled back into the light of day, as if from out of nowhere. This is precisely what Jesus was saying when He announced, "The time is fulfilled and

---

11 *Matthew* 13:34-35
12 *First Enoch* 1:1-2

the Kingdom of God is at hand!"[13] Though the world had experienced various degrees of awareness of God's existence until Jesus arrived on the stage
of history, the world remained in a perpetual state of spiritual dysfunction.
But upon being baptized by John—an event that was punctuated by a voice
from Heaven—the earthly ministry of Jesus was inaugurated and with it a
new era of enlightenment and awareness.

Again and again, the biblical authors spoke of God's deliberate pattern
of hiding and revealing His most important truths. In every age—from the
time of Adam, right up to the present hour—the world has ridden a veritable roller coaster of ignorance and awareness concerning the ebb and flow of
God's manifestation. Yet even in those most harrowing of days, when God
had withdrawn His presence because of mankind's utter disregard for Him,
there still remained a modicum of God-inspired revelation. In other words,
there is, and always will be, more than one level of truth that the Lord is in
the business of revealing. First, there is a general revelation of truth that all
humanity is capable of perceiving as described by Paul. "Since the creation
of the world, God's invisible qualities—His eternal power and divine nature—have been clearly seen, being understood from what has been made,
so that mankind is without excuse."[14]

In addition to this universal awareness of the Divine, there is another
aspect of understanding the reality of God, which is not something that can
be grasped by the general population. The reason for this is clearly spelled
out in *The Bible* so that there can be little doubt as to God's intention. Once
again, Paul, as the great interpreter of Scripture, said it best: "We speak a
message of wisdom, but not the wisdom of this age or of the rulers of this
age who are coming to nothing. We speak of God's *secret* wisdom, a wisdom
that God has *hidden* and destined for our glory before time began."[15]

When one begins to see the revelation of God's word in these terms,
which could be described as a cosmic bank vault with a time-specific point
of unlocking, it is much easier to understand that the role the apocryphal
literature has played throughout history is no aberration in the plan of God.

The knowledge of God, then, is not something that one is simply born
with or inherits from one's parents. It must be sought after with tremendous
effort and determination. Certainly, Solomon, renowned as the wisest man
in history, must have had this in mind when he declared: "God in His greatness has concealed many things, while kings have the honor of discovering
them."[16] The knowledge that *The Bible* speaks of is never merely surface-ori-
ented; it must be dug for much in the same way that precious metals must

---

13 *Mark* 1:15
14 *Romans* 1:20
15 *First Corinthians* 2:6-7
16 *Proverbs* 25:2

be unearthed. "If you cry out for insight and understanding, and search for it like you'd search for *hidden* treasure, then you'll begin to understand and find the knowledge of God."[17]

Ironically, however, not only must mankind search for wisdom, but the true Wisdom of God, Whom Solomon personified as a living force, also has the ability to search for us. "Wisdom calls out in the street. She shouts in the public squares; from the top of the walls and the gateways of the city, she cries out."[18] In this way, Solomon made it clear that the Wisdom of God is a thoughtful entity, capable of both pursuing and being pursued. As a result of this unique attribute of knowledge as an active, living force, God and mankind are in a veritable wrestling match when it comes to appropriating it. As so often happens, mankind foolishly spurns the advances of the very wisdom that reaches out to it:

> If you had responded to My rebuke, I would've poured out My heart and soul to you. But you rejected Me when I called, paid no attention when I reached out. You ignored all My advice and refused to listen to Me. So, I, in turn, will laugh when disaster overwhelms you. As you mocked Me, I will mock you when calamity overtakes you.[19]

In this, Isaiah further elaborated:

> I know how stubborn you are, with necks as unbending as iron. You're as hardheaded as bronze. That's why I told you ahead of time what I was going to do. That way you could never say, "My idols did it. My wooden image and metal god commanded it to happen!" You've heard My predictions and seen them fulfilled, but you refused to admit it. Now I'll tell you new things that I've never mentioned before, *secrets* that you've not yet heard.[20]

With all this in mind, it should come as no surprise that the average citizen of planet Earth thinks that God is either dead or not paying attention. Neither should one be surprised when the typical Christian doubts the possibility that the word of God could actually encompass more than the traditionally accepted sixty-six books. As one can detect from a brief scan of Scripture, truth as God defines it is simply not something that is easily or casually appropriated. For the most part, truth is a *hidden* thing — a *secret* that resides deep in the heart of God, Who apparently shares it only with those of His choosing.

---

17 *Proverbs* 2:3-5
18 Ibid. 1:20-21
19 Ibid. 1:23-26
20 *Isaiah* 48:4-6

So the next time some super-spiritual know-it-all starts pontificating about how the apocryphal books were not included in the Canon of Scripture because God declared them unholy or uninspired, just remind them that the Lord is always confounding the self-proclaimed geniuses of this world. "I thank You, Father, Lord of Heaven and Earth," Jesus said, "for *hiding* the truth from those who think themselves so clever and wise, and for revealing it to the child-like."[21] And be bold in your conviction, as you fearlessly remind them of the words of our Lord: "The Kingdom of Heaven is like a treasure that a man discovered *hidden* in a field. In his excitement, he *hid* it again and sold everything he owned to get enough money to buy the field—and to get the treasure, too!"[22]

Imagine that: How many people would even notice what is being said here? Admittedly, it is a subtle point, but for the purposes of our discussion it looms as an important subtlety, because contained in this parable is a clue for the existence of a body of *hidden* wisdom that someone discovered and then, after having gone to a great deal of trouble to find it, *hid* it again! If I am not mistaken this sounds exactly like the scenario surrounding the apocryphal literature with so much of its inherent mystery and intrigue. What else can this mean but that someone attained, by way of intense search, an understanding of God's long-lost kingdom and, having acquired this treasured awareness, then *hid* their discovery again in the hopes of recovering it at some future point in time?

Like echoes reverberating down through the corridors of time, this same idea resounds throughout the ages; from the days of Enoch, the scribe, down to that of Asaph, the psalmist:

> Oh, my people, hear my teaching; listen to my words. I'll open my mouth in parables, I'll utter *hidden* things from days of old—what we've heard and known, what our Fathers have told us. We'll reveal them to our children; we'll tell the next generation about His power, about the wondrous things that He's performed on our behalf. He decreed statutes for Jacob and established the Law in Israel, which He commanded our forefathers to teach their children so the next generation would know them, even the children who were yet to be born, and they, in turn, would tell their children. Then they'd put their trust in God and would not forget His deeds but would keep His commands.[23]

Then, from the mouth of Asaph, the words were reiterated by the Incarnate Word, Jesus, Who, contrary to popular belief, spoke in parables to veil

---

21 *Matthew* 11:25; *Luke* 10:21
22 *Matthew* 13:44
23 *Psalm* 78:1-7

the truth so they would remain ignorant of the *hidden* wisdom that the Lord chose to reveal to His elect ones. And just in case none of you believes that God is in the business of unveiling apocryphal wisdom, then simply revisit the words of Jesus as recorded by Matthew, Mark, and Luke:

> The disciples came to Him and asked, "Why do You speak to the people in parables?" And He replied, "The knowledge of the *secrets* of the Kingdom of Heaven has been given to you but not to them. Whoever has will be given more and he will have an abundance. Whoever does not have, even what he has will be taken from him.
>
> "This is why I speak to them in parables: Though seeing, they do not perceive; though hearing, they do not understand. In them is fulfilled the prophecy of Isaiah: You'll be forever hearing but never understanding. You'll be forever seeing but never perceiving. For this people's heart has become calloused. They hardly hear with their ears, and have closed their eyes. Otherwise they might see and hear, and understand with their hearts and turn, and I would heal them."[24]

Having set the stage this way, we next examine how a disparate set of ancient manuscripts, depicting long-forgotten worlds, was adapted so a modern audience can relate to them, followed by a brief history of the restoration of these manuscripts that were once thought to be lost forever. Then, you will be ready to digest the actual narratives in all their dramatic glory.

---

24 *Matthew* 13:10; *Mark* 4:10; *Luke* 8:9

THE TRANSLATION

The test of a translation, like the test of a book ... is not a line here and there but coherence, movement, action; not how easily we may pull it to pieces and what interesting pieces it makes but how it first interests us, then absorbs us, and finally sweeps us along.

James I. Cook, *Edgar J. Goodspeed: Articulate Scholar*

A Matter of Style

The Latent Message

ONE OF THE MOST difficult aspects in bringing these stories to life for the sake of a modern audience was the all-important decision concerning the style of translation employed in their retelling. Crucial to this process were certain considerations, the first being the original style of writing in which the stories had been presented in their various incarnations up to the present day. As previously stated, *The Book of Tales* is a work that has been synthesized from manuscripts some of which date from the remotest periods of antiquity, such as *The First Book of Adam and Eve*, *The Secrets of Enoch*, *The Book of Jasher*, *The Letters of Herod and Pilate*, and *The Gospel of Nicodemus*.

When I learned of the existence of these stories more than three decades ago, they only existed in collections that had been published in the 1920s, while these in turn were reproductions from even earlier versions of the original manuscripts. Upon my initial reading of them, I felt much like someone who encounters the unfiltered works of William Shakespeare for the first time. These were definitely not stories that one could simply breeze through. Poetic yet mystifying, inspiring yet exasperating, they were written in a style that was clearly as archaic and outdated as anything penned by the Bard of Avon. Nearly incomprehensible at first glance, the sublime meaning of the texts seemed to arise only after a great deal of reading and re-reading, which required many hours of study and contemplation. Over the course of time, however, I not only became enthralled with the stories in these books, but I also became convinced that they were literary treasures in their own right. Unfortunately, because of the convoluted style in which they were written, I could also see why most modern minds would remain unimpressed and untouched by the latent message embedded in them.

After several years of sharing these stories with friends and colleagues — with admittedly mixed results — I noticed that something unusual began to happen as I attempted to engage others with their contents. Gradually, as I continued to read the narratives aloud to those around me, I ceased to simply recite them verbatim as they were found in the books. I found myself "translating them on the fly" in order to better convey the meaning that I felt was trapped in their pages. Only then did people begin to become engaged, with the end result that they started offering remarks like: "These are some very interesting texts. They shed new light on questions I've always had about certain aspects of *The Bible*." And: "This is fascinating stuff. I wonder why we've never heard anything about these stories in church."

Finally, after countless readings of the stories, I came to the conclusion that they represented a startling, behind-the-scenes version of *The Bible*—an extended storyline that constituted an intriguing counterpart to the familiar versions of Scripture. Not only that, but at some point in my journey through this collection of *Tales*, I also began to see them as more than a collage of random texts. Slowly but surely, there emerged a distinct pattern of connectivity, which transformed this scattered compendium into a single, continuous timeline—one that literally pivots upon the little-known prophecy of The Great Five and a Half Days—with Enoch as the narrator of a series of stories, beginning with Adam and Eve, then Abraham and Nimrod, and finally Jesus and Pilate.

Unfortunately, there was still one seemingly insurmountable problem with my grandiose plan. Apart from biblical scholars and literary aficionados, I wondered: Who in this modern, skeptical world would ever take the time to decipher the content of these stories when they were trapped in a language frame that only hardcore Shakespeare fans could appreciate, let alone understand?

So, like every other author before me, the question remained the same: How could I go about creating believable dialog for characters who existed in some of the remotest chapters of human history? Would I simply resort to parroting the style of the *King James Bible* translators when attempting to depict the biblical past? For me, this would constitute the ultimate failure of nerve, because, quite frankly, I have never been satisfied with biblical movies that took this route. I mean, really, who in their right mind would ever believe that anyone in *The Bible* actually talked like people who inhabited the world of Elizabethan England? Does anybody think, for one second, that Jesus, Abraham, or Adam spoke in iambic pentameter? Of course not. So why should audiences continue to endure such artistic nonsense? To me, it has always been nothing less than a gross oversimplification that just because a story involves historical characters who inhabit worlds unlike our own they must be portrayed as speaking with dialects and accents in order to convey their unique time and place.

A Clarity of Language

WITH THIS AGE-OLD dilemma, one comes face to face with the next critical consideration in trying to present the most ancient of tales to a modern audience. Throughout the history of storytelling, authors have made a concerted effort to flesh out their narratives by means of presenting three crucial elements—the *time* when a story occurred, the *place* where it occurred, and the *characters* who existed when and where that story occurred. Primarily, the way in which the first two aspects of storytelling are portrayed, that is, the "time" and "place" of any given story, have been done in a fairly straightforward manner. Whether the author's presentation of such matters can be characterized as either profoundly poetic or merely functional in style, the conveyance of time and place is generally more an indication of the author's personal writing style rather than anything intrinsic to the story itself.

On the other hand, the one aspect of a story that exists apart from the author's style is the way in which the "characters" of a story are presented, which is done not so much by way of what they *do* but how they *speak*. In other words, regardless of the background and origins of an author, the characters of a given narrative—either fictional or nonfictional—should always speak in a way that is true to that character's unique background and origins. Whereas an author may depict the time and place of a story in a multitude of ways without altering it, the way that characters speak will inevitably alter the reception of that story. More than any other aspect of the story, how characters speak must ring true to the time and place that they inhabit, or else the audience might interpret everything they do as false or contrived. The depiction of the dialog of a story's characters, then, is the paramount hurdle with which an author must contend, and never more so than with a narrative like *The Book of Tales*, which attempts to portray characters that clearly have a specific historical setting.

A prime example of dialog that uniquely conveys the setting of a story can be found in the literary works of Mark Twain. Through his clever use of dialect, Twain not only conveys a character's personality but, with little or no back story at all, he also conveys their education level and position in society. On the positive side, Twain's use of dialect provides insight into his characters through a dialog that, by way of texture and sound, reveals a great deal about the setting of the story—one which conveys a truth far beyond the author's mere description of the time and place in which the characters exist. On the negative side, however, trying to read dialog that is steeped in a peculiar dialect is sometimes very difficult to decipher. Often narratives that resort to foreign dialects to convey the background of certain characters work on one level, but because the dialog is so stultified, the actual message of the work is literally lost in translation. As a result, books or movies with dialect-laden dialog might be applauded by one segment of the audience, such as critics or other artists, while the average patron winds up on the losing end because of the difficulties that arise from trying to decipher the dialog. Unable to follow the plot, the reader or viewer disengages from the narrative before they even have an opportunity to get involved with the story.

To avoid such a potential death knell to box-office success, many filmmakers have pursued an alternate route in attempting to convey the settings of their stories. Rather than employ characters that resort to hard-to-understand dialects, they use those who speak in the language of the people they portray while providing subtitles for the sake of the audience. Such is the case in films like *The Longest Day*, *Dances With Wolves*, and *The Passion of the Christ*. In *The Longest Day*, unlike most war films of that time, all the German and French characters speak in their own language, accompanied by English subtitles. *Dances With Wolves* has much of its dialog spoken in Lakota with English subtitles. And not to be outdone, *The Passion of the Christ* does not contain a single word in English. The entire film is comprised of characters who speak Aramaic, Latin, and Hebrew. Yet ironically, in order to convey its ancient message to a modern audience, the filmmakers chose to subtitle the film in what can only be described as "vernacular English."[25]

Therefore, when it came time to establish the style of dialog in this modern adaption of ancient tales, all of these potential pitfalls and possibilities loomed large in my mind. As a result, I decided to make every effort to avoid any of the aforementioned clichés. What kind of historian would I be, I asked myself, if I sought to make Enoch and his counterparts speak like characters who had just stepped out of one of Shakespeare's plays simply because audiences expected biblical characters to speak that way? Above all, I sought to achieve a clarity of language with this newly forged rendition. I was not content to simply convey the meaning of these stories in the same way that a literary scholar might do. More than anything else, I wanted these timeless tales to be expressed in a language that could be understood by every strata of society, from the scholarly critic to the ordinary individual.

As it turns out, I am not alone in such an effort. As a matter of fact, the same thing has been happening for many years in respect to updating the Elizabethan English of the *King James* Version of *The Bible*. Not until 1885, with the creation of the *Revised* Version, had any significant changes been made to it since its inception in 1611. Then, in the wake of the growing popularity of modern-day revisions, the twentieth century saw more and more similar endeavors, spearheaded by leading theological minds like Edgar J. Goodspeed, who, in 1939, published *The Bible: An American Translation*. Although these kinds of translations have always been met with a mixture of praise and criticism, Goodspeed insisted that such efforts constituted a necessary evolution in the language of *The Bible*. Said James I. Cook, in his biography of the man:

> Nothing horrified Goodspeed more than the popular notion that the modern *Bible* translator merely tinkers with the *King James* Version, replacing its archaic words with their modern equivalents. For him, the case for a new translation rested … upon the papyrus discoveries of the late nineteenth and early twentieth centuries. He was con-

---

25 *On the Film: The Passion of the Christ*, Wikipedia

vinced that these rendered intolerable, not simply the individual words but the entire linguistic style of the *King James* Version and its revisions. The papyri solved the problem of what kind of Greek was in *The New Testament*. It was not the classical or literary Greek of its own day... The papyri showed that *The New Testament* was written in the vernacular Greek of its time, the language of everyday life.[26]

This is why Goodspeed was so determined that despite all the well-intentioned protestations: "*The New Testament* must be retranslated if it is to reach the modern reader with anything like the force it had in antiquity."[27] And for Goodspeed that meant: "The only appropriate vehicle for such retranslation is the common vernacular English of everyday life."[28] Therefore, just as Goodspeed sought to make the canonical *Bible* more accessible by updating its language, I have sought to do a similar thing with the apocryphal books. Rather than assigning so many lines of ill-conceived dialog to the people in these stories, I chose to allow them to speak in a language entirely devoid of inappropriate dialects, which, in my view, contradicts an accurate depiction of reality. Let me explain what I mean by that.

Of Accents and Idioms

IMAGINE A CLASSIC film like *Gone With the Wind*, a drama set entirely in the Confederate South during the American Civil War. Because everyone in the story is a southerner living in the 1860s, the characters should all speak with a nineteenth-century southern drawl while invoking every known southern expression of that era. Right? But wait. Before you answer too quickly, take a moment to ask yourself one question, assuming that everyone reading this is also from a variety of ethnic backgrounds: When you converse with someone who possesses a mutual ethnicity as yourself, do you ever notice yourselves speaking with peculiar accents or idioms? I sincerely doubt it.

The only time that someone would ever detect such peculiarities is when there are people or, in this case, characters, who are interacting with individuals of *other* nationalities. In other words, only when a story depicts characters from different language frames should an author employ the use of unique accents and idioms. Unless the dialog is intended to reveal the cultural difference between their characters, as might occur in a war movie where an American soldier is talking to a German one, or in a Western that has a cowboy conversing with an Indian, there is simply no logical — let alone artistic — reason to invoke the use of accents or idioms. Yet invoke

---

26 *Edgar Johnson Goodspeed: Articulate Scholar*, James I. Cook, p. 24
27 *The Making of the English New Testament*, Edgar J. Goodspeed, p. 110
28 Ibid. p. 110

them they do.

Such is clearly the case in a "period piece" like the aforementioned *Gone With the Wind*. Do most of its characters speak in that southern drawl so indicative of the late nineteenth century in order to convey a sense of time and place? Not surprisingly, the answer is yes. On one hand, most of them invoke classic southern accents, like Vivien Leigh, with her perky exclamations of "fiddle-dee-dee" and "great balls of fire." On the other hand, Clark Gable,whose character stems from Charleston, South Carolina, exhibits barely a hint of an accent, as evidenced by his famous tag line: "Frankly, my dear, I don't give a damn!" Either way, it appears that screenwriters are just as guilty as most *Bible* translators in their clichéd attempts to telegraph the "who," "where," and "when" of their plots. Fortunately, though, this has not always been so — in the case of both Hollywood and Holy Writ.

The employment of non-archaic dialog in a "period piece" is never more evident than in the critically acclaimed film *Butch Cassidy and the Sundance Kid*. Though set at the turn of the nineteenth century, the movie does everything it can to avoid the sort of "countrified" dialog that is typically heard in most Westerns. As the story goes, this was a conscious, creative choice made by both the film's writer and director, William Goldman and George Roy Hill, respectively. Said Internet movie critic Eric D. Snider: "The dialog … is casual and nonchalant in a strikingly modern way, and their attitudes are not what you expect of people from the late 1800s… This is all by design. It's part of the reason the film was so popular with audiences at the time, and why it's still so well regarded today."[29]

Case in point: When Butch and Sundance are being pursued by a posse and are desperate to formulate an escape plan, Cassidy proposes that they go to Bolivia, but the Kid is far from enthusiastic about the idea. "You just keep on thinking of stuff, Butch," he replies with a mocking tone. "That's what you're good at." Frustrated, Cassidy grumbles back, "I got vision, and the whole world wears bifocals."

As it turns out, this is precisely the kind of thing that Edgar J. Goodspeed had in mind as he approached his updating of the Elizabethan English of the *King James* Version of *The Bible*, in his 1939 translation of *The New Testament*. His biographer, James I. Cook, described it this way: "Goodspeed's aim was to avoid translation English, which he regarded as almost no English at all, to exclude all echoes of the familiar '*Bible* English' of the older versions, and, in their place, to use American idiom."[30]

Another way of looking at this same problem might be to imagine two Eskimos having a conversation. If we, as English-speaking individuals, were listening in on this conversation, we would naturally detect accents

---

29 *What's the Big Deal?: Butch Cassidy and the Sundance Kid*, Eric D. Snider
30 *Edgar Johnson Goodspeed: Articulate Scholar*, James I. Cook, p. 28

and idioms that were very different from our own. However, from the point of view of the Eskimos who were speaking to one another, they would not notice anything unusual at all. To them, they would just be having a normal conversation. So, based on this assumption, if an author were to translate this conversation for their readers, then why, for Heaven's sake, would they resort to such illogical and unnatural gimmicks like foreign accents or peculiar idioms simply to convey the fact that they were Eskimos?

With all this in mind, then, I set out to depict the characters in *The Book of Tales* as individuals who are indigenous to the same world, whether it is Adam conversing with Eve or Abraham talking to Nimrod or Jesus speaking with Pilate. And, therefore, like southerners speaking with other southerners, or cowboys with other cowboys, or Eskimos with other Eskimos, the characters in this work have been deliberately stripped of dialect-laden speech so that the concise meaning of what they have to say can finally resound from their ancient origins and penetrate our own world of modern sensibilities.

Foreshadow and Payoff

IN ADDITION TO updating the language of *The Tales*, they have also been thoroughly "fleshed out" in admittedly "cinematic" terms. This was done for several reasons, the first of which is because there is such a clear parallel between the dramatic narratives found in *The Bible* and those in the theater, literature, and cinema. The second reason was because, considering the significance of the first reason, the fact that it had not been done yet seemed so incongruous. That is to say, it was done because, in the opinion of this writer, it was long overdue in terms of the development of the dramatic narrative as a cultural phenomenon. What does that mean? Consider this, if you will. Historically speaking, in both the sacred and the secular realms, the earliest examples of storytelling were confined to a much simpler and condensed format. Only since the birth of modern literature and its ancestor, the cinema, has a more expanded mode of expression evolved with the subsequent maturation of the secular narrative — one which was only hinted at in the theatrical productions of ancient Greece and medieval Europe. Conversely, the sacred narrative has traditionally lagged behind in terms of this natural progression, and they have undoubtedly done so because of the built-in resistance to what is generally perceived as "tampering" with the original narratives themselves. Such resistance is certainly the very thing that intrepid pioneers like Goodspeed experienced regularly, even as he correctly envisioned the potential boon to humanity as a result of his updating of not just the archaic language but also the outmoded narrative style of existing translations of *The Bible*.

The next reason for adding this new dimension to the original stories was because, even in their unembellished state, they were stories that were predominantly told through the actions and dialog of their characters as opposed to a litany of religious precepts or ideology. In other words, *The Tales* inhabiting the world of apocryphal literature were already steeped in dramatic elements so that one only needed to ask a few questions when deciding how to make them truly "cinematic." One example of this latent cinematic element appears throughout the original stories in that, much akin to earlier forms of the narrative, the "dialog" in them was usually expressed through extended "monologs." Such a mode of expression might have seemed perfectly natural in the past, but, typically, modern audiences find them tedious and artificial. Therefore, in order to bring these portions of antiquated storytelling into the present day, one simply needed to "translate" these *mono*logs into a scenario in which two characters are expressing the original content of the story in the form of *dia*logs. Mind you, though, the primary content of the original stories was never changed in this process of retelling them. Their inherent potential was merely "fleshed out." Altering their content—that is, the explicit intent of the original authors—was never an option. Instead, what we are talking about here is not a matter of changing their "content" so much as changing the conveyance of said content.

Another way in which these stories were updated hearkens back to our earlier discussion on the concept of parallel elements in both sacred and secular storytelling. By that I mean, because of the inherent similarity between the dramatic narratives found in Scripture and those in the theater, literature, and cinema, the potential for elaborating *The Tales* was always an obvious one. Though these two modes of communication have generally been viewed as being alien to one another, they are not so different after all. Consequently, in sacred terms, the dramas of *The Bible* unfold according to a principle known as "shadow and substance," while in secular terms, the dramas of the theater, literature, and cinema are conveyed by means of what has come to be known as "foreshadow and payoff."

What, exactly, does "foreshadow and payoff" mean? In filmic terms, foreshadow and payoff means that, in regard to both plot and character, the main body of a motion picture is in balance with its climax. In other words, through a filmmaker's clever use of plot details and character elements, a film's beginning and middle will naturally flow toward its inevitable end, and thus, from the audience's perspective, the finale will not seem to come "from out of nowhere." Otherwise, it does not matter how dramatic the ending of a movie is, without this proper balancing act of foreshadow and payoff, the audience will detect such foul play and quite rightly feel cheated by a finale that has clearly been tacked on simply for effect. Only when the "big ending" of a picture grows "organically," as it were, from all that has preceded its climax is that movie favorably received. This idea is never more evident than when one takes the time to see how this narrative device has been used in the proper way, in just the right doses, in some of the most successful films of all time. Generally, foreshadow and payoff are executed filmically in one of two ways—either through plot devices or thematic devices. Two films that have famously used plot devices to achieve this effect are *Jaws* and *Goldfinger*.

In *Jaws*, the finale comes when Chief Brody shoots and detonates the compressed air tank lodged in the shark's mouth, blowing it to kingdom come. But long before this occurs, it is cleverly foreshadowed in the main body of the film. During the early stages of the men's hunt for the man-eater, one of the oxygen tanks aboard their ship accidentally breaks loose and is quickly grabbed and secured. "Damn it, Martin!" exclaims the oceanographer Matt Hooper. "This is compressed air. You screw around with these tanks and they're gonna blow up!" With typical cynicism, Quint, the hard-bitten shark hunter, retorts, "Yeah, real fine gear you brought out here, Mister Hooper. But I don't know what that bastard shark's gonna do with it. Might eat it, I suppose. Seen one eat a rocking chair one time." At first, when this tension-filled dialog takes place, the audience experiences it as but a random flow of events that contribute to the mounting drama. In reality, however, it is all that and more; it also serves as an artfully planted clue that prepares the audience for one of the great climaxes in cinematic history, when Brody kills the shark by taking advantage of information that previously seemed incidental. Thus, the big ending does not materialize out of thin air but is a direct payoff of a foreshadowing event woven into the story entirely for the sake of the audience.

In *Goldfinger*, there are actually two instances of the foreshadowing of the demise of the villain—in this case, the sinister mute servant, Oddjob, as well as his boss, the namesake of the picture, Goldfinger himself. First, James Bond takes care of Oddjob by acting swiftly in connecting a loose electrical wire and electrocuting Oddjob as he is dislodging his deadly flying steel-brimmed hat from an iron cage. But prior to this, it was perfectly mirrored in the opening scene of the film when Bond outwits an assassin whom James shoves into a water-filled bathtub, then tosses a "live" appliance into the tub, also electrocuting him. In this way, the filmmakers not only demonstrate the inimitable Agent 007's resourcefulness in eliminating one of his enemies, but they also foreshadow the way he will eventually bring down one of his most famous opponents. As for the demise of Goldfinger: In another example of foreshadow and payoff, Bond is finally able to rid himself of this criminal mastermind when a stray bullet blows out the airplane's window and sucks the villain out, thus ending Goldfinger's tyranny. But before this happens, it, too, is adeptly foreshadowed. Having been captured, Bond is being transported by plane to Goldfinger's headquarters by his personal pilot, Pussy Galore, who holds him at gunpoint, saying, "Do you want to play it easy or the hard way?" Bond, however, cool as ever, replies, "Now, Pussy, you know a lot more about planes than guns. That's a Smith and Wesson .45, and if you fire at this close range, the bullet will pass through me and the fuselage like a blowtorch through butter. The cabin will depressurize, and we'll both be sucked into outer space together." So again, what initially appears to be just a passing remark actually serves to provide the necessary information to the audience when, in the final scene, the very thing that Bond had warned about occurs.

Apart from using plot devices, such as a particular action or piece of dialog to foreshadow a film's finale, another form of this principle of fore-shadow and payoff involves the use of thematic devices. As such, films that utilize this format are much broader in their technique. Instead of interjecting a' single foreshadowing event that results in an eventual payoff, these films rely on a whole series of subtle but potent moments throughout the picture, which, together, help build toward its climax. Famous examples of this type include such classics as *Shane*, *The Searchers*, and *The Godfather*.

In *Shane*, a mysterious drifter rides in from out of the desert and be-friends a family of desperate homesteaders, caught in the throes of a range war, sometime after the American Civil War. No sooner does Shane arrive on the scene, however, than he reveals that he is a man with a haunted past. At the slightest provocation—the young son's cocking of his toy rifle, the crunching steps of a stray deer outside the cabin window—and instantly, like a coiled rattlesnake, Shane is ready to draw his six-shooter on his imagined foe. Embarrassed by his own abruptness, Shane proceeds to exchange his buckskins and pistol for a pair of jeans and a pickaxe; in short, Shane the gunman becomes Shane the sodbuster. And although he quickly takes sides with this family, in opposition to Rufus Ryker, the heartless cattle baron who is hell-bent on running roughshod over every family in the valley, Shane seems just as determined to do it without resorting to gunplay ever again. Emboldened by Shane's apparent weakness, Ryker brings an even more menacing threat into the situation in the form of a hired gun by the name of Jack Wilson, who soon taunts one of the homesteaders into an obvious mismatch and ruthlessly guns him down in a mud-filled street. For the already-anxious homesteaders, this is the last straw, as more and more of them decide to pull up their stakes and leave. Still, Shane seems strangely unmoved. Only one man is willing to oppose Ryker, and that is the father of the family, Joe Starrett. In vain, his wife pleads with Shane to stop her husband from such a foolhardy enterprise, but the quiet stranger declines, much to the chagrin of the man's family. Only when Shane is informed that Ryker is drawing Joe into an ambush does he finally relent; only then does Shane put away his jeans and axe, and once again dons his buckskins and pistol, confronting Ryker and his hired gun in a final showdown. As Ryker looks on, Shane coolly stares down the malevolent Wilson—a man who is clearly unimpressed with the reticent drifter standing before him. Then it happens: The man haunted by his past, the man so reluctant to take up arms ever again, finally unleashes all his pent-up anger, and like the coiled rattlesnake that he is, explodes in a fury of gunfire, killing Wilson and then Ryker before they barely have time to pull their weapons. And just like that, every finely crafted moment in this classic film comes to a resounding crescendo—an absolutely perfect example of cinematic symmetry, if ever there was one.

In *The Searchers*, Comanche raiders kidnap Debbie Edwards, the young niece of Civil War veteran Ethan Edwards, initiating an intense and extended search for her by Ethan and her adopted brother, Martin Pawley. But what ostensibly begins as a rescue effort by Ethan and Martin changes over time. As the years roll on and they still have not been able to locate Debbie, Ethan's fierce hatred of all things Indian begins to blind him to his niece's humanity. Because Debbie has lived among the Comanches for so long, Martin comes to realize that Ethan feels she is no longer worth rescuing, and he must now do everything he can to rescue her before his uncle can do her any harm. When they finally find Debbie, Martin must physically shield her from Ethan, who menacingly aims his pistol, demanding that he step aside. But before Ethan can make good on his intentions, he is shot in the shoulder by a Comanche arrow, thus reprieving Debbie for the time being. Only later do the men track her down again in the camp of her kidnapper, fully realizing that if they do attack the Indian's camp, it means that Debbie will probably be killed by her captors rather than their relinquishing her. "That's what I'm counting on," rages Ethan, to which Martin protests vehemently, "She's alive, and she's gonna stay alive." Ethan then roars back: "Living with Comanches ain't being alive!" Only in the final sequence of this nightmarish search does Ethan catch up with Debbie, who, seeing the blistering anger in her uncle's eyes, recoils in terror. And then it happens: Upon seeing his niece face to face after all these years, Ethan is smitten and, disarmed of all his fury, his compassion overcomes his quest for vengeance. With quiet resolve, he tells her at last, "Let's go home, Debbie."

In *The Godfather*, Vito Corleone is the Sicilian head of a crime syndicate who rules with an odd blend of honor, justice, and vendetta. Known as the Don by his enemies who fear him and the Godfather by his family who respect him, he is a ruthlessly shrewd man who nonetheless displays great love and compassion for his three grown sons, each one with their own unique personality. Two are clearly destined for a life of crime—Sonny, the hotheaded firebrand, and Fredo, the ne'er-do-well oldest son, who cannot hold a candle to his younger brothers. Then there is Michael, the war hero who returns home on the day of his younger sister's wedding.

Dismayed by his family's reputation and openly critical of their activities, Michael insists to his fiancé that he has absolutely no intention of following in his father's footsteps. However, when Don Corleone is nearly killed in a failed assassination attempt, Michael inadvertently becomes ensnared by the very world that he had so adamantly refused to be a part of. At first, he is merely acting true to his nature by bravely guarding his father from further harm as the Don recuperates from his wounds, but then in a bold and impulsive move, he volunteers to strike back at the men responsible for his father's attack. After gunning down a rival crime boss and a corrupt police captain, Michael embarks on a completely new path, and as the years go by, he plunges deeper and deeper into the life that neither he nor his ailing father had intended for him. Upon Vito's passing from the scene, Michael masterfully orchestrates the assassination of all his rival crime bosses, and then it happens: As his incredulous wife looks on, the door slowly closes between her and the Godfather.

Now that this principle of foreshadow and payoff has been illustrated by way of a variety of films, one might naturally ask the question: How can any of this pertain to a discussion of adapting *The Book of Tales*? First and foremost, it should be noted that all five of the previously mentioned films were adapted from novels, which means that the source material, as such, contained more plotlines and characters than a movie is capable of sustaining. Consequently, the screenwriters who were adapting these novels into movie scripts were all faced with the same challenges that I faced in adapting *The Tales* from what they once were to what they are now. In other words, the primary task on both our parts was to sift through an array of events and personalities, and to forge them into a single, cohesive through-line story. To do this, the first order of business was to decide which aspects of each story, from among this plethora of information, were best suited for this framework we have just described, that is to say, a narrative that conforms to this filmic principle of foreshadow and payoff. Fortunately, this was not nearly as difficult as one might imagine, because these ancient narratives, even in their most primitive form, already possessed this innate potential. Like so many diamonds in the rough, these essential elements were just lying about, ready to be mined, cut, and polished in the hands of the master jeweler. And as it so happened, the key to unleashing this potential was to develop and adapt them in accordance to the aforementioned principle of foreshadow and payoff.

Still, in view of such elaborate alterations, one may ask the next series of inevitable questions: Do you not feel guilty "meddling" with what might otherwise be deemed sacred territory? After all, are you not in the process of trying to convince us that these apocryphal stories should be held on par with the canonical books? Why not simply stick to updating the stories from their archaic language into a more modern form while remaining faithful to the original stories, word for word, and be done with it? Why insert all this added business of foreshadow and payoff? Well, to answer such questions, I return to the thinking of Goodspeed, who was adamantly against this very thing when he said, "The most serious translation errors made in updating the language of *The Bible*, from Tyndale to the *Revised* Versions, was their adoption of a word-for-word method, with never a glance at the line of thought."[31] On this subject of updating the narratives of Scripture into those that were more suitable for a modern audience, James I. Cook had this to say about Goodspeed's thinking:

> A translation which was faithful in its individual parts but unfaithful in its total impression would be wrong in principle. That had been the greatest weakness of earlier translators. They had been more concerned with words than with phrases, with clauses than with sentences, with verses than with paragraphs. The test of a translation, like the test of a book, said Goodspeed, "is not a line here and there but coherence, movement, action; not how easily we may pull it to pieces and what interesting pieces it makes but how it first interests us, then absorbs us, and finally sweeps us along."[32]

Never has this advice been taken more to heart than in one of the finest examples of adapting a story from *The Bible* to the big screen, in the film *The Ten Commandments*. And just in case you think it sacrilegious to "add" to *The Bible* — a prohibition directed only to *The Book of Revelation*, by the way — imagine how this epic tale would have played out if those who had adapted it had not been audacious enough to "meddle" with its original storyline? Does this mean that those who did the "adding" were being disrespectful of Scripture when they chose to interject events and characters that were not already there? Fortunately, the end result and the test of time have answered both of these questions in resounding fashion. Clearly, they were more than respectful in their audacity; they were downright reverential. More to the point, they expressed this reverence by way of an overriding sense of foreshadow and payoff. Let us take a moment to revisit the movie in light of what we have just learned, and you will see exactly what I mean.

In *The Ten Commandments*, the film opens with Pharaoh's soothsayers warning the Egyptian king about an ominous prophecy concerning a Hebrew deliverer who will one day lead a slave revolt, declaring, "A star has proclaimed his birth." In starting the picture this way, with a scene that is nowhere to be found in *The Book of Exodus*, anyone familiar with the original story in *The Bible* is immediately struck by the fact that this rendition of Mo-

---

31 *Edgar Johnson Goodspeed: Articulate Scholar*, James I. Cook, p. 28
32 Ibid. p. 29

ses as Messiah is no longer simply an *Old Testament* story; it is also one that is deeply rooted in *The New Testament*. In other words, the film's payoff as Moses, the deliverer of Israel, is derived entirely from the way in which *The Bible* itself depicts the meaning of Moses' life as it is seen through the prism of Jesus, the Deliverer of humanity. As it is written: "By faith, Moses, when he was come to years, refused to be called the son of Pharaoh's daughter; choosing rather to suffer affliction with the people of God than to enjoy the pleasures of sin for a season, esteeming the reproach of Christ greater riches than the treasures of Egypt."[33]

And so, as the first scene of the movie goes in regard to Moses as Messiah, so goes the rest of the picture, and — I repeat — all made clear by way of the ingenious usage of this principle of foreshadow and payoff. For example, before Moses ever delivers the nation of Israel as a whole, he first rescues a pair of Hebrew slaves. One is a woman who just happens to be his aged mother, Yochabel, although Moses, as a prince of Egypt, raised in secrecy by Pharaoh's daughter, is still unaware of this fact; the other is Joshua, whom Moses sets free from a death sentence for striking an Egyptian while attempting to save Yochabel from being crushed by a quarry stone.

Later, when Pharaoh asks his son Rameses if he has learned the identity of the would-be Hebrew deliverer, Rameses insists that they do not need a deliverer because they already have Moses, who, even before God had ordained the people their Sabbath day of rest, had instituted a day of rest for the Hebrew slaves, much to the chagrin of Rameses. Then, when Bithiah, Moses' Egyptian adoptive mother, tries to persuade Yochabel to leave the country before Moses learns the truth of his Hebrew heritage, Yochabel resists her plea. When Bithiah challenges her priority as Moses' mother, Yochabel poignantly confesses that though she had yearned to reach out to her son, she resisted the urge, lamenting that she "dared not even touch the hem of his garment," a phrase that is clearly an allusion to Moses as a Christ figure.

When Moses finally does learn the truth about his Hebrew heritage, he is confronted by the two Egyptian women in his life whom he loves most, and in doing so, he must endure words of temptation as tearing as any offered by Satan to Jesus in the wilderness. First, Bithiah begs him to hide the truth that will only lead to certain servitude and hardship, asking plaintively, "Cannot justice and truth be served better upon a throne, where all men may benefit from your goodness and strength?" Then, his first love, the Egyptian princess Nefritiri chides Moses after retrieving him from the mud pits: "First Friend of the Pharaoh, Keeper of the Royal Seal, Prince of Thebes, and Beloved of the Nile God... A man of mud!" But when Moses takes it all in strides, Nefritiri scoffs, "Is this what you really want? To be a slave? If

---

33 *Hebrews* 11:24-26

you want to help your people, come back to the palace. Oh, Moses, the gods have fashioned you for greatness … and when you are Pharaoh, you can free your people." But just as *The Book of Hebrews* would later record, Moses summarily spurns their offers of instant gratification and chooses the more difficult path that God has personally laid out for him, forever turning his back on the throne of Egypt.

And again, to reinforce the Christ allusion, when Yochabel sees that Moses is willing to give up his Egyptian royalty in favor of pursuing his daring role as their destined deliverer, her words clearly echo those of another mother who would also come to realize the messianic role that was to be played by her son. That mother's name is Mary. Says Yochabel, "Blessed am I of all mothers in the land, for my eyes have beheld Your deliverer."

Still, before Moses ever takes on the mantle of deliverer, he first suffers in the mud pits alongside his fellow Hebrew slaves, where he is personally confronted with the brutality of their Egyptian taskmasters. When an old man is attacked for his dignified protest, the mortally wounded fellow reveals his lifelong wish to Moses, that of one day seeing the promised deliverer with his own eyes. With bitter irony, Moses asks under his breath, "What deliverer could break the power of Pharaoh?" "You!" barks the taskmaster to the others standing there. "Clay carriers. Throw this carrion to the vultures." Then the taskmaster snaps at Moses, "You. Take his place." And just as Jesus willingly took our place as the recipient of God's wrath for the consequence of the sins of all mankind, Moses, too, willingly and without a single word of protest steps down into the muck and mire of that muddy pit to stand side by side with his kinsmen slaves.

Finally, after receiving God's call from the burning bush, Moses explains to Joshua that he is to lead the Hebrews out of Egyptian bondage, and Joshua, like the Apostle Peter in his day, brashly looks to the sword for deliverance. But once again reminiscent of Christ, Moses declares, "It is not by the sword that the Lord will deliver His people but by the staff of a shepherd." In the end, it is this very staff that Moses stretches out toward the Red Sea, which temporarily bars the escape of the Israelites as Pharaoh's fierce charioteers move in on them. Then in one of the most memorable climaxes in cinema history, Moses, with staff in hand, confidently utters a mighty word of faith, as he and the people with him watch in awe as the waters part in a spectacular display of God's power, thus enabling the people to cross over through the midst of the sea as if it were dry land.

In foreshadow after foreshadow, then, this artful movie lays down its marvelous tapestry of clues that all eventually reveal the true depth of their meaning in the story's final payoff, as Moses slowly but surely rises to embrace his grand destiny. And just as God, the Ultimate Director of human history, must have surely directed the steps of the real-life Moses, Cecil B.

DeMille, the director of *The Ten Commandments*, in audacious stroke after stroke, masterfully directs the heroic life of his cinematic counterpart. More importantly, far from diminishing the message of faith and hope contained in Scripture, as some might argue, this classic film actually makes these biblically-inspired realities even more accessible, all through the unparalleled power of the dramatic narrative.

Thus, it was with all the foregoing ideas in mind that *The Tales* were reworked, that is to say, not just in the updating of their language but in the extent to which they could be infused with the same vital elements that are found in a modern-day narrative. And all with the utmost intention that this new adaption of *The Tales* should "first interest us, then absorb us, and finally sweep us along." In the final analysis, it will be this radically modern, dramatic approach to the reworking of these *Tales* that sets this work apart from any other in dealing with the subject of whether or not the so-called *Lost Books of The Bible* should be restored to their former status in the hierarchy of God's wisdom.

THE INTERLUDE

Men take it for granted today that in order to understand anything human ... they should search out its history... So pervasive has historicism become that we tend to forget it is itself a historical phenomenon.

Tom F. Driver, *Romantic Quest and Modern Query*

The Curtain Rises

Impossible Wonders

IN 1768, AN ANCIENT manuscript known as *The First Book of Enoch* was located in the mountains of Ethiopia. At the same time, Britain and America and, in effect, most of Europe were hopelessly embroiled in what was actually the first world war of ideas. Then, just when it seemed that our troubled world needed them most, more and more of these literary treasures from antiquity began to be rediscovered.

Ironically, though, after managing to recover these impossible wonders from the depths of oblivion, no one bothered to translate them. Rather than being seen as potential gems of spiritual wisdom, these priceless documents were relegated to the status of rare artifacts. So, for more than half a century, they sat unopened and unread on various museum shelves, simply gathering dust. But once the arduous task of decipherment had been completed, manuscripts like *First Enoch* began providing the West with a vivid, haunting glimpse into humanity's spiritual origins and destiny. Almost overnight, an entirely new way of understanding ourselves had been unveiled, as old as time itself.

Centuries of Suppression

STILL, AS MUCH AS these manuscripts have managed to illuminate the human condition, they have also sparked an inordinate amount of derision and controversy. Having survived for twenty centuries or more, these priceless documents depict events that reach far beyond normally accepted limits of prehistoric time. Most notable among these — besides *First Enoch* — are *The First Book of Adam and Eve*, *The Secrets of Enoch*, *The Book of Jasher*, *The Letters of Herod and Pilate*, and *The Gospel of Nicodemus*. Sadly, however, they have all generally been ignored, dismissed, or suppressed, presumably because of their provocative rendering of historical events and persons.

A typical example of this is *First Enoch*, which had been read and respected by Jews and Christians alike, and which had stood side by side with *The Book of Revelation* during the first four centuries of the Christian Era. While many of the Church Fathers, such as Clement, Ambrose, and Tertullian, endorsed it, others did not hold to this favorable view, and because of the efforts of influential opponents of the book, like Augustine and Jerome, who were critical of Enoch's description of those peculiar angels, or Watchers as they were called, the book was eventually deemed heretical. Along with other Enochic writings, it was banned from the mainstream

of Scripture. Shredded and burned, the book was lost to the West for over
a thousand years. Yet with remarkable persistence, many of these ancient
gems have, slowly but surely, made their way back into circulation. Today,
thanks to the efforts of a handful of men who were uniquely capable of
seeing beyond the veil of skepticism and doubt, nearly everyone has heard
something about these remarkable books.

Still, this never seems to answer the inevitable question: What relevance
could a bunch of ancient manuscripts provide for an increasingly cynical
world? The standard answer has always been that these books were designed so that a chosen few could understand them, but as to how this special remnant is supposed to assist in ushering in this awareness of God's
truth, the canonical record does not reveal; which brings us back to the subject of extra-biblical texts. With the unexpected occurrence of the Qumran
findings of *The Dead Sea Scrolls*, the notion of recovering "hidden" wisdom
literature has become more and more widespread. Consequently, it no longer seems so far-fetched that there might be other sources of biblical truth
not found amongst the traditional sixty-six books of *The Bible*. What is more,
these sources of truth are able to provide critical missing pieces to the biblical record. In this way, these remarkable texts are helping to answer questions that have puzzled scholars for hundreds, if not thousands, of years.

This is why, even before a place like Qumran could ever have been
imagined, when mere rumors of a surviving Enochic text began to surface,
the Scottish explorer James Bruce was eager to get his hands on a copy, no
matter the cost to him personally. So in 1773, Bruce endured an extremely
hazardous journey to Ethiopia, where he was able to secure three copies of
the rare book. Then in 1821, Dr. Richard Laurence, regius professor of Hebrew at Oxford, translated the work into English, providing the West with
its first glimpse into Enoch's "forbidden mysteries." No longer would we
remain a victim of centuries of suppression. No longer could the traditions
of men keep us in ignorance concerning the role of spiritual pioneers like
Enoch, the scribe.

As a result, we can study these so-called "apocryphal" texts for ourselves. Now we are free to digest the contents of these remarkable books on
our own. We can meditate on their mystical sayings and relive the fantastic
journey of Enoch, as easily as any described by the likes of Jules Verne or
H.G. Wells. We can now witness firsthand how God is still using Enoch as a
type of Christ, even after his supposed "death," from his being taken up to
Heaven, where he served as a divine mediator, right up to his reappearance
as one of the Two Witnesses described in *The Book of Revelation*.

Thanks to the courage and dedication of men like Bruce and Laurence,
who succeeded in restoring these ancient texts to our Western world, almost everyone who has ever studied biblical history has come to learn about

Enoch and the strange angelic beings called the Watchers. Their fabled story provides the building blocks for countless mythological motifs, particularly concerning their respective roles in the construction of The Great Pyramid of Giza. Since time immemorial, one civilization after another has told and retold its own version of a miraculously exalted hero, poised to usher in an age of enlightenment for the faithful. But what does tradition have to say about the rest of Enoch's life? Unfortunately, except for the brief passages in Scripture, tradition has very little to say. What really happened to Enoch during his ascension to Heaven? Did God simply spirit him away without leaving humanity a single word of explanation afterward? And why does there seem to be so little written about Enoch's role in the creation of *The Bible*?

Furthermore, how did Enoch react when an angel told him he was being recruited as a conveyor of the mysteries of God? What was the reaction of Enoch's family after he told them the news? What did his family do with the books he wrote? And could the accounts produced so long ago by Enoch and others like him finally be starting to prove their relevance, not simply to a few appointed people but to an entire world, ready and waiting for their lost message?

These are just some of the questions that this work, *The Book of Tales*, will attempt to grapple with, but it will do so in a way unlike any other that you have ever encountered. It will not seek to approach the issue in a strictly formal manner, and although many decades of scholarship have contributed to its creation, it will not attempt to do so in a purely scholastic way, either. Rather, the stories in this work will attempt to reveal a radical new approach to the key personalities and events of biblical history.

Admittedly, however, the unique approach to the historical events and persons contained in this work was not entirely my own creation. It came instead as an outgrowth of the development of mankind's evolving understanding of the nature of historicism itself and the subsequent pursuit of historical certainty. About this evolution of historical thought, Tom F. Driver, professor emeritus of theology and culture at Union Theological Seminary, said:

> Men take it for granted today that in order to understand anything human (often to understand natural phenomena as well) they should search out its history — its genesis and the processes by which it has come to its present state. For modern man, historical investigation is not only a method, it is very nearly *the* method, an approach to reality that conditions all modern thought. So pervasive has historicism become that we tend to forget it is itself a historical phenomenon. As a matter of fact, it revolutionized human thought

only in the nineteenth century and then only in those places where European culture was dominant.[34]

According to Driver, the most important pioneer in this revolution in historical thinking was the eighteenth-century Italian scholar Giambattista Vico. More than anything else, it has been Vico's philosophy of history, which Driver called "a theory of historical cognition,"[35] that ultimately provided the impetus for the present narratives found in *The Book of Tales*. Concerning this theory, Driver articulated Vico's belief that:

> Since man is native to history … man is capable of re-evoking the past in the depth of his own consciousness. Given a certain amount of historical data to begin with, man is able, through his imagination, to overcome the gap that separates the past from the present.[36]

This, in essence, is what this book sets out to do; it aims to provide the reader with all the necessary historical data that these ancient manuscripts have been offering all along. This data, however, is not reconstructed according to the dictates of intellectual inquiry alone. Instead, the persons and events depicted in them have been presented as a full-blown dramatic narrative, and it is this narrative that provides the ultimate foundation for the re-examination of said persons and events. In doing so, readers are invited to utilize their own God-given imagination to psychologically and emotionally bridge the seemingly insurmountable gulf between past and present. In other words, instead of the typical piece-meal approach so common to most historical treatises, *The Book of Tales* will provide a completely unique insight into many of the watershed moments of our collective history through the imaginative power of the dramatic narrative.

The Stuff of Legends

IN OUR FIRST installment, we witness firsthand Adam and Eve's expulsion from the Garden of Eden and God's reaction to their child-like response as they desperately try, again and again, to get back into His good graces. We see the establishment of the very first promises from God as He explains His plan to save them from a tragic fate.

For this wondrous tale, two men must be acknowledged for their selfless pursuit of biblical knowledge, men whose reputation in the Western world of theological studies was unimpeachable in their day. They are S.C. Malan, a British biblical scholar and linguist of Oriental languages, and W.R.

---

34 *Romantic Quest and Modern Query: A History of the Modern Theater*, Tom F. Driver, pp. xi-xii

35 Ibid. p. xiii

36 Ibid. p. xiii

Morfill, a British professor of Slavonic languages at Oxford. In 1882, Malan produced the first English translation of *The First Book of Adam and Eve*; and in 1896, Morfill gave us his translation of *The Secrets of Enoch*. Thanks to the efforts of this intrepid pair, humanity is able to once again partake of the long-forgotten world of the most famous couple of all time.

The story of Adam and Eve is literally the stuff of legends, from their prior glory in Eden to their disgraceful expulsion from the garden. Every culture the world over has incorporated some version of the Forbidden Fruit being offered up by some shape-shifting monster, poised to bring about the downfall of the first family of the clan. But what does tradition have to say about Adam and Eve after they were kicked out of Eden? Unfortunately, except for the brief passages in *The Book of Genesis*, it has little to say. What really happened to them during their exile experience? Did God simply abandon them to a life of hopeless despair? And why was nothing else written about the rest of their lives?

In *The Book of Tales*, we discover for ourselves how God continued to nurture Adam and Eve during every phase of their lives, from providing them with sheepskins for clothing, right up to His teaching them how to make their first offerings to Him. How did Adam and Eve learn to survive on their own after being deprived of direct access to God? What did Satan do in his attempt to thwart God's every effort in restoring them to their former state of grace and peace? How did Adam and Eve react when confronted with the idea of marriage? How many children did they have? What were their names? And could the woman that Cain was destined to marry actually have been his brother Abel's twin sister?

In our next installment, we begin in the palace of Nimrod, the first great rebel against God after the Flood. There, young Abraham is born to Nimrod's chief prince, Terah, as an awesome celestial event heralds his birth, thereby inaugurating the next phase of God's remarkable deliverance of Adam and his descendants.

For this adventurous tale, we Westerners are greatly indebted to one man: Moses Samuel, the British author and translator of Hebrew works, who, in 1838, gave us the first English translation of *The Book of Jasher*. Thanks to Samuel, we can now understand, like never before, what really inspired the one person, who, in the face of such opposition and peril, survived to spawn the mightiest lineage the world has ever known.

Nearly everyone has heard the story of the man whom God told to sacrifice his son. Their tale is an epic one, retold in countless ways, with nearly every culture ever since incorporating some form of sacrificial offering in order to ensure the clan's ultimate survival. But what does tradition have to say about why Abraham seemed so willing to do something like that in the first place? Unfortunately, except for the brief passages in *Genesis*, tradition does not have much to say. Did Abraham always have such unswerving faith? If so, then why was he so devoted to God? And if not, what enabled this one man, apart from all other men, to become the father of faith?

In *The Book of Tales*, we discover for ourselves how God guided Abraham throughout every stage of his life, from rescuing him as a young man from the furnace of Nimrod, right up to the time when He asked him to sacrifice Isaac on Mount Moriah. What role did Noah and Shem play in the development of Abraham during his formative years? What lengths did Nimrod take to kill Abraham before he could fulfill his world-changing destiny? How did Satan react to Abraham's attempts to sacrifice his son to God? Was Isaac really unaware of his father's intentions as he was being led up that mountain? And when Abraham told Pharaoh that Sarah was his sister was his story really so far from the truth, considering that she was his brother's daughter?

Finally, in our third installment, we come face to face with the most amazing chapter in God's rescue effort yet, the very hour when the ransom for that deliverance was to be paid in full. In it, we confront many of the lesser-known facts behind the trial and execution of Jesus of Nazareth, as well as the startling events that took place afterward, despite every attempt to erase them from the pages of history.

For this most pivotal tale of all, the Protestant West owes much to a trio of men. They are William Wake, a British clergyman who went on to become the archbishop of Canterbury; William Wright, a British Orientalist and professor of Arabic at Cambridge; and B. Harris Cowper, a British archeologist, historian, and translator. In 1693, Wake gave us the first English translation of *The Gospel of Nicodemus*, while in 1865, Wright gave us *The Letters of Herod and Pilate*, and in 1867, Cowper gave us *The Epistles of Pilate to Caesar*, *The Trial and Condemnation of Pilate*, and *The Death of Pilate, who Condemned Jesus*. Woven together into a continuous dramatic narrative, these texts combine to reveal an unparalleled glimpse into the hearts and minds of the players who took part in the most notorious trial ever recorded.

There is hardly a person alive who is not familiar with the scene of Pontius Pilate washing his hands before the angry mob that is demanding the death of Jesus. The story is renowned throughout the annals of world history, with every culture around the globe incorporating some version of the dying-and-rising hero providing his life for the sake of the group's continued existence. But what does tradition have to say about why Pilate really sentenced Jesus to die? Unfortunately, except for the brief passages in *The Gospels*, tradition has little to say. Did Pilate condemn Jesus because he was trying to avoid another bloody riot on his watch? Or was he really acting on orders from Rome, which required the pitiless end to all threats to the Empire? And when his wife tried to warn him about the innocence of the Man he was about to have crucified, did Pilate really believe her after all?

In *The Book of Tales*, we discover for ourselves why Pontius Pilate acted the way he did during his encounters with Jesus, from his early career as a ruthless politician, right up to his reaction to the machinations of the entrenched religious leaders in Judea at that time. Were the disciples of Jesus the only people who believed in Him or supported His cause? How did Satan react to Jesus' attempts to sacrifice His own life? What was Jesus really doing during the three days and nights prior to His resurrection? Was Jesus the only person Who was reported to have risen from the dead? And after everything was said and done, what was Pilate's real motive in turning Jesus over to a Roman crucifixion, even after he had openly declared Him innocent of every charge?

Beyond the Veil

THE BOOK OF TALES, then, is no ordinary rewriting of the same old stories. In this telling, for example, we find that, contrary to popular opinion, Enoch not only walked and talked with God, but he also left behind a written record of the history of all mankind's activities — past, present, and future. Adam and Eve were never totally abandoned by God just because He expelled them from the Garden of Eden. Isaac was very much aware of what his father Abraham was doing when the two of them made their way to the top of Mount Moriah. And Tiberius Caesar actually put Pontius Pilate on trial for allowing Jesus to be railroaded by religious leaders under his jurisdiction.

These are just some of the amazing things you will discover for yourself in *The Book of Tales*, where you will finally find answers to questions you have wondered about your whole life, not to mention a few that you never even thought to ask. Like marvelous links in a chain of time, these *Tales* provide an unprecedented view into our historic past, unlike anything you have ever experienced before. So prepare yourself for a starkly original journey beyond the veil of time and space; because instead of analyzing the past in a merely abstract manner, the reader of this book will experience firsthand the events of antiquity through the very lives of those who have inhabited our biblical past. As nearly as possible, these stories are authentic representations of a timeless wisdom that has been handed down from generation to generation. They are, in fact, stories from a land where all legends and lore collide. They are tales of forever.

The time has come, then. The players are assembled, the lines have been rehearsed, the stage has been set. All that remains is for you to begin the journey, one page, one chapter, one book at a time. And now, the curtain rises.

BOOK TWO

Oh, my children, listen to what I have to say, because I've been allowed to come to you today so that I may make an announcement, not from my lips but from those of the Lord Himself—all that is, and was, and will be, until the Day of Judgment.

Enoch the Scribe, *The Secrets of Enoch*

The Man from Forever

Adapted from
The Secrets of Enoch,
also called
The Slavonic Enoch
or *The Second Book of Enoch*

God took Enoch, Gerard Hoet, 1728

The Man from Forever

A Hole in Space and Time

THIS IS THE STORY of a man who soared through a hole in space and time, where space was without limit, and time stood still. There was only the man and his journey, and this journey took him to a land where all legends and lore collide, where the man found himself standing before the Face of God, the Lord of Eternity Who holds space and time in the palm of His hand.

When this man asked the Face why he was there, he was told simply that he should tell the tales of forever. Then he was given a pen of quick-writing and told to write them down as fast as he could. So for what seemed like but a moment, the man beyond time wrote down everything he heard. He wrote stories of everyone's lives, of those who *have* lived, of those who *were* living, and of those who *were yet to* live.

And after he was done writing, he awoke on his couch, wondering what he should do next. Until finally, he realized that he had no choice in the matter, because unless he did what he was supposed to do, no one else would ever know the tales of forever, because no one but him had witnessed the things that he had. So he looked in the mirror and understood what he alone had to do, because he recognized the face staring back at him, and it was the face of the man from forever.

Sparks and Secrets

IN THE SEVENTH generation from Adam, one of his sons became famous, not only for his skill as a master craftsman but also for his remarkable wisdom. His name was Enoch. Living before the Great Flood, in the days when people often lived more than nine hundred years, Enoch was still a young man at the age of three hundred and sixty-five.

One afternoon, he was at home, relaxing on his couch, when he fell fast asleep. As he slept, a horrible depression overwhelmed him, and he began to weep. Without warning, two angels materialized at the end of his couch. Their faces glowed like the Sun, their eyes flashed like beacons, and they had brilliant wings of gold.

"Wake up, Enoch," said one of them.

Confused and groggy, Enoch opened his eyes. Jumping to his feet, he stared oddly at the two luminous beings standing before him. "Hello, uh, how are you?" he stammered.

"Fine, thank you," replied the second one politely. "My name is Sariel,

45

and this is my associate, Raguel."

Enoch nodded nervously. "Nice to meet you both." Rubbing his eyes, he blinked widely.

"We're very sorry for intruding unannounced like this," said Raguel. "Did we startle you?"

"Oh, no, of course not." Enoch did his best to stay calm in the presence of this disturbing pair of visitors. "How can I help you two?"

"Relax, Enoch," said Raguel. "There's no need to be afraid. The Eternal God has sent us to tell you something."

"What is it?" asked Enoch, gulping in anticipation.

"Today," replied Sariel, "you'll be going up to Heaven with us."

"But how is that possible?" wondered Enoch, bewildered at the very idea.

Sariel extended his arm toward Enoch. "Take hold of my cloak and find out."

His eyes wide with anticipation, Enoch reached out his trembling hand and placed it on Sariel's luminous sleeve. Then the two angels abruptly extended their tremendous white wings, and up they went with Enoch in tow.

TO HIS AMAZEMENT, Enoch was instantly lifted through Earth's atmosphere, and rising upward to the first level of Heaven, he saw a vast crystal sea, even greater than that of the Earth's ocean.

Soaring onward to the third Heaven, with the aid of his winged escorts, Enoch caught sight of a beautiful garden with an amazing tree growing at its heart. Around the tree flew a swarm of bright, white angels, flitting about, limb to limb, manicuring the exquisite leaves and robust fruit, which resembled delicate grapes. From the lips of these angels came beautiful singing, more incredible than any human voice could have ever sung.

Enoch turned to his angelic guides. "Is that really what I think it is?"

The angels both nodded.

"Yes, it is," said Sariel. "The Tree of Life."

"And those are the three hundred angels," added Raguel, "who tend to the tree, day and night, without end."

The singing of those angels sent out such a hypnotic effect that Enoch became transfixed by it. "Remarkable," he murmured.

Onward, the two angels carried the awestruck Enoch, upward still, as yet another astonishing sight rolled past his eyes. Vast columns of warrior angels, armed with jewel-encrusted shields and swords, glided past the trio. They, too, sang a remarkably haunting song as they went by.

"This can't really be happening, can it?" Enoch asked incredulously. "I must still be asleep on my couch. I'm dreaming all this, right?"

"No, of course not, Enoch," replied Sariel.

"You are *seeing*." Raguel smiled back knowingly.

"And who are these troops I'm seeing, then?"

"These are the legions of the Almighty," said Raguel. "They all march under the banner of a single Ruler, the Omnipotent Lord, the King of Heaven."

Astonished, Enoch shook his head. "Simply amazing."

Still, the trio continued to soar upward, until they reached the seventh Heaven. Fiery archangels flew about everywhere, darting every which way. Wherever Enoch turned, he saw the same thing, row after row of dazzling thrones. Upon each of them sat a ghostly apparition staring down at him with smoldering eyes.

"What is all this?" asked a wide-eyed Enoch.

"These are the dominions of the Lord," Sariel said, quite casually. "From them proceed the order and government of God."

Enoch was dumbfounded as he watched cherubims, seraphims and other strange angelic beings, with numerous eyes wrapped around their heads, flying all around him. Turning to his two traveling companions, he asked, "Are you sure we're in Heaven?"

Sariel smiled reassuringly. "Don't worry, Enoch. We're getting very close to God's throne, that's all. This is no place for ordinary humans. Look!" The angel pointed up, and Enoch craned his neck to see.

Above them and still at a great distance, a brilliant purple light beckoned them onward.

"It's so beautiful," Enoch said quietly. "Is that God's throne?"

Together, the angels nodded reverently.

"It is," Raguel stated, quite matter-of-factly.

"Is that where you're taking me?" wondered Enoch.

"That is where *you* will be going, yes," Sariel replied with a benevolent smile.

"But I don't understand."

"Not everyone is as lucky as you are, Enoch," said Raguel.

"What do you mean? I thought you were taking me to see the Lord."

"Yes, Enoch, we have been taking you there," Sariel assured him. "But we've only been allowed to bring you this far, and no further."

"Beyond this point, we're not permitted to venture at this time," Raguel explained.

"But why?" asked Enoch nervously. "I don't understand."

A tremendous gust of wind suddenly blew the two angels off into the distance.

"No, wait!" shouted Enoch. "Don't leave me!" Looking about, he realized that he was very much on his own, while still, all about him in the air, the frenzy of angelic flight carried on.

"What is that strange smell?" grumbled a cherubim as it buzzed past

Enoch.

A seraphim then flew by. "I think it's this human."

"A *human*!" groaned the cherubim. "Who let *him* in here?"

"Don't ask me," the seraphim snorted. "How should I know?"

Terrified, Enoch began to panic. "Now what am I supposed to do? Why is this happening to me? Please, Lord, help me."

The fiery cherubim flew right up to Enoch, sniffing at him disapprovingly. "You're not supposed to be here! Who let you in?"

"I was brought here by angelic escorts," replied Enoch.

The seraphim buzzed back. "You're an intruder, I tell you!"

"Human flesh is not allowed here," growled the cherubim. "Get out of here right now, or we're going to kill you."

"No, you can't do that!" exclaimed Enoch with a shudder. "I told you, I was brought here by two of God's angels. Honestly."

The cherubim eyed him suspiciously. "You're lying."

"No. I was invited here; really I was."

"*You*?" scoffed the seraphim. "Why you?"

"But I'm not sure why. They didn't say, exactly. They just told me the Eternal God had sent them to bring me here."

"Enough of your lies, human!" barked the seraphim.

The cherubim drew out a fiery dagger. "I say we kill him, and be done with it!" He hovered closer to Enoch and raised his blade, poising it to strike. And then a hand grabbed hold of the cherubim's wrist.

"No," said an angelic voice. "You'll do no such thing. Nothing will keep this chosen vessel of God from fulfilling his destiny."

Enoch turned and looked up into the eyes of a handsome archangel.

"Gabriel!" howled the seraphim.

"What are you doing here?" the cherubim exclaimed, releasing his dagger.

"Mind your own business!" snapped Gabriel. "Now all of you get out of here this instant, or else I'll kill you instead." Gabriel shoved the startled cherubim several feet away. "You hear me?"

"Yes, Gabriel, of course," replied the cherubim, blinking wildly. "Anything you say."

The whole group of bewildered angels instantly darted off, and Gabriel turned to Enoch, who was still obviously traumatized from his close call. "It's all right, Enoch. They won't bother you anymore."

"Thank you so much. Gabriel? Is that what the others called you?"

"Yes, that's right. I'm Gabriel. I was sent to help you in the rest of your journey to see the Lord."

"Oh, thank God you got here when you did. I was so worried. First, these two angels brought me here, and then, suddenly, they were gone. I didn't know what I was going to do next."

"Yes, well, you can relax now. I'm here. Are you ready to see the Lord, then?"

Enoch thought about it for several tense moments. Taking a deep breath, he carefully replied, "Yes, I think so; I do believe I am."

"Good, because it's time," said Gabriel, who then took hold of Enoch by the arm and gently carried him upward. Like two leaves caught in a breeze, the pair soared up through two more levels of Heaven before they finally reached their destination.

"Well, Enoch, here we are," continued Gabriel as he set Enoch down, "the tenth level of Heaven."

"Thank you, Gabriel, for all your help."

"You're welcome." The archangel smiled radiantly. "Goodbye for now." There was another gust of wind, and just as suddenly Gabriel was whisked away, leaving Enoch all by himself again.

Looking around, Enoch finally saw what he had come for; right before his very eyes was the dazzling throne of the Eternal One. Awestruck, Enoch gazed up at the Face of God, like molten iron, emitting sparks as it glowed, a Face as awesome as it was beautiful.

"Welcome, Enoch," said the Lord with a crackle of thunder.

Trembling, Enoch fell to his knees and bowed to the ground. "Lord, I am most honored to be here."

"Don't be afraid, Enoch. Stand and talk with Me."

Suddenly another archangel appeared, carrying a luminous robe and a jar of light.

"Here; Michael will provide you with some things to protect you while you're in My presence. He'll dress you in a special suit of My divinity and anoint you with the oil of My Spirit."

Reverently, Enoch rose to his feet and the archangel wrapped him with a robe, as dazzling as God's throne itself. Then Michael reached out his fingertip, glowing with a brilliant purple light, and touched Enoch's forehead, leaving a dab of glowing ointment, which quickly absorbed into his skin. Then with an eerie flash of white light, Michael vanished as quickly as he had appeared.

Inhaling deeply and exhaling with a sigh, Enoch cautiously looked up into the glowing Face. "Thank You for that, Lord; and thank You for inviting me here. What can I do for You?"

"I want you to listen to Me very carefully, Enoch, because I'm about to tell you things I've never even told the angels."

"Yes, Lord, I'm listening."

"Good, because I've never told the angels about their origins or described My endless realm to them. They understand nothing about My creation; but I have decided to tell you about it."

"Me? Why me?"

"I'm telling you because I require someone who will be faithful in all I ask him to do. Will you be that man?"

"I will, Lord. Just tell me what You want me to do."

"Your mission is a very straightforward one. I want you to write down everything I tell you. That way you'll be able to hand down this wisdom to your descendants."

"But how will I ever remember everything You tell me?"

With a blur, another angel streaked into view and stood next to Enoch. Bowing gracefully, he said, "Hello, Enoch."

"This is Pravuel," said the Lord. "As you can see, the swiftness of his intelligence excels beyond all my other archangels. His lightning hand will assist you in preparing the books I want you to write."

Enoch bowed to the archangel. "Glad to meet you, Pravuel. Thank you. It will be an honor to work with you."

"Now," crackled the voice of the Lord, "bring Enoch the pen of quick-writing."

A seraphim fluttered over to Enoch, and handed him an odd-looking writing utensil. Fascinated, Enoch examined the pen thoroughly. He was particularly intrigued by the tip of the device, which emitted a faint, purple glow. Then, a cherubim floated over with an endless stack of paper and set it in front of Enoch, who looked up expectantly into the smoldering Face of God.

"Are you ready, Enoch?" asked the Lord.

"Yes, sir, I am."

"Good. Then listen very carefully and use the pen I've given you to write down everything I'm about to describe."

As the Lord began to speak, the archangel Pravuel reached over and placed his hand on Enoch's hand while He dictated. As swiftly as his hand could move, Enoch began to write, page after page, chapter after chapter, book after book, mesmerized by everything he was hearing. His eyes were glued on those scalding lips, emitting so many sparks and secrets as yet un-imaginable to any mere mortal.

WITH NO REAL WAY OF knowing how long the Lord had spoken, Enoch watched as the scalding lips uttered their final word, and then Pravuel lifted his hand from Enoch's hand. As if awakened from a powerful daydream, Enoch refocused his eyes. He shook himself and looked back up into the awesome eyes of molten divinity. "Now what, Lord?"

"Well, to begin with: I want you to apply your mind, Enoch, and realize Who is speaking to you so you'll always treasure the books I've had you write."

"Of course, Lord, thank you. I'm truly honored. I'll always treasure them far above all things."

"Good. Now I want you to go with Sariel and Raguel. Take your books with you to Earth, and when you get back, I want you to tell your children all about what I've told you and all that you've seen, from the lowest level of Heaven to the pinnacle of My throne room."

"Of course, Lord, but pardon me for asking: What if I tell them everything You've told me, and they think I've lost my mind? Maybe they say I'm making it all up. Then what?"

"Just give them the books you've written, Enoch. When they read them, they'll know Me for the Creator, and they'll realize, once and for all, I am the God of the Universe."

Enoch's eyes lit up. "Of course. Why didn't I think of that?"

"Then," continued the Lord, "I want you to distribute your books from person to person, from nation to nation, and from generation to generation."

Enoch was awestruck. "Lord, how will I ever carry out such a grand plan as that?"

"Don't worry. I'll give you an assistant: Michael the archangel. He'll help you preserve all the books you've just written."

Bowing reverently, Enoch smiled sheepishly. "Thank you, Lord. You are way ahead of me, as usual."

"And just think, Enoch, someday there will come a unique generation that will descend from your ancestors, faithful workers of My pleasure, who do not acknowledge My name in vain. And from among that generation, there will be One Who will finally explain the meaning of the books you've written. What's more, those whom He'll teach will be instructed in the guardianship of the world."

Enoch nodded knowingly. "Yes, Lord, it will be such a wonderful day. I can't wait."

"In turn, they will then communicate those truths to a future generation, and when those people have had a chance to discover them, they'll be blessed even more than those who had read them in the beginning."

"Thank You, Lord, for Your words of truth." Again Enoch felt compelled to bow.

"Now, Enoch, I'll give you a period of thirty days to spend at home with your family. Tell everyone in your household they can all hear about what I've told you. That way they'll be able to understand I'm the only God Who exists. Then maybe they'll keep My commandments and begin to read the books you've written."

"Whatever You want, Lord. Just say the word."

"And after thirty days, I'll send My angels for you again. They'll take you from Earth and from your children, and bring you back to Me. Are you ready?"

Enoch nodded. "Yes, Lord, I am."

"Good, then the time has come for you to leave."

Another angel appeared at his side, more terrifying than any that Enoch had seen up to that point. As this menacing creature stood next to him, Enoch took a good long look. Astonishingly, this fearsome angel was covered in frost and snow. The angel slowly reached out an icy finger and touched Enoch's face, instantly freezing it.

"Don't be alarmed, Enoch," said the Lord. "If your face isn't frozen like this, no one will be able to look at you when you return to Earth, because no mortal man can endure the terror of the Lord, just as it isn't possible to endure a stove's fire or the Sun's heat." Then Enoch turned to see that Sariel and Raguel were at his side once again.

"Now, you two," continued the Lord, "take Enoch back to Earth so he can prepare for the determined day."

The two angels immediately took hold of Enoch and headed back down to Earth. By then, Enoch was so exhausted from his ordeal that he lost consciousness as Sariel and Raguel cradled him in their arms.

ARRIVING BACK AT Enoch's home, the angels gently returned their human cargo to his couch, and there he slept soundly for quite a while, until quite abruptly, Enoch's son Methuselah came bursting into the room where his father was still fast asleep.

"Father, you're back! Finally!"

Groggily, Enoch sat up on the couch. "Good God, Methuselah; what is it now?"

"Thank the Lord above. Pop, you're home!"

Blearily eyeing his surroundings, Enoch muttered, "Well, I'll be. So I am." Then he turned to Methuselah. "Son, have I got something to tell you. In fact, I want you to get the whole family together. I have something to tell everyone."

"I'll say. We thought we'd never see you again. You had us worried sick."

"Worried? Why? What are you talking about?"

"You were gone so long. Everyone thought you'd been killed by wild beasts or taken captive. Who knew what had happened to you?"

"But I was only gone a short time, a couple of hours, maybe. The most amazing hours a man could ever hope to experience, and everybody has to complain because I go missing for a little while. What's the problem?"

"A couple of hours?" blurted Methuselah, staring back at his father, quite incredulously. "Are you kidding me? Are you feeling all right?"

"Of course. I feel fine. There's nothing wrong with me. What are you going on about?"

"Father, you weren't gone for a couple of hours. You were gone for two months."

Enoch squinted oddly at the thought.

"Are you sure you're feeling all right?" Methuselah asked.

"What did you say?" murmured Enoch.

"I asked if you were feeling all right."

"No, no, no. Before that."

"I said, you've been gone for two months!"

"But how is that possible?" A peculiar smile slowly crept across Enoch's face. "Remarkable."

"And Pop?"

"Yes, son."

"Why is your face covered in frost?"

Enoch touched his cheek and examined the tip of his finger, which he could see was lightly covered in snow. "Simply remarkable," was all he said.

THE NEXT DAY, ENOCH was surrounded by a large crowd of people, including Jared, his father, Methuselah, his son, and Lamech, his grandson, along with their wives and children. Cradled in Enoch's lap was a large book.

"My beloved family, I've asked you all here today to tell you about something very important." Enoch caressed the book lovingly in his hands. "So, I'm hoping you'll at least consider what I'm about to tell you, inasmuch as it is in accordance with the Lord's will."

"Of course, Father, we'll listen," said Methuselah, as if speaking for the entire group, who were all nodding, eager to hear what the patriarch had to say.

"Wonderful. Well, you see: These things I have to tell you about," said Enoch, hesitating nervously, his fingers playing lightly across the binding of the book in his lap. "What I'm going to tell you is simply what I've heard from the Lord's own mouth during my absence. To you, it seemed as though I was gone for two whole months, but from my perspective, it felt like just a few hours. You all remember, don't you?"

"Of course, son," said Jared. "How could we ever forget? We were worried out of our heads. We didn't know where you'd gone."

"Well, now I'm here to tell you, Father. But I'm afraid you'll never believe me when I do." Enoch paused thoughtfully again as he carefully scanned the group that was looking at him with such trusting faces. "Does anybody here think I would ever lie about something that concerns the Lord and His inscrutable will?"

"Certainly not, Pop," replied Methuselah. "What on Earth would make you think that?"

Embarrassed, Enoch shook his head. "Because I still find it so hard to believe myself. One moment, I'm sure it happened, then the next moment, I'm sure I dreamt the whole thing. It's all so confusing."

"Don't worry about us, Grandpa," insisted Lamech. "Who are we to judge what did or didn't happen to you?"

"Thank you, Lamech," said Enoch with a sigh of relief. "What a wonderful thing to say. I can't tell you how glad I am to hear that."

"So tell us, Father," prodded Methuselah. "Where did you go that whole time? Please, don't keep us in suspense any longer."

"Certainly, son. I went to Heaven."

"Y—*you* what?" sputtered Methuselah. "Did you say you went to *Heaven*?"

Enoch smiled radiantly, suddenly captured in his recollection of the place. "Yes, Methuselah, that's exactly what I said."

"But how, Grandfather?" asked Lamech.

"With the help of God's angels, that's how. Certainly you don't think I got there under my own power, do you?"

Methuselah and Lamech exchanged a peculiar look, as did everyone else there, including their two wives, who leaned in toward one another.

In hushed tones, Lamech's wife asked, "He didn't say he went to Heaven, did he?"

"No, of course not," Methuselah's wife replied quietly. "He said he *dreamt* he went to Heaven, that's all."

"Oh, okay," said Lamech's wife with a sheepish grin. "For a second, I thought he said he actually went there."

And together the two women laughingly shrugged it off.

"But Grandfather," blurted Lamech, who then hesitated when he saw that his father Methuselah was holding up his hand to caution him.

"Never mind, son, just never mind," Methuselah said calmly. "Just let it go. Can't you see your grandfather has been through enough already?"

Lamech nodded obediently, and Enoch, still flush with excitement, never even noticed that everyone there was quite oblivious to the true significance of what he was trying to tell them.

"So you see, my children," continued Enoch, "it's just that what I'm about to tell you is not something I made up from my own imagination. It comes straight from the Lord Himself. Do you understand what I'm trying to say?"

Methuselah nodded tacitly. "Yes, Father, we understand. Go ahead, please."

"Good. Then today I'll be reading to you from one of the books I wrote while I was in the Lord's presence. Would you like that?"

The group chimed in unison. "Yes, please."

"Yes, Grandpa, please read to us from your book, won't you?" added

Lamech.

Enoch smiled like a doting father. "And so I will, just as the Lord has requested." Opening the book, he carefully slid his hand over the surface of its pages. "In fact, what I'm going to tell you is all about the past, it's about the present, and it's even about the future, right up until Judgment Day."

A hush fell over the entire group. All eyes were fixed on Enoch; and slowly, confidently, he began to read aloud from the book, just as he had been told by God's own mouth.

Dawn of Time

Adapted from

The Secrets of Enoch,

also called

The Slavonic Enoch

or *The Second Book of Enoch*

and

The First Book of Adam and Eve,

also called

The Conflict of Adam and Eve with Satan

Adam and Eve in Paradise, Jan Gossaert, 1527

Dawn of Time

Of Light and Darkness

I N THE BEGINNING the void of darkness was everywhere, and in that darkness there was only silence, all except, that is, for the still, small voice of God, which said, "Before anything visible ever existed, only We, the Godhead, used to traverse the domain of the invisible."

THEN CAME THE DAY when God decided to create the Universe, so He said, "Let the very darkest regions produce a division between the visible and the invisible." Suddenly a tremendous light burst forth, and a great age began.

After that, God decided to produce something from this interplay of light and darkness, so He spoke again: "Let the waters congeal into a dense core of molten glass." And as He saw the light separate further and further from the darkness, God said, "Let an atmosphere encircle this fledgling planet I will call Earth. Out of the ocean waves, let volcanic rock emerge, and from the hardened rock, let the dry land pile up, and the depths of this Earth, I will call the Abyss, or the Bottomless Pit."

ON THE SECOND DAY God took a tremendous lightning bolt, composed of both fire and ice, which neither can extinguish, and He carved out a chunk of molten rock. Then God said, "Having received its remarkable nature from the gleam of My eye, let this firestorm produce the ten invisible orders of angelic troops, with weapons and clothing forged in flames, and let every one of them remain under their own commanders, even as I have decreed."

But among the hierarchy of angelic warriors there was one who grew restless with the existing order, so he turned to one of his companions and asked, "Why should god be the only one who has a throne? If I wanted to, I could place my own throne far above the clouds. Then, I, Lucifer, the Morning Star, could achieve equality with the lord, and nothing would be impossible for me. And if you join me, I promise we'll all have the kind of fame and glory that god thinks is his alone to possess."

So a great war broke out in the heavenly realms between Lucifer's minions and God's angelic warriors, with Lucifer lassoing one third of the angelic troops with his tail and dragging them into his diabolical service. The war raged on for some time as both sides pushed back and forth with the ebb and flow of battle, but before long, God personally intervened, ejecting Lucifer and his legions from Heaven. Like a tremendous cascade of lightning bolts, they all fell, crashing down onto the surface of the Earth, sending shockwaves to its very core as they landed. All across the globe, every mountain and every valley melted away as the planet shuddered violently.

"And there you will remain," declared God, "to fly continuously above the Abyss until Judgment Day. "But no longer will you be seen in the shimmering beauty of your original form as Lucifer, the Morning Star. From now on, you'll be transformed into the epitome of ugliness and filth, to be forever known as Satan, the adversary, and your angels will no longer continue in their prior state of elegance and grace, doomed as they are to become as grotesque and horrid as their despicable master."

ON THE THIRD DAY God turned to renewing and reshaping the devastated Earth, which had nearly been obliterated as a result of the Fall of Satan and his crashing minions, so He said, "Let the mountains and valleys be restored, and upon them let the seeds in the ground produce their plant life with incredibly lush grass and fruitful trees. And let there be a beautiful Paradise in the East, near the border of this world." Instantly, a colossal hedge grew around Paradise, completely enclosing it, except for an ornate gateway that served as an entrance. Then, darting through the air, a fiery angel streaked to the gate of Paradise and took up position at the entrance, where he raised a flaming sword, standing at attention with a menacing look stamped on his face.

THEN THE FOURTH DAY arrived. "Let the Sun appear for illumination of the day," said God, and a great fireball congealed above the blue sphere of the Earth. "And let the Moon appear in the celestial vault to shine at night, along with a vast array of stars." So the day gave way to night, and a cool white orb appeared out of the midst of the inky blackness, followed by countless stars, glimmering all around it.

WHEN THE FIFTH DAY came, God said, "Let the oceans bring forth fish, the sky, vast numbers of birds, and the land, animals of every species." And as they appeared, they all began to spread out in every direction, through the sea, across the sky, and over the landscape.

ON DAY SIX GOD SAID, "Now it's time for Me to create mankind. I'll make Adam by forming him with seven consistencies: One, his flesh will be made from the ground." Immediately, in the dirt, the shape of a human being began to form, first the torso, then the arms and legs, and finally a head. As God described His intentions, the form of this human gradually became whatever He said. "Two, his blood will be made of the dew." Moisture congealed from the air about this nascent creature and flowed into its form. "Three, his eyes will be made from the Sun." A tremendous beam of light flashed into the space that was slowly forming into a face. "Four, his bones will be made from stone." Rock jutted up out of the ground and into his members. "Five, his intelligence will be from the speed of the angels and the clouds." What seemed like part angelic presence and part cloudy substance swirled into the human's skull. "Six, his veins and hair will be made from the grass of the Earth." Blades of grass grew up into this developing body to form the human's circulatory system and the hair on his head and skin. "And seven, his spirit will be made from My breath and the wind." Just then, an ethereal human face appeared above the figure that was still embedded in the ground and hovered there, face to face with the human's prostrate form lying below it. A blast of energy flowed like a gust of wind from the mouth of the hovering face, and the now-living human sucked in a deep breath from this energy-flow. Opening his eyes, he slowly sat up and rubbed his eyes as though he had just awakened from an ancient slumber. The human—Adam—looked around, surveying everything around him. Awestruck, he marveled at all the animals as they made their way about the primordial landscape.

"And I gave Adam seven natures," continued God. "His flesh is for hearing." Adam tilted his head as he heard the call of the animals around him for the very first time. "His eyes are for seeing." He squinted oddly at their unexpected forms. "For the spirit, there is the sense of smell." Inhaling deeply, Adam felt the air flowing through his nostrils and deep into his chest. "There are veins for touching, and blood for tasting." Adam touched his own face, then put his fingers in his mouth, like an infant acclimating itself to its newborn existence. "He has bones for endurance." Adam stood to his feet and took his first, feeble step, testing the solid ground beneath him. "And finally, with his intelligence, there comes enjoyment." Feeling the dirt between his toes, Adam realized that there was a difference between it and himself. He smiled proudly as he made his way about this new world, inspecting each and every thing he encountered, from the tiniest insects to the largest mammals.

"So in the creation of this human, I'd conceived a cunning thing," continued God, "having formed him with both visible and invisible natures, and now his very being reflected that fact, too. He understood speech like a created being, and was fragile in his greatness, yet mighty in his frailty. I placed him on Earth to be a kind of 'second angel,' if you will. Regal and supreme, I appointed him to be king over this planet and to possess My wisdom. In fact, there was nothing like him among any of My creatures that I'd created to that point."

Looking skyward, Adam was amazed at the sight of so many stars, still faintly flickering in the early morning hours, stretching as far as the eye could see. "And because the name of this first human was derived from the four cardinal points of the Earth, I appointed four special stars for him." Then, four points of light, more brilliant than all the rest, streaked across the sky. A mesmerized Adam watched as each star took its new position, one soaring to the east, one to the west, one to the south and one to the north.

"Then I showed Adam two ways of life, one of light and one of darkness, and I explained to him what was good and what was evil so that I would be able to find out whether or not he really loved Me. I also wanted to find out who among his descendants would love Me or hate Me, because I understand all too well their true nature, even though they never have. Even worse, because they're so ignorant of their genuine selves, they'll sin even more, and in the end, what is left for them after they've sinned, except death?"

AFTER A BUSY MORNING of investigating his new surroundings, Adam sat down awhile, enjoying the afternoon breeze as it gently blew through his hair. Suddenly he grew so tired that he had to lie down.

"What's wrong with me?" wondered Adam. "I feel so strange."

Slowly closing his eyes, he fell into a deep sleep. As he lay there, a hand suddenly appeared next to his right side, which reached out with its forefinger and caused an incision to appear between Adam's fifth and sixth rib. Then from out of the incision came one of his ribs, which the hand set onto the ground next to the dozing man. Gradually, this rib absorbed into the ground and it, too, eventually expanded into the shape of a human being, filling in, bit by bit, in the same fashion as God had done with Adam.

"And finally I created a woman to abide with Adam," said God. "That way death would overtake him through her, and taking the last word he spoke before he fell asleep, I named her Eve, which is to say, *mother*."

ADAM SLOWLY OPENED his eyes, and to his amazement, he realized that there was someone lying next to him. The woman opened her eyes, too, and sat up. As soon as she saw Adam, she smiled. Adam stood to his feet, and taking the woman by her hand, he helped her up. For the longest time that first couple gazed at one another; and then Adam spoke his first words to her. "Why do I know your name?" he asked with a perplexed smile. "Even though I've never heard it before, I feel like I know who you are. Isn't that odd?"

Smiling back at him, she nodded. Noticing the scar on his right side, she reached out and gently touched it.

"Yes, that's right," said Adam, as if recalling a dream of how this woman had miraculously appeared next to him. In his mind's eye, he glimpsed how God's finger had opened his side and sealed it back up with merely a gesture. "You're bone of my bone, and flesh of my flesh. You are Eve."

Again she nodded with a smile. "Yes, I believe you're right. How strange. I am Eve. And even though I've never seen you before, I, too, feel as though I know your name." Her lips slowly formed a single word as it came lilting from her delicate mouth. "Adam."

"Yes, Eve, yes; I am Adam," he said, as he reached out to embrace her.

TOGETHER, THE COUPLE strolled, hand in hand, through the lush land-scape of their garden home without a care in the world. As they did, they marveled at every sight that came into view, like children seeing the world for the very first time. One by one, Adam pointed to each creature that they encountered. "Before you came into my life, Eve, God inspired me to name every one of them. Look, there's Horse, over there is Sparrow, and here is Butterfly."

LATER, AS ADAM AND EVE sat down to relax on that very first evening of their being together, they looked up at the starry sky.

"I opened the Heavens so Adam and Eve could see the angels singing," said God. "Radiant light never stopped shining for them."

A tremendous array of beautiful angels suddenly appeared above them. Flying down to greet the couple, the angels seemed genuinely intrigued by these two humans, who likewise felt the same way about meeting them.

"BUT BEFORE LONG," continued God, "Satan, who had been doomed to hover the Abyss, began to take notice of this new couple, who now inhab-ited the world that had, until then, been his, and his alone, to command."

Turning to his lieutenant, the devil grumbled, "God must be trying to create a new world, because this Adam now appears to be king of the Earth. Now he's controlling everything that's happening here instead of me."

"What should we do, Master?" asked the lieutenant.

"Well, I may be a fugitive from Heaven, and god may have altered me so I'm no longer like the rest of his darling angels, but the nature of my un-derstanding is still the same! I still understand all too well that we've been condemned for our crime."

"But, Lord, what does that mean?"

"It means god is never going to forgive us, you fool! It means that unless we do something about this Adam, even this miserable excuse for a planet is no longer ours anymore."

"You mean god will never restore us to our previous condition? And this Adam is going to be our king from now on?"

"That's exactly what I mean, yes! God's completely abandoned us, and now it seems he's starting over with these *humans*!"

"But isn't there anything we can do to stop it?"

Satan's hideous face instantly lit up with a sinister smirk. "Maybe there is one thing we can do?"

"What? Will you enlist the aid of this Adam like you did with the angels before him? Make a pact with him to wage war with god again?"

Satan shook his head. "No, I'm afraid that's no longer a viable option. Openly confronting god again might turn out as badly as it did the last time we tried that. Then god would certainly banish us to a place even worse than this one."

"Worse than the Abyss?" blanched the stunned lieutenant.

"Much worse, yes," growled Satan, still mulling over the new plan in his twisted mind. "No, I think what we need this time is a much more subtle approach."

"What?"

"I propose an invasion."

"An invasion? But if Adam and Eve aren't willing to cooperate, won't they simply enlist god's help in the face of an invasion?"

Then turning to his lieutenant, Satan flashed a malignant grin. "Not the kind of invasion I have in mind, no."

SO, DISGUISED IN the shell of a beautiful serpent, Satan's first act was to seduce Eve, without directly confronting Adam, or even God, for that matter. And offering up the Forbidden Fruit for Eve to eat, she unwittingly took a bite, and as soon as she had, she persuaded Adam to eat as well.

"And even though I warned them never to eat the Fruit from the Tree of Knowledge, they ate it anyway," God said with a tremendous mourning in His voice. "And when they did, their eyes were truly opened. At that very moment, they began to die. So what choice did I have but to curse ignorance? I refused to curse what I had already blessed, so I didn't curse Adam or the Earth or the other creatures, but I did curse Adam's evil deeds and their result. 'You're made of the ground,' I told him, 'so you'll return to it when you die. I won't be destroying you but simply returning you to where I took you from. Then when I return, I can restore everything that you've lost.'"

A Promise of Days

FINALLY, THE SEVENTH day arrived, and God said, "But because of what they'd done, I only allowed Adam and Eve to remain in Paradise for five and a half hours before I forced them to leave."

As Adam and Eve were leaving the Garden of Eden, they came to its gate and stood there, frozen with fear. To their utter dismay, all they saw was an alien expanse spread out before them. Slowly, the despondent couple made their way forward, step by cautious step. Every direction they looked the ground was covered with stones, large and small. Dirt was everywhere.

"Oh, Eve, what have we done?" groaned Adam. "Until now, all we've ever known is our garden home. But just look at this strange place. I've never seen anything like it before."

"It's horrible, Adam," whimpered Eve. "I don't think I can go through with this. My heart is breaking."

Seized by a terrible dread, they both fell flat on their faces and died. But the eyes of God were watching them as they lay prostrate at the garden's gate, and in an instant, a handsome Man appeared at their side. Gazing down at the couple, His eyes beamed with a love and compassion that seemed to transcend time and space. He bent down, took Adam and Eve by the hand, and lovingly helped them to their feet. Still disoriented from their experience, they stood up and gazed into the face of this marvelous Man standing before them.

"Who are You?" asked Adam, obviously sensing this Man was someone special.

"Actually, I have many names," He replied with a quiet reassurance, "as the time and circumstance dictates. In your case, you will know Me as the Word of God."

"What just happened to us?" asked Eve as she oddly examined her hands, then touched her face as if to confirm that she was really alive.

"I'm afraid you died," replied the Word, quite nonchalantly.

"Died?" wondered Adam. "But why? And if we died, how come we're talking to You right now?"

Amused, the Word smiled warmly. "Unfortunately, those are difficult questions to answer, but I'll try to explain all this in a way you might understand. First of all, you died because that's what God decreed for you and your children as soon as you ate from the Tree of Knowledge, and the reason you're talking to Me now is because I raised you from your state of death so you can fulfill the days God has decreed for you on this Earth."

Adam and Eve exchanged a peculiar look.

"So we actually died, but you restored our life again," said Adam, trying to work out this mystery in his confused mind. "Is that what You're saying?"

"It is, yes."

"Then does that mean You'll be restoring us to our garden home now, too?"

With deeply sad eyes, the Word gazed back at these two for several moments. "No, Adam, I'm sorry. Just because I raised you doesn't mean I'll be returning you to the garden right now."

"No?" Heartbroken, Adam nearly fainted. "But why not, Lord? You don't want us to die again out here in this wilderness, do You?"

"Oh, Adam, don't despair," replied the Word. "Rest assured; I haven't completely abandoned the two of you. I promise, someday I'll rescue you both from all of this, and then you can return to the garden home you love so much."

"Really?" said Adam with a tremendous sigh of relief. "Oh, thank You, Lord. Did you hear that, Eve? We're going to be rescued after all."

"Yes, Adam, I heard," replied Eve, sounding somewhat skeptical. "But when?"

"Someday, Eve," said Adam, shrugging his shoulders. "How should I know? Someday soon, I imagine."

"Until then," continued the Word, "I've appointed this Earth to have hours and days and years transpire upon it. And you and your descendants will live here until the determined time is completed. Then, I'll return to rescue you and all your faithful children."

"When, Lord?" wondered Adam. "When will that be?"

"After five and a half days, Adam."

Adam looked as confused as ever. "But, Lord, I don't understand what You mean by five and a half days. You mean we're going to be rescued after just five and a half days. Is that what You're telling us?"

"Not exactly, Adam, no," said the Word. "The days I'm speaking of represent days from My point of view. You and your descendants will experience these five and a half days from your perspective as 5,500 years. Then I'll come to rescue you and your righteous descendants. But I already told you all about this before, Adam, just as you two were leaving the garden. Don't you remember?"

Adam searched his mind, trying to recall what the Word was describing. "Not really, no." But mental images began to flash into view. "Wait, I do remember something."

In his mind, Adam could see himself, walking side by side with Eve as they were making their way toward the garden gate. As they walked slowly past the Tree of Knowledge, he remembered how it looked, recalling in vivid detail just how much it had changed. Now, it was withered and dry. Adam trembled as he approached the tree and fell at its foot, but suddenly the Word of God was there to gently pick him up.

"Yes, Lord, I remember now," exclaimed Adam. "I remember how You first told me about Your promise to rescue us after five and a half days." Then turning to Eve, he asked, "Don't you remember, Eve?"

"No, Adam, I don't."

"But you must. You were there, too."

But Eve despondently shook her head. "I'm sorry, but I don't remember."

Adam then turned to speak with the Word but found that He had vanished. "He's gone, Eve. Now what should we do?"

"How should I know, Adam? I'm just as confused as you are."

Quite reluctantly, the couple turned from the gate of their old home and started out into the forbidding landscape of their new home.

THE FIRST THING Adam and Eve noticed, having ventured eastward from the garden, was a vast ocean that stretched as far as the eye could see. Stepping up to the shore, they found the water was so clear that they could see into the very depths of the Earth.

"In fact," said God, "the water in this ocean was still so pure, one could even drink it, and if someone was completely stained, washing in it would make them as clean and pure as it was."

As the couple gazed out across the vastness of the sea, their eyes peered further and further into the distant horizon, where it appeared that this ocean was reaching upward to the edge of the sky, and from there it appeared to envelop the entire world in a tremendous canopy of water.

"For My own pleasure," continued God, "I created this sea because I knew that Adam and Eve would fall from grace, and after their banishment from Paradise, others would be born, and faithful ones from among them would die. But on the last day, I would reunite their souls with their flesh, and let them bathe in that ocean so they could all be cleansed from their sins."

Just then, an angel appeared and pointed for Adam and Eve to walk in the other direction. "I'm sorry to inform you, but God doesn't want you to stay here."

"But why?" asked Adam, shrugging his shoulders. "This seems like a perfectly good place to live."

"He's worried if you live here in the East, then you might try to wash yourselves in this ocean before the appointed time, and you'll be cleansed from your sins, forget the crime you've committed, and no longer contemplate your punishment."

Saddened by this, the couple turned and started walking the other direction.

AS THEY DREW NEARER to the garden, Adam and Eve could see two more angels, one standing at its northern edge and another to the south. Both were obviously poised as guards, and both were pointing the couple in a westerly direction.

"As for the northern or southern sides of the garden," said God, "I didn't want Adam and Eve to live there, either, because whenever the winds blew in their direction, it would have brought them the sweet smell of the trees in the garden, and smelling their lovely fragrance might cause them to forget about their disobedience, in which case they might never be cleansed from their crime."

Without a word of protest this time, Adam and Eve continued past the garden, traveling along the southern edge so they could at least catch a glimpse of the entranceway, and silently they continued onward to the western frontier of this new territory.

"FINALLY," CONTINUED God, "because I govern everything in a way that only I understand, I made Adam and Eve live on the western border of the garden, where the land was broad, in a cave, hewn out of solid rock."

Having arrived at this cave, Adam and Eve met another angel standing at the entranceway, but instead of barring their way, this angel was beckoning them to enter. "Welcome, you two. This is where God wants you to live. Come inside and make yourselves comfortable."

The couple cautiously stepped up to the mouth of the cave and hesitated as if frozen with indecision.

"Oh, Adam, I'm not so sure about this," moaned Eve. "Do we really have to live in there?"

"You heard the angel. This is where God wants us to live. So I guess that's all there is to it."

"But do we have to go in right now? Can't we look around a little while before we go inside?"

Adam shrugged. "I don't see why not. Let's go, then. Maybe we'll feel better about going in when we come back later."

Relieved, Eve nodded, and then the two of them turned and walked away.

ADAM AND EVE WANDERED aimlessly until, much to their surprise, they found themselves very close to the garden gate, where an angry looking cherub buzzed about with his flaming sword. The cherub glared fiercely at them with his sword raised, ready to strike.

"Hey!" shrieked the angel. "You two aren't allowed to be here! Leave this place before I kill you where you stand!"

Paralyzed by fear, the couple fainted, falling flat on their faces, but the cherub felt sorry for them, so he lowered his sword and flew up toward Heaven.

"LORD, I FOUND ADAM and Eve snooping around the entrance to the garden," said the cherub to the molten Face of God. "And when I ordered them to leave, they collapsed, dead away. Did I do the right thing?"

"You've done well, My faithful servant," replied the Face.

"What should I do now?"

"Return to your post, and I'll send My Word to resolve the situation."

SO THE CHERUB returned to the entrance of the garden, and suddenly the Word of God appeared where Adam and Eve lay prostrate. Sadly looking down at their motionless bodies, the Word shook His head. "What am I going to do with you two?" Then He reached down, restored their lives, and helped them to their feet.

"Lord, thank you so much for coming to our rescue," Adam said as he wiped himself off. "We were just wandering around, and before we knew it, we'd gotten too close to the garden gate. We're so sorry if we made You angry. Please forgive us."

"Never mind that now. Just promise Me you won't let this happen again."

"Yes, Lord, we promise," insisted Adam. "It's just that we're so miserable here in this new world. We miss our old home so much."

"I understand. But didn't I already tell you two I was going to save you after five and a half days?"

The couple nodded timidly.

"So relax," continued the Word, "and live in the cave like I asked you. Can you do that for Me?"

They nodded again and replied as one: "Yes, Lord."

"Good. Before you know it, everything you both desire will be restored to you again, and all the misery and sadness you're enduring now will just be a distant memory." And with that, the Word of God vanished.

Adam and Eve looked at each other and smiled reluctantly. "Did you hear that, Eve? I'm beginning to think God really is serious about rescuing us someday."

"Yes, Adam, I heard. The only problem is we don't know how long that *someday* is going to be, do we?"

Adam nodded meekly. "No, but still, something tells me it's going to happen. Our old life isn't so far away after all."

Enemy Within and Without

MEANWHILE, SATAN and his cadre of demons sat watching Adam and Eve from a distant hillside. "Can you believe those two?" groaned the devil. "What spoiled brats they turned out to be. I just don't get it. What does god see in them, anyway?"

"I think he just likes to make things that remind him of himself," replied his lieutenant, quite matter-of-factly. "You know, little versions in his own image that he can boss around and make do stuff."

Amused, Satan smirked. "Well, well, my infernal lieutenant. How clever you turned out to be."

Proud of himself, the lieutenant turned to one of his fellow demons and elbowed him in the side. "See, I told you I was smart."

"Tell me, then, if you're so clever," continued the devil. "What do you propose we do to rid ourselves of these despicable, little vermin before they infest every square inch of what's left of our Universe? Can you tell me that?"

For several tense moments, the lieutenant mulled the question over in his ugly mind. "Well, let's see, now that god has kicked them out of his presence, I say they're easy pickings. I say we go down there right now, rip their hearts out, and eat them while they watch."

Relishing the thought, the other demons howled with grisly delight. Satan, however, was clearly unimpressed. "And you think god will just sit back and let it happen, do you?"

"It's worth a try, isn't it? He is still angry with them, isn't he?"

"Of course he is. But if you've noticed, even after I went to all the trouble to get them kicked out of the garden, he's still helping them. What makes you think he won't just give them new hearts once you've eaten the old ones?"

"Hmmm, I never thought of that," mumbled the lieutenant.

"And if god did that for them," interjected another demon, "just imagine how grateful they'd be to him."

"You see?" blurted Satan. "Now that's exactly what I'm talking about! Open warfare is futile! How many times do I have to tell you that?"

"Well, if we can't overwhelm them with blatant violence," muttered the lieutenant, thoroughly vexed, "then what can we do?"

"We do the only thing we *can* do," the devil replied slowly, thoughtfully. "We go underground."

BACK TO THE ENTRANCE to their cave, Adam and Eve were still quite frustrated as they stood there, staring bleakly at its cavernous mouth, trying desperately to work up the nerve to go inside.

"Adam?"

"Yes, Eve. What is it?"

"Why do I get the feeling it wants to eat us alive?"

"What a strange thing to say." Adam turned to Eve with a peculiar look on his face. "What made you think of something like that?"

Eve shrugged. "I don't know. I just looked at it, and the thought struck me, that's all. Why?"

"Because for a moment, I felt the same way; as if it wanted to tear into our flesh and devour us."

"And now?"

"Now … it's passed. Now, there's just the sense of a mindless void … dark and lonely … waiting for us inside this cave."

"Oh, Adam. I'm not sure which is worse, being eaten alive or swallowed by the dark loneliness."

"Well, there's one way to find out," murmured Adam, and then he cautiously ventured forward through the craggy mouth of the cave, followed timidly by Eve.

Once inside, Adam was clearly dismayed by what he saw. "Just look at this place, Eve! It's so small! This place pales in comparison to the expanse of our garden."

"This isn't a home," Eve whimpered. "It's a prison."

"We used to have the Lord's mercy overshadowing us, but now all we have to shelter us is this slab of stone."

"And it's so dark in here. What's happened to our eyes? We used to be able to see angels singing in Heaven; but not anymore."

"Now our eyes are merely flesh, Eve. Now there's nothing but this gloomy cave to look at."

"Adam, do we really have to live in this cave for the rest of our lives? I feel like I'm going to suffocate."

"But we have to. God's ordered us to live here. And if we don't, we'll be in danger of being rebels all over again."

"Please, can't you at least ask God to let us live somewhere else while we wait for Him to rescue us?"

So Adam looked up at that rocky ceiling. "Oh, God, please release us from having to live in this cave. We don't want to stay under this overhanging rock anymore. We can't see the sky or any of Your creatures inside this place." Agonized, he began to beat his chest with such force that he abruptly dropped dead.

A devastated Eve began to weep. "Oh, God, it's true. We've gone from light to darkness all because of what I did, but please don't hold it against me forever. Just look at how Your servant Adam has fallen. Please restore his life, won't You? Don't leave me in this dungeon all alone. But if You decide not to raise him, will You at least take my life so I can be like him?"

She wept so miserably that soon she fell onto Adam's motionless body and died, too.

Then the Word of God appeared and, with merely a touch of His hand, revived Adam and Eve. Slowly, the couple got to their feet and wiped themselves off.

"Thank you, Lord, for coming to help us," Adam said with a sigh of relief.

"Have you come to take us somewhere else to live besides this cave?" asked Eve.

"I'm sorry, Eve, but that's not why I came."

Adam and Eve exchanged a distressed look.

"But why not?" moaned Eve.

"Stop it, Eve," said the Word. "What makes you think I'm not as upset as you are about all this? You think I'm happy you both chose to disobey Me? You think I wanted you to leave the garden?"

"No, I guess not," muttered Eve, sadly hanging her head.

"Of course not," He continued. "And now you'll simply have to get used to it. I didn't choose this destiny for you; you did. You defied Me because you wanted divinity and greatness, but I took away your luminous nature and made you come here. If only you hadn't eaten that fruit in the first place. I told you not to go near that tree, didn't I?"

Dolefully, the couple nodded.

"There were so many other trees in the garden!" lamented the Word. "But that damned Satan; he just had to make *that one* seem so much more appetizing, until finally you gave in and ate from it."

"But, Lord," groaned Adam, "how could eating something so small cause such a huge calamity?"

"Because when you ate, you were actually cooperating with Satan, a diabolical creature who, though originally created for an awesome purpose, chose instead to scorn Me and reject My first plan for him."

"You mean like us," mumbled Adam. "Don't You?"

"Yes, Adam, I'm afraid so. And because you listened to him, I've allowed the same suffering I unleashed on him to come upon you as well."

"So You do intend to wipe us out after all," replied Adam, thoroughly disheartened.

"Of course not, Adam; I'm the Creator. I would never create living beings simply for the sake of destroying them. But if they manage to make Me angry enough with their persistent rebellion, I will reprimand them with terrible plagues; that is, until they really want to change their ways."

"B—*but*, Lord, we *do* want to change our ways," stammered Adam. "We *have* changed. We realize how badly we've behaved and promise to never doubt what You tell us, ever again."

"Yes, Lord, Adam is right. We're so sorry we didn't trust You before. We really want to prove to You we can do better next time. Will You please give us another chance?"

"Of course, you two, you know I will," continued the Word. "Now remember: I've confirmed My promise with you, and I'll never forget it. But by the same token I can't let you back into the garden until after My contract of five and a half days is completed. So please, for your own sakes, stop trying to persuade Me to do something you know I won't do. Is that clear?"

Together, Adam and Eve replied, "Yes, Lord."

"And Lord," continued Adam. "Before we got kicked out of the garden, remember how all the animals were under my control?"

"Of course I do, Adam. Why do you ask?"

"It's just that ever since we disobeyed You I keep having the strangest feelings. It's like Eve and I are being watched or, worse, hunted. I'm worried one of these days an animal is going to try to eat us. Does that make sense?"

"Of course, Adam, I understand. And you're right. The world you're living in now is quite different from the one you used to know. Since your fall, the creation has suffered along with your rebellion. Even the animals have changed. But don't worry; I'll make sure they realize they're not to harm you or any of your righteous descendants."

TWO BY TWO, MALE AND female, the animals began to approach Adam and Eve, respectfully bowing before them. Among the more ferocious species came lions, bears, crocodiles, jackals, and wolves.

"Greetings, Adam," growled the lion. "God has instructed us to appear before you today."

"He wants us to give you our solemn assurance," grunted the bear. "So we will."

"As long as we're never attacked by you and your kind," snapped the crocodile, "you need never fear us."

"If you promise not to hunt us," yelped the jackal, "we promise never to harm you."

"If this is agreeable to you," snarled the wolf, "then we'll go in peace today with an understanding between us all."

In response, Adam and Eve bowed to the animals.

"We, too," said Adam, "pledge to never attack your kind without provocation, and we'll strive to co-exist in harmony as long as we remain together on this Earth."

"Agreed," the animals said with one voice. Then, they all left the couple in peace.

From a distance, however, the serpent was watching everything with utter disdain. "Just look at the way those pathetic creatures have all prostrated themselves before these humans. What a complete waste of time. What are they thinking? Who is Adam that we should bow down to him? Even God has abandoned him. He's nothing but a miserable animal like us now, just waiting for the day he becomes food; food for me, perhaps. What I wouldn't do to exact my revenge for what's happened to me."

"Revenge, you say?" asked a disembodied voice.

"Who said that?" snapped the startled serpent, his head darting about in an effort to locate the source of the voice. "Where are you? Show yourself this instant!"

Slowly, the hideous, black eyes of the devil materialized before the serpent. "Here I am, Serpent. Remember me?"

"You?" sputtered the serpent. "Why should I remember *you*?"

Then, as if to prepare the serpent for what he was about to see, Satan gradually materialized the rest of his body, bit by dreadful bit. Soon there stood before the dumbfounded serpent a monster of ghastly proportions. As though he were a twisted conglomeration of every ravenous animal rolled into one, the devil's skin was coarse like a crocodile's, his fingernails sharp like a hawk's, face ragged like a wolf's, eyes steely like a leopard's, teeth jagged like a boar's, horns crooked like a dragon's, and wings leathery like a bat's.

"Now do you remember me, Serpent?" sneered the devil.

Momentarily taken aback, the serpent gulped ever so slightly. "Good grief, no, I do not. I've never laid eyes on you before; and believe me when I say, by the looks of you, I'd certainly remember if I had. What manner of species are you, anyway?"

With a cavalier wave of his paw, Satan scoffed, "Ah, that's not important. The important thing is how you *feel* right now. Do tell, Serpent. What will you do with that unquenchable rage welling up in your belly, every day, every hour, every minute?"

"My belly? What do you know of my belly? Or my rage, for that matter? What makes you such an expert of me?"

"Because I know all about you, Serpent, that's why. I know very well how you were once the most respected animal in all of god's creation; that is, until he changed you, made you different, *cursed* you. I remember when you were one of the most beautiful animals in the world, so lovely all the others were awestruck in your presence."

The serpent's head tilted, his eyes thinned, his forked tongue flicked at the air. "Yes, as I still do, each and every moment I breathe."

"But now, I'm afraid, you're the ugliest animal of all," continued Satan, honing every word as sharp as a dagger. "Slippery, cold-blooded, forced to crawl around on your belly like a lowly, miserable worm. Instead of eating the best foods and living in the nicest places like you used to, now you eat in the dirt, live in the dirt, breathe the dirt."

"How I loathe the dirt," hissed the serpent through clenched fangs.

"Your home, once a place where every animal would gather, has now been abandoned, scorned. Before, everyone used to come and drink wherever the serpent drank, but ever since god's curse made you venomous, they all flee as they see the meanest creature alive approaching the drinking hole."

The serpent's eyes grew wide with rage. "Now none of them will drink with me. Now everyone hates me! But why? What did I ever do to them? Nothing!"

LATER, ADAM AND EVE were just sitting in their cave, staring blankly at the walls.

"Oh, Eve, when we lived in the garden our hearts soared. We saw angels singing in Heaven. But now just look at us, staring at the walls, with God's entire creation hidden from view! What's wrong with us?"

Then the Word materialized there in the cave with them. "You're no longer under My control, Adam; that's what's wrong with you. As long as you were, you had a luminous nature inside you. That's why you could see so many amazing things."

"And now that we've been banished," muttered Eve, "we'll never see things the same way again, *ever*."

"But why, Lord?" asked Adam.

"Because your luminous nature has been removed. Now, you're mere flesh and blood. So from now on, you'll only be able to see things close to you." Then the Word vanished once again.

"Did you hear that, Adam?" Eve moaned as she began to pace nervously about. "We've been reduced to mere flesh … *flesh*. Here we thought we'd become like gods, and what has become of us? Flesh."

"Eve, please, we've got to learn to relax. We can't keep worrying so much about things we can't control anymore."

Halting in her tracks, she turned to him. "What is that supposed to mean?"

"It means we've got to accept what's happened to us. If we're going to survive this mess we're in, then we're going to have to make the best of it."

"I suppose so," Eve replied with a heavy sigh. "What should we do now?"

"I say we go for a walk. See what we can see; I don't know. Anything is better than hanging around this miserable cave."

SO THE COUPLE wandered about aimlessly and again, without their even realizing what they had done, they ended up back at the garden gate. Approaching very close, they gazed longingly at its enclosed walls, comprised of dense, thorn-covered shrubs.

Eve abruptly burst into tears. "Oh, Adam, I thought we told God we wouldn't keep trying to get back into the garden."

"We did," Adam replied sheepishly. "And we're—*we're* not."

"Then why are we here again?"

"But we're not trying to get back in, Eve. We're just looking around, that's all. We're out for a walk."

They slowly stepped away from the gate and walked up a hill near the eastern edge of the garden. From there, they could see a river that flowed right past a huge tree at the heart of the garden and branched out into four rivers, which all made their way in every direction, north, east, south and west. As it so happened, one of those rivers flowed under the garden wall and right past the couple on its way to the ocean in the East.

"Look, Eve, it's the Tree of Life," blurted Adam as he eagerly pointed. "You see it?"

"Of course I see it, Adam. What about it?"

"There's water flowing from its roots. See?"

Confused, Eve shrugged her shoulders. "Okay, so there's water coming from the tree. So what?"

"Well, if water is flowing from the Tree of Life and it connects with this river that goes past us here, then maybe this water will restore us to life."

But as they looked closer, they could see that the water flowing from the roots of the Tree of Life was not moving in their direction; it was moving away from them, turning back toward the garden's interior.

"I'm afraid not, Adam. It doesn't connect with this river. It's going the other direction."

Deflated, Adam hung his head. "It's no use, then."

"But why? Water is water, isn't it? There's plenty of water flowing right past us. It comes straight from the garden. What's wrong with *it*?"

Adam then stepped closer to the water's edge in order to get a better look. "Nothing, I guess." As he stood there gazing at the river, Adam became hypnotized by its crystal-clear current flowing past him, swishing and gurgling, as if speaking some sort of secret language. "I think maybe you're right, Eve. Maybe this water really is special. Do you hear it? Do you hear what the water is saying?"

Stepping forward, Eve craned her neck. "Of course I hear the water, Adam, but I don't understand what it's saying."

Suddenly a thought struck Adam, and he began striking his chest with his fist. "Oh, Eve, why? Why did you have to bring such disaster on us? Why'd you do it?"

"Now what's wrong, Adam?"

"There *is* something special about this water, even if it's not the water from the Tree of Life. It was with us in the garden. It used to water every tree there, and now it's flowing right past us."

"So? What about it?"

"We never even noticed it back then, did we? But now, I can't stop thinking about what it means to us, means to our bodies."

"Adam, please," groaned Eve, who was becoming agitated. "What are you saying?"

"This water, Eve. This water is our life now. Without it, we'll die. Now, somehow, we're going to have to use it to help our bodies live."

Adam longingly stared down into the translucent waters where he could see fish swimming around. He leaned forward to get a closer look. "You see, Trout is smart enough to know he needs water to live." Then Adam jumped into the river and began flailing about.

"Adam, no!"

"Jump in, Eve. We need this water. Trust me."

So, Eve jumped in, too, and as soon as she did, she started flailing about as well. "Now what do we do, Adam?" she gurgled.

"How should I know? I just know we need this water to live."

Gasping for air, the couple began to sink, but fortunately for them the eyes of God were upon them as they slowly drowned. Soon an angel materialized at the river's edge, and pulling the couple out, he carefully laid their motionless bodies on the shore. The angel turned to see the Word of God appear next to him and said, "Lord, I'm afraid Your creatures have breathed their last breath."

Then the Word kneeled down next to Adam and Eve and, with a touch of His hand, revived them again.

Slowly, Adam stood up. "Lord, thank you so much for rescuing us."

"Adam, what were you doing in the water like that? You don't know how to swim, do you?"

"Not really, no. I just knew I needed this water somehow. I guess I didn't think it through."

"No, I guess not."

"It's just that while we were still in the garden we didn't even care about water. How come?"

"Because while you were under My control, you were like the angels, so you never *needed* to know anything about water. But now that you've disobeyed My order, you're never going to be able to live without it."

Adam turned to Eve with a knowing look. "See, Eve, I told you, didn't I?"

"If we need water so much," blurted Eve, "then what just happened to us? Water didn't seem to help us live at all."

Mulling this over, Adam turned to the Word. "She does have a point, Lord. How are we supposed to use this water, anyway?"

"You use it for drinking and washing. Drinking it will quench your thirst and help your bodies grow, and washing with it will cool you off and clean your skin. But now, because your bodies are just like the animals, you can't live in the water; only fish can survive in water without drowning."

"Like Trout, you mean?"

"Yes, like Trout." Then, the Word vanished.

Adam and Eve just stared at one another for quite a while.

"Oh, Adam, my mouth is so dry; my insides, too. What should we do? Should we at least try to drink some of this water?"

"I don't know, Eve," said Adam, skeptically shaking his head. "After what we just went through I don't think we should drink any of it."

"I guess you're right. Whether we throw ourselves in or whether we try to drink it, one way or the other we'll probably regret it in the end."

Nodding in agreement, Adam just walked away from the river without drinking, and Eve followed him without saying another word.

Fall of Night

LATER THAT DAY the serpent was slithering across the landscape, rooting about in the dirt. "I am so hungry. If only I had hands and feet like I used to, I could catch myself a decent meal." Frustrated, the serpent reared up on its tail and glared in every direction. "I've had it up to here with all this dirt. I'm so angry at those two humans, I could *spit!*"

"Then why not do something about it?" asked the disembodied voice.

"What's that?" The serpent's eyes darted in every direction. "Who's there?"

Once more the eyes of the devil slowly materialized before the serpent. "Just me again, Serpent."

"Good grief. Do you always have to make such a spectacle of yourself?"

With that, Satan faded completely into view, smirking with satisfaction. "So sorry; force of habit, I guess. But frankly, considering your own flare for the dramatic, I thought you, of all god's creatures, could appreciate it."

"What on Earth does that mean?"

"What with you being so special and all, so sophisticated; I thought you could appreciate my style."

"Style, yes, I see. Well, I suppose so. Tell me, then, what is the nature of your business? I'm very busy. I don't have all day to chit-chat, you know."

"Too busy groveling about in the dirt, you mean; too busy eking out a meager existence, subsisting on rats and sparrows."

"Enough already. I get your point. I still fail to see why you keep talking to me about all this. Why do you even care about my predicament?"

"I care because we have so much in common, because our fates are intertwined."

"Intertwined? Don't be ridiculous. I keep telling you. I don't even know who you are."

"Of course you do. We've been intimate, you and I."

"Intimate? Now you're getting downright revolting. Explain yourself before I bite your face off."

"Dear Serpent, you're hurting my feelings. I thought for sure you'd eventually remember me, but I guess I'll have to refresh your memory. I'm the one who made a pact with you to deceive the humans into eating the Fruit of the Tree of Knowledge. You were so jealous that Adam and Eve were getting all of god's attention you were more than willing to cooperate with me. Don't you remember?"

"You?" The serpent's eyes grew large and his tongued flitted frantically. "That was you? But you looked so different then. What happened? You were such a handsome fellow."

"Yes, well, sadly god and I have had our own falling out, much the same as you."

"And besides that, you lied to me!" the serpent snapped, suddenly furious. "You told me when Eve persuaded Adam to eat the Fruit that God would reject them! You said I'd be elevated in their place as a result. But look at me! Your plan was an utter failure. Now I'll never be the same again, *never!*"

"Well there's no use quibbling about it now, is there?"

"Then what *do you* propose I do in the way of restoring my old life, you impertinent fellow? Is there nothing you can offer me in the way of consolation?"

"As for restoring you to your old life, I'm afraid my hands are completely tied. But there is one other alternative I was hoping you might find appealing in lieu of that fact."

"And what pray tell might that be?"

"Revenge, dear Serpent, revenge."

MEANWHILE, AS THE couple sat in their cave, darkness slowly began to descend all around them. "Adam, what's happening to the light?"

"I have no idea," whispered Adam. "It seems to be fading away."

"But where is it fading *to*?"

"I wish I knew, Eve."

Before long, the couple could no longer see each other.

"Where are you, Eve?" Standing up, Adam groped around in the inky blackness.

"I'm here," she breathlessly replied as she got to her feet. "I'm standing right here. Where are *you*?"

"Oh, Eve, this is terrible."

"What do we do now?"

"Hold out your hand."

"Okay, I'm holding it out. Now what?"

"Now I grab hold of it. There. Now we sit down together and ask God to tell us what's happening."

"All right," continued Eve, through pursed lips. "Now we're sitting. God, are You there? Can you please tell us what is going on?"

But as the couple sat there in hushed anticipation, the darkness showed no sign of dissipating.

"Oh, Eve, remember how radiant we were while we lived in the garden? We never knew anything about this darkness. And remember the Tree of Life? The water flowing from it shimmered across the landscape. Can't you still see its awesome splendor?"

"Of course I can, Adam. But no sooner do we come to this strange place than this *darkness* overwhelms us."

"I wonder why this is happening."

"I don't know, Adam, but I'm scared. Tell me: What good is living a life in a world with no light, no happiness, no hope?"

"I wish I could tell you, Eve. We can only try to ask God to do something and to do it soon."

"I don't think He's going to do anything for us this time. Maybe He's too busy to worry about us anymore. Did you ever think about that?"

"Eve, don't say that. Don't even think it. If that's true, then we're doomed."

Thoroughly frustrated, Adam stood up and started groping around in the dark again, when suddenly he bumped into the cave wall.

"What was that?" exclaimed Eve.

"I just ran into the wall! I can't take this anymore, Eve!" And as he began to strike his chest, Adam threw himself to the ground and died. Hearing him fall, Eve felt around in the dark and eventually found his corpse. Horrified, she tried to scream, but her throat was so dry that nothing came out. Unable to make another sound, she simply clung to his side, weeping over his body.

EVENTUALLY, THE Word of God arrived, filling the cave with His luminescence, and again He revived Adam while at the same time opening Eve's mouth.

"Oh, Lord," moaned Eve as the couple got to their feet. "What happened to the light?"

"And where was that *darkness* before it attacked us?" asked Adam.

"Relax, you two," said the Word, touched by their lament. "As long as Lucifer was obedient to Me, he knew nothing about the darkness, either. He was covered with a bright light just like you, but when he violated My orders, I deprived him of that brilliance and threw him down to Earth. It was that darkness which first overcame him, and now the same thing has happened to both of you."

"I don't understand, Lord," said Eve. "Why was it so dark?"

"As long as you were living obediently to Me, My radiance covered you both, but when I heard about your crime, I took it away."

"Does the darkness come from us, then?" asked Adam. "Is that why it comes?"

"Oh, Lord, have we *become* darkness?" Eve wondered.

"No, no, of course not. I didn't turn you into this darkness. Turning you into darkness would have been like killing you, but in My mercy, I created you as you are, as human beings with bodies that experience heat and cold, light and darkness."

"And when we fell from grace," Adam continued somberly, "You drove us here to live in this cave."

"That's right," replied the Word. "And it was then that the darkness overcame you, just as it did to the one who first violated My order. So you see: This night has actually deceived you. It's not really going to last forever, as you believed. It will only continue for twelve hours. Then, when it's over, daylight will return as usual."

"You don't plan on tormenting us with the darkness from now on, do

You?" asked Adam.

"Stop worrying so much, Adam," replied the Word. "The darkness doesn't last forever. And quit thinking I'm trying to torment you with it. The darkness isn't a punishment. I did create the daylight for you, though."

"What do you mean, Lord?" asked Adam. "What did You create for us?"

"Because I knew you'd be sent to this place after your disobedience, I created the Sun and put it in place so you'd have light to live and work by. I never wanted your fall to cause your doom. Just because you had to leave the eternal light and enter this place of darkness, doesn't mean you have to start being afraid of *Me*. I'm not shutting you out completely just because you're here instead of the garden. I made you of the light, and I planned for Eve to give birth to children of light, just like the both of you."

Adam and Eve looked at each other in amazement.

"Oh, Adam, what have we done?" groaned Eve.

"Now, as I've already said," continued the Word. "I've made the day for you and your children to work, and the night for you to sleep. Nighttime will also be when animals come out to search for their food. But now very little of this night remains, Adam. Daylight will soon be reappearing."

"But, Lord," sighed Adam, "won't You please take us somewhere else? Don't let us live in a horrible place like this anymore!"

"Yes, Lord, we're begging You," cried Eve. "Take us anywhere there's no darkness!"

"Trust Me, you two. This darkness will pass, and it will do the same thing every day I've determined for you until My contract is made complete. Then I promise, I'll rescue you and bring you back into the garden again, into the place of light you desire so much, where there's never any darkness. In the meantime, none of this misery you've been burdened with is going to help you escape the clutches of Satan. But *I* will save you."

"But what does that mean, Lord?" asked Adam. "How will You save us?"

"By becoming one of your offspring, that's how. I, Who am without years, will be subjected to the reckoning of time. I'll be received as an ordinary human being in order to rescue you, and while in the flesh I'll suffer the same pain and anguish you're now experiencing, and the same darkness that overcame you in this cave will overcome Me in the grave." Then the Word disappeared, plunging the couple back into complete darkness.

Eve began crying. "Oh, Adam, we really won't be returning to the garden until the decreed days are fulfilled."

"No, Eve, I'm afraid not. But what's even worse is, in order to rescue us, the Lord Himself is going to have to suffer, too."

FINALLY, THAT FIRST morning began to dawn. Seeing the light was returning, their fears began to melt away as the darkness loosened its grip around them. Cautiously, Adam and Eve walked to the entrance of the cave and looked eastward. As the Sun gradually peaked up over the horizon with its brilliant, glowing rays, the couple began to feel its heat course over their bodies.

"Adam, look! I've never seen anything like it before. Have you?"

"No. What do you think it is?"

"I think it might be God!"

"I think you're right, Eve. God is a ball of fire!"

"Now that He's agreed to stop tormenting us with the darkness, I guess He's decided to send this fireball to scorch us instead."

Terrified, Adam and Eve fell on their faces.

"Lord," exclaimed Adam, "please don't torture us like this anymore!"

The Word of God returned. "Oh, Adam, this isn't God. It's just the Sun. And how many times do I have to keep telling you? I haven't sent any of these things to punish you. I created the Sun to provide light and heat for you and Eve. That's why I told you earlier that the dawn would be breaking soon and, with it, the light." And again the Word vanished.

Blood and Smoke

LATER THAT AFTERNOON, Adam and Eve left the cave, heading straight for the garden again. As they approached its southern border, they saw the serpent crawling in their direction. Moving toward the gate, it slithered along, despondently licking the dust. Then, when the serpent noticed Adam and Eve coming toward him, it rose up on its tail and swelled its tremendous head, preparing to strike. "I'm going to make you two pay for what you did, if it's the last thing I do!" With blood-red eyes and gaping fangs, the serpent went straight for Eve as she ran away, screaming.

"Help, Adam; it's after me!"

Momentarily, Adam just stood there, panic-stricken. "What do I do? Lord, help us!" Then, with a heart burning for Eve, he ran after the creature and dove for its tail. The serpent dragged Adam for several feet as he held on for dear life. Abruptly it stopped and turned toward him with dripping fangs. Terrified, Adam sprang to his feet.

"It's all your fault, Adam!" the serpent hissed. "Now, because of you and this woman, I have to crawl around on my stomach all the time!"

The serpent lunged at Adam and wrestled him to the ground. Wrapping its gigantic coils around his body, it poised to crush him. "I'll kill you for what you've done to me!"

But suddenly an angel appeared, and throwing the snarling creature away, he helped Adam to his feet.

"Thank you so much," Adam gasped, breathlessly wiping the dust off. "You got here just in the nick of time."

The indignant serpent glared at the angel. "What is the meaning of this outrage? Do you realize the misery these two have caused me?"

Then the Word of God materialized in their midst. "Of course he does, Serpent, but that doesn't give you the right to attack them, you miserable coward."

"How dare you speak to me like that," hissed the serpent. "This is an outrage! An outrage! Do you have any idea who I am, my good man?"

"Do *I* know you?" replied the Word with a hearty laugh. "Of course I do."

"Well, I doubt it. Because if you did, you'd treat me with some respect. After all, I am the wisest of all God's creatures."

"That may be true, but I'm the One Who created you with such wisdom in the first place."

"*You* created *me*?"

"I did, yes."

"Well then, if you're my creator, I have to assume it was you who changed me, forced me to crawl around on my belly; and for what?"

"Well, I may have forced you to crawl around on your belly, but still I never deprived you of everything. But from now on, you and all your kind will never be able to speak another word."

"Don't be ridiculous, you arrogant fellow. Why on Earth would you do something like that? What have I ever done to you?"

"It was *you* who first helped bring disaster to God's children, and now here you are trying to kill them, even though they've never wished you any harm, even after they were condemned because of what you did."

Enraged, the serpent's eyes thinned and his head swelled again. "Well, never in—"

But with a wave of His hand, the Word shoved the serpent's next word back down his throat, and following another gesture, a tremendous wind picked up the speechless creature and hurled him far away.

"See, Lord, I told You this would happen!" Adam exclaimed. "I told You the animals would attack us and try to eat us! Didn't I, Eve?"

Eve nodded, still trembling.

"Relax, Adam," said the Word. "The serpent was only angry at you because I cursed him for helping Satan deceive you and Eve, but none of the other animals have ever tried to harm you. Remember when I had them all visit you before? Remember how you all made an agreement to live in harmony?"

Reluctantly, Adam nodded. "Yes, I remember."

"I didn't invite the serpent, did I? Or else it would have attacked you then. I knew how vindictive it had become. That's why I never even let it get near you. So relax. Quit worrying so much. I'll still be with you until the end of the days I've determined for you."

"But, Lord, please," groaned Adam, "can't You take us somewhere else? Someplace the serpent can never reach us? Or else someday it might find Your servant Eve and attack her again. Its eyes were so horrible, so full of evil."

"From now on, you'll never have to worry about it. I've driven it far from this place, so it won't ever be coming near you again. In fact, none of the animals around here will ever attack you like that again."

"Thank You, Lord. If You hadn't come when You did, that thing would've killed us for sure. Where did You send it, anyway?"

"Right about now, I imagine it's slithering around, quite perplexed and angry, on some seashore far, far away, in a place called India." Then the Word disappeared.

The couple scanned the area with nervous eyes, and finally satisfied that the creature was nowhere to be seen, they returned to their investigation of the garden.

EVENTUALLY, THEY made their way up along a steep ridge facing the garden's western edge, but soon they began perspiring terribly. Exhausted, they stopped near a cliff and looked down at the garden from there. Eve suddenly broke into tears.

"What is it now, Eve?" asked Adam, vexed by her abrupt outburst.

"Oh, Adam, it's no use. Who are we kidding? We keep promising God we won't try to get back into the garden anymore, but just look at us. We're right back where we started."

"You're right, Eve. We'll never get our old life back if God doesn't see we can be honest with Him. Why would He want to save us? All we ever do is disappoint Him again and again with our lies."

Without warning, Adam flung himself from the top of the ridge.

"Adam, no!"

Careening down the mountainside, Adam's face was torn and his flesh ripped. Blood splattered everywhere. Crumpling at the bottom, he died in a heap. Eve stood at the edge of the cliff, screaming through her tears as she looked down at his shattered body.

"Oh, God, not again. I can't go on like this anymore. Adam's only doing this to himself because of me." Then she threw herself off, too. Lacerated and bruised, she tumbled to the bottom of the hill and died alongside Adam.

The Word of God returned again and raised them, sealing up all their bloody wounds in the process. "Oh, you two; punishing yourselves like this won't do a thing to eliminate My decree. It's not going to change the contract of five and a half days in the slightest."

"But, God, we're so sick of this place!" groaned Adam. "We're withering in this heat."

"I think I'm going to faint from all this walking around," Eve sighed. "And who knows how long it's going to be until You let us leave this place."

"Well, it can't be right now," said the Word. "But when the time does come, rest assured, I will bring you out of this dismal land. I promise."

"But, Lord," Adam moaned, "what good is a promise if we don't live long enough to see it fulfilled?"

"Having to live like this is unbearable!" cried Eve. "Ever since we came here, it's been nothing but one disaster after another."

"It's true, Lord, we admit it," said Adam. "We did freely disobey You. When we wanted to become gods like You, Satan was right there to deceive us. But please don't plague us anymore for one little sin. It's just not fair."

"Stop it, Adam. Now I've already told you that whatever you're going through I'll also be enduring for your sakes. Because you've endured fear and suffering and death in this world, I'll be experiencing the same things when I come to rescue you. So if I, Who have done no wrong, am willing to go through what you're going through, then I'm sure you'll survive just fine."

"God have mercy on us," said Adam. "Whatever You're willing to do, I want to do also."

Abruptly the Word vanished, leaving the couple alone once again. Captured in what seemed like an endless silence, Adam and Eve exchanged an agonized look.

"What was that all about?" wondered Adam.

Just as confused, Eve shook her head and said, "How should I know?"

"Come on, Eve; I have an idea." As Adam began walking around gathering stones, Eve stood and watched. Finally, he turned to her and impatiently said, "Don't just stand there. Help me."

"Well, what do you expect me to do?"

"What else, silly? Help me gather more stones."

So Eve started to pick up rocks with him, and when they had gathered a couple of dozen decent-sized stones, Adam began to arrange them into a crude, circular shape.

"Adam?"

"Yes, Eve."

"What are we doing?"

"We're building an altar."

"An altar? What's an altar?"

"Just wait; you'll see."

Then Adam started to pick up some of the leaves from the trees near the garden wall and began wiping up the blood that they had spilled on the rocks beneath the cliff.

"Now what are you doing?" asked Eve, still perplexed.

"Now I'm preparing an offering."

"A what?"

"Eve, I need you to stop asking me questions you know I don't have answers to. All I know is, it just seems like the right thing to do, that's all. Now will you please just help me?"

Together, they stacked up the blood-soaked leaves on the altar. Then Adam started banging two small, flinty rocks near the stack of leaves.

Puzzled, Eve asked, "What are you doing now?"

A perturbed Adam stopped momentarily and shot her a look of disdain.

"Never mind," was all she said as she stepped away, thoroughly confused.

Several minutes went by as Adam continued striking the two rocks together, until several cinders shot out and landed on the stack of leaves. Adam blew gently on the smoldering leaves and before long the whole pile of leaves was ablaze.

Mesmerized by what she was seeing, Eve wandered back to the burning altar. "Oh, Adam, how did you do that?"

But Adam shook his head. "I'm not exactly sure, Eve. I'm just doing what I see in my head."

"Oh, my. What are you going to do next?"

For several moments, Adam thought very hard and finally replied, "Now I think I'll pray to the Lord."

Eve smiled ever so slightly and nodded. "I think that would be wonderful, Adam."

So the two of them turned toward the glowing altar and lifted their eyes skyward.

"Please, Lord," began Adam, "forgive us for our disobedience. While we were still in the garden, our praises went up to You endlessly, like the smoke of this offering, but ever since we came to this strange place we've lost our powers of praise. Without our luminous natures, our perfect understanding is a thing of the past. So help us, Lord. Please look at our blood on these leaves and accept it, like the praise we used to offer You in the garden."

A fireball fell suddenly from the sky and consumed their gift. Adam and Eve stepped back cautiously.

"Adam, wh—*what* just happened?"

Wide-eyed, Adam shook his head. "I'm not sure."

"I hope God isn't mad at us again."

Then the Word of God returned. "No, you two, God isn't mad at you. Actually, quite the opposite is true. He's very impressed with your offering. He's amazed you did this thing without any specific orders from Him. Smelling the sweet savor of your offering, He sent this fireball as an expression of His mercy toward you."

Adam and Eve exchanged a look of tremendous joy.

"See, I told you I knew what I was doing," Adam said with an impish grin.

"And Adam," continued the Word, "just as you've bled, I will shed My blood someday, too. In fact, when I'm born as one of your descendants, I'll even die like you did. You offered your blood on an altar; I'll offer My blood on one, too. And as you asked for forgiveness on the basis of your blood, My shed blood will wipe away every transgression that's ever been committed."

"So what do we do until that day arrives, Lord?" asked Adam.

"In the meantime, whenever despair overwhelms you, make Me an offering, and I'll be kind to you."

Adam stared back, mulling the words over in his mind.

Then the Word continued, "But you have to promise me something, Adam."

"Yes?"

"I don't ever want you to kill yourself like that again. Is that clear?"

"But I *was* going to kill myself, Lord, at once!" blurted Adam. "Without Your radiance surrounding me, there's no point in living."

"Promise Me, Adam; I want to hear you say it."

"Oh, all right, I promise."

Then, the Word disappeared.

"What should we do now, Adam?" wondered Eve.

"Well, you heard Him, didn't you? God was happy with our offering. So from now on, we're going to make it a custom of ours to do the same thing every week."

"And you promise to stop killing yourself, right?"

"Of course, of course," he replied nonchalantly.

Unconvinced, Eve glared back. "Adam? You have to promise me, too. Say it."

"Oh, all right, Eve, I promise you, too."

Angel of Light

ADAM AND EVE HEADED back for their cave, but when they got close enough to see it from a distance, they got very depressed. The Sun was beginning to set beyond the western horizon.

"I hate to tell you this, Eve, but it looks like the Sun is starting to disappear again. The darkness will be returning soon, and we won't be seeing each other for quite a while."

"No, Adam, no," whimpered Eve. "Please ask God to help us."

So they spread their hands toward God.

"Lord, please, hold back the Sun," begged Adam, "and let it keep shining for us. We don't want the darkness to ever return."

"Yes, Lord," Eve lamented, "we'd rather die than endure such darkness again."

Then the Word of God returned. "Oh, Adam, I wish I could accommodate you, really I do, but if I did hold back the Sun, then the agreement I made with you could never be fulfilled."

"But why, Lord?" asked Adam.

"Because without the Sun, there would be no more hours or days or years. Then, I'm afraid, you'd remain banished from the garden. You and everyone you loved would be plagued by endless disaster, and no salvation would reach any of you, *ever*."

Adam and Eve exchanged a concerned look.

"So just try to relax and endure the nights until that time has arrived. Can you do that for Me?"

Eve began to weep. "Oh, Adam, what if something happens to us before the time comes?"

"I wish I could tell you, Eve; really I do," Adam replied sadly.

"You know, you two," continued the Word, "when I think of all the wonderful things you used to have, and why you had to leave them, I'm still more than willing to continue being good to you. But unfortunately, I can't alter the contract I've told you about, or else I would've already returned you to the garden."

Adam perked up. "Did you hear that, Eve?"

Eve nodded meekly as she wiped the tears from her cheek. "Yes, Adam, I heard."

"Until then," said the Word, "be patient and endure living in this cave, because the darkness you're so afraid of will only last twelve hours. Then the light will return, just as I've promised." And again the Word vanished.

UPON ENTERING THE cave, the couple held hands in dire anticipation.

"Oh, Adam, I'm terrified of the dark," groaned Eve. "Just the *thought* of it terrifies me. I'd rather die than endure another night of it."

"I know how you feel, Eve."

Slowly, almost agonizingly, the darkness descended around them.

"Please, Lord," Adam whispered, "be merciful to us throughout this night."

"We need Your help so much," added Eve.

Before long, the couple found themselves enveloped in utter blackness.

"Lord, we're begging You," Eve whimpered. "Please send the light."

THOROUGHLY DISGUSTED, Satan was watching their cave from a distance, even in the blackest of night. One by one, his demons gathered around him, as a murder of crows gathers about its leader.

"Just look at the little vermin, with their simpering prayers," grumbled the devil. "Won't they ever shut up? *God help us. Oh, please, please, please.* You'd think he'd eventually get fed up and blot them out. Why does he keep comforting them? I hate the very sight of them!"

"What will you do, Master?" asked his lieutenant.

"Well, if god insists on tickling their fancy with His shimmering light, then I can't wait to see the look on their faces when I hit them with my little lightshow."

AS ADAM AND EVE huddled together in the darkness, a peculiar singing began to filter in through the mouth of the cave, and trickling in with it was a beam of white light. When Adam and Eve saw it, they became transfixed. "Look at that light, Eve. I wonder what it could be."

"And that singing," added Eve. "It's so beautiful."

"I wonder where it came from. Do you think God is doing it?"

"Don't ask me, Adam; ask Him."

"Good idea. Lord, are there any other gods besides You Who can create a light as bright as this one?"

Suddenly an angel appeared before Adam and Eve, lighting up the cave with his own luminescence. "Don't be deceived, Adam. God isn't the author of the spectacle occurring outside your cave."

"Who is, then?" asked Adam as the couple got to their feet.

"This is the doing of the same one who hid in the serpent, the one who got you and Eve kicked out of the garden, but this time he's tried approaching you as an angel of light."

"But why?" Eve wondered.

"He was hoping you'd worship him. He wanted to mesmerize you, make you believe you were actually in God's presence. And if God hadn't sent me here, he may very well have succeeded."

Then, Adam and Eve followed the angel as he walked over to the mouth of the cave, where they found a group of angels singing their hauntingly beautiful melody. But as soon as this group saw that the couple was accompanied by one of God's angels, they ceased their singing. After a simple gesture from the angel, the group outside the cave was abruptly unmasked, revealing a cadre of hideous demons with their grotesque chief standing at their head. Adam and Eve gasped, as did the demons, who all painfully recoiled at the brightness of God's angel. Abruptly they scattered, leaving Satan standing there, frozen stiff, apparently unable to move.

"Who is this?" muttered Adam, squinting at the hideous creature standing before them.

"*What* is this?" Eve added, just as bewildered.

"This is Satan, your adversary," the angel replied. "Once, he was the most beautiful angel whom God had ever created; but not anymore."

Horrified and confused, Adam and Eve examined him from head to toe. They were repulsed by the very sight of him, with his reptilian skin, wolfen face and bat-like wings, his jagged teeth, claws and horns. As the couple gaped at him, the devil hissed lamentably, trying in vain to spit at them.

"What a despicable monster," said Adam.

"Why is he so ugly?" wondered Eve, almost in awe.

"He looks like this because God cursed him for rebelling against His divine rule. This is how he's appeared ever since he was kicked out of Heaven. Naturally, he knew you wouldn't invite him into your cave looking this way, so he transformed himself into a dazzling angel." Then God's angel grabbed Satan by the scruff of the neck and hurled him out of sight. "But God wants you to know," the angel continued, "you don't have to be afraid of him, because He Who created you will be your strength." And just as quickly as he had appeared, the angel vanished, plunging the couple back into darkness.

AS MORNING BEGAN to break inside the cave, the couple got up and stretched their weary muscles. "Lord, what should we do now?" asked Adam.

"I don't know about you, Adam," began Eve, "but I'd like to take a trip to the garden. I hope you don't think I'm being silly. It's just my heart yearns to go back. I know I shouldn't keep dwelling on it, but there it is; I said it."

"I don't think you're being silly, Eve. I feel the same way. We'll always be connected to it somehow. Just because we had to leave doesn't mean we have to stop thinking about it, right?"

Eve smiled at the thought. "Right."

AS THEY WERE WALKING along, Adam and Eve looked up and saw a dazzling array of angels flying toward them, soaring through the air like some kind of swirling, white cloud.

"Adam, do you see what I see?"

"I do, Eve. Angels of God. At least they look like angels."

"You don't think it's that monster in disguise again, do you? What was his name?"

"You mean Satan?"

"Yes, him. You don't think it could be him and his angels again, do you?"

Adam shrugged his shoulders as the cloud came closer and closer. "I don't know. He'd have to be pretty stupid to try something like that again. Let's find out what they want, though, before we jump to any conclusions."

"If you say so," Eve said suspiciously. "I just hope you know what you're doing."

Swooping down in front of the couple, the cloud of angels lit upon the ground and graciously bowed. "Greetings, you two," cooed one of the angels, who stepped forward to the head of the group.

"Hello," replied Adam. "Who are you?"

"I'm none other than an angel of the great and glorious God. Simyasa is my name, and these are His holy angels."

"Really?" said Eve. "Hello, Simyasa. What brings you here?"

"Why, God has sent us to help you, of course, in your quest to get back into the garden. Would you like that?"

"Would we ever," exclaimed Adam. "But how?"

"Well, naturally God can't allow you back inside the garden in your present condition, so he's asked us to help you prepare yourselves. Are you ready?"

"Of course," blurted Eve, suddenly eager and hopeful. "Tell him, Adam. Tell him we're ready."

"Good, then follow us," said Simyasa. "We're all going to go to the ocean, where you and Eve will be able to bathe. There, your bodies will be purified so you'll be able to return to the garden. How does that sound?"

His words sank deep into their hearts.

"That sounds wonderful," Adam replied.

Ecstatic at the thought, Eve touched Adam's arm as they exchanged a look of mournful longing. "Can it really be true, Adam?"

"It's time now," said Simyasa. "Let's get going."

BUT AS ADAM AND EVE followed the angels in their journey, they cautiously walked behind them, keeping their distance. They had walked only a short while before Eve leaned into Adam and whispered, "Are you sure we're going in the right direction? This isn't the way you go to get to the ocean."

EVENTUALLY, THEY CAME to the steep hill along the garden's northern perimeter, and there Adam and Eve stopped. Turning back toward them, Simyasa looked almost as perplexed as they did. "What's wrong?" he asked. "Why have you stopped?"

"We thought you said we were going to the ocean in the East," said Adam, who exchanged a nervous look with Eve.

"Yeah," added Eve. "Why are we going this direction?"

Simyasa took several steps toward the couple and held his arms out wide. "Oh, my dear ones, don't be alarmed. I'm merely taking you there by way of a short-cut. After all, you're not accustomed to all this walking about, now are you?"

Again the couple looked at one another, unsure how to respond.

"No," Adam said finally. "As a matter of fact, we *hate* walking. This place is nothing but dirt and rocks."

"You see, then," continued Simyasa. "What better way to get there than by way of a short-cut?"

"Yes, a short-cut," echoed Adam, however reluctantly, and turned to Eve. "What do you say, Eve? Wouldn't you rather take a *short-cut*?"

Eve shrugged again and said, "I guess so, sure."

TRUDGING THEIR way up to the peak of the hill, Adam and Eve were on the brink of exhaustion, when finally they were forced to stop in order to catch their breaths.

"Some short-cut this turned out to be," Adam muttered, huffing and puffing.

Simyasa and the rest of his group stopped and turned toward the couple.

"Don't stop now, you two," said Simyasa with a reassuring smile. "The hard part of our journey is nearly over. It's all downhill from here."

Simyasa waved them on, and the couple walked up to him where he stood very close to the edge of the cliff. Gazing out over the sprawling landscape, he turned to Adam and Eve. "How's this for a view?" he asked with a sweeping gesture of his hand. "Isn't God's creation a marvel to behold?"

Intrigued, the couple moved up to the cliff's edge and looked down. "Look how high we are, Eve," said Adam as the couple inched ever forward.

Still winded from their journey, Adam and Eve stared down, precariously close to the edge of the cliff, and as they did Simyasa surreptitiously stepped up behind them. "Undeniably, my friends, undeniably." He slowly stretched out his hands, preparing to push them.

But suddenly the disembodied voice of God roared from the void. "Satan, you scourge of the Universe! How dare you try to destroy My children!"

Terrified, Simyasa froze and, grunting in frustration, transformed into his true form as the devil. "Damn you, god, *not again!*"

Startled, the couple turned around to see Satan and his leathery claws stretched out toward them.

"What the—" Adam blurted.

To their amazement, the couple watched as the angels that were huddled about the devil were also unmasked, revealing their true demonic forms. Then, a tremendous gust of wind swept them all away, along with their hideous master, who hurled a steady stream of unspeakable insults as they went.

Confused and alone, Adam and Eve stood there looking around.

"Oh, Adam, we did it again."

"And this time God just let it happen."

"Well, what do you expect? We never bothered to ask Him if it was Satan or not, even after we knew better. Now what do we do?"

"What else can we do?" replied Adam, who raised his voice to the Heavens. "Lord, please forgive us for following Satan and his angels. Help us, won't You?"

Then the Word of God appeared. "Aren't you two ever going to learn? What were you doing up here, anyway?"

"We were looking for something to relieve our sadness," murmured Eve, "something to remind us of the life we used to have in the garden."

"Up here?"

Hanging their heads, the bewildered couple just shrugged their shoulders.

"Very well," continued the Word. "Maybe I can help you with that."

An angel appeared suddenly in their midst, and Adam and Eve looked up.

"Who is this?" asked Adam.

"This is the archangel Michael. I'm going to send him to where the ocean reaches India, to get some gold for you and Eve."

Then another angel appeared. "This is the archangel Gabriel," said the Word. "I'll be sending him to the garden, where he'll get you some frankincense."

Finally, one more angel materialized. "And this is the archangel Raphael. He'll be going to the garden to fetch you some myrrh."

The trio of archangels bowed humbly before the Word of God.

"Now go, you three, and be quick about it."

With the speed of the wind, the archangels darted out of view, leaving a vapor trail in their wake.

AS EACH OF THE archangels streaked to their divinely-appointed destinations, they encountered a barrage of demonic opposition. Each one had to slash his way through with the use of their flaming swords, slicing a pathway to their respective quarries. Eventually, Michael got through to the gold near the Indian Ocean, Gabriel made his way to the eastern border of the garden, where he retrieved the frankincense, and Raphael fought his way to the western edge of the garden, where he found the myrrh.

THE THREE ARCHANGELS then returned to where Adam, Eve and the Word of God were still waiting for them.

"Now, I want each of you to dip what you have in the Water of Life," said the Word with a gesture of His hand, and instantly the trio of archangels vanished again.

THE ARCHANGELS ALL found themselves at the Tree of Life in the garden, where they each kneeled down to dip their items in the crystal-clear water flowing from its roots.

THEN AS ABRUPTLY AS they had disappeared, they were back again where the couple still stood in anticipation.

"Now give what you have to Adam and Eve," said the Word of God.

Dutifully, the archangels stepped forward and, one by one, presented the awestruck couple with their gifts.

"So, you two," the Word continued, "you said you were looking for something to remind you of the garden, in the hopes that it might comfort you. Here you are, then. I'm giving you these three tokens to reassure you of My promise of the five and a half days."

And when Adam and Eve saw the gold, the frankincense and the myrrh, they became very happy.

"I'm doing this so you'll realize you can trust Me to keep My promise, because I really will come and rescue you someday."

The couple smiled at one another.

"When I arrive in the flesh, kings will also present Me with gold, frankincense and myrrh."

Adam's demeanor grew somber again, and he remarked, "Gold reminds me so much of the beautiful home we had to leave."

"That's because gold is a symbol of My kingdom," said the Word.

Adam continued, "This frankincense makes me think of the bright light that was taken from us."

"Because frankincense typifies My divinity."

"And this myrrh," observed Adam, "reminds me of all the despair we've been feeling since the day we had to leave."

"Because myrrh is reminiscent of My suffering and death."

Again the couple exchanged a concerned look.

"So Adam," added the Word, "I want you to keep these things with you in the cave. The gold will shed light by night, the frankincense will provide you with its sweet aroma, and the myrrh will help soothe you in your sadness."

"Thank you so much, Lord," Adam said, "we'll never forget Your kindness to us today."

"Yes, Lord," added Eve, "You've been most gracious. We can't thank You enough."

ADAM AND EVE SUDDENLY found themselves back inside their cave again. Looking around in amazement, the couple sucked in a deep breath and reached out to one another to steady themselves.

"Adam, what just happened?"

"I'm not sure; but I think we're back in our cave somehow."

"Yes, you two, God transported you to your cave," said a voice.

And when they turned to see who was speaking, they found Michael the archangel, standing there with everything that the archangels had retrieved at his feet. Bowing humbly, Adam and Eve began placing their new things in an appropriate spot. At the south end of their cave, they placed the gold, on the east side, the frankincense, and to the west, the myrrh.

"I hope this will help you both in your time on this Earth," said Michael. "May God richly bless you with His peace which surpasses all understanding." Nodding, he streaked out of view with a puff of smoke.

"You know, Eve, now that we have such nice things from God here in our cave, we should give this place a name to go along with this occasion. What do you think?"

"A name? What kind of name?"

"I don't know; like the Cave of Gold, the Cave of Treasures, something like that."

"Hmmm. I like that, Adam. Yes, the Cave of Treasures. That sounds nice. From now on, we'll call our home the Cave of Treasures."

"God knows if we do have to endure our new life within the confines of a cave, we should try to make the best of it."

AS ADAM AND EVE were acclimating themselves to their new surroundings, the molten Face of God looked down from His dazzling throne. "Did You hear that, Son? Adam and Eve have decided to name their residence the Cave of Treasures in memoriam of the gifts We've bestowed on them."

Then the Word of God turned to the Face. "Yes, Father, I heard. I think it's quite fitting, considering the fact that this is the third day since Adam and Eve have been expelled from their garden home."

"Yes," continued the Face. "And just as You will remain in the heart of the Earth for three days, they now have these three things as a pledge toward that someday."

Hollow

THEN CAME THE DAWN of the eighth day since they had departed from the garden, and for the first time, when Adam and Eve came out of their cave, they seemed happy.

"Oh, Eve, what a beautiful morning," said Adam with a tremendous yawn. "I had such a wonderful sleep last night. How about you?"

"I slept quite well, believe it or not," Eve replied, stretching her muscles. "These last few days I can actually say I haven't been so miserable."

"I think it's because of the sacred tokens the Lord gave us. Now our cave isn't so dark and dreary at night. It's starting to feel like a home instead of a prison."

"I wouldn't go that far, Adam. It's still a cave, you know. All the gold, frankincense and myrrh in the world won't erase that fact."

"No, I guess not."

"Can you believe it's been more than a week since we left the garden? My stomach feels funny."

"What do you mean, funny?"

"It's beginning to feel," said Eve, searching for just the right word. "I don't know." Then she turned to Adam with a mournful frown. "*Hollow.*"

"Hollow... Yes, now that you mention it, I'm beginning to feel hollow, too."

"I wonder what that's all about."

The couple exchanged a curious look and shrugged it off.

"What should we do today?" Eve asked.

"You know, Eve, I was thinking. We asked God to give us something from the garden, and He gave us those mementos."

"Okay. So what did you have in mind this time?"

"I don't know. Maybe God isn't so mad at us after all. Maybe He'd reconsider taking us back into the garden."

Eve nodded thoughtfully. "Maybe. And if He doesn't let us back in yet, then at least He could provide us with a nicer place to live than this one."

"Good, then let's go."

"Go? Go where?"

"Let's go to the ocean."

"Why the ocean?"

"I don't know. It seemed like there was something special about that place. Maybe if we went there to pray, God would see how serious we are about getting back into the garden."

SO THE COUPLE WENT to the ocean and stood by the shore, gazing out across the water.

"Now what do we do?" asked Eve.

"I want you to go down into the water, and I want you to start praying harder than you've ever prayed before in your life."

"For how long?"

"I want you to pray like that for forty days."

"Forty days? Isn't that an awfully long time?"

"Not at all, Eve; not if we really want to show God how serious we are about this. Pray with your sweetest voice. Pray that He please forgive us."

"Well, what about you? What are you going to do?"

"I'm going to walk further up the coast and do the same thing there. Then, after the forty days are up, I'll come back and get you."

"All right," said Eve with a skeptical nod, and slowly she waded into the water. "I sure hope you know what you're doing."

ADAM WALKED UP THE shoreline for quite a while before he, too, waded in and began praying. "Lord, please hear our prayer. We're so sorry for our crime against You and were hoping You might change Your mind about waiting so long to let us back into the garden."

SATAN AND HIS HENCHMEN, in the meantime, came buzzing about the Cave of Treasures.

"I wonder what Adam and Eve are doing today," grumbled the devil. "Begging god to do something else for them, I imagine."

"They're not here, Master," his lieutenant reported.

"I can see that for myself, you idiot!"

"But where can they be?"

"How should I know? You're supposed to be my lieutenant. You find them! If they're up to no good, I want to know about it!"

Splitting off in every direction, Satan and his despicable crew began searching.

WHEN THE DEVIL GOT to the ocean, he absolutely hated what he found there. "Here they are! But what are they doing just standing in the sea? Could it be? Why, yes. They're still begging god to let them back into the garden! What fools!"

Several demons streaked up to Satan's side and looked down at Adam and Eve as they stood praying in the ocean. "What are they doing now, Lord?" asked one of the demons.

"The pathetic, little replicas are begging god to be released from my control. What else?"

"Still? Don't they ever learn? What should we do to them? Just say the word, and I'll go down there right now and rip their hearts out!"

"Well, well, aren't we original? You're as bad as Adam and Eve when it comes to thinking of something new."

Then, when he felt a second demon next to him nudge him with an elbow, the first demon turned with an irritated scowl. "What is it now?"

Surreptitiously, the second demon put his finger to his pursed lips, as if to warn the first not to say anything more.

"What did I say that was so wrong?" mumbled the first demon.

AS EVE CONTINUED to pray knee deep in the ocean, she suddenly found herself with a visitor. A beautiful, little angel was flitting about her, as pleasant as a butterfly, smiling so radiantly. "Well, hello, my dear," beamed the tiny angel with a voice as tiny as itself. "I'm so glad I found you."

Intrigued, Eve smiled back. "Hello there. Well, look at you. I've never seen an angel so small. What's your name, little one?"

"My name is Suriyel. God has sent me to tell you He's heard your prayer, and He's forgiven you."

Eve gazed at him, suddenly perplexed. "He has?"

"Why, yes. First, He sent me to Adam, and I brought him the good news about your return to the garden. He was so excited about it he wanted me to come tell you right away."

"Is that so?" replied Eve with just a hint of skepticism in her voice. "So where's Adam now? Why didn't he come to tell me himself?"

"He wanted to; really he did. But he's already back at your cave, where he's worshipping God as we speak. That's why I was sent to tell you to come with me. So you can both be crowned with the same light you had before your fall."

But far from being overjoyed at the news, Eve still seemed puzzled. "I don't know. Are you sure it's all right?"

"Oh, dear, I can just imagine how you feel right now. Adam said you might react this way. So he told me that if you decided not to come with me to remind you about what you saw on the mountaintop. Do you remember how God transported you to your cave? How you laid the gold to the south, the frankincense to the east, and the myrrh to the west?"

Eve thought for a moment and nodded reluctantly. "Yes, I suppose so."

"Well, then, there you are. You see? There's nothing to fear. Certainly I'm nothing you should be afraid of. Now, come with me, dear Eve, won't you?"

Finally, Eve got very happy, so she came up out of the water and started to follow the tiny, fluttering angel.

THE ANGEL CONTINUED to lead her to the point where they were approaching Adam. As soon as she saw him still praying in the water, Eve frowned and said, "But you told me Adam was already back at our—" And turning to the angel, she found him gone. "Hey, where'd you go?" she exclaimed. Looking in every direction, Eve found that he was nowhere to be seen. Hesitantly, she waded into the water and stood next to Adam.

"And Lord," he intoned, still unaware that Eve was standing next to him, "I can't thank You enough for all the wonderful mementos You provided us." Then, turning toward her, Adam was horrified. "Oh, Eve, no." Striking his chest, he slowly sank into the water.

Just then, the Word of God appeared and dragged Adam to the shore. "Good, Lord," sputtered Adam as he blearily opened his eyes. "Oh, God, have pity on us, won't You?"

"Never mind that now, Adam," said the Word with the sternness of an older brother. "I want you to stand up like a man and explain to Eve what just happened. She's confused and needs to be able to look to you. She needs your sympathy right now. She doesn't need to be condemned. Do you understand Me?"

"Yes, Lord, I think so."

"Then go to her."

So Adam stood to his feet and walked over to Eve as she quietly wept. "Darling Eve, don't cry. Everything will be fine."

"No, Adam, it won't. I've ruined everything again, just when things were starting to get better for us."

Momentarily speechless, Adam turned to the Word, Who just nodded back as if to encourage him onward. "Don't say that, Eve," continued Adam. "It's all right. I promise: We're going to get through this. You'll see."

"Really?" murmured Eve, as Adam wiped the tears from her cheek. "You think so?"

"Of course."

"But I don't understand. Everything was going so well. We were so happy praying to the Lord, and then this little angel, this tiny wisp of an angel, looking as harmless as a butterfly, had to come along and spoil everything. Why would he do that?"

"An angel? What angel? What did this angel do?"

"A tiny angel came to me while I was praying in the water and said that God had heard our prayers, that He'd forgiven us, that we were finally going back to the garden. He said you were back at our cave, thanking God for His forgiveness, but he lied! He lied, Adam. He lied! Why would an angel of the Lord do something like that?"

"Oh, Eve, a true angel of God wouldn't lie."

"Well, that's what I thought, too."

"Eve, I'm afraid that wasn't one of God's angels. I think it was that damned Satan again. He probably saw us praying to God and decided he'd better stop us before the Lord had time to answer our prayers."

Like a bolt of lightning, his words sank into Eve's heart. "Oh, Adam, you're right. I can't believe I was so stupid. What was I thinking? Of course; that has to be it."

Then, Adam reached out and took hold of her hand. "Don't be so hard on yourself, dear. We're all bound to make mistakes with that despicable creature still lurking about."

AS THE SUN BEGAN to peek up over the eastern horizon, Adam and Eve stumbled out of their cave, looking weak and frail.

"It's been forty-three days, Eve, since we left the garden. Can you believe it?"

"Adam, my mouth is so dry. What's wrong with me?"

"Mine, too, Eve. And I'm so *hollow*."

WITH A FEEBLE SIGH, the couple sat down on the hilltop, just to the west of the garden, and there they looked out across the expansive landscape.

"My Lord and my God," said Adam, through parched lips. "You created me out of the ground and brought me into the garden on a Friday. Then You told me all about that tree, the one I was to avoid eating or even approaching. You told me, then and there, 'If you eat from this tree, you'll die.'"

"And when we did die on that very first day," Eve began, "just outside the garden gate, You could've left us like that, and You would've been perfectly justified. But no, in Your wondrous mercy, You chose to raise us so we could experience firsthand what a loving Creator You really are." Her words trailed off in tears.

"So, Lord," continued Adam, "could You help us again today? We're so empty. Our bodies are shriveling up. Our strength is withering away. What's wrong with us?"

Then the Word of God appeared. "Don't worry, you two. You'll be fine. You just need some nourishment, that's all."

Adam turned and meekly asked, "Nourishment? What's that?"

"Food for your stomach, liquid for your mouth; so you won't feel so *hollow* anymore."

"You mean we're not dying?"

"No, of course not. You're just hungry and thirsty."

"But why, Lord?" wondered Adam.

"It's because you don't live in the garden anymore. As long as you were there, you never knew a thing about hunger or thirst. How could you? You never experienced change or even had to sleep, but now you'll need to eat and drink to survive."

"Did you hear that, Eve? We just need to eat and drink, and we'll be fine."

"But we don't dare gather any of the fruit here," remarked Eve. "After all, look what happened to us when we tried that the first time."

"Relax, Eve," said the Word. "There are plenty of things to eat in this world besides the Fruit from the Tree of Knowledge. Feel free to have any of it to satisfy your needs." Then the Word vanished.

The couple exchanged a nervous look.

"But how will we know which is which?" asked Eve.

Adam just shrugged his shoulders.

Just then, the cherub responsible for guarding the entrance to Paradise flew over to Adam and Eve, and motioned for them to approach a fig tree. "Here, you two, God has instructed me to show you what is acceptable for you to eat. Now this is a fig tree, and these are figs."

The couple reluctantly plucked two figs from the tree, but in their weakened condition, they struggled even to hold them in their hands, considering the fact that these figs were, after all, much larger in those days, averaging the size of watermelons. Examining them closely, something struck them both at the same moment.

"Just look at these figs, Eve," groaned Adam, "and these *leaves*. Don't they look familiar?"

"Yes, Adam, they do look familiar; too familiar, I'm afraid."

"This is exactly the kind of fruit tree we tried hiding amongst when we realized we were naked for the first time."

And as if they were scalding hot, the couple dropped the figs and took a step back.

"We have no idea what kind of pain we'll feel if we eat these," sighed Eve.

Adam shuddered. "I don't even want to touch them anymore. Let's ask God if we can have some fruit from the Tree of Life instead."

So Adam and Eve walked away from the figs, and without knowing what else he could do, the cherub threw his hands up and flew back to his post at the garden's gate.

AS THE LATE AFTERNOON Sun began to inch its way toward the western horizon, Adam stood alone, just outside their cave. "Oh, God," he whispered, "it was the sixth hour of the sixth day when we defied Your direct orders. For just an instant, we disobeyed You, and this bitter struggle has been the result. But, Lord, don't be too harsh on us. Please, could You give us some of the Fruit from the Tree of Life to eat? We want to live again. We don't want to suffer like this anymore. After all, God, if anybody can fix a problem like this, it's You. Can't You please make these forty-three days of suffering equivalent to that one violation?"

Then the Word of God arrived. "I'm sorry, Adam, but I can't give you what you're asking for. I can't just give you the Fruit from the Tree of Life. At least not until the 5,500 years are completed."

Eve came out of the cave and stood next to Adam. "You can't give it to us?" she grumbled pathetically. "Or You won't?"

"Stop it, Eve," said the Word. "You know I would if I could, but there are just some things in this world that cannot be changed, no matter how much you wish them to be different. You're simply going to have to face up to that fact."

"Never mind, Eve, it's no use," insisted Adam. "We're just going to have to deal with it as is. And someday, we'll finally get what we're looking for."

"Someday," ranted Eve, "it's always *someday*. I'm sorry, Lord, but I feel like I'm losing my mind."

"I understand, Eve, really I do," said the Word. "But *someday* is still better than never."

"He does have a point, Eve," added Adam.

"And on that day, you and your righteous descendants will eat the Fruit from the Tree of Life and live forever. I promise."

Adam and Eve looked so disappointed.

"In the meantime, you two, I've already given you something to eat. You have your figs. So go ahead and eat them before you both die of hunger." And again the Word vanished.

So Adam turned to Eve and said, "Come on. I guess we should go back and get our figs."

Reluctantly, Eve nodded and started off with Adam on their journey.

The Fire That Burns

AROUND SUNSET, THE couple was back inside their cave, where they laid their figs down on the ground. Sitting down next to them, they stared at the figs for quite a while.

"Please, God," said Adam, "can't You satisfy our hunger without having us eat these things? I mean, what good will it do, really?"

"Just the thought of eating something again terrifies me," lamented Eve.

Then the Word of God arrived. "You know, you two, you never used to fast and pray like this before. How come? Why didn't you have this kind of apprehension before you violated My orders?"

The couple looked at each other, hoping that the other might offer some kind of reply.

"I'm afraid you're just going to have to get used to the fact that from now on your animal bodies can't survive without earthly food." And that quickly, the Word disappeared.

Slowly, then, Adam took his fig and placed it on the stack of gold. Eve put hers on the frankincense, and together they stood, praying silently well into the night.

AS THE SUN WAS RISING, Adam sat up and turned to Eve. "Come on, Eve, let's get going."

"Where are we going now?"

"I want to visit the spot where we could see the Tree of life, where the river splits in four directions. God may not be able to give us any of the Fruit from the Tree of Life, but maybe He'll let us drink some of the water flowing from its roots."

STEPPING TO THE river's edge, the couple turned their eyes skyward.

"Lord," began Adam, "while we were still in the garden we remember seeing the water that flowed from beneath the Tree of Life, but we never felt any need for it then. Now, here we are outside of Your mercy, and we see this water flowing right past us."

"We're dead, Lord; our flesh is so dry," added Eve. "We need the other water now more than ever. So, please, could You give us some of the Water of Life so we can live again?"

Then the Word of God appeared. "Why do you two keep asking Me for things You know I can't give you yet. The water from that tree is no different than its fruit. I can't give you either one. It simply isn't allowed until the day I descend into Hades to break the gates of brass and smash the kingdom of iron!"

"But when will that be, Lord?" blurted Adam.

"When the end of the world arrives, Adam; on the day I shed My blood on your head at Golgotha. Then, and only then, will that blood be the Water of Life for you. And not for you alone but for every one of your descendants who trusts in Me."

"But, Lord," groaned Eve, "I don't think we can wait that long."

"Relax, both of you. Now, I've provided you with food, but you refuse to eat. Fine. I won't force you to eat. And just because I can't give you the Water of Life, doesn't mean I'm not allowing you to drink from the water that's flowing past you. So, just as I've instructed you to eat when you're ready to eat, when you're ready to drink, feel free to drink, but I suggest you do it quickly." Then the Word vanished.

Adam and Eve stared longingly into the crystal-clear water for quite a while, but eventually, they left the river, still without drinking any of it, and headed back home.

AROUND NOONTIME, the couple approached their cave. As they did, they noticed a pillar of smoke rising near it. Startled, they stopped and stared, wide-eyed.

"Eve, why is there smoke coming from our cave? We didn't do anything to cause a fire like that, did we?"

"Of course not, Adam."

So the couple sprinted the rest of the way back to their cave, and when they got there, they were horrified to find a huge fire at its entrance.

"How could a fire like this have started, Eve?"

"I'm not sure we should even call it *fire*," she gasped. "I've never seen anything quite like it, except for when God sent that cherub with lightning in his hand. Remember?"

"That's right; this *must* be that same fire from the cherub's sword. He's trying to keep us out of our cave. God must be mad at us because we keep refusing to eat or drink!"

"Oh, Adam, it's true."

"But where will we live now?"

Eve clutched desperately at his arm. "And Adam, what if the darkness there is even worse than it is here?"

"Or worse still, what if He never wants to see us again? What then? All because we keep disobeying Him."

"Because we keep asking Him for so many things, that's why! And after we finally started to find some happiness here."

"Oh, Eve, if we travel even further away from God and the garden, how will we ever find Him again?"

"How will He ever be able to comfort us with His presence?"

"And if we can't find Him anymore, what's going to happen to the promise He made to us about the five and a half days?"

Helpless to do a thing, they just stood and stared as the blaze grew more intense with each passing moment.

UNBEKNOWNST TO ADAM and Eve, however, was the fact that Satan and his demons were at the heart of the matter.

"Quickly, my minions," snarled the devil, "bring me more material for our glorious fire!"

One by one, his demons threw tree branches and dry grass into the rear of the fire, fueling it with a tremendous crackle.

"Oh, my word," cooed Satan, utterly gleeful. "I can just see their pathetic faces as they watch their precious 'home away from home' burning to the ground, and there's not a damn thing they can do about it! Just the thought gives me goose bumps all over."

A sadistic laughter rang out among his legions.

"But, Master," interjected his lieutenant, apparently confused about something. "How come the blaze isn't destroying their cave? It seems to burn right up to its very edge but then no further. Is there some sort of shield protecting it from our fire? Or are my eyes merely deceiving me?"

"What?" blurted Satan, who turned to see what he was describing. "What are you babbling about now?"

Sure enough, as the devil hovered over to get a closer look, he could see for himself that the fire was burning right up to an inch or so from the cave. Reaching through the flames, Satan touched the wall of the cave with his hideous paw. "It can't be; but it is! Even though our fire burns as hot as the Sun, their filthy cave remains cool to the touch. What is the meaning of this outrage? Is there no justice to be had in this god-forsaken Universe?"

From within the thin barrier between the cave and the fire, a peculiar set of eyes suddenly materialized in plain sight.

"What is this, then?" growled the devil.

Then, along with the eyes, a face began to take shape, a cherub's face. "Don't be alarmed, Satan," said the cherub with a satisfied smirk. "It's only me."

Baffled, the devil inched forward, as did several of his confused demons alongside him. "M—Me?" stammered Satan. "Who the Hell is me?"

"I'm the cherub who guards the gate to Paradise. That's who."

"That scrawny, little puke I've seen buzzing about with his flaming sword? You mean that one?"

The face proudly nodded. "Undeniably, you foul creature. So glad to meet you, too."

"How dare you spoil my plans this way!" Enraged, the devil thrust his leathery fist in the direction of the cherub's satisfied grin, but because it instantly vanished, he only punched the wall of the cave. The devil let loose an angry, painful howl. "Ahhh!"

AS THE FLAMES continued to blaze out of control, Adam and Eve could only stand and watch the raging inferno, helpless and dumbfounded.

"Adam, are you sure we can't do anything? Can't we at least ask God for help?"

Adam shook his head. "I don't see why God would want to help us if He's already mad at us."

"Oh, that's right; I forgot. Then it's useless. We're doomed."

"There is one thing we could do, though."

"What?"

"If God won't help us put the fire out, maybe He'll at least tell us why the fire got started in the first place."

Eve nodded. "He might. So ask Him."

SATAN KEPT MOTIONING for his minions to continue bringing more tree branches and dry grass to throw into the fire. "I don't care how much that lousy excuse for a cherub tries to thwart me. I'm going to destroy this cave and everything in it, if it's the last thing I do!"

As his lieutenant proceeded to fuel the fire, he mumbled, "But are you sure it will do any good? The cherub said —"

"I don't give a damn what that little puke said! Bring me more branches, more grass! You hear me?"

"Yes, Master."

Buzzing into action, more demons followed suit and continued to stoke the fire, until the flames engulfed the entire cave. Still, the keen eyes of the cherub peered out from the invisible firewall as he intently watched Satan's futile attempt to breach his protective shield.

Finally, the Word of God appeared. "Enough already, Devil! Can't you see you're wasting your time?"

"This is an outrage, I tell you!" Satan screeched, sheepishly clutching a tree branch in his miserable paw, like a child caught with his hand in the cookie jar. "Why do you keep helping these two? What have they ever done to deserve your favor?"

"I'm sorry you don't understand, Satan, but I'm afraid you wouldn't believe Me even if I told you. Sadly, that is the curse of the liar. The liar doesn't know how to believe the truth, even when it's told to him."

Frustrated, the devil threw down the branch and stomped on it. "I am so sick of your double-talk! Why can't you ever say something I can understand?"

Slowly but surely, Satan's embarrassed minions began to retreat from view, one by one.

"You really are pathetic," insisted the Word. "You manage to deceive My servants and get them kicked out of Paradise, but that's not good enough for you. Now you won't stop until you destroy every last shred of their happiness, even if it means killing them."

"Well, what do you expect? Everything that used to belong to me is Adam's now! You know, if you're such a merciful god as you purport to be, you'd see your way to being kind to *me* once in awhile, too. Don't you think?"

"But I have been merciful to you. If I hadn't, I'd have already destroyed you and all your wretched minions. Instead, I've been patient with you, and will be until the end of the world. Now away with you, before I change My mind."

Satan fled angrily, and just as abruptly the Word vanished.

As soon as the devil and his crew withdrew, the fire began to subside. When Adam and Eve saw the blaze beginning to die down, they began to cautiously approach the cave. Without warning, the fire shifted and began moving toward them with its lashing flames. Horrified, the couple watched as it slowly encircled them.

"I guess God really is mad at us," remarked Eve. "Maybe that's why he doesn't tell us how the fire got started. He assumes we already know."

"I think you're right, Eve. Just look at these flames! Remember when we had the same thing inside us?"

"I do. But that seems like so long ago now. It used to yield to us; but not anymore, not since we've transgressed the limits of our creation."

"But this fire hasn't been affected at all!" shouted Adam, as the flames crept closer and closer. "Now it has complete power over us!"

As the couple moved to evade the fire, it moved to cut off their path of retreat.

"Oh, God," cried Eve, "just look at this inferno! It has a mind of its own. Wherever we turn, it's right there trying to scorch us."

"Lord, please, help us. This wall of flames won't let us get back into the cave that you ordered us to live in. Please tell us what to do!"

Then the Word of God appeared right next to them.

"Thank you, Lord, we're so glad to see You," cried Adam. "We thought You'd abandoned us for good this time."

Gazing into the flames, even the Word seemed mesmerized by the fire as it threw its sparks in every direction. "Just look at this fire, Adam! Do you see how different it is from everything else in the Garden of Delights?"

"Yes, Lord, I do. But why has it changed so much?"

"As long as you obeyed My command, it yielded to you, but as a result of your downfall, it's now able to attack you. So do you see how Satan has exalted you after all? Did you really think he loved you when he said he'd raise you On-High?"

"Then why did he do it?"

Turning from the flames, the Word looked Adam straight in the eye. "Why do you think? He wanted you to leave the light and stumble into darkness, to drag you down into slavery, to see your happiness turn into misery, and your peace become struggle."

"Oh, Eve," murmured Adam, unable to bear the searing eyes of the Word, turning back toward the flames, which were infinitely more bearable than the Lord's penetrating gaze. "Just look at this fire."

"That's right, Adam," continued the Word. "Take a good look at it, and see how it surrounds you. Then realize it will do the same thing to you and your descendants whenever you do things his way. He'll torment you with fire, and after you die, you'll go down to Hades. Then you'll see what it really means to burn in his fire."

Adam and Eve exchanged a terrified look.

"There, you and your descendants will stay until the time of My coming. So just as you're unable to enter your cave because of this inferno, you'll be imprisoned until I make a way of escape for you." Then the Word raised His right hand toward the flames. "Listen to Me, fire. I want you to make a pathway for My servants to walk through."

The fire began to slowly part in the middle. It continued to spread until a pathway opened up in its midst, and the couple cautiously started through the corridor. Then the Word vanished. As Adam and Eve passed through the gap in the fire, Satan's ugly face materialized and blew into the flames like a whirlwind, causing some of the flames to lash out and scorch their skin.

"Lord, save us!" cried Adam. "Please don't let us be swallowed by this fire!"

Again the Word returned, His arms spread wide, and extinguished the flames once and for all. This time, however, the wounds remained on their bodies.

"What happened, Lord?" asked Adam, grimacing from his burns. "We were so close to making it through unharmed."

"It was that damned Satan again. He couldn't resist one last opportunity to hurt you. So you see: The one who promised to give you divinity, instead burns you with fire. How fitting is that? Do you still believe Satan loves you?"

The couple solemnly shook their heads. "No, sir," they said in unison.

"But look, I'm the One Who created you. Do you realize how many times now I've rescued you from his attack?"

This time they both nodded with a sad smile.

"And Eve," continued the Word, "what did Satan promise you in the garden?"

She meekly replied, "He told us that when we ate from that tree our eyes would be opened, and we'd become like gods, knowing good and evil."

"Well, how is that for sweet irony?" asked the Word with an uncharacteristic smirk. "He's made you see fire's power over you; how it burns. And now you're seeing every evil that Satan has planned for you and your descendants! So, in fact, your eyes have been opened, haven't they?"

Then the Word vanished while Adam and Eve just looked at one another, utterly dismayed.

Rock of Ages

INSIDE THEIR CAVE, Adam and Eve were still trembling from their experience with the fire, still agonizing over the searing burns on their bodies.

"Oh, Eve, if fire burns our skin like this now, just imagine what it's going to be like when we're dead and Satan punishes our souls."

"And right now our rescue seems so far away. If only God in His mercy would come to fulfill His promise sooner."

Even as the daylight was fading the embers from the fire were still smoldering. Just then, a breeze fanned a tiny flame alive, and slowly it began creeping toward Adam and Eve. The couple exchanged a troubled look and cautiously backed away.

LATER THAT NIGHT, the couple walked up to the summit of the hill that overlooked the western border of the Garden of Eden. There they sat bathed in the light of a full Moon, just staring down at the garden, as the cherub buzzed about its perimeter, darting about, here and there, searching for possible intruders. Exhausted, the weary couple then laid back and fell asleep, quite peacefully, under that shimmering, moonlit sky.

BUT SATAN EVEN despised the sight of them sleeping. Like a persistent gnat that will not go away, the devil and several of his grotesque henchman hovered above the dozing couple. "I still don't get it," grumbled Satan. "Why does god keep promising salvation for Adam and Eve, but not me? He's never promised *me* a thing!"

"God isn't so good, after all, is he?" grunted his lieutenant. "If he were, then he'd save us, too. Where's our contract?"

"The goodness of god is meaningless, I tell you," Satan continued, his hollow, black eyes growing wider. "We're doomed to live in a Universe without hope! There's nothing left for us but an unquenchable demand for revenge."

"Then revenge is what you'll have, Master," growled his lieutenant. "What do you suggest?"

"Let me see," muttered the devil, mulling over his options. "Subterfuge has failed again and again. Even my old friend fire has failed me. So what else is left? There must be something we can do to get rid of these miserable humans."

"I say we just kill them and be done with it," replied the lieutenant. "Then the Earth will finally be rid of the pestilence of Adam and Eve."

"Of course," continued Satan, relishing the idea. "And once they're dead and gone, there won't *be* any descendants to inherit our old kingdom. It will be my exclusive domain once again! *Then* god will have to take me back."

With a puzzled look on his ugly face, one demon there turned to the fellow next to him. "I don't get it. Isn't that what I've been saying all along?"

The other demon glared back at him. "Fool, who are you to question the master's wisdom?"

"I'm not," grunted the first demon. "I'm just saying, that's all."

"Well, if I were you, I'd keep my filthy trap shut; unless you want to end up becoming food yourself."

"Forget I even mentioned it," he muttered. Then, returning his attention front and center, he burst out with a blood-curdling scream. "Death to Adam and Eve! Let's rip their hearts out and eat them!"

Inspired by his sadistic sentiment, the whole group resounded with a single, guttural howl. "Death to Adam and Eve!"

"Absolutely, my precious legions," growled the devil. Intoxicated by such a rousing display of bloodlust, he motioned to his minions. "Now, gather round."

As though drawn in by an invisible net, they all moved in closely.

"Our most malcontent Lord," scowled one of them, "what would you have us do?"

"I propose, hmmm, let me see," he began, scratching his furry chin, his malicious eyes scanning the eager faces before him. "Yes, I propose we find a huge rock and smash them into oblivion! That way there'll be nothing left of them for god to restore!"

The whole assembly let out a boisterous roar and eagerly swooped down to where Adam and Eve were still fast asleep. Turning to his lieutenant, Satan snarled, "And make sure the rock you choose has no craters or holes of any kind, or else they might escape being crushed. Is that understood?"

"Certainly, Master," replied the lieutenant. "Consider it done."

THE DEMONS SOON found a gigantic stone, wide and smooth. The group hovered about this stone, meticulously searching for any imperfections.

"This one is perfect, Master," said his lieutenant.

"Good," the devil replied. "Then pick it up and drop it on them! And be quick about it. The last thing we need is to have that misanthropic god of theirs showing up to foil our plans again."

Then, as if according to a single mind, the legion moved into action and together they hoisted the huge rock from its resting place.

"And I want you to make sure it doesn't roll off of them after it lands!" scowled Satan.

"Yes, Lord," grunted the lieutenant. "Your wish is our command."

So they took the colossal stone and maneuvered it directly over the sleeping couple. Then, they simply let go. The rock headed straight for them and landed with a tremendous thud.

"Good shot, you infernal bastards!" howled Satan. "I don't believe it! We did it! We've killed Adam and Eve. Be still my heart. We're free at last!"

A wave of horrid joy shot through the ranks of his legion. "We did it!" snorted one of them, turning to the fellow next to him. "Did you see that? We dropped that baby right on them, and there wasn't a damn thing they could do about it! Smash, boom, dead! Did you see it?"

Wide-eyed, fangs glistening, the other demon slapped him on the back with a hearty blow. "You better believe I saw it! And it was beautiful! What I wouldn't give to see the look on god's face right now!"

"Or Adam and Eve's faces, for that matter," replied the first. "If they still had faces!"

Their raucous laughter echoed for several moments while Satan continued to look down at the scene with such happiness. "I don't think I've ever seen a more beautiful rock in my entire, miserable life. I think I'm actually going to shed a tear." A sliver of a teardrop dribbled down his cheek, and he wiped it away in an instant. "Oh, there it was. My word, I haven't had a good cry like that in I don't know how long." But as the devil watched his demons frolicking about in such ecstasy, the look of joy suddenly washed away from his despicable face, to be replaced by his familiar scowl. "Enough already. The deed is done. Party time is over. We'd better vacate the premises before the meddler god shows up to check on his little darlings. We certainly don't want to be around for that." With a wave of his leathery paw, he shouted, "Now all of you, back to work!"

And just like that, the entire lot of demonic hosts jumped to attention and catapulted out of sight as if they had all been shot from a cannon.

FROM OUT OF NOWHERE, two angels appeared and flew down to the boulder. "Did you see what I just saw?" murmured the first angel.

"I'm afraid so, yes," replied the second with a painful grimace.

"Oh, dear, I can't believe those despicable monsters actually got away with it."

Inspecting the surface of the giant stone, the second angel noticed something. "Look, there's a crack in the rock."

"A crack?" asked the first. "How odd. A rock this size shouldn't have a crack in it after landing on a grassy knoll."

"It's not merely a crack, though. It's actually a small crevice punched straight through the slab."

"That *is* odd. Should we have a look?"

The second angel nodded eagerly and said, "Very well, then."

And together the two angels shrank down to the size of two insects. Then they walked straight through the crevice in the stone as if it were a very sizable doorway. Inside, they could hardly believe their eyes.

"Can it be?" gasped the first angel.

"Have you ever seen anything like this in all your days?" the second one said, quietly in awe.

"Absolutely not."

"But we both saw it with our own eyes, didn't we? The devil and his legions dropped a giant boulder on Adam and Eve while they lay sleeping, yes?"

"Yes, that's right; I saw it, too," insisted the first angel. "But it doesn't appear to be a boulder anymore at all, does it? It's…"

Mystified, the two tiny angels gaped upward at their strange surroundings.

"It—*It's* a canopy," stammered the second.

Sure enough, the angels gazed up, not at solid rock, as they had expected to see, but at a hollowed-out cavern, hewn out of the stone's core, and by the moonlight that peeked in through the crevice in the rock, they could also see two figures lying at the center of this, from their miniature perspectives, rocky cathedral.

"And those two figures on the ground there—"

"Are none other than Adam and Eve."

The couple woke up suddenly, and, sitting up, looked at one another, confused and groggy.

"Thank the Lord above," the first angel whispered.

"They're still alive after all," added the second.

And like two flying insects, the pair flitted back out through the crevice in the rock and disappeared.

"Eve?" mumbled Adam as he looked around, completely disoriented. "What is going on? Where are we?"

"You're asking me?" replied Eve, trying to shake the cobwebs from her mind. "How should I know?"

With eyes still weary, the couple peered through the dusty interior, lit only by the streak of moonlight filtering in through the crevice in the slab face.

Confused, Adam struggled to his feet and walked over to the stone wall. "Are we in some kind of cave?" Reaching out and touching the wall, he instantly drew his hand back as though he had been burned. His jaw dropped and he turned to Eve.

"Well," snapped Eve, "don't just stand there, Adam. Tell me. What's going on? Where are we?"

"We *are* in a cave, Eve, but it doesn't look like our cave. It seems more like we're inside a gigantic rock."

"Good Lord, Adam," exclaimed Eve, springing to her feet in a panic and moving to the wall to touch it for herself. "Last night we fell asleep under the stars; and now you're telling me we're inside a rock? How is that even possible?"

"I don't know, Eve. We've seen a lot of strange things since we left the garden, but this is definitely the strangest of them all."

"What did we do to cause a rock to bend itself over us like this? And what's next? Does the ground open up and swallow us?"

"Maybe God is mad at us because we left the cave without His permission. You know we only came here last night because we wanted to."

"We came here," insisted Eve, "because that fire wouldn't stop coming after us. You don't think God would be angry with us just because we tried to escape the fire, do you?"

"I don't know. Maybe God will tell us Himself."

"Then ask Him, Adam; ask Him now, please."

So Adam lifted his eyes toward the ceiling of that rocky cathedral. "Dear Lord, could You please tell us what has happened that we've now found ourselves under this rock? Are You mad at us for leaving the cave?"

Immediately, the Word of God appeared.

"Lord, thank you for answering our prayers," said Adam. "I can't tell—"

But before he could continue with another word, the Word put up His hand to stop him. "Never mind that now, Adam. I have an important question to ask you."

"Certainly, Lord. What is it?"

"Tell me, who told you to leave the cave and come to the hilltop overlooking the garden?"

The couple exchanged a worried look.

"See, Eve, I told you He was mad at us for leaving the cave."

"Don't talk to her, Adam, talk to Me. Now, who told you to leave?"

"No one, Lord," he meekly replied. "We only came here because of the heat from the fire. It wouldn't stop coming after us; not even in our cave."

"Really," said the Word, "you came here because a little flame chased you?"

"I'm sorry, Lord," interjected Eve, "but we're not sure if You're teasing us or what, because if You are, I don't think You're being fair. Adam and I were badly burned in that fire. Just the sight of it coming after us was very traumatic. And here you are chiding us for running away. What should we have done? Laid down next to it and gone to sleep?"

"Of course not, Eve, but seriously, if you're that disturbed by one night with the heat, how are you ever going to endure it while you're in Hades? Not to mention the fact that, by leaving your cave, you risked a fate far worse than the burning of your skin. Did you ever consider that for even a moment? Why didn't you just ask Adam to put it out, anyway? It wasn't that big of a fire, was it?"

"So that's why You covered us with this miserable rock?" wondered Adam. "A rock this heavy could've crushed us. Wasn't there any other way You could've taught us a lesson?"

"What makes you so sure I put this rock on you, Adam? I'm not the one who's trying to kill you, you know. This was Satan's doing. He's convinced himself that if he can kill you two, then I'll have no choice but to restore him to his old life."

"Satan?" exclaimed Adam. "But how?"

"His minions dropped a huge boulder on you, but in My kindness, just as the rock was falling, I told it to form this canopy over you."

Eve pointed down at their feet. "Look, Adam, He even lowered the ground beneath us."

"So You're not really mad at us?" asked Adam, embarrassed with himself.

"No, I'm not mad at you, but I am disappointed you didn't stand up for yourself in the cave. I'm disappointed you left without a fight. When are you two ever going to learn? With Me on your side, you can face anything, any storm, any attack, no matter how unsettling it may appear on the surface."

As His words sank into their hearts, they appeared deeply moved.

"Oh, Lord," muttered Eve, "I am so sorry for doubting You."

"Yes, Lord," said Adam, "we're both sorry for doubting You, and especially for not asking You to help us extinguish that flame."

"And thank you for turning this rock into a cave for us," added Eve.

"Of course, you two," said the Word. "I accept your apology."

"And, boy, were we scared when we woke up under this thing, Lord," Adam continued with a sheepish grin, trying to lighten up the somber mood. "You should have seen the look on Eve's face. But I guess You never have anything like this happen to You, what with You being the Lord and all."

"Don't be too sure of yourself, Adam. In fact, this very thing *will* happen to Me when I'm born on this Earth someday. Satan will stir up certain leaders among the Jews and drive them to put Me to death. Then they'll lay Me inside a cave, just like this one, where I'll stay for three days and nights, but on the third day, I'll rise again and provide salvation for you and your descendants."

Adam and Eve exchanged a puzzled look. They had no idea how to respond.

"Now, Adam, because you left the cave and came here without permission, I won't be letting you out from under this rock for three days. But don't despair; after the appointed time, I will set you free. Is that understood?"

Solemnly, the couple nodded.

"Yes, Lord," replied Adam. "We understand."

Then the Word vanished.

THREE DAYS LATER, an earthquake split the rock open, from top to bottom, and Adam and Eve slowly crawled out from underneath it. By then, their skin was extremely withered. Squinting at the Sun, the couple wandered around in a daze for quite a while.

"Thank God we finally got out of there," Adam said, stumbling slightly before righting himself. "I don't think I could've taken it much longer."

"I thought I was going to suffocate at any moment," added Eve, who sat down awkwardly, still trying to catch her breath.

LATER THAT AFTERNOON, the couple was back inside the Cave of Treasures, where the first thing they did was to go around making sure that all their mementos were still intact.

"Well," said Adam, "it looks as though everything is still here. Gold, frankincense, myrrh, all just the way we left it. You know, Eve, I hate to say it, but I've never been so glad to see this old cave as I am today."

"I hate to say it, too," said Eve with an embarrassed smile. "But after that fire nearly destroyed it and after three days under that rock, I feel the same way."

"Funny how something like that could happen, huh?" Adam said as he reached out and hugged Eve.

"Yeah, funny," was all she said.

Emblems of Hope

THEN CAME THE DAWN of the fifty-first day of their having been exiled from the garden, and when Adam got up early that morning, he said, "Come on, Eve, let's go and do some work. It'll be good for us."

"Work? What kind of work?"

"I don't know. I'm sure we'll think of something."

"I'll tell you what I'd like to do."

"What?"

"I'd like to find something to wear besides fig leaves. Do you think we can do that?"

"I don't see why not, if we try hard enough. Let's go."

SO THE COUPLE WALKED along the northern perimeter of the garden without really knowing exactly what they were searching for; they were just searching. Suddenly, Eve stopped and wiped her sweaty brow. Then, looking down at her dirty hands, she tried to wipe them off on her fig-leaf skirt. Finding her hands were no cleaner than they were before, she let out an exasperated sigh.

Watching her intently, Adam asked, "What's wrong, dear?"

"Oh, Adam, just look at us. We've spent so much time walking around in this heat, lying around in musty caves, rolling around in the dirt, we're filthy."

Adam shrugged. "Maybe God can help us figure out what to do about it."

Then the Word of God appeared. "Adam, take Eve with you and go to the seashore where you fasted before. There you'll find the skins of sheep that have been eaten by a lion. Now, just the skins remain. Take them and use them to make clothing for yourselves."

"Did you hear that, Eve? The Lord has clothing for us instead of these useless fig leaves?"

Eve nodded with a grateful smile. "That's nice, Adam. Thank You, Lord."

"And Lord?"

"Yes, Adam."

"What is *clothing*, anyway?"

"It's what you wrap around your body to keep it dry and clean, something you wear to protect it from the cold, the wind and the rain."

"That sounds like just what we're looking for. Thank You, Lord."

"NO, NO, NO, YOU'RE lying!" shrieked Satan. "I don't believe a word of it! You're a filthy liar!"

"But it's true, Master," insisted his lieutenant. "I've seen them with my own two eyes. There's not a scratch on them."

"But how? I watched them get smashed into oblivion! Certainly it must be some sort of illusion. God is playing a trick on me because he knows I've killed his little darlings."

"I don't think so, Lord. We just overheard god instructing Adam and Eve to go to the ocean, where they'd be receiving sheepskins they could turn into clothing, whatever that is."

"What am I going to do now? I thought for sure I'd gotten rid of them."
For the longest time, the devil fumed vehemently. Finally he turned ever so
slowly to his lieutenant. "When you picked out that boulder, I specifically
told you to find one with no holes in it, didn't I?"

"We did, Lord, and the rock was flawless. Trust me. I would never lie
to you, *never*."

"Flawless, my eye. And as for your not lying to me, let's not even go
there."

"But, Lord—"

"Enough! Off to the Abyss with you!" Satan simply waved his paw, and
the howling lieutenant was instantly sucked away into oblivion. Craning his
wolfen head, the devil looked around with a vicious scowl. "Now, who's
next in line?"

CURSING INCOHERENTLY under his breath, Satan was striding along the
seashore, heading straight for the sheepskins lying on the beach. "As usual,
when you want something done right, you have to do it yourself. What was
I thinking, anyway, asking a bunch of worthless rejects to do something as
basic as crushing a couple of humans with a boulder?" Stepping up to the
skins, his eyes thinned as he looked them over. "Now, as for these sheepskins, I still haven't decided. Should I throw them into the sea, or should I
burn them? Personally, I am so inclined toward burning."

But just as he was reaching down to grab them, the Word of God appeared. "Not so fast, Devil!"

"What the—" Satan sputtered, and before he even had a chance to put
up a fight, he found himself tightly wrapped in a brass chain. "Not you
again," he muttered, thoroughly deflated as he fell prostrate into the sand.

"Your new outfit suits you," said the Word with a wry smile. "I hope
you enjoy it." And then He disappeared, leaving the devil lying there next
to the sheepskins.

"Come back here, you coward!" grunted Satan.

EVENTUALLY, ADAM and Eve came walking along the seashore, quite
casually, when suddenly something caught Adam's attention. "Look, Eve,
there are the sheepskins God told us about."

But as they walked closer, they were confused by the added spectacle
of what they had never expected to see. "Adam, is someone lying next to
them?" wondered Eve. "What's he doing there?"

"It looks like he's chained up."

"I wonder who it is."

"Who," wondered Adam, "or *what*, you mean."

Then the Word of God returned. "Don't you two recognize your archenemy?"

The couple stared blankly at the prostrate figure awhile, before they shook their heads.

"Not really, no," said Adam.

"Of course, you know who this is," the Word insisted. "The one who tricked you by hiding in the serpent? Who fooled you by disguising himself as an angel? Remember?"

Adam turned to Eve. "Do you recognize this creature, Eve?"

"Of course you do," pressed the Word. "The one who promised you divinity?"

Eve shook her head in exasperation. "I'm confused, Lord. You say we should know him, but at the same time You say he's different things at different times. First he's a serpent, then he's an angel, now here he is looking like this hideous monster. What is he really? And how are we supposed to recognize him if he keeps changing his appearance?"

The couple expectantly stared back at the Word.

"She does make a good point, Lord," replied Adam.

"She makes a very good point, yes; but therein lies the rub. A creature that can appear as any one of these things *better* be recognized, and recognized quickly."

Then Adam turned to Eve. "Now He makes a good point." Thoroughly confused, Adam hung his head. "This is all very hard to take in, Lord. Could You please start over from the beginning? Who is this monster that we should know him?"

"This is the horror among the angels," continued the Word, "the source of all pride, the father of lies, the one who was responsible for your fall from grace. This is Satan."

Suddenly Adam and Eve's eyes grew wide with rage. "*Him!*" they said as one.

"You mean *he's* the one who tricked us into eating from the Tree of Knowledge?" sputtered Adam.

"*He's* the one who got us kicked out of our garden home?" screeched Eve.

"He's the one all right," added the Word, "lying here in all his miserable splendor. So much for his hollow promises now."

"But why don't You banish him, Lord?" Adam wondered, "like You banished the serpent, like you banished *us*?"

"I did banish him, but his banishment is of a different nature than that of the serpent's or yours, because Satan's nature is altogether different than any fleshly creature."

"Well if you banished him, how'd he get here?" asked Eve.

"He's here because in My providence I lured him here. He thought he could destroy the sheepskins I provided for you, but it was My intention to chain him until you arrived so you could see, once and for all, just how weak and powerless he really is. That is his true banishment, a banishment infinitely harsher than either you or the serpent will ever have to endure."

With just a wave of the Word's hand, the shackles fell away from Satan, and instantly he flew away, spewing his venomous curses as he went. For several awkward moments, Adam and Eve just stood there, and turning to the Word, they found Him gone again.

"Adam, why does He just disappear like that? Couldn't He at least say goodbye, or something?"

"Never mind that now, Eve. Let's just get our sheepskins and go back to our cave, before we get into any more trouble."

"Fine, but before we do, I'd like to wash up. If we're going to start wearing clothes, we should probably be clean before we put them on."

"Whatever you say, Eve. Let's hurry, though, and be done with it."

SO THE TWO OF THEM hastily washed up in the ocean, and before long they came out of the water cleaner than they had been in a long time. To the sheepskins, Adam stood and stared blankly at them for several moments.

"What's wrong now, Adam?"

"I'm sad thinking about how we got these skins, that's all."

"Sad, why?"

"I'm sad because these skins have come from owners who have died, and when we put them on, we'll be wearing emblems of their death."

"And someday," continued Eve, beginning to realize what he was saying, "we'll die just like they did, won't we?"

BACK INSIDE THEIR cave, Adam and Eve laid the sheepskins down, and again they dolefully stared at them for quite a while.

"Lord, now that we have these skins," said Adam, "could You please tell us what to do with them? How are we supposed to *make* clothes with them? We have no idea how to do something like that."

An angel suddenly appeared there in the cave. "Very well, then. God has instructed me to show you how to make clothes. Go get some palm thorns."

RETURNING WITH a handful of thorns, Adam handed them to the angel, who began to diligently work with the skins. First, the angel took a thorn and attached a long, thin string to it. Then, right in front of them, so they could both get a good look at what he was doing, he pierced the skins with the thorn and pulled the string through. So adept was this angel with his thorn that he wove his thread into those skins in such a way that the stitch was virtually invisible and that the entire thing was sown together with a single strand. Then he repeated the same process so that when he was finished he had created two complete outfits, one for Adam and one for Eve. Both were given loincloths for their waists, while Eve received a slender top to cover her breasts. The couple eagerly put them on.

"How does it look Adam?" asked Eve, twirling about the cave in her new outfit.

"It looks great, Eve."

"I love the way it fits. Thank you so much. You really are an angel sent from above."

"You're welcome," he replied. "It's been a pleasure to serve you. Goodbye now."

"Goodbye," said Eve.

Then, the angel streaked out of view.

"See, Adam, the angel says goodbye when he leaves. Why doesn't the Lord?"

"Maybe because when the Lord leaves our presence, He's not really gone. He's still right here in our midst."

Intrigued, Eve nodded. "You know, Adam, I think you might be right. What a comforting thought." Walking over to him, she planted a kiss on his cheek. "I never thought of it that way before. Thank you for that."

Obviously proud of himself, Adam smiled.

As a Roaring Lion

THE NEXT MORNING, the couple got up and surveyed the world from the mouth of the cave.

"Lord, bless us today," said Adam, "and help us to know what we should do so You'll always be proud of us."

"Very good, Adam. What would you like to do today?"

"I don't know," he replied with an innocent shrug. "I was just thinking, since we still have no idea what's off in the West, it might be nice to see what's out there."

HEADING INTO THE West, the pair had not gone very far, when Satan spotted them from a distance. "What have we here? Two wandering doves, I see, helpless as can be." And landing behind a bush, the devil transformed himself into a lion. "My word, this body of mine is absolutely ravenous. I feel as though I haven't eaten a thing for three days. I wonder what's on the menu."

Appearing on the horizon, the unsuspecting Adam and Eve began to approach Satan's position. "Ah, if it isn't the main course," growled the devil, "headed right this way."

With barely a sound, the lion darted out from his hiding place and started to charge Adam and Eve. Instantly, the couple saw him coming. Eve let out a blood-curdling scream, and Adam instinctively stepped in front of her, acting as a shield. "Lord, save us!" he cried.

Still, the lion galloped closer and closer, until finally, just a few feet away, the Word of God materialized in his direct path toward the couple. Too close to stop, the lion tried to swerve around the Word, but with just a touch from His hand, the lion was catapulted into the surrounding brush, where he became thoroughly entangled. Terrified, Eve fell into Adam's arms.

"It's okay, Eve. The danger's passed. The Lord's prevailed again."

"Thank God," murmured Eve, "I thought for sure we were dead."

"Thank You, Lord," said Adam. "What would we ever do without You?"

Still trembling, Eve gaped at the prostrate lion as it struggled to extricate itself, to no avail. "But why, Lord, why did this lion attack us? Didn't they pledge to not attack us as long as we never tried to harm them?"

The Word nodded. "They did, yes, but this is no ordinary lion." And with a wave of His hand, He caused the lion to transform back into its true appearance.

The horrified couple took a step back.

"Satan," was all Adam said.

"That's right, Satan," echoed the Word, "lurking about as a roaring lion, seeking whom he may devour."

"No wonder it attacked us, Eve," said Adam, as Eve still clung firmly to him. "But see, just like I told you, the Lord never left us for a moment."

"Now away with you, Devil!" shouted the Word, and after another wave of His hand, Satan's entanglement loosened and fell from his body. Without a sound, he flew away in a whirlwind of dust.

Then the Word turned to the couple and smiled reassuringly. "I'll bet that's the first time you ever saw the devil completely speechless."

Forcing a smile, they both nodded.

"So tell me, Adam," the Word continued. "What are you doing out here in the West? Isn't your home east of this place?"

"Yes, Lord. Eve and I were just out here exploring. We were curious to see what lay in this direction, that's all."

"I see. You almost paid a very dear price for the sake of curiosity, didn't you?"

Timidly, Adam nodded. "We did, yes."

"You've got to be more careful, Adam. I warned you before, to never go wandering off like this. But still, you don't seem to realize how precarious your situation is. As long as you reside where I've designated, you know you're safe. But when you choose to go wherever you please, then this is the result. Is that what you really want for you and Eve?"

Adam shrugged his shoulders. "Of course not, Lord."

"Then go back to your home and stay close. I don't want you to allow any more opportunities for Satan to attack you."

Then the Word vanished, leaving the couple still trembling from their experience. Once again, without a word, they slowly headed toward home.

BY THE TIME THE couple got back to the Cave of Treasures, their strength was clearly failing.

"Eve, I am so sorry. If it wasn't for me, we'd never have found ourselves in that predicament."

"Don't blame yourself, Adam. It was the devil who attacked us, not you."

"But you heard the Lord. *I* was the one who put us in harm's way. I could never forgive myself if I lost you like that. Damn this insatiable curiosity of mine. I'm sick of this world. What good is it, anyway, if we always have to worry about being attacked by that renegade?"

"But what can we do about it? We keep asking God to let us back into the garden, but all He ever does is tell us to wait."

"I know, Eve, but we can't wait. We have to think of another way."

"Like what?"

"I don't know, but I'll think of something."

THE NEXT MORNING, Eve woke up, and turning to see Adam, she found that he was gone. "Adam, where are you?"

"I'm here, Eve."

Springing to her feet, she met him at the mouth of their cave. "Don't scare me like that. For a second there I thought something had happened to you. Where were you?"

"Out wandering."

Relieved, Eve hugged him tightly, when suddenly she noticed something. "Adam, you're bleeding. What happened?"

Looking down, Adam saw it, too. A trickle of blood was dribbling down his wrist. "Oh, that? It's nothing. I slipped and fell climbing a rock, is all." He bent over, and grabbing a handful of grass, he then wiped the blood away with it. "See, all gone," he said with an innocent smile. "Now, what do you say, Eve; are you ready to go for a walk with me?"

TOGETHER, THE COUPLE was strolling along the southern border of the garden.

"Where are we going, Adam?"

"I told you; for a walk."

"I know that, but where to?"

"You'll see."

Eve started to open her mouth but thought better of it and simply followed Adam.

SOON, THEY CAUGHT a glimpse of the gateway to the garden.

"Adam, look, the cherub's gone. The entrance is clear. Where could he be?"

"Doing his job, I hope," replied Adam with a peculiar look in his eye. Single-minded in his intensity, he stared straight ahead at the empty gateway leading back into the garden.

"I don't get it," murmured Eve. "You *want* the cherub to do his job? Why?"

Still staring at the vacated entranceway, Adam put his finger to his mouth and started toward the garden gate. "Don't say a word, Eve. Just follow me."

MEANWHILE, THE CHERUB responsible for guarding the gate was flying along the northern perimeter of the garden, inspecting the thorny hedge that surrounded it. Suddenly he noticed something. "What have we here?" Streaking down to take a closer look, he was disturbed by what he saw. "If I didn't know better, I'd say someone has been tampering with this hedge." Sure enough, the cherub then found a section where a huge hole had been partially torn into the thorny exterior. "Oh, thank Heaven, it doesn't go all the way through. At least no one has penetrated the wall here." And looking closer still, the cherub was shocked at what he saw on one of the branches. "Blood?"

BACK AT THE GATEWAY, Adam and Eve were drawing near to the entrance, stepping very cautiously so as to not make a sound. Just a few feet away, they were closer to getting back in than they had ever been before, when suddenly the cherub swooped down in front of them, wielding his sword of fire.

"How dare you!" screeched the cherub. "You know you're not allowed back in! Are you two trying to get me in trouble, sneaking around behind my back like this? It's not right, I tell you!"

Rushing forward, the cherub raised his fiery sword to strike them, but before he could, the terrified couple collapsed. Then the cherub's flaming sword flickered and dimmed. "What's this?" muttered the cherub. Inspecting his sword, he found that it was no longer emitting flames, not even a spark. "What's happened to my sword?"

Suddenly an earthquake rumbled through the landscape, shaking the garden walls in its wake, then, just as quickly as it had commenced, it was over. In a flash, a cherubim flew down to the garden gate to see what was happening. Noticing the confused cherub hovering over the two motionless bodies, he flew over to him. "What's all this, then?" asked the cherubim.

"I'm not sure," replied the cherub. "I was making my rounds about the garden's perimeter, when I discovered a potential breach in the wall, and when I returned to my post, I found Adam and Eve trying to sneak back inside."

"So you killed them?"

Bewildered, the cherub shook his head. "That's just it; I never got the chance. When I raised my sword to block their way, they collapsed, and just like that, my sword fizzled out."

"Fizzled out? What do you mean, fizzled out?"

"I don't know. It just went out, as if I'd dipped it in a cold stream. One moment it was a flaming sword, then *whoosh*, it fizzled out."

"I wonder how something like that could have happened. Do you think God might have decided to be merciful to Adam and Eve, even though they nearly outsmarted you?"

"Outsmarted me? What's that supposed to mean?"

"Maybe instead of allowing you to kill them, He chose to spare them, considering it was your fault for nearly allowing them to get back inside."

The cherub earnestly considered his words. "Oh, dear, I never thought about it that way. What should we do now?"

"We? There is no *we*, my dear fellow. This is your responsibility, not mine."

"Then what do you suggest I do? Certainly you could offer me some sort of council in this matter. I can't just fly back to Heaven and ask God. He might still be angry with me for nearly letting them back in."

"Yes, that is a distinct possibility. You've certainly gotten yourself in quite a predicament, haven't you?"

Then a group of angels came down to where Adam and Eve were lying, and where they discovered the cherub and the cherubim staring at one another, quite perplexed.

"What is going on here?" asked one of them.

"That's just it," replied the cherubim. "We're not exactly sure. This fellow was supposed to guard the garden gate so Adam and Eve couldn't regain entrance. And just now he found them trying to sneak back in."

"No!" cried the angel, gaping at the prostrate couple.

"Yes!" blurted the cherub.

"So you killed them?" exclaimed another of the angels.

"No. I never had the chance!" insisted the cherub, holding his cold sword out for them to see. "Look, my sword doesn't even work anymore. I couldn't harm a flea with this thing."

"It's true," interjected the cherubim. "When he tried to stop Adam and Eve with it, his sword, *whoosh*, mysteriously extinguished."

"*Whoosh?*" echoed the first angel.

"Whoosh," said the cherubim with a knowing nod.

The angels all exchanged a curious look amongst themselves.

"Well, that's wonderful news," exclaimed yet another of the angels. "God must have changed His mind about letting Adam and Eve back into the garden. Or else why would he have prevented the cherub from striking them down?"

But the first angel remained unconvinced as he stared down at the couple's motionless bodies. "I don't know. They don't look so good to me. There's no way their death in this place could've been an accident. If you ask me, I think God killed them for trying to get back in without His permission."

Then the Word of God appeared in their midst, to the amazement of all the angels. "Don't worry, everyone. I'll handle this."

And with that, the whole group scattered; all except for the cherub, that is. Embarrassed, he just hung his head, rolling his dim sword about in his hands, as if unsure of what to do with it.

"Relax, Cherub. This wasn't your fault. You've done your job well."

The cherub's head popped up with a grateful smile. "Oh, thank You, Lord. I'm so relieved to hear it."

Then, with a wave of His hand, the Word reignited the cherub's sword. "There you are; now, feel free to resume your duties."

"My sword!" exclaimed the cherub, who then cheerfully buzzed out of sight.

Turning to Adam and Eve, the Word reached down and revived them once again. The couple slowly opened their eyes and realized who was standing over them. Reluctantly, they stood up and wiped themselves off, exchanging a serious look as they did.

"So," began the Word, "you two want to get back into the garden that badly?"

Adam innocently shrugged his shoulders. "Who, us? No, of course not, Lord."

"No?" blurted Eve, glaring back at him. "What are you saying, Adam?" She grabbed his arm in desperation. "Tell Him the truth. Tell Him: We *do* want back in. Tell Him we're tired of being attacked by falling rocks and hungry lions and flaming swords."

"But I thought we already covered all that," said the Word.

"Yes, Lord, we have," replied Adam, "more times than I can count, I'm afraid."

"Be reasonable, you two. You know you never have to worry about being attacked when you stay within your designated domain. The only time you ever have a problem is when you choose to stray. Isn't that right, Eve?"

Considering His words for a moment, Eve finally nodded. "Yes, Lord, I guess so; when You put it that way."

"Good, now please try to stick with the plan, will you? I really hate to see all this needless suffering you're putting yourselves through. This world is tough enough without your having to add to your own misery." And again the Word vanished.

Just then a strange fluttering sound began to emanate several feet from Adam and Eve.

"Eve, do you hear what I hear?"

"I do. What do you think it is?"

"It sounds like the beating of angels' wings."

"What could it mean?"

"I don't know," Adam replied as he took several steps in the direction of the sound, "but there's one way to find out."

"Be careful, Adam. And for Heaven's sake, don't get mixed up with the devil again, please."

As the fluttering sound continued, it slowly began to spread, until it reverberated in the air all around them.

"Oh, angels who wait upon the Lord, have pity on us," Adam said, flinging his hands about in an effort to grab hold of something tangible. "We used to sing praises just like you, but now, even though we know you're there, we *still* can't see you. You angels of God, you could help us, though, couldn't you?"

"But what could we possibly do for you?" asked an odd, little voice.

Turning toward the voice, Adam and Eve were stunned by what they saw. "Look, Eve, a pair of eyes staring back at us."

Sure enough, a pair of disembodied eyes blinked back at them both.

"Are you really an angel of the Lord?" wondered Eve as she cautiously took several steps toward the eyes.

"I am."

"Then why don't you show yourself?" asked Adam, moving forward to Eve's side.

"I don't wish to be seen, that's why."

"By whom?" asked Eve.

"By Satan, of course. He watches you constantly, seeking any opening, any weakness, never sleeping, never ceasing."

"If you're really an angel of the Lord," said Adam, "then you're committed to serving God's purposes. Isn't that so?"

"Just what are you getting at?" the voice murmured suspiciously.

"If you serve God, then you should want to help Eve and I."

The eyes blinked repeatedly, as if thoughtfully considering his words. "If I were you I wouldn't be so eager to twist me toward your selfish purposes. We've already had that game played on us before, thank you."

"What game is that?" asked Adam, suddenly growing impatient.

"The devil's game, of course," replied the voice, "a subtle game, whereby you propose that your aims are undoubtedly the aims of God. We've seen it all before, I assure you."

"Tell us, angel, what have you seen, and when?" insisted Adam.

"Before you ever got kicked out of the garden, Satan was kicked out of Heaven after he tried to convince God's angels it was in our best interest to help him, too. Sound familiar?"

The couple exchanged a frustrated look.

"Go on, angel," said Adam.

"First, Satan promised us all kinds of incredible things, like invincibility, divinity, immortality. Some were foolish enough to think he was telling the truth, so they bowed to him and renounced the majesty of God."

"But you didn't believe his promises?" wondered Eve.

"Of course not. I knew they were all lies."

"Didn't you at least consider his offer for a moment?" asked Adam.

"Absolutely not!" snapped the voice. "I flatly refused him."

"What happened next?" pressed Eve.

"What do you think happened? Satan unleashed his troops on us! If it weren't for God's intervention, we'd never have been able to drive him out of Heaven. And when he fell from among us there was incredible happiness, because had he been allowed to stay not a single one of us would have survived. So you see: When you try to persuade me to believe your ends are God's ends, you merely dredge up old wounds, unforgivable wounds, and you very nearly make me regret why I ever felt sorry for you in the first place."

Adam and Eve looked at one another, extremely disturbed by this.

"Forgive us, angel," said Adam. "We're sorry for our selfish behavior. You were right to doubt our motives after all. Truly you are an angel of the Lord."

"I understand," replied the angel, his eyes slowly fading from view. "Peace be with you, Adam and Eve. I promise we will do everything in our power to help you in your time on this Earth."

The angel's voice then began to ring out in a hauntingly beautiful song. "Dear Lord, our most merciful Creator, we, Your faithful servants, humbly beg You to protect Adam and Eve as the devil seeks to destroy them. Never let the jealousy of the Evil One come between them and Your kindness, and please bear with them until the ultimate fulfillment of Your promise. So be it until the end of time."

Then the Word of God returned. "What a beautiful song that was," He said.

"Yes, Lord, it was," added Adam with a melancholy nod.

"And just think, if only you two had obeyed Me, You'd still be with the angels right now, singing right along with them. But no, you had to cooperate with Satan, and now you're living among his angels, demons more evil than you can imagine."

Adam and Eve exchanged a troubled look.

"Lord, please," Adam groaned. "Why are you torturing us like this?"

"Adam, how can you say that?" asked the Word. "I've done nothing but rescue you, time and time again. But if you think I'm being too harsh, maybe you can ask the devil to help you instead. Ask him to give you the divine nature he promised. Do you think he can make you a garden like I did?"

"I don't know, Lord, can he?" asked Eve.

"Of course not, Eve," replied the Word. "He's incapable of keeping a single promise he's ever made to you. I, on the other hand, am capable of fulfilling every one of My promises. Now hurry, get away from here, or else the cherub will come back and try to kill you again."

Vigilance

SATAN CASUALLY WALKED up to the Cave of Treasures, where he stood at the entrance and called out contritely. "Adam, please come outside. I'd like to have a word with you."

"Adam," said Eve, "do you hear that? Someone is calling you."

"Calling me? Who's calling me?"

"How should I know? Someone is outside our cave calling for you. Why not find out for yourself."

Curious, Adam jumped to his feet and headed for the mouth of the cave. "Maybe it's an angel bringing us a word from the Lord," he muttered, half to himself.

But when he got outside and saw the hideous figure standing there, he took a cautious step back. "Oh, it's you," he said with obvious disdain. "What do you want?"

"I just wanted to talk to you, that's all."

"Since when do you just talk?"

"Since now."

"All right," replied Adam cautiously. "Start talking. In fact, I'd like to know something while you're at it. You told Eve if we ate from the Tree of Knowledge, we'd have our eyes opened and that we'd know what God knew. Isn't that what you told us?"

Satan tilted his head. "I vaguely remember saying something like that, yes."

"And you told her we'd receive a divine nature. Isn't that what you said?"

"I suppose so."

"Well, what happened to all that? When are we going to get what you promised us?"

Satan grinned sheepishly. "I'm so sorry. Did you *actually* think I was going to do something for you just because I promised I would?"

"I'll bet you can't even make us a garden like God did, can you?"

"Me? Certainly not, you pathetic mongrel."

"So tell me. Have we gotten a single thing you ever promised us?"

Then the devil's smirk turned to a scowl. "Of course not. And you never will. So how do you like it?"

"I think it stinks!"

"Good," grunted Satan as he extended his grotesque paw in a mock gesture. "Then let me officially welcome you to the club, because I'm never going to get what I'm asking god for, either!"

"Then why'd you do it? Why'd you lie to us? Why'd you have to go and ruin *our* lives?"

"I did it because god ruined my life and replaced me with you!"

Adam shook his head in disbelief. "Well, that doesn't make any sense. We didn't do anything to you. Why not punish God? Why do you have to take it out on us?"

"That's a damn good question; but sadly it's a question I don't plan on answering."

"Well, why not?"

"Because god is much too uncooperative to reason with, but you, on the other hand," spewed the devil, his eyes black with hatred, "*you* are infinitely more manageable. And now that you're under my control, *I'm* going to be your king from now on! So the fact is: I don't have to answer any more of your silly questions, no matter how clever you think you are."

"And this is what you came here to talk to me about?"

"As a matter of fact, yes; it is."

"Eve, did you hear? This miserable liar isn't going to keep *any* of the promises he made to us in the garden."

Cautiously, Eve stepped to Adam's side, shuddering at what she saw. "Not you again."

"Did you hear that, Eve? He says *he's* our king now. Can you believe it?"

"I don't know what to believe anymore, Adam. God only knows. He created us; maybe He can tell us if it's true or not."

"God?" scowled the devil. "God doesn't give a damn about you. If he did, he'd never have allowed you to fall into my clutches in the first place. And while you mull that bombshell over in your pathetic, little minds, consider this: If you think you're going to inherit *my* kingdom, you've got another thing coming, because I'll *never* cease my quest to destroy you! Not for a day, not for an hour, not for a minute! I'll see you both dead, if it's the last thing I do! How do you like that?"

Then, Adam and Eve joined hands and lifted their eyes skyward.

"Lord, please help us," exclaimed Adam. "Save us from the Evil One. Don't let him destroy us before You've had time to fulfill Your word. Please, drive him far away, won't You?"

Suddenly an angel appeared. "Satan, the Lord rebuke you. Leave this place immediately before God destroys *you* instead."

And like a bolt of lightning, the devil streaked out of sight, leaving a cloud of dust in his wake. Turning to the angel, the couple found that he was gone, too.

Adam then turned to Eve. "Well, now we've heard everything. First, God tells us we're safe as long as we stay put, then the devil shows up on our doorstep, telling us about his plans to murder us; and in broad daylight, no less. It doesn't make any sense. Why would God let him do something like that?"

"I don't know, Adam. Nothing about this upside-down world makes any sense to me. Everything keeps changing, shifting from one day to the next. How will we ever know the difference between the truth and the lies?"

"The only time we really know we're listening to the truth is when the Lord is right in front of us. Then all the lies disappear."

"Yeah, but you know as well as I do," countered Eve, "He never sticks around long enough to keep it that way."

"Maybe if we asked God to help us learn the difference for ourselves, maybe He'd show us the way."

"What makes you think He'll do that?"

"I don't know," Adam groaned in frustration, "but it's certainly worth a try. Otherwise we'll never feel safe in this world."

"What did you have in mind?"

"I say we set up a vigil in our cave. We sit right down and pray like we've never prayed before, and this time we do it for the full forty days."

"But you know we already tried that at the ocean."

"I know, but this time we won't make the mistake of splitting up. This time we stick together till the bitter end, even if it kills us in the process. Agreed?"

Eve nodded. "Anything, Adam, anything. As long as it keeps that miserable devil from ruining the rest of our lives."

So Adam and Eve walked back into their cave and sat down.

"Dear Lord," began Adam, "we thank you for sending your angel just now and rescuing us from the wrath of the devil, but frankly we're a little concerned that his attacks are becoming bolder by the day. Is there any way

You could help us learn how to prevent these random acts of his violence before they occur?"

MEANWHILE, SATAN and his minions sat watching the Cave of Treasures from a distance, and for the longest time the devil just sat there, staring, without a shred of emotion displayed on his sullen face.

One of his demons leaned over and whispered into his neighbor's ear. "He's been sitting like that for days. Whatever could he be thinking?"

"I imagine he's planning something. Great minds like his are always planning things."

"Oh, of course. How right you are. Something absolutely diabolical, I imagine."

"Simply diabolical."

"I wish he'd tell us what he's thinking, though. I hate the suspense. We don't dare go wandering off. You know as soon as we do, he'll decide to rally us to his cause, or some such thing."

"So shut up, why don't you? And let the great one think."

Satan slowly turned his wolfen head toward them and growled, "Yes, do shut up and let me think, you infernal chatterboxes. How do expect me to come up with something worthy of my diabolical genius, if you're both constantly flapping your ridiculous jaws?"

Startled, the demons looked down contritely.

"Forgive me, Master," mumbled the first demon. "So sorry to disturb you."

"Yes, Master," added the second, "a thousand pardons."

"Oh, don't mention it," replied the devil. "It won't happen again." And with a wave of his paw, Satan sent the pair of hapless demons careening off into oblivion. Turning to his lieutenant, he asked, "What is the weather like in the Abyss this time of the year, anyway?"

The petrified lieutenant just shrugged his shoulders, unable, or unwilling, to utter a single syllable.

"AND THANK YOU, LORD," intoned Adam, "for always hearing our prayers and gracing us with Your presence. Amen." Then he looked over at Eve. "Would you like to say something, dear?"

But Eve vacantly shook her head. "No, you're doing just fine." Then she grimaced ever so slightly as the faint sound of gurgling came from her stomach.

"What's wrong?" asked Adam. "Are you getting bored with all this praying?"

"It's just hard to concentrate, what with all that's going on in my stomach."

"Why, what's wrong with your stomach?"

"You know very well what's wrong with my stomach. It's *empty*. And I'm sure by now yours is just as empty as mine."

"Yes, but now is no time to think about something like that. This is too important."

"Naturally," replied Eve, obviously unimpressed.

"Besides, I thought we both agreed to stay put until the forty days were finished. It's the Lord's will that we remain wherever he's told us is safe. Remember?"

"Sure, but didn't the Lord also tell us that we should eat and drink something before we died of starvation and thirst? Why can't we do both?"

"I thought you were afraid to eat anything."

"I am, but that doesn't mean that eventually I might have changed my mind. Did you ever consider that? This world isn't the only thing that changes around here, you know."

"But what made you change your mind?"

"The emptiness in my stomach, Adam. What did the Lord call it? Hunger? Thirst? It's becoming unbearable. Don't you feel it, too?"

"Of course I feel it, but I'm trying my best to ignore it. I just don't want anything to spoil our plans this time. Now, maybe if you lead us in our next prayer, the emptiness will go away."

STILL, SATAN WATCHED and waited from his perch, like a buzzard sitting on a tree branch waiting for its dying victim to succumb. "Those two have been in that damned cave of theirs for three straight weeks now, and not once have they even bothered to poke their miserable heads out! I don't like it one bit. What are they up to this time?"

"Last time we checked, Master," replied his lieutenant, "they were praying."

"Praying? Praying for what? What could possibly take this long to pray for?"

"From what we've been able to gather, they've committed themselves to a forty-day vigil, hoping to convince god to reveal more about our strategy. They realize we want nothing more than to see them dead, and they're begging him to expose our tactics."

"What?" Taken aback, Satan grabbed his lieutenant by the throat. "A prayer vigil, you say?"

The lieutenant nodded timidly.

"For forty days?" croaked the devil.

His lieutenant could only nod again with a hand wrapped around his throat.

"Then why wasn't I informed about this sooner?"

Struggling to speak, the lieutenant gurgled in response.

"What are you saying, you damned fool?"

The lieutenant frantically pointed at the hand clenched around his throat.

"Oh, very well," snapped Satan as he relinquished his chokehold. "If you insist."

"But, Master," sputtered the lieutenant, "we've only just ascertained this bit of intelligence and were waiting for the appropriate time to convey it to you. Naturally, we didn't want to disturb your ... *thinking time*."

"Naturally," grumbled the devil. "So the pathetic, little replicas want to learn more about our tactics, eh? So they think that will do them any good. Well, we'll see about that. Maybe it's time we put them and their god to the ultimate test!"

"But, Lord, what can we do? Until now they've been impervious to our attack in the cave. And now they seem quite determined to stay there until god reveals our secrets to them. What if he actually consents to their request? What if he arms them with a defense we'll never be able to breach? Then what?"

"Enough with your revolting fears! I will never succumb to such pessimism! That is the human's weakness, not ours. Ours is to seek the vulnerable, exploit the opening. And believe me, there is always an opening which is vulnerable to our kind. Now find it and find it quickly, before I find someone else who can. Is that clear?"

"Of course, Lord. I understand all too well."

AS ADAM AND EVE continued their prayer vigil in the cave, it was apparent that they were growing weaker by the moment. "Lord, please, Eve and I are running out of strength. We don't know how much longer we can continue like this. We know you've instructed us concerning our need to eat and drink, but with the devil ever vigilant, we were desperately hoping You could equip us with some way to detect his presence, some way to discern his plan of attack. Otherwise, how will we ever know when we're in danger or, for that matter, when it's safe to eat or drink? For all we know, we might end up eating the wrong thing all over again, and then we'd be right back where we started."

From out of nowhere, the sound of swarming, angry insects began to reverberate in the distance.

"Adam, what's that sound?"

Startled, Adam struggled to his feet. "I'm not sure, but it sounds like it's heading right for us."

"I'm scared, Adam. What should we do?"

"Brace yourself, my dear, brace yourself."

The swarm then streaked into the cave and covered the screaming couple like a dense, dark cloud.

"Hornets!" shouted Adam. "Thousands of angry hornets!"

"And their stingers are all over me!" cried Eve.

In actuality, these fierce, little creatures were no ordinary hornets. Upon closer inspection, they were none other than tiny demons, as minuscule as buzzing insects. With their razor sharp swords, like thousands of painful stingers, they all stabbed at Adam and Eve, until finally the couple collapsed in a heap. Then, just as quickly as they appeared, the malicious horde darted off into the night, leaving the pair for dead.

WHEN THE WORD OF GOD arrived, He not only raised Adam and Eve, but with a wave of His hand, He also healed all their wounds. Stunned, the couple examined their flesh, hardly believing their eyes.

"Lord, what was that all about?" Adam muttered. "And what happened to our wounds. We were just stung to death by the angriest swarm of hornets I've ever seen."

"I'm sorry, you two, but those weren't hornets that just attacked you."

"They weren't?" gasped Eve. "Then what were they?"

"They were thousands of demons, the size of flying insects."

"But how, Lord?" groaned Adam. "How could they attack us in our cave? I thought you told us as long as we remained where You told us to, we'd be safe from the devil's assault."

"I did say that, Adam, yes, but unfortunately that doesn't just apply to your physical location. In and of itself, this cave is no different than any other cave in the world. What I've been telling you all along is that when you're in obedience to My word, wherever and whenever you go, *then* you can be sure that you and Eve will be safe from Satan's attack. Does that make any sense?"

Both Adam and Eve struggled to grasp the meaning of His words.

"Not really, no, Lord," Adam replied. "Apart from just being attacked by a thousand demonic hornets, Eve and I are so weak from hunger and thirst, it's making things much more difficult to understand."

"And that's exactly the point I'm trying to make. That's how Satan was able to penetrate your shield. Even he was shocked when he realized he could overcome you in your cave. Even he thought you were impervious here. And it was true, as long as you obeyed My command. But when you kept refusing to eat and drink the things I've already designated as good and safe for you, that's when you, once again, fell from My grace. That's when you afforded the devil an opening to strike."

Shaking her head in disgust, Eve glared at Adam. "You see, this time I was right, and you were wrong. I knew it was finally time to eat and drink. Why wouldn't you listen to me, Adam, for once?"

"Oh, Eve, this is no time to blame each other," insisted the Word. "Defying My order for you to eat or drink wasn't the only thing that left you two vulnerable."

"It wasn't?" asked Eve, suddenly embarrassed.

"No, just as great a sin as it was to refuse to eat or drink was the moment when you and Adam came to a disagreement between yourselves. Like a wedge that drove you from Me and My power, your division drove a wedge between you and Adam's power."

"You mean I have power, too, Lord?" blurted Adam.

"Of course, Adam. As water has power to cut its course into a riverbed, the spirit I've given you has a similar residual power, and as the riverbed supports and controls that course of strength, so does your individual human will direct your power as well."

"Did you hear that, Eve? I have power, too."

"But never forget, Adam. It's still only a power too easily limited by your own hopes and fears and choices, ones that occur during every moment of your existence."

"Eve, darling Eve, let's agree to never quarrel with the will of the Lord again, all right?"

"I agree, Adam, and I'm sorry for arguing with you, too."

"Just think, you two, if only you had have acted this way before you fell from grace, you wouldn't be going through any of these difficulties right now. So, now that we have this understanding between us, how would you like to do something for Me?"

"Anything, Lord," exclaimed Adam. "Anything at all."

"I'd like you and Eve to finish your prayer vigil in the cave, and as soon as you're done, I want you to eat and drink the things I've designated for you. Can you do that for Me?"

Together, the couple nodded wholeheartedly.

"We can, and we will," replied Adam.

Brother of Mine

NINE DAYS LATER, Adam and Eve had very little strength left as they nervously paced back and forth in their cave.

Eve stared dejectedly down at her palms. "My hands, Adam; they're so shriveled. They look awful." Then she turned to Adam, disturbed by what she saw. "Just look at us. We're nothing but skin and bones."

"Oh, Eve, I'm not sure what I want to do more, eat or drink. How about you?"

"I know how you feel."

Overcome by exhaustion, they both collapsed in the cave.

"How much more of this do you think we can take, Eve?"

"Not much, I'm afraid."

"But we're so close."

"How long has it been now?"

"We've been praying for thirty-nine days, as far as I can tell."

"Thirty-nine days? I can't believe it. You mean we only have one more day to go?"

"As far as I can tell."

Just then, a middle-aged gentleman, immaculately dressed in dapper sheepskin clothing, complete with staff in hand, wandered up to the entrance of their cave. "Oh, dear me, is this the place? Hello? Is there anyone in there? Hello, anyone?"

Venturing several steps into the cave, the man peered in and caught a glimpse of Adam and Eve, lying there quite still.

"Adam, is that really you?" wondered the man. "And Eve, could it be you, too?"

The couple exchanged a perplexed look, almost too exhausted to respond.

"Yes, we're Adam and Eve," replied Adam. "Who are you?"

"Oh, dear, I'm not exactly sure how to put this," said the man, thoughtfully considering his words. "My name is Dakar; and Adam ... I'm your older brother."

"What?" blurted Adam and Eve with one voice, and as if they had just been invigorated with some new source of strength, they scrambled to their feet and quickly walked over to the man.

"Y — *you can't* be serious?" stammered Eve. "You're Adam's older brother? But that's impossible."

"But look," insisted Dakar, holding out his hand for their inspection. "I'm made of flesh and bones just like you. See?"

Bewildered, Adam shook his head. "This is the craziest thing I've ever heard. If you're my older brother, then how come I've never seen you before?"

"That's because after God created me, He placed me in a garden of my own, located far to the north, at the very top of the world."

"But that still doesn't explain how Adam came to be your younger brother," insisted Eve.

"That, I'm afraid," said Dakar, "is where things get a little *tricky*."

"Tricky?" Adam echoed. "What do you mean, *tricky*?"

"Well, you see," continued Dakar, a bit awkwardly, "one day, a long, long time ago, God put me into a very deep sleep and brought you, Adam, out of my side."

"Adam?" blanched Eve.

"Yes, Eve?"

"Did you hear what he just said?"

"I did, yes."

"I wonder if he's telling the truth," she muttered.

"Of course, I'm telling the truth," Dakar said as he pulled away his sheepskin, offering them a look at his side. "Look for yourself. I have a scar on my side just like Adam's."

The couple leaned forward in bittersweet anticipation and, sure enough, saw the scar on Dakar's right side, directly between the fifth and sixth rib.

"Oh, my God, it's true, Adam," whispered Eve. "He does have a scar like yours."

The couple reached out together to touch it.

Confused, Eve turned to Adam and said, "I thought you said God made you out of the ground."

"That's what I thought, too," he replied, thoroughly bewildered. "So, if I came out of your side Dakar, then how come God never told me about you?"

Dakar smiled so benevolently. "You know, that's what I wanted to know, too, but, unfortunately, He refused to tell me. For some strange reason, He just wouldn't let you stay with me. He took you away from me and placed you in a garden all your own."

"Well, what did you do after that?" asked Eve.

"After that, I got very depressed. I missed you so much, Adam."

"Then what did God tell you to do?" pressed Adam. "You prayed to Him about it, didn't you?"

"Oh, yes, of course. But you know how God is. He just told me to quit worrying and to not interfere with what He was doing with you because He'd already brought a companion out of your side as well. He insisted you were perfectly happy on your own. So what else could I do?"

"That's terrible," grumbled Eve. "Why would God let something like that happen?"

"So if I'm your brother," Adam continued, "then how come you never came back to find me?"

"I never came looking for you because until God just told me, I had no idea where you were living. I certainly had no idea you were enduring such misery and pain; all because you disobeyed God and cooperated with Satan. And now just look at you two, suffering this way."

"So why did God send you to us now?" asked Adam.

"Well, as you know," replied Dakar, "it's been a very long time since you left the garden, and now, God has instructed me to come here to take you home with me. He wants me to keep Satan away from you from now on."

"God did that for us?" wondered Adam.

"Oh, yes. He doesn't want you to be attacked anymore."

"He actually said that?" pressed Eve.

Dakar smiled back. "Of course He did. I mean, just look at the two of you, barely clinging to dear life."

"Did God tell you anything else?" asked Adam.

"Oh, yes. That's the best part. God has ordered me to personally give you fruit and water from the Tree of Life."

"Really?" Adam's eyes opened wide.

"Is that all?" asked Eve.

"As a matter of fact, no," replied Dakar calmly, calculatingly, "then He told me I was to restore you to your original state of grace and to restore all the powers you used to have prior to your unfortunate fall."

Adam and Eve smiled at one another, and reaching out, they held hands.

"Eve, did you hear that?"

"I can hardly believe my ears, Adam."

"Oh, Adam," continued Dakar with such melancholy in his voice. "It's so good to see you again and to finally meet Eve. I've missed you so much. I just couldn't stand the thought of what you two were going through."

"So when you came here to rescue us," asked Eve, "did Satan try to attack you, too?"

"Oh, my word, of course he did. He is such a nasty fellow, isn't he?"

Adam and Eve nodded back in agreement.

"What did you do?" asked Adam.

"Did you ever think about giving up on us?" asked Eve.

"Certainly not," insisted Dakar, putting his hand to his breast as though he were swearing allegiance. "I'd never do something like that, not when it concerned my own dear brother."

"Come on, you can tell us," chided Eve. "You were scared to fight the devil, weren't you?"

"Well, alright, I admit it," replied Dakar, rather sheepishly, "I did at first tremble upon hearing the name of Satan. I thought: Maybe I shouldn't venture out by myself. What if he traps me like he did the two of you? So I prayed: 'Oh, God, Satan's going to meet me on my way to rescue Adam and Eve. He'll challenge me just like he did them.'"

"What did God say?" pressed Adam.

"He told me: 'Don't be frightened. Take this staff for protection, and when Satan confronts you, strike him with it. But whatever you do, don't be afraid of him, because he can't really hurt you. After all, you've been around a lot longer than he has.'"

"Then what happened?" asked Eve.

"I said, 'Lord, I don't think I can go. Please, send Your angels to bring them here instead of me.' But God replied: 'Certainly they won't agree to come with angels. They're not the same as Adam and Eve. They'll never trust them. But I've chosen you because you're Adam's older brother. You're just like him, so he'll listen to what you have to say.'"

"Interesting," said Adam.

"Positively," replied Dakar, smoothly confident. "Then do you know what God said to me?"

Adam and Eve looked at each other, hoping that the other one might respond, but neither of them could think of a response, so they turned back to Dakar and shrugged their shoulders.

"No, what?" replied Adam.

Dakar beamed back his benevolent smile. "Then He told me: 'But if you don't have enough strength to walk there, my son, I'll send a cloud to carry you. It will drop you off at the entrance to their cave, and if they agree to come with you, I'll send the cloud back to return you all safely to your garden home.'"

"No," said Adam.

"Yes," insisted Dakar. "I'd never lie to you. God actually commanded a cloud, which picked me up and brought me straight here to you."

"That's amazing," said Eve.

"So, my brother, my sister," continued Dakar, "I've traveled so far to get here, and now the time has finally come. We're all going to a wonderful place of peace and tranquility. What a marvelous time we'll all have, finally, together at last." Then, Dakar began to weep so much that tears poured down his face like water. "Oh, dear, I told myself I wasn't going to do this."

Touched by his emotional outburst, Adam and Eve stepped closer to get a better look at him.

"Look at him, Adam; he really does look just like you. Doesn't he?"

"Of course he looks like me." Adam nodded proudly. "We're brothers."

Wiping his tears away, Dakar smiled at them and held his hands out. Slowly, Adam and Eve each took hold of one, and then Dakar began to lead them away from their cave.

THEY HEADED STRAIGHT for the hill that overlooked the western edge of the garden, where the couple was so fond of going.

As they walked along, Eve leaned into Adam and quietly said, "Adam, what about the cloud Dakar told us about? I thought *it* was supposed to take us where we were going."

"Oh, that's right, I forgot," replied Adam, who then turned to ask, "Please, Dakar, we'd like to know: Where's the cloud you told us about? Eve and I are tired of walking. I don't think we can take another step."

"Certainly, my brother, I understand," he replied. "Don't worry. It's just around the bend. You'll see."

MAKING THEIR WAY up the hilltop, the couple continued to follow Dakar, until finally they saw it, extending out from the edge of the cliff, a shimmering cloud, spreading out like an iridescent flying carpet.

"Look, Eve, there it is," said Adam. "There's your cloud, just the way Dakar described it."

"See, you two?" said Dakar confidently. "What did I tell you?"

"It's beautiful," murmured Eve. "But it looks so delicate. Are you sure it'll hold us?"

"Certainly," insisted Dakar. "Just climb abroad, and before you know it we'll be off to your new garden home. Soon, all this misery and suffering will simply be a thing of the past."

The couple inched their way, closer and closer, toward the edge of the cliff, where the dazzling cloud awaited them.

"That's it," said Dakar. "You're almost there. Just step out onto the cloud, and we'll all get going."

To the very edge of the cliff, Adam and Eve looked down at the luminous cloud and then at one another. They were filled with an exhilarating sense of both anticipation and dread.

"Oh, Adam, I'm so nervous. Are you sure we can do this?"

"Sure we can, Eve, if it means a new life far away from this miserable place. Don't you want to go?"

"Of course she does, Adam," said Dakar. "Here, let me help you. All you two really need is a bit of encouragement." And stepping past the couple, Dakar walked right onto the shimmering cloud and turned back toward them with his hands held out. "See how sturdy it is? There's nothing to fear. Now, come, it's your turn to join me, won't you?"

The couple inched nervously forward and reached out to take hold of Dakar's outstretched hands, but instead of walking onto the cloud, they fell straight through it.

"Oops," sneered Dakar, who then transformed into the devil and burst out laughing. The screaming couple fell helplessly through space, headed straight for the bottom of the ravine, but just before they landed, Adam and Eve abruptly stopped short of the ground. Confused, they looked around as they dangled just a few feet above the ravine floor.

"What the—" muttered Adam.

Looking down from his vantage point, Satan was completely baffled by the sight of Adam and Eve suspended in mid-air. "What is it this time?" he snapped, and swooping down to investigate, he was incensed by what he saw. To his utter amazement, he found that the couple was being held up by two glittering clouds of their own. But of course these were no ordinary clouds. As the devil moved in closer still, he found that these clouds were actually comprised of thousands of miniature angels. Gently, they began to lower Adam and Eve down to the ground, where they were finally able to stand on their own. Then, like a billowy swarm of shimmering butterflies, they fluttered past the devil.

"Are you kidding me?" Satan growled. "What do I have to do to get rid of these two pests?"

Then the Word of God appeared.

"Well, well," snarled the devil, "if it isn't the meddling god, right on time as usual. I see that two can play at this game, can't they? How fitting you've rescued your little replicas by the same means with which I nearly destroyed them; and how *infuriating!*"

Looking Satan dead in the eye, the Word pointed toward the horizon. "Just go, you miserable excuse for an adversary. Go tell your minions how well you did here today. I'm sure they're just waiting to congratulate you on your latest achievement."

"Yes, yes. No need to rub it in, my good man. I already know the drill." And with a cloud of dust in his wake, Satan streaked out of view.

The Word then turned to the couple, who stood there, relieved and embarrassed. "Oh, Adam," He said, disappointed, "what just happened? You were so close. Why did you leave your cave this time?"

"But, Lord, excuse me for saying this," sputtered Adam, "but seriously, You are not going to believe what just happened to us."

"Really? Tell Me, then. I'd be very interested to hear it."

"Well, You see, we were in our cave praying like You told us, when quite unexpectedly this strange man came to visit us."

"See, I warned you, didn't I?"

"But this was no angel of light, Lord. This was a man, a real man; but not just any man. This was a man with a scar in his side, a scar just like mine. And this man told us a story about how You'd taken me from his side, just like Eve had been taken from mine. He said he was my brother, my older brother, in fact."

"And you believed him?"

"But he showed us the scar in his side, Lord," interjected Eve. "We touched it with our own hands. It was real. It was all *so* real."

"But was it real after all?"

Adam hung his head in shame. "Everything but the cloud, I'm afraid."

"So now you realize who you were dealing with, right?"

"Don't tell me it was Satan again?" asked Eve.

"Of course it was Satan, Eve."

"But he looked just like us, Lord," grumbled Adam, as if he were genuinely disappointed. "How could it have been the devil?"

"Didn't I tell you he was the father of evil arts? He's tried everything else, so this time he thought he could accomplish his goal by appearing to look like you. And he was right, wasn't he?"

"But he was so convincing, especially that scar of his," insisted Adam. "And just the way he told us his whole story about being my brother. He even said he was going to take us to his garden home where we could find some peace and quiet for once in our lives."

"Of course he'd say that, Adam. He's going to tell you exactly what you want to hear. That's how he got you kicked out of the garden in the first place. Now he's doing everything he can to eliminate you, because he thinks if he succeeds I'll have no choice but to take him back."

"Where's Satan now, Lord?" asked Adam.

Nervously, the couple looked around to see if he might have returned without them noticing.

"Relax, you two. He's long gone for the time being."

"Thank you, Lord," said Adam with a sigh of relief.

"Now, Adam, take Eve back to your cave and stay there until tomorrow. Then, after your forty-day vigil is completed, I want you both to go to the eastern edge of the garden, where I'll give you further instructions."

THE FOLLOWING MORNING, Adam and Eve were waiting patiently at the eastern border of the garden.

"Lord, please give us new strength," said Adam, almost breathless. "We're famished."

"Could we please have something to satisfy our terrible hunger?" asked Eve, ever so frailly.

Exhausted, they fell down, unable to lift a finger.

Again the Word of God arrived. "Adam, Eve, get up. Go home, get the two figs I put in your cave and come back here as soon as you can."

The couple exchanged a serious look. Slowly, they got to their feet and headed back toward their cave.

AS USUAL, SATAN AND his cadre of henchman were watching everything from a distance.

"I am getting so sick of watching god help that miserable pair," grunted the devil. "I still don't get it. Why does he do it?"

"Is there anything I can do to help, Lord?" asked his lieutenant.

"*You*? I certainly doubt it. But go ahead; try me."

"Well, let's see, we tried deceiving them. Oh, that was beautiful how you got them kicked out of their garden, Master."

"Yes, yes, flattery will get you nowhere. A lot of good that did me."

"All right, I was just saying. Okay, so we tried deception. Then we tried blatant violence."

"Keep going, keep going. Tell me something I don't know."

"Begging your pardon, Lord," said the lieutenant as he furled his malicious brow, trying desperately to come up with a decent idea. "Just give me a second; I'll think of something. Have we ruled out blatant violence yet?"

"Yes, we have, you infernal dolt! What we need is a different method to rid ourselves of these two, and preferably one where god doesn't get more credit if he rescues them again."

"All right, then. So what's left? Adam and Eve just spent forty days fasting and praying, and now they're on the brink of starvation. Why? Because they keep refusing to eat or drink anything."

Just then, a twinkle appeared in the devil's beady, black eyes. "Wait a second; wait a second. What did you just say?"

"I asked if we'd ruled out blatant violence."

"No, no! After that, you idiot!"

"I said Adam and Eve were on the brink of starvation."

"Yes, that's it! If we simply oblige them in their persistent refusal to eat or drink, then maybe they'll die of their own accord. Certainly god won't force them to eat or drink anything. He apparently values freedom far too much for that, the sentimental fool."

"What a perfectly diabolical idea, Master. I think you might be onto something." Then turning to Satan, his lieutenant found him missing. "Master? Master? Where did the master go?"

LIKE A STREAK OF lightning, the devil was already hurling through space; and the place he was going to was the Cave of Treasures. Arriving before Adam and Eve had time to get there, he went inside and found the two figs that the couple had left for safe keeping. "Well, well, what do we have here? Morsels, just ripe for the picking."

Stepping outside with the figs securely in his grasp, the devil searched the horizon. "Now, tell me, where are my insolent minions? You mean to say that no one is with me today."

"We're with you, Lord," rattled a guttural voice. "We await your command."

Turning his wolfen head, Satan was happy to see that a swarm of his demons had followed him on his journey. "Good, very good. Now quickly, bury these damned things, and bury them so deep that Adam and Eve can never find them again."

IN NO TIME, HIS CADRE of demons had dug a huge trench in the ground, and dumping the figs into the hole, they filled it in, taking turns to stomp the ground into a solid mass.

As he watched with tremendous satisfaction, the devil let out a raucous laugh. "Wonderful! I can't wait to see the miserable look on their faces when those two realize their precious figs are gone forever!"

But no sooner had the figs been planted in the ground than they rapidly grew up into a pair of fig trees, complete with dozens of tender young figs hanging from their branches. Horrified, the devil and his henchmen stared at the trees in utter disbelief.

"How did that happen?" grumbled the lieutenant.

"Well, don't just stand there gawking," Satan snapped, "hack the miserable things down, you pathetic worms!"

But as his minions slashed away at the tree, they found that their fiery swords were useless. Each time a demon hacked at a branch, the blade merely bounced away.

"Now what's wrong?" demanded the devil.

"I have no idea, Lord," blanched the lieutenant. "These trees are impervious to our blades, no matter how hard we swing them!"

"No, no, no!" howled Satan. "How could this be happening again? I'd have been better off leaving those damned figs where they were!"

"God is mocking us, Master! What should we do now?"

"God hasn't merely mocked us, my legions, he's turned our brilliant plan inside out! Now I have no idea how to get rid of this revolting *food* of theirs!"

Food for a Change

STROLLING UP TO their cave, Adam and Eve noticed the two large fig trees for the first time. The puzzled couple examined the fruit on them. They also noticed how the trees were now providing such nice shade for their cave.

Confused, Adam shook his head. "I think we're lost, Eve. These two trees weren't here before, were they? We must have gotten off course somehow. What do you think?"

Eve just shrugged her shoulders.

"I say we check inside to see if the figs are in there," continued Adam. "If this *is* our cave, then they should still be there. If not, then we'll know it can't be our cave."

So they went inside and looked all around. Every square inch of the cave was inspected, but still they found no sign of the two figs. They did, however, find the gold, frankincense and myrrh. Stepping outside again, the couple sat down, exhausted from their desperate search.

Adam turned to Eve with a puzzled look on his face. "I give up. Everything else is still in our cave; so where'd our figs go?"

"I wish I could tell you, Adam, but I just don't know what to think anymore. I'm so hollow and dry inside, I can't think straight."

Adam struggled to his feet. "God, You ordered us to come here to get our figs, but we can't find them anywhere. Did You take them?"

"We're so confused, Lord," whimpered Eve. "Where'd they go?"

"Please explain this mystery, Lord," said Adam. "Where did these trees come from?"

Then the Word of God returned. "Well, you two: As you can imagine,

Satan is up to his old tricks again."

"What?" blurted Adam. "What did he do this time?"

"When I sent you to get your figs, Satan went ahead of you. He got here first and buried the figs outside your cave."

"But why?" asked Eve, almost painfully.

"He thought burying them would destroy them, and that by destroying them you'd die of starvation, but I caused them to grow into the fig trees you see here."

"You're kidding," said Adam. "You mean our two figs are now these two trees? Satan must've really gotten mad when he saw that."

"Is that why you made the trees grow, Lord, to anger the devil?" wondered Eve.

"Of course not, Eve," replied the Word.

"Then why *did* You do it?" asked Adam.

"I did it because in My mercy I wanted them to grow for your sakes. That way you'd be able to have their fruit close by, not to mention having the shade from their branches and leaves."

"You did that just for us?" asked Eve.

"Certainly," insisted the Word. "I wanted you to see an example of My power, and I *especially* wanted to show you how cruel and vengeful Satan is. You know, he hasn't stopped trying to hurt you since the day you came out of the garden. Not for a single moment!"

Adam and Eve exchanged a knowing look.

"But remember," continued the Word, "I still haven't given him complete power over you. So from now on, the two of you can enjoy the fruit from these trees whenever you get hungry, and rest under them whenever you get tired or hot. Now each of you may have a fig."

"Now?" asked Eve.

"Yes, now," replied the Word, "before you die of starvation." Then He vanished.

Timidly, the couple each picked a fig from its branches. They went inside their cave, and sat down with the figs.

"What should we do now, Eve?"

"I guess we're supposed to eat them."

"But how do we do that?"

"How should I know? I've never eaten figs before. Just the thought of eating something terrifies me."

"Me, too. What if they make us sick?"

"What if we actually *like* this food. What then?"

So they just sat there, staring at the figs for the longest time, when suddenly an angel appeared before them. Smiling, he sat down in front of Adam and Eve.

"God has sent me here," began the angel, "because He wants you to know you can't go on living without eating something. Now take the figs and peel some of the skin off to get to the pulp inside. Scoop some out, put it in your mouths, and chew. Then, when you've chewed sufficiently, you swallow. Understand?"

Cautiously, Adam and Eve each picked up a fig. They slowly proceeded, just as the angel had instructed them, and began to eat.

"Mmm," said Eve, "this is good. How's yours?"

"Not bad, not bad." Nodding, Adam chewed some more. "I think I like this, eating."

Eve noticed some of the juices running down his chin. "Drooling. Uh, Adam, you're drooling."

Adam wiped his chin with a sheepish grin. "You're one to talk. Look at you."

Smiling playfully, Eve wiped her chin, too. "Sorry."

THAT EVENING, THE couple sang hymns of praise to God, and when they were done, they slept quite soundly because of all the food they had eaten.

THE NEXT MORNING, however, when they got up and left their cave, they felt sick to their stomachs. Pacing frantically in front of the mouth of their cave, they were both terribly distressed.

Adam bent over, trying to catch his breath. "Oh, Eve, I wonder what's happening to us. Why are we in so much pain?"

"We've really done it this time, Adam," gasped Eve as she stumbled to the ground, stabbed by a stomach cramp. "Oh, God. We'd have been better off dying of hunger than to have eaten those figs!"

"At least we'd have kept our bodies from being contaminated with food."

"We never experienced anything like this when we were in the garden."

Dropping to his knees, Adam put one hand to the ground to prop himself up. "My insides feel like they're about to explode!"

On her side, Eve curled into a ball and whimpered, "Lord, no. I don't want to die like this, please, not when I finally started to believe You'd actually fulfill Your promise to us."

"Lord, please help us," groaned Adam. "I realize You may not be ready to keep Your promise just yet, but please don't abandon us now."

At once, something happened to Adam and Eve, something that relieved them of all their pain. As quickly as it had struck them, the stabbing in their gut was no longer there. Equally puzzled and relieved, the couple stood to their feet, cautiously touching their stomachs, as if to check where the pain had gone.

"Eve, what happened? The pain. It's gone. Thank the Lord above."

"You're right, Adam. I feel normal again. God must've answered our prayers."

"Of course He did." Adam nodded with a tremendous sigh. "What other explanation is there?"

AS THE SUN SLOWLY SET, the couple sat at the cave's entrance, trying to relax, when Adam noticed a troubled look on Eve's face as she dolefully held her hand to her stomach.

"What's wrong, Eve?" he asked. "Are you feeling sick again?"

"No, I'm fine."

"But you don't look fine. Something has you upset. What is it?"

Eve stared straight ahead, obviously caught up in some sort of inner turmoil. "Well, as it turns out, ever since the pain left my stomach, it seems as if it's decided to take up residence somewhere else. And though what I felt in here hurt me terribly…" Pausing thoughtfully, she removed her hand from her belly and placed it to her breast, "it's nothing compared to the unbearable ache I now feel in my heart."

Adam nodded with a look of understanding. "I know exactly what you mean, Eve. Our bodies won't ever be the same now that we've eaten *food*. God would never want us back in His garden now, not with earthly bodies with such peculiar functions as ours."

Pitifully, Eve nodded and began to cry. "Which means all our hopes and dreams of getting back into the garden are completely gone now!"

"We just don't belong there anymore," Adam added lamentably.

"From now on, we're nothing but dirt, just like every other creature living in this miserable world."

Adam gazed longingly out across the landscape. He saw the animals roaming about in the murky twilight, and looking up he saw the stars and the Moon. "For as long as I can remember, I've always felt like a genuine part of God's creation, as if I were actually one with everything in it. You know?"

"I do, yes." Eve nodded sadly and dried her tears. "But now?"

"But now," Adam continued, "with every day that passes, I feel more and more like a stranger on this Earth. Do you realize it's been ninety-four days since we left the garden?"

"Ninety-four days," murmured Eve. "Ninety-four days, and what has it gotten us? We've become nothing but strangers … *strangers* in a world we call home."

Bread from Heaven

THE COUPLE WOKE UP the next morning and looked at each other expectantly.

"What should we do now, Adam?"

"Well, we asked God for something to eat and He gave us those figs, so now let's ask Him for a drink of water."

STANDING AT THE riverbank where they had previously thrown themselves in, the couple stared longingly down at the water as it flowed past them.

"Please, God," began Adam, "could You send us Your Word to tell us if we can drink some of this water?"

Then the Word of God arrived. "It's all right, Adam. Now that your body is merely flesh, it requires water. So go ahead, both of you, drink and give thanks."

So the couple stepped closer to the river, and dropping to their hands and knees they began to drink from it.

"Oh, this is so good, Eve."

"You're right, Adam. I can't believe we waited so long to do this."

IN THE MORNING, Adam and Eve went to where they had stored their leftovers, and to their absolute amazement, they found that the figs had been restored to their original size and condition, just as perfectly shaped and plump as they had been the day before.

"Can you believe it, Eve? It's as though we never even ate any of it."

"Maybe these figs have miraculous qualities, Adam. Maybe that's how our bodies were transformed."

"I think you're right. I say we put them in a safe place and find something else to eat."

Eagerly, Eve nodded her approval. So the couple took the two figs, along with the leaves, and hung them up on the wall of their cave.

"This way we'll always have these as a memorial of God's blessing," said Adam, "and someday our children will be able to look at them and remember all the wonderful things God has done for us."

For several moments, the couple proudly inspected the new memorial that graced their cavern wall.

Then Eve turned to Adam with a peculiar look on her face. "Adam?"

"Yes, Eve."

"You said someday our *children* would look at this memorial."

"Uh, yeah, I did, didn't I?"

"What are *children*?"

Tilting his head and squinting his eyes, Adam thoughtfully considered her question and finally shrugged his shoulders. "How should I know?"

OUTSIDE THE CAVE, the couple wandered here and there, searching the landscape.

"Lord," Adam said, "please show us where we can find something else to eat."

Then the Word of God returned. "Adam, I want you to travel west from here, until you reach a land of dark soil. There, you'll find more food."

JOURNEYING WESTWARD, the couple eventually came to a land where the ground was covered in a dark, rich soil. They found wheat growing there, full-eared, ripe and ready to harvest. They even found more figs, too, which they ate right away, so happy with their discoveries.

Again the Word of God appeared. "Take this wheat, Adam, and make bread with it. Eating this bread will also help nourish your body."

THE COUPLE EAGERLY began uprooting the wheat with their bare hands until there was enough to form several large piles. Then Adam began to grind the grain with a flat stone, adding a little water to the mix until it turned to dough. This dough, in turn, he then cooked over a fire, and when it was cooked, the first loaf of bread was broken up by the happy couple and eaten until both of them were full.

"Oh, Adam, I couldn't eat another bite. That was delicious. How did you learn to make—what did the Lord call it again?"

"Bread."

"Right, bread. How'd you ever learn to make bread like that?"

"I'm not sure, Eve. It just came into my mind, that's all."

"It must have been God Who inspired you to make something that good," she replied with a heavy yawn. "Oh, wow. I am so sleepy after all that work. I need to lie down awhile. How about you?"

Adam nodded with a weary, contented smile, and together they found a shady tree and plopped down under it, where a cool breeze fanned them into a deep sleep.

SATAN AND HIS MINIONS, meanwhile, were watching the dozing couple from a distance.

"Damn those two!" snapped the devil. "I had such high hopes the little replicas were going to starve themselves to death. Now look at them, so fat and content with their *food!*"

"Don't despair, Lord," said his lieutenant, "all is not lost yet. There must be something we can do to end their reign of peace."

"First, god provided them with figs to eat," Satan grumbled, "then he caused fig trees to grow up, then he gave them water to drink. Now he's gone and given them wheat, too! Damn their miserable hides!"

"Wheat? What's *wheat*, Master?"

"Wheat! You know, wheat! Humans make bread with it."

"But what's *bread*?" wondered the lieutenant, turning to the other demons, who all in turn just shrugged.

"Apparently, it's what humans use to make a new kind of food, you idiot. Now stop asking me such ridiculous questions! They still have a huge pile of this wheat left over from their efforts!"

"What should we do, Lord?"

"I want you to destroy it, of course," the devil growled impatiently. "And I want it done before they try to eat any more of it. If we're ever going to starve these two into extinction, we must cut off their food supply! Is that understood?"

"Naturally, Master, your wish is our command. It does appear they're still fast asleep from all their hard work. We could attack them right now."

"Good, then hurry before that miserable pair wakes up. Go and burn their grain! *Now!*"

"Yes, Lord; we'll burn it all this instant!"

"And can you believe it?" chimed in another demon. "Now Adam and Eve have a bucket to carry water, too."

"A bucket?" spewed Satan. "Where did that come from?"

All eyes turned toward this demon, who started to reply, but much to his dismay the words stuck in his throat. Both frustrated and horrified, he tried to shrug it off with a pathetic, toothy grin.

"Well," snapped the lieutenant, "you heard the master. Where'd they get it?"

"I—I—I," croaked the demon, suddenly jolted back to speech. "*I'm* afraid I have no idea, sir."

Turning to his lieutenant, Satan shrieked, "Enough already! Never mind how they got it! Do something, damn you!"

Pointing to another demon, the lieutenant snapped, "You there!"

"Who, *me*?" replied the unsuspecting one.

"Yes, you," barked the lieutenant. "Get down there now, and take care of that bucket."

"Yes, sir. Consider it done."

"Good," replied the lieutenant. "Now get going!"

"Yes, that should do the trick," cooed Satan. "Then maybe we can kill them with thirst!"

"And if we're lucky," howled the lieutenant, "maybe they'll curse god, and he'll destroy them for us! Then we'll finally be rid of Adam and Eve, once and for all!"

SO THE DEVIL AND HIS horde bellowed with revolting glee as they began to hurl fireballs down onto the remaining piles of wheat, which in turn rapidly engulfed the entire field in flames. Startled, the dozing couple woke up and saw the fire all around them.

"Oh, Lord, not again!" shouted Adam, who reached for the bucket of water next to him but found it tipped over and empty. The terrified couple retreated from the blaze and stood at some distance, helplessly watching their beloved field go up in flames.

"No, Adam. There goes our beautiful field. Now what are we going to do?"

"I guess we have no choice but to go back to our cave."

SMUDGED WITH SOOT from head to toe, the traumatized couple had traveled several miles before finally, too exhausted to continue, they slumped down into the dirt.

Then the Word of God appeared. "Are you two all right?"

"I guess so, Lord," muttered Adam, rubbing his soot-covered forehead. "But all our wheat is gone. Even our bucket of water got dumped out."

The Word calmly replied, "It seems that Satan and his henchmen have been up to no good as usual."

"But how could this happen?" asked Eve. "Did we do something wrong again?"

"Oh, my poor Eve," continued the Word. "That's not an easy question to answer. Sometimes, no matter what you do, the rain is going to fall on the just and the unjust alike."

"What does that even mean, Lord?" asked Adam. "Pardon me for asking: But did we or did we not do something to deserve this?"

"In this case, no. Actually, you could say that the only thing you did *wrong* was follow My instructions."

"I am so confused," Adam said, shaking his head. "Now what are You telling us? Bad things can happen to us even when we do the *right* thing?"

"I'm afraid so, yes."

"But why?" blurted Eve. "That doesn't make any sense."

"Unfortunately, it makes perfect sense when you consider that you've already willingly handed your kingdom over to the devil by following his advice to eat from the Tree of Knowledge. He is, after all, the king of this world."

Adam and Eve just looked at each other, thoroughly frustrated.

"Now do you understand what I'm saying?" asked the Word.

"Yes, Lord, I think so," replied Adam with a heavy sigh. "What You're telling us is: Satan is just as angry, if not more so, when we do follow Your instructions."

"Now you've got it, Adam."

"So if bad things are just as likely to happen to us if we do the right thing," interjected Eve, "then why should we even bother to do it?"

"Because when you do what is evil, I'm against you, but if you do what is right, then only the devil is against you. And never forget, when he attacks you, I'm still more than willing to protect you, but if I'm against you, there's no one in the Universe who can save you from My wrath."

WITH HEAVY HEARTS and still covered in soot, Adam and Eve were silently on the move again. They walked like that for quite a while before Eve finally turned to Adam. "So what's the point of going back to that field if all the wheat has been burned to the ground?"

"The point is," Adam blurted impatiently, "God told us to go back, so we're going; end of story."

"All right, all right. Are you mad at me now?"

"I'm sorry, Eve; I don't mean to be angry with you. It's just that every time we turn around we have something completely unexpected thrown in our faces. I'm losing my mind, I think."

With a knowing look, Eve nodded. Then she stopped and pointed as a peculiar expression swept across her face. "Adam, look! Our field!"

"Can it be real, Eve? Or is it just another of the devil's illusions?"

Having arrived back to the wheat field, they were amazed to discover that it had been completely restored to its original condition. Together, they ran, with outstretched hands, through row after row of full-grown stalks of wheat.

"But it can't be an illusion, my love," shouted Eve. "I feel every grain of wheat flowing right through my fingertips."

"You're right, Eve. And look, here's our bucket, full of water again."

They even found a stout, full-blossomed bush with a fluffy, white substance sprouting from every branch.

"That's strange, Eve. I don't remember seeing this bush before."

Eve shook her head, dumbfounded. "Me neither."

Intrigued, the couple stood and stared at it.

"What kind of fruit is this, Adam?"

"How should I know? I've never seen anything like it before in my life."

"It's manna," came a sweet, clear voice.

Turning to see who was speaking, Adam and Eve found an angel standing next to them.

"Manna?" replied Adam. "What's manna?"

"It's bread from Heaven," the angel said with a serene smile.

"You mean like the bread that Adam made for us?"

"Better."

"Better?" blurted Eve. "Impossible."

"If you don't believe me, then go ahead and try it yourself."

The couple cautiously reached out, plucked a handful, and touched it to their lips.

"Mmm, it's sweet," said Eve, who put it in her mouth and chewed. "Oh, Adam, he's right, it *is* better than your bread, and you didn't even have to bake it."

So Adam took a bite, too, and happily nodded in agreement.

SATAN AND HIS MINIONS, as usual, were watching the couple and the angel from a distance.

"This is so infuriating," grumbled the devil. "Every time we come up with a way to strike misery and fear into the hearts of those two, it completely backfires on us. What can we possibly do to counteract something like that?" Silently brooding for several moments, Satan finally turned to his lieutenant. "Well, what do you have to say for yourself this time?"

Stunned, the devil could not believe his black, cold-hearted eyes, because instead of looking into the face of the lieutenant, he was staring into the face of the Word of God, which sat curiously atop the shoulders of his faithful lackey, a totem of astonishing dimensions.

"Wh—*what kind of trickery* is this?" stammered the devil as he rubbed his eyes with his leathery paws.

"What's wrong now, Satan?" replied the Word, sporting a sardonic grin. "How does it feel to doubt what your eyes tell you?"

"Please, state your purpose, if you don't mind. The sooner you tell me why you're here, the better."

"As you wish, Devil. I'm here to warn you."

"Warn me? Warn me about what?"

"I trust you love your minions."

"Love my minions? What's that supposed to mean?"

"Your minions. Do you love them?"

"Love is such a strong word. I hardly think it's a word that even exists in my vocabulary."

"Then you enjoy their company. You love what they can do for you."

"Oh, I see what you're getting at. Of course, I do, yes. Why do you ask?"

"From now on, for every stalk of wheat you destroy, I will banish one of your minions to the depths of the Abyss. Is that clear?"

Satan's eyes thinned as he considered this proposition, and then, without a word, he nodded with a nearly imperceptible groan.

"Very good," said the Word, and just like that His handsome face faded from view, giving way to the lieutenant's grotesque visage.

As if waking from a deep sleep, the lieutenant's eyes rolled back into their sockets and focused on Satan's angry gaze. "What?" mumbled the lieutenant, barely coherent. "Why are you looking at me like that?"

The Perfect Sacrifice

AS THE SUN SLOWLY set behind the mountain where Adam and Eve had brought their first offering of blood, the couple was preparing some grain as an offering. Placing the oblation on the same altar, they burned it. As they stood nearby, they watched as an incandescent pillar of smoke began to rise from the fire.

"When we were in the garden, Lord," began Adam, "our praises rose like the smoke of this offering, and our innocence ascended to You just like incense. So, God, please accept this offering from us, and don't turn us away without Your mercy."

Then the Word of God appeared. When Adam and Eve spotted Him, they walked over and joined Him. "Lord," said Adam, "we're so honored You could be here with us."

"You've done well, Adam. I'm proud of you."

The couple smiled at each other.

"Hear that, Eve? We did something right for a change," he remarked, looking in every direction. "And see, the devil is nowhere in sight."

The Word smiled knowingly. "That's right, Adam, because he can't stand the sight of what you've done here today."

"Why, Lord?" wondered Eve.

"Because you've offered this thing of your own free will. To the devil, it's repugnant, but in the sight of God, it is most precious; so precious, in fact, He's decided to make it My body when I'm born on this Earth to save you. And I'll cause it to be offered continually upon an altar to provide forgiveness and mercy for everyone who partakes of it properly."

Suddenly a fireball hurled down upon their offering, engulfing the whole scene with a tremendously bright light. The astonished couple stepped back.

"What's happening, Lord?" asked Adam. "What's that light?"

"God has accepted your offering and has sent this light to illuminate your hearts with grace and peace."

Then, from out of the flames of their offering, a strange figure began to rise from the altar. It was the figure of a dove slowly ascending into the evening sky.

"What's that, Lord?" Eve asked quietly. "It's so beautiful."

"You two are most honored, because today God has sent the Holy Spirit to visit you and your offering."

In awe, the couple looked at one another in the flickering moonlight.

"Oh, Eve, can you feel it? It's as though the love of God is coursing through every fiber of my being. What an amazing thing. I've never known anything like it in all my days."

"I do feel it, my darling. And you're right, the only way I can describe it: It's as if God's love, His peace, His warmth, is flooding my innermost being. I feel so alive."

Completely transfixed, Adam and Eve stood there, basking in the iridescent glow of that special moment.

"Oh, Lord," sighed Adam, "if only this moment could last forever. Eve and I could be happy even in this darkened world. Please tell us You can make it so."

As the couple watched with such yearning, the dove of the Spirit continued to ascend with majestic wings of light. Gliding upward, further and further, it eventually became a mere speck of light in the celestial vault and then vanished.

"It's gone, Eve," murmured Adam, "gone, all too soon." Then turning to Eve, he saw tears streaming down her face. "Oh, Eve, don't cry, it'll be all right."

"But I'm not crying because I'm sad, silly. These are tears of joy, tears of longing, tears of hope."

Overwhelmed, they embraced and as they did Adam peered over her shoulder to the Word looking on with such happiness. "Thank You, Lord, for this moment. You really have blessed us beyond measure today."

The Word nodded. "You're welcome, Adam."

"If only this sort of thing could happen again and again," said Eve with a contented sigh.

"But what makes you think it can't?" asked the Word.

Amazed at this, the couple turned to the Word. "What are You saying, Lord?" asked Adam. "You mean this could happen again? But how?"

"Whenever you make a free will offering to Me, you're turning from yourselves and the misery of this fallen world. In that moment, when you offer yourselves in this way, it provides a delicate yet powerful conduit into the Divine, a kind of 'new beginning,' if you will, whereby God has the ability to renew your dead selves."

"You mean it's as if, in that brief moment, our old life," mused Adam, "the life we used to have in the garden, is restored."

"Yes, that's exactly what I'm saying."

"Did you hear that, Eve? All we have to do is make an offering whenever we're overwhelmed by pain or depression, and God will fill us with His — what did you call it, Lord?"

"The Holy Spirit."

"Right, the Holy Spirit."

ADAM WAS STILL SO excited the next morning he could hardly contain himself. Vaulting out of their cave, he was a man possessed with a new mission in life. "Eve, Eve, my darling Eve. What a beautiful day this is."

Eve smiled, too, as though she did not have a care in the world. "You're right, Adam, it is a beautiful day. I don't know when I've ever felt better. God knows, this place is no Garden of Delights, but somehow that doesn't seem so important anymore. Somehow the thing I wanted so badly doesn't seem so far away after all. Isn't that odd?"

"Then it's settled. We're going to make a free will offering, just like we did yesterday, three times a week. We'll do it every Wednesday, Friday and Sunday, and we'll keep on doing it that way for the rest of our lives."

Suddenly the Word of God arrived. "Hello, you two. I've come to tell you God is very pleased about your commitment to bring your offerings on a weekly basis."

"That's great news, Lord," replied Adam.

"And because of your resolve to do this thing, you've now determined your fate for both you and your descendants."

Adam and Eve exchanged a curious look.

"Is that a good thing?" wondered Adam.

"Of course it is. It simply means that when I come as a human being and suffer for your sakes, it will happen in such a way as to fulfill the meaning of all your sacrifices offered from this point onward."

"But I don't understand, Lord," Adam said, shaking his head. "I'm afraid I don't follow Your meaning."

"Don't worry about that now, Adam. Someday you'll understand. All I'm saying is that when I come to give My life as a ransom for many, it will also take place on a Wednesday and proceed through the preparation day of Friday. And then, just as I created everything in the beginning and raised the Heavens high above the Earth, so once again, My rising again on Sunday will create joy for everyone Who trusts in Me. So, you two, just remember to continue bringing these offerings to Me for the rest of your lives, and everything else will take care of itself."

ADAM AND EVE APPROACHED their altar again, where they piled their meal offering in a large heap and set it ablaze. As they stepped back, the fire crackled intensely, sending a shower of sparks skyward, shimmering upward in the shape of a dove. "Look, Eve, there's the Holy Spirit. God has accepted our offering again. Can you feel His love flowing through our veins?"

Eve nodded contentedly.

"Can you believe it? We've been bringing our offerings to God for seven whole weeks now, and it seems like we're growing closer and closer to Him every day."

Again, with her sweet smile, Eve just nodded. Then abruptly she withdrew a flinty dagger from beneath her sheepskin loincloth and began slashing into Adam with her blade of stone, piercing him squarely in his right side, causing him to shudder with each blow.

"Eve, no."

Ripping into his side with stab after stab, Eve then threw the bloody knife at his feet as she watched blood and water gush out of his wounds.

"Oh, Eve, what've you done?" gasped Adam. "How could you?"

Slumping at the foot of the altar, Adam died. Eve just stared at his lifeless body, oozing its strange mixture of fluids. Then, slowly lifting his corpse, she placed it up on the altar, extinguishing its flames. With a peculiar look in her eye, she moved her face very near to Adam's and gently pressed her lips against his. Slowly, Eve's countenance transformed into that of the devil's, and his grotesque lips finally withdrew from Adam's mouth.

"So, Adam," sneered Satan, "how does it feel to offer yourself up as a living sacrifice to your beloved god? Not all it's cracked up to be, is it?"

BEHIND THE CAVE OF Treasures, Eve lay prostrate on the ground, her mouth wrapped securely with a sheepskin muzzle. She desperately struggled to break free from the cords that bound her hands and feet. Just then, a pair of hands untied the muzzle.

"What is going on?" gasped Eve as she turned to see that an angel was untying her hands and then her feet.

"There is no time for a lengthy explanation, my dear," he said. "Suffice it to say that Satan and his angels abducted you in an effort to stop Adam from bringing any more offerings to the Lord."

"Adam! Is he all right? Where is he?"

"He's at your altar, Eve, and he needs you more than ever."

Jumping to her feet, Eve bolted away.

"Go quickly, young lady," exclaimed the angel. "Run like the wind!"

ARRIVING AT THE altar, Eve found Adam lying dead on it.

"Oh, Adam, I'm too late." Trembling and crying, she pulled his corpse from off the altar. As she did, blood oozed out over the embers of the smoldering sacrifice. Setting his body on the ground, Eve kneeled down next him, just as the Word of God appeared a few feet away.

Tears streaming down her face, Eve turned and asked, "What happened, Lord?"

"The devil, dear Eve, disguised himself as you and stabbed him."

"As *me*? But why?"

"Why does Satan ever do anything to you two? He's jealous of the peace and tranquility your offerings have brought you. He can't stand the thought of you and Adam growing closer to the heart of God, while nothing he does prevents it from happening."

Turning back to Adam, she fell onto his corpse, weeping uncontrollably. "Poor Adam, how you must have suffered. Please, Lord, please bring him back to me, won't You?"

The Lord reached out His hand toward Adam, and slowly all of his stab wounds sealed back up.

Sucking in a deep breath, Adam sat up, wild-eyed. "Eve, why!"

Dismayed, Eve jumped to her feet, looking to the Word for moral support.

"Relax, Adam, don't be alarmed. Eve didn't attack you. It was the devil again. He transformed himself to look like Eve so you'd never suspect how close your attacker was."

"Oh, thank You, Lord," gasped Adam. "For a second there—"

Obviously offended, Eve protested. "Adam! What are you saying? Did you seriously think for one second I could've done something this despicable?"

"Never mind, Eve," insisted the Word in a reassuring tone. "Appearances can be deceiving. Don't be so hard on him. He was, after all, just killed by a woman. That in itself will always try a man's soul."

"He makes a good point, Eve. You can hardly blame a guy for jumping to conclusions."

"Very funny, you two," smirked Eve.

"Now, go ahead, Adam," continued the Word, "I want you to finish up here with your offering. Just realize how precious this is to God. In fact, the same thing is going to happen to Me while I'm on Earth."

"What, Lord?" asked a confused Adam. "What's going to happen to You?"

"I, too, will be pierced in My side, and blood and water will also flow from My wound, and that blood that is spilled will be the true offering, one that will be laid upon an altar as a perfect sacrifice."

A Message from God

THE COUPLE WALKED westward from their cave early the next morning. They went to the field of wheat and rested under the shade of a large tree. No sooner had they sat down than a pack of wolves appeared from the bushes and moved in toward the relaxing couple. Growling maliciously, fangs extended, the animals crept forward, preparing to rush at them. The startled couple sprang to their feet, and Eve instinctively hid behind Adam.

"What's the meaning of this, wolves?" asked Adam as he boldly stepped forward.

Stepping ahead of the rest of the pack, the lead wolf snarled, "We're hungry, and lately our hunting has been scarce. Provide us with food, and we'll leave you in peace."

"I wish we could help you, Wolf, really I do."

"What, then, should we tell our hungry families when we return to them empty-handed again?" asked the wolf while the pack slowly crept forward several more feet.

Adam put up his hand in protest. "Wait! Certainly you remember the oath we all took to never harm one another. Why would you do something like this?"

For a moment, the wolves hesitated and looked at one another.

"Are you aware of making such a pact with these humans?" asked the lead wolf of his companions.

"I am not," replied one of them.

Turning back to address Adam, the lead wolf shrugged his furry shoulders. "It seems my brothers and I took no such oath. Now, provide us with something to eat. Or else!"

"But we have no food for your kind," replied Adam.

"Then prepare to *become* food, humans!" growled the wolf, and lunging ahead the pack rushed forward along with him.

"Adam, do something!" screamed Eve.

"Into the tree, Eve, quickly!" Adam nimbly hoisted Eve into the branches of the tree and scrambled up after her, just as the furious pack, fangs extended, swept past them with their snapping jaws. Circling back around, the pack gathered at the base of the tree and began scratching at it, frantically trying to jump up after the couple.

"Now what do we do, Adam?"

"We go higher, Eve, higher."

So climb they did, moving upward from branch to branch. Finally, one of the wolves managed to claw his way up into the lowest branch of the tree. Eve was desperately trying to reach the branch above her when the one she was on suddenly broke. Managing to grab her wrist as she fell past him, Adam held on tightly. But as her feet dangled, the wolf in the tree was very close to reaching her with his vicious fangs.

"Get the female!" snarled the lead wolf as he tried to climb into the tree with his companion. "Get her!"

Eve struggled mightily to hoist herself upward while the branch supporting Adam creaked loudly. Unable to hold their combined weight, the branch finally snapped, sending the pair down onto the wolf in the branch just below them. "Adam, no!" Eve screamed.

Together, all three came spiraling down out of the tree, scattering the pack below. Landing in a heap, Adam and Eve looked at each other and then at the wolf they had landed on. Fortunately for them, the wolf just laid there, quite unconscious. Struggling to their feet, the couple looked frantically about, only to find that the pack, which had temporarily backed away, was now returning to stalk their prey.

"Step aside everyone," said the lead wolf. "Allow me to show you how this is done."

Obligingly, the pack parted to let him forward, and before Adam and Eve had time to react, the wolf was sprinting toward them. Frozen with fear, the couple just stood there.

"Lord, help us, please," whispered Adam.

Just as the wolf began his leap, an angel appeared in front of the trembling couple, and having simply been touched by this angel, the wolf floated past Adam and Eve and fell harmlessly to the ground with a thud. Grumbling angrily, the wolf laid there, huffing and puffing, but obviously incapable of any real movement. Just as abruptly, two more angels appeared and stood before the pack of wolves. They, too, simply motioned to them, and without a whimper the pack scattered and disappeared into the landscape, leaving their immobilized leader to fend for himself.

"Thank you so much, angel," said Adam, still trying to catch his breath. "And not a moment too soon."

As furious as she was terrified, Eve moved forward to examine the prostrate wolf, still lying helplessly on the ground. "Why would you do something like this, Wolf?" she snapped. "We made a pact with you and your kind. How could you?"

"He did it, Eve," began the first angel, "because he is no wolf at all."

Confused, the couple stared at the trio of angels.

"Not a wolf?" blurted Adam. "Then…" A strained look of realization swept across his face. "Oh, no. Don't tell me it's him, *again*?"

And after a simple gesture from the first angel, the startled look on the couple's faces revealed that the answer had become all too apparent.

"Satan," said Eve, blanching at the hideous creature on the ground, no longer looking like the wolf that had just attacked them.

"Yes," replied the angel, quite calmly. "Satan. Doing what he does best, deceiving you with his myriad disguises. And if it were not for the fact that God is so concerned about your safety, he might have succeeded with his clever ruse."

"No wonder, Eve," said Adam. "Of course, the animals would never have attacked us this way. I should have known all along. How stupid of me."

The other two angels stepped over to them, looking down at the monster with equal parts disgust and dismay.

"Don't be too hard on yourself, Adam," said the second angel, "anyone could have made a mistake like that. A creature like this, with the ability to take on any form he chooses, is simply impossible to anticipate."

"Now, be gone, Devil!" snapped the third angel, "and count yourself lucky that God doesn't destroy you for trying to destroy his beloved children!"

And with a cloud of dust, Satan streaked out of view.

Sighing heavily, Adam turned to the trio of angels. "You three certainly look familiar. Have we met before?"

"Of course, Adam," replied the first angel. "We're the archangels who brought you gold, frankincense and myrrh."

"Oh, right," said Adam. "I remember now. What were your names again?"

"I'm Michael. I was the one who brought you the gold."

"I'm Gabriel, and I brought you frankincense."

"And I'm Raphael. I brought you myrrh."

"That's right," said Adam as he turned to Eve with a smile. "Remember, Eve?"

"Of course, I remember, Adam. We're so grateful to the three of you; then and now."

"It is our pleasure to serve you, my dear," said Michael with a perfunctory nod.

"The Lord bless you and keep you always," added Gabriel.

"So tell us," continued Raphael, "have you enjoyed the gifts we brought you in the name of the Most High?"

"More than words can say," replied Adam. "We'll cherish them forever."

"So glad to hear it," said Michael.

"You bringing us those tokens," interjected Eve, "was the first nice thing that had ever happened to us in this miserable place."

"Tell us, then, angels," continued Adam, "is there any chance you might have something more for us from the Lord?"

"You mean apart from rescuing you both from Satan's attack just now?" asked Gabriel, smiling playfully.

"Oh, Adam," said Eve, clearly embarrassed. "Haven't they done enough for us yet?"

Adam sheepishly hung his head.

"Don't worry, Adam," added Raphael, "the Lord always has more for those who trust Him without reservation. Do you trust Him?"

Looking up with a tremendous smile, Adam replied, "Of course I do, with every ounce of my being."

"Good," said Michael, "because today is a special day, you two. Not only has the Lord rescued you from the jaws of death, but He has also asked us to bring you a very important message."

"Really," mused Eve. "What could it be?"

"Oh, it's nothing really," quipped Michael. "Still it is a message from God. Are you willing to listen and perform it?"

Adam nodded. "Tell us so we can receive it."

"Then you have to promise you'll do it. You have to swear."

"But I don't know how to swear," replied Adam.

"Then I'll show you," said Michael, holding out his hand. "It's easy. Give me your hand."

Adam then placed his hand in Michael's hand.

"Now, say this," continued Michael. "As God lives and speaks and is rational, Who raised the Heavens in space, established the Earth on the waters, and created me out of the ground, I, Adam, will never break my promise, nor renounce my word."

Adam repeated the oath.

"Very well, then," said Michael with an earnest nod. "You know it's been a long time since you came out of the garden, and in all that time you've never done anything wrong. Now, God wants you to take Eve, who came out of your side, and marry her."

"Marry her?"

Adam and Eve exchanged a curious look.

"But what does that mean?" asked Adam.

"It's when two humans are joined together as one," said Michael, quite matter-of-factly.

"Really," muttered Adam, mulling the idea over in his confused mind. "Do I really have to marry my own flesh and blood now? Wouldn't that mean I'd be committing adultery against myself? God would really want to destroy me then."

Michael blanched. "Adultery? Who said anything about adultery?" Turning to the two angels with him, he asked, "Did either of you hear me say anything about adultery?"

Both of them shrugged and together said, "No."

All eyes returned to Adam, who still looked very confused.

"There, you see?" said Michael with a reassuring smile. "Marriage just means that you and Eve will be able to bear children to comfort you in your sadness. Doesn't that sound like something that would appeal to you?"

"Adam?" interjected Eve.

"Yes, dear?"

"Ask him to tell us what *children* are."

But Adam put up his hand in protest. "Hold on, Eve. We'll get to that in a minute. First things first. What I want to know is: If God exiled us and deprived us of our luminous natures because we ate fruit from a tree, what do you think He'd do to us if we consented to this thing you called—what was it again?"

"Marriage," said Michael.

"Yeah, marriage. I bet He'd wipe us out if we do something like that!"

"But I'm telling you," insisted Michael, quite adamantly, "there is nothing wrong with what God is proposing."

"Wait a second!" blurted Adam, suddenly suspicious. "God never told us anything about what you're saying. Maybe you're not one of God's angels after all. You're really the devil and his henchmen in disguise again, aren't you?"

With that, Michael opened his mouth to reply, but strangely enough, although his lips were moving, no sound came out. Puzzled, the trio of angels turned to one another and tried to converse amongst themselves, but still, though they were all mouthing their words, nothing could be heard from any of them. Nervously, they looked back at Adam and Eve, and then took several cautious steps backward.

"Damn you, Satan!" exclaimed Adam, "get away from us right now, in the name of the Lord!"

Suddenly the three angels transformed into their true appearances as Satan and two of his hideous demons.

"But—*but how*, Adam?" stammered Eve. "Didn't we just see Satan as the wolf? And now here he is again. What is going on?"

Adam and Eve stepped back, but the devil did not advance toward them. Instead, he made a hasty retreat, spewing obscenities, with his demons following close behind.

THE DEPRESSED COUPLE sat in their cave, late into the evening, just staring at each other.

"Oh, Eve, did you see that?" groaned Adam. "I just swore by God's name and shook hands with the devil."

"I know, Adam, but you have to stop beating yourself up like this. It's not your fault. Those disguises of his are impossible to figure out."

"Please, whatever you do, don't ever tell anyone about this. All right?"

So Eve remained silent while Adam spread his hands toward God. "Oh, Lord, please forgive me for what I've done. I never meant to cooperate with the devil again."

ADAM CONTINUED TO stand and pray like that, day after miserable day. Disheartened at the sight of what Adam was putting himself through, Eve approached him and held out a slice of bread.

"No thank you, dear," said Adam. "I'm busy right now."

"But, Adam, I'm worried. You haven't eaten for over a week now. You need your strength. Please eat something. I made you some bread, just the way you like it."

"I'm sorry, Eve, but I just don't feel like eating right now."

"Please, for me? You know, it's one thing to pray for God's forgiveness, but it's another thing altogether to starve yourself in the process."

"I'm sorry, Eve, really I am; but I need to keep praying until the Lord responds."

"But you know that takes forever sometimes."

"If He never responds, then so be it. I'll die of starvation. Then, without me to take care of you, the Lord will have to let you back into the garden."

"But I don't care about the garden anymore, Adam."

With a look of disbelief, Adam turned to Eve. "What did you say?"

"I said, I don't care if I ever get back into that silly, old garden."

"Oh, Eve, don't say that, not even in jest. Don't you want our old life back?"

"Not if it means losing you, no. I don't even know what I was thinking before. What do I need with a garden, anyway, when we have each other, when we have God, the Word and the Holy Spirit? What more do I need beyond that?"

"Wow, I'm not quite sure how to respond to that. Now, would you please just let me get back to my prayers?"

"Fine," she said, and then sadly turned and walked away.

STILL REFUSING TO eat or drink after several more days of determined prayer, Adam, overcome by exhaustion, finally slumped to the ground, very near death.

Lamentably, Eve looked down at his motionless body. "Lord, please, help us. I'm afraid Adam doesn't look so good."

Then the Word of God appeared and revived Adam again, helping him to his feet. "Oh, Adam, what am I going to do with you?"

"I don't know, Lord," replied Adam, hanging his head in dismay. "I feel just terrible about all this."

"You swore an oath by My name."

"I know, Lord. How could I have done something so stupid?"

"And you made another agreement with Satan."

"I know, Lord. What was I thinking?"

"But, for the very first time in your life, you saw through his deception, rebuked him, and caused him to flee without any help from Me at all."

"I know, Lord. I feel so ashamed. Wait—*what*?" Confused, Adam looked up at the Word. "What did You say?"

"I said, you saw through his deception and caused him to flee without the slightest bit of help from Me. I'm very proud of you, Adam. You're finally beginning to grow into a genuine knowledge of God."

Adam and Eve exchanged a relieved look and a smile.

"Did you hear that, Eve? The Lord is proud of me."

Eve happily nodded.

"Oh, Lord," exclaimed Adam. "I can still hardly believe what happened. There were ravenous wolves. And there were these angels who looked just like the ones who brought us the gold, frankincense and myrrh. And then there I was shaking hands with the devil!"

"But you sent them all packing in the end, didn't you?"

"I did, didn't I?" replied Adam, getting more and more excited.

Quite pleased, the Word nodded and put up His hand as if to calm an excitable boy. "But never forget, Adam. You still have to be very careful with Satan around. Now more than ever actually, since he'll be seeking to exact his revenge for your having outsmarted him for the first time. Will you do that for Me?"

With this sobering thought in mind, Adam quickly calmed down and solemnly nodded. "Of course I will, Lord."

Then the Word disappeared.

Relieved, Adam turned to Eve. "I am so hungry, Eve. Is there anything to eat?"

Beauty and the Beast

ADAM WOKE UP THE next morning and, rolling over, he watched Eve with an intense longing as she lay sleeping.

Slowly opening her eyes, Eve became startled by his scrutinizing gaze. "Adam, why are you looking at me like that?"

"No reason. I'm just looking. Have I ever told you how beautiful you are?"

Bewildered, she shook her head. "No, you haven't."

"Well, then, I'm telling you now. You are very beautiful, my darling; your eyes, your hair, your face, all lovelier than the most beautiful sunset I've ever seen."

Taken aback, Eve stared at him with a peculiar look on her face. "Why, thank you, Adam. What has gotten into you?"

WALKING ALONG THE river on the eastern border of the garden, Adam and Eve got to its bank and sat down. Enjoying a pleasant breeze, they gazed out over its peaceful, flowing waters.

"Tell me, Eve: Do think God would be angry with me if I wanted to marry you?"

Thoughtfully, she considered the question for a moment, then turned to him with her most charming smile. "I don't know. Have you ever thought about asking Him?"

"Frankly, it's all I *can* think about."

SATAN AND HIS MINIONS, of course, were watching the couple from a distance as they were often in the habit of doing. The devil scratched his furrowed brow, staring, brooding, plotting. "What to do, what to do? Those disgusting, little replicas are really starting to drive me crazy. Now they're even beginning to see through my most elaborate schemes."

Seated at the devil's right hand, his lieutenant's face suddenly lit up and his eyes opened wide. He eagerly raised his bony finger and his lips slowly parted, as if he were about to say something significant.

Noticing him, Satan turned his ugly face and sneered, "What is it now, you insufferable dolt?"

Deflated, his lieutenant closed his mouth, lowered his finger, and frowned.

"Just as I thought," grumbled the devil. "Can't anyone offer me anything in the way of a workable plan to convince god to destroy these two troublemakers?"

Then, as if his lieutenant had something else occur to him, he raised his crooked finger again.

"Yes, yes," mumbled Satan. "Out with it already."

"Well, Lord, I was thinking."

"Do tell."

"Well, as I see it, even though Adam has been repeatedly protected from our attacks, there would be no one to protect him if he incurred the wrath of god."

"Naturally, you idiot, that's a given. But how do we accomplish such an aim?"

"But you've already figured it out yourself, Master."

"I have?" muttered Satan, trying to figure out what it was. "Oh, yes, of course I have." Turning to his lieutenant, the devil leaned toward him in anticipation. "What was my idea again?"

"When you persuaded Adam to shake your hand, it revealed his innermost desire to have relations with the female. It revealed his vulnerability to something their god has never given them permission to do."

Mulling over his words, Satan's eyes thinned. "Yes, I see what you're saying. If I can just trick Adam into marrying Eve without receiving permission from god, then he'll kill them for us."

"Precisely, Master! That's exactly what I'm saying."

"Oh, my word. I am diabolically clever, aren't I?"

With an oppressive howl, the whole group of demons shrieked their approval.

Then, as the din slowly simmered down, Satan turned to his lieutenant and quietly asked, "Now, remind me again how I plan to carry out this grand scheme of mine?"

TRYING UNSUCCESSFULLY to relax, Adam sat with Eve on the riverbank, but obviously he was growing more and more agitated about something.

"So what do you think, Eve? How do you feel about marrying me?"

"Marrying you? Why do you want to marry me?"

"Because I love you; isn't that reason enough? Don't you love me?"

"Of course I do, sweetheart. You know that."

"Well, then, marry me. What do you say, Eve, you want to marry me?"

"I don't know," she replied with a sheepish grin, obviously embarrassed by his impetuousness. "What does this marriage involve, anyway?"

Leaning over to her, Adam kissed Eve amorously on her neck. "It involves being in love; you know, being together."

"No, I don't know," she said, pulling away, suddenly uncomfortable. "And what makes you such an expert on marriage? Has God told you something I don't know about?"

"Not in so many words."

"What's that supposed to mean? Has He advised you about marrying me, or not?"

Frustrated, Adam turned away. "No."

And for quite a while, the couple just sat there without a word, unsure of what to do next. Then something caught their eye from the shoreline.

"Adam, what's that in the water?"

Rising from the depths of the river, ten women, exotic, naked and sensuous, came up slowly, not more than fifty yards in front of them.

"I don't know, Eve," said Adam, his eyes widening, much to the chagrin of Eve. "But I think they're women, *beautiful* women."

The entire group of ladies effortlessly made their way through the rivers current. Reaching the shoreline, they stepped out of the water and up to the couple.

"Hello there," said the tallest of the women. "What's your name?"

Adam and Eve exchanged a stunned look, and then returned their wide-eyed gaze back to this group of exquisite visitors.

"My, uh, my name is Adam. And this is Eve. Who are you?"

"Hello, Adam, Eve. My name is Lurana, and these are my sisters."

"Does this mean there's another world beneath our own?" asked Adam. "And is everyone living there as beautiful as you?"

"Why, yes, of course," Lurana replied, her dark, seductive eyes fixed squarely on Adam. "We are an abundant race."

"But how do you multiply?" asked Eve.

"How else does anyone multiply?" replied Lurana, quite nonchalantly. "We all have husbands who have married us, of course. Aren't you and Adam married?"

Eve shook her head, thoroughly confused. "No."

"You mean to tell me you have no children?" asked Lurana.

"Children?" echoed Adam as he shot a furtive glance at Eve. "What are children?"

Clearly taken aback by the question, Lurana replied tersely. "You know, progeny, offspring, *children*."

"But where, exactly, do these children come from?" asked Eve.

"By way of birth, of course," replied Lurana with an awkwardly charming smile. "All my sisters and I have given birth to many children, who then grew up and in turn got married and had children of their own. Of course, if you don't believe us, we can always prove it to you."

So the whole group of women turned toward the river. "Husbands, children, come to us now!" Lurana shouted. "Come and greet your neighbors of the dry land!"

Quite to their surprise, Adam and Eve watched while ten men and twenty children ascended out of the river. Every one of them walked straight to one of those lovely, young ladies and stood next to her.

"You see?" continued Lurana. "Here are our husbands, our sons and our daughters. Say hello, everyone. This is Adam and Eve, our neighbors."

"Hello," said the group as one.

"Hello," echoed Adam and Eve together.

"Just think, Adam," continued Lurana, "you and Eve could get married just like we did, and you could have children of your own." Then, she fell silent. Allowing some time for her words to sink in, Lurana fixed her sensual gaze firmly back on Adam.

Considering her advice, Adam grew even more agitated. "Eve, darling, didn't I tell you? Just think what it would be like to be married, to have children of our own. Wouldn't that be something?"

"But, Adam, what would God say?" Eve said slowly, half to herself, half to him. "Are you sure He wouldn't be angry with us if we got married without His permission?"

"All right, Eve, all right," grumbled Adam, thoroughly frustrated. "Have it your way." So he stood and turned his eyes skyward. "Lord..."

Lurana tilted her head oddly. "But why do you need God's permission to do something so natural?"

Adam adamantly shook his head. "Because if we don't get His permission, He may be angry with us for doing something like this."

"Nonsense. We never required permission to marry, and look at us. God didn't kill us, did He?"

"I'm sorry, but we have to ask God for His advice. Now, please, stop interrupting me." Again Adam lifted his eyes skyward. "Lord, Eve and I would like to get married, but we don't want to make You so angry with us that You'd wish to kill us. Could You please tell us what You think about all this?"

With that, the entire group of exotic visitors exchanged a peculiar look and cautiously stepped back.

"Wait," exclaimed Adam. "Where're you going? You have to stay until the Word of God comes to tell us His decision."

But Lurana resolutely shook her head, and without another word, the entire group walked back to the river, where they slowly descended, one by one, into its depths and disappeared from view.

BACK IN THEIR CAVE around evening time, Adam and Eve were trying to go about their business as if nothing unusual had just happened, but because Adam continued to pace incessantly about, Eve got annoyed. "Adam, would you please sit down and relax? You're not helping this situation with all your pacing."

"But why won't God answer us? Why won't He let us know what to do? I've never been more confused about anything in my life. I can't stop thinking about marrying you. So many thoughts are surging through my mind, my body. I can't take it anymore."

"I'm sorry, but I'm exhausted. I'm going to sleep. You deal with it on your own. I'll see you in the morning. Good night."

But even after Eve had long since fallen asleep Adam was still pacing back and forth.

AT THE BREAK OF DAWN, Adam woke Eve up. "Come on, Eve, hurry. It's time to get up."

Sitting up, bleary-eyed, Eve gaped at Adam. "Did you even go to sleep last night?"

"Sleep? How do you expect me to sleep with so many questions gnawing at me? Now get up; we've got to go."

"Go? Go where?"

"We're going to the hilltop where we received the gold, frankincense and myrrh. I need to ask the Lord about this thing."

Still half asleep, Eve laid back down. "But I'm tired, Adam. I'm not ready to go anywhere right now. Just leave me alone."

"Are you kidding? I need the Lord to explain what it means to marry you! I'm telling you, Eve, those people at the river have set my heart on fire! I can't stop thinking about what they told us! Thoughts of their sensual lives keep racing through my mind! But I refuse to just take you without God's permission, or else He might destroy us for sure!"

"But why do we have to go to the hilltop?" asked Eve, struggling to sit up, yawning and stretching her tired muscles. "Why not just pray to God here in our cave? He'll tell us if marriage is a good idea or not."

Adam then turned his eyes toward Heaven. "Oh, Lord, would You please tell us about this thing called marriage? If it's okay with You, then let us know, but if it isn't, then order us to resist our desires, because if You don't give us permission soon, we'll be overpowered for sure! We'll be following Satan's advice again, and You'll have no choice but to reduce us to nothing!"

Then the Word of God appeared. "Just think you two. Do you realize that if you had been this cautious in the beginning, you'd have never been forced to leave the garden in the first place? You've certainly come a long way since then."

Smiling, Eve stood up and took hold of Adam's hand. Suddenly the three archangels who had brought them the gold, frankincense and myrrh appeared next to the Word.

"So that you won't think this is a mere illusion, I've asked Michael, Gabriel and Raphael to join Me before you now. Above all, I want you to be absolutely sure that I am blessing your union together, and in order to explain everything that you'll need to know about your impending marriage, I'll leave you two in their capable hands."

Adam smiled proudly at Eve. "Did you hear that, sweetheart? The Lord has blessed our marriage."

Smiling back, she nodded.

Then the Word vanished, leaving the angels standing before the happy couple.

"Now, Adam," began Michael, "take some of the gold you were given and present it to Eve as a wedding gift."

So Adam took a sliver of gold and placed it on Eve's sheepskin blouse, just over her heart. "This I give you, Eve, as a pledge of my undying love."

"Then," added Gabriel, "pledge yourself to her by giving her some of the frankincense I brought you."

As Adam handed Eve some of the frankincense, he said, "This I give as an assurance that I will always be there for you, Eve, to protect you, to shelter you, to care for you all the days of my life."

"And when you present her with the myrrh," said Raphael, "you'll be engaged."

Finally, Adam presented her with some myrrh. "And this I offer you, Eve, so you may know that when we two become one, it will not merely be a oneness in flesh alone, but it will be in spirit and in truth as well."

"Well done, Adam," said Michael. "You two are now officially engaged."

"Now, God wants you both to fast and pray for the next seven days," continued Gabriel, "and after that, Adam, you may go in to Eve, your wife, because then it will be a pure union, a sacred union."

"Then, you are to have children," added Raphael, "who will multiply and replenish the entire planet."

Adam and Eve happily nodded to the archangels.

"We'll do everything just as you've told us," said Adam, "as though it were straight from the mouth of the Lord Himself."

THE COUPLE REMAINED in their cave for several days, fasting and praying, when suddenly four visitors appeared at the mouth of their cave. It was Lurana, with her husband, son and daughter. But much to their chagrin, Adam and Eve refused to even speak to them. The couple simply pointed them in the opposite direction. Reluctantly, the dejected visitors from the river turned and walked away. Kissing Adam on his cheek, Eve proudly smiled and watched as he resolutely strolled back into the cave.

AS THE SUN ROSE THE following morning, Adam rolled over and gently shook Eve awake. "Dear Eve, wake up. It's time."

Opening her eyes, Eve gazed longingly up at him. "Don't tell me, my love. Is it really the morning of the eighth day?"

Happily, Adam nodded, stood up, and helped Eve to her feet.

FROM THEIR VANTAGE point, Satan and his minions watched from a distance, miserable and helpless, as Adam and Eve, flanked by Michael, Gabriel and Raphael, stood reverently before the Word of God. Then, Michael handed a ring of gold to Adam, who gently placed it on Eve's finger.

"I now pronounce you man and wife," said the Word. "Adam, you may kiss your lovely bride."

And as Adam took Eve in his arms and kissed her, the Word and the archangels slowly dissolved from view, just leaving the married couple quite alone and quite in love.

"What a touching sight," said the devil as a lone tear trickled down his furry cheek.

Noticing the desperate look on Satan's face, his lieutenant leaned in toward him and whispered, "Are you all right, Master?"

"I'm afraid," mumbled the devil with a pathetic sniffle, "weddings make me cry."

"Really?" wondered the confused lieutenant. "But, Lord, when have you ever seen a wedding before?"

Irritated, Satan glared back at him. "You idiot! This is all your fault!"

"Me? Why me?"

"It's been two hundred and forty days since I managed to get Adam and Eve kicked out of that horrid garden of theirs, and what've you accomplished in all that time? *Nothing!*"

"B—*but, Master*, please. I'm not the only one who's failed. You're not being fair."

"Fair! Who said anything about fair? This was a war, you insolent worm! A war for our very existence! A war with an entire kingdom on the line, and you want fair? Fair has nothing to do with it!"

"But all is not lost."

"You fool, *it is lost,* I tell you! Our direct war with Adam is over! We have no more tricks, no more deceptions, no more tactics. *It's over!*"

"But, Lord, you said yourself, we must never give in to doubt and pessimism, never give in to merely human weaknesses. Remember?"

"I said that?"

Meekly, the lieutenant gurgled, "Y — *yes*, M — *Master*, y — *you did*."

"Damn your pathetic hide," screeched Satan with a wave of his wretched paw. "How dare you contradict me!"

Then, with an eerie rush of wind and a whimpering howl, the terrified lieutenant was swept away into oblivion. Still fuming, the devil turned to his trembling cadre of demons and eyed them with the blackest eyes they had ever seen. "So tell me, did any of *you* hear me say something like that?"

A Change of Heart

FOR A WHILE AT LEAST that very first couple lived peacefully on the Earth. Then one day as Eve was bathing in the river, she stopped and tilted her head curiously. Holding her hand to her bulging stomach, she turned with a strange look on her face. "Adam?"

"Yes, dear, what is it?"

"Come here, please," she said quietly.

"Right now?"

"Yes, Adam. Your pregnant wife would like to see you *right now*. Hurry, please."

"Are you all right?" he asked, stepping into the river with her, looking rather concerned. "Is something wrong?"

"Not at all."

"Then what is it?"

"Here, give me your hand," she replied as she took his hand and placed it on her stomach. Confused, Adam went along with her but suddenly jerked his hand away.

"Wh — *what* was that?"

"That was your child kicking inside me."

"No."

"Yes."

"If I didn't know better, I'd say there was a wrestling match going on inside there."

"There is, Adam. And do you know what else?"

"What?"

"It was exactly one year ago today that we were married."

"Is that so?"

"It is, yes."

"A year ago already, wow. How time flies."

"And you're still happy that we got married?"

"Of course Eve, it was the best decision I've ever made. The best decision I will ever make. Right after trusting the Lord, that is," he said with a wry smile. "And you?"

"What about me?"

"Are you still happy we got married? No regrets, I mean? No more imagining what it would be like to have things the way they used to be? To be back in the garden again?"

For just a moment, Eve hesitated and then said, "No, not really."

"Not really." Then with just a hint of skepticism in his voice, he asked, "You mean to tell me that you're still not pining for your old life back? I find that very hard to believe. Tell me, then: If God decided to change His mind tomorrow and offered to let us back into the garden? Wouldn't you want to go, just a little?"

"Of course, silly, but…" Eve paused again, as if unsure of her next words.

"But what?" pressed Adam.

"But if He's doesn't, I'm okay with that, too. I won't be upset. Not any-more. I already told you: What do I need with a garden, when I have every-thing that was *in* the garden, right here, right now?"

"You make a good point, as usual."

"But what about you?" she asked. "Are you really okay with all this, too?"

"Well, I admit, there are still moments when I miss our old life, sure. The time we spent in the garden was like a dream, a sweet, beautiful dream, filled with cool breezes and the smell of nectar, but…" Pausing, Adam's gaze drifted from Eve and wandered far into the distant horizon.

This time Eve pressed the issue. "But now?"

"But now," said Adam, slowly mulling the words over in his mind, "af-ter all the time we've spent here together, building a new life by the sweat of our brow, the labor of our hands, I'm beginning to feel like this is more real than all that other stuff ever was. And if life in this place means learning to cope with the hardships we face, with your help and the help of the Lord and His angels, then I'm with you, Eve, all the way. Besides, what good is thinking about the past, when it keeps you from living in the present?"

"Good, I'm so glad. I needed to hear you say it for yourself. Now, please, can you get me some more of that delicious manna? I'm really craving some-thing sweet right now."

AS THE COUPLE TRIED to sleep in their cave, Eve tossed and turned so much that finally Adam sat up. "Eve, dear, are you all right?"

"No, Adam, I'm not."

"What's wrong? Is the baby kicking again?"

"No."

"What is it, then?"

So Eve sat up, too. "It's our cave."

"Our cave? What about our cave?"

"It's just that I'm going to have a baby soon, and this cave, well, it's a sacred cave. I mean, because of all the miraculous things that have happened here. You know?"

"Sure, Eve, I understand. What about it?"

"Well, I just don't think it would be proper for me to give birth here, that's all."

"Where should we go, then? Where else *can* we go?"

"Maybe we should go to the rock Satan dropped on us. God did turn it into a perfectly good awning over us, remember?"

Adam nodded. "Of course, it formed a natural cave, didn't it?"

"It did, yes. So, how about we go there? You could fix it up in no time; make it a kind of 'home away from home.' Please?"

ADAM AND EVE THEN went to stay in that sheltering rock until the time of her delivery approached, and when that day arrived, Eve cried out in agony. Adam felt so badly because of what she was going through that he prayed like he had never prayed before.

"Oh, Lord, have mercy. Please, stop torturing Eve this way."

Then the Word of God appeared.

"Lord, I think Eve is dying."

"No, Adam, she's not dying."

"What's wrong with her, then? Have we angered You in some way again?"

"Don't be alarmed. It's true, Eve is experiencing tremendous pain at this moment, but it's not because of anything you've done recently."

"Then why is she going through this?"

"It goes back to the beginning, I'm afraid, when you first disobeyed the command of God, and the Lord cursed your evil deed. She's going through this so God's word to her will be fulfilled: 'In pain and suffering, you'll bear your children.'"

Eve let out a lamentable scream. "Oh, Adam, the pain; it's unbearable!"

"Do something, Lord," begged Adam. "Don't let her suffer like this anymore."

"Don't worry, Adam. Soon, the agony of childbirth will subside, and when the twins are finally born, it will all be a distant memory."

"*Twins?*" Bewildered, Adam turned to the Word. "Good God, what are twins?"

EVE'S CRIES OF AGONY eventually gave way to the crying of her newborn son, and along with him came a daughter, too.

Holding the children in her arms, Eve was feeling much better.

"Oh, Eve, there are two of them, two of them. I can't believe it. No wonder there was such a wrestling in your belly."

"Say hello to your new son and daughter, Adam," whispered Eve, tired but happy. "How does it feel?"

Adam beamed a proud smile. "Wonderful."

FORTY DAYS LATER, Adam brought a meal offering to the same stone altar that they had built with their own hands, and watching from a distance, Eve held her two infants while Adam set fire to the offering.

"Lord," began Adam, "we come here today to consecrate the birth of our two children, Cain and Luluwa, and to ask that You watch over them, protect them, guide them, just as You've done with Eve and I."

A beam of light suddenly came streaming down from Heaven, which shone down on the altar. Amazed, Adam motioned to Eve, and slowly she walked to him with the children. Then with Cain in Adam's arms and Luluwa in Eve's arms, the couple stood before the altar, basking in the glow of the divine lightbeam and the warmth of the fire.

"Do you feel the love of God, Eve?" asked Adam with a serene sigh.

"I do, my darling, yes."

"And you're happy?"

"Happier than at any time in my life."

MEANWHILE, AS USUAL, Satan and his minions were watching what that first family were doing, and they looked thoroughly disheartened. With equal parts disgust and dismay, the devil moaned, "And I have never been *less* happy than at any time in my hateful existence." Turning to his new lieutenant, the devil asked with a grim scowl, "Tell me, then, my latest recruit, what miserable news might you have that could cheer me up today? In light of this tragic turn of events, that is."

After thinking very hard for several moments, the lieutenant raised his scrawny finger and emphatically declared, "You are still king of this world, Master, and we are all your obedient and willing slaves."

"Good grief. Tell me something I don't know."

Then a new idea ignited a spark in the lieutenant's sinister eye. "The children, Lord."

"The children? What news concerning those crying brats could cheer me up?"

"Their names, Lord."

"Names? What about them, you babbling idiot?"

"It seems that Adam, as he so often does, has discerned something unique about his future, in this case, his newborns. Before it's come to fruition, I mean; something that you might find very interesting."

"Really?" Satan leaned in, his eyes thinning and nostrils sniffing. "In what way?"

"Well, you see, he named the female Luluwa, which means *beautiful*, because apparently Adam believes she will be even lovelier than her mother."

"Ahhh," grunted the devil. "How in Hell is that supposed to cheer me up?"

"Wait, wait, Master, there's more. He named the male Cain."

"Yes, of course, Cain." Mulling this over in his malicious mind, the devil shrugged his leathery shoulders, shook his wolfen head, and hissed through clenched teeth. "So what."

"But, Master, he named him Cain. Don't you see?" The lieutenant's beady eyes opened wide. "Cain means *hater*, because he hated his own sister, even while he was still in his mother's womb."

Then, as if a bolt of lightning had hit him, Satan swooned, and donning his most malicious grin yet, he growled, "Oh, that is delicious. Now I see what you're saying. Yes, I do believe I can do something with that one. Good work, Lieutenant, very good work."

EVENTUALLY, EVE GAVE birth to another set of twins, again a boy and a girl, and as she held the babes to her breast, she looked up at Adam with a serene smile.

"Say hello to your new children, Papa."

"Hello, my dear son; hello, my darling daughter."

"And have you decided on names for them yet?" asked Eve.

"I have, yes. Our son is called Abel, and our daughter is Aklia."

ADAM MADE AN OFFERING for Abel and Aklia forty days later, and as a beam of light cascaded down upon the couple and their four children, they huddled together around the offering that burned so brightly against the night sky. And for that first family, yet another year had transpired, which meant they were at least that much closer to the time when God would finally rescue them and bring them back into the garden home they had longed for so very much.

Day of a Thousand Years

ENOCH CLOSED his book and looked out over this gathering of his family. By then, there were more than three times as many people listening to him since he had begun telling the story. He smiled graciously at the blossoming crowd. "Well, well, everyone. What did you think? Did you all enjoy the story of the Lord's creation and our very first parents?"

"Very much, Papa Enoch," chirped a child, around ten years old, in the front row.

"Good, Eli. That's very good. Did anyone learn anything from their example?"

Then Lamech stood up. "Of course, Grandfather. I learned that the Lord is faithful to all His promises, whether for good or for bad."

Enoch smiled proudly. "Excellent, Lamech."

"I must admit, Father," said Methuselah, "I also found your story to be most intriguing. If I didn't know better I'd swear you were telling the story as though you'd been there yourself."

"But that's what I've been trying to tell you. I was taken up to Heaven where I stood before the Face of God. Like molten iron, it glowed like the Sun. I've seen it with my own eyes. I've heard His voice with my own ears. Now everything He told me is in the books I've written for you."

Again everyone exchanged a look of consternation. Only Lamech's wife seemed sure of herself as she leaned in to Methuselah's wife, who looked just as perplexed as everyone else. "See, I told you he said he went to Heaven," Lamech's wife said quietly, much to the chagrin of her aunt.

Enoch grew suddenly melancholy. "But now He's only given me thirty days to tell you about it in person. It just doesn't seem fair somehow."

Baffled, Methuselah shook his head. "Please, Father, try and relax. You've obviously been through a very trying ordeal. You need your rest. You're delirious."

"Nonsense. I'm fine. It's just that what I'm trying to tell you is so important, and I don't have much more time to tell you." Enoch sprang to his feet, setting the book down in the seat behind him. "If only I could somehow get you to see what I've seen, hear what I've heard. Doesn't anyone here understand what I've been through in the slightest?"

Methuselah hung his head. "I wish I did, Father, really I do; but I'm afraid I don't."

"Well, then, try to imagine something for me, if you can. You've all seen me using my compass, haven't you?"

Methuselah looked up and, with the rest of the family, nodded. "Of course, Father, more times than I can count. You're a master craftsman."

"Yes, well, then try to imagine seeing the world from God's point of view: A Universe stretched out using the Lord's perfect compass. With it, I analyzed the Sun's orbit and counted off the hours it marks with its arc. I investigated everything concerning the Earth, every plant, every flower, every blade of grass. I discovered where the clouds live and how they create raindrops. I even saw the way of thunder and lightning, and how angelic guardians protect the Earth by restraining their power so their violent nature, harnessed in the thunderheads, won't destroy everything on the planet."

"Please, Pop, we understand," said Methuselah. "Now, have a seat, will you? You look tired."

"Tired? But I keep telling you: I'm fine! I've never felt better in my whole life!"

"What else did you see, Papa Enoch?" asked little Eli.

"Well, I saw the treasure houses of wind and ice, where I discovered the secrets of the wind, how they're brilliantly balanced throughout the globe to prevent earthquakes. I observed the key to the changing seasons, and I measured all the mountains, hills and rivers, all the fields and trees, right down to the very last stone."

"That's amazing, Grandfather," sighed Lamech. "And you say there are more books where we can read about these things?"

"That's exactly what I'm saying, Lamech, yes. If I saw it, I wrote about it, from the exalted Heavens, down to the depths of Hades and the place of judgment, where I saw tortured prisoners who all understood the nature of their judgment. I made a record of everyone being sentenced by the Eternal Judge, everything the accused have done, as well as all the verdicts. And that's when I saw *them* for the first time."

"Them?" blanched Methuselah.

"Yes, my son. *Them.*"

"What did you see, Grandpa?" asked Lamech in hushed tones.

"I saw the gatekeepers of Hades, huge serpents that had faces like extinguished lamps, with eyes of fire and teeth sharp as razors."

"Awesome," whispered Eli.

Aghast, Eli's mother stepped forward. "All right, Grandfather, enough with your spooky stories, really. The children will be having nightmares for weeks."

Taken aback, Enoch stared at her. "Nightmares? Why? From hearing the truth about God's creation? Nonsense, I tell you. It's good for them."

"So scaring children is a good thing now, is that it?" quipped Eli's mother.

"If having the privilege of understanding the Lord's actions is a scary thing," Enoch replied with a defiant nod, "then yes, I guess it is."

"It's all right, Grandfather," Lamech chimed in. "We're not scared. We appreciate what you're doing. You're a great man. The Lord has blessed you above all others by choosing you to be His mouthpiece."

"Oh, my dear boy," sighed Enoch. "God bless you for that. But now just look at me. What do you see? You see the Lord's eyes shining through me, like the Sun's rays, filling every one of you with awe." He then turned to the youngest member of the family. "I'm not frightening you, am I, Eli?"

"No, Papa Enoch," said Eli with an impish grin. "Not really."

"Of course not. God is wonderful. In fact, I saw how His actions are always good, unlike that of mankind, who sometimes does good and other times bad, and through this work of God, the heart of every evil person will be revealed for what it truly is."

"Then how come God didn't let Adam and Eve back into the Garden of Eden after five and a half days like He said He would?" The voice came from yet another young man, around the same age as Lamech, who stepped forward from out of the crowd.

"What's that, my boy?" Enoch squinted at the young man. "I'm sorry, my son, but I seem to have forgotten your name."

"My name is Jubal," said the young man.

Eli's mother nodded. "He's Lamech's cousin, twice removed."

"Oh, of course, yes," said Enoch apologetically. "The resemblance is most striking. You two could pass for brothers, twins almost. What was your question again, Jubal?"

Jubal calmly looked Enoch straight in the eye. "Didn't you tell us God promised to rescue Adam and Eve after five and a half days had transpired? So God never really did keep His promise to them, after all, did He?"

"Excuse me, Jubal, but I distinctly recall saying God promised to rescue Adam and Eve after five and a half of *His days*, not the kind of days you're thinking of."

Jubal shrugged his shoulders. "I still don't follow your meaning."

Not getting the response he was looking for, Enoch paced about for several moments. "Hmmm, let me see, maybe if I put it another way. I want you to stop and think about something for me, all right?"

Everyone except for Jubal respectfully nodded, but Enoch never even noticed him, having become so absorbed in his attempt to explain what was on his mind. "Good. Now, everyone remembers how God told Adam that he'd die the day he ate from the Tree of Knowledge, don't they?"

Again everyone but Jubal nodded in agreement.

"But he didn't die the same day, now did he? No. In fact, Adam actually went on to live to the ripe old age of nine hundred and thirty years before he finally died. Can anyone tell me why?"

Dumbfounded, the group stared back as they silently tried to figure out the answer.

"Come now, everyone?" urged Enoch. "How long do God's days last?"

"A thousand years?" said Lamech timidly.

"That's right. Now you're getting it. So, if God's days last a thousand of our years on Earth, then what?"

His eyes growing suddenly wide, Lamech raised his hand like an eager student.

"Yes, Lamech," said Enoch, nodding in approval. "Have you figured it out?"

Lamech smiled proudly and said, "Then, when Adam died at the age of nine hundred and thirty, it means that he still died on the first day of creation from God's perspective."

"Very good, Lamech. And that means?"

"And that means that when God told Adam that He'd rescue him after five and a half days, He was actually saying that He'd rescue him after 5,500 years had transpired."

"Exactly, Lamech, that's right! Very good, my boy. You're most observant. What's more, the Lord even went so far as to confirm this same promise to Adam and Eve's third son, Seth. When he was old enough to understand the truth, God also told him that He'd rescue Adam and his faithful descendants after 5,500 years. But that's not all, everyone. Do you know who else God personally told about His promise of five and a half days, besides Adam and Seth, I mean?"

Everyone there sat quite still, thinking the question over in their minds. Some of them looked to the person next to them to see if they knew, while others shrugged their shoulders or shook their heads, revealing that they had no idea.

"I know the answer, son," said Jared, quite matter-of-factly, as all eyes then turned to him.

"You, Grandfather?" wondered Methuselah. "How come you know who God told about His promise of days?"

"I know, my boy, because it was me. After God told Seth ... many, many years later, God told me about it."

A subdued hush rippled through the crowd.

"Wow," sighed little Eli. "That is so amazing. But Papa Jared?"

"Yes, Eli."

"How come *you* never told us about the five and a half days?"

"But I did. I told you all about it. Don't you remember?"

"You did?" Looking rather puzzled, Eli squinted curiously. "You told me?"

"Of course, I did; certainly."

"But when did you tell me?"

"Just now. I told you about it just now."

"No you didn't," said Eli with an amused, little grin. "That was Papa Enoch who told us about it."

"Well, who do you think told him all about it, my boy?"

Then turning to his mother, Eli smiled precociously at her. "Papa Jared is being silly, isn't he, Mama?

"He is, my love," she replied with a smile of her own. "That he is."

"So what do you think of that, everyone?" asked Enoch. "Now all of you know about God's promise of days, too. How exciting."

"Thank the Lord above," shouted someone from the crowd.

"Thank God for His faithfulness, from generation to generation, and throughout all time," added Lamech.

Impressed, Enoch looked at his grandson for quite a while, deep in thought. "You know, Lamech, something has occurred to me."

"What, Grandfather?" asked Lamech.

"What you just said reminded me of something else God told me. And now I think I'd like to tell you all another story, and I want you to pay close attention to what your earthly father is telling you. If you think I'm difficult, just imagine how terrifying it is to appear before the Ruler of Heaven?"

Methuselah then chimed in. "We'll listen, Father. But will you please do us a favor?"

"What is it now, my boy?" Enoch replied, growing weary with trivial interruptions.

"Would you please sit down while you tell us your next story?"

All the children giggled, and Enoch smiled awkwardly. "Certainly, son." And turning to pick up his book, he plopped back down into his chair. "But don't expect me to lean back and put my feet up while I do."

"No, we'd never think that, Pop," said Methuselah with a wry smirk. "Not in a million years."

"Good; because more than anything else, the Lord wishes that you cheerfully endure every difficulty in life, all for His sake. That way you'll be sure to find your reward in the Day of Judgment, because on that day everything will be exposed on the weighing-scales and in the books."

"Tell us, Grandfather," Lamech pleaded. "What do the books say?"

"Yes, Papa Enoch," peeped little Eli. "Please tell us."

"Very well, my children. I'll tell you another story from the books of the Lord."

And again a hush fell over the crowd.

"Next week, that is." Enoch grinned at the disappointed looks on all the faces of everyone in the group, which obviously wanted to hear more.

"Next week?" groaned Lamech. "Why next week?"

"So people from far and wide can come to hear the same stories you're lucky enough to hear. Why else?"

"But why do we want that, Papa Enoch?" asked Eli.

"Well, why should you be the only ones to hear these remarkable stories? Don't you think the Lord would want others to hear them and learn to trust Him, too?"

Everyone nodded in agreement; all except for a sullen Jubal, that is, who surreptitiously withdrew from the front of the group and disappeared into the crowd.

"Certainly, Father," said Methuselah. "We understand now. The mercy of the Lord is available to anyone who will trust Him. Is that what you're saying?"

"That's right, son."

"Then that's what we'll do, Grandpa," added Lamech. "We'll invite everyone everywhere to come and listen to what God has shown you and told you."

ONE WEEK LATER, Enoch was seated before a huge gathering of people, and just as he had done before, he reverently cradled a large book in his lap. Scanning the entire group, he saw that not only were all of his sons there, sitting right in front, but his elders were there, too.

"Welcome, welcome, everyone," began Enoch. "I'm so glad to see that, in addition to Methuselah, the rest of my fine sons have decided to join us today. There's Regim, Riman, Uchan, Chennion and Gaidad. Good to see you boys."

They all nodded in recognition of their father, and Regim stood up and bowed on behalf of his brothers. "Thank you, Father, for inviting us. We're honored to be here."

"Don't mention it, son," replied Enoch with a wink. "Not only that, but I'd also like to express my gratitude to our beloved elders who have come to graciously offer their support today."

Even at their advanced ages, these men all still possessed a keen eye. Every one of them nodded, one by one, as Enoch acknowledged their presence. "Seated with my father Jared, there's my grandfather Mahalaleel, my great-grandfather Cainan, my great-great-grandfather Enos, and my great-great-great-grandfather Seth. Thank you, gentlemen. I'm more honored than you can ever imagine."

"You're welcome, my boy," replied Seth. "We're very pleased that you've invited us to hear what you have to say today."

With that, Enoch looked out across the hushed crowd. "In fact, it's good to see all of you today. Now, can anyone tell me why we're here?"

Again Regim stood, as if for the entire group this time. "Yes, Father, we've all come to hear everything the Lord of Heaven and Earth told you when He spoke to you face to face."

Enoch nodded benevolently and slowly opened his book. "Very good, Regim, thank you. Then listen closely, everyone, because I know all too well about the things I'm about to describe for you. Of all the people in this world, I was there when the Lord's voice thundered from the midst of swirling clouds."

Fire and Blade

Adapted from

The Book of Jasher,

also called

The Book of the Upright

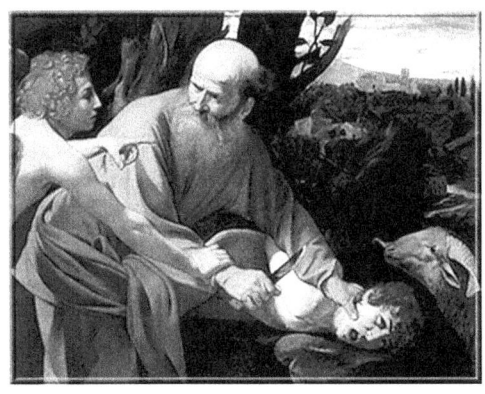

Sacrifice of Isaac, Caravaggio, 1603

Fire and Blade

Shooting Star

IN THE YEARS AFTER the Great Flood, Cush, the son of Ham and grand-son of Noah, got married. He was getting to be an old man so when his wife gave birth to a son, he loved the child very much. They called him Nimrod, saying, "Once again men have begun to rebel against God."

In no time at all, the boy grew up, becoming a fine young man, and one day Cush presented him with a gift so special that he made sure to give it to him in the secrecy of his own tent.

With a tremendous smile of satisfaction, Cush handed Nimrod a pack-age and said, "Here, my son; this is for you."

The young man eagerly reached out to take it. "Thank you, Father; but what's it for?"

"It's to honor your twentieth birthday. You're a man now, and because you're so special to me and your mother, I wanted you to have this."

Wide-eyed, Nimrod stared at the package. "What is it?"

"Why not open it and find out for yourself."

Tearing into the package, Nimrod found a loincloth made of sheepskin inside. Quite puzzled by them, he asked, "What's this?"

"It's a very special garment, my son."

"Oh?" said Nimrod, not entirely convinced. "What's so special about it? Did Mother make it just for me?"

Cush chuckled. "No, no. That's not why it's so special. It's special be-cause this garment was the same one that God provided for Adam after he was expelled from the Garden of Eden."

Nimrod's eyes lit up. "No."

"Yes, it's true."

"But how did you get it?"

"Well, like you, my father … your grandfather, gave it to me when I was your age."

Running his fingers across the sheepskins, Nimrod smiled proudly. "Really? And how did Grandfather get it? Did God give it to him?"

Cush hesitated at this, momentarily taken aback. Clearing his throat, he continued. "Well, not exactly, no. You see, son, the story of these sheepskins goes back a very long way, as you can imagine."

Nimrod looked up at his father, quite expectantly. "Please tell me, Fa-ther. I want to know all about it."

"Of course, Nimrod, I'll tell you. To begin with, the garment was orig-inally handed down to Enoch, the son of Jared, after Adam's death. Then, just before Enoch was taken up to Heaven by God, he gave it to his son Methuselah, and after he died Noah inherited it."

"Amazing. Then what?"

"When the time came, Noah wore it when he brought the animals into the Ark."

"Father, didn't you say these skins were special?"

Cush nodded. "Yes, son, I did. Why do you ask?"

"Oh, nothing; I was just wondering. Could that have been how Noah was able to control all the animals? Otherwise, how could he have gotten them all to cooperate with him?"

"Why, yes, Nimrod, it is. But how could you have possibly known something like that?"

Nimrod shrugged his shoulders. "I don't know. It just came into my mind, I guess."

Dumbfounded, Cush just stared back at his son for several moments.

"Is something wrong, Father? Have I made you angry?"

"No, of course not. As a matter of fact, I'm very pleased you've discerned this thing on your own. It's a tremendous omen. It can only mean one thing."

"It means the God Who walked and talked with Adam and Enoch and Noah is with me as well. Doesn't it, Father?"

Cush beamed back a smile, as proudly as any parent could. "Yes, my son, I do believe it does."

"Then just imagine what God has in store for me when I begin to wear these skins."

With that, Cush turned to leave. "Certainly I have imagined it for you, Nimrod, more than you can possibly know. Since the day you were born it has weighed heavily on me to do this thing, sensing somehow that this was what my father had mind ever since he received it from Noah."

As Cush neared the door of the tent, a peculiar look flashed across Nimrod's face and his eyes thinned. "Don't you mean, ever since Grandfather *stole* it from Noah? Isn't that what you meant to say, Father?"

Startled, Cush turned back toward his son. Nodding cautiously, his lips barely parted. "Yes, Nimrod, that's right. Now, is there anything else I've failed to mention?"

"Of course, Father; it seems you forgot to remind me to keep your gift of these skins a complete secret, even from my own dear mother."

Cush nodded nervously. "Naturally," he whispered and then slipped out through the tent door.

TRUE TO NIMROD'S own prediction, when he began to wear the sheepskin garment of Adam, he became empowered by them. He quickly became a formidable hunter, using his bow and arrows with tremendous prowess.

Then, he would reverently sacrifice many of the animals that he had killed on an altar. Lifting his eyes skyward, Nimrod exclaimed, "I pray that the Lord of Heaven and Earth accept this offering as an expression of gratitude for His care and protection."

AS ONE WARRIOR AMONG many in his clan, Nimrod slashed away at his enemies with his terrible, swift sword, whirling and stabbing, as if he already knew what his opponents were going to do before they did. If an opponent swung at him with his sword, Nimrod ducked well ahead of time. When an opponent whirled about in a different direction, he was already there with his blade to cut the man to pieces. And this happened in battle after battle as Nimrod steadily rose within the ranks of his family. He moved from the flanks of their battle array to the point where he entered the fray at the right hand of the leader, until finally he was the one leading the charge into enemy lines.

AT THE CONCLUSION of yet another of these conquests, Nimrod stood tall at the head of his troops, bloody sword raised in triumph, and let out a thunderous shout. "What say you to this, my brothers? God has helped me in so many battles, I've become invincible!"

Echoing his battle cry, the roar of his troops rippled through their ranks like an irresistible tidal wave.

"May God always help us, just as He does Nimrod," yelled one of his fellow warriors, "a mighty hunter before the Lord, invincible in battle!"

AS NIMROD SAT ONE day contentedly honing the blade of his sword, several of his soldiers came to him with heavy hearts and bowed.

"My Lord," began one of them, "I'm afraid to report the children of Japheth have attacked our people, and several members of your family have been captured."

"What fools," sneered Nimrod. "Don't they have any idea who they're dealing with? Very well, send word to mobilize every available warrior at once. We'll strike our enemies so swiftly, so brutally, they'll wish they'd never started this war with us."

WITHIN TWENTY-FOUR hours, Nimrod and his army were on the move, arrayed head to toe in their most formidable battle armor and every imaginable weapon of bronze.

As they marched toward the battlefield, Nimrod assured them. "Don't worry about a thing, men. With God's help, we're going to easily defeat our enemies, and you'll be able to do whatever you want with them. Trust me."

And with just five hundred warriors at his side, Nimrod smashed into Japheth's army, conquering it within hours of the engagement. Besides the hundreds of men they had killed in battle, Nimrod's troops had taken thousands of prisoners; among them, even women and children were led away in chains.

TEARFULLY REUNITED with his family, Nimrod and his troops headed for home. So grateful was his family for rescuing them that as soon as they got back they unanimously chose to make him king over them all. There and then, they placed a crown on his head. Equally intoxicated by the sting of battle and ecstatic at his meteoric rise to power, Nimrod raised his sword exultantly. "What say you now, my *people*?"

"All hail, King Nimrod," shouted one of his princes, "the mighty warrior of God!"

And the people roared back with a single voice, "All hail, King Nimrod!"

IN NO TIME, NIMROD could be found sitting on his gilded throne, entertaining a steady stream of dignitaries; among them was one man who stepped forward and bowed.

"And how is my new kingdom doing these days, Terah, my prince?" Nimrod asked.

"Very well, My Lord," replied Terah. "As you've requested, many of your princes, governors and judges have been set up in places of authority over your subjects, even as it is the custom among the kings throughout the land."

"Excellent," said Nimrod with a satisfied smile. "And above them all, I've placed you, my favorite prince."

Again Terah bowed. "I'm humbled by such an auspicious appointment, Sire, an appointment that, I must confess, still has me somewhat baffled."

"I don't understand. You mean to say you don't know why I've appointed you to such a position of authority."

"Not really, My Lord, no."

"Then maybe I appointed the wrong man."

Terah put up his hand in protest. "No, no, Sire. I mean, I think I might know why you've appointed me; that is to say, for all my years of dedicated service, my cunning administrative skills, my ruthless attention to detail."

Nimrod smiled slyly. "You've answered well."

"Then I'm correct in assuming you've promoted me because of these things?"

The king nodded with a smirk. "That, and the fact that your father is Nahor the First, of the line of Shem, the brother of Ham, my grandfather; which means you're from the good side of the family. Now, do you, or do you not, want to be chief prince over my army?"

"Of course, My Lord," replied Terah, bowing again. "I cannot thank you enough, and I forever pledge my loyalty to you, Great King."

"Yes, yes. Then quickly remove yourself from my sight, and proceed with your duties, before I grow weary with your groveling and change my mind."

CONVENING A MEETING with his princes, governors and judges, Nimrod eagerly leaned forward and said, "I've called you all here today because I've decided it isn't proper that a king of my stature and reputation should reside in such a puny, little province as this."

"What would you like us to do, Great King?" wondered Terah. "I, and all your loyal subjects, stand ready to execute your will."

"Good, because I want you to build me a city, a magnificent city with a majestic palace, one befitting your … *great king*."

LED BY TERAH, HIS princes immediately spread out across the landscape, where they found a large valley facing westward and there construction began.

SURVEYING THE WORK of building, Nimrod nodded in approval. "I think I'll call this city of mine Shinar, because the Lord has vehemently shaken and destroyed all my enemies."

ONCE THE CONSTRUCTION of his city had been completed, vast numbers of people came to live with him on the plains of Shinar. They bowed to him and presented him with a tremendous assortment of gifts.

"Oh, Great King," said one man, bowing graciously and placing his gift at the foot of Nimrod's throne, "your fame has spread throughout the world; you are indeed the lord and master over all the sons of Noah. Now, everyone is following your advice, and before long the whole world will be speaking a single language, the language of your people."

NIMROD WENT OUT one morning, amongst the plains of Shinar to hunt for game with his bow and arrows. When he returned with his quarry, he sacrificed some of the animals he had killed on an altar, but this time, it was not an altar he had built for the God of Heaven and Earth but one made for idols fashioned by his own hands. "I pray these gods of wood and stone will accept this humble offering as an expression of my thanks for their care and protection."

Then, he turned and motioned to some of his family members, and they, too, came and laid their sacrifices on the altar. Following their lead, his princes came and did the same thing. Eventually, all of his subjects began to follow suit, until everyone was following in Nimrod's footsteps, sacrificing and bowing to idols made of wood and stone.

IN THE MEANTIME, Terah met and fell in love with a beautiful woman, and before long, the day of their marriage arrived. In a tremendous wedding ceremony, Terah and his bride were lavished by everyone in Shinar. Presided over by Nimrod, his princes, governors and judges, the event was attended by dignitaries from miles around. They all came to show their respects to Terah and his new wife. Sitting to Terah's right, as part of the wedding party, were two young men who bore a striking resemblance to him. They each picked up a cup of wine and stood together.

"Attention, everyone," said the man standing next to Terah. "Time to toast the happy couple." Then turning to his right, he asked, "Do you want to go first Nahor, or should I?"

"By all means, Haran, you're the oldest by fifteen minutes," quipped Nahor with a hearty grin. "So, first in birth, first to toast!"

"Very good," replied Haran, who proudly held up his cup. "I'd like to offer this toast to our father and his beautiful new bride. May they know only happiness together, and a long and prosperous life."

"Absolutely, brother," said Nahor, who then raised his cup. "We love them both very much, and wish a future for them that will bring everything they've always desired."

"May it come true," intoned all the guests with one voice as they held up their cups.

"Very nice, boys," said Terah, who then stood and hugged his two sons.

Then the king raised his glass to the happy couple. "Here's to the chief prince of my army and his lovely bride, Amthelo, the daughter of Cornebo. May his next child grow up to be even mightier than his father."

"Let it be so," exclaimed one of Nimrod's governors, "even as the king has proclaimed!"

And with a blast of music, the celebration kicked into high gear.

SOON TERAH'S WIFE bore him a son. As the midwife held up the screaming child, she turned to Terah. "Congratulations, My Lord, it's a boy. Have you decided on a name?"

"His name is Abram," replied Terah, beaming like the proudest father in the world, "because the king has promoted me far above the rest of his princes."

That whole day, Terah's family, along with Nimrod's people, celebrated the birth of Abram. Terah's house overflowed with guests as they happily ate and drank with him. Trays filled with an assortment of food were passed around, as was cup after cup of wine, which the guests all happily consumed well into the evening.

AS THE PARTY GUESTS began to say their goodbyes and depart, some of the king's sages and sorcerers were walking with them. Just then, one of them looked up into the night sky and saw something that absolutely astonished him. A huge star, shining very brightly, was soaring across the sky, traveling from east to west.

"Look!" exclaimed the sage, pointing skyward. "A shooting star!"

"It's an omen!" shouted a sorcerer.

Together, they watched as that single shooting star streaked through the night sky in four different directions, swallowing up four other stars in the process. Everyone watching was mystified by the spectacle; the sages and sorcerers, however, were more disturbed than amazed by what they saw.

"An omen?" wondered one of the onlookers. "Is it a good omen?"

The sages and sorcerers all exchanged disturbed looks amongst themselves.

"No, I'm afraid it's not," said one of the sages with a look of grim concern on his face. "This speaks of none other than the child that was born to Terah tonight."

"But what does it mean?" pressed the onlooker. "Why is this a bad omen concerning Terah's child?"

"Because the shooting star we just saw gobbled up four stars from the four corners of the night sky," insisted one of the sorcerers.

"So?" asked the onlooker with a shrug of his shoulders. "What's wrong with that?"

"An omen like this clearly foretells that when this child of Terah's grows up, he's destined to become very powerful," continued the sage. "In time, he'll flourish into a vast race of people, his children will kill great kings, and as a result will inherit all their land. Eventually, they'll acquire the entire world by means of their invincible power and will own it forever after."

Everyone there gasped.

"I don't know," continued the onlooker. "Maybe it was all just a trick of the light. Maybe we had too much to drink. Have you considered that?"

Perplexed, the group began to disperse, still obviously undecided about the true nature of what they had just seen. The sages and sorcerers, however, were going away with no such doubts in their minds. Far from being divided in their interpretation of this nighttime spectacle, they were unanimous in their appraisal. To a man, they were all clearly overwhelmed with a foreboding sense of dread and doom.

Child of Destiny

ASSEMBLED IN THEIR sacred hall the next morning, the king's sages and sorcerers looked just as concerned as they had the night before.

"Of course," began one of the sages, "the king has no idea about what happened last night at Terah's house. Am I correct in assuming this, gentlemen?"

"That is correct," replied one of the sorcerers. "No one's told him a thing. But you know, if he does find out someday, he's going to ask us why we kept the truth from him."

"He'll have us all killed then, for sure," muttered another of the sages.

The sorcerer scratched nervously at his flowing beard. "I say we go right now and tell Nimrod everything we saw."

"Should we tell him about our interpretation of the event?" asked one of the sages.

"Of course," insisted the sorcerer. "We should *especially* tell him about our interpretation! That way we'll all remain innocent of the matter."

APPEARING BEFORE Nimrod, the whole group reverently bowed before him.

"Long live the king of Shinar," said a sorcerer, who slowly stepped forward.

"Yes, yes, what is it?" asked the king, annoyed with the interruption.

"Well, My Lord, it appears that a child was born to Terah, son of Nahor the First, the chief prince of your army."

"I'm aware of that. What about it?"

"But, Sire, there's something else you may not be aware of yet."

"Really? What?"

"As we were leaving Terah's house, we observed a great star, soaring from the East, and this star swallowed up four other stars from the four corners of the night sky."

"Interesting," said Nimrod as he sat up in his throne. "What was your reaction?"

"We were all quite astonished, of course, even a little terrified."

"Yes, I see. Have you arrived at an interpretation for this event?"

"Certainly, Your Highness," replied a sage, who came forward and stood next to the sorcerer. "Our verdict of this matter was quite unanimous."

Nimrod leaned forward in anticipation. "Well, then? Tell me now!"

"Sire," continued the sage, "we're fully convinced this thing involves the child that was born to Terah! This portent of the star devouring the other stars signifies that he'll flourish and become incredibly powerful. He'll kill every king on Earth, and his descendants will inherit their land forever."

Nimrod's eyes became as big as saucers. "You mean to tell me this child, this son of Terah, is going to kill every king in this world, including *me*?"

"I'm afraid so, yes."

Nimrod gritted his teeth at the thought. "You've done well bringing me this news."

"Thank you, My Lord, for saying so. You see how we've faithfully reported everything concerning this child."

"Yes, yes, of course. Well done. You'll all be rewarded accordingly."

Nimrod sat there for several agonizing moments. "Now, on to the question of what should be done to this son of Terah."

"Well, Sire," continued the sorcerer, "we think you should kill Terah's child before he ever has a chance to grow up, because if he's allowed to establish himself in our country, we'll all die for sure."

Mulling over the idea, Nimrod was obviously disturbed by such an outcome. He grimly nodded and said, "Very well. Have Terah brought before me immediately."

AS TERAH STOOD AT attention, Nimrod scrutinized him from his throne. "My dearest prince, I've just been told that when your son was born the other day, astounding things were seen in the Heavens, all because he's supposed to be special; so special, I'm told, it's prophesied that when he grows up, he'll conquer the whole world. Is this true?"

Terah timidly nodded. "Yes, My Lord, I suppose it is."

"Then I want you to give me the child right now."

"Give him to *you*? Then what will you do with him?"

"Naturally, I'm going to kill him before he has a chance to destroy us all," the king replied, quite matter-of-factly. "Of course, I'll pay you handsomely for your trouble. In fact, I'll fill your entire house until it overflows with silver and gold."

"Excuse me, Sire," said Terah, trying to remain calm. "I hear what you're saying, and of course I'll do anything you want. But, please, can I first tell you about what happened to me the other day? Then maybe I'll be able to better respond to your generous offer."

Nimrod stared thoughtfully at his favorite prince for several tense moments. "Very well, my friend, go ahead."

"Well, you see, uh, last week, an associate of mine came to me and said, 'Give me the beautiful horse the king gave you, and I'll pay you well. Just name your price.' But I told him, 'Not so fast. Wait until I ask the king about your offer, and I'll do whatever he decides.' So, Your Highness, now that you've heard my story, what do you think I should do?"

"You idiot! How could you even *think* of selling the fine horse I gave you? That horse is priceless! There isn't another one like it in the whole world!"

"But, Sire, that's exactly what you're asking me to do with my son."

A look of recognition swept across Nimrod's face as he suddenly realized Terah was using this parable to talk about him. Initially embarrassed, the king next became infuriated.

"But, of course, My King," continued Terah, "everything I have is still in your power. Do whatever you want with me. Yes, even my son is in your power, without receiving anything in exchange for him. Even his two older brothers are yours, too."

"No, no, of course not," said Nimrod, settling back down in his throne, somewhat appeased. "Don't be ridiculous. I only want to purchase your youngest son."

"Then, please, Your Highness, could you at least give me three days to consider all this for myself? Allow me the chance to talk with my family about what you're asking me."

"Fine, I'll give you three days. But only because I hold you in such high esteem."

"Yes, Benevolent One, of course," said Terah, bowing graciously. "Thank you so much. I can't tell you —"

"Enough already. You know I hate when you grovel."

THREE DAYS LATER, the king's official deputy was pounding on Terah's front door. "Terah, chief prince of Nimrod, the king says your time is up! You must comply with the royal decree to send your son for the price he spoke about, and if you don't hand him over, everything in your house will be slain, and not even a dog will be left alive."

Terah quickly ran into the back room, where he took one of his concubine's newborn sons and gave the infant to the deputy, who paid him handsomely.

DELIVERING THE CHILD to the king's court, the deputy handed him over to Nimrod. As he held the child in his arms, Nimrod wrestled in his mind for a moment. "Tell me, Deputy, are you sure this child is the one my sages and sorcerers predicted would topple my kingdom?"

"He is, Your Highness. I saw Terah retrieve him from his house with my own eyes."

Having satisfied himself, the king then took the baby and, with all his strength, smashed his head into the ground.

UNDER THE COVER OF night, Terah spirited little Abram away, along with his mother and nurse, and concealed them in a cave.

"Now, I want the three of you to stay here awhile," said Terah, "and I promise, you'll all be safe from the wrath of Nimrod."

"Wait, what about you?" blurted Amthelo. "You're not going to just leave us here all alone, are you?"

"But I have to return to my duties, dear, or else the king will get suspicious. Besides, who better than me to ensure the necessary provisions are delivered to you every month?"

"Don't *dear* me, husband. How can you be so callous, abandoning us like this?"

"I'm sorry, Amthelo, but I don't see that we have much choice in the matter. If I don't return, then we merely put the boy back into harm's way.

Now, I promise, in six months this whole thing will blow over, and Nimrod and his men will forget it ever happened."

LATE ONE EVENING, Terah came to visit his wife in the cave. After warmly greeting her, however, Terah found that she was not nearly as pleased to see him as he was to see her. But Terah just shrugged it off.

"I can't tell you how good it is to see you, Amthelo," he began. "Things have been damned difficult back at the palace. You don't even want to know how hard it's been to get away from there, let alone manage to have all your supplies delivered without the king's knowledge. I trust my men have been faithful in that regard, have they not?"

Unimpressed, Amthelo nodded while a young boy, around ten years old, stood just behind her, as if he were using her as a shield. "They have," she grumbled reticently.

"Good, good," said Terah with an awkward smile. "After all, you're both very important to me. Just because I'm not here in person doesn't mean I'm not thinking about you two all the time. Always remember that." Terah took several steps forward, obviously trying to get a better look at the boy. "Hello, son; how've you been? He looks well enough. What is Abram now, anyway? Seven, eight years old?" Looking back to his wife, Terah was met with a frown.

She snapped, "He's ten."

"Ten years old?" Terah exclaimed proudly, still trying to avoid the fact that his wife was so irked. "Really? And he's still being a good boy for you, I hope, living here like this."

Growing more perturbed by the moment, Amthelo nodded sternly. "Well, yes. Considering he hasn't had a father all these years, he's been a very good boy."

Terah stepped over to his son and bent down to give him a perfunctory pat on the head. "What do you mean he's never had a father? Of course he has a father. Who else has been taking care of him all these years? Isn't that right, son?"

Young Abram, however, just stared back at Terah, as if he were a complete stranger.

"I mean a *real* father," scoffed Amthelo. "What happens when he starts to become a man? What happens when he starts asking me why his father is never around? Then what?"

Terah turned to his wife and, in hushed tones, said, "Then we'll deal with that when it happens. Until then, I've decided that maybe it would be best if we took the boy to live with Noah and Shem."

"Oh, thank God," said Amthelo with a tremendous sigh of relief. "It's about time. Anything would be better than living here in this miserable cave."

AMTHELO, YOUNG ABRAM and his nurse soon left the cave and, accompanied by half a dozen men, traveled quite some distance before they eventually reached some foothills.

Turning to one of the men with them, Amthelo asked, "Are you sure you know where you're going?"

"Of course, ma'am. The home of Noah and Shem lies beyond these hills, hidden away in a mountain stronghold, in a land forgotten long ago by the world." As the man spoke, he turned his eyes north toward a foreboding mountaintop beyond the foothills where they stood. "To this day only a handful of followers remain loyal to the great patriarch and his son, while the rest of mankind has completely abandoned the ways of the Most High."

Amthelo took a long look at the mountaintop he was referring to and then turned back to him with her nervous eyes. "You mean, we're going up there?"

"Yes, ma'am. Those were my instructions. Do you wish to turn back?"

Amthelo and Abram's nurse exchanged a concerned look while the rest of the men continued on, unaware of their reluctance.

"Somehow I don't see we have much choice," murmured Amthelo and, taking hold of Abram's hand, haltingly started after the group.

ARRIVING AT THE HOME of Noah, they were greeted right away by Shem. Kneeling down, he shook young Abram's hand. "Hello, Abram; welcome. It's good to see you, son. Did your mother tell you who I am?"

Abram nodded bashfully. "You're my great, great, big grandfather."

"Very good. What a fine boy you're growing up to be," he said, nodding to Amthelo, who beamed the smile of a proud mother.

NIMROD AND HIS subjects, meanwhile, continued to bring their burnt offerings to their endless array of idols. Doing exactly as Nimrod had taught them, the people reverently bowed to these idols, and even though they were incapable of responding in any way, they persisted in sacrificing their animals to them. In Terah's house, there were twelve idols, one for each month of the year. Most of them were quite large; some were made of wood and some, of stone. And when Terah finished preparing his sacrifice, he would proudly bring his meat offering to his idols and lay it at the foot of one of them, depending on the month.

IN THE HOME OF NOAH and Shem, however, young Abram would sit for hours and listen to a very different kind of teaching.

"Whatever you do, Abram," said Noah, "never forget there is a God Who rules the Earth and all its inhabitants, a God Who alone is worthy of our praise and sacrifice, a God Who lives in the Heavens above, a place of incorruptible majesty."

"Can you remember that, Abram?" asked Shem.

Abram nodded eagerly. "Yes, Father Shem. The Lord of Heaven and Earth is the only One Who is worthy of our sacrifice and praise."

"Not only that, Abram," continued Shem, "but the Lord of Heaven and Earth is the only One you should ever obey. Anyone who tells you to do something that your Heavenly King would disapprove of isn't worthy of your allegiance or obedience, no matter how many thousands or tens of thousands bow down to that man."

"Do you understand?" asked Noah.

Again young Abram nodded. "Yes, Father Noah. No earthly king should ever stand in the way of what the King of the Universe wants me to do."

"Good, Abram, very good," continued Noah. "The Lord is very proud of you and everything you're learning."

"Do you have any questions, son?" asked Shem.

"Yes, Father Shem, I do," he replied with a precocious gleam in his eye.

"Well, Abram, go ahead," prodded Noah. "What is it?"

Slowly, the words formed in Abram's mouth, and then they came out. "What does God look like?" he said with a smile, revealing the missing tooth in his childish grin.

Noah and Shem burst out laughing, causing young Abram's smile to grow even bigger.

AS ABRAM WENT OUT into the fields one day, he was accompanied by his dog. As the two of them wandered aimlessly, something sparked Abram's curiosity. "Hey, boy," he said, squinting up at the Sun. "Did you ever notice the way that great ball of light glows as it moves across the sky? I wonder if that's God. Maybe we should serve Him."

So Abram sat down with his faithful companion, and together they basked all day in the warmth of the Sun, but when evening came, the Sun set and disappeared. "Hey, where'd it go, boy? I guess that wasn't God after all. I wonder Who did create the Heavens and the Earth. Where could He be?"

Soon the night darkened around them, and looking up, Abram noticed the Moon, lit brightly against the starry sky. "Of course, that must be the God Who made the Universe. And look, those are His servants all around Him."

So they sat and stared all night at the Moon and the stars, but as the evening dragged on, Abram grew too tired to continue, so he fell fast asleep.

THE NEXT MORNING, Abram was rudely awakened by his dog licking his face. Sitting up, he realized that the Moon had disappeared and the Sun had returned, and with it, the daylight. Abram looked around, and surveying his surroundings, he exclaimed, "Of course, boy, none of those things were God. None of them made the world or the people in it. They're all just God's servants. I'll bet you anything He lives somewhere else."

Overjoyed, Abram jumped to his feet and started to walk back home. "I can't wait to tell Father Shem and Father Noah, boy. They'll be so proud of what we figured out." And before Abram had taken more than three steps, he broke into a full run, followed by his faithful companion, who galloped happily alongside him, wagging his tail the whole time.

Tower of Folly

NIMROD'S PRINCES, along with the most influential men from his family, came together for a meeting. This time, though, it was Nimrod's father, Cush, who presided over the gathering.

"Welcome, everyone. It does my heart good to see you've all dragged yourselves here today!" exclaimed Cush, eliciting a boisterous cheer of approval from the group. He motioned proudly to three men to his right. "Even my kid brothers Phut, Mizraim and Canaan have managed to join us!"

"Thank you, big brother," said Canaan with a hearty salute. "Glad to be here."

"Good. Now, as you all know, for many years the mighty Nimrod has been ruling his kingdom with an iron fist, and he's been doing it from this great and glorious city of Shinar. But today I'm here to tell you, it's time to build another city, an overflowing city, one that will extend the fame and glory of our kingdom into all the Earth! So, I ask you, here and now: Who is with us?"

Everyone enthusiastically thrust their swords skyward. "We are!" roared the group in thunderous unison.

"Good, because not only do we intend to establish a new city, but we also plan to construct a magnificent tower in the very heart of it, a tower so huge, so colossal, it will reach Heaven itself! Our enemies will be so dismayed, they'll never even think about going to war with us again! We'll rule the world, and our names will go down in history forever!"

Again the group burst out with a resounding cheer.

CUSH AND HIS THREE brothers next went to Nimrod's palace, where the king sat smugly on his gilded throne.

"Then it's agreed," said Nimrod with a satisfied grin. "It's time to unleash the full potential of my kingdom, until no one is beyond my command. Send a thousand men to look for a place to build our new city, somewhere suitable to construct this mighty tower."

LIKE A THOUSAND milling insects searching for a morsel of food, a vast array of men fanned out across the countryside, inspecting every square foot for miles around.

CANAAN SOON RETURNED with a report for the king. "I believe we've found a suitable location for your mighty ambition, nephew."

Nimrod smiled approvingly. "Very good. You've done well, Uncle Canaan. Where?"

"A lush valley, just two days east of Shinar."

"Then let the work begin. And may this kingdom of ours never be the same again."

"Certainly, my nephew, My King," said Canaan, bowing reverently. "Let it be so, even as you have decreed."

THE LAND BEGAN TO swarm with determined workers, moving in every direction, like a vast colony of single-minded ants, making their way back and forth from a central hub in the valley. One group of workers set about excavating clay, which was scooped in huge quantities from hillside after hillside. The next group placed the clay, mixed with sand and straw, in tens of thousands of wooden moulds. Once removed from these moulds, the wet bricks were set out in row after row, to dry in the heat of the noonday Sun. Another group hauled these naturally-dried bricks to crude kilns, where they were fired and cooled into finished bricks, while yet another hauled the bricks to an enormous circle that was forming around this central hub, which was at last used by those who did the actual construction of the city and the tower.

Within six months, the foundations of the city and the tower were complete, and a little more than a year later, so was the city itself. But long after the buildings were finished, the tower continued higher still, brick by brick and layer by layer. Eventually, huge ramps were built to hoist the workers, along with their bricks and mortar, to the next layer of the tower, which then became the next level and, in turn, the next section.

A BURLY CONSTRUCTION worker stopped what he was doing with his brick and mortar one day and asked the man next to him, "Hey, you ever worry that what we're doing here is wrong?"

Confused, his co-worker mumbled, "Wrong? What do you mean, wrong? I don't get you."

"This tower; you know, a tower built to reach Heaven, and all. Don't you ever wonder if god might get mad at us for doing it?"

"God? Which god?"

"How should I know?" he replied with a shrug of his huge shoulders, and thinking better of it, he went back to laying his next brick. "Never mind. Forget I even mentioned it."

SO THE TOWER CONTINUED to rise, slowly but surely, higher and higher. As it did, Cush and his three brothers watched proudly, as though on a sacred vigil.

"Just think, brothers," said Cush with tremendous satisfaction, "someday we might even be able to start a war with god himself."

"You might be onto something, brother," remarked Phut. "At this rate, the tower will be high enough to reach the gates of Heaven before you know it."

"And when it is," boasted Mizraim, "we'll strike down every last one of god's pathetic angels with our fearsome arrows."

"Then no one will stop our warriors from invading his kingdom," swore Canaan, "and when we have, we'll set up our own gods of worship."

THE TOWER EVENTUALLY soared to such a tremendous height that it took a full year to carry the bricks and mortar to the top. Some men ascended, while others descended. And when a brick fell from their hands and broke, they would weep over it, but when a man fell and died, none of them would pay the slightest attention to him.

AT NOAH AND SHEM'S home, meanwhile, Abram was growing up nicely, continuing to learn more and more from his two mentors.

"So, Abram, do you have any questions about the Lord?" asked Shem.

Nodding, Abram smiled precociously, "Yes, sir, I do. I still want to know what God looks like. Doesn't anybody know?"

With a tilt of his head, Shem turned to Noah. "He is a persistent one, isn't he?"

"That he is, my boy, that he is," replied Noah, who patted Shem on the back and turned to leave. "He sprang from your loins, didn't he?"

"Where do you think you're going?" Shem asked plaintively. "The boy is posing a good question here. He needs an answer."

But Noah just kept on walking. "Not to worry, son. I'm sure you can handle it. After all, it's only the most impenetrable mystery of creation. Consider it a personal challenge."

Shem shook his head, partly in amusement, partly in frustration. "Great," he muttered, then turned to gaze into the face of young Abram, who was still patiently waiting for an answer.

"Well, Father Shem?" persisted Abram. "Hasn't anybody seen the Face of God? I mean besides the people who've died and gone to Heaven?"

"Sure, Abram, I guess so, if you put it that way. There has been one man in the history of our people who's been fortunate enough to see God and live to tell the tale. But that was a long time ago."

"Tell me, tell me," exclaimed Abram, his face lighting up. "Who was he?"

"His name was Enoch, and he was a great man whom God deemed worthy to translate into His very presence without ever tasting the bitterness of death."

"Really? But why him?"

Again Shem stared back for several moments, stumped for a response.

"Well, unfortunately, that's still a mystery, my boy. I don't think we'll ever know for sure why God chose Enoch. It's hard to say why the Lord chooses anyone for that matter. The most obvious answer, of course, is because Enoch had tremendous faith in God. He worshiped the Lord no matter how much the rest of mankind refused to obey Him."

"Did he tell anybody what God looked like?"

"Certainly, Abram. He told his whole family, and then he wrote all about it in books he gave to his descendants, like you and me."

"So what did he say? I mean, about how God looked."

"According to Enoch, his description of what he saw in Heaven was of a remarkably awesome Face."

"A Face?"

"Yes, a molten Face of God, with brilliant sparks that shot out every which way."

"Was Enoch scared?"

"Sure, at first. Fear of the Lord is, after all, the beginning of wisdom. But once God spoke to Enoch, he immediately realized He was also a Supreme Being of tremendous compassion and love."

"Oh, Father Shem, thank you so much for telling me all this," Abram said, stepping forward to hug Shem. "I hope someday the Lord will deem me worthy of some great mission for His sake; if not as important as Enoch's, like being translated into His presence and writing books about it, then at least in some small way to serve such a majestic God as Him."

"You're welcome, Abram," replied Shem with a sigh of relief. "And I hope the same thing for you as well. God bless you, son."

HIGHER AND HIGHER, Nimrod's tower continued to grow, when one day his men took a break from their arduous task. From the uppermost section of the tower, they shot arrows into the sky, and when they fell to the ground, they were covered in blood. Examining one, a man triumphantly shouted, "I think we just killed someone in Heaven!"

"Hurry," roared another. "Let's build faster!"

So, intensifying their efforts, they continued building the tower, until the years eventually turned into decades.

AS THE MOLTEN FACE of God looked down on their construction project, He turned to the seventy angels who stood nearest to Him. "For nearly forty years," said the Face, "I've watched the building of this tower, reaching higher and higher, till finally it's risen more than a mile and a half above the plain of Shinar. But now, I've grown weary with their folly. Come, it's time to go down and confuse the language of everyone who's building that infernal tower. That way no one will be able to understand what anyone is saying anymore, and work on the tower will grind to a halt."

"As You wish, Lord," replied one of the angels.

SWOOPING DOWN FROM Heaven, the seventy angels began to pass imperceptibly through the ranks of the builders. With a single invisible touch, the workers were, one by one, plunged into a state of utter confusion. Whenever a builder wanted something from a co-worker, like a hammer, he tried asking for it. But what came out of his mouth sounded like gibberish, so his co-worker would hand him something he had not asked for, like a brick. When he found that it was not what he wanted, he would simply throw it away, and invariably, the thing he tossed aside would then strike another one of the builders somewhere down the line, either maiming or killing them in the process.

QUITE A NUMBER OF MEN were struck down that way, and dismayed by such mayhem and chaos, the men building that tower eventually began to go insane. Some men began wandering around as brute as apes, while others turned against one another with their bows and arrows. The rest of the builders who witnessed these horrors began to abandon their work, little by little, dropping their tools and walking away.

A VIOLENT EARTHQUAKE suddenly struck the place, and the ground opened up, swallowing a third of the tower. Not only that, but fire fell from the sky, too, burning up another third of it. As a result, so many men died at that tower that when the onlookers came to survey the devastation, they could hardly walk without stepping on the corpse of one of the construction workers. Only a third of the tower remained, jutting up out of the ground, left as a grim reminder of the folly of those who attempted to defy the God of Heaven.

WHEN ABRAM HAD GROWN up to be a fine-looking young man, a messenger came to the home of Noah and Shem. Noah read the letter and sadly handed it over to Shem, who was also deeply moved by the news.

"What is it?" wondered Abram. "Is there something wrong?"

"It appears that one of your forefathers has died, Abram."

"Died?" said Abram. "Who died?"

"Your grandfather, Nahor the First, son of Serug, has died," murmured Noah.

Shem hung his head in mourning. "But he was still so young."

"How old was he?" asked Abram.

"Nahor was only three hundred and four years old," replied Noah. "It seems as though men are simply not living as long as they used to. What a pity."

"That's terrible," exclaimed Abram. "How old are you, Father Shem?"

"Who, me?"

Noah grinned at Shem. "Old Shem, here; he's a middle-aged man, now. Or at least what used to be considered middle-aged."

"Really?" said Abram. "How old is that?"

"I'm four hundred and thirty-nine."

Abram's eyes widened. "Wow, that is old."

Shem smiled reluctantly. "You think I'm old? Father Noah has us all beat. He's more than nine hundred years old."

Astonished, Abram turned to Noah. "Really, Father Noah? Are you really that old?"

"That's right, my boy," he replied with a weary nod. "And soon, I'll be standing before the Face of God, too, just as Nahor is at this very moment. So as difficult as it is for us to accept the absence of our loved ones, it's actually a blessing for those who have passed from this life to the next."

"So what you're saying is," Abram slowly said, trying to visualize what he was hearing, "Grandfather now knows firsthand what I've been seeking to know my whole life."

"That's right, Abram," added Shem, proud of his student. "Today, he knows what God looks like."

IN THE AFTERMATH of the earthquake at Nimrod's tower, the king and several of his princes stood on a nearby hilltop, surveying the devastation.

"How the mighty have fallen," muttered Nimrod, half to himself, half to his men.

"What's that, My Lord?" wondered Terah.

"Oh, nothing, really. I was just contemplating how, in a matter of minutes, a magnificent city like this could simply vanish from the face of the Earth."

"What will we do now, Sire?"

"We'll rebuild, of course. What else can we do?"

"Naturally, My Lord. Then we'll commence to rebuild the city at once." Terah whirled about and turned to leave.

But Nimrod raised his hand. "Wait, wait; something has just occurred to me."

Stopping, Terah looked back in anticipation. "What is it, Your Highness?"

"I've decided I must respond to this disaster in a manner befitting my great kingdom, a manner that will commemorate, for all time, the adversity I and my people have endured in this misbegotten place."

Terah nodded thoughtfully. "Very good, My Lord. What will you have us do? Should we make the city even larger and mightier than before?"

"No," replied Nimrod with a capricious twinkle in his eye. "Where there used to be a single city, I want *four new ones* built to replace it."

Befuddled, Terah considered the king's declaration. "I see, Sire," he mumbled.

Irked, Nimrod growled, "What's that? I didn't quite hear you, Chief Prince of My Army?"

"I said, I'll see to it right away, Sire," exclaimed Terah as he turned again to leave.

Quite pleased with himself, Nimrod grinned from ear to ear.

THE SURVIVORS FROM amongst the construction workers of that tower soon spread out across the landscape, where they began their monumental effort of not simply rebuilding one city but four of them in its place.

AS WAS HIS CUSTOM, Nimrod stood with Terah and his associates at his side, atop a nearby hillside, supervising the rebuilding efforts. "Tell me, my princes, what do you think of my ambitious project now? Did any of you actually think it could have been accomplished so quickly?"

"Most impressive, My Lord," replied one his princes. "You've outdone even yourself."

"Thank you, Chedorlaomer. And what about you, Arioch?"

"Who would have thought that less than a decade ago, this land lay in complete ruin?" said Arioch. "But today, here it is in all its glory, a testament to your enduring legacy."

"And you, Tidal, what's your opinion?"

"Truly magnificent, Your Highness. Lying before us are nothing less than four more jewels in your illustrious crown of achievements."

Nimrod nodded proudly, exhaling a satisfied sigh.

"Have you decided what you will name your new cities, My King?" asked Terah.

"I have, yes," he replied with an impish grin, "and according to the practice of our day, I'm naming them in memory of what we've all experienced as a result of building our mighty tower to Heaven."

Puzzled, Terah and the other princes exchanged a nervous look amongst themselves.

"Really, My Lord?" Terah said cautiously. "And what, may I ask, have you decided upon?"

"The first city I've named Babel because god confused the language of everyone there. The second city is called Erech because god scattered the people from that place. The third is Eched because there was a tremendous battle with god in that land. And the fourth is Calnah because I provoked god, and as a result, my princes and warriors were consumed there."

For several, intense moments, his princes stood there, unable to respond, until finally, apparently bored with the spectacle, Nimrod began to walk away. "Now, my princes, I bid you all, good day. Carry on with your duties. I'm sure there's still a lot of work to be done."

No one moved a muscle as they all watched the king leave. Then, when they were sure that he was no longer within hearing distance, Chedorlaomer turned to the others and grumbled, "The arrogance of that man. God crushes his ill-conceived tower, nearly wiping out an entire civilization, and then he has the audacity to mock us by trivializing the matter."

"What could he be thinking," blurted Tidal, "naming cities to commemorate such a black day in the history of our people? And cities, mind you, built upon the backs of these same people."

"Well, I, for one, have had it," continued Chedorlaomer. "If he insists on bringing us all down with his reckless abandon, I think we'll have to give *him* a name to commemorate his stupidity in building that damned thing!"

"Then so be it," said Arioch, raising his hand in a mock salute. "From this day forward, ignominious King of Shinar, you will be known as Amraphel because your princes and warriors fell as a result of your foolishness at that tower. All hail, King Amraphel!"

Together, they all followed suit, raising their hands with him, exclaiming, "All hail, King Amraphel!"

BACK HOME IN SHINAR, Nimrod resumed his favorite pastime of sitting on his gilded throne, receiving a steady stream of dignitaries.

As one foreign prince came bearing gifts, he humbly bowed before Nimrod. "Greetings, King Nimrod, I wish to congratulate you on this the inauguration day of your four newest crown jewels. And I especially wish to commend you on the naming of your latest cities, built to extend your fame and glory throughout the entire world."

Benevolently, the king nodded. "You've spoken well, sir. Your gracious words are much appreciated."

"It is particularly heartening to see that since the destruction of that abominable tower, you've chosen to memorialize God's judgment to the benefit of all mankind. The Lord, I'm sure, is most pleased you've honored His actions in this way."

Tilting his head oddly, Nimrod sat up on his throne and glared down with furrowed brow. "Excuse me, my good man, but I think you've completely misunderstood my motive in the naming of my new cities. My intention was not to honor some unknown god who capriciously hides behind a mask of anonymity but to mock the mindless fates that inexplicably struck down my heroic efforts."

"B—*but I* don't understand. I thought for sure, after such a crushing blow, I mean—"

"You thought *what*?" barked Nimrod, who became increasingly irritated. "That I'd lost my nerve, that I'd repented of my decision to honor the gods of my own choice?"

"Why, yes, what else would I have thought?"

"Well, then, my deluded friend, you are sorely mistaken, aren't you? Now, before I lose my temper and demonstrate what divine retribution is really like, I suggest you leave my presence immediately."

ABRAM WAS HAVING lunch with Shem and Noah several months later.

"Well, Abram," began Shem, "it's hard to believe, but it's been forty years since you came to live with Noah and I."

"My word," Noah said wistfully. "It seems like only yesterday. How old are you now, anyway?"

"I just turned fifty, sir."

"Ah," said Noah with a playful smile, "you're still just a child."

"But, sir, I've grown up in more ways than you can imagine."

"It's true, Father," said Shem. "Abram is a grown man now, a man in whom God has given a unique heart of understanding."

"Is that so?" Noah asked thoughtfully. "Then tell me, Abram, what's the most important thing you've learned in all your years with us?"

Abram pondered the question for several moments and then confidently replied, "I've come to realize that all the efforts of this idolatrous generation are as useless as their false gods."

Proudly, Shem looked at Noah and winked. "See, Father, I told you he was ready."

IN THE NEIGHBORING territory of Elam, another king was, at that same time, holding court with several of his princes, and this king was none other than Nimrod's own prince, Chedorlaomer.

One of his princes graciously bowed. "King Chedorlaomer, we came as soon as you called. How may we serve you today?"

"I've made a rather momentous decision today, and in light of recent developments, I believe the time is ripe to act upon it."

"Tell us, My King, what have you decided?"

"Well, you all know how I've faithfully served King Nimrod as one of his chief princes for many years. Without question, I've obeyed his every command. Even when he decided to build that damned tower of his, I never hesitated to supply him with as many men and materials as he desired. But it's been ten years since the confusion of tongues, and our kingdom has never been the same since."

"I heartily agree, My Lord. It's taxed all my skills as an administrator just to reorganize and maintain our standing army."

"Tell me, then; how would you rate your efforts? Is my army ready for action?"

"They are, yes. They thirst for action. Men like that grow restless with nothing to test their mettle."

"Excellent."

"What did you have in mind?"

"One last thing," replied Chedorlaomer, carefully considering a new thought. "And please be frank with your response. I'll hold your answer in the utmost confidence, of course."

"What is it, Sire?"

"Have you heard what the people are saying about Nimrod? Behind his back, I mean."

"Naturally, My Lord, news of such a nature always spreads like wildfire. Any man who seeks to uphold the highest position in the land is always a target for this sort of derision."

"What have you heard, then?"

"I've heard that since the rebuilding of his cities, his own people have begun to call him by a new name, that of Amraphel, because his princes and warriors were struck down at that tower because of his foolishness."

"What does that tell you?"

"It tells me the once and great king of Shinar has lost his grip on the hearts and minds of the very people who have faithfully served him. It tells me that, just as you have said, the time is ripe."

"So it is, yes. The time is at hand to put an end to the tyranny of Nimrod."

"And not a moment too soon, My Lord. Have you heard what's being said of his own son?"

"What? That his son Mardon is proving to be an even greater menace than his father?"

"But it's true. Men have even begun to spread a proverb concerning his evil ways. Are you aware of it?"

"I am. 'From wickedness proceeds even more wickedness.'"

"Exactly."

"Then it's settled. We must uproot this weed before another one has a chance to grow up alongside it, one even more pernicious than the first."

"Will we be attacking Nimrod head on, then?"

"Certainly not. We're still in no position to take the bull by the horns yet. We'll attack the Five Cities of the Plain, Sodom and Gomorrah and her neighbors. Once we've brought them under our sway we'll consolidate our power. Then we'll be ready to bring down the tyrant, once and for all."

"An excellent idea, My Lord."

"Then make the necessary arrangements. Let my army prepare itself for battle. Let all my people know what we have decided today. Let everyone know that the time for revolution is upon us all."

CHEDORLAOMER'S ARMY was on the move before long, and with terrible swiftness, it struck into the heart of the Cities of the Plain. With hacking swords and flying arrows, the warriors of Chedorlaomer fanned out through the five cities, besieging the inhabitants with remorseless fury.

WHEN HIS TROUBLED messenger came and bowed before him, Nimrod was, as usual, relaxing on his gilded throne. Concerned by the look on the man's face, the king sat up in anticipation.

"Tell me, messenger; you have bad news for me, don't you?"

"I'm afraid so, Your Highness. Your great kingdom has suffered a terrible blow today. What's worse, this treachery has been dealt upon you by none other than one of your very own princes."

Bolting to his feet, Nimrod was incensed. "What prince of mine would dare such a thing? Tell me his name, and I'll blot him out of existence."

"It's Chedorlaomer, and he's attacked the Five Cities of the Plain. As of this moment, the army of Elam appears unstoppable. Sodom and Gomorrah have already fallen, and the other three are on the verge of complete collapse."

Disheartened, the king sat back down and slowly sank into his throne. "My power, my power," he whispered, "what is happening to my power?"

"What's that, My Lord? I couldn't hear you."

"Never mind." Nimrod looked back at his messenger with hollow eyes. "I wasn't addressing you."

"Then what should I tell your princes? They look to you for guidance, Sire. They wonder when you will organize them in a counter-attack."

But the king remained unmoved. "Tell them," he continued, simmering to a boil, "*tell them* I've grown weary with their incompetence."

Confused, the messenger stood there, mouth agape. "Excuse me, My Lord? You want me to tell them that?"

"Yes, yes, tell them exactly that, word for word," snapped Nimrod with a wave of his hand. "Now, leave me, before I grow weary of your services, too."

The Homecoming

WHILE TERAH WAS relaxing at home one day, his servant entered and said, "Excuse me, My Lord, but you have a visitor."

Obviously deep in thought, Terah waved him off. "Tell them to go away. I'm much too busy to entertain guests right now."

"I told him the same thing, sir, but he refused to leave. He insisted you would want to see him, immediately."

Curious, Terah sat up in his chair. "He did? Who does this man think he is, barging into my home this way?"

"The man," said a voice from beyond the doorway, "thinks he's your son."

"My son?" As Abram entered the room, Terah stood, trembling. "Abram?"

"Yes, sir, it's me, Abram. Tell me, Father; am I still your son, even after all these years?"

Terah smiled and opened his arms wide as Abram ran forward to embrace his father. "My son; of course, Abram, you'll always be my son. Welcome home, my boy. I've missed you so much."

TO CELEBRATE HIS son's homecoming, Terah and his entire household had a tremendous feast. Open fire pits roasted wild boar, filling the night air with a thick, smoky haze. Dozens of servants lavished Abram and his guests with tray after tray of food and flagons of wine. Exotic dancers sensually moved to the beat of lilting musical strains that filtered through the crowd.

Sitting next to Abram and Terah were two more men. One of them heartily slapped Abram on the back. "Just look at our little brother, Nahor. He's all grown up now."

"That he is, Haran," said Nahor. "You're looking quite well, Abram. It's good to have you home."

"Thank you, Nahor. It's good to be home."

"So, Abram," continued Haran, "what have you got to say for yourself after all these years?"

Feeling a little tipsy, Abram smiled. "I am well, Haran. How've you been?"

"Oh, as well as can be expected, I guess. And how are old Noah and Shem doing these days? Did they take good care of our kid brother?"

"They're fine. And yes, they did take care of me, very good care of me, in fact. Everything I needed to know about serving the Lord of Heaven and Earth, I learned from them."

As one of the beautiful dancing girls swiveled her way closer to Abram, Haran grinned at his brother's obvious uneasiness. "But tell me, brother, did Noah and Shem ever teach you in the ways of love?"

Abram timidly shook his head. The woman danced so sensually between the two brothers that it made Haran swoon.

"Ah, love so sweet it takes your breath away," Haran continued. "Did they teach you about that?"

"No, brother, they did not," replied Abram with an embarrassed gulp.

"I didn't think so," grunted Haran, clearly intoxicated. "What a shame. Then I'm afraid they might've been wasting your time after all."

Seeing the uncomfortable look on Abram's face, Terah leaned in. "Relax, Haran, leave your brother alone. He hasn't been home two days, and you're already making trouble for him."

"Don't worry about me, Father," insisted Abram. "I can handle my own battles."

"Well, listen to you," added Haran, amused by his brother's gumption. "Hear that, Father? Abram can handle himself. By the gods, my brother's become a man, and now he's come home to take his rightful place among his real family."

"Well, it's about time!" spouted Terah proudly.

"A toast!" blurted Haran, who thrust forward his cup of wine. "A toast to my dear brother; the wandering sheep has finally come home to stay!"

SEVERAL DAYS LATER, Abram ventured into an ornate chamber in his father's home, where he discovered twelve idols, each standing in its own miniature temple. Abram was clearly shocked by what he saw. "Good God, what is this?" Seeing his brother walking down the hall, he called out, "Haran, come here, please."

"What's wrong?" Haran asked, stepping to the doorway.

"Have you seen all this?"

"Seen it? Of course I've seen it," he proudly replied. "Everything you see here, I helped Father build with my own two hands."

"But I don't understand. What are you saying? What is this room?"

Confused by his question, Haran shrugged his shoulders. "This is Father's room for our gods. What did you think it was?"

"Your what? Your gods?"

"Our gods, yes, you brainless idiot," Haran replied, giving Abram a gentle tap on the back of his head, "one god for each month of the year. Now, if you're done wasting my time, I'd like to go. I have things to do." And turning to leave, he left Abram standing there with his mouth hanging open.

"And he calls me a brainless idiot?" mumbled Abram. "The man fashions idols with his own hands and then has the nerve to call them his gods? I don't believe it. As the Lord lives, I refuse to stand by and watch my father and brothers destroy their own souls with a bunch of useless idols."

Abram stormed out of the chamber and went to the living room, where he found Terah sitting with his brother, Nahor. Abram sat down next to them. "Father, please answer a question for me, won't you?"

"Of course, Abram; what is it?"

"Where is the God Who created everything and everyone?"

"Why, of course, the gods who created us are right here in this house."

"Then, please, sir, could you show me?"

"Certainly, son," said Terah, who then led him into his chamber of idols, with its twelve statues. "See, here they are. These are the gods who created you and me and all mankind." Bowing to them, Terah then left the room.

DEEPLY TROUBLED, Abram went to see his mother.

"What's wrong, son?" asked Amthelo. "You look like you've just seen the devil himself."

"I'm afraid you're not too far from the truth, Mother."

"Tell me, then. What happened?"

"Father just showed me the gods whom he claims made the Universe."

"Oh, them. So you finally got to see his beloved chamber of idols."

Dolefully, Abram nodded.

"So what did you think of it?"

"It made me sick, absolutely sick. To think that my own father could actually believe a bunch of idols created the Universe. It's more than I can take, I tell you."

"What are you going to do about it?"

"What am I going to do? I'm going to give them a meat offering; that's what I'm going to do. And you're going to help me."

TAKING SOME SAVORY meat, Abram laid it at the feet of one of his father's idols. Then, he sat there all day, watching and waiting, to see what they would do with it, but, of course, they did nothing in response. "Well, well, I guess Mother's cooking wasn't as good today as what you're used to getting. Or maybe I just didn't serve enough to suit any of you. Maybe that's why you didn't eat anything. Tomorrow, I'll bring you an even bigger and better meal than this one; then we'll see what happens."

WITH ANOTHER PLATE of succulent meat, Abram returned the next morning to his father's chamber of idols. He approached them and placed the offering in front of the largest one there. Again he sat and watched them well into the afternoon. Still, none of them reached out to eat a thing. Springing to his feet, Abram began to anxiously pace back and forth, growing more agitated by the moment. Lifting his eyes toward Heaven, he cried out, "Lord of Heaven and Earth, please tell me: What should I do?"

Suddenly an eerie wind blew into the room, gusting through his hair and into his nostrils. Inspired by the whirlwind, Abram shouted above the din, "My father and this wicked generation are all doomed! They serve idols with mouths that can't speak. They have eyes and ears and hands, but still they're completely useless, just like the people who made them!" As if seized with a tremendous insight, Abram's eyes began to gleam with a curious shimmer. Grabbing a hatchet, he started hacking away at his father's idols.

Hearing the sound of the hatchet from outside his home, Terah ran inside to see what was happening. As Terah was heading for his chamber of idols, he passed Abram casually walking down the hall in the other direction. And when Terah went into the room, to his absolute horror, he found that all of his idols had been smashed to pieces; all except one, that is. Much to his chagrin, this remaining idol was standing there with a plate of food in front of it, and stranger still, this idol was holding Abram's hatchet in its hand. A stunned Terah ran into the living room, where he found Abram, lounging with his brother, Nahor.

"Abram, by the gods," blurted Terah, "what have you done?"

"What's wrong, Father?"

Wringing his hands in abject frustration, Terah then pointed down the hallway toward his chamber of idols. "M—*my gods*, someone's destroyed them! Didn't I see you coming from their room just now? You did this thing, didn't you?"

"You say they've *all* been destroyed?"

"All but one, yes. They're completely smashed. Tell me, son, before I lose my temper. Why'd you do it?"

"But I have no idea what you're talking about, Father," replied Abram, as calm as can be. "I only brought them a meat offering in your honor, but when I came closer, they all tried to grab the food before the biggest god had a chance to eat any of it."

"Nonsense."

"No, Father, really. Didn't you say they'd all been destroyed except one?"

"Yes, you know I just told you that."

"Well, there you are. It's just like I told you, really. You should've seen it. The biggest god was so angry he became violent. He took a hatchet and smashed them all before I had a chance to stop him. As I recall, he's still got the thing in his hand. Check for yourself, if you don't believe me."

"Never mind that now, Abram." His father's frustration abruptly turned to anger. "You're lying! You're nothing but a filthy liar!"

"No, Father," said Abram in earnest, looking his father right in the eye. "That's where you're clearly mistaken. Tell him, Nahor. Tell him his son is no liar."

But Terah was too angry to wait for Nahor's response. "You actually expect me to believe these gods have the power to do what you've just described? What kind of a fool do you take me for?"

"What are you saying, then? You mean your gods aren't capable of such a thing?"

"Of course not. How could they? They're just wood and stone. I should know; Haran and I made them ourselves."

Astonished, Abram gaped at his father. "Then, for Heaven's sake, why do you worship them?"

"Because, well, because..." Terah blanched, momentarily taken aback. "Because that's what we've always done, why else?"

"Do they hear your prayers?"

"H—*how* should I know?"

"Will they fight any of your battles? Can they rescue you from your enemies?"

"Of course not." Terah obstinately crossed his arms. "Please, son, now you're just being ridiculous."

"You know, Father, I'm sure this can't be good for you or my brothers. Only a fool would serve an idol, or worse, a rebel against God."

"Enough already! You're overreacting, son. There's no way that God could be that concerned about how we choose to live."

"But that's just it; He does care. Don't you remember? Our forefathers sinned like this in the past, and the Lord wiped them out with the Flood!"

Terah defiantly shook his head. "Oh, Abram, that was then; this is now. The Lord would never do something like that again, not to us."

"I don't know, Father. Are you really so eager to find out? You actually want to risk inciting the anger of God just so you can worship a bunch of useless idols?"

"Abram, please. I still say you're overreacting to this whole thing."

"For God's sake, Father, put an end to this madness right now, before it's too late! You don't want to bring disaster to your own family, do you?"

Abram then sprang to his feet and started back toward the chamber of idols.

"Abram, son, where do you think you're going?" Turning to his other son, he pleaded, "Nahor, don't just sit there; do something! Your brother's gone insane!"

"*Me*? What do you expect me to do about it? He's your son."

"Abram, wait!" Bolting down the hall, Terah ran through the doorway just in time to see his son approaching his one remaining idol. "Son, I forbid you to come in here anymore!"

"I'm sorry, Father, really I am; but all this has to end, so help me God."

Abram strode to the idol, took the hatchet from its hand, and raised it, ready to strike.

"No, son! Don't!"

And after hacking Terah's last idol into so many bits of firewood, Abram ran out of the room, leaving his father just standing there, stunned and speechless.

Into the Fire

APPEARING BEFORE Nimrod, Terah humbly bowed. The king was puzzled by the troubled look on Terah's face. "What's wrong, my friend?"

"Please, Sire, I have something very important to discuss with you."

"Go on, tell me. What's troubling my favorite prince?"

"Well, you see, it's been many years since one of my sons was born to me." Terah paused, trying to find just the right words.

Nimrod leaned forward. "Yes, and now?"

"And now you wouldn't believe what he's done to me and my gods. And the things he keeps telling me; I don't understand. I'm at my wits' end. He's gone insane, I think."

"I'm sorry to hear it, Terah. How can your king be of assistance?"

"I'm afraid I have no choice but to have him brought before you, My Lord, so you can judge him according to our Law. That way maybe you can put an end to his evil; otherwise, we might all succumb to his madness."

SO ABRAM WAS BROUGHT to stand before Nimrod, who was sitting with his princes and governors, and, of course, Terah was seated there, too.

The king looked at Abram, perusing him from head to toe. "What's your name, young man?"

"My name is Abram, sir."

Upon hearing this, the king had a peculiar look flash across his face. "Abram? Hmmm, Abram, yes. Why does that name sound familiar?" Turning to Terah, the king saw his favorite prince just shrug his shoulders. "No?" muttered Nimrod, dismissing his suspicion with the wave of his hand and returning his intense eyes back upon Abram. "Do you know who I am?"

"Of course I do. Everyone knows who you are. You're King Amraphel, right?"

An audible gasp swept through the ranks of everyone in the room as Nimrod's eyes thinned. "What did you call me?"

"I called you King Amraphel. I'm sorry. Isn't that what people call you nowadays?"

"How dare you address me like that. Don't you realize I hold your life in my hands? Your own father has brought you here to suffer the consequences of my judgment. Still you have the audacity to mock me to my face?"

"Really," said Abram as he glanced over at his father, who looked away, unable to face the scrutinizing gaze of his son. "That's why I've been brought here?"

"That's right, young man. You stand accused by your own father. Now tell us, what have you done to his beloved gods?"

Abram calmly replied, "I, sir, have done nothing to my father's *idols*. The damage he described was caused by his chief idol when *it* became jealous that the others were receiving more attention than they deserved."

"Ridiculous," scoffed Nimrod. "Certainly you don't expect me to believe Terah's chief god has the power to do something like that."

"Then what are you telling me? If they're powerless, why do you serve them? Do you actually think they can rescue you?"

"Don't be absurd. The gods are fickle and beyond our understanding. They do whatever they want, whenever they want, whether we like it or not.

Who are you to expect them to do your bidding?"

"Then why not serve the God of the Universe? He created you. He controls your life. He's the only One Who can both annihilate and sustain life."

"Just who is this god of yours, anyway? I've never met him."

"What an ignorant king you turned out to be. Shame on you. Instead of teaching your subjects to do the right thing, you've infected the world with your rebellious attitude."

The king slammed his fist down on the arm of his gilded throne. "How dare you! Your father was right. You are an insolent, little bastard!"

"Oh, stop. It's time to end this madness, or you'll all die miserable deaths." Abram then lifted his eyes toward Heaven. "The Lord sees every wicked person and judges them all."

"Enough! Seize this man and throw him in prison until I decide what to do with him!"

Nimrod's guards immediately grabbed Abram, dragged him to his jail cell, and slammed shut the iron bars.

NIMROD SOON ASSEMBLED his sages and sorcerers, along with all his princes and governors from each of his provinces.

"Have you heard about what Terah's son, Abram, has done?" snorted the king.

"He's a disgrace, I tell you!" shouted one of the princes.

"That's exactly what he is, yes," sneered Nimrod. "And when I ordered him to appear before me, he insulted me to my face; so I threw him in prison!"

"Prison is too good for him, Great One," chimed in one of the governors.

"Then tell me," continued the king. "What should I do to a man who mocks me this way?"

Stepping forward, the governor declared, "The man who defies his king should be crucified!"

"But that's not all he did!" cried one of the sages. "He's insulted our gods, too! And for that, the Law states he should be burned to death. So if it pleases the king, we can make a fire in your brick furnace and let it burn all day."

"Then we'll throw Abram into it!" added the prince.

Nimrod nodded, motioning to his servants. "Then it's settled. Prepare the furnace of Chaldea. But don't let it burn for just one day; let it burn for three full days. Then notify me when it's ready."

"As you wish, My Lord," replied one of his servants.

ABRAM WAS MARCHED from prison three days later, flanked by two of Nimrod's guards. Every one of the king's princes, governors and judges came to watch him get put into the furnace, not to mention a swarm of spectators. Women and children crowded onto rooftops and towers to see what was happening, and even though so many people had to watch from a distance, there was hardly a person in the country who did not come to see the spectacle that day.

As soon as Abram arrived, Nimrod's sages and sorcerers discerned who he was. "Why, of course, My Lord!" shouted a sage. "This must be the same man who was born into the House of Terah so long ago, just as we told you."

Frantically, they crowded around the king. "Yes, Your Highness," weighed in one of the sorcerers. "This is undoubtedly the man who was born when the great star swallowed the other four stars! But we already told you about this thing some fifty years ago!"

"I don't understand," Nimrod said, growing agitated. "What are you saying?"

"This man, Abram," continued the sage, "it appears he was born into the House of Terah after all. Apparently, you didn't kill his son as you believed so many years ago."

"*What*?" grunted Nimrod. "You mean to tell me Terah's son survived?"

"Yes, Sire," the sorcerer continued, "it seems that Terah defied your decree!"

"But I distinctly remember killing the little monster with my own two hands! How can this be?"

"He must have given you a different child," said the sage. "You must have killed *it* instead of Abram!"

"Of course, of course," murmured the king, "but why didn't I see this thing for myself? How could my insight have failed me so miserably, just when I needed it most?"

DRAGGED BEFORE THE king, Terah straightened his disheveled clothes and looked up at Nimrod, who was as frustrated as he was angry.

"So, Terah, Chief Prince of My Army, have you heard what my sages and sorcerers have said about you?"

Terah nodded timidly. "Yes, My Lord, I have."

"Tell me, then, my old friend. I must hear it from your own lips. It's not true, is it?"

"It's true, Sire. Everything the sages and sorcerers have told you is true."

"How could you?" asked Nimrod, truly disappointed. "You disobeyed my direct order?"

"Yes, My King. I'm afraid so."

"You gave me a child that wasn't yours?"

"In my defense, Sire, the boy was mine, born to me by one of my concubines."

"Still, the boy you gave me was not the one I asked for, the one I paid a great deal of money for. Is that correct?"

"It is, Great King, yes."

"But why you? Why would you, of all people, betray me like this?"

Befuddled, Terah shrugged his sagging shoulders. "I don't know. I guess my love for him overwhelmed me at the time."

"At least tell me it wasn't your idea to deceive me like this. Tell me someone else persuaded you to do it. Tell me now, and I promise: You won't have to die for this crime."

A terrified Terah stared back at the king for several agonizing moments. "Uh, yes, well, Haran … my oldest son … as a matter of fact, he was thirty-two years old when Abram was born … and, yes, he was the one, you know … who told me to do it. Come to think of it, it *was* him."

"Very well, then. You, my dear prince, will live, and for telling you to do this thing, Haran, your son, will stand in your place; he will receive the death penalty instead of you. He will die for concocting this insufferable lie that now jeopardizes our entire kingdom! He will die with Abram in the furnace of Chaldea."

"Wait, *what*? Wait, not—" Terah gasped, suddenly finding it difficult to breathe. "No, not *both* my sons, please. Oh, dear God, no… What have I done?"

MEANWHILE, HARAN was at home, having lunch with Amthelo, who looked quite worried as she sat there, just playing with the food on her plate.

"Mother, you haven't had a single bite," said Haran. "Please eat. It won't do Abram any good for you to waste away on his account. Everything will be all right. Trust me."

Amthelo glared up at Haran. "That's easy for you to say while you sit there in the security of your comfortable home. But what I want to know is: Why doesn't your father do something? What good is being the king's chief prince if he can't even save his own son?"

"I wish I could tell you, Mom, really I do."

"Is that all you have to say for yourself? You know, you may not want to admit it, but I know you admire Abram, even if he is your kid brother. Deep down you wish you had his guts, his conviction. I see the way you are around him, always trying so hard to keep your thoughts to yourself, trying to act so unconcerned, but you don't fool me. I may not have given birth to you, but I still have a mother's instinct, you know."

Haran nodded. "Of course I'm concerned by this. And you're right. I do have tremendous respect for Abram; so much so, in fact, I've made a very important decision."

"A decision. What's that supposed to mean? You're going to say something to your father? Is that it?"

"Not exactly, no."

"What, then? What's this big decision of yours?"

"I've decided it's time to follow Abram in the ways of the Lord, assuming he survives his ordeal with the king. I figure if God sees His way to rescuing Abram, then He must be worthy of my commitment, too."

Amthelo stared at him in disbelief. "That's it? That's your momentous decision?"

"Well, what else can I do?"

"For one thing, you could talk to your father. Demand he intervene on your brother's behalf. Now *that* would be the brave thing to do. And what if God doesn't save Abram from the wrath of Nimrod? Then what?"

"Well, naturally, I'll follow the king instead."

Disgusted, Amthelo jumped to her feet and bumped her plate of food from the table, sending it crashing to the floor. Just then, there was a knock at the door. Haran got up and opened it. Standing on the doorstep were several of Nimrod's soldiers.

"Are you Haran, son of Terah, the chief prince of Nimrod's army?" asked the lead soldier.

"Yes," replied Haran with a suspicious nod. "What's this about?"

"By order of King Nimrod, you are under arrest."

"For what?" asked a befuddled Haran.

"For treason against His Majesty, King Nimrod. Now come with us peaceably, sir, or we'll have to take you by force."

The soldiers stepped forward and seized Haran.

Horrified, Amthelo sprang to Haran's side. "No! There must be some mistake. My son is absolutely loyal to the king. By whose testimony does this charge of treason come?"

"By no less than Terah's himself."

"My husband did this?"

"It appears so, ma'am."

Haran and Amthelo both gasped. "God, no," said mother and son together.

A RESTLESS SEA OF onlookers had swollen to the point that there was standing room only along the thoroughfare where Nimrod's servants were leading Abram and Haran, who were both stripped down to their underwear, hands bound with linen cords. Together they were hoisted and thrown into the furnace. Within moments, Haran, screaming in agony, burned to ashes, but miraculously, Abram was not even singed by the inferno. Only the linen cords that bound his hands burned up, so Abram continued to walk around, quite unharmed, inside the furnace. As several of Nimrod's stunned servants peered inside, flames spewed out, killing a dozen of them.

ABRAM WAS STILL wandering around the next day, inside the furnace, as if nothing unusual was happening to him. Nimrod's bewildered servants stood and stared, frozen with fear and indecision.

"What should we do?" asked one of them. "We can't just stand around doing nothing."

"What do you expect us to do?" asked a second.

"Someone has got to go to the king," insisted a third. "Someone has to tell him what's happening here. Don't you think?"

"And tell him what?" blurted the first servant. "He'll think we're making the whole thing up and order *us* into the furnace."

"He has a point," said the second to the others. "So what *should* we do?"

"I say we tell the king and take our chances," continued the third. "One way or the other we're in big trouble. But if we don't say a thing, we're dead men for sure."

"He's right," said the second. "If we tell the king, and he doesn't believe us, then at least we'll die knowing we did everything we could to avoid it. And who knows, maybe he'll come here and discover the truth for himself."

The other servants all nodded in agreement.

"I think you're right, yes," added the second. "Either way we have to tell him."

WHEN ONE OF THE servants appeared before the king, Nimrod was naturally surprised to see him. "What are you doing here?"

"Excuse me, Your Highness," replied the servant, "but what I'm about to tell you is too impossible to believe."

Nimrod leaned forward in anticipation. "Yes, yes, what is it?"

"Well, when we threw the two brothers, Abram and Haran, into the furnace, the older one died in a matter of moments." The servant shook his head, searching for just the right words. "But Abram. H—h—*he's* walking around inside the furnace like it's nothing!"

Nimrod's heart sank. "Are you insane? That's impossible. Has everyone in my kingdom lost their minds?"

ARRIVING AT THE furnace of Chaldea the next day, two of Nimrod's princes carefully approached it and peered inside. Seeing Abram walking around in the midst of the fire, they turned to one another with a look of complete disbelief.

"It's impossible," muttered the first prince.

"Oh, it may be impossible," said the second prince, scratching his head, "but there it is, right in front of us. Now what do we do?"

"You have to tell the king."

"*Me*? Why me?"

"Never mind. We'll both tell him, then."

THE TWO PRINCES reluctantly returned and appeared before Nimrod, who sat up in anticipation.

"Well," snorted the king, "what have you two got to say for yourselves?"

The two men exchanged a nervous look.

"Don't just stand there, staring at each other. Tell me what you've seen."

"It's true, Great One, we've both seen it with our own eyes. Abram *is* still alive, wandering about in your furnace, unharmed and unperturbed."

"Nonsense! I don't believe it! I won't believe it; not unless I see it for myself!"

SURE ENOUGH, WHEN Nimrod went to the furnace and looked inside, he saw Abram casually walking back and forth through the flames. Noticing the charred remains of his brother, the astonished king waived to his servants. "Get Abram out of there, this instant."

But the men just stood there, frozen with fear.

Frustrated, the king motioned them toward the furnace and growled, "Do it, you cowards, or else."

Finally, a trio of servants nervously made their way to the door. One of them quickly unbolted it and ran away. The door slowly swung open, and as soon as it did the fire breached the confines of the furnace and lashed out, forcing the other two men to withdraw.

"Hurry up!" Nimrod shouted above the roar of the flames. "Get Abram out of there right now, or I'll have you all thrown in with him!"

Again several of his servants moved toward the door of the furnace. This time the flames rushed out so violently that eight more men were engulfed and killed.

Nimrod cautiously stepped forward. "Abram, Servant of God," said the king in as pleasant a voice as he could muster, "won't you please come out of this furnace and stand before me now?"

With that, Abram walked out of the firestorm, through the open door of the furnace, and casually made his way over to the king.

The bewildered Nimrod examined Abram from head to toe. "B—*but how*? I don't understand. How on Earth did you survive inside that furnace, while your brother … my servants … all burned to a crisp?"

Abram calmly smiled. "The God I trust, the God of All Power, rescued me from your fire."

EVERYONE WHO HAD witnessed how Abram had endured the furnace of Chaldea soon began coming to see him up close.

"Obviously, this man is blessed of the gods," said one woman, who reached out to touch him.

One spectator, however, was more amazed than all the rest; and that was Abram's father, Terah. He watched in utter disbelief at all the people who came to bow down to his son, including many of Nimrod's princes. Even more startling, he watched as Nimrod, much to the amazement of the crowd, kneeled before Abram.

But Abram frantically raised his hands in protest. "No, no, no. Don't do that! Only worship the Lord above! *He's* the One Who saved me from the fire. I didn't do anything."

Rising to his feet, Nimrod motioned to his servants and princes, who showered Abram with a staggering assortment of gifts, including cattle, sheep and goats; wine, dates and olive oil; gold, silver and jewels.

"Here you are, Blessed Man," said Nimrod, "the finest gifts my kingdom has to offer. I even want you to have my chief servant, the absolute best servant I've ever had, in fact. His name is Eliezer."

The fellow came before Abram and bowed. "I'd be most honored to serve you, Master Abram."

Embarrassed, Abram nodded back. "That's quite all right, Eliezer. Thank you, you're most gracious."

"I'd especially like to hear more about this God of yours," said Eliezer. "You say *He* was the One Who rescued you from the fire?"

"Yes, He was. And I'd be very happy to tell you more about the God of my fathers, you and anyone among you who wishes to know more about Him."

"Now, Abram," interjected Nimrod, "if you'd like, you're free to go."

Abram was pleasantly surprised. "You mean, I'm really free to leave? Just like that?"

"Most assuredly, yes; you and anyone else who wishes to follow you and your god," replied Nimrod with an awkward smile, "just like that."

SO WHILE THE SAME people who had come to watch him die in Nimrod's furnace now hailed him as a conquering hero, Abram triumphantly marched out of the town square, followed by some three hundred of the king's people who joined him that day.

Out of Chaldea

THE FIRST PLACE Abram went after regaining his freedom was his father's home, where a forlorn Terah greeted him as he approached.

"Oh, Abram, I am so sorry. Will you ever be able to forgive me for what I've done?"

Looking into his father's eyes for several moments, Abram mulled over his response. "Of course I forgive you, Father, but the real question is: Will you ever be able to forgive yourself?"

Cut to the quick, Terah averted his eyes and kicked at the dirt. "Would you like to come inside?"

"This is still my home, isn't it?"

"Certainly, Abram. You'll always be welcome here."

"So you're not still angry with me for destroying all your beloved idols?"

"What, that? I've already forgotten about that. Besides, you were just trying to protect your old man, right?"

"Of course, Pop; you know I was."

Turning from his father, Abram started toward the front door.

"Abram, wait a minute, will you?"

"What is it, Father?"

"I need to ask you for a favor."

Stopping, Abram turned back toward his father, who then walked over to him with a grim expression. Terah continued in hushed tones, "Haran's two daughters are here for his memorial service, and I'm worried they might start asking questions."

"Questions?"

"Yes, you know, about their father; how he died."

"You mean *why* he died, don't you?"

"Something like that, yes."

"You're afraid they might find out it was you who implicated him, trying to save your own skin. Is that what you're telling me?"

"Please, son, just tell me you won't say anything about my role in all this. I'm afraid it'd break their hearts if they found out I was involved."

"I'm sorry, Father, I thought I made it quite clear. I'm no liar. And I certainly don't plan to start becoming one now. Not for anyone in this world."

"But, son, be reasonable. You said yourself that when you told a white lie about destroying my idols, you did it because you were trying to protect me from myself. Can't you do it one more time for my sake?"

Taken aback, Abram hesitated for a moment, then countered, "That was different."

"How was it different?"

"It was just different, that's all." Then, Abram turned and headed for the front door.

"Please, Abram, if you won't do it for me, then at least do it for the sake of the girls. It would break their hearts, I tell you."

Almost to the door, Abram hesitated, as if he might respond, but thinking better of it he opened the door and stepped inside. He immediately caught sight of his brother Nahor and beside him two young women who were trying in vain to hold back their tears.

"Abram," began Nahor with a sigh of relief, "it's so good to see you still in one piece. We've been so worried about you. It's hard to believe you survived such a gruesome ordeal."

Hardly paying any attention to his brother, Abram fixed his gaze on the two women, and his heart sank when he did. "I'm all right, Nahor, but please, I'd rather not talk about it; not in front of the girls, anyway."

Turning to the two women, Nahor became embarrassed. "Oh, I am so stupid. I'm sorry, Sarai. I don't know what I was thinking. Milcah, will you forgive me?"

"It's okay," replied Milcah as she lovingly embraced Nahor. "We're all at our wits' ends right now. You don't have to apologize because Father didn't survive Nimrod's fire."

"Milcah's right," said Sarai, "you didn't mean any disrespect. We're all a little out of kilter. We're grieving."

Abram dolefully stared at Sarai and then stepped over to her. "I'm so sorry about what happened, Sarai. How are you holding up?"

"I'll be all right, Abram," she said, falling into his arms. "I just can't believe Father is gone."

She gazed up at him with such beautiful, tear-filled eyes that Abram nearly swooned. "You'll be okay, Sarai. I'm here for you."

"Thank you, Abram," she murmured, hugging him tightly. "I just wish someone could tell me how this could have happened. It just doesn't make any sense."

Just then, Terah walked in and saw Sarai in Abram's reassuring embrace.

"I mean," Sarai continued tearfully, "Uncle Nahor told us why the king was angry at you, but why did Father end up in that furnace? What did he do to make the king condemn him like that? Do you have any idea, Abram?"

Considering her question for several agonizing moments, he looked first at his father standing there, breathless with anticipation, and then back at Sarai, who was likewise looking to him in hopeful expectation. Slowly, reluctantly, he replied, "I wish I could tell you, Sarai, really I do... But, unfortunately ... I don't, no." And hugging her, he blankly looked at his father, who turned away with an imperceptible sigh.

A DOUBLE WEDDING ceremony soon had Abram and Sarai standing together alongside Nahor and Milcah.

BY THE FOLLOWING year, Milcah and Sarai were both holding crying babies. The two women appeared quite happy, as did Nahor and Abram, who both looked on proudly.

"Congratulations, Nahor," said Abram. "Your sons are beautiful."

"And what lungs those two have," remarked Nahor. "Can you believe it? Twins! Who would've thought."

The two men stepped into the other room. "Oh, that's much better," continued Nahor. "I'm not so sure I'm cut out for fatherhood."

"Ah, you'll get used to it."

"So what about you, brother?"

"What about me?"

"How are you and Sarai getting along? Any children in the works for you, I mean?"

"Of course we want kids. But as you can see, we haven't had any luck in that area yet."

"Give it time. Besides, you don't want to get tied down too early in your marriage."

"What's your excuse, then?"

"Well, I don't count. I'm a lot older than you. I'm at the point in my life when I'm ready for something like this. But you? I just don't see you as the childrearing type."

"What's that supposed to mean?"

"Relax, Abram, don't get offended. I just meant that you strike me as a man who's going places, a man with a mission, you know? Sometimes a man like that finds a family holds him back from what he needs to do."

Abram considered his words for a moment and said, "But what if that mission involves children? Then what?"

"If that's the case, then, naturally, they'll come. But until that day comes, I wouldn't lose any sleep over it." Wincing at an outburst of crying from his twins, Nahor glibly smiled. "Ah, blessed sleep, something I'm afraid I won't be getting much of for quite some time."

AS NIMROD SAT ON HIS throne in Babel, he fell into a deep sleep. He dreamt that he was standing with his troops and subjects in a valley located directly in front of the furnace of Chaldea. Suddenly Abram vaulted out of the fiery furnace, and with sword in hand, he came and stood before Nimrod. Without warning, Abram swung his sword at the king who fled, terrified. As he ran away, Abram threw an egg at Nimrod, which broke on the king's head. From the broken egg, water poured out. A trickle at first, it quickly became a stream, and then a raging river, which proceeded to drown all his soldiers and subjects in a torrent of water. Nimrod looked around and was horrified to find that only he and three other men had survived this deluge. As Nimrod waded through the floodwaters, the three men ran after him. After this trio caught up with him, the king could see that they were also dressed in princely attire. Then, from out of nowhere, an eerie gust of wind began to blow into the river, causing its waters to reverse their course and flow back into the broken egg, which inexplicably reassembled itself and sealed back up. Bewildered to see the egg intact again, Nimrod blanched at the sight of another crack splitting the egg open. This time the egg released a hawk, which came out and flew straight at the king. With outstretched talons, the bird lunged at his head and plucked out his eyes. With a blood-curdling scream, Nimrod woke up and found that he was lying at the foot of his throne, clearly as embarrassed as he was terrified.

ALL OF NIMROD'S SAGES and sorcerers quickly assembled before the king. "Now that you've heard the contents of my dream, can any of you explain it to me?"

"Yes, My Lord, I believe I can," replied one of the sages.

"Ah, yes, Anuki, my esteemed sage. Come forward and tell me what you think."

Stepping to the head of the group, Anuki humbly bowed. "I believe what you're seeing is none other than the evil of Abram and his descendants making itself known again."

"What?" Nimrod eyed his sage suspiciously. "Are you sure?"

"Yes, Your Highness, there's no doubt about it."

"Tell me, then. What's the meaning of my nightmare?"

"It speaks of the day when Abram and his family will start a war with you. They'll destroy your troops, your subjects, your entire kingdom."

"My kingdom? Destroyed? But what about me? What will happen to me?"

"As you recall, My King, three men escaped with you in your dream, three men you saw dressed like yourself."

"Yes, yes. I remember. What about it?"

"Well, you see, that means you'll escape with three other kings out of all your allies in battle."

"I see, good," said Nimrod, somewhat relieved. "Then my life is to be spared."

Anuki exchanged a nervous look with one of the sorcerers, and Nimrod sat up. "What? Is there something you're not telling me? Out with it, or I'll have you all torn to pieces!"

"Well, My Lord, in your dream you described a river that turned back into an egg. Is that correct?"

"Yes, yes, that's right." The king leaned forward. "And?"

"And that's when a hawk plucked out your eyes?"

"Yes, yes! But what does it mean? Tell me!"

"My Lord, I regret to inform you this means a descendant of Abram is going to kill you someday."

"What? Don't be ridiculous."

Anuki bowed humbly before Nimrod. "But I assure you, My King, this is your dream and its interpretation, both of which are entirely true."

"Impossible, I tell you!"

"But, Sire," interjected one of the sorcerers, who took a cautious step forward, "certainly you remember it's been more than fifty years since we first warned you about your fate, a fate which was clearly written in the stars even then."

Nimrod glared back at his sages and sorcerers. "Of course I remember, but what should I do about it?"

"Abram must be killed, of course," continued the sorcerer.

"Kill him, you say? But I already tried that."

"Yes, My Lord, and, with all due respect, you must not stop trying. As long as Abram is allowed to live, neither you nor your kingdom will survive."

"Very well. Then find Abram and bring him back to me. Maybe this time we'll have better luck."

Fortunately, Eliezer, Abram's chief servant given to him by Nimrod, was in the hallway eavesdropping on the conversation. As soon as they were finished, he slipped out of the palace.

ABRAM LISTENED INTENTLY as Eliezer spoke in earnest, "So you see, sir, I'm afraid you have no choice. Nimrod is more determined than ever to try to kill you."

"And you say this is happening because of a nightmare the king had?"

"That, and the advice of his sages."

"Those fools. When will they ever learn?"

"What are you going to do?"

"I'm not sure." Abram shrugged his shoulders. "But I'm not going to panic."

"Of course not, My Lord. After all, you are the same man I saw survive the furnace of Chaldea. What can a mere man like Nimrod do to someone like you?"

"It's not me I'm worried about, though. I still have to worry about what Nimrod can do to my family. I survived that fire, but for whatever reason, my brother Haran didn't."

EVENTUALLY, THE king's soldiers went to Terah's home, and one of them banged loudly on the front door. "In the name of King Nimrod, open this door!" shouted the commander, "or we'll have no choice but to break it down!"

A FRONT DOOR OPENED wide, and Shem stood there surprised by what he saw. "Well, hello," he said, "what are you all doing here like this? This is no time of the year to be traveling in these parts."

Standing on the doorstep of Noah's mountain hideaway were Abram and Sarai, accompanied by half a dozen men. "Sorry, Father Shem," said Abram, "but we had no choice. It was an emergency. May we come in?"

"Of course, of course. Get in here, everyone, before you catch your death of cold."

APPEARING BEFORE Nimrod, his soldiers stood at rapt attention.

"So, Commander," grumbled Nimrod, "what do you have to say for yourself? Have you found Abram yet?"

"We regret to inform you, Your Highness," said the commander, "Abram was nowhere to be found. For three full weeks we've searched everywhere we could think of, but none of my men can locate him."

Disappointed, the king hung his head and put his hand to his furrowed brow. "Why am I not surprised?"

TERAH EVENTUALLY came to see Abram at Noah's place. "Well, son, are you ready to come home yet?"

Abram stared back at his father in disbelief. "Are you kidding? *Your king* is trying to kill me. Or have you forgotten?"

"Abram, stop. You're overreacting, as usual. I guarantee Nimrod has already forgotten about the whole thing."

"Oh, Pop, please. Stop kidding yourself. You know that bunch of old, snaggle-toothed sages will never stop feeding Nimrod their bad news. And if that beloved king of yours can't kill me, then you know he wouldn't mind killing my entire family just to spite me."

A deflated Terah hung his head and frowned. "Yeah, I guess you're right. I just wish there was something I could do."

"But there is something you can do."

Terah looked up expectantly. "What?"

"Well, unless there's something holding you back, I recommend you leave with us right now."

"Leave? Leave and go where?"

"To the land of Canaan."

"But why do I need to go with you?"

"Have you already forgotten what happened to Haran because of your king? Do you want the same thing to happen to Mother, to Nahor or Milcah, to your grandchildren?"

"Of course not. But how can you expect me to abandon everything I've worked so hard for? My privileges, my status, the love of my king, all wiped away on a whim?"

"*A whim*? I'd hardly call it a whim, Father. Don't you realize? Nimrod doesn't give you privilege or status because he loves you. He showers you with gifts for his *own* benefit, not yours. Besides, what good is all the wealth in the world when you and your family are all dead?"

Terah took several moments to let his son's words sink in. "Fine. Then tell me what we should do."

"We pack everything we have and go to Canaan right away, out of Nimrod's reach, where he can never hurt any of our loved ones again."

"Right now? But I need more time. I have to arrange for my gods to go with us."

"No, Pop, I'm sorry. There's no room for them; not anymore, not *ever*."

Terah started to respond but thought better of it.

"Please, Father, just throw away all the useless things you've been pursuing. Serve the Lord Who created you, then everything will be all right. You'll see."

No sooner had he finished speaking than Shem stepped forward from out of the shadows. "It's true, Terah. Everything Abram is telling you is true. Go to Canaan as soon as you can, before it's too late for all of you."

DETERMINED TO GET beyond the reach of the king of Shinar, Abram gathered his entire household as quickly as he could. Soon he and Sarai, along with Terah, Amthelo, Nahor, Milcah, their two children and all their servants were on the move, followed by everyone who had joined Abram after the incident at Nimrod's furnace. Traveling in a tremendous caravan, there were more than four hundred people in the group, not to mention their various herds of cattle, sheep and goats.

They marched for several weeks before coming to a fertile outcropping in the middle of an otherwise arid landscape, nestled alongside a meandering river, and there they stopped to set up camp.

"What do you think of this place, everyone?" asked Abram. "Beautiful, isn't it?"

"Where are we?" wondered Nahor.

"First we establish camp, my boy," said Terah. "Then we find out where we are."

"There's so much room here," added Amthelo. "And plenty of water for our herds and people."

"This place is perfect," said Nahor. "I say we christen it after Haran, to honor the memory of what happened to him in the furnace of Chaldea. That way our children will always have something to remember him by, and his name will never fade from our history. What do you say, Abram?"

Considering his suggestion with a satisfied smile, Abram nodded. "I like that, Nahor. I agree. We'll call this place Haran. But don't anyone forget: This isn't our final destination. We're just stopping here awhile en route to Canaan."

"I just hope the people living in these parts are friendly," interjected Sarai.

"We'll find out soon enough, my dear," said Abram. "But I'm sure with the Lord on our side we'll have no trouble winning the people over."

STROLLING THROUGH a lush pasture one pleasant evening, Abram was tending to his flock of sheep, when suddenly a shimmering purple light materialized several yards in front of him. From within this sphere of light, a radiantly handsome Man stepped forward and stood before Abram.

A startled Abram blanched at the spectacle, sucked in a deep breath, and exclaimed, "What the — *Who* — *How*?"

"Don't be alarmed, Abram. I've just come from the presence of the Lord."

"Excuse me? You what? You came from where?"

"Certainly you've heard of Heaven, haven't you?"

"Of course I have. I've just never met anyone *from there* before."

"I see. Well, now you have."

"What should I call You?"

"I am the Word of God, the Mediator between Heaven and Earth, the One Who rescued you from the furnace of Nimrod."

Abram gulped at the news. "Oh, dear. And what have I done to deserve such an auspicious visit as this?"

"You, Abram, are a man who has tremendous faith in the God of your fathers, Noah and Shem. Are you not?"

"I am. Since before I can remember, I've sought to know the God of my fathers, to know His will, to know His ways."

"You've done well, my friend. Now you'll have what you've desired of the Lord, and if you simply do what I tell you, Abram, I'll vanquish all your enemies. Your descendants will become as numerous as the stars and the sand, and I'll bless everything you do so you'll never need a thing."

Overwhelmed, Abram kneeled in a gesture of obedience. "My Lord and my God, thank You so much for this. Mere words could never express what I'm feeling right now."

"Now, Abram, take your wife and your group to Canaan. Stay there, and I'll be your God and will bless you." Then the Word of God vanished, leaving Abram alone again, except for the bleating sheep that gathered around him in the night.

ABRAM AND SARAI MADE preparations to leave Haran several days later, but when he went to his father's tent, he was disappointed to see that Terah, Amthelo, Nahor, Milcah and several others were just casually sitting around.

"Father, what's going on?" asked Abram "Why aren't you guys packed and ready to leave? We're wasting daylight."

Terah hesitantly explained, "I'm sorry, son, but your mother and I have decided not to go along this time. Maybe we'll catch up with you later."

"Not going? But why?"

Amthelo interjected, "Don't worry about us, Abram. It's just that I'm so tired of being uprooted every time I turn around. Your father and I like it here in Haran. The past few years have been so nice here. I don't mind telling you, this place makes me feel right at home. Besides, Canaan is no place for people like us. You go there with Sarai and your people. Visit us when you can. You understand, don't you?"

"Sure, I guess so."

Then, Nahor stood up with a look of melancholy on his face. "Dear brother," he began, "I'm sure going to miss you."

"Nahor, you? You're not coming, either? What is wrong with everybody? It was never our plan to stay here. We were always supposed to continue on to Canaan. What's happened to you guys?"

"I'm sorry, Abram, but frankly, Mom and Pop are done with this whole *mission* thing you've got us involved with. You know as well as I do, they're not as young as they used to be, and they need someone to look after them."

"You mean *you.*"

"Yes, me. Look, little brother, I realize you supposedly had some kind of epiphany and all, inspiring you to pack up and leave everything behind, *again.* But that's just not for me right now. I'm sorry; you're on your own, buddy boy."

Turning to one of the other young men there, Abram asked, "And what about you, Lot? Sarai will be heartbroken if her kid brother doesn't go with us. What's holding you back? Don't you want to seek the Lord's call? We have a wonderful destiny just waiting for us. Don't you want to find out what it is?"

Lot just sat there, trying to think of something to say, but before he could, Terah stood and walked up to Abram. "Don't worry about him, son. You have enough to worry about with your own group. Lot is still a young man. He's not like you."

"Like me? What's that supposed to mean?"

"Well, you know, you've always been one to seek the higher road, with your head in the clouds."

"I'm sorry, Uncle Abram," Lot said hesitantly. "Life is too short to get so serious all the time. I want to live a little; you know, sow my wild oats. Someday I'll come and stay with you guys; you'll see. But right now, I'm just not ready for all this *destiny* stuff."

Thoroughly deflated, Abram just hung his head.

A House Divided

ONE MONTH LATER, Abram and his overflowing entourage, comprised of more than five hundred people and their herds, arrived at the outskirts of Canaan, where the landscape was dotted with orchards of fruit trees and fields of grain.

Turning to Eliezer, Abram said, "This looks like a good spot to stop for now. Tomorrow, you and I will go into the city with some of the men and find out what the people are like. In the meantime, pass the word that everyone is to set up camp here for the night."

"Yes, sir, right away."

ABRAM, ELIEZER AND half a dozen men made their way by foot into the midst of the city, where they came across a large bazaar displaying goods and wares of all kinds, including wine, dried fruits and grain. Hawkers selling their wool products, dyed a deep purple, beckoned Abram and his group as they passed by. Intrigued by what they saw, two of Abram's men stopped to examine an area with several rows of tools and weapons of every sort. As Abram paused to give his men a chance to look at some of the swords on display, a dirty-faced urchin boy approached him, holding out two arms covered with ornate bracelets.

"Hello, good sir," said the little boy, "would you like some beautiful jewelry today? Your wife would love some, no?"

"Well, well, what have we here?" mused Abram, who leaned forward to examine the goods. "And how much will you take for one of those bracelets you have there, my boy?"

"How much have you got, sir?" asked the boy with a toothy grin.

"I'm not sure," replied Abram, who then withdrew his moneybag and opened it to look inside. "Let me take a look."

Without warning, another boy, considerably older than the first, bolted from out of nowhere and snatched the bag from Abram's hand.

"Quick, get that little thief!" shouted Eliezer, who started to run after him, followed closely by several of Abram's other men. Darting through the crowd, the men had a difficult time maneuvering past the people in the way. As they ran after the youngster with Abram's moneybag, they knocked several people over, not to mention numerous carts filled with various fruits and vegetables. Suddenly the fleeing youth collided with an unsuspecting shopper and crashed to the ground, where Eliezer and the men finally caught up with him.

DRAGGING THE YOUNGSTER back to Abram, Eliezer returned his moneybag to him. Opening the bag to inspect its contents, Abram was satisfied. "Hmmm, everything seems to be here. No harm done. You may release the lad."

"But, sir," muttered Eliezer, "I'm sure there's a law against this sort of thing, isn't there?"

Overhearing the conversation, a Canaanite woman stepped forward and snapped, "He's right, you know! Our Law metes out a very fitting punishment for a thief like this!"

Several Canaanite men moved in and wrestled the youngster from Eliezer's grasp.

"We'll take over from here, sir," barked one of the men. "We know exactly how to handle this sort."

"No, please, I'm so sorry," cried the youth, who then turned to Abram. "My mother is very sick and needs medicine. We had no money left, good sir. Please don't let them do this to me."

"Oh, well, why didn't you say so in the first place," grumbled the Canaanite man. "You little fool; what do you take us for? Now hold out your hand. Your mother may not be getting the medicine she needs today, but we certainly have the kind that'll cure your ailment."

The men forcibly dragged the boy to the nearest countertop and stretched his arm out across it. Withdrawing his sword and raising it, the man turned to Abram and said, "Now, all that remains is for you, sir, to pass judgment on this street rat."

"Me?" gasped Abram.

"Yes, of course, you. You're the man who was injured at the hands of this crook, aren't you?"

"But I haven't been injured in any way, my good man. No money was lost in the exchange. I have no quarrel with the boy. If there's any judgment to be meted out, I'm sure the God of Heaven is perfectly capable of doing it."

The confused Canaanite man lowered his sword and walked over to Abram. "You actually want this little thief to go unpunished? Don't you realize you only have to say the word, and he'll receive a just penalty for his crime?"

"You mean, if I simply give my consent, you'll chop off this defenseless boy's hand, is that it?"

"Naturally, it is the Law," replied the man, confused as ever.

"But it's not my Law, sir."

"Then what do you propose I do with this pest?"

"I say let God judge him."

"God? Which god?"

"Why, the God of my fathers, Noah and Shem."

Eying Abram suspiciously, the man stepped even closer. "You're not from around here, are you, mister?"

"Certainly not."

Frustrated, the man turned to the others, who were still struggling to restrain the youth. "Very well, release him." Turning back to Abram, the man grunted, "But if this unsavory brat is ever caught stealing again, I'll hold you personally responsible. You hear me?"

"I understand completely, yes. Now, good day to you, sir. Thank you for your concern."

And just as quickly as they had appeared, the three Canaanite men disappeared into the crowd, leaving the youth just standing there, quite speechless. He stood there for the longest time, staring dumbfounded at

Abram, who began to get uncomfortable.

"Well, son, what have you got to say for yourself? Certainly you don't plan on standing there all day with your mouth hanging open, do you?"

"No, sir, it's just that…"

"It's just that *what*?"

"It's just that I'm so grateful you're such an understanding and compassionate man. If it wasn't for you, I'd have suffered terribly at the hands of those men. How can I ever thank you?"

"Don't thank me. Thank the God I serve. He's the One Who's so understanding and compassionate. I'm merely His servant."

The youngster slowly stepped up to Abram and humbly bowed. "Then, please, sir, would you be so kind as to tell me more about this God you serve?"

"I'd be glad to, my son. I don't think I caught your name?"

"My name, sir?"

"Yes, lad, your name. What do they call you?"

"Nicu. They call me Nicu."

"Very good, Nicu. Now, if you don't mind, I'd like to ask you for a favor."

"Anything. Just say the word."

"I need a place to accommodate a large number of people and herds. Do you know of such a place?"

"I do, sir. Follow me, if you please."

ABRAM AND HIS GROUP were soon setting up camp in the very heartland of Canaan. As evening began to fall around him, Abram stood alone on a nearby hillside, overseeing the operations of his tremendous entourage of people and animals, when suddenly the Word of God appeared next to him.

"Lord, hello," said Abram, somewhat startled, "it's good to see You again."

"Hello, Abram. I see you finally made it to Canaan. How do you like it here?"

"I like it very much. There seems to be more than enough room here to sustain the group You've so generously blessed me with."

"That's good, Abram, because this is the land I've given to you and your children."

"You're giving this place *to me*? Really?"

"That's right. Not only that, but in time I'll also make your descendants even more abundant than the herds and flocks you see before you. Someday, your descendants will be as numerous as the sand and the stars, and this land will be given to them as an inheritance forever."

Kneeling before the Word, Abram bowed his head to the ground. "Thank You, Lord. I'm truly grateful for all You've done for me and my family. We'll honor You all the days of our lives."

"You're welcome, Abram. And be sure to continue teaching everyone you meet to follow in the ways you've received from your fathers, Noah and Shem, and it will be well with them, too."

"You mean like the young man we encountered last week in the bazaar? If men like that are willing to receive Your Word, then even they'll be included in this promised inheritance?"

"Yes, Abram, even them." Again the Word vanished, leaving Abram staring out across the landscape where his people and animals wandered about in every direction.

ABRAM BUILT AN ALTAR of stone, then and there, sacrificing one animal of every kind from among his flocks and herds.

"Dear, God, I thank You for all Your blessings. From this day forward I will call on the name of the Lord, seeking You daily and endeavoring to teach everyone concerning Your marvelous ways. And in the years to come, they will all commemorate this moment in time, and they'll remember this place, this Bethel, this House of God, from generation to generation and throughout the ages to come."

ARRIVING AT ABRAM'S camp in Canaan, a messenger delivered a letter to the patriarch. Upon reading it, Abram became deeply disturbed. When Sarai saw the troubled look on his face, she hurried over to him. "What's wrong, husband?"

"I'm afraid that after living some nine hundred and fifty years on this Earth, the wise old man of our clan has died."

"Noah died?"

Abram nodded mournfully and began to weep. "Yes, my dear, my beloved teacher and father has gone to be with the Lord."

Touched by his lament, Sarai embraced him. "Oh, my love, don't cry. He lived a good, long life, and now he rests peacefully with our forefathers."

"Yes," whispered Abram. "And together they're all gazing upon the Face of God."

NIMROD WAS SITTING on his throne, as usual, entertaining another foreign dignitary. Abruptly interrupting their meeting, his messenger burst into the room.

"I'm sorry to disturb you, Your Highness, but we just received word you will definitely be interested in."

"This better be good. Out with it."

"Apparently, after paying Chedorlaomer, king of Elam, an annual tax for more than a decade, the Five Cities of the Plain, led by Sodom and Gomorrah, have begun a revolt against his rule."

Intrigued, Nimrod sat up on his throne. "A revolt? Against my old friend and adversary, Chedorlaomer?"

"It seems that way, My Lord."

"Well, well," muttered the king, half to himself. "I guess your plans of conquest are finally beginning to unravel, my old prince. How does it feel now that the shoe is on the other foot for a change?"

"What should I tell your princes, Great King? They await your command."

"Tell them the day of revenge is at hand. Tell them to assemble my troops at once and prepare their weapons of war, and when they're ready to march, tell me at once."

SOME SEVEN HUNDRED thousand armor-clad warriors congealed in the valley of Babel to form a massive sea that was Nimrod's army. They gathered there between Elam and Shinar, preparing to clash with Chedorlaomer, whose forces, stationed along the hilltops, were dwarfed in comparison to their opposition. One of Chedorlaomer's princes came to him with a concerned expression.

"Why the troubled look, Commander?" asked Chedorlaomer.

"My Lord, our estimate of Nimrod's army is nearly three quarters of a million men."

"And your point is?"

"Sire, our present force stands at a mere five thousand warriors. We're outnumbered a hundred and forty to one. Far too many of our troops are tied up at the moment trying to suppress the revolt of the Five Plain Cities."

"I see, and what would you advise at this time?"

"My advice would be to wait until we can recall some of our troops. Bring them up from the south to support our exposed flank. We'd stand a much better chance with their numbers added to ours."

"Your point is well taken, Commander, but right now we hold the high ground, while Nimrod's men lie below us in the valley. If we wait for reinforcements, we run the risk of losing our present strategic advantage. Not only that, but should we allow them the opportunity to strike first, it could prove to be even more suicidal than attacking them with our inferior numbers. You certainly see my dilemma."

"Yes, My Lord, I do. But the look in your eye also tells me you have another strategic advantage you haven't mentioned yet."

"Very perceptive, Commander. I commend you on your astuteness." There was a subtle gesture from Chedorlaomer, and a shadowy figure slowly emerged from his group of warriors. "Gentlemen," exclaimed the prince to his men, "meet our tactical advantage. His name is Anuki; and he's come to us straight from the court of King Amraphel himself. Here to bring us news of our foreordained victory, news of the once invincible king's defeat, news that has actually been written in the stars for the entire world to see."

ARMED WITH THIS DIVINE foreknowledge, Chedorlaomer and his warriors hurled themselves with reckless abandon upon Nimrod's troops down in the valley of Babel. Arrows flew, swords clashed, and bodies collided, as a great mass of howling warriors swirled in a blood-curdling dance of death. The fighting lasted all day. By nightfall, Nimrod's army was struck down by the sheer audacity of the attack, with nearly six hundred thousand of his men having fallen in battle. Among them was Mardon, the king's own son, who was killed in a hailstorm of arrows.

WHEN NIMROD CAME upon his son's corpse, bloody and arrow-riddled, he was devastated. "No, no, no; not my son," he moaned, dropping to his knees and weeping over his lifeless body. "My god, my god, why have you forsaken me? How could you let this happen to me? To me, the mighty hunter before the Lord?"

Several arrows abruptly swished past, barely missing the king, and Nimrod's soldiers quickly swooped in and grabbed him by both arms, wrenching him away from his son's body. "Your Highness, you have to leave this place," insisted one of the soldiers, "or else you'll be lost as well. Please, Sire, you must live to fight another day."

Reluctantly, Nimrod relented. As they led him away, he glared at the men who were escorting him. "To live another day, you say? Tell me, you misbegotten mongrels, tell me: What have I done to deserve such a miserable fate as that?"

SITTING AT THE CENTER OF a large gathering of people who all eagerly nodded at his every word, Abram said, "So you see, the Lord of Heaven and Earth is not just the God of a single people, He's also the God of everyone who will trust Him, of everyone who will follow His ways. Thank the Lord for His loving-kindness and mercy to a thousand generations. Amen."

And all the people there echoed Abram, saying with one voice, "Amen."

"Now," continued Abram, "unless there are any more questions, that will be all for today."

Everyone rose and slowly dispersed, when a young man stepped up to Abram. "Excuse me, sir, but there is one more thing, if you don't mind."

Looking up at the man, Abram smiled. "My dear Nicu, just look at you. I still can't believe it's been twenty years since we met you in the dusty, unfamiliar streets of Canaan."

"Yes, sir, I still can't believe it myself."

"What can I do for you, son? You have a question?"

"Not so much a question as a request."

"Out with it, then," said Abram with an impish grin. "Neither one of us is getting any younger, you know. And just seeing how old you're getting to be is beginning to make *me* feel old."

"Old?" said Nicu. "You're not that old, are you, Master Abram?"

Another voice suddenly intruded into their conversation. "Not if you call a man of seventy-five old, no; he's not old at all. He still has a lifetime of adventures ahead of him."

Turning to see who was speaking, Abram and Nicu saw a man standing next to them.

Abram's face lit up with excitement. "Lot! Is that really you?"

"Of course it's me, Uncle Abram."

"What on Earth are you doing here like this, so unexpectedly?"

"I'm sorry I didn't warn you in advance, Uncle, but I didn't want to spoil the surprise."

"Of course, Lot, I understand. Is this just a visit, or have you decided to come stay with us for good?"

"I'm not sure. Do you want me to stay?"

"Certainly, my boy; nothing would make Sarai happier. And you know that whatever makes her happy, makes me happy, too."

"Fine. Then it's settled. I'll stay."

Turning to Nicu, Abram exclaimed, "Quickly, my boy, can you do me a favor?"

"Anything, sir."

"Tell me what your request was."

Confused, Nicu tilted his head. "Sir?"

"Before Lot showed up just now, you wanted to ask me something. What was it?"

"Oh, right, I almost forgot. It was just that I was hoping to be more than just a student of your teaching. I was hoping you might find me a place of employment, working for you and your family, that is; even if it means being a servant."

"Consider it done, young man; you're hired. Now, for your first assignment: I want you to find my wife and tell her we have a very special guest. Can you do that for me?"

"Yes, sir, thank you. Of course I can do that."

"Good, then run as fast as you can, Nicu, and tell her the good news. Tell her to prepare a feast today because her dear brother Lot has come home to stay with us for good."

THE WINE FLOWED and the food was served that evening, as everyone celebrated with Abram and Sarai at the homecoming of Lot and his wife. Music played and dancers danced, and the night air was filled with the sweet smell of roasted meat and herbs.

"Oh, Ado, my beloved sister-in-law," said Sarai with a serene happiness. "You've never looked more beautiful. How do you do it?"

Coyly, Ado smiled back. "Ah, Sarai, you can't fool me. You're just saying that because I brought your brother back to you in one piece."

Sharing a hearty laugh, the two women clinked their cups together, spilling some of their wine as they did.

From Feast to Famine

BUT SADLY, THE FESTIVE mood of this joyous homecoming soon turned to mourning as the land of Canaan was, within a matter of months, seized by famine. In the spring, the air had been filled with the scent of succulent meat roasting in the fire pit, but by summer it was filled with the stench of rotting animal carcasses strewn about the landscape, hapless victims of drought and disease.

"Oh, Abram," groaned Sarai, "just look at how quickly our happiness has turned into misery. Everywhere we look death stares us in the face. Once, this land was flowing with milk and honey, but now it's a place oppressed by hunger and thirst."

As Abram and his family watched helplessly, droves of people were on the march, trudging past them in makeshift carts, filled with their meager belongings.

"Where are they all going, Master Abram?" asked Nicu.

"From what I understand most everyone is headed for Egypt. Word has it the land to the south has, so far, remained untouched by famine."

"Then what are we waiting for, Uncle Abram?" said Lot. "Let's pack our things and get down there as fast as we can, before we lose any more of our herds."

Abram hung his head in defeat. "As much as I hate to leave the place God has chosen for us, it seems we have no choice. Send out the word. We leave for Egypt right away."

ABRAM AND HIS BAND of several hundred men, women, children and animals were once again on the move, heading south for greener pastures.

FATIGUED FROM THE journey, the group paused at the Mizraim River, where they watered their herds and rested awhile. As Abram and Sarai strolled along the river's edge, the weary husband turned to his wife. Noticing his intense gaze, she asked, "Abram, why are you looking at me like that?"

"Tell me: When was the last time I told you how beautiful you are?"

Tilting her head and wrinkling her brow, she replied with a suspicious tone, "Husband, what is going through that mind of yours?"

"Nothing, really. It's just I'm concerned about our journey to Egypt."

"Concerned about what?"

"I'm afraid God made you so beautiful the Egyptians might kill me and steal you for themselves."

"Oh, please."

"No, I'm serious. You know very well the fear of our God doesn't exist there."

"So what do you plan on doing about it?"

"Well, I think the best thing for us would be if anyone asks about you, then we should tell them you're my sister. What do you think about that?"

"You think lying to people about my being your wife will keep them from killing you and abducting me? Is that what I'm hearing?"

"It's not that far-fetched, if you think about it. After all, you are my brother's daughter. You have to admit there is a family resemblance."

"Oh, Abram, I don't know."

"I'm telling you, it'll work, as long as we all stick to the same story."

"But it seems so underhanded. It just doesn't sound like something I'd be comfortable with, living a lie like that."

"You have a better idea?"

Sarai stared at Abram for several intense moments. "And since when did you start lying to get what you want? This doesn't sound at all like the man I married."

"Sarai, please, don't be so naïve. Even a man like me will do almost anything when it comes to protecting the ones he loves."

"I don't understand. I've never known you to tell a lie before. But now you're telling me you *do* lie if it suits you?"

"That's not what I said, Sarai," replied Abram, getting frustrated. "I was referring to the fact that I was willing to abandon our home in Canaan to ensure the survival of my loved ones, even if it meant leaving the very place God had given us."

Sarai started to raise her hand in protest but thought better of it.

ABRAM ADDRESSED HIS gathered group. "So, do we have an understanding amongst ourselves? If the Egyptians ask you about Sarai, what are you supposed to tell them?"

Timidly, Nicu raised his hand.

"Yes, Nicu, go ahead."

"We tell them that Mistress Sarai is your sister."

"Good, very good."

THIS GROUP OF WAYWARD travelers eventually began their final approach to the Egyptian border, but still Abram seemed deeply troubled.

Noticing the worried look on his face, Sarai asked, "What is it now, husband?"

"I'm sorry, my dear, but I just have a bad feeling about this. I can't seem to shake it. Something is going to happen. I can feel it in my bones."

"But, Uncle, what more can we do?" wondered Lot.

A strange look flashed across Abram's face. "Stop the caravan. I have an idea." Turning to Lot, he said, "I want you to find the largest trunk we have, empty it of all its contents, and bring it to me as fast as you can."

"But why, Uncle?"

"Don't argue with me, Lot. Just do it. Hurry!"

Sarai glared suspiciously at her husband. "Abram, what are you up to this time?"

BRINGING THE TRUNK to Abram, Lot opened it, revealing that it was empty.

"Now, Sarai, I need you to do me a favor."

Staring back in disbelief, she stammered, "I'm not getting in that thing, if that's what you're suggesting."

"But I need you to do this, sweetheart, please."

"Don't *sweetheart* me. I'm not doing it. I'll suffocate in there."

"But it's only until we make it through the gate. Once we're past the guards we'll have you out in no time."

Sarai adamantly shook her head. "No, Abram, no. You can't make me do it. I might die in there. I won't."

ARRIVING AT THE border, Abram and his entourage were halted by the king's chief officer.

"Give a tenth of what you own to the Pharaoh of this land," said the chief officer. "And then you may enter our country."

Abram and everyone with him were more than happy to comply, and once they did they all entered with their cargo and herds, but once inside the king's chief officer noticed how Abram and Lot were paying a great deal of attention to another chest they were transporting. Suspicious of their behavior, he approached them.

"Hey there, you two!" he shouted. "What are you doing with that chest?"

"Who, us?" Abram surreptitiously asked, trying his best to remain calm.

"Yes, you. I don't remember inspecting this chest when you came in. What's in it? I demand you open it immediately and give a tenth of everything inside to the Pharaoh."

Abram and Lot exchanged a nervous look.

"But, sir, I *can't* open this one," sputtered Abram. "I'll pay you whatever you want to insure its safe passage. Please, just name your price."

"Aha! There is something suspicious about this chest. It's full of precious jewels, am I right? Then give us a tenth of them, or else you'll have to turn around and leave at once!"

"Please, I'm begging you. I'll give you anything you want, but don't open this chest."

"Enough!" the king's officer snapped, motioning to two of his deputies, who then came and pushed Abram aside. Stepping to the chest, the deputies hesitated, looking at one another, as if unsure of what to do next.

"Don't just stand there, you fools. Open it!"

"Please, gentlemen," blurted Abram. "This chest contains very precious cargo. Whatever you do, be careful!"

Forcing the chest open, the deputies peered inside and then looked at one another quite perplexed.

"Well, what's inside?" demanded the king's officer.

"It's a body," muttered one of the deputies.

"Of a pretty lady," added the other.

"A woman's body?" exclaimed the dumbfounded officer, who then turned to Abram. "What kind of nasty business are you up to, sir? Why are you trying to smuggle a body into the country of the great Pharaoh?"

Horrified, Abram and Lot bolted to the chest, and to their utter dismay, they found Sarai was unconscious.

"Sarai, no!" Abram shouted. "Quick, Lot, get her out of there!"

Abram and Lot hoisted her from the chest and gently laid her on the ground.

"Sarai, dear Sarai," moaned Abram. "Please, wake up." He began to shake her in an attempt to revive her. "Somebody, get some water!"

Someone then handed Abram a cup of water, and he splashed it over her face. Instantly, Sarai gasped and opened her eyes. Wiping her face, she looked around, baffled at the sight of everyone hovering about her, gawking in anticipation. Then, turning to Abram, she grumbled with an angry scowl, "I'm going to get you for this."

THE KING'S CHIEF officer soon came and dutifully bowed before Pharaoh.

"I was told," began the king, "you're here to report an unusual border incident that occurred yesterday. Is that right?"

"Yes, My Pharaoh, I am. While attending my duties as chief inspector of the main gate, I encountered a visitor from Canaan, a man who came here seeking refuge from the famine that's raging in that land."

"I'm well aware of the famine, yes. What about this visitor?"

"Well, among his cargo was a chest we considered suspicious in nature, so we searched it, much to the chagrin of this fellow and his family."

"I see. And what was in the chest?"

"At first we thought he was smuggling a body in it."

"A what?"

"A body, a woman's body. And the strangest thing about it was that even in death this woman seemed to be the most beautiful woman my men had ever laid eyes on."

"Well, what can one expect from such laggards?"

"But, My King, with all due respect, I saw her myself. The men, I can assure you, are not exaggerating in the least. She really is that beautiful."

"This dead woman, you say?"

"But that's just it. She wasn't dead after all. She'd merely fainted while having been concealed in this man's treasure chest."

"What on Earth was she doing in a chest?"

The king's officer shrugged his shoulders. "No one knows for sure, but I have to assume the strangers were concerned for her safety."

"I've never heard of such a thing before. This woman must be truly exceptional for a man to go to such lengths to hide her away like that. I'd like to meet her. See to it that she's brought to me at once."

AND WHEN SARAI MADE her appearance before him, Pharaoh was so smitten by her beauty that it nearly took his breath away.

"Well, well, my dear lady," said the king, "it's been brought to my attention that you endured a most unfortunate incident while entering my fair city."

"I did, My Pharaoh," replied Sarai, who curtsied politely.

"But I trust you've made a full recovery?"

"I have, thank you."

"Good. I'm glad to hear it. Why were you in that infernal chest in the first place?"

With an embarrassed smile, Sarai murmured, "My family was worried about my safety. They meant no harm."

"Your safety? What were they trying to keep you safe from? Certainly there were no bandits lurking about the gate to my country, were there?"

"No, My Pharaoh, I'm afraid it was just a big misunderstanding. Sometimes my family can be a little overprotective."

"Naturally. A woman of your exceptionally rare beauty should be protected by any means possible."

"Why, thank you, My Lord. I don't know what to say."

"Say you'll do me the honor of accompanying me for dinner this evening."

Nervously, Sarai bowed. "Of course, My Pharaoh, how could I possibly refuse such a charming invitation?"

ABRAM HAD A VISITOR before too long. It was Nicu, and he had a rather grim look on his face.

"What's wrong, son?" asked Abram. "Where's Sarai? Didn't she return with you?"

"I'm sorry, sir, but Mistress Sarai will be detained a little longer than expected."

"What's that supposed to mean?"

"Pharaoh has invited her to stay for dinner, and unfortunately—"

"Don't tell me she accepted."

"But what choice did she have, sir? After all, he is Pharaoh."

"All right, all right, let's try not to panic. I mean, what harm could there be in her having a little dinner with the king, right?"

SITTING IN PHARAOH'S private chamber, a deeply troubled Sarai lifted her eyes toward Heaven. "Dear God, you told Abram to go to Canaan, so we did. We left our home and our family, and went to a strange place. Then, because of the terrible famine, we had to come here. And now this happens! Please, Lord, save us from this predicament."

Just then, Pharaoh entered the room. Turning to see him walking toward her, Sarai was stunned to see an angel hovering a few feet behind him, though unnoticed by the king.

"Don't be afraid, Sarai," said the angel. "The Lord has heard your prayer." With that, he vanished from view.

Making his way across the room, Pharaoh sat down next to Sarai. "Hello, my dear," he said. "I hope you enjoyed your dinner."

But Sarai was still too upset to respond, so she simply nodded politely.

Undaunted, the king pressed on. "Please, Sarai, don't be upset. You've done nothing wrong. In fact, quite the opposite is true. I find everything about you to be quite remarkable." The Pharaoh gazed longingly at Sarai, waiting for some response from her. Again she could only think to politely nod. The frustrated king sat back, thinking for a moment. "Very well, then. Tell me this, if you would. About the man who brought you here to Egypt: What is he to you? Is he your husband, your fiancé, perhaps?"

Staring at the spot where the angel had appeared, Sarai was hoping to catch another glimpse of him. "What?" she muttered and then turned to Pharaoh. "Oh, no, of course not. Abram's my brother."

"Wonderful. I'm so happy to hear it. Then of course it's my responsibility to do everything I can to make him important in my country. I'll make him a dignitary; give him whatever else you can think of."

QUITE MISERABLE IN his tent, Abram stared off into space, when suddenly there was a tapping at his door. "Hello, Abram," said a man's voice. "I know you're in there. Would you please come outside? I need to speak to you about a very important matter."

With a tremendous sense of dread, Abram slowly stepped outside. To his chagrin, he was greeted by none other than the same chief officer of Pharaoh who had ordered the opening of the chest containing his wife.

Abram was obviously dismayed at his appearance. "You again? Haven't you caused me enough trouble already? What do you want now?"

"Oh, my dear sir," replied the officer, smiling as though he were addressing an old friend. "I am so sorry if we got off on the wrong foot the other day, but you must understand I was only following orders."

"Yes, yes, how commendable. Just tell me why you're here. No, let me guess. You found more of my belongings, and now I have to pay your king a tenth of them. Is that it?"

Amused with Abram, the officer burst out laughing. "Oh, that is a good one, my friend. You are a funny, funny man, I think. No, no, that is not why I am here."

"Then tell me, before I go back inside. I also have important business to tend to, if you don't mind… Truth is: I'm not feeling very well right now."

"Of course, my friend, then maybe this might help you feel a little better." The Pharaoh's officer then stepped back and clapped his hands. "Look and see your great reward from His Majesty, the Pharaoh!"

A swarm of Pharaoh's servants jumped into action, delivering several baskets of gold, silver and jewels at the feet of Abram. Looking around in amazement, he saw a dozen more of the king's servants step forward, each of them leading a head of cattle behind them. Overwhelmed by what he saw, Abram muttered, "What is all this?"

"Why, of course, this is a royal gift for you, sir. These are your riches, your cattle, your servants, all compliments of the Pharaoh himself."

"But why? What have I done to deserve all this?"

"Because you have brought great happiness to the one and only Pharaoh of this mighty land, by presenting him with your beloved sister Sarai as his new bride!"

Abram's knees buckled, and he very nearly collapsed. "Oh, God, no," he mumbled under his breath. "Now it's time to panic."

A DISCONSOLATE Abram made a token appearance before Pharaoh, as he was regaled in a lavish prenuptial celebration, presented in honor of the brother of the king's bride-to-be. With Sarai at his right hand, Pharaoh proudly nodded at Abram, who tried his best to keep a straight face, even while his wife never looked lovelier sitting there in her Egyptian betrothal gown. Naturally, it was all that Abram and Sarai could do to keep from having a nervous breakdown during the otherwise boisterous festivities, considering how torn their hearts were at that moment.

PHARAOH WENT TO Sarai's room the next day and found her sitting on the bed. He casually walked over and sat down next to her. Reaching out to caress her cheek, he received quite a shock when an invisible force slapped his hand away. Confused, he jumped to his feet and took a step back.

After a while, the king took a cautious step forward and again reached out to touch her cheek. Again the unseen power knocked his hand away. Pharaoh stood there, flabbergasted, trying to comprehend what was happening.

Screams suddenly began to echo throughout the palace. Bewildered, the king sat back down next to Sarai. For several disturbing moments, he listened to the sounds of terror resounding in the background, but eventually he found that he could no longer resist. Once again he reached out to touch her face. This time the invisible force violently shoved him off the bed, sending him crashing to the floor.

"That does it!" blurted Pharaoh. Jumping to his feet, he dusted himself off and headed for the door. "I don't know what's going on around here, beautiful lady, but I have a strange feeling it has something to do with you!"

RETURNING TO HER ROOM later that evening, even as intermittent screams could still be heard echoing throughout the palace, the king spoke to her as pleasantly as he could. "Sarai dear, please, can you tell me anything else I might need to know about this man Abram? Is he some kind of sorcerer?"

"Who, *him*?" replied Sarai, quite sheepishly. "A sorcerer? Certainly not, My Pharaoh. My husband is no sorcerer, I can assure you."

"Your husband? Did you say your *husband*?"

Sarai reluctantly nodded. "Yes, I did."

"Then why on Earth did you tell me he was your brother?"

"I only told you that because we were afraid someone might kill him to get to me. I did try to warn you my family was overprotective when I first met you, remember?"

Perplexed and dismayed, the king turned and left her room, and when he did the haunting shrieks began to subside throughout the palace. As the cries slowly died down around him, a peculiar look washed across his face. "I knew it," he mumbled as he scratched his furrowed brow. "But how is this possible?"

ABRAM STOOD CONTRITELY before Pharaoh. Glaring at him for several intense moments, the king finally broke the uneasy silence. "Well, well, if it isn't the deceiver, here to tell me another amusing story at the expense of me and my people."

"Please, sir, I can understand why you'd be furious with me, but believe me, I never intended for anyone to get hurt."

"Tell me, then. What could you have possibly thought to gain by telling me Sarai was your sister? I want to hear it from your own lips."

"I did it because I thought it would help me live longer."

"You may think you're an amusing fellow, but I do not. You knew very well I was taking steps to take her as my wife, yet you did nothing to prevent me from making a complete fool of myself, not to mention endangering the lives of everyone in my palace."

"And for that I am truly sorry," Abram solemnly replied.

"Never mind that now," grumbled Pharaoh as he motioned to his servants, who brought Sarai out and led her to Abram's side. "Here's your wife back. Take her and leave my country before someone dies."

Again Pharaoh motioned to his servants. This time they brought out several more baskets filled with gold, silver and jewels, and presented them to Abram.

"Here, take this with you as well. Call it an expression of my gratitude for leaving my country still in one piece."

Abram bowed perfunctorily. "Certainly you're a most gracious king."

Pharaoh, however, was clearly unimpressed. "Yes, yes, of course. Don't mention it."

After another gesture from the king, a servant girl walked over to Abram and Sarai, and bowed dutifully before them.

"My dear, Hagar," Pharaoh said, addressing the girl, "I believe it would be better for you to be a slave to this man and his wife than to stay with me as a mere concubine. Please, go with them and be blessed by the power of this man. I have no idea how he's accomplished the things he's done in our land, but I do hope that somehow you may live your life as a recipient of his miraculous gift."

"Thank you, My Pharaoh," replied Hagar, who curtsied toward Pharaoh and then turned to Sarai and curtsied to her. "Ma'am, it seems I'm now in your service."

"So, I bid you all a fond farewell," said Pharaoh with a sardonic smirk, "and just to show you there are no hard feelings between us, I'll have my guards escort your entire group to the border. That way no one will bother you in any way, which means Abram will have no further need of securing his poor wife in a chest while traveling through our fair country."

A Parting of the Ways

RETURNING TO CANAAN, the first thing that Abram and his group saw was a dried-up water hole, littered with the bones of several dead animals, a stark reminder of the famine which had had such a devastating effect on the territory prior to their departure no less than a month earlier.

Undaunted, the group eventually arrived back at Bethel, going to the very spot where Abram had built his first altar. There, he and his entourage set up camp.

Laying a burnt offering on the altar, in the sight of all his people, Abram lifted his voice to Heaven. "Dear God, we've returned to the land You've promised to me and everyone who follows me in Your ways of truth and righteousness. We now humbly ask You, Lord, please restore this land of plenty to what it once was and heal it from this horrible famine before there's no one left among us to serve You and Your holy name. Amen."

And the people echoed his salutation together with one voice, saying, "Amen."

IN DUE TIME, THE famine loosened its grip upon their country, and eventually Abram and Lot had nurtured their surviving heads of cattle, sheep and goats back to their previous numbers. The two of them bred so many animals, in fact, that they began to have a difficult time coexisting. Now there were too many animals and people, and simply not enough land to go around.

WHEN ABRAM'S shepherds took their flocks out to feed in the fields, they never allowed them to cross over into their neighbor's land to graze, but Lot's men never bothered to do the same, allowing their flocks to graze in other people's fields all the time.

"Hey there, you!" cried one of the neighboring Canaanite shepherds.

"Who, me?" Lot replied, sounding so innocent.

"Yes, you. Why are you letting your herds graze on my property? You're supposed to stay in your own territory."

"All right, already. Don't get yourself in an uproar. How am I supposed to control where my herds graze? They're just animals, you know. They have a mind of their own. Don't blame me."

AT THEIR WITS' END, the Canaanites went to Abram to plead their case.

"Abram, Abram," began one of the Canaanite shepherds, "what are you going to do about your nephew's herds? They're allowed to graze on our property without any concern for the consequences. This can't go on much longer. Please speak to your nephew, won't you?"

"Of course, my friend," replied Abram. "I'll take care of it right away. I promise it won't happen again."

A FRUSTRATED ABRAM then confronted his nephew, who was busy tending to his herd. "Lot, my boy, what are you trying to do? Our neighbors are furious with me."

"What's wrong, Uncle?" groaned Lot, annoyed at the interruption.

"You know perfectly well what's wrong. Your shepherds keep allowing your flocks to feed in my neighbor's fields."

"But how do you expect me to keep track of where my flocks decide to graze?"

Unconvinced, Abram shook his head. "No, no, no; that's no excuse. What you're doing is wrong, and you know it. We should be trying to live in harmony with these people, not stealing from them. Have you forgotten? We're still technically strangers among the Canaanites."

"Then maybe you should start worrying more about your own family instead of a bunch of strangers." With that, Lot turned and walked away.

"Oh, Lot, my dear boy," murmured Abram, truly disappointed. "Why are you doing this?"

BUT NO SOONER HAD Abram stated his case than Lot's shepherds were up to their old tricks again, allowing their herds to roam freely, grazing wherever they wandered, much to the chagrin of Abram's Canaanite neighbors.

THOROUGHLY EXASPERATED, Abram again confronted his nephew. "Lot, how long are you and your men going to be a nuisance to my neighbors? I'm begging you."

"But I already told you, Uncle. My herds are hungry, and my family has to do whatever it takes to survive. I'm sorry you don't see things my way, really I am."

"Look, this is getting tedious. Let's not argue about this anymore. We're family."

"Then maybe you should quit sticking your nose in my affairs, Uncle."

Stung by his nephew's rebuff, Abram bluntly replied, "Fine. If that's the way you want it, then maybe it's time we parted company."

"Fine," said Lot without a shred of remorse.

"Then I suggest you find another place where you and your people can live with your herds."

"Fine."

"But just make sure your group keeps its distance from ours. Is that clear?"

For just a moment, Lot's resolve wavered. "So now you're going to disown us, is that it? What happens if everyone else attacks us once they've seen we've had a parting of the ways?"

Abram resolutely shook his head. "I'm sorry, Lot, but you chose this course of action for yourself, and you'll have to face the consequences of that choice. Now, are you, or are you not, prepared to leave on your own terms?"

Several more tense moments passed as Lot thought hard about his uncle's proposition, then came his terse reply. "Fine."

"Good, then I want you to get your things and move out as soon as possible." Abram felt a sudden twinge of remorse as he looked upon his beloved Sarai's brother. "And, no, I'm not going to abandon you completely. If anyone attacks you, just let me know, and I'll gladly avenge your cause."

But Lot was barely listening by then. He was already gazing longingly out across the well-watered plain of Jordan. Without the slightest response to his uncle's offer, Lot just walked away, and Abram sadly watched him leave.

LOT QUICKLY GATHERED his family, his herds and everything he owned.

"But, Lot, where will you go?" asked a heartbroken Sarai as she embraced him, her eyes filling with tears. "When will I see you again?" Turning to Abram, she said with a lamentable sigh, "Oh, Abram, don't make him leave, please. Why are you doing this?"

"I'm sorry, my dear," said Abram, shrugging his shoulders. "I tried to resolve this situation in a reasonable manner, but—"

"Please, Sarai, don't cry," interjected Lot. "We're not going that far. Before you know it we'll all be together again. As soon as we get settled we'll send word. Then you can come visit us, all right?"

Drying the tears from her eyes, Sarai nodded with a sad, little smile.

BEFORE LONG, LOT AND his group, which now included Nicu, were all on the move in their trek for new frontiers.

As they traveled along, Lot said to Nicu, "I'd like to thank you for joining us, Nicu. I know it wasn't easy for you to part ways with Master Abram."

"No, sir, it definitely was not. I love him very much. If it wasn't for him, I wouldn't be the man I am today."

"Do you mind my asking why you did it, then?"

"I did it because Mistress Sarai personally asked me to do it."

"Really? Did she give you her reasons?"

"She asked me to go along with you as a special favor to her, because she hoped I might serve you as faithfully as I've served the both of them."

"And will you?"

"As much as it is in my power, yes; I pledge myself to you and your wife as if it were to Master Abram and Mistress Sarai. Does that answer your question?"

Without another word, Lot nodded, obviously humbled by the man's fierce loyalty.

ALONG WITH ALL THEIR cattle, sheep and goats, Lot and his entourage of about a hundred and fifty people traveled across the plain of Jordan, where they eventually came to a lushly vegetated, well-watered expanse. Surveying the land, far and wide, Lot said with great satisfaction, "Well, everyone, I think this might be just the place for us." Noticing a traveler wandering by, Lot called out, "You, my friend, can you tell us where we are? You there, do you hear me?"

Finally realizing that he was being spoken to, the man turned and suspiciously eyed Lot's group. "Yes, sir. I hear you just fine. Why do you ask?"

"Because I and my group are adventurers, seeking new lands, new pastures for our herds and flocks."

"I see. Then I'd advise you to keep on traveling. Strangers aren't welcome in these parts. Best you just keep moving along, if you know what's good for you."

Lot and his wife exchanged a peculiar look.

"But I don't understand," replied Lot. "Certainly the people here wouldn't turn away a man like me, would they?"

"You? What makes you so special?"

"Just look at the tremendous herds and flocks at my disposal. Don't the people here require such things to live? If we chose to live here, we wouldn't be a burden at all. On the contrary, we'd be a blessing and a boon."

Considering his words for a moment, the man reluctantly nodded. "I suppose so."

"Good, then it's settled."

"Suit yourself," said the man as he turned to go. "But don't say I didn't warn you."

"Wait, sir."

"What is it now?" he grumbled impatiently, looking back and squinting into the Sun.

"You still haven't told us the name of this place."

"Sodom," the man grunted and turned to leave. "This place is called Sodom."

Turning to his wife, Lot declared, "Welcome to your new home, my dear Ado. Welcome to Sodom."

How the Mighty Have Fallen

MEANWHILE, CHEDORLAOMER, king of Elam, was sitting on his gilded throne, sulking with his dark, brooding eyes. Standing at attention before him were three men, all dressed in royal attire: Tidal, king of Goyim, Arioch, king of Elasar, and Nimrod, king of Shinar.

"Good afternoon, gentlemen," began Chedorlaomer. "I trust you've all been well."

"We have, Your Majesty," Tidal replied with a slight bow of the head.

"Naturally, you're all wondering why I've summoned you here today."

"We've heard rumblings, Sire," remarked Arioch with a respectful nod. "Rumblings of another rebellion."

"Really? What have you heard?"

"Word has it that after more than twelve years of paying you tribute," Nimrod replied, "Sodom and Gomorrah are planning another revolt against your rule."

"And what about you, Nimrod?" asked Chedorlaomer. "Are you eager to join them again in their revolt against me? Do you still thirst for revenge for my rebellious actions so long ago?"

"I think not, Your Majesty. Since the death of my son Mardon, I've lost much of my former zeal for battle. I'm now quite content to serve my people of Shinar on your behalf."

"How touching, how noble, how wise. You've spoken well, King Amraphel, even if it has taken disaster upon disaster to bring you to such a conclusion. Then you'll join my cause as an ally this time. Is that what you're telling me?"

Nimrod nodded dutifully. "I will, My King. I, and all my warriors, are at your disposal."

"And what about you Tidal?"

"The same goes for me and my warriors, Your Majesty."

"Arioch?"

"Of course, Sire. My men and I are always at your service. Just say the word."

"Very good," said Chedorlaomer, raising his clenched fist. "Then together we'll crush this revolt, once and for all!"

SO ALL FOUR KINGS, Chedorlaomer, Tidal, Arioch and Nimrod, led a tremendous wave of their warriors, about eight hundred thousand strong, plundering everything they could get their hands on, and as this great swarm of soldiers marched, they left a wake of sheer terror in their path, killing every man they found along the way.

AT THE SAME TIME, the two kings of Sodom and Gomorrah were conferring in their royal tent, overlooking the Valley of Siddim, when a royal messenger arrived.

"Excuse me, King Bera, King Bersha," said the messenger, bowing graciously, "we've received word that Chedorlaomer and his combined forces are proceeding toward the Siddim Valley to oppose us with more than three quarters of a million men under their command."

The two kings exchanged a serious look.

"Thank you, messenger," replied Bera, "then prepare to send word to our commanders in the field to prepare our armies for the impending invasion." Turning to his fellow king, he then said, "Bersha, tell me: You're sure the kings of the other Cities of the Plain are resolved to join us in battle."

"They are, Bera. Rest assured, my friend: We five stand as one. Shinab, Shemeber and Bela have all declared their absolute allegiance with us in this matter."

"Good. For all our sakes, I hope they are, or else we're doomed for sure."

"Don't worry about them," said Bersha. "They've all assured me they feel it's far better to fight and die in battle than to continue serving the infidel Chedorlaomer as mere slaves."

ALONG WITH THEIR overflowing armies, those nine kings came together in a resounding clash of men and arms in the Valley of Siddim. Arrows flung in every direction, striking targets with deadly effect; swords savagely swung left and right, hacking off innumerable appendages. After a fearsome, bloody battle, a tremendous loss of life was suffered on both sides, but in the end, the warriors of the Five Plain Cities, outnumbered and outmaneuvered, proved to be no match for Chedorlaomer and his combined forces, and eventually they were struck down, having been reduced to row after row of bloody carcasses.

FOR GOOD MEASURE, the warriors of Chedorlaomer pursued the kings of the Plain Cities, who sought refuge in the lime pits that were so common along the borders of Siddim Valley. What survivors there were ran every which way, fleeing into the mountains for safety. Still, the war-weary Elamite forces refused to relent, pursuing their quarry to the very gates of Sodom. They seized everything and everyone, even capturing Lot and Nicu, who both became prisoners of war, along with thousands of their fellow countrymen.

INTOXICATED BY THEIR victory, as well as the copious amounts of wine they had seized in battle, the Elamite troops drank themselves into a complete stupor that night, eager to celebrate their achievement. Fortunately, Nicu found himself working as a wine steward that evening, having been commandeered by one of Tidal's field commanders. One by one, the soldiers drank themselves to sleep, and eventually Nicu saw his opportunity for escape.

TRAVELING ALL NIGHT and well into the next day, Nicu made his way to the home of Abram and Sarai. Confused by his unexpected arrival, the couple anxiously greeted him. As Nicu proceeded to tell them what had happened to Sodom and how Chedorlaomer's forces had captured Lot in the process, Sarai fainted dead away at Abram's feet.

ABRAM IMMEDIATELY marshaled his forces, gathering around three hundred fighting men from his group. "Now, everyone," Abram began, "I realize that what I'm asking of you might seem like an impossible task. We're greatly outnumbered, in fact. But there is still one thing even more important than this, and that is the Lord of the Universe is on our side today, because the same God Who protected me in the furnace of Nimrod, spoke to me personally and, in no uncertain terms, promised me He'd vanquish all my enemies. So, I stand here this fateful, dreadful moment and I say to all of you who, with me, trust in the God of Heaven and Earth: Trust now in His awesome power, and go forth today as His warriors in a righteous cause, and He will lead us to certain victory!"

Amidst a tremendous hurrah from his men, Abram set out after those Elamite kings and the remnant of their armies.

JUST BEFORE DAWN, Abram gave the signal to attack, and in a tremendous display of selfless courage, his men struck swiftly and violently, slinging arrows and swinging swords with deadly accuracy. From the start, the Elamites, hung over and bleary-eyed from their night of revelry, were thrown back on their heels by the sheer audacity of Abram's men. Not only that, but they were also joined by thousands of Sodomite prisoners of war, who were just waiting for a chance to avenge their shameful loss. In fact, the disoriented Elamite troops were in such disarray that they even killed many of their own fellow warriors in the panic and confusion.

THE COMBINED FORCES of Abram's men and the freed Sodomite prisoners soon cut down every last Elamite soldier. The only survivors were their four kings, Chedorlaomer, Tidal, Arioch and Nimrod who all fled like cowards. As the vanquished kings were running for their lives, Nimrod found himself in a strangely familiar situation. Suddenly he began to remember the dream he had had, many years earlier, warning him of this very day when Abram would cause his downfall. Haunting images of that horrific dream began to flood his mind, images of the mysterious egg that had cracked open and released a hawk. Nimrod blanched at the sight of that screeching hawk as it flew straight for his head with outstretched talons, and plucked out his eyes. Seized by an uncontrollable madness, Nimrod screamed wildly as he clutched at his face. Abruptly splitting away from the other three kings, he then ran off in his own direction, muttering incoherently under his breath as he went.

HORRIFIED BY THE carnage he saw along the battlefront, Abram shook his head in disbelief, but very quickly all was forgotten when he turned to see Lot walking toward him. His grief instantly turned to joy as soon as he was reunited with his nephew. Letting bygones be bygones, the two men embraced.

"Uncle Abram, what a sight for sore eyes you are."

"Lot, my boy, it's good to see you, too."

"Is it true? You led this task force?"

"It's true."

"Just to save me?"

"To save Sarai."

Lot hung his head. "Of course, sir, I should've known. How can I ever thank you?"

"Don't thank me. Thank the God I serve. He's the One Who brought us this victory today. Without Him, we'd never have had the slightest chance of success."

Looking up at his uncle, Lot dolefully nodded. "Then, from this day forward, I owe my life to both you and—" Looking over Abram's shoulder, Lot blanched. "God, no."

A perplexed Abram turned to see what was affecting his nephew, and that was when he saw it for himself. "Nicu," he murmured, as one of his men walked toward him with his friend and servant dangling in his arms.

Stepping up to Abram and Lot, the man laid Nicu down at their feet. "He's barely holding on, sir. I'm afraid he's been badly injured. He insisted I bring him to you."

Kneeling down, Abram leaned forward to examine Nicu's blood-stained body and whispered, "Oh, no, my dear Nicu, not you. What happened?"

With great difficulty, Nicu feebly replied through bleeding lips, "We fought a good fight, didn't we, Master Abram?"

"We did at that, my son. And because of your tremendous courage, my wife will have her brother restored to her."

"Good. I'm glad to know it," he replied, reaching up with his right hand to embrace Abram, who then saw that the man's hand had been severed at the wrist.

Heartbroken at the sight, Abram groaned, "Oh, Nicu, I'm so sorry."

Turning to see what he was looking at, Nicu grimly smiled. "Oh, that. Funny, how things turn out."

"Lord, why? Dear Nicu, believe me when I say I never wanted anything like this for you; not you."

"You don't have to apologize, sir. You were the one who restored my life. Without you ... that thing would've been gone a long time ago."

As tears began to roll down Abram's face, he shook his head with a sad, reluctant smile. "Dear, silly boy."

"Thank you, Master ... for all you've done for me... Because of you, I've lived a wonderful life ... a life worth living."

"Oh, Nicu, please don't talk like that. And whatever you do, don't call me master. Don't you know? You're much more than a servant to me. In my heart, you'll always be my son. Do you hear me? My son."

Nicu coughed, sputtering a mouthful of blood and nodded. "I hear you ... Father." Then with his last syllable, Nicu died.

Devastated, Abram embraced him and wept uncontrollably.

RETURNING FROM THE battlefield, a grief-stricken Abram and his weary men passed by the lime-pits there, and as they did Bera, Bersha and their men came out to meet Abram.

"Greetings, Abram of Canaan. I am Bera, king of Sodom, and this is Bersha, king of Gomorrah. We want to personally thank you on behalf of all the people of the Plain Cities for what you did for us."

Nodding amicably, Abram solemnly replied, "That's quite all right, gentlemen, but naturally I didn't do it for you. I did it to save my wife's brother and his family."

"Naturally," added Bersha with a thoughtful nod. "But that still doesn't change the fact that we're forever indebted to you for your heroic actions. It's remarkable what your people accomplished today in the face of such overwhelming odds."

"What we did, we did with the help of the Lord of Creation. Make no mistake about it. If you're indebted to anyone, you're indebted to Him, not me."

"As usual, my favorite student has spoken well," said a familiar voice.

The group turned to see who was speaking, and Abram's face lit up. "Father Shem!"

"Abram, my son; just look at you now, the mighty warrior of the Lord."

An embarrassed Abram shook his head. "No, the Lord Himself deserves all the credit for this victory. How could I ever lay claim to such a success?"

"Nonsense, Abram. Obviously, the God of Strength helped you in your efforts. That goes without saying. But it's just as true that He couldn't have won the battle if you didn't lead the way. So God may be the author of this victory, but without a willing pen to cooperate in the effort, there still remains an empty page."

Pleased with this accolade from his beloved teacher, Abram finally broke into a reluctant smile. Bera and Bersha then stepped forward and bowed before Shem.

"If I'm not mistaken, sir," continued Bera, "you are Shem, king of Jerusalem."

"I am. However, I stand here today not as the king of an earthly city but rather as Melchizedek, a priest of the Most High, come today to bless my son Abram, to consecrate him and assist him in honoring the Lord Whom he has served since the days of his youth."

Again Bera and Bersha respectfully bowed.

"Then if it pleases the priest of the Most High," added Bersha, "we stand ready to assist the man Abram in whatever way he deems acceptable."

So Shem turned to his charge and asked, "Well, Abram, what do think? Do you consent to having these men participate in today's ceremony?"

"I have no objections."

"Very well, then," replied Shem with a clap of his hands. "Let the festivity of the bread and wine begin."

EVERYONE THERE SOON received a piece of bread, which was broken from dozens of loaves and passed from person to person. Then, copious amounts of wine were quickly handed out to all the men.

Shem reverently raised his cup of wine in one hand and a piece of bread in the other, and began to intone, "We praise You, oh, God of Heaven and Earth, Author of life and death. We come together this day to honor a great victory, one that You've accomplished through the hands of your servant Abram. I pray You consecrate his life from this day forward in all he does in Your great name, and I ask this of You, as I stand here today, worshiping Your majesty, as one who is called Melchizedek, priest of the Most High. And all the people said: Amen."

Together, everyone echoed his words, saying, "Amen." And eating their piece of bread, each one of them drank their cup of wine.

"ABRAM, FRIEND OF GOD," exclaimed Bera, "how could we have been so fortunate as to have had your nephew Lot among our people? Certainly there must be some way we can repay you for your tremendous act of self-lessness."

"All our goods recovered from the battle are naturally at your disposal," added Bersha. "Take whatever you wish. We'd consider it a great honor to relinquish all of it in exchange for restoring our lives and our freedom."

"As the Lord lives, gentlemen," insisted Abram. "I want nothing from you. The Creator of the Universe redeemed our lives and defeated our ene-mies. What more do I need from you?"

"But we insist," continued Bera. "After all, it's only right that you should be rewarded for helping us."

Abram adamantly shook his head. "Thank you, but no. I require noth-ing for myself. Of course I would like to see that Anar, Ashcol, Mamre and my men receive something for their efforts in this battle. I do think they're entitled to their fair share of the spoils."

"Of course," said Bera. "Anything you wish."

"Your deeds here will never be forgotten, Abram," chimed in Bersha. "I only wish we could do more to express our gratitude."

"Well, now that you mention it," replied Abram. "I do have one final request."

"Anything," replied Bera. "Just name it."

"I want Shem to receive one tenth of everything we recovered, and by that I mean, not just what was restored to you from the plunder of Sodom and Gomorrah but one tenth of everything Chedorlaomer lost as a result of his defeat. Agreed?"

The two kings exchanged a determined look and then nodded.

"Agreed," replied Bera and Bersha as one.

The Sand and the Stars

HAVING RETURNED TO his home in Hebron on the plains of Mamre, Abram was relaxing one afternoon, watching over his herds and flocks, when suddenly the Word of God appeared next to him.

"Lord, it's You," sputtered Abram, who sprang to his feet.

"Hello, Abram, how are you today?"

With a solemn, calculated tone, Abram replied, "I'm well, as is my family, thanks to You, of course."

"Good. I want to commend you for honoring the priest of God the way you did. I can see that his words of truth have not been wasted on you."

"Thank you, Lord, for saying so."

"And someday, Abram, because of your obedience to the words of your beloved teacher, you'll receive a tremendous reward from Me. I'll bless you and make your descendants like the sand and the stars, so numerous you won't be able to count them. Not only that, but I'll also give this land to them as an eternal inheritance. Just be courageous and sincere with Me always, and everything I've promised you will come to pass."

"Descendants, Lord," replied Abram, thoughtfully mulling over the words in his troubled mind, "like the sand and the stars?"

"Yes, Abram, that's right."

"Lord, forgive me for saying this, but…" Abram tried in vain to get the next words out of his mouth. He futilely hung his head in despair.

"You're thinking of Nicu, aren't you?"

"Yes, I am. If only he was still with me, I could be as happy and proud as any father could be about a son."

"Don't despair, Abram; all is not lost. As surely as I live, Nicu has found his reward in Me, and he's asked me to tell you how grateful he is to you and Sarai for rescuing him and showing him the only true kindness he had ever known, until now."

With a sparkle in his eyes, Abram looked up with tremendous joy. "Nicu said that?"

"He did, yes."

"Oh, Lord, thank you so much for that. You don't know how happy it makes me feel."

AS THE DARKNESS OF night began to settle in around him, Abram sat by the door of his tent, gazing out across the landscape. He casually picked up a handful of sand and watched the granules slip through his fingers. He did that again and again, and then he turned his eyes toward the night sky, looking up at the stars as they appeared, one by one.

Noticing what he was doing, Sarai walked over and sat down with him. "Is something bothering you, husband?"

As if coming out of a trance, Abram turned and focused his eyes on her. "What's that, my dear?"

"You've been so distant lately, moping around, staring off into space. Are you all right?"

"I'm fine. I've just been thinking, that's all."

"About Nicu?"

"I do think about him, yes; very often, as a matter of fact."

"He loved us so much, and we loved him, too."

"He was the closest thing we've ever had to a son, and now he's gone."

"I'm so sorry, Abram. This is all my fault, isn't it?"

"What? Of course not. Why would you say something like that? It wasn't your fault that Nicu was killed."

"No, that's not what I meant."

"Well, then, what are you saying?"

"I meant that if only I could be a real wife to you, a wife who could give you a son, your own son, then maybe I could help heal this emptiness in your heart."

Touched by her lament, Abram reached out and took hold of her hand. "Oh, Sarai, my dear, dear wife. Don't worry. The Lord will provide some-day. You'll see."

"HAGAR," SHOUTED SARAI as she busily stoked an open fire one cool, breezy afternoon. "Hagar, where are you, young lady?"

"I'm right here, ma'am," replied Hagar, sticking her head out of the tent.

"It's time to bring the meat."

"Right away, ma'am."

BUSY WATCHING OVER his flocks, Abram suddenly became distracted. Sniffing at the air, he muttered, "Oh my, something smells good. It must be lunchtime."

SIDLING UP TO SARAI, Abram found her ladling a rack of sizzling meat with a creamy mixture of butter and herbs. Swiping at the meat with an ea-ger finger, Abram then sucked on his flavorful fingertip. "Oh, that is good. How thoughtful of you, my dear. You're making my favorite."

"Hey, you; stop that. Go away. It's not done yet. And don't thank me, thank Hagar. She prepared the spices especially for you."

"Really?"

"Yes, really. She wanted to surprise you."

"My goodness. This is a surprise. I suppose compliments to the chef are in order. She certainly is a quick study, isn't she?"

"She is at that. We're very lucky to have her. There's nothing I've tried to teach her that she hasn't taken to practically overnight."

"Clearly, she's a chip off the old block."

Sarai flashed a wry smile at her husband. "Clearly."

Intrigued, Abram remarked, "You know, Sarai, if I didn't know better, I'd say there was something else going on in that head of yours. What are you thinking?"

"I want a baby, Abram, and I want one now."

"Excuse me."

"You heard what I said."

"But, Sarai, we've already been over this. When God wants you to have a child, you'll get pregnant. Until then, there isn't much else we can do."

"Oh yes there is."

"There is?" Abram stared at his wife with a confused look. "What might that be?"

Hagar then stepped up to the couple as they stared at one another with a peculiar look on both their faces. "Excuse me, ma'am; is there anything else I can do for you?"

"Yes, Hagar, as a matter of fact there is." And taking hold of Hagar's hand, Sarai placed it into Abram's. "I want you to give me a child I can hold on my lap."

"*What*?" replied Abram and Hagar together.

"You know, a child, a baby, *a son*," Sarai said emphatically, squeezing their hands together. "I'm tired of waiting for God to make this happen, so I'm taking matters into my own hands."

Pulling his hand from Hagar's and Sarai's, Abram shook his head. "Oh, Sarai, I don't know about that. Have things really become that desperate?"

"You mean, have *I* become that desperate? Isn't that what you're asking? Well, the answer is yes. And besides, you said yourself that she's a chip off the old block."

"Oh, Sarai, how could you? That is so unfair to use my own words against me like that."

"I'm sorry, but my mind is made up. You're not getting any younger, you know."

"For God's sake, wife, I'm only eighty-five years old. My father was seventy when he had me. So what are a few more years going to—"

"Uh, ma'am, sir," Hagar interjected, "I'm still standing right here. You're making me feel very uncomfortable talking about me as if I'm not."

Suddenly embarrassed, Sarai turned to Hagar. "I'm so sorry, Hagar, how rude of me. I hope I didn't offend you with my bluntness."

"No need to apologize, ma'am. I realize how depressed you've both been since Nicu's death. It's only natural. You were so close, as close as any son could ever be. I don't blame you for what you're asking, really I don't."

"Thank you, Hagar," Sarai sighed. "So you'll at least consider my proposal, then?"

Hagar dutifully nodded. "You and Master Abram have been so kind to me ever since Pharaoh sent me away. I'd have to be completely heartless not to at least consider it; if only to provide you both with as much happiness as you've provided me."

Turning back to Abram, Sarai asked, "And you? What about you? Won't you at least consider it, for my sake?"

And Abram nodded, too. "For your sake, my dear, of course I'll consider it."

FINALLY THE DAY CAME when Abram relented to the persistent pleading of his wife. Slowly, he entered Hagar's tent, where his servant girl stood awkwardly smiling. He hesitantly stepped up to her and kissed her tenderly, first on her forehead, then on her cheek, and finally full on her mouth.

AS DAYBREAK WASHED away the darkness of night, Hagar was carrying two pails of water from a nearby well. Stepping up to where Sarai was working with a roll of cloth, Hagar poured the contents of one of her pails into several smaller vessels. A strange expression suddenly rippled across her face, and just as abruptly, she grabbed the bucket that she had just emptied and vomited into it.

"Hagar," exclaimed Sarai. "Are you all right?"

"Forgive me, ma'am. I'm afraid I haven't been feeling well the past few mornings."

With a worried look, Sarai handed a small towel to Hagar, who then wiped her mouth.

"Mornings, you say?" murmured Sarai. "You're sick in the mornings? But the rest of the day?"

"The rest of the day, I'm fine. I can't imagine what's wrong with me."

"Hagar. You don't think?"

"What, ma'am?

"You don't think you're pregnant already, do you?"

"Pregnant? No, of course—" But no sooner had the words slipped out than she vomited again into the bucket.

"My God, you are pregnant."

AS HAGAR CELEBRATED with several other servant girls who were lavishing her with hugs and kisses, Sarai coolly watched them from a distance.

"Congratulations, Hagar," said one of the girls. "God has blessed you tremendously."

"How lucky you are," added another, "and how happy Master Abram must be with you for conceiving his child so quickly."

Receiving another hug from her friends, Hagar's joyous expression melted away when she noticed that Sarai was watching her. Suddenly smitten with an intense sadness, Sarai turned and walked away, unable to bear the sight of their celebration any longer.

"GOOD GOD, ABRAM," grumbled Sarai, "you should see what a spectacle Hagar is making of herself, carrying on like she was the queen of the hive."

"Sarai, what's gotten into you? I thought this was what you wanted."

"I wanted a son, yes; but this is more than I bargained for."

"But I don't understand. What's got you so upset?"

"That servant girl of yours obviously thinks she's better than me now. That's what has me so upset!"

"Don't be ridiculous. She doesn't think that. Not Hagar... You think?"

IN NO TIME AT ALL, Hagar's belly was beginning to show signs of the child within her. One evening as Abram and Sarai were having dinner in their tent, Hagar poured some water into their cups. Hagar gasped suddenly, and seeing her clutch at her stomach, Abram stood and held her arm to steady her balance.

"Hagar," exclaimed Abram, obviously nervous about her condition. "Are you all right?"

"Of course, sir. It's just the baby kicking inside me again." Taking hold of his hand, she placed it on her stomach. "Here, feel for yourself." Readily complying, Abram slid his hand across her swollen belly, and then he flinched.

"Oh, I felt that," sputtered Abram. "Good Lord, woman, sit down this instant. Sarai, get her a chair. I refuse to have Hagar waiting on us like a common servant girl anymore."

Sarai reluctantly cooperated, and Hagar slowly sat down with them at the table.

"There, that's better," announced Abram. "How do you feel now?"

"Much better, thank you."

"No, no, thank *you*, my dear. You are most welcome. After all, you're going to be the mother of my child soon. Isn't that right, Sarai?"

Turning to her, Abram and Hagar were both confronted with a mildly suppressed, though unmistakable, scowl.

"Please, ma'am," said Hagar, "don't be angry just because God has seen fit to provide me with a child so soon. You can't blame *us* just because you haven't been able to conceive yet … can you?"

SARAI CONFRONTED Abram the next morning while they were alone in their tent.

"This is an outrage, husband!" Sarai growled as she paced about like a stalking lioness. "How come you didn't pray for *me* to have your child?"

"Sarai, sweetheart, please be reasonable. You know perfectly well I've prayed long and hard for you to have my child."

"Reasonable? Reasonable? How do you expect me to be reasonable? Now, whenever I talk to Hagar in your presence, she mocks me; all because she's carrying *your child!*"

"I don't know what you expect me to do."

"I expect you to say something to her."

Abram shook his head in frustration. "It's a little late for that now, isn't it?"

"You infuriating man!"

Abram shrugged his shoulders. "Now what did I say?"

"I hope this all comes back to haunt you someday!"

"Sarai, please, you have to stop taking this out on me. This was all your idea in the first place. Why do you act as if *I* were to blame?"

"Well, you didn't exactly have to be whipped into her tent, you know."

"Oh, Sarai, that is so unfair. Now stop this nonsense. I've had quite enough of your ranting for one evening. In the meantime, Hagar still belongs to you, so you do whatever you want with her. I don't want to hear another word about it."

A PAIL OF WATER WAS dropped to the ground, spilling its contents.

"Hagar!" snapped Sarai. "How could you be so clumsy? Now pick that up."

But Hagar just stood there, glaring back in defiance.

"Young lady," Sarai continued, "I'd advise you to stop looking at me like that. Stop this nonsense immediately, and quit acting like a spoiled child."

"Funny, your husband didn't think to treat me like a child when he came to visit me in my tent."

"How dare you!" Cut to the quick, Sarai slapped Hagar square across the face.

Hagar blanched, wide-eyed and, quite abruptly, turned and ran away.

TRUDGING THROUGH the desert in the heat of the day, Hagar grew more exhausted with each step she took, until finally she came to a well. She eagerly pulled on the rope and drew up a pitcher of water, which she drank right away. Then without so much as a sound, an angel suddenly appeared next to Hagar. Startled by its unexpected arrival, she took several steps back, eyes darting every which way as though she were about to run.

"Hagar, wait," said the angel. "Don't be afraid."

"Who are you?" she replied, looking the creature over from head to toe. "*What* are you?"

"I'm an angel of the Lord."

"So I'm dead; is that it? Is that what you're telling me?"

"No, no; you're not dead."

"Then what do you want from me?"

"I'm here to inform you the Lord has seen the way your mistress has

mistreated you, and He wants you to know that He's with you in your distress."

"*He* would help *me*?"

"He would, yes. In fact, the Lord has promised to make your family
flourish, too, even as He's promised to bless all the children of Abram. Soon
you'll have a son. Call him: Ishmael. But for now, you need to return to Sarai
and submit to her."

"Submit? To that woman? I'd rather die first."

"Fine," replied the angel as he surveyed the barren landscape all around
them. "But just remember, when you die, alone in this wilderness, the legacy of your son dies with you. Is that really what you want?"

HAVING RETURNED TO Abram's tent, Hagar, in due time, gave birth to
a son.

"Your son, Master Abram," said the midwife, holding the baby up for
Abram and Sarai, who came in to see how mother and child were getting
along.

"A boy," exclaimed Abram, proud as he could be, much to the chagrin
of Sarai. The midwife handed the baby over to Hagar, and very quickly, the
child nestled upon her breast and fell asleep.

"Have you decided on a name, sir?" asked the midwife.

For several moments, Abram thought about it.

"Ishmael," whispered Hagar, exhausted and spent.

"What's that, Hagar?" wondered Abram.

"The angel told me to name our son Ishmael."

Exchanging a puzzled look between themselves, Sarai remarked to
Abram, "The woman is obviously delirious. What do you expect?"

"MA'AM, YOU CALLED for me?" asked Eliezer of Sarai, who had her back
turned to him as she busily prepared the afternoon meal.

"Yes, I did, Eliezer, two hours ago," Sarai replied impatiently, then
turned to face Eliezer with a frown on her face. "When I ask for you, I don't
expect to have to wait so long. Where have you been this whole time?"

"Begging your pardon, ma'am, but one of the lambs wandered off from
the flock, and the ewe apparently went looking for it. By the time we caught
up with them, a wolf had them cornered in a ravine."

Sarai's anger instantly turned to grief. "Oh, no. What happened?"

"We got there just as the pack started to converge. We were able to scatter them, but the mother was left to shield her lamb from the first wolf."

"So you managed to save them?"

With downcast eyes, Eliezer replied, "The lamb was unharmed, but the
ewe, I'm afraid, was not so lucky. She tried to drive the beast away, but in
the end she gave up her life to save her lamb."

A heartbroken Sarai grew weak in the knees. "Dear God, no." Suddenly she could not seem to catch a breath as she reached to steady herself.

Eliezer rushed to her side and helped her to sit down. "Steady, ma'am, steady. I'll run and get the master."

But Sarai's plaintive eyes kept him from moving. "Eliezer, no. Please don't do that. I'll be fine, really I will. There's no need to concern my husband."

"But ma'am—"

"But nothing, Eliezer," she replied, holding her hand to her breast, still trying to steady her breathing. "I'll be fine, I tell you. Now I need you to do something very important for me. Can I depend on you?"

"Certainly, ma'am, always. What is it?"

"I need you to pick two good men and go to Sodom for me. I need to find out how my brother Lot and his family are doing. The rumors I keep hearing about that place have got me worried sick. I need to know if they're true or not. Can you do that for me?"

"Yes, ma'am, of course."

"And not a word about my little spell to Master Abram. Is that understood?"

Eliezer nodded solemnly.

Reign of Terror

NO SOONER HAD THEY arrived in Sodom than Eliezer and his two companions witnessed an altercation between two men; one fellow was well-groomed and dapperly attired, while the other fellow was, quite in contrast, severely unkempt and bedraggled.

"Please, sir," muttered the bedraggled man to the well-groomed man, "I'm a stranger to these parts, and I have nowhere else to turn. Won't you help me?"

"What do you expect me to do for you?" asked the dapper Sodomite, obviously irritated with the intrusion.

"I'm so hungry," muttered the man as he feebly held out a handful of silver and gold coins. "Please, won't you sell me some food?"

"Oh, I see, why didn't you say so?" said the Sodomite, who then casually dropped a silver coin into the man's hand. "Here you are."

Dumbfounded, the pathetic, little man stared at the coins in his hand. "But, sir, what am I supposed to do with more money? What I need is something to eat."

"Then I guess you're out of luck, my dear fellow." With that, the local man turned to leave.

In a fit of desperation, the stranger dropped his handful of coins and grabbed the Sodomite by the sleeve. "No, wait, please. I'm at my wits' end.

I have to eat something, or else I'm going to starve to death."

The Sodomite coldly stared down at the dirty hand clutching his sleeve. "How dare you put your grubby paw on me, you filthy foreigner. Release me, this instant."

"Please, sir, I just need something to…" The man spoke with ever-increasing difficulty. "Something, anything, to eat. Please, I need…"

As Eliezer and his two companions stood some distance away, they watched in horror as the Sodomite cruelly grasped the stranger's hand and, with considerable force, wrenched it from his sleeve. "What's that, you miserable worm? You say you need a good thrashing?" The Sodomite slowly twisted the offending hand, forcing the stranger to drop to his knees. Then quite abruptly, he landed a swift blow to the head of his supplicant victim. The man's eyes rolled into the back of his head, and he collapsed to the ground in a dusty heap. Then, to add insult to injury, the Sodomite proceeded to rip the man's coat from his body, leaving the poor fellow with just his tattered trousers. To the amazement of Eliezer and his two companions, the spectators who had gathered to watch applauded the Sodomite as he triumphantly walked away with the man's coat securely under his arm.

Eliezer immediately ran over to the bedraggled man and helped him to his feet. "Are you all right, sir?"

The poor fellow shook his head, trying desperately to clear his mind. "I'm not sure. What just happened?"

"That man just struck you on the head and took your coat."

As if waking up from a bad dream, the stranger focused his eyes on Eliezer and mumbled, "Will *you* help me, my friend?"

Bolting into action, Eliezer then ran and caught up with the Sodomite. "Hey, you there!"

Stopping in his tracks, the Sodomite turned. "Who, me?"

"Yes, you. How could you do something like that? Striking a defenseless man that way, and then stealing his coat. You should be ashamed of yourself."

The Sodomite defiantly glared back at him. "What are you saying to me? Was that man your brother? Is that what has you so upset?"

"No."

"I take it the people of Sodom have made you a judge. Is that it?"

"Of course not."

"Then I suggest you stop pestering me. This man is obviously none of your business."

"But there's no need to treat a man like a worthless dog."

"Is that so? Well, for your information: He's a vagabond, an out-of-towner. And around here, people like him aren't welcome. He got what he deserved; no more, no less."

"That's ridiculous." Eliezer stepped up to the Sodomite with his hand held out. "Now, be decent about it, and give the man his coat back. Come on."

"Who are you, anyway?"

"I'm nobody; just a man who hates to see injustice done to any human being."

"Justice? What do you know about justice?" said the Sodomite, who casually leaned down to pick up a rock. "Personally, I think you're suffering from a very serious malady, an acute imbalance of the head. Here, let me help you with your delusions."

The Sodomite then struck Eliezer in the forehead with the rock, and instantly blood gushed from the wound.

"Now that that's been taken care of," said the Sodomite, quite matter-of-factly, "pay me for helping you get rid of all this bad blood."

"What?" blurted Eliezer, wiping the blood from his forehead. "Are you insane?"

"How dare you speak to me like that," replied the man, who then grabbed Eliezer's arm. "Now pay me what you owe, or else!"

Looking at him in utter disbelief, Eliezer pulled his arm free. "You mean, you've wounded me, and now you want *me* to pay you for it?" Refusing to speak to him any further, Eliezer turned to walk away, but the Sodomite grabbed his arm again.

Just then another man, dressed in flowing black robes, strode from the gawking crowd.

"Hold on, hold on," grunted the man in stentorian tones. "What's all the excitement about?"

As soon as the Sodomite saw this man, he released Eliezer and respectfully bowed. "Excuse me, Your Honor. We're most humbled by your presence here today."

"Never mind, never mind. Just tell me what this is about."

"Who are you?" asked Eliezer, pressing the wound on his forehead in an effort to stop the bleeding.

The Sodomite wrinkled his brow. "Who is *he*? Why, this is Shakra, of course, esteemed judge of Sodom."

"A judge?" said Eliezer. "Oh, thank God; finally someone who can sort this out."

"Tell me, then," continued Shakra. "What seems to be the problem?"

"With all due respect, Your Honor," began the Sodomite. "You wouldn't believe what's transpired here today. I struck this delusional man with a stone so that the bad blood flowed from his forehead, and still he's unwilling to pay me for my services."

So the judge turned to Eliezer. "Well, what's wrong with you?" he asked with a perfectly straight face. "You heard the man. Pay him what you owe."

"Excuse me?" asked a flabbergasted Eliezer.

"I said, pay this man for services rendered. He is, after all, perfectly within his rights."

"Pay him? For what?"

"Now, see here, you," interjected the Sodomite. "I'm quite well known for my services in Sodom. How dare you question the efficacy of my work."

"Your work? What on Earth are you talking about? What kind of work do you do?"

"Why, naturally," continued Shakra, "this man is a highly esteemed doctor of spirits. People pay him dearly for his skill in removing the bad blood that is responsible for quite a number of ailments."

"Is that so?" Eliezer replied.

"That is so, yes," said the Sodomite matter-of-factly.

Thoughtfully nodding, Eliezer bent down to pick up a stone, and then he threw it at the judge, hitting him squarely in the forehead and producing a sizable wound that instantly started to bleed. "Fine, Your Honor," Eliezer said to Shakra. "If this is the Law around here, then please pay this man what I owe him!" And with that, he dashed off.

"Stop!" howled the judge. "Don't let that man get away!"

"By your own decree," Eliezer yelled back as he ran away, followed by his two companions, "you're getting exactly what you deserve; no more, no less!"

Several bystanders just stood there, without so much as moving a muscle.

"Are you just going to stand there while he gets away?" asked the bewildered Sodomite, addressing the bystanders.

"But he does offer a perfectly good argument, sir," replied one of the apathetic bystanders, who innocently shrugged his shoulders.

Thoroughly frustrated, the Sodomite shook his head in disgust as several other bystanders stepped forward to help the wounded judge try to stop the bleeding from his forehead. Disgusted with their feeble efforts, Shakra gruffly waved them off and, whirling about, disappeared into the crowd. As everyone began to disperse, there was still one young woman who stood there, apparently deep in thought.

"FATHER?" ASKED THE young woman, having returned home.

"Yes, Paltith. What is it?" replied the man, who just happened to be Lot.

"I was downtown this afternoon picking up some things for Mother, when I witnessed an altercation between a pair of out-of-towners and some of the locals."

"What happened?"

"I saw one out-of-towner try to defend another out-of-towner after a local man beat the first man and stole his coat."

"Good God, Paltith, you didn't get involved, did you? You know you're not supposed to have anything to do with out-of-towners."

"I know, Father. It's just so sad to see the way the locals continue to treat them. Why do they have to be so cruel? What crime have they ever committed?"

Overhearing their conversation, Lot's wife, Ado, walked over to her daughter and hugged her. "My dear, sweet Paltith, so innocent, so compassionate."

"Mother, please. Stop treating me like a child. You know how much I hate that."

"Well, then, it's time you stop acting like one, isn't it? The world is a harsh, unpredictable place. People do not just accidentally wander into town for no reason. Maybe these men were thieves or con men looking for easy money. You just don't know."

"Oh, hardly. You know perfectly well not everyone in this world deserves to be treated with suspicion and contempt."

"That's not for you to decide, young lady. Now, I don't want to hear another word about it. The rules are the rules, and as long as we live in this city we have to abide by them. Do you understand me?"

"You mean just because the locals refuse to sell food to an out-of-towner we're supposed to go along with it, even if it is a crime against God?"

"Rules are rules, Paltith," insisted Ado. "We didn't make them."

"But don't you think it's a barbaric practice? We refuse to sell a morsel of food to these poor souls, but we'll give them gold and silver instead. Then, because no one will sell them a thing to eat, they eventually drop dead from starvation, and everybody takes back their money. Who would devise such a wicked scheme, anyway? It's sick, I tell you, absolutely sick!"

"Young lady, I've had just about enough out of you! I'm still your mother, and I won't have you speaking to me as though I'd instituted this policy myself."

Thoroughly frustrated, Paltith turned to Lot. "Daddy, please."

But Lot adamantly shook his head. "I'm sorry, Paltith, but there's nothing I can do about it. Now, obey your mother. She only has your best interests in mind. Best not to pursue the issue any further."

"Oh, all right," she replied, skulking, and walked away.

HAVING MANAGED TO make his way out of the downtown area, the bedraggled stranger found a shady tree and sat down under it. Still, he feebly held out his handful of coins. "For Heaven's sake, won't somebody please sell me something to eat?" But all he ever got were more coins from the occasional passersby, so he just sat there, thoroughly frustrated, staring at the growing collection of coins in his hand. Then, unexpectedly, a piece of bread dropped into his hand. Hardly able to believe his good fortune, the stunned stranger slowly looked up into the most compassionate eyes he had ever seen; they were the eyes of Paltith.

"Are you an angel?" asked the stranger, who gratefully devoured the piece of bread.

Paltith smiled warmly at the sad, little man. "Of course not, silly." And handing him a cup of water, she happily watched him gulp it down all at once.

AS THE STRANGER continued to sit under the shade of that tree, his demeanor no longer reflected that of a man in distress. Instead, he was resting quite comfortably with a serene smile on his face, and as the people of Sodom made their way past him, they glared at the man with a growing suspicion.

"I wonder why this out-of-towner is still alive," commented one man. "I've never seen anyone conquer starvation for so long."

"And why isn't he still begging us for something to eat?" grumbled one woman.

"Something isn't right here. This man looks too happy, and I don't like it one bit."

"How do you think he's doing it? Could someone be helping him?"

"I have no idea, but I aim to find out."

Shaking their heads in disbelief, the disgruntled pair continued on, muttering incoherently under their breath, until finally they disappeared around a corner.

HEADING BACK TO THE well with her pitcher, Paltith paused to give some bread and water to the stranger. Quickly gulping down the water, he began to eat the bread, when suddenly the suspicious Sodomite man peeked around the corner.

"Aha!" he exclaimed as he bolted into action, marching over to the unsuspecting pair. "So you're the one who's been helping this foreigner! That's why he hasn't starved! That's why he hasn't died like all the rest!"

Then, before the stranger could get another bite of his bread, the Sodomite snatched it out of his hand. Tossing it to the ground, he stomped on it, grinding it to powder.

PALTITH WAS SUMMARILY brought before Judge Shakra, much to the dismay of her parents. Lot and Ado helplessly watched the proceedings from amidst a mob of angry spectators.

"She's the one all right, Your Honor!" snapped the Sodomite man. "I caught her red-handed supplying bread and water to a filthy out-of-towner."

As he sat so smugly in his regal black robes, Shakra gazed down at Paltith. "Tell me, then, my dear, is this man telling the truth about you?"

With downcast eyes, she meekly replied, "He is, Your Honor, yes."

"But why would you do such a thing? Aren't you aware of our civil code prohibiting the feeding of foreigners?"

"I am."

"Then why did you do it?"

"Your Honor," interjected Lot, "if I may offer a word in this girl's defense."

"You? Who are you?"

"I'm her father."

"I'm sorry, sir, but you're not on trial here today; this young woman is. Permission denied. Now answer the question, young lady. Why did you feed an out-of-towner when you knew it was in clear violation of our Law?"

"Law?" said Paltith, raising her head in plaintive defiance. "What kind of law condemns someone to death for no other reason than that they're from another country? I'd hardly call it a law at all, Your Honor. I think what you mean to ask me is: Why was I unwilling to commit a crime in the name of Sodom?"

At this, a tremendous outcry rose up from the angry crowd.

"You insolent brat!" growled a man. "How dare you question the wisdom of our Law!"

"Clearly this woman has violated a sacred trust, Your Honor!" bellowed another man. "She must pay for her crime, or else we'll all suffer the consequences!"

Shakra impatiently pounded his crudely fashioned stone gavel. "Silence! Silence! I will have order in my court, this instant!"

The incensed crowd slowly simmered down to a quiet boil, and the judge returned his attention to Paltith. "I can see from your arrogant attitude, young lady, you remain unrepentant of a crime you freely confess to committing, and unfortunately, a violation of this nature strikes at the very heart of our city's existence. If allowed to continue, we would certainly be overrun with an endless stream of foreigners, swarming about like so many locusts in search of food. Therefore, you leave me no choice but to sentence you with the strictest penalty our Law allows, and that sentence is death." Again Shakra slammed his stony gavel down with a tremendous thud. "Sentence to be carried out immediately."

"No!" screamed Ado. "You can't kill my daughter just for having pity on an out-of-towner! This is an outrage, a crime against God!"

Another man turned and glared at Ado, pointing his bony finger in her face. "Oh, yeah? Well just watch us, lady! And there ain't a damn thing you can do to stop us! Not you, and certainly not any *god* of yours!"

Overwhelmed with grief, Ado staggered, and Lot had to hold her up.

THE PEOPLE OF SODOM soon built a huge bonfire in the middle of one of their streets, and slowly they led Paltith toward it. To the absolute horror of Lot and Ado, they watched as their daughter was thrust into the flames; and although she screamed miserably as she died, burning to ashes in a matter of minutes, no one there but her family pitied her in the least.

BUT PALTITH'S CRIES did ascend to Heaven, as the molten Face of God looked down with incredible anger and said, "Never has it been truer said: From the wicked proceeds even greater wickedness. For so long now the people of Sodom and Gomorrah have provoked Me with their evil deeds, even though they've been blessed with a beautiful land, one with plenty of food and water to sustain them. And even though Abram, My servant, rescued them from the bondage of Chedorlaomer and his forces, they still refuse to share any of the resources I've given them. But now the time has come to end their reign of terror and greed. Something must be done about their crimes against humanity, once and for all."

One of the seventy angels then turned to the Face that was gazing down with such righteous indignation, and asked in great anticipation, "What, Lord? What will You do?"

"Wait and see," was all He said.

A Father of Many Nations

ABRAM WAS SITTING alone on a hilltop one evening, just as the stars above and the crickets below were beginning to make their presence known. Gazing thoughtfully across the landscape, he surveyed the meanderings of his numerous cattle, sheep and goats while his men were busy corralling them for the night. As he sifted a handful of sand through his fingers, his eyes inevitably wandered upward to the night sky, where he saw more and more of the twinkling lights coming into view. Abruptly the Word of God appeared before Abram, diverting his attention from the Heavens. A startled Abram jumped to his feet and sucked in his breath. "As long as I live, Lord, I don't think I'll ever get used to You showing up like this."

The Word smiled warmly. "Hello, Abram, how've you been?"

"Fine."

"Fine? Really?"

Embarrassed, Abram looked away. "Oh, what's the use. There's no point in trying to hide anything from You, is there?"

"Not really, no."

"Then what's the point of asking if You already know what I'm feeling?"

"The point is to always be honest with Me, to know you can trust Me in all you do, to believe I'll listen to whatever you need to say, no matter how difficult it is to understand why you're going through it. Does that make sense?"

"Yes, Lord, it does. So if I said I was frustrated with how things were going for me, You'd understand?"

"Of course I would."

"Frustrated with how things have turned out for me and Sarai, I mean. You wouldn't hold it against me?"

"Certainly not. In fact, that's why I've come here tonight."

"Really?"

"Yes, Abram, I've come to let you know about My intentions to make a contract between you and Me so that before long you and Sarai will have more children than you can possibly imagine."

"Like the sand and the stars?"

"That's right, Abram, just like the sand and the stars. So from now on, your name will no longer be Abram, but it will be Abraham, because I'll multiply your family to such an extent that your descendants will comprise many nations, and your wife will no longer be called Sarai, but her name will be Sarah, because kings and queens will descend from her."

Abraham bowed reverently. "Thank you, Lord. Thank you very much."

"And as a sign of our agreement, you and every male child among you will be circumcised, and this contract, which will be testified to in your flesh, will bind us together, forever."

ENJOYING THE HEAT of the day, Abraham was sitting uncomfortably outside his tent. Then, as if from out of nowhere, three men appeared not more than a few hundred feet from where he sat; and they were headed straight toward him. Grimacing painfully, he got up to greet them.

"Hello, gentlemen, how are you all doing today?" Abraham asked.

"We're hungry, thirsty and tired from our extended journey," replied one of the men.

"I know exactly how you feel," said Abraham, squinting up at the Sun. "I've spent many years myself traveling from one country to another. Where are you folks from, if you don't mind my asking?"

"We've come a very long way, Abraham," the second man replied. "Further than you can possibly imagine."

"Is that so?" Wrinkling his brow, the patriarch stared back for several moments. "You know who I am, then?"

"Why, certainly," said the third man. "The reputation of a man like you travels far and wide."

"You don't say," Abraham said thoughtfully as he fixed his eyes on the third man standing before him, to the exclusion of his two companions. "Because until recently, I was known by my former name, Abram. I've only just recently taken on the name of Abraham. Could it be that we've met before, sir? Could that be why you seem vaguely familiar to me?"

The trio exchanged a peculiar look amongst themselves, then shrugged innocently.

"Like we said," continued the first man, "news travels far and wide."

"Interesting," said Abraham.

"So Abraham, father of many nations," continued the second man with a wry smile, "where are all your children?"

"Oh, them?" he mumbled. "I only have one son at the moment."

"Pity," replied the first man, "for a man called Abraham, I mean."

"One can always hope and pray, though, can't they?" he replied.

"Always," echoed the third man, supremely confident.

"Who knows, Lord willing," continued the second man, "maybe someday your name will inspire God to provide you with the many children you've been hoping and praying for."

"Yes, Lord willing, I do hope so," Abraham said with an awkward smile. "Now, if it's all right with you, gentlemen, won't you join me for lunch? That is, if you're still hungry and thirsty."

"It would be our distinct pleasure, Father Abraham," said the third man, who nodded respectfully.

ABRAHAM'S GUESTS ate and drank everything that had been set before them. After they finished their meal, the third man turned to Abraham and quietly remarked, "You know, my friend, I have a very good feeling that by this same time next year, I'll be returning to find that Sarah has given birth to your child; a son, in fact."

Amazed at this, Abraham beamed a huge smile at the man. "Oh, that would be nice. You say you have a good feeling about it?"

The man nodded confidently. "Yes, a very good feeling. So much so, I can guarantee it will happen."

Abraham's eyes lit up. "Really? I can only hope you're a true prophet of the Lord, sir." Turning to the two other men, he playfully asked, "Hey, can you two vouch for your friend here? Is he really a prophet sent by God to deliver such good news to me?"

Without hesitation, the pair nodded.

"Yes, sir, he most certainly is," said the first man.

"He's all that, and more," added the second.

Then the trio stood to their feet.

"And on that note," continued the third man, "we must be on our way. We have another very important mission to take care of."

Abraham sat there, unable to think of anything to say. He just waved goodbye and watched silently as the trio departed. As they moved off toward the horizon, Sarah stepped over to her husband, who sat there still watching the men in the distance with the most peculiar expression on his face.

"What did that man say, Abraham?" asked Sarah. "I don't think I heard him correctly."

"He said you're going to bear me a son next year."

But Sarah just laughed. "I think you were all sitting in the Sun too long, that's what I think. Either that, or you were drinking the good wine."

Abraham shook his head, as if awakening from a deep sleep, then he smiled at his wife. "Oh, Sarah, never underestimate the wonders this life can bring. Never. After all, you're still as beautiful to me as the day I married you."

Sarah smiled back at her husband. Then, as they returned their gaze back to the landscape, they saw that their trio of guests had split up along the way. Two of the men continued their journey, while one of them veered off by himself and abruptly vanished into thin air. Abraham and Sarah exchanged an odd look and, as if to signify they had not seen anything unusual, simply shrugged it off.

Sodom and Salt

AS THE HEAT OF THE day began to bear down on the plains of Sodom, Lot was sitting just inside the gate to the city, fanning himself with a palm leaf. Staring blankly out across the plain of Jordan, he suddenly caught a glimpse of Abraham's two visitors as they approached him. With great anticipation, Lot watched the pair as they walked right up to where he was sitting. Rising to his feet, he graciously bowed before the two strangers. "Greetings, gentlemen, glad to meet you."

"Likewise, I'm sure, my good fellow," the first man said.

"Looks like you two have traveled a long way," continued Lot. "Where'd you come from?"

"Canaan," replied the second man.

"Canaan?" blurted Lot, excited by the news. "You don't say. Canaan. Beautiful place, that's for sure. I have family living in Canaan."

The two visitors nodded vacantly, staring past Lot and toward the heart of the city.

"Is that so?" muttered the first man, apparently only half-listening.

"Why, yes, my sister, actually," Lot continued. "You know, not many strangers like you come around here anymore. What brings you to Sodom, anyway?"

The two looked at each other, as if wondering how to respond, but before they could say a word, Lot excitedly raised his hand like a knowing child in class.

"Of course, of course, how stupid of me. You two must be here to participate in one of our famed annual festivals. Am I right?"

"Festival?" asked the first man. "What festival?"

"The festival of the Moon, naturally."

Again the pair looked at each other, then back to Lot, shrugging their shoulders, obviously unfamiliar with what he was talking about.

"Four times a year," continued Lot unabated, "the people of Sodom gather together to celebrate the various degrees of the Harvest Moon. There's wine and women, there's music and singing. It's a time of wild revelry, where many a man lays with his neighbor's wife. I've even heard tell of some taking their virgin daughters this time of year."

The two visitors exchanged a disturbed look, and seeing their strained expression, Lot quickly added, "Er, uh, well, that is, if one indulges in that sort of thing. Not that I do, you understand."

"I should hope not, sir," said the first man.

"No, friend," continued the second man, shaking his head, "we're certainly not here to attend a festival like that."

"What does bring you here, then?" Lot asked, clearly confused. "Decent folk like you shouldn't be wandering through a place like Sodom unless you know somebody here or have some real purpose. If not, then this place is liable to eat you alive and spit you out."

"Yes, Lot, we understand," said the first man. "But you don't have to be concerned for our safety. That much we're certain of."

"Hey, how do you know my name? I don't remember telling you yet. Who are you guys, anyway?"

"That's not important, Lot," replied the second man. "What is important, is our mission."

"Mission? What mission?"

"Never mind that right now," said the first man. "You'll find out soon enough."

Confused at this, Lot shook his head, as if to clear the cobwebs from his melancholy mind. "You'll have to excuse me. I haven't been myself lately. I've recently suffered the tragic loss of my dear daughter."

Without further delay, the two men started past him, heading down the main thoroughfare that led to the city's center. "We know, Lot," said the second man, quite matter-of-factly. "That's why we're here."

Lot oddly tilted his head. "Excuse me?" Then seeing they had started without him, he hastily followed after the pair. "Hey, are you two thirsty? You can come to my home for something cool to drink if you want."

The two men stopped, turned to Lot, and nodded perfunctorily. And when he made his way past them, they followed. "And if you're hungry, you might have dinner with us, too. How does that sound?"

Again the pair nodded graciously and continued to follow Lot.

AS LOT AND HIS TWO visitors walked along, the lilting strains of music began to fill the air. A crowd of men, women and children appeared from out of nowhere, dancing and singing as they went. Passing by Lot and the two men, several people from the group paused to address the trio.

"Well, hello, gentlemen," said one Sodomite man, pleasantly inebriated. "How are you this fine afternoon?"

"We're well, neighbor," Lot replied.

"Wonderful. And are you here today to celebrate with us?"

"We are not, good sir," the first visitor stated perfunctorily.

"How disappointing," said the Sodomite as he pulled a beautiful woman forward to stand next to him. "Are you sure there isn't something you see that might change your mind?"

A mortified Lot stepped between the Sodomites and the two visitors. "We thank you for your generosity, friend, but I'm afraid these men are not interested in that sort of thing."

"Not interested?" wondered the bleary-eyed man, who looked at the woman next to him and back again at the trio of men. "Not interested in this? That's the stupidest thing I ever heard. Are you people out of your minds?"

"But he speaks the truth, sir," insisted the second visitor. "We seek something altogether different."

"Well, why didn't you say so," said the Sodomite, who then stepped over to a young girl around fourteen years of age. Taking her by the hand, the man led her up to the trio and spun her around like a toy doll on display. "Then maybe I can interest you in my daughter, guaranteed virgin soil, if you know what I mean."

The two visitors exchanged another serious look and turned to Lot for support.

"Gentlemen, please," interjected Lot, "we're most grateful for your selfless offer, but really, my friends and I will pass."

Upon hearing this, the Sodomite became irritated. "What are you saying, then? We're not good enough for you, neighbor?"

"That's not it at all, sir," the first visitor said. "It's just that our mission involves something entirely different."

"Mission? What do you mean, *mission*? Say, who are you people, anyway?"

Finally losing their patience, the two visitors stepped past the Sodomite man, followed quickly by Lot, leaving the entire group of Sodomites with the strangest look of bewilderment on their faces.

TO HIS TENT, LOT and his two guests found Ado inside, sewing one of his shirts while their two young daughters, twins about sixteen years old, looked on. Turning to see Lot enter, the girls ran and embraced him.

"Papa, you're home," exclaimed one of the girls.

"Well, hello you two. I'm glad to see you as well."

Looking up at the two visitors, the other girl asked, "Who are you?"

"These are my new friends. Can you say hello?"

"Hello," said the girls together.

"They've just arrived from Canaan."

"Really," replied Ado, who turned from her sewing and, with a suspicious tone, continued, "And just like that you've decided to invite your *new friends* into our home? Out-of-towners you've only just met?"

"Yes, my dear, that's right. I understand your concerns, but there's something special about these men," Lot insisted with an awkward smile. "I'm not quite sure how to put it, but something about them compelled me to make their acquaintance."

"Compelled you?" echoed Ado, obviously unconvinced.

Uncomfortable with her scrutinizing gaze, the two visitors turned to Lot.

"We're sorry if we've caused you any inconvenience, Lot," said the first man. "We'll leave at once if you wish."

"No, no, don't be silly," he replied. "Don't mind my wife, please. As you can imagine, living in a place like Sodom, a place so suspicious of foreigners, she's just looking out for the safety of her family."

The two men bowed perfunctorily.

"Certainly," said the second man. "And we can assure you, ma'am, your safety is of paramount importance to us as well."

"You see, Ado?" continued Lot. "There's nothing to be afraid of. I'm telling you, these men are our friends. I can feel it in my bones."

"Tell me, then," Ado said. "Have your friends told you why they've come to Sodom?"

"Naturally, my dear. They're here on a very important mission."

"A mission?" wondered Ado. "In Sodom? What kind of mission could you possibly have in a place like this?"

The two men dutifully bowed again.

"Time will tell, good lady, time will tell," insisted the first man.

Ado turned to Lot with a puzzled look. "They certainly are a mysterious pair, aren't they? I sure hope you know what you're doing, Lot."

WHEN ADO PUT DINNER on the table, the pair dug right in. Ado furtively glanced at her husband. "Mission, eh?" she said to Lot with a wry smile. "And you're certain that this mission of theirs isn't to eat us out of house and home?"

THE NEXT MORNING, the two visitors approached Lot and Ado.

"It's time now for us to carry out our mission," said the first man, quite calmly. "Are you ready?"

"Ready?" asked Lot, turning to Ado. "Who us?"

"Yes, of course, you, your wife, your daughters."

"But what do we have to do with your mission?" asked Lot.

"*You are* our mission, Lot," replied the second. "The Lord has sent the two of us to rescue you from the destruction that's about to overtake this evil place. Very soon the judgment of God is going to rain down upon this land. Very soon Sodom will be obliterated from the face of the Earth."

"You're kidding," blurted Lot.

The two men looked at one another, obviously confused.

"I'm sorry, Lot, but we never kid," remarked the first man.

"And that's another thing," Lot said. "You never did tell me how you knew my name before I told you."

"How else do you think?" asked the second man. "The Lord Himself sent us here. Now, do you, or do you not, want us to save you?"

"Save us from what?" Ado sputtered. "What are you people talking about?"

"We already told you," said the first man, growing impatient. "The Lord is about to destroy this place!"

"Destroy?" exclaimed Lot. "What do you mean, *destroy*?"

Looking oddly at his partner, the first man then shifted his gaze back to Lot. "Eradicate, annihilate, *destroy*," he continued, apparently unsure of the question. "What don't you understand about this word, destroy?"

Lot shook his head in exasperation. "No, no; of course I understand what destroy means. Look, I guess you just caught me by surprise."

"God knows, Sodom can be a terrible place to live sometimes," added Ado, "but it's still our home, like it or not."

"Well, I, for one, am sick to death of it," Lot said with a lamentable sigh. "After what they did to our Paltith, this whole God-forsaken country can burn to the ground, for all I care."

"Lot, this is crazy," Ado interjected, "we don't know these men. How can we be sure they're telling us the truth? For all we know they're going to lead us off on some wild goose chase while their partners move in and ransack our home of all our valuables."

Mulling her words over, Lot turned to the two men and asked, "What do you gentlemen have to say to that? Is there any way you can prove you've been sent by God?"

"Yeah," continued Ado, "tell us something only God would know about us. And if you can't, I want you out of my home right now."

The two men exchanged another serious look.

"You see, Lot?" snapped Ado. "They can't do it. They're frauds, I tell you."

"Paltith," said the first man, "your daughter."

"Paltith?" wondered Ado. "What about Paltith?"

"Besides your immediate family," the first man continued, "does anyone know why you named your daughter Paltith?"

Lot and Ado looked at one another and shrugged.

"Not that I'm aware of, no," replied Lot.

"Well, apparently after Abraham rescued you from Chedorlaomer and his army, you wanted to pay tribute to God for delivering your family, so, on the very day that Ado announced to you she was pregnant, you decided to honor that miraculous event by naming your daughter Paltith."

Again Lot and Ado looked at each other, but this time, they appeared more astonished than anything else.

Ado's legs grew weak. "But I don't understand."

"I'm right, aren't I?" asked the first man.

Feebly, Lot and Ado nodded in tacit confirmation.

"It's not possible, I tell you," Ado muttered. "How could you know something like that? *Why* do you know something like that?"

"Because, for the sake of Abraham and his family," replied the second man, "the Lord is watching over you to avenge their cause."

Turning to the visitors, Lot said with unflinching resolution, "When do we leave?"

"As soon as possible," replied the second man. "There isn't much time left. Gather your two daughters, whatever you can carry, and prepare to leave at once."

Ado clutched at her husband's arm. "Lot, wait! Not so fast." Looking to the two men, her look of desperation was downright heartbreaking. "We have two more daughters, married daughters, who don't live with us anymore. What about them?"

"Go," said the first man without hesitation. "Find them. Persuade them to come with us, *now*. Go quickly, before it's too late!"

UNFORTUNATELY, THOUGH, when Lot arrived to plead with his daughter, she raised her hand in protest. "I'm sorry, Father," she said, quite unsympathetically, "but you must be out of your mind. You think God is really going to destroy our city? How could you even suggest something like that?"

ADO, TOO, FARED NO better with their other daughter. "Oh, Mother," she stubbornly said, "I can't just uproot my family at this point in our lives. And for what? Some ill-conceived exodus? And to where? Out there, to wander and die in the wilderness? I'm surprised at you, really."

WHEN THEY RETURNED home, Lot and Ado understood all too well what the look of despair meant on the face of the other. So without a single word between them, they gathered their two youngest daughters and whatever they could carry, and left their home, accompanied by their gracious visitors.

ALONG THE WAY, LOT'S family and their escorts encountered the same group of Sodomites they had met the day before. The head of the group suspiciously stepped up to block their path.

"Well, well, look who we have here," said the Sodomite man. "If it isn't our old friends, too busy to spend any of their precious time with us during this happy time of festival, as if we were something to be shunned, or worse, to be *despised*."

"Please, sir," the first escort began, "we meant no disrespect to you or your family."

Obviously a little tipsy, the Sodomite turned to his companions. "How noble. Isn't our new friend as noble as the day is long?"

Another of the Sodomite men there was quite amused at his friend's antics. "How noble," he echoed with a drunken nod.

Turning back to Lot and his escorts, the first Sodomite noticed the bags that they were carrying. "And just where do you folks think you're going with all this stuff?"

"Please, sir," interjected the second escort, "we have no quarrel with you. Just let us pass, and there will be no trouble between us."

Undeterred, the Sodomite man stepped up to the escort who had just addressed him. "Trouble? Trouble from who? From you? Don't make me laugh. Now, if you know what's good for you, we can make a little deal. I understand you may not be interested in our wives or our daughters. No harm done. But I *am* very interested in yours. So hand them over to us right now, or, if you prefer, I might be persuaded to accept all the goods you're carrying instead. Which do you prefer, friend?"

At a complete loss, Lot and the others exchanged worried looks all around.

"Well," snarled the Sodomite, "don't just stand there gawking at each other. What'll it be? Your women, or your goods?"

"I'm warning you, sir," continued the first escort, "we don't have time for this. Now step aside, or else."

Wrinkling his brow, the Sodomite tilted his head. "Or else *what*?"

Suddenly the two escorts transformed into a pair of luminously beautiful angels who stretched out their wings in an awesome display of power. Gasping in disbelief, the group of Sodomites took a collective step back. The two angels then simply waved their hands, and every last one of those Sodomites were instantly struck with blindness.

"What did you freaks do to me?" screeched the first Sodomite. "I can't see a thing!"

The terrified Sodomites all began clutching at their eyes and groping around, as if they had been plunged into utter darkness.

"Now, hurry!" said one of the angels to Lot and his family. "We've got to get out of here as fast as we can."

"If we don't leave this place right away," continued the second, "you'll be consumed along with the evil of this entire city!"

So Lot, his family, and the two angels immediately began to run.

THICK CLOUDS BEGAN to congeal in the atmosphere above the Five Cities of the Plain, turning into angry, blood-red thunderheads as far as the eye could see. Then, a crimson drop of rain fell, followed by several more drops, which quickly turned into rainfall. This steady rainfall turned into droplets of magma, which then became a torrential downpour of liquid flame. With relentless force, it came down upon Sodom, Gomorrah and the surrounding Plain Cities, until the entire region was being consumed in a vast conflagration of fire and brimstone.

Breathless and exhausted, Lot and his family made their way beyond the outskirts of Sodom, still accompanied by their two angelic escorts. In anguish, Ado turned to her husband and groaned, "Oh, Lot, I'm so worried about the girls. What's going to happen to them?" Turning back to witness the destruction of the doomed cities, she froze in her tracks, horrified by the sight of the great cloud of smoke and ash that rose up from the plain. And as soon as the stark realization of the devastation struck at her, heart and soul, Ado instantly transformed into a pillar of salt.

My Laughter

SITTING CASUALLY by his tent, one lazy, hazy afternoon, Abraham was watching Sarah as she walked by. Noticing his scrutinizing gaze, she smiled and stepped over to him. "Abraham, why are you looking at me like that? I always know you're up to no good when I see that look in your eyes."

"But Sarah, dear."

"Don't *dear* me. What's going on?"

"I was just thinking."

"Thinking?"

"Yes, thinking."

"And?"

"Well, we've been living in Canaan for what, twenty-five years now?"

"Around that, yes. What about it?"

"It's just that we've done just about everything we can do in this place, and I'm growing restless for new horizons."

"New horizons? You actually expect me to believe that? You mean, this has nothing to do with the fact that you're on the verge of your one hundredth birthday?"

"Oh, all right. There's no use trying to put anything past you. Yes, I've been thinking a lot about that lately."

"Abraham, what are you so worried about? You know perfectly well how long Noah lived. Shem is what, well past four hundred? And he's still going strong. Eber, Reu, Serug, all past two hundred. Compared to them, you're barely middle-aged, for Heaven's sake."

Abraham's frown turned to a smile. "My sweet Sarah; you always know how to cheer me up."

"Now, what were you saying about new horizons?"

"Who, me?"

"HELLO, SARAH," SAID a quiet voice.

Startled, Sarah, who was folding clothes inside her tent, turned to see who was speaking to her. It was the Word of God. With her hand to her breast, she hesitantly replied, "Oh, dear, hello there. Where did you come from?"

"I'm sorry if I startled you, Sarah."

"Excuse me, but have we met before?"

"Not exactly, no. But I have met with your husband before."

"Really?"

"As a matter of fact, yes; on several occasions."

"So you're here to see him again?"

"No, not today."

"You two are friends?"

"Yes, very close friends."

"That's nice. I don't think he's ever mentioned you before. Who are you?"

"I am the Word of God, the Mediator between Heaven and Earth, the same One Who told you last year that I'd be returning with word of Abraham's son. Don't you remember?"

"That was you?"

"It was. And do you remember when Abraham told you about your conceiving a son? *Your* son, Sarah? Do you remember what you did when you heard the news?"

An embarrassed Sarah smiled awkwardly. "I laughed."

Then, right before her eyes, the Word vanished, leaving Sarah standing there with the most peculiar look on her face. Quite unconsciously, she reached down and placed her hand on her stomach.

Abraham walked into their tent. "Sarah. Are you all right? You're not ill are you?"

With her hand still on her belly, she replied, "No, of course not. Why do you ask?"

"You should see the look on your face. What's wrong?"

"The strangest thing just happened. A man was just here."

"Here? Just now? A man?"

"Yes, a man. But not just any man. He said he was the same man who came to visit us last year, the same man who told you I'd be giving birth to your son. First, he was standing right here talking to me, then suddenly he was gone, just like that."

"Sarah, no."

"I'm afraid so, yes. If I didn't know better, I'd say the summer heat has finally drained me of all my senses."

With an odd smile, Abraham stepped up to her. "Oh, Sarah, don't be ridiculous. You've never made more sense in all your life."

"What?" Sarah gaped at her husband, thoroughly perplexed. "What are you saying? You mean I haven't lost my mind?"

"Of course not, my darling."

"But how can you be so sure?"

"Because the same Man you've just described has been appearing to me in exactly the same way, over and over, throughout my entire adult life. One moment He's there, and the next, *poof*, He's gone."

"*Poof?* Just like that."

"Just like that." A strange look then flashed across Abraham's face. "Sarah, do you know what this means? The Man Who came here last year to tell us about our son was not just any man; it was Him. It was the Lord Himself Who came to bring us such good news. No wonder He seemed familiar to me that day. No wonder."

With a sigh of relief, Sarah exclaimed, "Well, why on Earth haven't you told me about any of this before?"

"Oh, I see. It's not enough that I've dragged you from one end of the country to the other, on nothing more than an apparent whim." And looking down at Sarah's hand resting on her stomach, Abraham smiled impishly as he placed his hand on hers. "Now you want me to give you even more reason to think the father of your child is completely insane."

THE MUFFLED CRIES of a baby echoed through the night, causing Abraham to turn in the direction of the sound. As he did, a midwife came out of his tent. "Congratulations, My Lord," she said wistfully. "That's the healthy cry of your newborn son."

"My son? *Sarah's* son?"

"That's right."

"How are they?"

"They're both fine. Go inside and see for yourself."

Stepping into his tent, Abraham proudly smiled at the sight of Sarah and their newborn son. As she held the crying baby close to her heart, Sarah whispered, "Hush, hush, my child; there's no need to cry. The days and nights of weeping are over, and now they've become laughter; my son … my Isaac … my laughter."

AS THE SUNLIGHT FADED from view and the crickets began to chirp all around, Nimrod and several of his men entered their makeshift camp. With an exhausted sigh, they relinquished their kill of antelope and wild boar from their stout shoulders, dropping them just beyond the perimeter of the fire pit.

"Have the cook prepare our meal right away," Nimrod said. "I'm hungry, and I'm tired."

"As you wish, Sire," replied one of his men. "I'll see to it at once."

"In the meantime, I'm going to warm myself by the fire. Let me know as soon as dinner is ready."

SEATED SEVERAL YARDS away from the crackling fire, Nimrod yawned and stretched his tired muscles. As he sat there, his weary eyes flitted from the flames jumping up out of the fire pit, to the bustle of activity of his men hurrying about the camp, and back to the fire again. Hypnotized by the flickering of the fire, he was unable to resist closing his eyes, but when he heard the sound of footsteps very close to him, he quickly opened them. He could hardly believe what he was seeing.

"Abraham," blurted Nimrod, whose eyes grew wide with surprise, "what are you doing here? How did you get past my men?" Looking around, he saw that no one except Abraham was standing before him. "Where *are* my men, for that matter?"

"It seems as though they've all abandoned you," came Abraham's calculated reply.

"That's absurd. Why would they do that?" A glint of steel reflected from the hand of Abraham, causing Nimrod's eyes to open wider still. "What's that in your hand?"

"What?" Abraham asked nonchalantly as he held out a sword. "This?"

"Yes, that." Nimrod's uncharacteristically nervous eyes darted about, his hand surreptitiously taking hold of his sword lying next to him.

As Abraham held his sword up and examined it with a peculiar look in his eye, he replied, "This, my friend, is an instrument of divine justice. Apparently your rebellion against the God of Heaven has finally overtaken you."

Abraham abruptly lunged at Nimrod with his sword, striking down at him just as the king rolled out of the way. With sword in hand, Nimrod sprang to his feet and swung back at Abraham, who adeptly evaded his blade. The two men then stood face to face and sword to sword. Still Nimrod's eyes furtively searched the landscape that flickered in the light of the campfire.

"Quit wasting your time wondering where your men have gone, King Amraphel," insisted Abraham as he raised his sword, preparing to strike again. "You alone must stand as the recipient of God's wrath." And with a furious growl, Abraham rushed at Nimrod, swiping his blade with reckless abandon. Barely ducking the tip of his opponent's sword, the king slashed back and, with one clean stroke, cut off Abraham's arm. Sliding cleanly off his shoulder, it fell to the ground with a thud. As Nimrod turned to look, however, he no longer saw Abraham but only his bloody right arm, which was lying on the ground in front of him.

With a satisfied grin, Nimrod said, "Well, well. So much for the retribution of God."

For just a moment, he stood triumphantly over the severed appendage of his foe; that is, until the arm began to writhe and twitch in the dust. The bewildered king watched as the bloody arm then transformed into a huge serpent, which rose up before him. Frozen with fear, Nimrod dropped his sword just as the creature, with blood-red eyes and dripping fangs, lunged forward, and clamped its tremendous jaws down on his head.

WITH A BLOOD-CURDLING scream, Nimrod sat upright, sweat pouring down his face. His wild eyes swiveled in every direction as he quickly realized he was still seated by the campfire with all of his men staring at him, perplexed by his anguished outburst.

"CLEARLY, SIRE, THIS was another vision of Abraham's destiny involving your demise," intoned one of Nimrod's black-robed soothsayers.

"My demise," Nimrod sputtered with a sarcastic grimace. "Quit mincing words with me, soothsayer. You mean my *death*, don't you?"

"Forgive me, My King. My intention was not to offend you."

"Then stop treating me like a simpering child. I have to know the truth about this vision. What does it mean?"

"I believe the vision speaks of the fact that, despite all your efforts, typified by your cutting off his arm, Abraham will still, one way or the other, wind up causing your death."

"You mean to say that Abraham himself will be the one to kill me with his own hands? Is that what you're telling me?"

"Of that, I'm afraid, no one can say for sure. The fact that his right arm became the serpent that killed you might indicate an offspring of Abraham will carry out the act, a son or maybe a grandson. It's difficult to say."

"Difficult? The only difficult thing around here is trying to decipher your flimsy explanations. If Abraham and his sons don't put me out of my misery, listening to all your vague interpretations will surely be the death of me."

"A thousand pardons, Your Highness," muttered the soothsayer, hanging his head. "Please believe me when I say, we're doing everything we can to assist you in this matter."

"How commendable. Then tell me: What do you suggest I do to rid myself of this scourge of Abraham? So far, all our humanly efforts have failed miserably. Can't one of you cast a spell on him? Smite him with dumbness or madness? Conjure up the dark lord of the underworld? Anything! What good are you people if all you ever do is offer me a bunch of useless interpretations?"

With a thoughtful nod, the soothsayer said, "We'll look into it right away, Sire."

WHEN ISAAC WAS AROUND five years old, he was sitting by the door of the family tent, quietly playing with a small wooden toy. Nearby was Ishmael, who was nineteen by then. As Isaac played by the tent door, Ishmael was diligently practicing with his bow and arrows, taking shot after shot at a tree marked with a bull's-eye. Quite skilled with his bow, Ishmael managed to nearly hit his mark, missing it by only a few inches.

Eventually getting bored with his target practice, Ishmael walked over and stood just a few feet away from his younger brother, staring oddly at him for several moments. "So you like playing with your toys, do you, Isaac?" he asked.

Isaac looked up at his brother with a smile and a nod. "Papa made it for me. Papa loves me very much."

With a peculiar look in his eye, Ishmael replied, "Is that so? Well, I have a toy of my own, little brother." And taking another arrow from his quiver, he slowly drew it back in his bow, taking direct aim at little Isaac.

Walking past the tent, Sarah caught sight of what Ishmael was doing with her son and screamed, "Ishmael, no!" Horrified, she ran and got between his poised bow and Isaac. "Stop, Ishmael! Put that thing away, this instant! What do you think you're doing?"

Ishmael lowered his bow in frustration and walked away, muttering under his breath. "Ah, I didn't mean nothin' by it. I was just playing around."

OUTRAGED AND TREMBLING, Sarah went to Abraham. "You will never believe what I caught Ishmael doing just now."

"Good Lord, Sarah. What?"

"He had this crazy look in his eyes, like a wild animal, and he was aiming an arrow at Isaac!" Sarah began to weep as she relived the moment. "He was going to kill my baby! My God, I can only imagine what might have happened if I hadn't been there to stop him."

Abraham reached out and pulled his wife into an embrace. "Oh, Sarah, thank God you did. I'll go right now and talk to that boy."

"Talk to him?" snapped Sarah as she abruptly pulled from his arms. "Are you kidding me? You can't talk to that one anymore. You should've seen the look in his eyes, Abraham; so hollow, so remorseless."

"But what else can I do, Sarah?" replied Abraham, confused by his wife's stark anger. "Ishmael is my son. He'll do what I tell him."

"This is the last straw, I tell you. I want him and that mother of his out of my home!"

"But I can't just kick them out like that, can I?"

"That woman is still our slave, isn't she?"

Begrudgingly, Abraham nodded. "Of course."

"Then I want her and her son gone from this place, right now! Her son is not going to be heir with mine! Not after what I just found him doing!"

Speechless, Abraham hung his head in despair.

THE VERY NEXT DAY, a deflated and distraught Abraham gathered twelve loaves of bread and several flasks of water, and gave them to Hagar and Ishmael. Then he reluctantly sent them, along with a large number of cattle, sheep and servants, into the wilderness of Paran.

OVER THE COURSE OF time, Ishmael grew into a skilled archer and eventually married an Egyptian woman. With his wife, his six children and his mother, Ishmael traveled throughout this wilderness, pitching his tents and nurturing a huge number of flocks and herds as they went.

ONE DAY, ABRAHAM was sitting with his wife in their tent. "You know, Sarah, it's been a long time since I've talked to my son Ishmael. I think I'll take a trip to see him."

So Abraham rode his camel into the wilderness of Paran, searching for his son.

ABRAHAM ARRIVED AT Ishmael's tent around noontime. Unfortunately, his son was nowhere in sight. Only Ishmael's wife was there, sitting inside with three of their six children. Remaining on his camel, Abraham called out, "Hello? Anybody? Can someone tell me where Ishmael is?"

"He's gone hunting!" came his wife's gruff reply from within the tent.

"My dear woman, could you please get me something to drink? A bit of water would really help me right now. I'm so thirsty from my long journey."

Remaining inside the tent, Ishmael's wife responded with an obvious edge of irritation to her voice. "We don't have any water, or bread, for that matter."

Still Abraham sat patiently on his camel as he listened to the various sounds of Ishmael's wife and children moving about inside the tent. Then suddenly there came the muffled sound of a child's face being slapped, followed by a young boy's scream.

"Stop it, you good-for-nothing brat!" howled Ishmael's wife. "How many times have I told you not to do that? But what could I expect, considering you were born of that misbegotten father of yours!"

Even from inside the tent, her grating voice bellowed so loudly that it embarrassed several passersby and absolutely offended Abraham. Finally losing his patience, Abraham's typically pleasant demeanor turned to an angry scowl. "Excuse me, young lady. I must insist that you come out here and speak to me directly."

"Oh, for God's sake," Ishmael's wife grumbled. After several awkward moments, she finally exited the tent, looking quite annoyed, and stood before him with her arms crossed. "What do you want now?"

"I take it you're Ishmael's wife?"

Nodding impertinently, she replied, "Yes, yes, what about it?"

"My dear woman, can you please tell me with whom am I speaking?"

Ishmael's wife grunted, "What?"

"Your name, your name. What do I call you?"

"Oh, Meribah," she replied suspiciously. "My name is Meribah. What's it to you?"

"Well, then, Meribah, I need you to tell something to Ishmael when he comes home. Can you do that for me?"

Reluctantly, the woman nodded. "Yes, I suppose so."

"Good. Then I want you to tell him an old man from Canaan came to see him, but when he arrived, I never asked him who he was, or offered him any refreshments for his long journey. Finding you gone, he said, 'When Ishmael returns, tell him the old man said to discard the nail you're using for your tent, and put another one in its place.'"

Then Abraham turned and rode away on his camel.

ISHMAEL, HAGAR AND the three oldest boys, ages fifteen to twenty, returned later with an assortment of game they had acquired during a fruitful day of hunting.

With considerable disdain, his wife informed him, "Ishmael, an old man from Canaan came here today looking for you."

"From Canaan? An old man, here for me? Who?"

"How should I know? He never told me his name."

"Well, didn't you ask him?"

"I guess it never occurred to me, no. He just kept asking for food and water."

"And did you give it to him?"

"Well, of course not. What am I, the maid?"

"Did he tell you what he wanted? Besides food and water, I mean."

"I already told you: He was looking for you."

"Meribah, what did he do when he found out I was gone?"

"When I told him you'd be out hunting all day, he told me to give you a message."

"Okay, then. Please, tell me what he said."

"Just a lot of nonsense, that's all."

"Like what?"

"He told me to tell you the nail to your tent was no good, and that you should replace it. Isn't that the most ridiculous thing you ever heard?"

And when Ishmael heard this, he was so smitten that he turned and walked outside, where he hung his head, deep in thought. Troubled by her son's reaction, Hagar followed him outside.

"Ishmael, what's wrong? Do you know who this man was, or why he came here?"

"Of course I do, Mother."

"Tell me, then. I want to know what has you so upset."

"Don't you see? The old man from Canaan was Father. He came to see me today, but we weren't here to greet him."

"Your father?"

"Yes, yes, Father. And what's worse, my silly, stubborn wife failed to honor him properly. She gave him nothing to drink, nothing to eat. She just sent him away empty-handed, in her typically hospitable way. It's a disgrace, I tell you."

"Oh, dear. That's too bad. And what was all that about a nail in your tent? Is that supposed to mean something?"

"What else? It was Father's subtle way of breaking the bad news to me."

"Bad news? What bad news?"

"That Meribah is unfit to be my wife, and that she should be replaced with a better one."

THREE MORE YEARS passed by, and one day Abraham grew restless again.

"What's wrong, husband? You've been so preoccupied lately."

"Oh, nothing, my dear. I'm fine. It's just I was thinking how long it's been since I've seen Ishmael. Maybe I should take another visit to try and see him."

SO ABRAHAM RODE OUT into the wilderness again, on his camel, finally reaching Ishmael's tent around noon. Seeing no one around, he called out, "Hello? Could someone tell me where Ishmael is?"

This time a different woman came out of the tent and smiled at him. "I'm so sorry, sir, but he isn't here right now. He's gone hunting with Mother and the boys."

"Hello, my dear. And who might you be?"

"My name is Malchuth. I'm Ishmael's wife."

Abraham's face lit up. "Oh, how nice to meet you, Malchuth. How are you this fine day?"

"I'm very good, sir. Won't you please come inside? Have something to eat. You must be exhausted from your journey."

Abraham shook his head. "No, thank you, my dear. That's all right. I won't be stopping. I'm in a terrible rush to continue my journey; but I would like some water. I'm so thirsty."

Malchuth ran into the tent and brought out a cup of water and a piece of bread. She urged him to enjoy, and so he happily ate and drank.

"God bless you, my dear, for your kindness. Now, when Ishmael comes home, can you tell him something for me?"

"Why, of course, sir. Anything you like."

WHEN ISHMAEL, HAGAR and the boys returned home with their game, Malchuth came out of their tent to joyfully greet them. "Hello, husband. How was your day?"

"Oh, not bad. How about you? Did anything happen while I was gone?"

"Not much. Oh, I almost forgot; someone came to see you, now that you mention it."

"Someone came to see me? Who?"

"You know, I'm not really sure. When I asked him his name, he just told me to tell you an old man from Canaan came to see you, but you weren't here, so I brought him bread and water, which he happily ate and drank, and when he left, he said, 'Tell Ishmael the nail of your tent is very good. Don't ever remove it.' Isn't that strange? I wonder what he could have meant by that."

Gratified and relieved, Ishmael beamed a tremendous smile. "Thank you, sweet Malchuth. You've done my heart good today. Did you hear that, Mother? An old man from Canaan came to visit me today, and he said the nail of our tent is a very good one."

"I heard, son," she said with a proud smile. "I'm so glad to hear it."

ISHMAEL THEN GATHERED his household and all his flocks and herds, and journeyed to see his father in Canaan, where he was met with Abraham's tearful embrace.

"Ishmael, my son," Abraham said wistfully. "It's good to see you again. I've missed you so very much. Please, won't you stay with us awhile?"

"Of course, Father, if you insist. I'll stay."

A Line in the Sand

ISAAC WAS GROWING up nicely under the tutelage of Abraham, when one day a messenger arrived outside the tent where father and son were conversing. Seeing the messenger depart and noticing the sad look on her husband and son's faces, Sarah immediately went to them. Before she even had time to ask, Abraham told her, "Bad news from Haran, I'm afraid."

"What's happened?" she asked.

"It seems as though Grandfather has died," Isaac replied, "at the age of two hundred and five."

"Terah?"

"Terah," Abraham quietly said with a somber nod.

TRAVELING TO THE city of Haran were Abraham, Sarah, Isaac and Ishmael, who together with Nahor and Milcah, mournfully tended to Terah's funeral service.

Watching the solemn proceedings from a distant hilltop was a shadowy, hooded figure, standing alone against the murky night sky. From out of the darkness, someone stepped up and stood next to the figure.

"What is it, Commander?" asked the shadowy figure, obviously annoyed with the interruption.

"Sorry to disturb you, Sire," he replied, "but I'm afraid our scouts have been detected. Should I order our withdrawal?"

With a dissatisfied sigh, the man reached up and pulled back his hood, revealing that he was none other than Nimrod. "Fine. Have the men withdraw at once."

"As you wish, My Lord," said the commander, who turned and slipped back into the darkness.

Still, Nimrod stood gazing at the funeral service. "Your days of running are over, Terah, my prince, my old friend," he murmured. "Your days of strife are finally at an end. How I envy you."

Abraham and Nahor stood side by side, grieving over their father's grave, when someone surreptitiously moved up to Abraham, whispered in his ear, and pointed in the direction of the shadowy figure far off in the distance. Head still down, Abraham merely shifted his eyes to catch a glimpse of the figure that finally turned and disappeared behind the hilltop.

ISHMAEL WAS VISITING Isaac in his tent one afternoon. "You know, when I was thirteen years old," Ishmael began, "the Lord told Father to circumcise us. I gave my life to Him then, and ever since, I've never disobeyed."

"Why brag to me about something like that?" asked Isaac, obviously unimpressed. "You cut off a piece of your skin because the Lord told you to. As the God of Abraham lives, if He told Father to cut me into pieces and sacrifice me as a burnt offering, I wouldn't hesitate. I'd gladly consent."

THEN CAME THE TIME when the seventy angels arrived to place themselves before the molten Face of God, and when one angel, looking more beautiful than all the rest, caught the Lord's attention, He immediately addressed him. "So, the renegade has returned to the 'scene of the crime,' as it were."

Graciously, the angel nodded. "Greetings, Eternal One."

"And just where have you come from today?" asked the Face.

"Why, from traveling back and forth throughout the Earth, as I so often do."

"And what do you think of the people living there?"

"Well, I'm particularly amused by the ones who serve you," cooed the angel, whose eyes suddenly turned black with hatred. "Whenever they need something, that is!"

Startled by his outburst, the angels next to him cautiously moved away to a more suitable distance.

"You don't say," replied the Lord matter-of-factly.

"Yes, and then, when you give them what they want, they ignore you again!" continued the angel through clenched teeth, as his beauty and brilliance began to fade, slowly revealing the sinister features below the surface. "Just like that, doing things your way is completely abandoned."

"Well, well, the Morning Star has spoken. How ironic that Satan would think himself capable of righteous judgment. Then tell me: What about Abraham, the son of Terah?"

"What about him?" scoffed the dark angel with a wave of his hand, shedding the last vestiges of his disguise, grotesque as ever now, grinning with his hideous fangs exposed for all to see. "You think he's special? He's no different from all the rest."

Finally realizing who was sitting amongst them, the rest of the angels moved even further away, leaving the devil alone in his stand against the smoldering Face of God.

"Really?" said the Face, quite casually.

"Yes, really. First, he lied to his own father about destroying his idols, he lied to Sarah about Terah's involvement in the death of her father, Haran, and then he lied when he tried to convince everyone his wife was his sister. In my book, that makes him a low down, filthy liar. There's no telling what he'll lie about next."

"I see. Is that all?"

"Well, how about the fact that when he had no children he prayed to you, day in and day out, building altars to you, and proclaiming your name to everyone he met? But now just look at him. Ever since that brat Isaac was born, he's completely abandoned you."

"But are you so sure you've considered My servant Abraham thoroughly? There really isn't anyone quite like him in the whole world."

"Then how come when Isaac was born he didn't offer you any of the animals he killed that day? Not one of them was brought to you. No burnt offerings, no peace offerings, not an ox, not a lamb, not even a goat! *Why*?"

"Offerings? How dare you speak to Me about offerings. What do you know of genuine sacrifice? Your rabid hatred of anything sacred blinds you. Abraham is a noble man, one Who reveres Me and hates evil, but you only see what you want to see. You don't really think you fool Me with your self-righteous facade, do you? Since the day Abraham was born, you've done nothing but stir up the hatred and jealousy of Nimrod and his people. But in the end, all your efforts will fail, just as they failed when you tried to thwart My plans for Adam, his forefather."

"How touching, how sentimental, how *sickening*. Still, nothing you've said will change the fact that ever since Isaac was born your so-called 'servant' hasn't built you a single altar! All because you *gave* him what he wanted! And now, for thirty-seven years, he's forgotten you, just like all your other pathetic, little replicas!"

"Ah, you may think you know Abraham, but I'll bet if I told him to bring Me his son Isaac as a burnt offering, he would even do that."

"Then say the word!" growled the devil with blood in his eyes. "Tell him to do exactly that! Then we'll see, once and for all, if he has the guts to go through with it!"

SO THE WORD OF GOD went down to Earth and visited him. "Abraham?"

Startled at his abrupt appearance, Abraham stood there for several moments. "Yes, Lord, what is it?"

"I've come to bring you another important message. Will you receive it?"

"Of course, I will. What is it this time?"

"I want you to take Isaac, your only begotten son, and go to Moriah. Sacrifice him there on one of the mountains to which I will lead you."

"You want me to do what?" asked a confused Abraham.

"I want you to offer up Isaac as a burnt offering. Will you do that for Me?"

"I suppose so, Lord, if You insist. But how will I know which mountain to go to?"

"Above it will be a cloud filled with the splendor of the Lord. That's how you'll know."

"And what should I tell his mother? How will I ever be able to tell her I'm sacrificing the son You provided for us in our old age?"

"Why not try telling her the truth? Are you afraid of what she might think of you if you follow the command of God?"

"Forgive me, Lord, but this is nothing compared to my ordeal in Nimrod's furnace or my battle with Chedorlaomer. After all, back then, I hardly had time to even think about the dire nature of my predicament, so compelled by the audacity of youth as I was."

"But now?"

"But now, so many years later, after so much living, so many worries, so many disappointments, things are different. And this isn't something that just involves me and my decision to defy a king. This involves my son and my wife."

"I see. Is that all?"

"Of course not, Lord. This time it involves not just an earthly king but an eternal one. May I ask what I did to deserve such a fate?"

"In due time, Abraham, all in due time."

"Meanwhile, what choice do I have in the matter, really? Who am I to defy the Lord of Glory?"

"Well said, my friend."

"And perhaps God will protect my son from the blade the same way He protected me from the fire of Nimrod."

"Certainly, Abraham, time will tell; time and the inscrutable decision of the Lord above."

Then the Word vanished, leaving Abraham standing there, more confused than ever.

ABRAHAM PENSIVELY entered his tent and sat down with Sarah. "You know, my dear," he began, carefully choosing his words, "Isaac is grown up now, and it's been a while since he's studied the service of God. So tomorrow I'm taking him to see Shem and Eber."

"Really?" replied Sarah. "What for?"

"So they can teach him what they know about the Lord. Maybe they have a thing or two to tell him I haven't thought of, something I might have overlooked. Who knows. Then he'll know how to serve God even better than before."

"Well, I suppose so; if you feel that strongly about it. Just don't keep him too long, though. You know how connected we are."

Abraham sighed. "Oh, Sarah, let's pray for the Lord to do great things with us."

March to Moriah

AS ABRAHAM AND ISAAC left their tent, along with Ishmael, Eliezer and several of their servants, a distraught Sarah followed some distance behind them.

"Be a good boy, Isaac," Sarah called out, barely able to speak the words. "And come home safe and sound, you hear?"

"Please, Mother, I'm not a child," he replied, annoyed with all the fuss. "I'll be fine."

But just hearing the sound of her son's voice, Sarah started crying. Abraham began weeping, too, and so did Isaac. Everyone there, in fact, had to fight back their tears because they were all so affected by Sarah's emotional outburst.

Unable to resist any longer, Sarah ran to Isaac and grabbed his hand, holding it tenderly to her face. "Who knows if I'll ever see you again, my son?"

"Mother, you're embarrassing me in front of everybody. Would you please go home? Everything will be fine, honestly."

Abraham could hardly stand it. "Please, Sarah, you don't have to worry. Of course you'll be seeing Isaac again. Before you know it, he'll be back in your arms. I promise. The Lord, I'm sure, will see to it Himself. Now, stop your crying please, my dear, or else we'll never be able to leave."

Nodding mournfully, Sarah wiped the tears from her face and finally let go of Isaac's hand. Then with the help of some of her other servants, she reluctantly walked away.

AS HE WAS SO OFTEN in the habit of doing, Satan watched the whole scene from a distant hillside, flanked by his lieutenant and several of his minions. "Well, well," he croaked. "It looks like that old fool Abraham is going to call my bluff after all. And worse still, it looks as though that addle-pated son of his is going along with god's absurd plan."

"What should we do, Lord?" asked his lieutenant.

Satan slowly turned to him with his angry, reptilian gaze. "*Do*? What do you think we should do? We do whatever we can to stop them, you brainless idiot! Why would you even ask me such an asinine question?"

The lieutenant shrank back in abject fear. "Forgive me, Master, I was just trying to help."

"Help," grumbled the devil, thoroughly disgusted, as he turned his lurking black eyes back upon his quarry. "What do you know about *help*? I suppose your idea of help would be to openly terrorize them with fear and intimidation. Is that it?"

The lieutenant then turned to the demons next to him and asked quietly, "What else is there?"

ABRAHAM'S CARAVAN, consisting of a dozen men, was plodding along at a slow but steady pace. Most of them were walking alongside their camels, which were laden with supplies, as was Abraham who was walking some distance behind the others, thoroughly absorbed in his own thoughts, when suddenly he realized that an old man he did not recognize was walking alongside him.

"Good day, sir," exclaimed the stranger. "How are you this glorious morning?"

"Well, hello there, friend," replied Abraham, apparently relieved with the diversion. "I'm fine. Thank you for asking. I hope all is well with you."

"It is, thank you. But, sadly, there is one thing troubling me."

"Oh, and what could that be?"

"Well, sir, I have to admit. I'm very confused by your actions here today. I mean, are you really such a heartless man after all?"

Confused at this, Abraham asked, "What in the world are you talking about?"

The old man, however, remained undeterred, shaking his head knowingly. "Ah, don't play coy with me. You know very well what I'm talking about. I'm talking about your son."

"My son? What about my son?"

The man grinned back sardonically, revealing that several of his teeth were missing. "I just want to know why? Is that too much to ask? Why would you do it? I mean, really."

Beginning to get irritated with the stranger, Abraham blurted, "Why what?"

"Why would a supposedly good man like you do something so evil as to kill his own son?"

Momentarily taken aback, Abraham slowly mustered his reply. "Look, I don't know who you are, but I am only doing what the Lord has asked me to do. What could be wrong with that?"

"You mean to tell me it's all right to murder the son that God gave you and Sarah in your old age as long as it's because He asked you to? Is that really what I'm hearing? I take it back; you're not heartless, you're crazy."

Abraham swallowed hard at this. "How dare you, sir. Who are you, anyway? A sorcerer? How do you know so much about me and my family?"

"Ah, that's not important. What's important is why you won't answer my question. Why is a good man like you leading his own son to the slaughter?"

"I already told you: Because the Lord asked me to, that's why!"

"Has Isaac done something wrong? Is that it?"

"I never said he did."

"Yet you still insist on destroying him. You are insane, aren't you?"

"If that's how you see it, then, yes, I guess I am."

"But don't you realize the Lord would never ask someone to do something this evil? He'd never ask a man to kill his own child."

Thunderstruck, Abraham stopped dead in his tracks and turned to the old man. "You know, *friend*, something has just dawned on me."

"Really, what?" asked the old man, stopping with Abraham.

"You never did say how you knew so much about me. If you really were a sorcerer, you would've had no problem admitting it, but you didn't, did you? No, of course not. So you must be someone else, or *something* else, for that matter."

The old man tilted his head in a curious way. "What the Hell is that supposed to mean?"

"Yes, that must be it. When I was a young man, my forefathers, Noah and Shem, used to tell me stories about beings who were capable of such a thing."

"Beings? What are you going on about now?"

Abraham stared intently into the eyes of the old man, mesmerized by the train of thought that came flooding into his mind. "Yes, shape-shifters; that's what they called them, malignant beings who could transform themselves into any form they desired."

The old man shook his head in disbelief. "Have you lost your mind, sir? Or have you just spent too much time in the Sun today?"

"And the most evil of them all was their leader, a diabolical creature who, for some inexplicable reason, still had limited access to the heavenly realms."

"You really have gone insane, you babbling fool," said the old man, who took several steps back from Abraham, obviously disturbed by what he was hearing.

"No, sir, not at all. In fact, I've never been clearer about anything in my life, as if an arrow has just been shot directly into my heart. It is you. That's how you knew so much about me, my family, my mission here today."

With a wild look in his eye, the old man moved back some more, but Abraham kept pace with him with each step. "Certainly not," he insisted.

"Yes, of course," pressed Abraham, raising an accusing finger. "I can see right through you now. You're the Evil One himself, the very one who was thrown down from the heights of Heaven. Satan, get away from us, this instant! I won't allow you to stop us!"

The old man held his hands over his ears. "Shut up, you raving lunatic! I won't be spoken to like that!" And quite abruptly, the man turned and walked away, furiously kicking at the dirt.

Finally, Isaac came over to investigate. "What was that all about, Father?"

"Nothing to worry about, son," replied Abraham, who anxiously put his hand on Isaac's shoulder to steady himself.

"Are you all right?" asked Isaac.

"I'll be fine. No worries. Everything is perfectly fine now."

"Who was that man?"

Abraham thought for a moment about how to answer. "Just a wanderer, I suppose."

"He seemed so angry," Isaac said, staring in the direction of where the old man had disappeared. "Do you think he poses a threat to our journey?"

"No, Isaac; he's nothing more than a thundercloud with no rain, something to be seen but never heard from again, I hope."

With that, Abraham and Isaac, along with the rest of their group, continued their journey.

BEFORE TOO LONG another stranger wandered up to them. This time a handsome young man came up alongside Isaac, who, like his father before him, was straggling some distance behind the group, lost in his thoughts.

"Hello, my friend," said the young man with a gracious charm. "How are you on this wonderful day?"

Vacantly nodding back, Isaac was apparently not as happy with the intrusion as his father had been. "Fine, thanks," he muttered. "And you?"

"Oh, I can't complain. There is one thing puzzling me, though."

"Really," said Isaac, hardly paying attention. "What?"

"Do you have any idea why your father is taking you on this trip?"

"Well, yes, I have my suspicions," replied Isaac. "But I don't think he wants to tell me because he's afraid I might not go along with his plan."

The young man was flabbergasted. "*What*? You mean your father hasn't even told you what he's up to?"

"Not in so many words; but the Lord and I both know I'm ready for this. I've declared my intentions to God, and I believe He's found me worthy of such a mission."

"But don't you know your silly, old father is wasting his time by killing you today?"

Isaac turned with a peculiar look. "Who said anything about me being killed?"

But the young man grinned back knowingly. "Ah, not so fast, not so fast. You know as well as I do, there are some people in this world who can sense what others fail to recognize. Get my drift?"

"So you're telling me you're one of those people. Is that it?"

"That I am, my friend, that I am."

Not sure how to respond, Isaac frowned and turned away.

Satisfied with himself, the young man pressed on. "So that's it? You have nothing more to say for yourself?"

"Look, friend, I don't have to explain myself to anyone, least of all you."

"Aha," exclaimed the man. "I knew I was right. Admit it. You are having second thoughts about this harebrained scheme of your father's, aren't you?"

"Not necessarily," replied Isaac as he flashed the young man a keenly determined look. "If the Lord told my father to do this thing, then who am I to argue with what they've decided?"

The young man grew agitated at this. "But don't you see? Your father is senile. He's lost what little mind he has left."

"No, you're wrong," Isaac insisted. "He's a good man, and he knows what's best for us."

"Oh, please, stop. Certainly you must know you were made for better things. I mean, honestly, what purpose could it possibly serve to throw your life away like this?"

"But I'm not throwing my life away. I'm obeying the God of Heaven."

"You poor, ignorant fool. You actually think your life is that precious to God? Who do you think you are, anyway? Out of all the people in this world, what makes you so special? Tell me that."

Fed up, Isaac started to walk faster until he caught up with Abraham. "Father, have you heard what this man has been saying to me?"

Abraham stopped and turned. "No, son; what?"

"He thinks we're wasting our time doing what God has told us to do. He says I shouldn't bother throwing my life away for His sake."

"What? How dare you say such a thing to my son."

The young man walked up to them and innocently shrugged his shoulders. "But I'm only saying: How do you really know you're doing the will of God today? You could just be wasting your time serving a figment of your own imagination. Have you ever thought of that?"

Abraham took a step closer to the man and looked him straight in the eye. "My God, are you back again?"

Uncomfortable with Abraham's piercing gaze, the young man moved several steps back. "What?" Turning to Isaac, he asked, "Why is he looking at me like that?"

Isaac shrugged back. "How should I know?"

As Abraham stared him down, the young man slowly withdrew. "What is wrong with you people?" he grumbled.

"It *is* you," Abraham insisted.

"Who, Father?" asked Isaac. "Who is he?"

Abraham held up his hand, as if to caution his son. "Be careful with this one, Isaac. Don't listen to another word he says. This may be hard to believe, but this man isn't who he appears to be."

"What is that supposed to mean?" blurted the young man.

Abraham pointed an accusing finger. "He's actually the archenemy of God and all His sacred purposes."

"But how can that be?" Isaac wondered. "He's just an ordinary man."

"No, I'm afraid not, son. Thank God our forefathers taught me all about him. Since time immemorial there have been malignant creatures, diabolical shape-shifters who walk among the living. And whether or not you're willing to accept it, this so-called 'ordinary man' just happens to be the granddaddy of them all."

"You *are* crazy, you old coot," snapped the young man, who grew more agitated by the moment, "you and anyone else who believes in your wild stories."

"Father, please," intoned Ishmael, "I don't mean to sound disrespect-ful, but you don't really expect us to believe such nonsense? You're talking gibberish."

"Really, sir," Eliezer added. "You don't want to say anything you'll re-gret later. I'm sure this young man will leave us alone if we ask him. We don't have to make up outrageous accusations, now do we?"

Abraham defiantly shook his fist. "Fools, all of you. You have no idea what you're dealing with."

"Father, you're scaring me," continued Isaac. "What are you saying? Who do you think this man really is? Some sort of demon?"

Turning to Isaac, Abraham implored, "Not just any demon, son, but the chief of all demons, the most evil spirit of them all!"

"You mean the devil?" asked Isaac, wide-eyed at the realization. "You're saying this is actually Satan himself?"

"Yes, Isaac, it's Satan, disguised as this young man. He was here before. Don't you remember that old man earlier today?"

"Of course I do. What about him?"

"That was him, too. And now he's back again, trying everything he can to lure us away from what God wants us to do!"

Ishmael and Eliezer, still unconvinced, however, just hung their heads in embarrassment.

But an undeterred Abraham again pointed an accusing finger at the young man. "Satan, I rebuke you in the name of the Lord Who created you. Leave this place immediately, you foul creature!"

The young man covered his ears and threw his head back as though he were in excruciating pain. "Shut up, you crazy bastard!" Abruptly the man transformed into his true form as the devil, hideously grotesque, sniffing and clawing at the air. Craning his wolfen head back around toward the men, Satan focused his reptilian black eyes on Abraham and growled, "No one talks to me like that, filthy human, especially you!"

Equally awestruck and terrified, Ishmael, Eliezer and the rest of the men blanched at the sight of this malignant creature, while Abraham and Isaac resolutely stood their ground.

"Silence, Devil!" thundered Abraham. "And leave us at once! I don't ever want to see you again, do you understand?"

As agonized as he was furious, Satan howled through his jagged fangs and, extending his leathery, bat-like wings, turned and flew away in a whirl-wind of dust. Then, as if nothing unusual had just happened, Abraham and Isaac calmly wiped themselves off and resumed their journey, but Ishmael,

Eliezer and the other men stood like statues for quite a while, shaken and bewildered. Then, realizing that Abraham and Isaac were moving on without them, followed by the camels and all their supplies, they began to stir into action.

"What are we doing dawdling around in this God-forsaken place?" Eliezer exclaimed. "And whatever you do, don't talk to any more strangers for the rest of this trip. You hear me?"

REACHING A POINT in their journey where they saw a large brook flowing across the road, Abraham and his group started across. Casually wading through it at first, the men quickly found the water reaching up over their knees. Venturing further still, they were soon in up to their midsections. Eventually, the group became very concerned that the water was by then up to their necks. Not only that, but the current's strength was increasing with every step. Desperate to reach the other side, the men and their camels struggled through the ever deepening and ever more powerful river.

"Wait!" shouted Abraham. "I know this place! There was never any river here before! Now I understand what's happening! It's that damned Satan again, doing all he can to keep us from finishing what we've started!" Defiantly shaking his fist over his head, he roared above the din of the river's flow. "Stop this, Devil! We have to do what God wants! The Lord is going to punish you! Get away from us right now, or else you'll suffer the consequences!"

Suddenly the place where they had been struggling through a coursing river became dry land. The group exchanged troubled looks all around as they examined themselves in total disbelief.

"We're not even wet," muttered Ishmael. "But how?"

"B—*but*," stammered Isaac, who, when he turned to his father, was met with a knowing look, "but we were just up to our necks in raging waters."

"*Why* aren't we wet?" blurted Ishmael, his voice trembling. "What on Earth is going on? This is sheer madness!"

"I don't know," grumbled Eliezer, "and, frankly, I don't want to know."

Then without another word between themselves, the dismayed and confused group started off again, headed for their destination.

ON THE THIRD DAY of their journey, Abraham looked up and saw a remarkable fire burning on a distant mountaintop. Even from afar, he could see that its smoke rose into a shimmering, iridescent cloud.

Abraham pointed. "Isaac, do you see what I see rising above that mountain?"

"I see fire and smoke, Father," he replied, obviously awed by what he was seeing. "And above that is a cloud filled with the splendor of the Lord."

Abraham then turned to Ishmael and Eliezer. "What about the two of you? What do you see on top of that mountain straight ahead?"

"I see a mountain," said Ishmael, "like any other mountain on Earth. What else would I see?"

Eliezer shrugged. "I see a mountain, too. An ordinary mountain, that's all. Why?"

Abraham confidently nodded at Isaac. "Then the Lord has revealed His decision, just as He promised." Turning to Ishmael and Eliezer, he said, "You two, wait here with the rest of the group. Isaac and I will go to the top of Mount Moriah, where we'll worship the Lord, and when we're done, we'll return again. Is that understood?"

"But, Father," said Ishmael with an uneasy tone, "there's no telling what might happen to us while you're away."

"Please, sir," added Eliezer, sounding just as nervous. "I wholeheartedly agree with Ishmael. We have no desire to part ways with you now. Not after everything we've endured to this point."

"I'm very sorry," replied Abraham. "Really I am. But this is the way it has to be. Besides, I'm quite sure nothing further will threaten you down here."

"But how can you be so sure, Father?" asked Ishmael.

"Because if anything is going to happen, it's going to happen on the next leg of our journey," said Abraham, who returned his gaze to the ominously glowing mountaintop, "on our way up there."

IT WAS EARLY AFTERNOON by the time Abraham and Isaac had nearly reached the mountaintop. Along the way, Abraham began picking up pieces of wood, and one by one, he handed them to Isaac, who carried them for his father.

Finally to the top, Abraham pointed to a suitable clearing, where Isaac dropped his load of wood and then stood watching while his father knelt to make a small campfire with some kindling he had whittled with his knife.

"Father, I see the fire, and I see the blade, but where's the lamb we need for our burnt offering?"

"Oh, Isaac, my dear son," Abraham said as he dolefully stared into the fire. "I'm afraid the Lord has chosen you to be the burnt offering, not a lamb."

Isaac tried his best to smile. "Yes, Father; I suspected as much."

"What?" An amazed Abraham turned to his son. "You knew? But how? I never told a soul."

"You didn't have to. I declared my intentions to the Lord, and He obviously heard me."

Confused, Abraham got to his feet and walked over to his son. "What are you saying, Isaac? You spoke to the Lord about what He's asked me to do?"

Isaac nodded. "I have, Father, yes, and I'll happily do whatever He wants."

"You mean, you don't think what we're doing is wrong? Just tell me, son, if you have any doubts about this. I'll understand."

"As the Lord lives, Father, nothing is going to keep us from doing what God wants. I'm completely resolved. In fact, I thank God for choosing me to be a burnt offering for Him."

With a heavy sigh of relief, Abraham hugged his son, and together they began to gather stones. As they built up their stones into a crude altar, the two men quietly wept. After placing a stack of wood on the altar, Abraham began tying Isaac's hands and feet with linen cords.

"Make sure the rope is good and tight, Father, so I can't roll around. I don't want to ruin the offering by breaking loose when your knife cuts me."

Abraham nodded sadly and tightened the cords around his son's hands and feet. Then he carefully placed Isaac atop the pile of wood.

"And Father, please, promise me you'll take some of my ashes to Mother. Tell her: 'This is the sweet-smelling savor of Isaac.'"

Abraham dolefully nodded again. "I promise, son."

"But make sure you don't tell her if she's sitting near a well or anywhere high up. I don't want her throwing herself off trying to come after me."

Cut to the quick, Abraham cried even more, spilling his tears onto Isaac, who also began to cry uncontrollably.

"Don't worry, Father, we'll be all right. Outwardly, our eyes are weeping, but inwardly our hearts rejoice."

Abraham smiled awkwardly. "Yes, my son, I can't explain it, but I feel the same way, too."

Isaac stretched out his neck. "Hurry, Father, do what God told you to do."

"My dear, sweet boy, I love you so much. My only consolation in all of this is knowing that, even before I do, you will look upon the magnificent Face of God."

Then, Abraham raised his blade, preparing to slash his son's throat.

AT THAT VERY MOMENT, the seventy angels appeared before the Face of God.

"Lord!" exclaimed one of them. "You're such a compassionate King. Do You see how Abraham's son is tied down like an animal prepared for slaughter?"

"I do see, yes," replied the Face.

"Dear God, can You imagine how Abraham and Isaac are feeling right now as they carry out Your orders?"

"I can imagine. What would you like Me to do?"

"Lord, please, won't You provide a ransom for Your servant, Isaac?"

"Very well, go."

IN A FLASH, THE ANGEL appeared next to Abraham at the altar. "Abraham, stop!" shouted the angel, grabbing his hand just as it lunged toward Isaac's outstretched throat. "There's no need to harm Isaac. Now God knows for sure you really trust Him, even to the point of sacrificing your own son for His sake."

Looking up, Abraham saw a ram with his horns caught in a thicket.

"Take the ram you see," the angel continued, "the ram that God prepared on the first day of His Creation, created for this very moment when you'd sacrifice it as a burnt offering to the Lord in place of your son."

Running to the ram as it struggled to break free, Abraham discovered a disembodied hand, leathery and grotesque, hidden amongst the thick branches, where it had ensnared the ram's horns with its talon-like fingernails.

"What is this?" asked an astonished Abraham.

"It's the devil again," the angel said. "He's trying to thwart God's purposes to the bitter end. This ram was actually advancing toward you, but when Satan heard God was providing a substitute for your son, he entangled his horns in these bushes, hoping you might kill Isaac before it got to you."

As Abraham wrestled with Satan's horrid claw, the ram struggled to break free with all its might.

"I told you before, Devil," Abraham bellowed, "I didn't ever want to see you again, even if it is just your miserable paw. Now be gone in the name of the Almighty Lord! Away with you!"

Immediately, the hand vanished, and, that quickly, the ram was released from the thickets. Abraham led the animal to the altar, and untying Isaac, he helped his son down. With the same linen cords that had been used on Isaac, Abraham securely tied up the ram, and placing it on the pile of wood, he killed the ram instead of Isaac. Sprinkling some of the ram's blood over the altar, Abraham intoned, "This was done in place of my son. May it be regarded as his blood." And after each and every thing he did at that altar, Abraham announced: "May the Lord accept this instead of my son."

MEANWHILE, THE seventy angels looked down from Heaven, as did the smoldering Face of God.

"Tell us, Lord, if You would," began one of the angels. "Did you honor the sacrifice of Your servant, Abraham?"

"I did, yes," the Lord replied. "In fact, everything Abraham did with the ram at his altar has been counted as though it had been done with Isaac ·himself. And as a result of Abraham's actions, I'll pour out My blessings on him and his descendants, and will continue to do so from this day forward until the end of time."

Sweet Sarah, Why?

BACK HOME, SARAH anxiously paced back and forth inside her tent, waiting for some news about her husband and son.

With a sad, downcast face, an old man stepped up to the door of her tent. "Hello, Sarah?" he called out. "Sarah? Are you home, my dear?"

Finally realizing that someone was calling her, Sarah turned and stepped to the door of her tent. Upon seeing the man, she graciously nodded. "I am, sir. And who might you be?"

Gently kicking at the dirt, he muttered, "Who, me? Oh, that's not important. Let's just say I'm a concerned party."

"Really?" Sarah took a closer look at this strange man.

"What is important is I have some very bad news for you."

"Bad news? What news? About my husband? My son? Tell me."

"Well, you know that husband of yours," the man said, shaking his head pitifully.

"Yes, yes," gulped Sarah. "What have you heard? Just tell me."

"Oh, dear, it seems he went and built himself another one of those altars he's so fond of building. You know the kind."

"Yes, and?"

"Well, then God told him to take Isaac and kill him on it."

"What?" Sarah gasped. "No!"

"Yes. He actually offered him up as a living sacrifice, just because God asked him to. Can you believe it?"

"But how could he do such a thing?"

"You know, I haven't the slightest idea. And no matter how much Isaac wept as he begged his father to spare his life, Abraham refused to even look him in the eye. All the compassion he ever had for his son was completely gone at that moment."

Then, the old man shrugged his shoulders, turned and walked away, disappearing around one of the tents.

As Sarah stood there, agonizing, one of her servant girls ran to her side. "What's wrong, My Lady? What has you so upset?"

"That old man," muttered Sarah, growing breathless, as though a tremendous weight was crushing her chest.

"What about him? Who was he?"

"I don't know; he didn't say. But I think he was one of the men traveling with my husband and son when they left on their trip. That much I do seem to remember."

"But what did he do to get you so upset? Did he say something?"

"He told me Abraham had sacrificed my boy as a burnt offering to the Lord?"

"A burnt offering? Isaac?"

Still trying to catch her breath, Sarah nodded as tears began to well up in her eyes.

"But why?" asked the girl.

"He said, God asked him to do it."

"What? Well, that doesn't make any sense. Are you sure that's what he said?"

"My dear, sweet Isaac, dead." Bursting into tears, Sarah's legs grew weak, and she fell to her knees. "Oh, my son, if only it could have been me that died, not you!"

"My Lady, please don't despair."

Weeping miserably, Sarah threw dirt over her head. "My heart is breaking, my boy. I was so happy to raise you, but now just look at how my joy has turned into mourning."

"Try to think of the good times, ma'am," said the girl, who kneeled next to Sarah and tenderly embraced her. "You two shared so much love and happiness together."

For a moment, Sarah's mind shifted. "Yes, how I remember those special days. How I wept and prayed to God to even have you at my age." Then suddenly a wave a grief seized her again. "But now, after all that, it turns out you were made just for the fire and the blade."

"Please, My Lady, be strong."

"Still, I can console myself with your memory, my son, and with the time we had."

"And by doing this marvelous thing, your husband and your son have faithfully carried out God's plan."

"But how?" asked Sarah through her cascading tears.

"I wish I could tell you, ma'am, but I just don't know. How can we ever hope to understand the mind of God?"

Sarah meekly nodded. "And who could ever resist doing what the Lord wants? He controls every living creature."

"Lord God, everything You do is perfect," Sarah's servant girl added.

"So now I, too, will celebrate Your decision, and even though I'm crying on the outside, inwardly I will rejoice." With that, Sarah gently laid her head on her servant girl's shoulder and became as still as a stone.

AFTER GATHERING HER wits, Sarah began to scour the area, approaching anyone she passed by. "My husband, Abraham, have you seen him?"

"No, Sarah, I'm afraid I haven't," replied one woman.

UNFORTUNATELY, EVERYONE she met along the way just shook their heads as she continued her desperate quest. Accompanied by some of her servants, Sarah traveled for miles, unwilling to stop even when someone offered her a cup of water.

"I think it's time we split up so we can cover more territory," Sarah said to one of her male servants.

"Begging your pardon, ma'am," he replied. "I don't think that would be wise. Not in your condition."

"I don't care what you think!" snapped Sarah. "Just do it! We need to find my husband, now!"

Reluctantly, the man bowed. "As you wish, My Lady."

Then, while her servants went off in one direction in their search, Sarah turned and went the other way.

EVENTUALLY, SARAH encountered the same old man who had come to her tent earlier that day. There he was again, smiling, greeting her as cordially as ever. "Sarah, my dear, I am *so* sorry. I'm afraid I spoke too soon earlier. It turns out I was wrong about your son."

"Now what are you saying?"

"It's Isaac. He's not dead!"

"What? But how?"

"I guess Abraham didn't sacrifice your son after all! God was just testing him. Isn't that marvelous?"

"Are you serious? My boy isn't really dead?"

"No! I'm telling you: Isaac is *alive!*"

Sarah was ecstatic. "That's wonderful!" But within a matter of moments, her wild elation quickly turned to agonizing sorrow. A terrified look swept across Sarah's face. Her breathing became labored, and she started clutching at her chest.

The old man's eyes widened. "Dear lady, what's wrong? You don't look so good."

Dropping to her knees in a cold sweat, Sarah murmured, "God, no, not again; not now." And after several desperate, gasping moments, she slumped to the ground and died. As the old man stood over her body, he transformed into his true appearance. Once again it was Satan. Laughing sadistically, he flew away before anyone noticed what had happened.

BACK AT MOUNT MORIAH, Abraham and Isaac returned to where Ishmael, Eliezer and the rest of the men were still waiting at the base of the mountain. Then, they all headed back home for Hebron.

BUT WHEN ABRAHAM and Isaac arrived back at their tent and found that Sarah was gone, they began searching everywhere for her.

Abraham found one of his servant girls. "Where's Sarah? Have you seen her?"

"But, sir, she's not here."

"What do you mean, she's not here? Where is she?"

"She went looking for you."

"Looking for us? Why?"

"She heard you'd sacrificed Isaac as a burnt offering, so she was desperate to find where you'd gone."

"What? How on Earth did she find out about that? I never told her a thing about my plans."

"She said an old man who'd been traveling with your group came and told her."

"An old man, here?"

The distraught servant girl nodded.

"My God, not again," Abraham growled.

"Do you know who the old man was?"

"I'm afraid I know exactly who the fiend was, my dear." Abraham frantically turned to see Isaac. "Quickly, son; we've got to find your mother before it's too late."

"Too late? What do you mean, too late?" he blurted.

"There's no time to discuss it, Isaac. We've got to hurry. Now let's go."

ACCOMPANIED BY SEVERAL of their servants, Abraham and Isaac searched the countryside for Sarah with ever-increasing desperation. Eventually they were greeted by two men. "Abraham, Abraham, I'm so glad I found you," one of them said, obviously depressed. "I'm afraid I have some very bad news."

"Sarah," gasped Abraham. "Is she all right?"

"Follow me, old friend. I'll take you to her."

WITH A DEEP SENSE OF foreboding, Abraham and Isaac were led to the tent where Sarah was lying in state. When Isaac saw his mother's body, he ran to her side, fell to his knees, and put his cheek to hers. His tears flowed down over her face. "Oh, Mother, Mother, where've you gone? How could you leave me like this? Why, God? Why did You let this happen?"

Heartbroken at the sight of both his deceased wife and his grieving son, Abraham buried his tear-stained face in his hands. "My sweet Sarah, why?"

WITH THE POMP AND circumstance observed only for royalty, Abraham and Isaac then set out to bury Sarah, having dressed her in wonderfully ornate garments. Shem and his great grandson Eber, along with Anar, Ashcol and Mamre, all walked alongside her casket as the carriage made its way to the burial cave.

A HAND LIGHTLY TOUCHED down on Abraham's shoulder as he sat quietly weeping. "I'm here, Abraham. You wanted to see me?"

Abraham dolefully looked up. "Yes, of course, Father Eber." And sucking in his breath in an attempt to regain his composure, he wiped a tear from his eye. "I'm so glad to see you."

"How are you holding up, son?"

"Not very well, I'm afraid. My heart breaks all over again every time I think of my Sarah just lying there, gone like that."

"I can imagine. We were all devastated when we heard the news. It was so completely out of the blue."

"It just doesn't make any sense. How could God have let something like this happen?" Hanging his head, Abraham could not hold back his tears any longer.

Deeply touched by his lament, Eber put his arm around him.

"And thanks again for coming on such short notice," Abraham murmured as he fought to regain his composure again.

"Of course, Abraham, you know you can always count on me. We all share in your loss. Sarah was a good woman, such a spirited girl. I can't believe she's really gone. She was still so young. What was she, all of a hundred and twenty?"

"A hundred and twenty-seven last April."

"Do you have any idea what could have caused her untimely death?"

"I do, yes. In fact, that's why I've asked you here today."

Eber sat down and looked deep into Abraham's mournful eyes. "What is it, son? I sense something stirring deep within your soul."

"It's Isaac. I believe he's in terrible danger."

"Tell me, Abraham. What can I do?"

The Woman at the Well

"BUT, FATHER, I STILL don't understand," Isaac grumbled as he and Abraham stood waiting on the doorstep of the home of Shem and Eber. "Why can't I stay with you?"

"Isaac, Isaac," replied Abraham, trying to remain patient, "we've already gone through this before. My mind is made up. I want you to spend time with Shem and Eber so they can teach you what they know about the Lord."

"But why can't you keep teaching me?"

"I'm sorry, son, but this is how it has to be. Besides, you know very well that my father did the same thing for me when I was a boy. So, please, don't make this any harder than it has to be."

Then Shem and Eber came out to greet them. "Abraham, Isaac," exclaimed Eber. "So good to see you."

Abraham turned and lit up at their appearance. "Father Shem, Father Eber; how are you?"

But Isaac just frowned.

"Isaac, please," Abraham pleaded. "Stop acting this way. You're embarrassing me. Say hello to your elders. They deserve your respect."

"Hello, Father Shem, Father Eber," said Isaac with a perfunctory smile. "How are you both today?"

"There's a good boy," Abraham sighed. "See, Isaac, before you know it, you'll be having the time of your life."

"I don't know, Father," he grumbled, obviously unconvinced. "Why do I get the feeling there's something else you're not telling me about?"

Shem and Eber exchanged a knowing look.

Eber leaned in to Shem and quietly said, "Clever boy, that one."

"Chip off the old block, if you ask me," murmured Shem.

"What are you saying?" sputtered Abraham, who looked to Shem and Eber, hoping for some moral support. "Of course not, Isaac. Don't be ridiculous."

"Isaac, my boy," interjected Shem, right on cue. "Did your dad tell you how much Father Eber and I have been looking forward to this? These are important days in a young man's life, and I was really hoping I could do for you what I once did for him. How would you like that?"

Isaac turned to Shem and reluctantly smiled. "Well, I guess so, sir; when you put it that way."

"Then you'll be all right with them, son?" ventured Abraham hesitantly.

"Don't be silly, Father. Of course I'll be fine. I'm not a child anymore, you know."

Thoroughly amused, Shem and Eber both grinned from ear to ear.

THOUGHTFULLY GAZING out across the sprawling landscape, Abraham watched the bustle of that afternoon's activities as people purposefully moved about in every direction.

"You called for me, sir?" asked a voice.

Looking up, Abraham forced a smile. "Eliezer, yes, I did. Thank you."

"How are you today, sir?"

"Oh, as well as can be expected, I suppose."

"That's good to hear. We've been so worried about you lately."

"Worried about me?"

"Of course. I mean, it's bad enough you haven't seen your son in ages, but on top of that you've had to endure the deaths of your nephew Lot and your beloved brother Nahor. It's a great deal for any man to handle, even a man like you."

"Nahor, yes, Nahor," he replied with a distinct air of melancholy. "It's true. A day hasn't gone by that I haven't thought about my brother's passing. Even though I know he's been reunited with our forefathers, it still saddens me to know I can no longer see him in this present life."

"But certainly you can rejoice in the fact that he led a good, long life."

This time Abraham replied with a more relaxed smile. "Yes, Eliezer; you're quite right about that. For one hundred and seventy-two years that scoundrel gave the world all it could handle, didn't he?"

"That he did, sir, that he did. Now, what can I do for you today?"

"What's that?"

"You called for me, sir. What did you want?"

"Oh, of course, I forgot. I'm getting so old, I lose my train of thought sometimes."

Eliezer smiled back politely.

"In fact," continued Abraham, "I'm getting so old, who knows, my death may come at any moment."

"Please, sir, don't talk like that. You still have many more years left. I'm sure of it."

"Yes, well, that may be true, but with so many of my loved ones having passed from the scene, I'm not sure I want to keep on living. Only Isaac, the light of my life, and Ishmael, that rascal, hold me fast to this life on Earth."

Eliezer nodded with another smile. "Of course, My Lord."

"And even you, my dear Eliezer, if the truth be told. Certainly you know how much I love you. You've always been like a son to me."

"And you, sir, have always been like a father to me. So you see: There are at least three reasons to go on living after all. Now, please, tell me: How can I be of service?"

"It's my son, Isaac."

"Isaac? What about him?"

"I need you to help me find him a wife; someone who isn't from this place, I mean. Lord knows I do not want him marrying a daughter of the Canaanites."

"But what can I do? Where would I go?"

"I need you to go back to the city of Haran, where the rest of my family still lives. Find a wife for my son there. Can you do that for me?"

Eliezer shrugged his shoulders. "But Haran is such a large city. How will I ever hope to succeed in something like that, without having any idea where to look?"

"Ah, don't worry about that. The God of the Universe has led me my whole life. I'm sure He can do the same for you if we just ask Him."

Eliezer perked up. "You think so?"

"Of course, Eliezer. I'm quite confident that with God's help there's no way you can fail. This way you'll be sure to bring Isaac a wife who comes from our own family."

"Then I'll be leaving right away, sir."

"Good. There's no time to lose."

"But what if the woman I find for your son isn't willing to return with me? Then what? Should I take Isaac back there?"

"No, no, no!" insisted Abraham, his eyes growing as big as saucers. "Whatever you do: Don't ever take my son back there! Do you understand?"

Eliezer dutifully nodded.

"Good," Abraham continued. "Now stop worrying. I already told you: The Lord Who has been walking with me my whole life will help you in your mission."

GATHERING TEN OF Abraham's male servants and ten of his camels, each heavily laden with baggage, Eliezer headed out.

"God of my master, Abraham," whispered Eliezer. "If You can hear me now, please bless this journey of ours and guide us to Haran, the city of Nahor, the brother of Abraham. Amen."

A MESSENGER ARRIVED at the home of Shem and Eber one afternoon and delivered a letter to them. Eber read it immediately.

"What does it say, son?" asked Shem.

"It's word from Abraham. He says the danger that was threatening Isaac's safety has apparently passed, for the time being, at least. Now it's time for us to return him home. He says he's planning on getting him married."

"Married?"

"That's what it says. Married."

"Here I thought you said the danger had passed," Shem said with a wry smile. "Sounds like the danger is just beginning for that young man."

The two men burst out laughing. Hearing the commotion, Isaac walked into the room to investigate, and as soon as he did, the men ceased their laughter. Puzzled, Isaac saw the strangest look on both men's faces. "What is going on?" he asked suspiciously.

Quickly regaining his composure, Shem replied, "Your father has sent word that we're to send you home."

"Home?" he wondered. "Did he say why?"

"So you can get married," said Eber, in mock congratulatory fashion. "Our best regards to the happy bridegroom this fine day. We salute you."

"Married?" blurted Isaac. "That's the craziest thing I ever heard."

"You're telling me!" chided Shem with an impish grin. "I didn't think you even knew what a woman was."

"But I don't," Isaac stammered. "I—I mean, of course I do. Of course I know what a woman is! I am forty years old, you know."

It was all that the two men could do to suppress any more laughter, as Isaac just stood there with a bewildered look on his face.

AS THE SUN REACHED its zenith in the noonday sky, Eliezer and his ten men arrived in Haran. Parched and weary, the group stopped by a watering hole just inside the city gates so they and their camels could drink their fill of water. As the men and their camel's were resting, Eliezer slipped away by himself. "God of Abraham, please lead me in the right direction so I can find a wife for Isaac from his own family. Amen."

Just then, a young woman around sixteen years old came and began drawing water from a nearby well. Intrigued, Eliezer walked over to her. Seeing him approach, she curtsied.

"Hello, young lady," Eliezer began, "I hope you don't think it too forward of me, but I felt compelled to meet you."

"Good day, sir," she said. "Compelled, you say?"

"Yes, isn't that odd?" he continued with a peculiar, faraway look in his eyes.

"If I didn't know better, I'd say you had dishonorable intentions," the girl said in a playful tone. "Should I run and fetch my brothers before it's too late?"

A startled Eliezer then looked directly at her. "Heavens, no. My intentions are absolutely honorable; on behalf of my master, that is."

"I see. So you weren't waiting to draw water from this well?"

"Oh, no, child," he replied, motioning to the water hole, "my men and I have already had our fill for the time being, but thank you for asking. Besides, there was no one around to obtain permission to access this well."

"That's very noble of you. Most people around here would have simply drawn water without any thought of permission. What's your name, if you don't mind my asking? I've never seen you around here before."

"That's because I'm not from around here."

"Then that explains your manners," she replied with a wry smile.

"My name is Eliezer." Smiling back, he was clearly charmed by her precocious wit. "And I've traveled here from Canaan on a very important mission. And who might you be?"

"My name is Rebecca, daughter of Bethuel."

Eliezer's ears instantly pricked up at the sound of that name. "Bethuel? Do you mean to say your father is Bethuel, the son of Nahor?"

"Yes. That's right."

"Then your father is the nephew of Abraham? From the land of Canaan?"

"Yes, of course. Why do you ask?"

"Because Abraham is my master, the man I spoke to you about earlier. It's on his behalf that I've come here."

"Abraham of Canaan is your master?"

"Yes, he really is, young lady."

"I see. Then maybe you'd like to come to our home, where you can speak to my father personally."

ACCOMPANIED BY Rebecca, Eliezer, followed by his ten men, rode up to her family's tent, where they were met by none other than Bethuel and his wife, who both came out to see who was arriving. Eliezer got off his camel and reached out a hand of greeting to Rebecca's father.

"You must be Bethuel," said Eliezer, smiling graciously. "I'd recognize the family resemblance anywhere."

Intrigued, Bethuel looked at his wife, then back at Eliezer. "You know who I am?"

"Of course; you're Bethuel, son of Nahor, nephew of my master, Abraham of Canaan."

Bethuel nodded with a craggy grin. "Yes, that's right. And you say you're a servant of Uncle Abraham?"

"Not just any servant, mind you; his chief servant. My name is Eliezer."

"Well, well, Eliezer. How is it that you've come to me on this fine day?"

"That's the astonishing thing, I must admit, because I came to this land without a clue as to where I was going, or with whom I would meet. Master Abraham simply told me I should come here to seek a wife for his son, Isaac. And even though I had no idea what I'd find, he assured me his God would lead me to where I needed to go."

"A wife, you say?" muttered Bethuel, who again glanced at his wife.

"That's right. And, as you can imagine, I was quite amazed when we stopped, purely by chance, at the well where your daughter came to draw water. It's an absolute miracle that our paths crossed so unexpectedly."

"A miracle, you say," echoed Bethuel.

"Yes, I do say. Certainly the Lord has blessed us all today."

As his eyes began to wander, Bethuel took a closer look at the entourage of men and camels that were gathered around Eliezer. "And what is all this, anyway? It looks like you have an awful lot of stuff. Looks like you're planning to go a long way still."

"Oh, forgive me, I nearly forgot," Eliezer said, shaking his head, as if he were scattering the cobwebs from his mind. "How foolish of me. No, we have no other destination in mind but this one. All this is for you and your family. It's my master's dowry on behalf of Isaac."

"For me, you say?" wondered Bethuel, his eyes widening at the thought of what might be amongst the cargo that took so many men and camels to transport.

"Yes, that's right; all of it's for you, if, of course, you're willing to provide a wife for my master's son."

With that, Bethuel turned and, clutching his wife's hand, led her back into their tent. After much discussion in hushed tones, the two of them came back out and bowed respectfully before Eliezer.

"It is agreed," intoned Bethuel. "Tell Uncle Abraham that we accept his gracious, and most generous, offer."

"Wonderful," Eliezer exclaimed, exhaling the breath he had been holding in anticipation. "Do you have any idea who the young lady will be?"

"We do, yes," Bethuel's wife replied, glancing at her husband with a happy smile.

Bethuel nodded back with his craggy grin and continued, "May we present you with our beloved daughter on behalf of my uncle." Together, he and his wife turned to see a young woman coming out of their tent.

"Rebecca," said Bethuel and his wife with one voice.

"Rebecca," echoed Eliezer. "You?"

Curtsying as graciously as she had when they first met at the well, she smiled sweetly and replied, "Yes, Eliezer. It's me."

AS SOON AS ELIEZER and his group returned to Canaan, Isaac came out to greet them. Beaming with pride, Eliezer led Rebecca by the hand and walked her right up to Isaac, who already appeared star struck by her beauty.

"Rebecca," began Eliezer, "I'd like you to meet my master Abraham's son, Isaac; Isaac, this is Rebecca, daughter of Bethuel, the son of Nahor and nephew of Abraham of Canaan."

With barely a thought, Isaac reached out, took her delicate hand, and lovingly kissed it. "Hello, Rebecca. I am so glad to meet you."

Embarrassed, Rebecca turned away, looking to Eliezer, unsure of what to do next, and he nodded back, as though urging her to respond. Turning back to Isaac, who still held her hand, anxiously awaiting her response, she curtsied and said, "Likewise, I'm sure. I'm pleased to meet you, too, Isaac."

In that moment, the pair locked eyes and, for quite a while, stayed like that as if there were no other people in the whole world except them.

The War Within

TWENTY YEARS WOULD pass by before Rebecca would conceive, and when she did the children inside her began to struggle. This caused her so much pain, in fact, that at times all her strength would drain away. Bewildered and fatigued, she paid a visit to one of the other women in her village. "Has anything like this ever happened to anyone you know?" Rebecca asked.

"No, never," came the woman's solemn reply.

"But why am I the only one?"

THEN SHEM AND EBER came to see how Rebecca and Isaac were getting along.

"So how's our mother-to-be?" Shem asked Isaac. "We've heard she's been having quite a time of it."

Isaac was clearly consumed with concern for his wife. "I don't know, Father Shem. I'm afraid for her life. No one has any idea what could be wrong with her."

"Don't be alarmed, son," said Eber. "The only thing wrong with your wife is she's going to give birth to twins."

"Oh, my Lord, *twins*?" Isaac blurted, nearly as breathless as his poor wife.

Eber nodded knowingly. "That's right. Even now the children inside her are struggling for supremacy, as each one tries to outwrestle the other. From this pair, two great nations will emerge. Naturally, one of these nations will be stronger than the other, but, as it turns out, the more powerful of the two will end up serving the younger one."

IN DUE TIME, THE DAY to deliver her children arrived. Kneeling down, Rebecca proceeded to give birth to twin sons. The first child came out as though he were wearing a hairy garment.

"Look at this one!" exclaimed the midwife. "We should call him Esau. He was already complete even before he came out of the womb."

Then, after Esau had been pulled out, his twin brother reached from their mother's womb and grabbed Esau's heel.

"And this one must be Jacob, the heel-catcher."

"YOU WANTED TO SEE me, Father?" asked Isaac, who upon entering his father's tent was stunned by the riches he saw surrounding the aged Abraham who was comfortably reclined on his bed.

"Pop, what's all this?"

"Ah, this? It's nothing. A small sample, really. And now it's all yours, Isaac."

"Me? But why? What did I ever do to deserve this?"

"You came into this world, my boy. By God's grace, you've blessed your mother's heart and mine, and what you're seeing here is just a part of your inheritance when I die."

"Father, don't talk like that."

"Oh, son, don't worry about me. I've lived a good, long life. One hundred and seventy-five of the most thrilling years a man could ever hope to live. But before I leave this present life, I have a few things to settle."

"Like what, Pop?"

"Like some things I've been meaning to tell you about, important things that need to be said before it's too late."

"All right. I'm listening."

A great melancholy suddenly washed over Abraham as though his whole life were flashing before him. In his mind's eye, images from his past came flooding back to him. First, he saw himself destroying his father's idols in a fit of rage, and then he found himself in the furnace of Nimrod again. But much to his dismay, although he miraculously survived the ordeal, he remembered all too clearly how his brother Haran had died in such agony. Then he remembered how, to make matters worse, he had lied to Sarah as she mourned his passing.

"Father, are you all right?" asked Isaac as he watched his father slipping away before his very eyes.

"Promise me, son," whispered Abraham.

Leaning forward, Isaac asked with an odd tilt of his head, "What, Father?"

"Promise me."

Then came more images into the patriarch's weary mind, all-too-fleeting glimpses of his beloved Sarah, of the time he went so far as to hide her in a chest in his attempts to deceive the Pharaoh, and of the time he lied to her concerning his plans to do God's bidding in sacrificing Isaac. Especially vivid was his recollection of how Sarah had wept when she had to say goodbye to her son for the last time, although at the time none of them could have ever known it really was the final moment they would spend together in this life.

"Just promise me, Isaac, promise," moaned Abraham, on the verge of tears.

"Anything, Father, anything. What's wrong? Please tell me."

Then, as if wrestling free from the grip of those bitter memories from so long ago, Abraham refocused his eyes back upon his son and wiped away the tear that slowly trickled down his cheek. "Oh, my dear son, Isaac. Please forgive me. I'm such a fool."

"Don't say that, Pop. You're a good man; no, you're a great man, a man in whom the Lord of Hosts has entrusted the fate of the whole world. Who else can lay claim to such a thing?"

Still clearly unhappy, Abraham shook his head. "But at what price, my son, what price? Never forget, serving God comes only at a tremendous price. Do you hear me?"

"I hear you, Father."

"Never forget that, Isaac. Never deceive yourself for a single, solitary moment. In order to do the things that God requires, one can never underestimate the lengths to which our humanity will stoop, will sink, in order to preserve itself in response to the Lord's call. The human heart is pernicious and cunning and never stops fighting us for even a moment, as it continually seeks to undermine the higher good." Struggling to sit up, Abraham became extremely agitated. "Do you understand what I'm trying to say, Isaac?"

"Hold on, Father, hold on," he replied, stepping forward in an effort to keep him from springing headlong out of bed. "Relax. Everything's going to be all right."

"Then you'll follow my advice, son?"

"Of course. You know I've always done whatever you've asked me. Haven't I?"

Somewhat appeased, Abraham settled back into his bed. "Certainly, Isaac, yes, always. You're a fine man. Now, there's just one last thing I need you to do for me."

"Name it, Father."

"Promise me that whatever you do, you won't ever let the earthly treasures you see before you take the place of God in your life. Always remember, the Lord of Heaven and Earth is the only lasting treasure you should seek in this life. Can you do that for me?"

"Of course, I promise."

"He's the One Who gave me every earthly delight, the One Who delivered me from the furnace of Nimrod and led me here, Who promised to give this land to my descendants whenever they did things His way. So you have to remember to always follow Him, and never let anyone lead you astray from the commands of God."

"I'll remember, Father. There's no One but Him."

"Good. And never forget, my son, always teach your children to do what He says. That way things will always go well with them, too. Above all, teach your children about the Lord and His way of doing things. Always, always remind them."

"I promise, Father. I'll do everything you've asked of me."

"Good, very good. Then I'm ready."

"Ready for what, Pop?"

"After a lifelong quest to penetrate the greatest mystery of the Universe, I'm finally ready, my son, finally ready to look upon the Face of God for myself."

THEN, IN THE FIFTEENTH year of Jacob and Esau's life, Abraham died. Immediately, Isaac and Ishmael set out with heavy hearts to bury their beloved father, along with their wives, Rebecca and Malchuth, accompanied by the twins, Jacob and Esau. There to show their support as well were all of Abraham's relatives from Haran, including Bethuel and his family, and as they led the great patriarch's coffin in a lavish royal procession, the Canaanite kings, princes and noblemen all joined in to pay their respects, too.

The Hunter Becomes the Hunted

THE MID-MORNING SUN began to wipe away the dew of the previous night as several antelope raised their heads, startled by the sound of tall grass crumpling very near to where they were feeding. Young Esau poked his head through the lush blades, but before he even had a chance to draw his bow, the antelope bolted away, much to his chagrin.

Meanwhile, at the opposite end of the same field, less than a hundred yards away, Nimrod, in spite of his advanced age, was also hunting with his bow and arrow. Accompanied by several of his fiercest warriors, the wily king caught sight of Esau, who was quite oblivious to their presence.

"Well, well, what do we have here?" Nimrod muttered, obviously more interested in this human quarry than he was in the animal prey that ran for cover as his men fanned out across the landscape. "If it isn't Esau, the grandson of my old nemesis. Just look at him strutting about. So he thinks himself a mighty hunter, does he? What a foolish, arrogant child."

EXHAUSTED AND empty-handed, Esau came home, only to find Jacob cooking a pot of beef stew over an open fire. He eagerly sniffed at the air like a wild animal in desperate search of prey. "That smells delicious," he growled. "What are you cooking? I'm famished."

"No luck hunting, eh?" asked Jacob, grinning at the pathetic look on Esau's face.

"Afraid not. Scarce pickings out there today. No thanks to Nimrod's men, of course. They always grab the best territory for themselves."

"Of course."

Esau wandered closer toward the pot of Jacob's simmering stew. "You are such a wonderful cook, brother. May I have some?"

"How come you're only my friend when I'm making something good to eat?" he replied mockingly. "Why is that?"

"Jacob, my twin soul, how could you say that? Talk like that hurts my feelings."

"Hardly."

"Well, what do you expect?" said Esau with a miserable groan. "I've been hunting all morning, with nothing to show for it except an empty belly. I'm hungry, no, I'm starving to death, right before your very eyes. Please, dear brother, have pity on your own flesh and blood, won't you?" Reaching around Jacob, he scooped out two fingers full of stew and instantly gobbled it down.

"Hey, you pig! Get your filthy paw out of my food!"

"You know, someday somebody's going to give that Nimrod the lesson he deserves."

"Yeah, then why don't you give it to him?"

"Who, me?" scoffed Esau. "Yeah, right. With all his men surrounding him wherever he goes? Are you nuts?"

"His power doesn't lie in his men, you know," Jacob assured him.

Esau licked his fingers of every drop of juice. "What are you babbling about now?"

"His power."

"Yeah, what about his *power*?"

"It's not what you think, that's all."

"And what makes you such an expert?"

"Don't you remember? Fathers Shem and Eber told us about it when we were kids."

"You mean, those old wives tales, don't you?"

"Not the part about the garment of Adam. They didn't make that part up, did they?"

"Garment? What garment?"

"God provided sheepskins as clothing for Adam, and it was handed down to Enoch and then Noah. Don't you remember?"

"Oh, sure, those," he cynically replied. "I remember now. And I suppose that's why they had power over the animals. Adam named them all, Noah brought them into the Ark, that sort of thing."

"Exactly," exclaimed Jacob, as if he thought Esau actually believed what he was saying. "But after the Flood, Ham stole the garment and gave it to his son Cush, which was how Nimrod got it. That's how he became the mighty hunter before the Lord. In fact, the garment not only gave him power over the animals, but it also made him invincible in battle. That's why his people made him king; that's why he nearly conquered the entire world. That is, until the confusion of tongues at the Tower of Babel disintegrated his kingdom. Don't you get it?"

Esau shook his head. "My dear, demented brother, you are so naïve. Honestly, if I thought for one second that that garment Nimrod is wearing actually turned an ordinary man into a world conqueror, even I'd try to steal it from him."

ESAU WENT HUNTING again in the fields where Nimrod often went, but this time, he saw the king and his warriors before they noticed him. As luck would have it, Esau discovered that only two of his bodyguards were with Nimrod, while the rest of Nimrod's warriors were all some distance away, off in their own search for game. So, before anyone had a chance to see him, Esau hid behind the surrounding bushes and began stalking his prey. As Nimrod and his two guards wandered past him, Esau leapt into view, adeptly brandishing his sword. Nimrod's two men instinctively withdrew their blades and prepared to rush at Esau.

"Wait!" Nimrod exclaimed. "Stand down, you two. This ends, here and now."

"But, Your Highness," said one of his bodyguards, "certainly you're in no position to defend yourself alone."

"How dare you question me. I may be two hundred and fifteen years old, but I'm not dead yet!"

"Forgive me, Sire. As you wish."

The two bodyguards obediently returned their swords to their sheaths and stepped back several feet.

"*This* is between me and the boy," said Nimrod, who then withdrew his own sword.

"Who are you calling a boy?" Esau grumbled.

"What are you, all of seventeen, eighteen?"

"I'll have you know, sir, I'm twenty years old."

Nimrod tilted his head oddly. "How fitting. I was the same age when I took on the responsibilities of a man."

"So it's man to man," said Esau, supremely arrogant. "Is that it?"

"As a matter of fact, yes, it is. Before you stands not a king, not a rebel, but a man, a man who refuses to wrestle with phantoms in the night any longer." Slowly, Nimrod held up his sword with one hand and motioned to Esau with his other, beckoning him to commence their engagement.

With his sword drawn, Esau charged at Nimrod. "Then prepare to taste the vengeance of the God of Abraham!"

Nearly upon him, Nimrod inexplicably lowered his sword.

"This is for Uncle Haran," spewed Esau, "you miserable bastard!" And with a single, furious slash of Esau's blade, Nimrod's head rolled off his shoulders and his body fell limply to the ground. Stunned by what they had just witnessed, Nimrod's two bodyguards let out a vicious howl and charged Esau with flashing swords. Spinning to avoid their attack, Esau furiously slashed away, killing them both with two swift strokes of his blade.

THE REST OF NIMROD'S warriors, who were out hunting in different parts of the wilderness, heard the distant cries of the two bodyguards and started to run to see what had happened.

ESAU KNELT DOWN NEXT to Nimrod's body and removed Adam's garment from around his waist, tightly wrapping them around his own. From a distance, he saw Nimrod's men coming toward him, so he ran as fast as he could with the priceless garment now securely in his possession.

RUNNING INTO THE CITY with the garment, Esau finally came to his father's tent. To the point of exhaustion, Esau approached Jacob, who was cooking a steaming pot of lentil stew, and wearily sat down next to him. "What a wonderfully delicious aroma," he sighed, still trying to catch his breath. "My God, I am ravenous."

"Don't tell me. You've been out hunting again?"

"You know me so well, brother."

"And let me guess. You had no luck again with the game today, all thanks to your old nemesis, Nimrod."

"Ah, yes, the game. Well, you see, today it turns out that the game actually went all my way."

An intrigued Jacob turned to look at his brother and was instantly shocked by the sight of the sheepskins wrapped around Esau's waist. "Good God, you did it? You got the garment?"

"You mean to tell me you knew this was Adam's garment just by taking one look at it?"

"Something like that, yes, I suppose I did."

"Must be nice. Now, before I die of starvation on this very spot, would you please give me something to eat?"

"Something to eat?" Jacob asked incredulously. "You have the garment of Adam in your possession, and all you can think about is your empty belly?"

The hairy one shrugged. "What else is new?"

"Fine, I'll feed you." With a wicked twinkle in his eye, his brother added, "For a price, that is."

Grinning from ear to ear, Esau waved his hand in a friendly gesture. "Of course, brother, anything for you; just name it. After all, if it wasn't for you, I would never have known this garment was—"

"I want your birthright," Jacob interjected, quite casually.

Esau's grin immediately turned to a scowl. "But I'm about to die, right here and now. How could you be so mercenary at a time like this?"

The heel-catcher shrugged. "Sorry; not my fault. So … what'll it be?"

"You dirty scoundrel, you conniving rat. You really are my twin brother, aren't you?"

"That's right, brother," Jacob cooed as he held out a bowl of his most delicious lentil stew. "So tell me. You want some … or not?"

"Of course, I want some … brother," he replied with a snide grin. "What do I need with my birthright, anyway, now that I have Adam's garment?" And grabbing the bowl of stew from Jacob's outstretched hand, Esau hungrily gobbled its contents.

TRANSPORTING NIMROD'S body back to his own city of Shinar, the king's warriors buried their dead monarch amidst great pageantry and lamentation. And after reigning for one hundred and eighty-five years, the king of Shinar died shamefully by the sword of Esau, killed by a descendant of Abraham after all, just as Nimrod had seen in his own dreams and just as his sages and sorcerers had predicted so many years ago.

The Mystery of the One

ENOCH SLOWLY CLOSED the book in his lap and looked up at everyone. As before, the crowd had continued to swell as he had been reading his story aloud. The pleasantly surprised patriarch scanned the group of eager listeners. "Well, everyone, now I want you to think carefully about what I've been telling you, because it really does come to you straight from the Lord's own mouth."

"Thank you, Father," said Methuselah. "That was another incredible story. How do you do it?"

Enoch smiled contentedly. "Tell me, then. Did anyone learn anything from this story of the father of faith? And what about the children of faith who followed in his footsteps? Did they teach you anything?"

Lamech stood up. "Well, I learned that each and every person has to have faith for themselves. No one else can do it for you. The faith of a single individual, that's what the Lord responds to. Is that right, Grandfather?"

For several moments, he gazed at his grandson before breaking into a smile, like a teacher satisfied with his student. "Very good, Lamech. Yes, that's correct."

Then Jubal stood up and boldly took a step forward. "You mean to tell me one person's faith really does all that? I'm sorry, Grandfather, but it seems to me you're filling everyone's head with a bunch of silly old wives tales."

Enoch turned slowly. "Young man, I do believe you still have a great deal to learn. In the meantime, I'd advise you to avoid saying anything you'll regret later."

"I beg your pardon, sir." Jubal reluctantly bowed to the patriarch. "I meant no disrespect. I just fail to see the moral of your story, that's all. How can the faith of one person accomplish everything you've just described?"

"My dear, Jubal." Enoch knowingly smiled. "You mean to tell me you don't know about the mystery of the One?"

"The mystery of the One?" Jubal shrugged. "No, sir, I'm afraid not."

"Oh, yes, the mystery of the One. As one year is more honorable than another year, so also is one person more honorable than another. One person may have tremendous wealth, while someone else may be very poor. One person may be quite intelligent, while another is not so bright. One person is famous for their silence, another for their cleanliness, one for strength, another for sensibility. But let it be heard and understood by everyone here, there is no one better than the one who respects God. In the time to come, that person will be more glorious than all the rest."

"That's it?" replied Jubal, clearly mystified. "That's the mystery? I don't get it."

"I guess that's why they call it a mystery, cousin." Lamech smiled sarcastically.

The entire group chuckled, but Jubal, unamused, scornfully glared back at Lamech.

"What's so difficult to understand, my son?" Enoch continued. "It's simple. The one who respects the principles of his forefathers is blessed, but the one who perverts the decrees of his forefathers is cursed."

Jubal shook his head impatiently. "Yes, yes, of course, I get all that, but what about the angels and the thrones? Can't you tell us more about them? What about the gatekeepers, serpents with eyes like lanterns and teeth like razors?"

"The one who imparts peace and love is blessed," Enoch persisted, "but the one who disturbs those who love their neighbors is cursed. The one who is humble in speech is blessed, but the one who speaks peaceably, while harboring murder in their heart, is cursed. The mystery of the One is just like that. Do you see what I'm saying?"

"Of course I do, yes," replied Jubal, nodding his head in frustration. "That's all very commendable. I see that. But, please, why won't you tell us more about the treasure houses of ice and snow? Or about the secrets of the wind."

"Blessed is the one who refuses to hold a grudge," Enoch continued patiently, "the one who helps the injured, the condemned, the brokenhearted, who gives to the needy, because on Judgment Day every weight and measure will be as it is in the marketplace. That is to say, they'll be hung on scales so that everyone can inspect the truth for themselves, and according to this measure, they'll receive their reward."

"Fine, yes, well," said Jubal, clearly exasperated. "Then I guess you're not going to answer my question. Never mind. I'm sorry I even asked. Good day to you, sir." And bowing dutifully, Jubal turned and walked away, disappearing back into the crowd.

"Don't mind him, Papa Enoch," urged Eli's mother. "He's a handful, that one. Headstrong like his mother, I'm afraid."

Enoch nodded amicably. "I understand all too well, my dear."

"So, Pop," interjected Methuselah, trying to steer the conversation in a new direction, "what else do your books have to say?"

"Ah, yes, of course. Let me see: Well, the one who brings an offering to the Lord will have God Himself assist in the blessing of that gift, but the one who approaches Him without sincerity will not have his treasures increased in Heaven. And when God demands an offering of bread or cattle or any other sacrifice, for that matter, it's nothing compared to what He's really looking for."

"And what's that, Grandpa?" asked Lamech.

"A pure heart, my boy. Sincerity, honesty, call it what you will. In fact, a pure heart is so important to God that He uses all these other things just to test the heart of each and every man, woman and child. That's the mystery of the One. Don't you see?"

"Is it even more important than the secrets of the wind and the snow and the stars?" wondered Eli's mother.

"Yes, my dear, much more. Listen, everyone. Understand something very important here. If anyone brings a gift to an earthly ruler while harboring disloyal thoughts in his heart, and the ruler finds out, won't he be angry with him?"

"Of course he would," Lamech replied.

"And wouldn't that same ruler also refuse to accept any of his so-called 'gifts'? Wouldn't he then hand him over to a swift and severe punishment?"

"Of course," chimed in Jared. "That goes without saying."

"That's right, yes. Then there's your answer. The mystery of the One is like that, too."

Methuselah's wife squinted her eyes, trying to wrap her mind around what Enoch was saying. "I'm still not sure if I understand what you're telling us, Father."

"That's all right, my dear. There's no shame in admitting you don't understand right away. These things take time. That's why it's so important to take the books I've written for you and read them for yourselves. Take your time getting to know what's in them."

"We'll do just that, Grandpa," Lamech said. "How many books are there, anyway?"

"Oh, my, there are hundreds of these wonderful books, just waiting for you all."

"Hundreds?" chirped little Eli in amazement.

"Yes, hundreds. Right there in black and white for everyone to see, answers to all your questions, about everything that took place long ago in the beginning of God's creation, right up until the End of Time."

"Well, Pop," said Methuselah, "now that you've finished with your story, what will you do next? And when do we get to see these books of yours with our own eyes?"

"Soon, my boy, very soon. In the meantime, I have one last story to tell you before I return to God."

Methuselah looked puzzled at this statement. "Now, when you say return to God, what, exactly, do you mean by that?"

"Well, it means I have three weeks left before the Lord sends his two angels, Sariel and Raguel, to return me to where He is."

Methuselah and Lamech exchanged a concerned look.

"Father, please," replied Methuselah, "let's not talk about that right now. I think it's time for a break, don't you?"

Enoch wearily nodded. "Then we should all agree to meet back here again next week at this same time, and I'll tell you another story. How does that sound?"

"Very good, son, we're looking forward to it," said Jared, who turned to the rest of the elders seated there with him. "Isn't that right, everyone?"

To a man, they all nodded.

JUBAL AND HIS TWO brothers, Hiram and Tubal, were loitering the next day down the street from Enoch's home. To the casual passersby, there was nothing at all sinister about this unassuming trio, but to those in the know, it clearly represented a worrisome moment for Enoch and his group.

Hiram lustily licked his lips. "Boy, would I love to get my hands on one of Enoch's books. How about you, Jubal?"

Grinning back, Jubal sneered, "That's exactly what I was counting on, brother."

"What?" wondered Hiram, who suddenly realized what Jubal just said, "Wait. You were?" He then turned to his other brother. "Tubal, what do you think Jubal means by that?"

"I'm not sure, Hiram. Jubal, are you saying what I think you're saying?"

"I might be," he replied with a malicious twinkle in his eye.

"Uh, Tubal," said Hiram suspiciously. "I do think our brother is up to no good again. I've seen that look in his eyes before."

"What look is that, brother?" Jubal asked, quite innocently.

"You know very well, Jubal," replied Tubal. "The look of desire."

"He's right, Jubal," Hiram groaned, as Jubal looked at them as if offended. "When I see that look in your eyes, I see the eyes of robbery staring back at me."

"What is wrong with you two?" Jubal scoffed. "What harm could there be in borrowing a few books? Have you both lost your nerve? It's not like we'd be taking anything of value. They're just books."

Hiram and Tubal exchanged a troubled look.

"Besides," continued Jubal as his eyes veered off into the distance, "we'd just be borrowing them for a little while. Then, after we've had a good look at them for ourselves, they would, quite mysteriously, find their way right back to where we found them."

"All right, all right," Tubal said. "I admit it. The thought of seeing one of Enoch's precious books with my own eyes has begun to gnaw at me, too."

"We haven't lost our nerve, have we, Tubal?" wondered Hiram.

"Of course not, Hiram," insisted Tubal.

"Good, then it's settled," murmured Jubal, consumed by his thoughts.

"Together we hatch our plan, together we execute that plan, and together we discover for ourselves exactly what's inside those books." And turning to his two brothers, he donned a malicious grin. "When the time is right, that is."

ANOTHER HUGE CROWD surrounded Enoch, who sat happily with his book perched in his lap, gazing out over several hundred eager faces. From his sons and daughters, and his fathers and mothers, to his aunts and uncles, and his nieces and nephews, everyone was there to listen that day. And in their midst, Jubal, Hiram and Tubal sat like hawks watching a field mouse from across the field, just waiting for an opportunity to strike.

"Well, hello, everyone," Enoch began. "I'm so glad to have this chance to tell you all about the wonderful books the Lord has asked me to give you."

"Thank you, Papa Enoch, for having us today," said Eli's mother.

"Of course, my dear, my pleasure. Now, I want you all to know that after I'm gone, you'll be able to give these books to your children, too, throughout all your generations."

"Tell us, then, son," asked Jared, "these books you're going to give us, will they be intended for our nation alone?"

"No, Father, of course not. The Lord is the Ruler and Judge of the entire Universe. Anyone who respects God will be allowed to read them. That way everyone will have a chance to come to love these books, more than any mere earthly delight. Does that make sense?"

"Certainly," Jared replied. "It does, yes."

"In the meantime, everyone, don't be deceived," continued Enoch. "There really is a place that's already prepared for each and every person. How do I know?" Looking around at the crowd before him, Enoch gazed deeply into their eyes. "Does anyone here know how I know?"

Everyone just shrugged their shoulders.

Enoch then turned to Jubal. "Do *you* know?"

But Jubal never even flinched.

Tubal surreptitiously looked over at him. "Is he talking to you, Jubal? He's looking right at you, isn't he?"

"Would you shut up?" muttered Jubal. "And quit looking at me, you idiot."

Enoch gazed intently at Jubal as he continued. "I know because I've already described everyone's life in all the books that God had me write, that's why."

Hiram mumbled under his breath. "You don't think he suspects us, Jubal, do you?"

Enoch proceeded. "I assure you all, even before you were born, each and every one of you had a place prepared for you. Not only that, but God has measured out a unique set of trials and tribulations which are designed just for you and your specific nature."

"He doesn't know a thing, I tell you," whispered Jubal. "The man is a charlatan."

A stern woman sitting next to Jubal and his two brothers leaned in toward them, grumbling indignantly. "Would you please be quiet? Show some respect."

The trio immediately snapped to attention, trying, however clumsily, to conform.

Enoch's words continued to flow like water from a mountain stream. "Analyzing every person's accomplishments and failures throughout their lifetime, I wrote corresponding judgments to go along with those specific deeds." Again and again, the patriarch's eyes kept returning to Jubal, resting his intense gaze on him. "In fact, there isn't a single person born on Earth who can hide from this kind of scrutiny, ever."

Hiram muttered to Jubal out of the corner of his mouth. "So tell me again, brother, why he keeps looking at you."

"Hush!" snapped the stern woman.

Again the trio of brothers snapped up, front and center, trying their best to look like they were paying attention to the storyteller.

"And when the Lord sends a great light," Enoch continued in reverential tones, "there will be judgment for the just and the unjust alike, because no one among us can ever hope to escape from being held accountable by Him." The wistful patriarch slowly opened the book in his lap. "And so it continues, this mystery of the One."

Trial by Fury

Adapted from

The Letters of Herod and Pilate,

The Epistles of Pilate to Tiberius Caesar,

The Trial and Condemnation of Pilate,

and The Death of Pilate, who Condemned Jesus

and

The Gospel of Nicodemus,

formerly called

The Acts of Pontius Pilate

Behold the Man, Antonio Ciseri, 1871

Trial by Fury

Teachers and Tyrants

CANAAN, OR PALESTINE, *as it was later called because of the Philistines living there, would become known by yet another name after its conquest under Joshua: Israel.*

These were the words on a chalkboard inside a room full of raptly attentive Jewish schoolboys, ranging in age from thirteen to seventeen, where a neatly clad teacher strode back and forth.

"So, class," beamed the proud teacher, "are you ready for today's history lesson of how we, as a proud and mighty nation, came to be in this land of ours?"

"Yes, Professor Ada," the class chimed in unison.

"Very good, then let us commence. It all began about fourteen centuries ago, when Joshua led the Twelve Tribes of Israel in the conquest of Canaan. This was followed by a period of some four hundred years, in which the land was ruled by judges, such as Gideon and Samson. Then, a little more than a thousand years ago, a loose but powerful confederation of all the tribes was welded together under King David, who ultimately catapulted our nation to its zenith of glory. Sadly, however, the kingdom divided some seventy-five years later, when the last portion of our great nation ceased to exist as an independent territory, and for the next several centuries, two kingdoms struggled for survival where, before, there had been just one. Both the House of Judah to the south and the House of Israel to the north would then become minor provinces in a succession of larger empires. Yet try as they might, none of these fierce nations, not Assyria or Babylon, not Persia or Greece, none could extinguish the indomitable spirit of our people."

As Professor Ada paced back and forth in front of them, the enthralled students tried very hard to envision the scene as he was describing it.

"Then, about ninety years ago, Roman barbarians took control of our beloved homeland when their expanding domain overflowed eastward and Julius Caesar's most effective general, Pompey, subdued Jerusalem in a horrific three-month siege."

A VALIANT BATTLE raged in the mind of every schoolboy there, as each one imagined how their brave ancestors had fought in that not-too-distant past. Arrows flew and swords clashed, with warriors on both sides squaring off in brutal hand-to-hand combat, district by district and street by street.

"Sadly, though, in spite of the valiant efforts of our fighting men, our proud nation fell again to the merciless hand of the foreign usurper, and for nearly twenty years the land and its people lay waste and desolate. But finally, after having revived from the bitter slumber of servitude, the spirit of patriotism was rekindled and civil war broke out."

In their unbridled fury, droves of ordinary Jewish peasants, armed with nothing but crude shields and swords, managed to break through a formidable blockade of Roman soldiers.

"Hoping to quell the chaotic situation, the Roman Senate appointed a client-king over Palestine, choosing a man who'd been governor of Galilee for six years."

Above the chaos of strife and revolt, a new king arose.

"Known as Herod the Great, he was given an army that eventually helped him re-establish Roman order in Jerusalem. Total victory was achieved in three years, and as a result of the ongoing support he received from Rome, Herod's rule there remained unchallenged for the next four decades."

Overwhelmed by the sheer volume of Roman soldiers, many proud Israelite warriors were led away in chains, to the absolute horror of their onlooking families.

"Naturally, in the years following the fall of Jerusalem, the Jewish nation chafed bitterly under Herod's yoke, despising this puppet-ruler because of his complete insensitivity to their religious and political concerns."

Their shields and swords taken from them, these Jewish prisoners were handed picks and shovels, and summarily whipped into action.

"Turning many of the cities in his domain into Roman civic centers, Herod tried unsuccessfully to introduce a way of life the people of Judea would forever detest."

Digging away the rubble, the Israelites were forced to rebuild new edifices where the war had reduced the old ones to piles of rock and burned-out lumber.

"But what made matters even worse, Herod the Great was an Idumaean Jew, from the nation of Edom, which had descended from Esau, the hated twin brother of Jacob."

As his forced laborers toiled to rebuild the city, Herod the Great supervised the work from the safety of his palace stronghold.

"And ever since Esau was tricked by Jacob out of the birthright blessing, there has been perpetual distrust and division between the two clans. So for the nation of Israel to be made subject to anyone with Edomite blood, well, as you can just imagine, class, this was an insult too great to bear."

Although they had been deprived of their traditional weapons of war, the servile Israelites were not beneath turning their construction tools into implements of revolt. While their overlords were not paying attention, they diligently sharpened their picks and shovels into razor-sharp condition.

"So for Rome, the threat of a Palestinian revolution would be a constant concern, for them and for anyone given the task of ruling over a nation prone to such religious fervor."

Many an unsuspecting Roman construction supervisor or legal magistrate would be subdued by the Israelite slaves, thereby forcing the position to be refilled with another man; each time with someone even more apprehensive about the role than the last person.

"Then, approximately thirty years ago, in an attempt to decentralize the troubled territory, the Roman emperor Augustus Caesar split up the kingdom, dividing it among an ailing Herod's three sons."

The solitary puppet-monarch, Herod the Great, slowly faded from the scene and was replaced by three vassal-kings, each ruling from his own lavishly decorated palace.

"Philip was given jurisdiction over Bethsaida and Paneas, Archelaus controlled Samaria and Idumea, while Herod Antipas presided over Judea and Galilee. A decade later, Tiberius Caesar, the stepson of Augustus, ascended as emperor of Rome."

Handing away his sword and receiving a royal scepter in its place, this proud monarch was crowned amidst a lavish Roman parade.

"Having already distinguished himself as one of Rome's greatest generals, Tiberius proved more adept still as an administrator, successfully strengthening the Roman economy and ensuring that even his far-flung provinces were properly governed. But Tiberius was personally unpopular because of his austere ways."

As the parades and celebrations came to an abrupt end, this somber king retreated to his solitary existence securely behind the walls of his palace in Rome.

"Still primarily a soldier at heart, Tiberius abhorred indulgent living and public spectacles. So, after just eleven years on the throne and in opposition to the advice of his counselors, he withdrew from public life, temporarily leaving behind the political intrigue of his power-hungry relatives. Retaining his emperorship, however, he left the administrative details to someone else, the commander of the Praetorian Guard, Lucius Sejanus."

Mortified and incredulous, his family and associates cringed as Tiberius handed over his royal scepter to one of his most decorated soldiers. With great satisfaction, Sejanus raised the scepter while the only people celebrating this stroke of imperial whim were his fellow soldiers amongst the ranks of the Praetorian guards.

"Once in place, Sejanus had no problem at all getting his friend and ally appointed as the governor of Judea. His friend's name was Pontius Pilate, a Roman knight from the Samnite clan of the Pontii, hence his name Pontius."

A new man then came to the forefront, striding onto the scene with his robes of imperial power wrapped securely around him.

"Thoroughly confident of the skills of his old friend, Sejanus was certain that Pilate, a ruthlessly efficient administrator, would have no difficulty in restoring much-needed order in his new role as governor of this volatile territory."

Strutting his way through the streets of Jerusalem, Governor Pilate was followed stride for stride by his cadre of stalwart Roman soldiers.

"But for all of Pilate's prior successes as a seasoned soldier and cunning politician, he seemed unusually incapable of cooperating with Jewish sentiments. In fact, his very first act as governor brought on needless turmoil. In an ill-conceived attempt to honor his patron Sejanus, he installed images of Emperor Tiberius throughout Jerusalem, images which portrayed Caesar as a god. To the Jews, a graven image like this was utter sacrilege."

Wherever Pilate and his soldiers went, they left plaques in their wake, which caused every Jewish citizen who gazed at them to react with disgust.

"Then Pilate began to mint coins bearing pagan religious symbols."

Without warning, imperial soldiers invaded every one of the market places in Jerusalem, where they dumped out jars of Roman coins. Then having emptied their jars, the soldiers absconded all the Jewish money from their places of business, refilling the jars with the money they had just seized.

"Soon, the entire city was in an uproar."

As Pilate complacently sat on his governor's seat, a surging crowd of Jewish peasants clamored around his palace.

"They begged Pilate to remove these objects of sacrilege from their sacred capitol but were adamantly refused."

The demonstrators tried their best to push their way forward, but the heavily armored Roman soldiers stood their ground, injuring numerous protesters in the process.

"Even if the governor couldn't understand these strangely zealous people, he would at least have the satisfaction of ruling over them with a firm hand of imperial authority, and thanks to the protection of his friend Sejanus, Pilate was assured of at least that much."

As a result of so many injuries amidst the jostling throng of demonstrators, a lamentable howl rose up, which Pilate could hear even from inside the palace. Finally losing his patience, the governor sprang to his feet. "Enough already!" he shrieked. "Tell this obstinate bunch to disperse or suffer the pain of my soldiers' hardened blades!"

A pair of his men bolted out onto the balcony overlooking the city square. Brandishing his sword for all to see, one of them leaned forward and barked, "Governor Pilate wants you to know that if you don't leave immediately, he'll have you all cut down where you stand!"

A hush swept across the crowd, and for several tense moments, everyone there looked to the person next to them. Then, from out of the midst of the crowd, a solitary protester hissed, "Do your worst, you filthy dogs! We're not intimidated by your threats."

Then, as if with a single mind, the protesters all held out their necks in bitter defiance. Puzzled by this peculiar display, the two soldiers looked at each other, then went back inside and stood at attention before Pilate, unsure of what to tell him.

Obviously pleased with himself, the governor gloated. "Well, well, they certainly simmered down after that, didn't they? They're disbanding, then?"

"I'm afraid not, sir," said one of the soldiers.

"What?" blurted Pilate, who looked to the other man in frustration.

"He's right, Governor," the second soldier added. "In fact, they seem more determined than ever to die for their cause."

"Ridiculous," spewed Pilate, who went out to witness the spectacle for himself, flanked by his soldiers. Incredulous at the sight of so many people postured in mock submission, he leaned over the balcony rail and bellowed, "What is wrong with you people? Don't any of you value your lives? What about your families? Doesn't the prospect of their grieving over your corpses concern you at all? And for what? A bunch of plaques and coins paying tribute to your king?"

"Caesar is not our king!" screamed one man from the crowd. "We'd all rather die than see such a violation of our sacred city."

Baffled, Pilate threw his hands up. "You're obviously all insane." Turning in disgust, he went back inside, followed by his men.

"What should we do now, sir?" the first soldier asked. "Should we give the order to disperse the crowd by force?"

"No," Pilate murmured.

"Then what do we do?" wondered the second soldier, half to himself.

A deflated Pilate slowly replied, "I want you to remove the plaques and return all the money you confiscated, and I want it done immediately."

The two soldiers exchanged a confused look.

"Yes, Governor Pilate," said the first soldier. "Right away."

As the pair left his presence, Pilate dropped heavily into a chair, stewing in his own juices. "What kind of madhouse have I gotten myself into?"

EVERY YOUNG MAN in that classroom watched in eager anticipation as Professor Ada paced back and forth in front of them like a caged lion. "Then, just four years ago, Tiberius Caesar, emperor of Rome, uncovered a plot to seize imperial power. And the man attempting to overthrow him was none other than Pontius Pilate's friend and protector whom Caesar had personally placed in charge of his kingdom. Now, does anybody here remember the name of the man that Tiberius left in charge?"

One of the boys instantly raised his hand, furiously bobbing it about until finally the professor pointed to him. "Yes, Zachariah; do you remember?"

The boy excitedly jumped to his feet. "Yes, sir, I think I do."

"Go ahead, then. If you'd be so kind, tell the class for us."

"Lucas Sojourner."

Several of the boys giggled, and Professor Ada smiled. "Very good, Zachariah. That was very close, actually. In fact, class, that man's name was Lucius Sejanus. And in no time at all this man, who presumed to corrupt the authority he'd been granted, was summarily executed, along with many of his supporters."

LED BEFORE TIBERIUS Caesar, who was back again on his gilded throne, Lucius Sejanus had been stripped of every vestige of his illustrious military status. Forced to kneel at the hands of a captain of the Praetorian guard, Sejanus glared defiantly up at Tiberius.

"Do you have any last words in your defense, old friend?" Caesar asked.

Sejanus just shook his head, choosing instead to bow his head in silent resolve.

"How noble of you," said Tiberius sarcastically, and after a subtle gesture from the king, the captain of the guard sliced off Sejanus' head with a single swipe of his sword.

A YOUNG MAN'S HAND was again bobbing up and down with great excitement.

"Yes, Zachariah, what is it now?" Professor Ada asked.

"Why didn't they execute Pontius Pilate, too?"

"Well, class, that's a very good question, isn't it? Unfortunately, though, no one really knows for sure. Somehow, I guess, fortune just happened to be smiling on Pilate that day, because for whatever reason he was never implicated in the plot to overthrow the emperor. But, of course, that didn't mean his situation continued without further controversy. Far from it, actually. Not long after that, Pilate was up to his old tricks again, inept as he was in governing such a political hotbed as Judea."

ROMAN SOLDIERS FANNED out across the city.

"Again the governor tried to display commemorative shields dedicated to Caesar, but this time, he made sure the shields bore no images, just the names of the emperor and himself."

Everywhere they went the soldiers posted these shields engraved with the names of Tiberius and Pilate on them.

"But because Caesar was universally worshiped as a god throughout the Roman Empire, the Jewish population soon took up arms in protest."

A swarm of demonstrators again overflowed the city square, buzzing about like a dense cloud of angry hornets, surrounding Pilate's palace and eventually forcing the centurions below Pilate's balcony to abandon their posts.

"This is an outrage, Governor!" screamed one of the protesters. "We refuse to sit back and let you persist with your damnable worship of Caesar!"

EVEN HEROD'S THREE sons, Philip, Archelaus and Herod Antipas appealed to Pilate.

"How many times do we have to go through this, Governor?" Philip said. "It's simply not in our best interests for you to continue meddling in areas you know so little about."

"How dare you come here and tell me what I can and cannot do," snapped Pilate. "This is still Roman territory, and none of you rule here without the authority of Rome. Or has your loyalty suddenly grown stale?"

"Don't be ridiculous, sir," Archelaus replied. "Our loyalty to Rome is unquestionable, but in the interest of both your nation and ours, we insist that you remove the shields from this holy city."

"But I won't remove them, I tell you," insisted Pilate. "Not unless I receive direct orders from Caesar himself. Now, either you gentlemen leave of your own free will, or I'll have my soldiers escort you to the door. Which will it be?"

The brothers exchanged angry looks and without another word turned and left.

THE FOLLOWING WEEK, Pilate received a letter by royal messenger. Disgusted by its contents, the governor threw the letter down at his wife's feet.

"What's wrong now, husband?" she asked.

"Can you believe it, Procla?" fumed Pilate. "The emperor of Rome has taken sides with these Jewish foreigners. Those three traitorous sons of Herod have gone behind my back and reported me to Caesar himself. Now he's rebuked me on their behalf and ordered me to remove the shields I posted in *his* honor."

Procla gasped. "By the gods, this is awful. It's bad enough those puppet-masters have managed to best you in a contest of wills, but now Caesar has begun to take sides against you. Dear husband, I can't tell you what a dangerous precedent this is."

As if he had just suffered a physical blow, Pilate's knees grew weak, forcing him to sit down on his bed. "It now seems, with the execution of Sejanus," Pilate grumbled painfully, "my situation as governor of Jerusalem is on even shakier ground. Now I know how a caged animal feels. It appears I can no longer sweep my actions so easily under a rug, no matter how well-intentioned they are."

Touched by his lament, Procla moved to his side and sat down, placing her hand on his. "My husband, do you realize what this means? If there's ever an investigation from Rome, they'll certainly uncover an endless list of atrocities, acts of corruption and plunder, your unmitigated cruelty and murder of people who've all been condemned without the benefit of a trial."

Cut to the quick, Pilate sprang to his feet and stepped away from her. "Thank you for that, my dear. As usual, I can always count on your complete frankness."

A STUDENT'S HAND popped back up.

"Yes, Zachariah; go ahead," said a mildly frustrated Ada.

"Has Pontius Pilate ever done anything good in his life?"

"Unfortunately, no," the professor replied.

Then another hand popped up.

"Yes, Tobias. Is there something you'd like to add to the discussion?"

"My father told me that, one time, the governor built an aqueduct to supply water to Jerusalem. Isn't that a good thing?"

Ada shook his head with a wry smile. "Oh, he built it all right, but unfortunately he did so using sacred money from the Temple treasury. So even when Pilate tried to do something positive for the city, he did it with a complete lack of understanding as to how his methods might affect the people he was governing. As you can imagine, when the people of Jerusalem found out about Pilate's underhanded dealings, they were outraged."

THOUSANDS OF ANGRY demonstrators were again trying to push their way into the governor's square, and because the area was too small to accommodate them all, the rest milled about the outskirts of the palace grounds.

"We demand an end to this project, Governor!" yelled a protester who stood just below Pilate's balcony.

"You foul dog, you're not worthy of your position!" screamed another.

"Why not just cut your own throat and be done with it, you scum, before we have to do it for you!" bellowed another.

Inside the governor's palace, Procla stood at her husband's side as they both listened intently to the commotion from the safety of its interior.

"By the gods," murmured Procla," what have you done this time, husband? The people are on the verge of an all-out riot."

"Relax, Procla. I have everything under control."

"Control?" she blurted, cautiously stepping out onto the balcony. "Somehow I fail to see what you mean by that."

Following her outside, Pilate walked past her and moved to the edge of the balcony. As he looked down upon the overflowing mob, he pondered his next move.

"Do you hear us, you filthy swine?" another disgruntled protester growled. "Put an end to your treachery, or we'll burn your palace to the ground."

Aghast, Procla leaned into her husband. "What are you going to do about all this?"

"Just watch," he calmly replied. Then, after a simple hand signal from Pilate, what appeared to be ordinary civilians in the midst of the crowd jumped into action. Dozens of men began beating the protesters, causing a tremendous cry to rise up, as chaos instantly ensued. Unwilling to give in so easily, though, the angry protesters began to fight back. Spurred on by the unexpected resistance of the crowd, the aggressors then withdrew daggers from beneath their robes and began to indiscriminately stab the demonstrators. Unarmed and outmanned, many of the protesters were killed or wounded.

Horrified by all the bloodshed, Procla turned to her husband. "What on Earth just happened? Is this your idea of having everything under control?"

"Absolutely not," Pilate croaked, as though he were being reprimanded by his own mother. "I only had my soldiers infiltrate the crowd in disguise so they could rough them up. I never ordered them to draw blood. Honestly, I had no idea that something like this would happen."

"Unbelievable," snapped Procla, who, disgusted and disappointed, turned and walked back inside. "This is the last straw, for sure."

Watching her disappear back into the palace, Pilate then turned to his men and motioned for them to cease their assault. "Enough!" he roared. As the noise of the tumult slowly died down, the governor haplessly gazed out across the disheveled crowd. Disheartened by the debacle of death that lay before him, he turned away and muttered beneath his breath, "What have I done this time?"

"THEN, SOMETIME during those dark days," Professor Ada continued, "a series of startling eyewitness reports began to circulate throughout Palestine, reports that threatened to overthrow not only the Roman Empire but the nation of the Jews as well."

The professor's hand etched out another word on his chalkboard; just one.

Martyrdom.

"In some cases they were reports that these eyewitnesses were to seal with their very lives in martyrdom." Ada turned back to address his students. "Now, class, can anyone tell me what this word means?"

Several hands popped up, and the professor pointed to one student. "Yes, Nathaniel."

"Martyrdom is when someone is killed for a sacred cause, when a person gives their life for a purpose greater than themselves."

Professor Ada smiled like a proud parent. "Very good, Nathaniel. I couldn't have said it better myself." Then, hesitating for several moments, he thoughtfully scanned his audience of eager students. "Now, the reason I bring this up is because I wish to delve into a very important aspect of our current society, one which may be viewed as too controversial for boys of your age. But considering the caliber of students I seem to have, I feel very confident you can all handle this kind of adult subject matter."

Returning to the chalkboard, he underlined the word he had just scratched out and reiterated in a solemn tone, "Martyrdom." Professor Ada turned back to his students again. "So now that we've defined this word: What does the notion of martyrdom mean to us in the context of today's lecture concerning the history of the Jewish people in Palestine? And to answer that question we have to begin examining a radical new sect of Judaism, one which has actually had its beginnings in our very own territory here in Galilee. And the leader of this new sect is a wise Man called Jesus. Have any of you heard of this Man before?"

Several hands timidly rose into the air, and Professor Ada pointed to one. "Yes, Nathaniel; you've heard about this Man?"

"Yes, sir, I have."

"Good, and what have you heard?"

"Well, my father talked about him once, but he said he was just a madman who believed the impossible about himself."

"Really?"

"Yes, and that's why the Romans killed him."

Ada smiled awkwardly. "Ah, but that's where you're wrong, my boy. The Romans didn't kill him."

"Then who did?" wondered Nathaniel.

Again Ada tried his best to smile. "Well, you see, unfortunately, that's where things get a little tricky, and what we're confronted with, in the end, is the irony of life's most fickle human trait, that of the power to rule and those in our society who've been entrusted with that power."

"What does that even mean?" Nathaniel asked, thoroughly confused.

Ada scratched his brow. "Oh, dear, maybe I should've thought twice about proceeding with this after all."

"No," yelped Zachariah. "We want you to continue, Professor. My mother says this Jesus was a wise Man, that He was the most special Man Who's ever lived, considering all of the amazing things He did."

Intrigued at this, Ada smiled.

But Nathaniel, obviously unimpressed, rolled his eyes. "If he was so special, Zachariah, then why was he crucified?"

Zachariah shrugged his shoulders. "How should I know?"

"He was crucified, Nathaniel," blurted Ada, suddenly caught up in the moment, "because the religious authorities considered Him a threat to their vested positions of power."

"But my father said he was a fraud," retorted Nathaniel, "and that he led the people astray."

"No," Zachariah insisted. "My mother said He was a good Man."

"Your mother doesn't know what she's talking about," replied Nathaniel, as cold as ice. "But my father does, and he told me the man was nothing but a heretic."

"Nathaniel, no," Ada countered. "I'm sorry to have to tell you this, but that's where your father is wrong. He *was* a good Man, a Teacher of the kind of men who gladly received the truth, Jews and Gentiles alike. He was undoubtedly the Christ, and when Pontius Pilate, at the behest of our own religious leaders, had Him condemned to die on a cross, He appeared alive again after three days in the grave."

An audible gasp rippled through the classroom.

"What did you say?" asked Nathaniel, his mouth hanging open in disbelief.

With firm resolution, the professor looked him right in the eye. "I said, He rose from the dead after three days in His tomb. As a matter of fact, this same Jesus confirmed everything our divine prophets have been foretelling our people since the beginning of time."

A stunned Nathaniel rose to his feet. "Well, sir, I'm sorry to have to tell *you* this, but I think you've lost your mind. And I'm going straight home to tell my father the terrible lies you're spreading at school." Bolting to the door, Nathaniel flung it open and ran out as fast as he could, leaving everyone there in a complete state of shock.

An Eye for an Eye

AS PONTIUS PILATE was intensely scanning an assortment of documents late into the evening, he was interrupted by one of his servants.

"Excuse me, Governor," said the servant, "but you have a very important visitor."

"An *uninvited* visitor, you mean," replied an exasperated Pilate. "At this hour?"

"I'm sorry, sir, but it's Herod Antipas, and he wishes to see you right away."

"The king of Judea? Here, now?"

"I'm afraid so, yes."

"But why?"

"He wouldn't say, sir. He just said it was urgent."

"Very well. Send him right in."

"Thank you, Governor," said the servant, who dutifully turned and left.

In a matter of moments, the regal figure of Herod Antipas stepped inside and stopped, hovering there between light and shadow. "Greetings, Governor Pilate," he said through a suppressed yawn. "I regret the intrusion at this late hour, but unfortunately it couldn't be helped. I hope everything's going well with you at least."

"Why, hello," replied Pilate, trying to mask his uneasiness with the unexpected visit. "Why didn't you let me know you were coming? I could've made adequate preparations for your arrival."

"You can dispense with the diplomatic posturing, Governor. I have much bigger problems on my hands."

Pilate nodded tacitly, eyeing his visitor as though he were sizing up an opponent in battle. "Yes, of course. If you insist. Please, come in, have a seat, make yourself at home."

Herod then took several steps forward and wearily replied, "That won't be necessary. I'm not staying long."

Now that the monarch was that much closer to him, Pilate could see that he clearly looked as though he had endured too many sleepless nights.

"You know," said the governor, "you really don't look so good. What's wrong?"

"Wrong? What hasn't gone wrong for me lately? That's the question."

"So tell me: What has you so upset?"

"My daughter, Herodias," he replied, almost incapable of uttering the words, "my dear, sweet child."

"Your daughter? What about her?"

"She's dead," whispered Herod.

"Dead? How?"

"An accident. She was playing on a pool of water covered over with ice. Then without warning the ice beneath her broke, and her little body fell through. Her head was cut off instantly, before anyone had time to even blink."

"No," gasped Pilate.

"Oh, yes. And her head? Yes, well, it just laid there on the surface while everyone just stood around, frozen with fear, hoping somebody would do something, anything."

"That's terrible. I'm sorry for your loss. How are you and your wife holding up?"

"Not so good, I'm afraid. You should have seen my poor wife, sitting there for the longest time, just holding our daughter's head in her lap. Our home will never be the same after this."

Even Pilate seemed genuinely moved. "Is there anything I can do for you?"

"I need a favor, Governor."

"Of course, anything. Just say the word."

"Well, as you know, ever since I heard about the man Jesus, I had a desire to see him for myself, one on one. I wanted to hear his words firsthand to find out for myself whether or not they were like those of any other ordinary man."

A suddenly smitten Pilate turned away as he tried to gather his wits. "Yes, of course," he muttered, awkwardly clearing his throat. "I do know; I know exactly how you feel, in fact."

"But now," interjected Herod, hardly noticing Pilate's suppressed reaction, so distraught by his own personal ordeal, "because of all the evil things I did to John the Baptist, and because I mocked the Nazarene for believing he was the Christ, I'm receiving the rewards of my corruption."

"What?" gasped Pilate, turning back again. "You actually think that's why your daughter was killed? It was a freak accident. You can't blame yourself."

"But what else can I think? You know as well as I do, I've spilled way too much innocent blood with these hands. Don't you see?"

Pilate stared back at Herod for several tense moments, then mumbled, "I see."

"So it appears that God's judgment is perfect after all," Herod continued blankly, beyond the point of grief, nearly drained of all human emotion, "because every man receives according to his thoughts."

"Then tell me," said Pilate, confused and shaking his head, "if you're convinced this is some sort of divine retribution for your evil deeds, then why are you asking *me* for a favor? Why not go knocking on the door of your local temple?"

"Because you were worthy to get to know that God-Man, that's why," he replied, his face suddenly going flush. "Now, it's only right and good that you've agreed to help me. You did say you wanted to help me, didn't you?"

"So let me get this straight. You're here because I've personally encountered this God-Man, as you called him, and because I've apparently survived unscathed? Is that it?"

"I know it sounds absurd; I know it. But I also know that something evil, something unspeakable, has attached itself to me and my family."

"And you believe it's because of this man?" Pilate hung his head in disbelief, stepping away to clear his mind of the sheer weight of this avalanche of thought. "Oh, Herod, I just don't know. I have to be honest with you. This is the last thing I would've expected from a man in your position, coming to me with all this. I don't know how to respond. I'm not a priest; I'm a politician."

"Well, do you have a better explanation?" Herod continued, beginning to work himself into a frenzy. "Even as we speak my son Azbonius lies in agony on his deathbed. He'll be dead before very long. I, too, have been doomed to an appalling fate. I'm miserable with the dropsy now, and all because I persecuted John, the one who introduced baptism by water. Don't you get it?"

Pilate was dumbfounded. "I'm finding this very hard to take in. Do you realize what you're asking me to believe?"

"Believe whatever you want. All I know is: My wife is blind in her left eye, mourning day and night for our daughter. Why? Because we wanted to blind the eye of righteousness. So you see, it all makes perfect sense: A verdict from God really is a just sentence."

"I don't know. If you say so. I suppose your answer is as good as any."

"There's no peace for an evil person, just as the Lord says," muttered Herod.

"If what you're saying is true, then why are you the only ones suffering from this curse?"

"But we're not the only ones, you fool! Tragedy has already overwhelmed the scribes and priests of the Law because they delivered the Just One to you! The consummation of the age has come upon us, and now the Gentiles have become heirs of the promises. The children of light will be cast out, having rejected the things preached concerning the Lord and His Son."

"I still can't believe I'm hearing all this from the king of Judea. Why don't you proclaim this recent insight of yours to your own nation?"

"Are you insane? Do you have any idea what you're suggesting? And since when did you start caring about my nation, anyway?"

"But I don't. I was just curious."

"Then stop being such a hypocrite, will you? The fate of my nation is already sealed, regardless of what I might say or do… Now, it's time for you and your wife Procla to face a similar destiny; depending on your response, that is."

"What's that supposed to mean?"

"It means that now it's time for you to commemorate this Jesus, because the kingdom is being handed over to you, the Gentiles."

"But why?"

"What a ridiculous question. I can still see you have a lot to learn about the people you're governing. This kingdom of ours is now available to you because we, the Chosen, have scorned the Righteous One! What do you think I keep trying to tell you?"

"Fine. Just for the sake of argument, let's say you're right. So I embrace this kingdom of yours, fine, it's mine now. What good does that do you? You still haven't answered that question, have you?"

"Well, at least it might leave you with a change of heart; I don't know. Maybe then you could see your way to doing some good in this life for a change."

"For someone like you, you mean?"

Herod nodded eagerly. "That's right, yes, even for someone like me."

"So, what? Now I'm supposed to start doing good in this life to make up for all my evil deeds in the past? Is that what you're suggesting?"

"Well, naturally. Is there anything wrong with that?"

"Then spit it out. What do you want from me?"

"I want you, as the acting governor, to see to it that my family and I are properly buried."

"That's it? You want proper burials? That's why you've come here under the cloak of night?"

"That's right. My wife, my children and I; we all deserve to have dignified ends, don't you think?"

"Well, of course. You all deserve treatment worthy of your status, but don't your priests have some sort of predetermined ritual to take care of things like that for royalty such as yourself?"

"No, no, no! I already told you. The priests are all doomed! Revenge will soon be overtaking every last one of them!"

"Revenge? When?"

"At the return of the Christ, of course, just as the Scriptures declare."

Pilate frowned. "I don't know. I still think you're overreacting to all this."

"Just promise me that you'll arrange decent burials for me and my family, and I'll leave you alone in peace. Can you just do that for me?"

Pilate paused again to scrutinize Herod, who waited for his response with great anticipation. "Yes, of course, I can do that. I promise to make sure you and your family receive proper treatment when the time comes."

"Thank you, Governor," he said with a sigh of relief. "Then I'll be leaving now. Say goodbye to Procla for me, will you?"

Pilate nodded vacantly. "Certainly."

"Oh, and I'm sending you my daughter Herodias' earrings, as well as one of my own rings."

"What on Earth for?"

"Let's just say I'm giving them to you as a memorial of my death. Even now my body is being consumed from the inside out. So you see: I'm already receiving a form of divine justice."

"Maybe you've just lost your mind. Maybe you're in shock because of the tragedy of your daughter's death. Have you ever considered that?"

"More often than you can imagine, my old friend and adversary. But losing my mind isn't what disturbs me. The scary thing is the thought of losing my soul. Tell me: Has a man like you ever worried about a thing like that in your life?"

Pilate wearily shrugged his shoulders. "I don't suppose I have, no."

"Then consider this: Lose your mind, and you still might be fortunate enough to find it again someday; lose your soul, and you're never able to restore it in your own strength, *ever*."

With that, Herod turned and left, disappearing into the darkened corridor, as surreptitiously as when he had arrived.

This Man from Galilee

CAREFULLY WEIGHING each and every word as he spoke them, Pilate began to dictate a letter to his scribe. "Greetings from Pontius Pilate, governor of Jerusalem, to Herod Antipas, king of Judea: I certainly hope you and your family are feeling better in this terrible time of crisis. But please remember that from the first day you delivered Jesus to me I took pity on myself, even going so far as to demonstrate my disapproval by washing my hands of the whole affair. So, concerning the Man's fate, I'm innocent of every charge. After all, I only did to Him what you wanted me to do. It was you who asked me to cooperate with His crucifixion. But no sooner had He been killed than His executioners began testifying to me that He'd risen from the dead. And believe me, I've gone to great lengths to confirm the things I'm about to tell you."

As Pilate recounted his tale, his thoughts drifted back to those fateful events, his mind shot through with the startling images that would forever change his life.

FIRST AND FOREMOST was the image of Jesus, a gentle, confident soul, who stood amidst a crowd of baffled onlookers, unsure if what they were seeing was real or not.

"Because according to innumerable eyewitness accounts," continued Pilate as he proceeded to dictate his letter, "this Man reportedly appeared in Galilee, looking just as He always had prior to His crucifixion. He boldly continued to teach about His resurrection and a kingdom that would last forever."

Then there was Pilate's wife, who strode through the landscape of his troubled mind, looking as determined as ever, accompanied by an entourage of Roman soldiers.

"Even Procla, my wife, became convinced of the visions that came to her at the same time you asked me to deliver Jesus to those spiteful Jewish leaders. So, as soon as she heard He'd risen, she enlisted the efforts of Longinus, the centurion, and several of the guards at His tomb, and they all went to see the risen Christ, as if they were going to witness some kind of grand spectacle."

Entering the city, Procla and her group found Jesus with His disciples. Awestruck, they all stood and stared at Him.

"What is it, Procla?" asked Jesus. "Do you believe in Me, too?"

Procla nodded. "Yes, Lord, I do believe. What would you have me do?"

"Are you aware of the agreement that God made with the Fathers, where it's written that everyone who dies will live again through My death?"

"I am, Lord."

"Good for you, Procla, and now you've seen it with your own eyes. I'm alive, even though I was crucified. I suffered many things, until I was put in a grave, but I broke down the gates of Hades and destroyed the power of death, and someday I'll return again in all My glory."

"Thank you, Lord, for allowing me to see Your mysteries unfold. What should I do now?"

"I want you to believe in My Father Who is in Me. Can you do that?"

"Yes, Lord, I can."

AS PILATE SAT GRIMLY postured before his scribe, he continued to dictate his letter. "After that, Procla came home and told me everything she and her group had experienced, and they wept as they did because they felt so badly that they had originally been against Him, even going so far as to plan every horrible thing they had done to Him."

DRIFTING THROUGH the darkened corridors of his memory, Pilate was no longer clad in his flamboyant governor's robe but in a drab cotton garb.

"I, too, was cut to the core by a sickening guilt and the deepest depression I'd ever known. Dressed in a garment of mourning, I took fifty soldiers with me and my wife, and headed for Galilee so I could see Him for myself."

With a melancholy look in his eye, Pilate led his own entourage, which included Procla and a very determined group of Roman soldiers, who were likewise clad in rather modest outfits, also quite in contrast to their stations in life.

"And while we were on our way, I testified that you, Herod Antipas, had ordered the things I did, forcing me to arm myself against Him, to judge Him Who judges everyone, and to scourge the Innocent One, the Lord of the Just."

Eventually, Pilate and his somber group arrived in Galilee, where they found Jesus, standing and talking with His disciples. The Lord turned and stared directly at Pilate.

"Then and there," continued the governor with his dictation, "I also realized that this Man you had delivered to me really was the Creator."

Pilate and his companions all fell face-down at His feet.

"I've sinned, Lord," Pilate told Jesus. "I helped condemn You, the One Who avenges everyone in truth! At first, I only saw Your humanity and not Your divinity, but now I realize You're God in the Flesh, the Son of God Himself. Herod and those Israelites forced me to do this despicable thing to You. Please, have pity on me, God of Israel!"

Procla lamented, too. "Dear God of Heaven and Earth, please don't punish me for what Pilate or those Israelites did to You, and please don't be too hard on my husband."

Stepping up to Pilate, the Lord helped him to his feet, along with Procla and the soldiers, too. Looking closely at Him, they all marveled at the sight of the scars of the cross that were clearly evident in His body.

And Jesus calmly said, "Everything the righteous Fathers could only hope to see actually took place in your lifetime. The Lord of Time, the Son of Man, the Son of the Most High Who is forever, has risen from the dead and is glorified."

SOON PILATE'S MESSENGER delivered his letter to Herod Antipas, who immediately read it. Obviously disturbed, he crumpled it and threw it to the ground, and for the longest time Herod sat there brooding, rubbing his bearded chin, trying to decide what to do next.

Day of Reckoning

MEANWHILE, BACK IN Rome, Tiberius Caesar was lying in bed, groaning softly. In obvious discomfort, he rolled over and rang a small bell.

Within moments, his royal steward appeared at his door. "I'm here, Sire. How are you this morning?"

Tiberius sat up, grimacing painfully. "Terrible. If I didn't know better I'd have thought that one of Hannibal's elephants slept on me all night."

"I'm so sorry to hear that. Is there anything I can do for you?"

"Yes. I want you to send for Cadmus immediately."

The royal steward dutifully nodded and left.

A SHADOW APPEARED in Tiberius' bedroom doorway as Caesar lay dozing on his side.

"I'm here, My Lord," said the shadow.

Tiberius slowly opened his eyes with a scowl. "Cadmus, it's about time. Get in here. What took my most trusted counselor so long to get here?"

The man stepped forward, out of the shadows, and humbly bowed. "A thousand pardons, Sire. My wife is in labor with our second child. I came as soon as I could."

"Of course. How is she?"

"All things considered, she's doing well."

With great difficulty, Tiberius sat up in his sickbed. "Good. I just wish I could say the same for myself."

"How can I serve you today, My Caesar? Do you wish me to consult with your physicians?"

"Certainly not. I've had it with my physicians. They're all useless as far as I'm concerned. You're here today for a far different sort of consultation."

"I see. What about?"

For several moments, Tiberius pondered his reply. "Tell me, Cadmus, do you believe in the intervention of the gods?"

The counselor tilted his head thoughtfully. "I myself, Sire, remain undecided. But naturally, in your case, I would not rule it out."

"Why is that?"

"Because you're Caesar, of course. You are the embodiment of the deity itself. If ever there was someone with whom the gods would wish to intervene, you would certainly be that person."

Intrigued, Tiberius nodded. "Good, because I wish to make a very special request of you."

"Certainly, My Lord. How may I be of assistance?"

"It just so happens that I've recently gotten wind of some very peculiar reports. Of course these reports only circulate in the darkest of shadow, and of course the people spreading these reports wish that no one else knows what they're saying, but still I hear about them anyway."

"I see, and these … peculiar reports are why you called me here?"

"Yes, Cadmus, it is," snapped Tiberius, growing impatient. "And stop playing coy with me."

Taken aback, Cadmus offered a conciliatory nod. "Certainly, Great Caesar. I meant no disrespect. Please, Sire, help me understand what you're trying to say."

"Fine, fine," he replied with a weary wave of his hand. "I just want you to tell me honestly: What do you know about certain reports concerning the work of a unique physician in Jerusalem, a man by the name of Jesus of Nazareth who supposedly heals every disease just by speaking. Tell me: What do you know about this man?"

A befuddled Cadmus tried to respond. "I—*I*, uh—"

"Come on, out with it, preferably before I expire on the spot. Are you, or are you not, aware of the rumors concerning this man? And if not, then I want to know why I continue to employ you as my counselor?"

"Yes, of course, Sire, I've heard about the man, but as to vouching for the veracity of these accounts, I cannot say one way or the other."

"I didn't ask you to vouch for them. I want to know what you *think* of them?"

"Think, My Lord?"

"Yes, considering the sheer impossibility of these reports, do you think there's even the slightest chance that they might be true? For a man like me, in my condition, that is."

"As I alluded to before, I remain undecided on issues like this, but I can tell you, there is one way to find out, once and for all."

"Really? How?"

"Bring the man here as fast as our swiftest vessels can deliver him. Jerusalem is under our control. As you know, Pontius Pilate is the governor there. Dispatch your royal messenger Volusianus to fetch him, and then you'll find out for yourself just how true these rumors are."

Tiberius considered his answer for a moment. "So you don't think I'm insane for believing this man might actually provide me a divine cure?"

"Certainly not, My Lord. I'd never presume to make such a judgment. I am merely your humble counselor. You, on the other hand, are Tiberius Caesar, the divine emperor of Rome."

"Good. Then let's make sure we keep it that way. Are you sure Volusianus is the right man for a task like this?"

"I am, My Lord. I believe Volusianus is more than up to it."

"Then speak to him about the delicate nature of his mission, and have him set sail for Jerusalem immediately. It's time my friend and servant Pontius Pilate make good on his appointment there. Tell him that more than anything else in this world I wish for him to hand over this physician to me so I can also have my health restored."

EMBARKING UPON HIS quest, Volusianus traveled first by ship and then by royal caravan, eventually arriving, after a lengthy journey, in Jerusalem.

THERE, VOLUSIANUS appeared before Pontius Pilate, who sat auspiciously in his ornately decorated governor's seat.

Volusianus bowed graciously before Pilate. "Greetings, Governor Pilate, my name is Volusianus, and I am the royal messenger sent here by your most omnipotent master, Tiberius Caesar, emperor of Rome."

"Really? The emperor of Rome sent you here to see *me*? But why?"

"It seems that Caesar has heard the rumors circulating in your country about a remarkable physician, one who's been performing a tremendous work here."

"A physician? This country has all sorts of physicians. Which one is Caesar looking for? Just give me his name, and I'll see to it that he's immediately sent to our great and illustrious emperor."

Volusianus hesitated for a moment, trying to decide how to articulate his unusual request. "Uh, well, let me see. It seems as though Caesar is looking for the physician who heals his patients simply by speaking to them."

"Oh, that one," replied a deflated Pilate.

"Then you know who I'm talking about?"

"Yes, I'm afraid I do."

"Good; because Caesar is very eager for you to send him to Rome as soon as possible. He wants his disease to be healed, too."

"But the man you're talking about was accused of being a criminal," sputtered Pilate, whose gruffness was merely an attempt to mask his inner terror. "People from his own nation insisted he was fomenting revolution against the Empire. How was I supposed to know he was innocent of every charge? I'm just one man here, trying to maintain order in this madhouse. You have no idea what I've been dealing with here! No idea at all!"

Volusianus eyed him suspiciously. "So what are you trying to say, Governor? Where is this man now?"

Dumbfounded, Pilate just sat there.

"Well, where is he?" pressed Volusianus. "In exile? In prison? Tell me."

The governor's words came out with great difficulty. "I'm afraid that after discussing the matter with the city's spiritual leaders it was decided he should be crucified."

"Crucified," Volusianus groaned as if someone had punched him in the stomach. "But why?"

Pilate just shook his head, unable to reply. Staring at the floor, the mortified governor sank down in his seat and put his hand over his brow as though he were hoping he might simply disappear. Head in hand, a grief-stricken Volusianus just turned and walked away.

ON HIS WAY BACK TO the ship that would return him to Rome, a sullen Volusianus, burdened with the responsibility of conveying the bad news to Caesar, encountered a noble woman.

"Excuse me, good lady," Volusianus said, "but could I have a moment of your time?"

"Veronica," replied the woman with a charming smile.

"Ma'am?"

"My name is Veronica."

Obviously distracted, the messenger nodded. "Of course, Veronica, pardon me. I am Volusianus, royal messenger sent here from Rome by His Majesty, Tiberius Caesar."

Seeing the regal caravan that was traveling with him, the woman was intrigued. "Certainly, sir. What can I do for you today?"

"I was just wondering. I know this may strike you as odd, but considering the importance of my mission here, I feel compelled to ask."

"Go right ahead, young man. Ask me anything."

"You see, it seems there have been rumors going around, rumors that we, even in faraway Rome, have been hearing."

"Rumors?" echoed Veronica with a curious tilt to her head. "What rumors?"

"Rumors that there was a remarkable physician in this country who healed his patients simply by speaking to them. Is it possible you might know who I'm talking about?"

"Oh, yes, of course, my dear boy," she said as her face lit up at the mere mention of Him. "I know all about the Man you're describing. Why do you ask?"

"Well, as it turns out, I was sent here specifically to look for this special man on behalf of my master who's very sick and seeking a cure from his disease."

"Oh, dear, I'm so sorry to hear that," Veronica replied, truly touched. "What do you want to know?"

"I want to know why anyone would've killed a man like that. What could have possibly driven a people to such hatred, such madness?"

"Oh, my dear sir," moaned Veronica, who began to weep. "He was crucified because they were jealous of Him, that's why."

"Jealous?"

"Yes, jealous," she replied, fighting back the tears. "Ordinary folks loved Him, but corruption in high places wouldn't stop until they saw Him dead."

"But I was supposed to return this man to the emperor of Rome. He was hoping so much that he could help cure him." Volusianus hung his head. "Now I'm afraid I'll never be able to accomplish my royal mission."

Veronica slowly regained her composure. "Maybe you still can."

Confused and intrigued, Volusianus looked up at her. "Pardon me? I'm afraid I don't understand. What are you saying?"

"It just so happens that after Jesus finished teaching in our town, He had to leave, so I wanted a painting of Him. That way I'd have His likeness to console me while He was gone."

"That seems natural enough, yes."

"So just imagine my surprise when: Who do you think I happened to meet on my way to see an artist?"

"No." Eyebrows raised, Volusianus gaped. "You don't mean—"

"That's right, Jesus."

"What did he do? What did he say?"

"Well, when He found out where I was going, He asked me for my canvas."

"Yes, yes. Then what?"

"Then He gave it back to me, and…" Veronica choked up, unable to continue.

"And?"

Veronica opened her mouth, but nothing would come out.

"And what?" Volusianus' eyes grew wider.

"Oh, you wouldn't believe me if I told you," murmured Veronica, obviously embarrassed.

"But I would, honestly. Tell me: I'll believe you, and I'll personally make sure that Caesar himself hears what you have to say."

"Well, I could hardly believe my own eyes," she continued, slowly measuring out her words, "but incredibly, the canvas He handed back to me was no longer blank. Now it had a picture of His marvelous face painted on it."

"What? I'm sorry. Could you say that again for me? I don't think I heard correctly."

Veronica sheepishly smiled. "You heard me. There was a picture of His face on it."

"Astonishing. Caesar will definitely have something to say about this."

"What will you do now?"

"I'll return to Caesar with the news. But only the gods know for sure if I'll find him still fit enough in mind or body to receive it."

"I wonder what would happen if your master were to see this painting for himself."

"What do you mean? Take your painting to Caesar and present it to him in person?"

"Yes, that's right. Maybe if he looked at it, you know, maybe he could experience His healing power, too."

Volusianus was thunderstruck by the mere suggestion. "Yes. I do think you're on to something. Would it be possible to buy a picture like this with gold or silver?"

"No, of course not," replied Veronica, smiling sweetly. "But I will go with you, and together we'll take the painting to Caesar."

IN THE MEANTIME, Pilate sat with his scribe and began to dictate another emotionally charged letter. "Greetings from Pontius Pilate, governor of Jerusalem, to Tiberius Caesar, emperor of Rome: Your Majesty, although I was quite opposed to it and went to great lengths to stop it, a bitter punishment was recently inflicted on Jesus of Nazareth by the will of the people. But, in fact, no age has had, or ever will have, a Man so good and so disciplined. Yet the people made an incredible effort with all their leaders, scribes and elders, to conspire in crucifying this Ambassador of Truth, and they did it even though their own prophets, like the Sibyls among us, warned them not to."

FROM HIS DISTANT vantage point, Pilate watched the gruesome spectacle, a scene forever emblazoned in his tortured memory. First, Jesus was nailed to the crossbeam using a pair of iron nails that were mercilessly pounded through His wrists, and with the sound of each hammer blow and each agonized groan, the governor flinched.

"And believe me, Great Caesar, when I tell you," continued Pilate to his scribe, "if there hadn't been such a threat of revolt amongst the bloodthirsty rabble, this Man would probably still be living among us."

A trio of Roman soldiers then banded together to hoist Jesus, securely nailed to the horizontal beam, onto the upright section of the cross. With an eerie thud, it dropped into place, and lastly, one of the soldiers nailed His feet in place, much to the delight of the gawking onlookers who let loose with an approving howl.

"But being compelled by my loyalty to you, rather than by my own desire, I never tried too hard to prevent the sale and suffering of righteous blood, even if it was guiltless of every accusation. An injustice to be sure, these were the actions of malicious men, although, as their own Scriptures foretell, it will eventually work to their own destruction."

PAINED AT THE RECOLLECTION of that fateful day, Pilate enunciated each word as his scribe, who seemed similarly affected by the governor's account, wrote it down as fast as he could. "Just as everyone there will testify, when He was hung on that tree, supernatural signs appeared, which, in the opinion of the philosophers, threatened to destroy the entire world."

AS SOON AS VOLUSIANUS arrived back in Rome, he was ushered in to deliver his report to Tiberius, who sat precariously on his throne, obviously still in a state of poor health.

"Oh, Great Caesar," said Volusianus, "I regret to tell you that Jesus, Whom you've wanted to see for so long, was crucified by Pilate and the Jewish authorities. Quite illegally, of course."

"What?" Stunned, then furious, Tiberius struggled to his feet. "But why?"

"According to every report I've gathered: It was jealousy that nailed Him to the cross!"

"You mean to tell me a simple case of political intrigue has deprived me of meeting this remarkable physician?"

"I'm afraid so, Majesty. But fortunately, a gracious lady has returned with me to Rome."

Then Caesar's expression turned from anger to incredulity. "By the gods, first you tell me the treachery of cowards has denied me my request, and now you think I'll be appeased by the company of some strange woman? Is that what I'm hearing?"

"Certainly not, My Lord. That's not what I meant at all. What I'm saying is: I believe you'll be pleasantly surprised with something she's brought you."

"Seriously?" Exasperated and exhausted, Tiberius dropped down into his seat, too frustrated to continue looking at his royal messenger. "What could she have brought that could possibly interest me at this point? A potion, perhaps?"

"No, Your Majesty, a gift."

"A gift," grumbled Tiberius, deflated merely at the thought. "What do I need with more gifts? I need a cure."

"Well, a talisman, really."

"I see, go on," said Caesar, still unimpressed. "Surprise me, then."

"It's a miraculous painting of the same Jesus Whom you've been seeking. I think if you look upon it, there's a chance that your health might be restored."

"Miraculous, you say?"

WITH THAT, CAESAR'S royal servants draped his entire room with marvelous silk cloths in preparation for the occasion. As the king lay expectantly on his bed, Volusianus slowly entered with Veronica's painting. With great anticipation, he stepped forward and held up the sacred talisman for his ailing emperor to gaze upon, and as soon as he looked at it, Tiberius' entire being was transformed. Flushed with a look of sheer ecstasy, Caesar jumped to his feet, and turning to Volusianus, he gave him an affectionate bear-hug, much to the amazement of everyone there.

Fury of the Gods

PILATE'S LETTER WAS delivered several days later to Caesar, who was sitting quite contentedly on his throne. No longer looking ill, he exuded a healthy, confident glow, but after reading the letter, his expression darkened, and he became incensed. With a renewed vigor, Tiberius shot out of his royal seat like a man half his age. "Summon my scribe immediately," he growled.

WITH AN INTENSITY that made his scribe uncomfortable, Caesar dictated his letter with a steely glint in his eye. "Greetings from Tiberius Caesar, emperor of Rome, to Pontius Pilate, governor of Jerusalem: Pilate, my servant, tell me: Who was this man that such complaints were lodged against him? And why would the men of Palestine have ever crucified someone like him? If the majority demanded what was right, it would have been proper to consent to them, but if what they were requesting was unjustified, then how could you have so blatantly violated the Law?"

WHEN PILATE FINISHED reading the letter from Tiberius, he limply dropped his arm to his side and released the tattered page, allowing it to slip through his rigid fingers. Eyes glazing over, he watched it flit about in the air until it landed on the ground.

IT WAS NOW PILATE'S turn to respond. The words he spoke to his scribe were brimming with an ominous dread. "Greetings from Pontius Pilate, your administrator of the eastern province, to the most potent and divine Tiberius Caesar: My most excellent emperor, I'm writing to you with great apprehension in order to report what has happened here recently. It's true: Jewish religious leaders did deliver the Man called Jesus to me, accusing

Him of all sorts of terrible crimes, but they were never able to convict Him of a single thing. All they did was charge Him with heresy because He insisted the Sabbath wasn't their true rest, but in my opinion this was an incredibly flimsy basis on which to accuse someone, especially when you consider all the remarkable things the Man had done up to that point."

AS JESUS MADE HIS way through a clamoring crowd of sick people, who all pressed in toward Him, a mere touch of His hand healed each and every one of them. "He restored sight to the blind," continued Pilate to his scribe, "cleansed the lepers, healed the paralyzed."

A hunched, bedraggled fellow wandered aimlessly through the desert. "Still others were severely tormented by demons, forced to live among wild beasts." The man's hair and beard were matted and gnarled, eyes yellow with fear and pain. He gnawed at his own bloody fingers. Startled, the man sniffed at the air like an animal and turned to see Jesus, flanked by several of His disciples. "Once vexed by foul spirits, these people were all restored with just a word from this amazing Man." Within moments, the man's beast-ly appearance melted away, and the crooked creature that had just been so deformed gradually stood up straight before Jesus, looking as handsome and complete as any human being could.

"Then, there was a poor woman who had had an issue of blood for so many years her bones could be seen through her glass-like skin." A feeble wisp of a woman crept to her window. "All her physicians had completely dismissed her, refusing to offer her any hope of recovery." The woman in question was none other than Veronica, teetering at her window, a mere shell of the beautiful lady who had so proudly ventured to Rome with Volu-sianus. Looking out her window, she saw Jesus was approaching, followed by a group of people vying for His attention. "But once, while Jesus was passing by, this woman saw her chance for the impossible thing her doctors told her she would never have." As Jesus made His way past her home, Veronica somehow pressed through the crowd and, with her last ounce of strength, reached out with her trembling hand. "She merely touched the hem of His garment, and all her strength returned." Instantly healthy again, she began to run about as though she had never been sick at all.

"Not only that, but sometime later this same Jesus did something even more powerful, something unheard of even among our gods. He raised a dead man named Lazarus, a man who had been in his crypt for four days, and He did it just by speaking to him." As a group of onlookers mourned and wept, Jesus stretched His right hand toward the grave. "Lazarus, come out!" exclaimed Jesus. "And so Lazarus, smelling of sweet perfume, came bounding out of his tomb like a bridegroom running to greet his beloved bride."

AS PILATE DICTATED his letter, he noticed the odd look on his scribe's face, obviously uncomfortable with what he was writing. An irritated governor sat up in his chair and affirmed, "And as hard as all this is to believe I can absolutely assure you everything happened the way I'm describing it. I even saw Him perform some of these miracles with my own eyes. Still, the only complaint the Jewish leaders could offer was that Jesus did these things on the Sabbath. That was when He was handed over to me by Herod Antipas and the priests Annas and Caiaphas. And even though they condemned Him, I refused to cooperate with them, but in the end, because the people threatened to start an all-out riot, I reluctantly consented to His crucifixion. But no sooner had He been killed than I realized I'd made the biggest mistake of my life."

AS JESUS DANGLED ON the cross, struggling for every breath, a midday eclipse began to blot out the light of the Sun. "Because even as this Man was slowly dying before our very eyes, the world was mysteriously plunged into darkness, as if it were expiring with Him. The Sun disappeared, even though it was still daytime, and the sky became black as pitch, and although the stars became visible for a time, even they refused to shine with their typical luster."

The inhabitants of Jerusalem became quite agitated at the dark spectacle of the sky as they wandered the streets like lost sheep, gawking upward and bumping into one another in the darkness. "But I'm sure I don't have to remind you, Your Majesty, about how we had to light our lamps at noon and keep them going until the evening. It seemed like the Moon was covered in blood. Even though it was full, it was barely visible, as if Orion and all the stars were openly mourning the crimes of the Jews."

HEAD HUNG SLIGHTLY, the lamentable Pilate paused, unsure of how to proceed. His scribe looked up from his writing, waiting expectantly for the governor to continue, and finally, with obvious difficulty, he did so. "And as if that were not strange enough, three days later, on the first day of the week, around nine o'clock in the evening, the Sun suddenly reappeared, shining at night as it had never done before. It was then that a swarm of angels appeared above us, flashing like lightning in a storm."

A MYSTIFIED GROUP of spectators cowered at the sight of a massive cloud of angelic beings, hovering above them in the night sky.

"Glorify God above everything else!" one of the angels shouted. "Peace has finally come to mankind! You who are chained in the depths of Hades, come out!"

PILATE'S VOICE BEGAN to quiver, and his scribe flinched ever so slightly as he wrote down the governor's words. "The hills and valleys shook with the blast of the angel's proclamation, and as if in response to that cataclysmic voice, an earthquake unleashed its fury across the landscape. Boulders cracked, tremendous chasms formed in the ground, the very regions of the Abyss opened up."

AS THE GROUND LET loose beneath their feet, several men tumbled headlong, screaming, into these chasms, cavernous openings in the ground that belched smoke from their depths. "Amazingly, the Jews who suffered most were the same ones who'd spoken against Jesus. Only one of their synagogues remained in Jerusalem, because all of those that had conspired against Him were overwhelmed in the disastrous events of that day." Then the governor's lips uttered the impossible, almost choking on the words as he did. "And suddenly the most astonishing thing of all began to occur. As if it weren't enough that the ground had opened up to swallow men whole, but then having devoured one group, it proceeded to regurgitate another. No sooner had men sunk into the Abyss, never to be seen again, than those same depths began to spit out others who had previously been imprisoned there."

THE SCRIBE STOPPED writing and looked up at the governor, who was obviously lost in his thoughts. Clearing his throat, the scribe timidly muttered, "Excuse me, sir, but I'm not sure I understood that last part. Could you please reiterate?"

Looking his scribe squarely in the eye, Pilate seemed oddly plaintive. "What didn't you understand? Was I stuttering?"

"No, sir."

"Then proceed with your dictation, and, by all means, make your description as explicit as possible. Is that understood?"

"Yes, sir, but I'm simply not sure what it is I'm being explicit about."

"Dead men," murmured a distraught Pilate.

The scribe tilted his head and squinted his eyes. "*Dead men*, sir?"

"That's correct, scribe, *dead men*. Right before our very eyes we began to see dead men rising again, rising from the ground, rising from their graves."

ONE BEWILDERED MAN pointed and, barely able to utter the words, stammered, "L—L—*Look*, there's Abraham and Isaac and Jacob!"

Sure enough there stood Abraham, flanked by his son Isaac and his grandson Jacob, all looking as healthy as can be, as though they were still in the prime of their lives.

Abraham boldly proclaimed, "The Lord God has raised us from the grave, even as He brought me out of the furnace of Nimrod! He's conquered death and plundered Hades, restoring the dead back to life again!"

"But how is that possible?" asked the bewildered man's wife. "These men have been dead for two thousand years!"

"Don't ask me," replied the man, shrugging his shoulders. "All I know is, there they are. I've even heard reports that others have seen Noah and Job and Moses, all alive again, healthy as can be!"

Awestruck by everything he was seeing, Pilate wandered past the gawking couple. "Even I, My Caesar, saw many of these dead men who had appeared alive again in the flesh." The governor stepped up to one fellow, looking dazed and confused, and asked him, "Are you all right?"

The man nodded blankly, as though he had just awakened from a dream, and replied, "I'm not … quite sure. Where am I?"

"Jerusalem."

"Jerusalem?" blanched the man, who stared at Pilate in complete disbelief. "But I don't understand. One moment, I was sitting in the midst of the shadow of death, and then suddenly I was here."

"That's it? That's all you remember?"

For several seconds, the man strained his mind in an effort to answer, and then his eyes opened wide. "I think I *do* remember something else, yes."

"What?"

"A tremendous light, yes, I remember now; purple and gold, streaming into our darkened world, lighting up every recess, and…"

"Yes, and then?"

"And then … there was a Man."

"Who? Who was this Man?"

"Yes, a Man," muttered the fellow, who then proceeded to wander away from Pilate as though he no longer had any idea that he was having a conversation with the governor. "A Man with the strangest scars in His body," he sighed, as his voice faded in the distance.

With that, Pilate looked as confused as the man who had just wandered away. In whichever direction he looked, he was met with an astonishing sight: People stumbling around, obviously wondering how they had gotten there; others who were staring at them, looking just as confused as they were. Still others, both the living and the undead, were weeping and wailing over the magnitude of the destruction of their once-magnificent city. "In fact, Glorious Caesar, so many inexplicable wonders had overtaken me that day that I was gripped with the most terrible dread I had ever known. That was when I ordered a written account of everything that happened, and it is this very record that I've sent to you."

AS CAESAR SAT IN HIS illustrious auditorium, amidst his Senate and soldiers, a tremendous chattering rippled throughout the crowd.

"So that's what happened?" blurted one of his senators. "Who would have thought that something so far away, involving such a backward, superstitious people, could have had its effects felt even in distant Rome?"

"But there you have it, Rufus," replied Tiberius, quite matter-of-factly, "you just heard it for yourself. The solar eclipse, the earthquake, the evening light, all of it having a direct impact on our beloved capitol; all of it did, unmistakably, occur because of what happened in the land of those backward, superstitious people."

"Besides the tremendous loss of life and property caused by the earthquake," Rufus continued, "the resultant tidal wave that swept through the Mediterranean devastated the southern coasts of Cyprus, Crete and Rhodes. Even Achaia and Sicily were not beyond the reach of this disaster. Initial reports have it that untold thousands perished in its wake, but, of course, it will be several months, maybe years, before its true impact can be fully ascertained."

Then, for the longest time, everyone in the auditorium fell silent. Tiberius, at the center of it, sat brooding, scratching his brow, obviously deep in thought. Sitting up, he drew the eager attention of everyone there. Finally, he began again. "But as tragic as this devastation is to the physical order of things, which is to say, the loss of life and property, actually the most devastating thing about these cataclysmic events is how they force us to re-evaluate the nature of this misbegotten world of ours. Clearly, the fury of the gods was incited at the death of this innocent Man called Jesus, but as to why the gods would've willingly conspired with this Crucified One is a mystery that will haunt us all for a very long time."

"Quite true, My Lord, and considering this question of re-evaluation, if I may be so bold."

"You may, Rufus. Speak your mind."

"Obviously the otherworldly nature of these events can only be ascribed to the intervention of the gods. That much is beyond question. But based on this most recent report, a report which, for all intents and purposes, constitutes an explicit confession of guilt, it appears that all of it was due to the negligent actions of a man who was supposedly an ally of Rome."

Tiberius nodded thoughtfully. "Yes, I see what you're saying. Your point is well taken."

"So tell me, Great Caesar, if you don't mind my asking: What should be done to someone who readily confesses to a crime of this magnitude? In fact, what *must* be done to the man who, as you've said yourself, triggered what can best be described as a 'cosmic conspiracy,' if you will, a conspiracy of world-shattering proportions?"

"Why, of course, such a man will be arrested and brought to Rome, where he'll personally answer to me for his negligence." Then Tiberius stood to his feet and, with fists clenched, snarled, "And mark my words, all who hear the sound of my voice, I will utterly destroy the one who nearly destroyed our world!"

The Sky is Falling

THE AUDITORIUM WAS buzzing with a cacophony of hundreds of conversations, but all that ended when the hall doors swung open. Immediately, a hush fell throughout the crowd, and Pilate, bound in shackles and clad in a meager linen robe, was led into the room. Made to stand at the bar of judgment, the governor contritely looked up at Tiberius, who sat poised upon his throne, looking as menacing as ever. Seething with rage, Caesar stood up and took a step forward. Barely able to withhold his inner fury, he opened his mouth to speak.

But inexplicably, at that moment, all of his anger melted away and his face reflected a charming glow that he usually only exhibited in his happier moments. As gently as a lamb, he said, "Well, hello, dear Pilate, my old friend. I'm so sorry to see you looking like this. Tell me: Were my soldiers kind to you? If not, just say the word, and I'll have them flogged, this instant."

Dumbfounded, Caesar could hardly believe the words that came out of his mouth, as was everyone else in the auditorium. Struggling to lift a finger, Tiberius motioned to his men. "Please, guards, would you be so kind as to take this poor man out into the hall," he said through pursed lips.

And as soon as Pilate had vacated the room, Caesar's fury returned with a vengeance. "By the gods, what on Earth just happened? Why didn't I strangle that man with my own hands? What was I thinking? Bring that child of death back in here right now so I can tell him what I really think of him!"

The bewildered guards retrieved Pilate, and as soon as they marched him back in, Tiberius' anger, once again, simply melted away. "Pilate, my friend, what a terrible injustice it is to see you in this state. I can't tell you how sorry I am. After all, it wasn't your fault that Jesus was crucified, now was it?" Completely flabbergasted by this, Tiberius put his hand over his own mouth. His senators gasped in disbelief. Even his guards looked at one another, amazed by what they were hearing and seeing.

Then one of the Roman soldiers promptly stepped over to Senator Rufus, who was sitting in the front row, and whispered something into his ear. Immediately, the senator sprang to his feet and motioned to Tiberius. "Sire, please, may I have a word with you, in private?"

Caesar, however, was in no mood for subterfuge. "Come here, Rufus, please," he replied, struggling with a peculiar smile that formed on his otherwise bewildered face. "Share your secret with me, here and now. Whisper in *my* ear, too, won't you?"

So the senator moved to Tiberius' side and whispered in his ear, at which point, apparently struck with an idea, the emperor, still sounding as pleasant as ever, said, "Guards, if you don't mind. Would you kindly remove the prisoner's robe?"

"Your Majesty?" replied a guard, obviously confused by the request.

"The prisoner, my good man. His robe. Strip him of his robe, this instant."

"Here?"

"Of course, here. Do you have a problem with that?" asked Tiberius with an odd grin.

"No, Majesty," replied the embarrassed guard, who finally jumped into action and stripped Pilate of his linen robe, leaving the governor naked and barely able to cover himself with both of his hands in shackles.

Immediately, the original fury of Caesar's mind rushed back into him. His face went flush with rage. "Thank you, guard! You've finally given me a reason *not* to have you executed alongside this prisoner. Now, before I change my mind again, remove this sorry excuse for a Roman governor from my sight, and take him to his cell while I decide what to do with him."

Bolting into action, the guard dragged Pilate out of the room as the emperor just shook his head.

Perplexed by the preceding spectacle, another senator slowly rose to his feet. "With all due respect, Great Caesar, could you please tell us what just happened here? Since when does a mere governor of Rome possess the power of a magician?"

Looking back at the senator, Tiberius started to reply but thought better of it. Turning to Rufus, he nodded to him as he turned and stepped through the door to his private chambers.

"Apparently, Rubellio," began Rufus, "the source of Pilate's magic lay in the fact that he was wearing the seamless robe of Jesus of Nazareth."

"Absurd," scoffed Rubellio. "Miraculous healings, flying angels, walking dead men; and now a magical robe? How much more of this nonsense are we expected to endure?"

"I sympathize with you, my dear fellow, but you saw what just happened here with your own eyes, didn't you? Do you have a better explanation?"

"You know very well, Rufus, I do not. So tell me: If what you say is true, how could anyone even know something like that?"

And just as Caesar had done before him, Rufus simply turned to the Roman soldier who had first whispered into his ear and nodded.

"Because I was one of the centurions who stood guard when Jesus was crucified," said the man with sullen, resolute eyes. "That's how."

"You, Longinus?" asked Rubellio. "How did you come into possession of the robe?"

"Of all the people in the world, I happened to win the robe when some of my fellow soldiers and I decided it would be fun to gamble for it."

"I see. But that still doesn't explain how Pilate got hold of it."

At this, the steely-eyed centurion blanched momentarily, as if teetering upon a precipice in his own mind.

Growing impatient, Rubellio pressed on. "Longinus, what is your problem? Are you worried your testimony might implicate the governor? Did Pilate, in fact, confiscate the robe in the hopes of commandeering its alleged powers of persuasion? Is that it?"

Longinus shook the cobwebs from his mind and looked the senator straight in the eye. "No, sir, he did not. I gave him the robe of my own free will."

"But why?" interjected Rufus. "After what we all witnessed just now? Why would you give something like that away? I would've thought a talisman of this nature would be very useful in the hands of an imperial warrior like yourself."

Again Longinus hesitated, clearly disturbed by what he was thinking. "But it wasn't like that at all, Senator. It's not some kind of magic wand, if that's what you're thinking."

"Then enlighten us, dear Longinus, if you please," Rufus insisted sarcastically. "We're all dying to know why you so willingly gave it away."

"Because once it was in my hands, I was seized by a terrible dread, all right?" snapped Longinus, clearly embarrassed by his abrupt confession. "As if every act of war, every act of violence I'd ever committed, came flooding into my mind; as if every drop of blood I'd ever spilled in the almighty name of honor and valor was drenching my soul. I couldn't stand it anymore. I *had* to get rid of the robe; I had to get rid of it. Don't you see? What else could I do?"

Drained of all emotion, Longinus just hung his head. The two senators exchanged a troubled look, and the auditorium fell as silent as a tomb.

PILATE WAS BROUGHT before Caesar once again as the king sat in the Temple of the Gods, above the Senate and his soldiers, displaying the complete array of his power, and there at the bar of judgment, the governor stood, in chains and rags.

"Pontius Pilate, you profane ass!" growled Tiberius. "When you heard that this Jesus was doing such remarkable things, how could you dare allow Him to be crucified? Don't you realize? Your treacherous act almost ruined the whole world!"

"Oh, Great King," Pilate sputtered, "I'm not the guilty one! It was those Jewish leaders who instigated this whole thing! They're the guilty ones, not me!"

"Just who are these men?"

"Herod Antipas, Archelaus and Philip, along with Annas, Caiaphas and many of their so-called 'religious authorities.'"

"But why did you carry out their plan?"

"Their nation has always been subversive! You know that! They're all rebels who never submit to your authority!"

"You fool! When they delivered Him to you, He should've been protected, then sent to me, but under no circumstances should you have agreed to crucify such a Man! Even *I* was restored to health just by looking at His painted image. Obviously, all these miracles prove that not only was this Jesus the king of the Jews, but He also was undoubtedly the Christ!"

Suddenly a tremendous rush of wind blew into the auditorium, causing all the statues of the gods, perched high above, to tremble and shake. Panic-stricken, people began to scatter in every direction. Caught in the vortex of the whirlwind, the statutes cracked into pieces and toppled to the ground in a heap of rubble and dust. Most escaped with their lives, but many were not so lucky, having been crushed to death by the falling debris. One man, pinned by a gigantic hand, lay disfigured and bleeding. With his dying breath, he whispered, "Surely the lips that uttered the name of Christ have vanquished the power of our gods."

Tiberius stood gawking at the destruction and mayhem all around him and mournfully shook his head. "Who is this Jesus of Nazareth? And what kind of Man could cause such devastation at the mere mention of His name?"

CAESAR AND HIS ENTIRE Senate were now assembled in the Capitol Building, and again he began to fiercely interrogate Pilate. "Because of your infamy against this Jesus, our sacred temple has been reduced to rubble! So I want you to tell me right now, you impertinent ass, just Who was this Man you crucified?"

"But I already told you," the governor whimpered. "I didn't want Him to be crucified. I had no choice."

"Enough of your lies! Your evil crimes have begun to infect Rome itself! Earthquakes and tidal waves have devastated the continent. And now the mere utterance of His name has toppled our gods!"

"Well, I, for one, can vouch for the accuracy of what people say He did. Even I became convinced by what I saw. He really is greater than all the gods we worship."

Tiberius slammed his fist down. "You fool! If you admit that you realized Who this Man was, then why did you allow Him to be treated in such a despicable manner?"

Pilate shrugged his shoulders pathetically. "I have no idea, Sire, but I can tell you I am truly sorry if any of my actions have brought shame upon either you or Rome."

"Yes, yes, how touching. Maybe you were hoping to capitalize upon this Man's notoriety. Maybe you were really trying to undermine my government, like all the rest. Is that what you were up to, Governor?"

"Of course not, Your Majesty."

"Has anyone from my family contacted you?"

"No, Sire. No one."

"Then you wish to cause my downfall in order to avenge the execution of your friend and protector Lucius Sejanus! Is that it?"

"No, of course not! I did it because those rebellious Jewish leaders forced me to crucify Him! Let the public record show that *I* was His greatest advocate!"

"Nonsense." Tiberius shook his head in disgust.

"But it's true. I'm *begging* you, Great Caesar, please let the record be read before you as my only witness, and before God as my final testimony."

Tiberius scowled, then reluctantly nodded and gestured to one of his soldiers who hastily left the building. "Very well," he said with a vindictive sneer. "All I've got to say is, this better be good."

Moments later, the soldier returned with a large book and handed it to Senator Rufus, who stepped up to the bar of judgment next to Pilate. Setting the book down, he opened it and cleared his throat. "As it turns out, Your Majesty, this book was discovered at Jerusalem, in the Hall of Pontius Pilate, just as the governor has testified." Looking down, Rufus began in stentorian tones to read it aloud. "It states that all the things written here took place in the nineteenth year of Tiberius Caesar, emperor of Rome, in the seventeenth year of Herod Antipas, king of Judea, son of Herod the Great."

A Most Improbable Ally

AT THAT TIME, A GROUP of disgruntled, black-robed Jewish religious leaders appeared before Pontius Pilate. "Greetings, Governor Pilate," began one of them, nodding graciously. "As I'm sure you're already aware, I am Annas, chief priest at Jerusalem, and these, my esteemed colleagues, have all joined me today in a most holy cause on behalf of our nation."

"Naturally," Pilate replied with a hint of sarcasm in his voice.

Gesturing to the man next to him, Annas said, "This is Caiaphas, our current high priest."

"Of course," said the governor as Caiaphas nodded respectfully.

"My fellow priests, Summas and Datam," continued Annas, motioning to the other members of his group. "And from our supreme council, the Sanhedrin: Representing the Pharisees are Gamaliel, Judas and Levi, and from the Sadducees are Alexander, Cyrus and Nepthalim. With us, too, are various elders, scribes and doctors of the Law. First of all, we would like to express our gratitude for your providing us this opportunity to meet with you personally."

For several intense moments, Pilate stared at this group of men who were all looking at him with such stern faces. "Certainly, Annas, but before you continue, at least do me the honor of putting away any false pretense of diplomacy. I'm well aware of what to expect today. Some moral outrage has you all in an uproar, as usual. Am I right?"

With that, Annas' amicable demeanor washed away, having been replaced by an offended scowl. "As you wish, Governor. Forgive me if I offended you with any ill-conceived attempt at civility."

Pilate nodded, apparently satisfied with his pyrrhic victory. "And don't think I'm not aware of your illustrious history, Annas. Not only were you once the residing high priest of your people, but you've also been father to no less than three more. In fact, the present high priest, Caiaphas, the man standing at your right hand, is your son-in-law."

Annas and Caiaphas exchanged a serious look.

"But, Governor," interjected Caiaphas, "I fail to see what that has to do with today's proceedings."

"Really?" Pilate quipped. "Well, from where I sit, it has everything to do with them. Never forget, gentlemen, a man in my position, as governor of Jerusalem, must always see through to the truth of any matter I'm forced to confront. So, when a group of men like you suddenly appears on my doorstep, it's absolutely critical for me to know who's pulling the real strings of power. You get my meaning now?"

Annas reluctantly nodded. "Of course, Governor; I do, yes."

"Good, then quit wasting my precious time, and state your business before I throw you all out on your sanctimonious asses."

"As you wish, sir," said Annas, trying to remain calm in the face of Pilate's abrasive manner. "We've come here today to discuss a very serious concern of ours; one which will no doubt concern you as well."

"Me? What could you possibly have to say that would concern me?"

"You have a revolutionist in your midst, Governor," blurted Caiaphas, "a seditious man who threatens the peace and tranquility of the entire nation of Israel!"

Obviously unimpressed, Pilate rolled his eyes at the mere suggestion. "Please, not another revolutionist. Don't you people ever learn?"

The black-robed men all exchanged nervous looks as Pilate yawned apathetically.

"But what do you propose to do about it?" Annas pressed "And what if Caesar finds out that, when given the chance to intervene, you instead allowed things to escalate because of your failure to act?"

"How dare you imply I'd ever shirk my duty to Rome; and just who is it this time that has you all in such a fit? You're usually the first ones to spearhead this kind of rebellion. What's so unusual about this man?"

"This time the rebel in question seeks to not only undermine our way of life but also the authority of Rome."

Still obviously unconcerned, the governor said, "Really. And just what is the name of this rebel?"

"His name is Jesus of Nazareth," continued Annas, "and he is a criminal of the highest order."

"You don't say. And what could he possibly have done to make me think he's a threat to Roman authority?"

"The man declares himself to be king of the Jews," Annas replied.

Pilate blankly stared back at the group. "Well, is he?"

"Of course not!" exclaimed Caiaphas. "The man has lost his mind. He's even gone so far as to declare himself to be the Son of God. But, of course, it's common knowledge this Jesus is merely the son of Joseph and Mary."

Pilate grinned, amused by such antics. "So the man has gone insane. So what? He hardly sounds like a threat to the imperial majesty of Rome. Would any of Caesar's loyal subjects actually switch sides for the likes of such a man? Is that what you're suggesting?"

The men exchanged more nervous looks all around, growing frustrated with Pilate's blatant sarcasm.

"But he's trying to destroy the sacred Law of our Fathers!" blurted Annas. "And if he's allowed to continue, unopposed, you might very well have another riot on your hands. Is that what you want? More bloodshed?"

Pilate grew serious at the mere mention of another riot. "Of course not. So tell me: What is he saying? What's he trying to destroy?"

The Pharisee Gamaliel stepped forward. "Our Law that forbids the performing of cures on the Sabbath."

"But still he insists," barked Summas, the priest, "on curing both the lame and the deaf!"

"And those tormented with palsy and blindness," grunted another priest, Datam. "Not to mention lepers and demoniacs!"

"All on that very day!" yelped Alexander, the Sadducee.

"And all with diabolical methods!" growled Annas.

"Hold on, hold on. One at a time, people," Pilate said with his hand up in protest. "Now obviously, I'm no expert in religious matters, but even I fail to see the logic in what you're telling me. How can this man be doing all these good things by diabolical means?"

"Because he's a sorcerer, that's how!" snapped Caiaphas. "He casts demons out by the power of the prince of demons. That's why everything is under his control!"

Pilate shook his head. "Casting out demons doesn't seem to be the work of an evil spirit. These things have to come from the power of the gods."

"Please, sir," said Annas, "summon this Jesus to appear before your tribunal and listen to him for yourself. Then you'll witness firsthand the true nature of our grave predicament."

APPEARING BEFORE Pilate, a solemn messenger dutifully bowed. "Greetings, Governor, how may I serve you today?"

"Tell me," said Pilate. "Are you familiar with this man Jesus of Nazareth?"

Pilate's messenger nodded. "I am, sir."

"Good. I need you to figure out some way to get him here without causing a huge scene. Can you manage that for me?"

"I believe so, Governor, yes."

"Very well. Go, then, and bring him here as soon as possible."

MAKING HIS WAY through the city streets, the messenger soon found Jesus. Bowing, he worshiped Him. "Lord, I've been sent by no less than the governor of Jerusalem, Pontius Pilate himself, who's requesting an audience with You."

Jesus nodded calmly. "I see. Would you like Me to come with you now? Is that it?"

"With all due respect, Lord, yes. Thank You."

"Then lead the way," He said, smiling graciously.

ESCORTING JESUS TO the door of the Assembly Hall, the messenger spread his robe on the ground. "Lord, please walk on this as You enter."

But the Jewish authorities were milling around outside, and when they saw what the messenger had done, they were outraged.

"How dare you, young man!" shrieked Caiaphas. "You were ordered to summon this heretic, not to grovel before him as though he were some sort of royal figure!"

Then turning to Jesus, Annas pointed a crooked finger at Him. "You stay here. We'll deal with you later. Right now we're going to see to it that this boy is dealt with first."

THE YOUNG MAN WAS immediately corralled into the presence of Pilate.

Glaring defiantly at the governor, Annas snarled, "Why didn't you give Jesus his summons through an official bailiff, and not just by simple messenger?"

"What is wrong now?" wondered an exasperated Pilate.

"Apparently, this messenger of yours worships Jesus," snapped Caiaphas. "He laid his robe down for him to walk on, and said, 'Lord, the governor anxiously awaits your arrival.'"

Turning to him, the governor asked, "Is this true?"

The messenger nodded timidly.

"Why on Earth would you do something like that?"

"I did it because I saw other people do it."

"When?"

"Well, sir, it was not too long ago, when you sent me to deliver a message to Herod's nephew, Alexander. As I made my way through Jerusalem, I saw Jesus riding majestically on a she-ass. The Hebrews called out to Him: 'Hosanna!' And that's when I saw the people there spreading their clothes before Him in the street and saying: 'Please, save us, You Who are from Heaven! Blessed is He Who comes in the name of the Lord!'"

Many of the Jewish leaders began grumbling in protest.

"Those people were speaking Hebrew!" Summas exclaimed. "You're Greek! How could you understand them?"

"Because I asked one of the men there: 'What are those people saying?' So he told me."

Pilate turned to the angry Jews, who were suddenly speechless. "So, is it a crime now to do what a bunch of Hebrews were first seen doing?"

The Jewish leaders looked amongst themselves, hoping someone would offer something in their defense.

"I'll assume your silence means you've changed your minds about my messenger's so-called 'guilt' in this matter. Again I ask you: What has he done that was so wrong?"

But the men remained silent.

"Fine. Then if we can put this matter behind us, we can proceed." The governor turned to his messenger. "Go ahead. Bring Jesus in now."

AS JESUS ENTERED the Assembly Hall, where twelve standard-bearers held up the royal insignias of Imperial Rome, the tops of the standards bowed down as He walked past them. Taken aback by this bewildering sight, Pilate had the most peculiar look on his face. The Jewish authorities, however, reacted quite differently.

"Wait, wait, wait!" Annas bellowed. "Now your standard-bearers are bowing before this criminal! I must insist, Governor, that you put an end to this sort of thing immediately!"

Pilate shook his head, still unsure of what he had just seen. "Look, gentlemen, I realize it wasn't pleasant for you to see the standards bow to Jesus all by themselves, but why get angry with the standard-bearers as though *they'd* bowed before him?"

Caiaphas fumed. "But we *did* see them bowing before Jesus!"

The governor motioned to one of the standard-bearers to come to him. "Why'd you just do that?"

But the man shrugged, clearly perplexed by all the fuss. "But we didn't do anything, sir. We're pagans. We worship the gods in the Temple. We have no reason to bow to this man."

Satisfied with his explanation, Pilate then turned to the leaders of the synagogue. "Now I want you to choose the strongest men from amongst yourselves and have them hold up the standards. Then we'll see if they bow down by themselves or not."

SO THE TWELVE STRONGEST men that the Jewish authorities could find had the standards handed to them, and these new men proceeded to hold up the royal insignias.

Pilate told them, "By the life of Caesar, if you men don't keep the standards held up properly when Jesus enters, I'll have all your heads cut off. Is that understood?"

"It is, Governor," replied the first man in line.

"Good. Now have Jesus brought back in."

And when Jesus came in and walked past the standard-bearers again, the royal standards bowed down, just as they had before.

Equally amazed and confused by this, Pilate sat contemplating his next move, when suddenly his wife Procla, who was standing some distance away, motioned to her own private messenger. She whispered something in his ear, and then the messenger ran to her husband.

"Begging your pardon, sir," said the messenger, "but I have an urgent word from your wife."

"Yes, go ahead."

"She says: 'Please, don't harm this innocent Man. I've suffered horribly because of a night vision involving Him.'"

"See, didn't we tell you he was a sorcerer?" Summas barked. "Now he's caused your wife to have some kind of nightmare!"

Pilate turned to Jesus. "You hear their testimony against you, yet you still offer nothing in your defense. Why?"

But Jesus just calmly replied, "If they hadn't been given the power of speech, they'd never even be able to speak, and since they're all capable of making their own decisions, they'll just have to work it out for themselves."

"What do we have to work out for ourselves?" scoffed Annas. "We already know more than enough about you. First of all, you were born through fornication!"

"And because of the reports of your birth," Caiaphas said, "the male infants in Bethlehem were all slaughtered."

"Even your mother and father fled into Egypt," added Datam, "because they couldn't trust their own people."

But a man named Antonius stepped forward from out of the crowd. "Well, we know His mother Mary was married to Joseph at the time, so you can't say He was born through fornication."

Pilate glared at the Jewish leaders. "Then your account is false. Men from your own nation have testified that he wasn't born through fornication."

Annas glared back. "But you'd better pay attention to the ones who insist that he *was!*"

"The only ones denying this charge are his converts and disciples," insisted Caiaphas.

"Who are these converts?" Pilate asked.

"They're the children of pagans," groaned Summas. "They aren't real Jews. They're just some of his followers, that's all."

But several more Jews stepped forward, including Eleazer, Asterius, Caras and Crispus.

"We're not converts," Eleazer said. "We're Jews, and we're telling the truth."

"We were present when Mary and Joseph became engaged," added Asterius.

"I charge you to swear by the life of Caesar!" growled Pilate. "Are you sure you're telling me the truth?"

"Certainly we are, sir," Caras insisted. "But our Law forbids us to swear because it's considered a sin, so if *they're* willing to swear by Caesar that what we told you is false, then we'll gladly submit to execution."

Disgusted, Annas shook his head. "These men will never believe what we know to be a fact. The man was born a bastard."

"No matter how much he pretends to be the son of God and a king," Caiaphas added with a shudder.

"Enough already," snapped Pilate. "I want everyone out of here immediately; everyone, that is, except for the men who are sympathetic to the Nazarene."

ALONE WITH JUST the group of sympathizers, Pilate turned to them. "Why are men from your own nation, religious men, no less, why are they so determined to condemn this Jesus? It doesn't make any sense."

"They're angry," Crispus began, "because He cures people on the Sabbath Day, our holiest day of the week."

"Excuse me?" muttered Pilate with a peculiar tilt of his head. "You can't be serious. You mean to tell me that they'd condemn a man for doing *good* just because he did it on a so-called 'holy' day?"

"Yes, sir," Crispus mournfully replied. "It seems they would."

STORMING INTO THE outer hallway where the Jewish authorities were milling about like a cloud of angry bees, Pilate fiercely confronted them. "I call you all to witness. This man has done nothing wrong. How dare you bring him to me thinking I'd cooperate with the likes of you!"

"Hold on now," persisted Annas, who stepped forward to face the governor, "if this man were not a criminal, we'd never have brought him before you."

"Don't be absurd! If this man has committed a crime against your nation, then take him away and try him according to your own Law."

"But it's against the Law for us to put anyone to death," Gamaliel replied.

"Oh, I see," grumbled Pilate, "so the commandment: 'Do not kill,' belongs to you but not to me, eh?"

BACK INSIDE THE Assembly Hall, Pilate addressed Jesus in private. "Tell me: Are you really the king of the Jews?"

"Are you asking this for yourself? Or have the Jewish leaders told you this about Me?"

Pilate shrugged. "What do I care? Am I a Jew? Your own religious leaders have delivered you to me. What have you done, anyway?"

"My kingdom is not of this world. If it were, My servants would be fighting for Me right now, and I'd never have been turned over by these men."

"Are you really a king, then?"

"You say that I'm a king. That's why I was born into this world. My purpose is to bear witness to the truth, and every person of the truth recognizes My voice."

"What is truth?"

"Truth is from Heaven."

Pilate seemed genuinely disappointed. "Then what are you saying? Truth is nowhere to be found on this Earth?"

"Believe Me when I tell you: Truth is on this Earth whenever those with the power of reason are governed by truth and make correct decisions."

Thoroughly frustrated, Pilate hung his head with an exasperated sigh.

ADDRESSING THE JEWISH leaders again Pilate insisted, "I'm sorry, gentlemen, but I can't find a single crime this man is guilty of."

"But he said, 'I can destroy the Temple of God,'" Cyrus grumbled, "'and rebuild it again in three days.'"

"What kind of temple was he talking about?" asked the governor.

"The kind that took Solomon forty-six years to build!" barked Datam. "The man is a raving lunatic!"

Pilate shook his head in disbelief. "But that's no reason to condemn him. I'm sorry, but I'm innocent of his blood, I tell you. You'll have to work this out amongst yourselves."

But Summas persisted. "Let his blood be on us and our children!"

"Gentlemen, please. Stop acting this way. I keep telling you the man hasn't done a thing that deserves the death penalty. He certainly shouldn't be killed for curing sick people on the Sabbath."

"By the life of Caesar," blurted Levi, "if anyone is a blasphemer, he is worthy of death, but this man blasphemes the Lord!"

ALONE WITH JESUS, Pilate gazed at Him for quite a while. "What am I going to do with you?" wondered the governor.

"Do what is written," He replied.

"What is written?"

"Moses and the prophets prophesied a great deal about My suffering and resurrection."

Eavesdropping at the door to Pilate's chamber, the Jewish leaders became furious again. Caiaphas banged the door with his fist and bellowed, "Why will you continue to listen to this man's blasphemy?"

An enraged Pilate swung the door open and confronted them. "If what he just said is blasphemy, then you'll have to take him to your court and try him according to your Law!"

"Our Law says he should receive thirty-nine stripes by whipping," said Gamaliel, "and if he continues doing the same thing, he should be stoned to death."

"Well, if you think that speech of his just now was blasphemy, then I guess you'll have to put him on trial, won't you?"

Gamaliel continued. "But our Law orders us to not murder anyone."

"So we want *you* to crucify him," Alexander grunted, "because he deserves to die on a cross!"

Pilate adamantly shook his head. "No. It isn't right that he should be crucified. Just whip him publicly, and send him away."

And when the governor looked around, he saw many of the Jews in the crowd were crying. "Well, well, not all your people want his death, do they?"

"We *all* came here," croaked Summas, "just for the purpose of seeing him die!"

"But why should he die?" asked Pilate in amazement.

"Because," Annas said, "he declares that he's the Son of God."

"And a king," added Caiaphas.

Angry and exasperated, Pilate motioned for his soldiers to usher everyone out of the hall again. Court was adjourned, and, for the time being at least, the Assembly Hall fell completely silent.

In His Defense

THE JEWISH LEADERS were together again, appearing before a disgruntled Pilate in his Assembly Hall. This time a pair of temple guards led Jesus in, and when the governor saw that His hands were in shackles, he became particularly agitated.

Still another black-robed Jewish leader came forward and stood before Pilate. "Oh, righteous judge, please allow me to say a few words."

"And who are you now?" the governor asked. "Another detractor here to berate the good man?"

"My name is Nicodemus, and although I'm a leader among the Pharisees, no, I'm not here to rail upon the good Man, as you call Him."

"Really." Intrigued, Pilate nodded. "Go ahead, then. I'm interested to hear what you have to say. By the gods, I've certainly had my fill with trumped-up charges thus far."

So Nicodemus proceeded to state his case, slowly and confidently. "Very good. Then hopefully I will divert you today with my fresh testimony, because I've just recently come from a meeting where I spoke quite frankly with a group of our elders, scribes and priests who are all gathered in Jerusalem for our Passover festival. I talked to them about this Man Who has performed so many miracles, unlike anything anyone has done or ever will do again, and I asked them: 'What, exactly, are your plans for this Man?'"

"How dare you disturb the esteemed governor's official business like this, Nicodemus," interjected Annas.

"Excuse me," Nicodemus replied calmly, "but I've been given permission to speak here. Do you mind?"

Pilate perked up. "Ah, don't pay any attention to them. You go right ahead."

"You silly, old fool," Caiaphas interjected. "What in Heaven's name do you expect to gain from all your pathetic groveling, anyway?"

"I was hoping the governor would agree to release this Man, before He falls victim to your unmitigated hatred and envy."

"Well, how about that," said an astonished Pilate, who turned to Caiaphas with a wry smile. "One of your own leaders thinks this Jesus should be released. What do you say to that?"

"Preposterous, blasphemous!" Caiaphas howled. "This man should be ashamed to call himself a spiritual leader of our people!"

"Oh, please," scoffed Nicodemus, "what's all the fuss about, honestly? If this Jesus is a mere mortal as you people claim, then you have nothing to worry about if He's released. His so-called 'miracles' and 'divine cures' will simply come to nothing all by themselves."

"But what if he really has been sent by your alleged God, then what?" asked Pilate, leaning eagerly forward, as if to get a better view of the fistfight that might ensue at any moment.

"If He does come from God," Nicodemus continued, "then His miracles will be unstoppable no matter how hard you try to prevent them."

"Ridiculous!" growled Annas. "What this man is suggesting is completely absurd."

"No, that isn't true," countered Nicodemus. "A similar thing happened when God sent Moses into Egypt to perform his miracles. Pharaoh's sorcerers, Jannes and Jambres, could do some of the same miracles Moses performed, but in the end their power proved to be no match for Moses."

Pilate turned to Annas and Caiaphas. "Were either of you aware of this fact from your own Scripture?"

"Of course they're aware of it," insisted Nicodemus, sensing that the governor might prove to be a potential ally after all. "Any teacher in Israel would remember the stories about those sorcerers. They'd also be very aware of what happened to all the people who believed in them."

"What did happen to them?" asked a wide-eyed Pilate with an almost child-like enthusiasm.

Caiaphas awkwardly cleared his throat. "They all died untimely deaths, naturally."

"Naturally," echoed Nicodemus.

The governor flashed a lusty smile at this, much to the chagrin of Annas and Caiaphas.

Seeing Pilate's favorable reaction, Nicodemus pressed on. "So, Governor Pilate, may I be so bold as to appeal to your sense of propriety and justice. Please, release this Man right away. Obviously, anyone can see that the miracles He's performed have come from God. The last thing He deserves is to be executed for them."

But Annas coldly replied, "So now you're making eloquent speeches on his behalf, are you? Have you become one of his disciples, too?"

Nicodemus, however, remained unruffled. "Certainly you're not suggesting that Governor Pilate has become one of His disciples, simply because he also makes speeches in His defense?"

"You traitor!" bellowed Alexander, shaking his fist at Nicodemus. "You just go ahead and believe everything he taught you is true! I hope you end up with him!"

"Yes, I do accept everything He taught me as the truth," replied the unflappable Nicodemus. "And, yes, I do hope I end up with Him as well, just as you say. Thank you."

"All right, everyone," said Pilate, who put up his hand in protest. "Enough already. Both your sides have been well represented. Now, is there anyone else who can offer something new to this discussion?"

Another Jewish man timidly stepped forward and quietly said, "Yes, sir, I can."

"Really now, and who are you?"

"Oh, my name is unimportant, sir. Unlike these other important men,

I am just an ordinary man. But I can promise you I have an extraordinary story to tell."

"Then, by all means, tell it."

"For thirty-eight miserable years, I laid by the sheep pool at Jerusalem, struggling with a terrible disease. Year after year, I sat there waiting for a cure brought whenever an angel of God would come and disturb the water so that whoever stepped in first, after the stirring of the waters, was healed of whatever illness they had."

"Yes, yes," Caiaphas groaned impatiently. "We're all aware of the legend. Please make your point."

"Well, you see," the man continued, "Jesus saw me languishing there, so He asked me: 'Would you like to be healed?' But I answered: 'Sir, I have no one to put me into the pool when the water is disturbed.' Then He said, 'Get up and walk,' and immediately I was healthy again."

"It's a lie!" yelped Caiaphas. "Certainly the testimony of this scoundrel cannot be admitted before this grand tribunal!"

"But I'm telling you the truth, Governor," he insisted. "I swear it. That very moment I got up and walked away, completely healed."

"But, sir," Annas grunted, "ask him what day it was when he was cured of his disease."

"On the Sabbath Day, of course," murmured the man. "Why do you ask?"

"See," cried Caiaphas, "didn't we tell you this Jesus performed his cures on the Sabbath? And all by the power of the prince of demons!"

Then, a disheveled man slowly stepped up and bowed before the governor.

"Who are you?" Pilate asked.

"My name is Bartimeus, and I was born blind. My whole life, I was a prisoner to darkness, but one day, as Jesus was walking by, I called out: 'Son of David, have mercy on me!'"

"Then what happened?"

"Jesus stopped, of course, and told me: 'Receive your sight,' and instantly I could see for the very first time in my life. And I've been following Him ever since."

"He just *told* you to receive your sight?" asked the incredulous governor. "And then you could see again?"

"Yes, sir, that's exactly the way it happened?"

An astonished Pilate darted a look at Annas and Caiaphas, who both looked as skeptical as ever.

"Preposterous, I tell you," Caiaphas sneered.

Another man then stepped up.

"What's your story, young man?" asked Pilate.

"Me? Oh, well, I used to be a leper."

"And you also encountered this man called Jesus."

"Yes, Governor, I did, and when I met Jesus, He told me: 'I want you to be healed.'"

"And you were healed?" asked Pilate. "With just a word from this man?"

Shaking his head, still in disbelief himself, he replied, "I know it sounds absurd, sir, but it's true. Jesus simply told me to be healed, and just like that, I was healthy again."

"Please, Governor," Caiaphas grumbled. "How much more of this rubbish do we have to listen to?"

A woman pressed forward through the crowd. "Governor Pilate, Governor Pilate, please. I also have a story to tell."

The governor nodded amicably. "Go right ahead, young lady. Tell us."

Trying to hold back her tears of joy, she said, "I am a daughter of Abraham, and I was severely deformed. My back was so crooked it was impossible for me to stand up straight."

"Don't tell me," scoffed Caiaphas. "You also had an encounter with a mystical healer calling himself the son of god."

"That's right," came her charming reply, completely undeterred by the high priest's cynicism. "And with just a word, He straightened my back. I've been able to live a normal life ever since."

Another woman, her eyes downcast, then came forward and stood contritely before Pilate. Slowly lifting her head, this beautiful lady beamed a radiant smile, a familiar smile, the smile of the same woman who previously had in her possession a remarkable painting of the Man she now sought to defend. "Hello, Governor Pilate. My name is Veronica, and for twelve miserable years, I was afflicted with an issue of blood. My doctors gave me no hope of recovery. To a man, they were unanimous as to the certainty of my fate. For all intents and purposes, sir, I was a walking corpse, withering away, day after wretched day, just waiting for the day of my blessed release … my death … the only thing I was told that would free me from my deadly affliction. Until the day, that is, I was somehow able to press through the crowd surrounding Him, and that was when I merely touched the hem of His garment, and then…" Veronica choked up, unable to continue.

Pilate leaned forward in anticipation. "Yes, and then?"

Regaining her composure, Veronica looked him straight in the eye and replied, "And then the bleeding stopped that very moment; and I've been healed ever since."

"Excuse me, Governor," Gamaliel interjected with a disgruntled scowl, "but our Law forbids women from being allowed to offer evidence in court."

"You don't say," said Pilate, who, upon seeing the sour look on the face of the prosecution, glibly smiled. "Too bad for you that you neglected to mention it until now."

So another man came forward. "Then I guess I'll have to testify to what I saw, sir."

"Of course, go right ahead," urged Pilate. "You also encountered this man?"

"I did, yes. I was at a wedding celebration in Cana where Jesus and His disciples had been invited."

"When was that, young man?" asked Annas.

"Oh, I'd say right around the time there was a wine shortage in Galilee."

"I see," mused Annas. "Can you please tell us what happened at this wedding?"

"Yes, well, after we drank all the wine, Jesus ordered the servants to fill six clay pots with water."

"Water?" chimed in Caiaphas. "You ran out of wine, so this man told you to fetch *water*?"

"Yes, that's right."

"Then what happened?" Pilate asked.

"The servants filled the jars to the brim, just as they'd been ordered."

"With water?" quipped Annas.

"Yes, with water, and then He blessed it."

"Great," snickered Caiaphas. "Then you served holy water to a bunch of disgruntled wedding guests. Is that about it?"

"No, sir, that's not how it happened at all."

"Young man," intoned Annas, trying to remain patient, "would you please just get to the point of your story?"

"Well, then, the servants poured drinks for everyone there, and to our absolute amazement, the water had turned into wine."

"What?" moaned Caiaphas. "You're joking."

"No, sir. I can assure you I saw the whole thing with my own eyes: Water went into the jars, and then wine came out of them. We all drank it together, and celebrated well into the night. Honestly."

"Ridiculous, I tell you." Caiaphas crossed his arms, quite indignantly.

"I know it sounds crazy," the young man said, thoroughly apologetic. "We could hardly believe it ourselves, but I can assure you, it really did happen."

Then another gentleman stepped forward. "That's nothing compared to what I saw."

Pilate leaned forward. "You saw something more amazing than that?"

"Oh, yes, sir. I saw Jesus teaching in the synagogue at Capernaum. A man with a demon yelled at Him: 'What do You want with us, Jesus of Nazareth? Have You come to destroy us before our time? I know You're the

Holy One of Israel, the Son of God!'"

Annas turned to Pilate with outstretched hands. "Please, sir, do we have to listen to any more of this nonsense? Now we have to be subjected to stories about demons? Really?"

But Pilate glared back at him. "I'll decide what is, or is not, considered nonsense." Then the governor turned his attention back to the gentleman. "Now, continue. What makes you so sure this man had a demon speaking through him?"

"Well, I don't really know how to answer that, sir. All I know is that, when Jesus said to him: 'Shut up, demon! Come out of this man, right now!' I mean, instantly, some kind of evil spirit flew out of his chest, and just like that, the man was completely normal again, as though he'd just woken up from a bad dream."

"What?" asked a stunned Pilate. "Is he all right? Where is he now?"

"Oh, he's fine. Back to work, as usual. Like nothing ever happened to him at all."

Another young man slowly stepped forward and awkwardly cleared his throat.

"You?" blanched Caiaphas. "Jonathan? Don't tell me you're here to testify on this man's behalf, too."

The man resolutely nodded. "Yes, sir, I am."

"But, Jonathan, why?" asked the high priest, horrified and distraught. "Why on Earth would you do something like this?"

Intrigued by the palpable tension between these two, Pilate sat up in his seat. "Wait a minute, Caiaphas. Just who is this man?"

The high priest almost choked on his words as he reluctantly replied, "He's my nephew."

"Your nephew?" exclaimed Pilate, clearly amused with Caiaphas' dilemma. "Oh, that is a good one."

"Not only is he my nephew, but he's also a man who until recently was in training for the priesthood, a fledgling Pharisee, as I understood it from my sister."

"Well, well, so the story gets even more interesting," the governor continued. "So, then; Jonathan, is it?"

"Yes, sir, that's right."

"So, Jonathan, what's your story?" he pressed. "You're not studying to become a priest anymore? No longer interested in joining the vaunted ranks of the Pharisees?"

"No, sir, I'm not."

"But why? Why the sudden change of heart?"

"Because ever since I encountered the Nazarene, I could no longer bring myself to continue following a path that, for me at least, had no meaning, no purpose, no hope."

An audible gasp rippled through the ranks of Caiaphas and his colleagues.

"Jonathan, how could you?" grimaced the high priest. "We all had such high hopes for you."

"I'm sorry, Uncle, but I didn't choose any of this for myself. It happened *to* me, I'm afraid."

"And here you are," Pilate continued, "not only willing to risk your future in the ministry of your so-called 'Chosen People,' but you also stand here willing to risk being spurned by your own family."

"Yes, it does appear that way, doesn't it?" replied Jonathan with utmost resolve.

"Why, Jonathan, why?" Caiaphas asked again, bitterly disappointed.

"Because I, too, saw vast numbers of sick people come to Jesus, from Galilee and Judea, from the seacoast and many of the countries around Jordan. Wave after wave of the sick followed Him wherever He went. The anguished, the dying, the hopeless, all besieged with every kind of disease that no doctor, no medicine, no ritual could cure. But in this Man's presence alone, they found a remedy. They found in Him the answer to all their desperate prayers. In Him, they discovered the truth about what made them sick, in body and in spirit, and through His benevolent intervention, everyone who came to Him in faith and hope was miraculously healed."

"No, no, no," groaned Caiaphas. "That's just not possible. You've lost your mind, I tell you; your soul, for that matter. This carpenter's son has deluded all of you by the power of Satan."

"No, Uncle, that isn't true," Jonathan insisted. "I saw it all for myself, and there's nothing you'll ever be able to say or do to persuade me otherwise."

Then a Roman soldier stepped forward. This time it was Pilate who sat up, suddenly curious. "Centurio, what are you doing here?"

"Well, sir, I saw Jesus in Capernaum, too."

"That's your hometown, isn't it?"

"Yes, Governor, it is."

"Don't tell me. You're here to tell us about some miraculous encounter you also had with this man?"

"I am, yes."

"This man healed you, too? Is that it?"

"Not me, sir, my servant. For the longest time my servant was bedridden with the palsy. You remember, don't you?"

"Yes, of course. I do remember something about that, now that you mention it. And you're telling me this Jesus came to your hometown?"

"He did, Governor."

"What happened?"

"I begged Him to heal my servant, and right away, He told me: 'I'll come and cure him.' But I said, 'Sir, I don't even deserve to have You come to my house. You just say the word, and my servant will be healed.'"

"Interesting," mused Pilate. "And then?"

"Then He told me: 'Go now. You'll receive just as you've believed.' And my servant was healed from that very hour."

Amazed at this, Pilate flashed a peculiar look of dissatisfaction at Annas and Caiaphas, who both had to avert their eyes, unable to bear his scrutinizing gaze.

Then a nobleman came forward and stood before the governor. "I had a son in Capernaum who was on the brink of death."

"Another person from Capernaum?" mumbled Caiaphas. "Haven't we heard enough from that part of the country yet?"

The man hesitated at this and looked to Pilate, unsure if he should continue.

"Ah, don't mind them," the governor said with a wave of his hand. "I, for one, am very interested in hearing your story. Go right ahead."

"Well, sir, one day, I had heard that Jesus was in Galilee, so I went there on my son's behalf, and I asked Him if He could possibly heal my boy, too. And He said, 'Go home, your son is fine now.'"

"Just like that?" said Pilate, snapping his fingers.

"Yes, sir, just like that," came the man's unflinching reply. "And when I returned to my home in Capernaum, I found that, just as He had assured me, my son really had been cured."

Another young man stepped forward. "Of course He's the Son of God, sir. How else could He cure every disease by merely speaking?"

"Obviously this power only comes from God!" declared an old man.

"The demons are all completely under His control!" said another woman with an emphatic conviction that made the governor raise his eyebrow.

Pilate then turned to His accusers. "And why aren't these demons subject to the power of your doctors?"

"The power to control demons can only come from God," Datam replied with a smug arrogance. "Men simply don't have the kind of power these people are describing, especially a mere peasant like this good-for-nothing Nazarene."

"But I saw Jesus raise Lazarus from the dead with my own eyes," interjected Nicodemus, "even after he'd been dead for four days. That doesn't sound like something an ordinary person can do, does it?"

Pilate shuddered and again turned to the prosecution. "So tell me again, gentlemen: What, exactly, do you seek to gain by shedding the blood of this innocent Man?"

Lamb Led to the Slaughter

THE EXASPERATED governor stood on his balcony, gazing out over a mob of Jewish protesters. With each passing moment, the crowd was swelling to the point of overflowing the square below him. Furious spectators waved their fists in the air, and someone even went so far as to throw their sandal in the direction of one of Pilate's guards who was standing near the balcony rail.

Barely ducking out of the way of the hurling object, the guard turned to Pilate. "Sir, how long will you permit this crowd to roam free? They grow more unruly by the minute. Say the word, and we'll clear the square in no time flat."

"Stand down, soldier, stand down. No one ever lost his life at the point of a sandal. I'll let you know when I want you to take action. Is that clear?"

"Yes, sir."

"Pilate, you filthy pig!" shouted one of the spectators. "If you're not willing to execute the Nazarene, in the name of your almighty Caesar, hand him over to us! We know how to take care of scum like him!"

Shaking his head in disgust, the governor muttered under his breath. "And they say we Romans are the bloodthirsty ones."

INSIDE, PILATE ADDRESSED Nicodemus and the Jews who had stated that Jesus was not born through fornication. "This whole thing is creating a riot among your people," the governor began. "If something isn't done quickly, there's liable to be more blood on my hands besides that of your Jesus. Isn't there some way to reason with these fanatics?"

"I'm afraid, Governor," Nicodemus said, "that the people you're dealing with are no longer acting in accordance to reason. They've been deluded by the powers that be that it's in the nation's best interest to sacrifice one decent man for the sake of their collective peace and tranquility."

"But all this flies in the face of my experience to this point. Certainly I've dealt with my share of anarchists before, believe me, but I've never known insanity like this; and from the very people you'd think would benefit most by a revolutionist like Jesus. Frankly, I'm at a complete loss. Can't any of you offer me a viable solution?"

Crispus shook his head. "We don't really know what to tell you anymore, Governor. Maybe you should let the ones who are in such an uproar decide."

"Tell me you're joking. Tell me you're not actually suggesting I allow that mob out there to decide this man's fate, because not only does his fate rest on my next act, but so does mine. And not in Caesar's eyes alone but certainly in the eyes of the One who's responsible for all of the miracles this man's been performing."

A DISHEARTENED PILATE walked out onto the balcony and took his position at the railing, where he again faced the tumultuous throng of Jewish protesters. With him were two of his guards, both of whom escorted a prisoner bound in chains. To his right was a resolute Jesus, beaten, bruised and bleeding, who stood serenely looking out over the angry crowd. To his left was a brutish man, grimy, wild-eyed and menacing, who took one look at the man guarding him and defiantly spit at his feet.

With every ounce of dignity that remained in him, Pilate raised his hands in an effort to silence the crowd. Slowly but surely, the clamoring mob simmered to a low boil. "Listen up, everyone, and listen well. As you all know, we've established a custom among your people where I'm allowed, by virtue of imperial decree, to release one prisoner from among you during this festival known as Passover. Presently, I have here a notorious criminal, a man by the name of Barabbas, the leader of a rapacious gang of thieves responsible for unspeakable mayhem, with so many murders to his credit it would be impossible to catalog them all. And I have here a man by the name of Jesus, whom many call the Christ, a man who doesn't deserve to die for any reason, someone responsible for so many deeds of kindness and mercy that to catalog them all would prove just as impossible. Therefore, keeping this in mind, I put it in your hands: Which man does your conscience bid you to return to your community? Will you unleash the beast, Barabbas, back upon your wives and children? Or would you rather set free the Innocent One, Jesus? Tell me now: Which one should I release?"

Momentarily smitten, everyone in the crowd glanced at his neighbor with a nervous look, and then returned their eyes back upon the governor. The crowd roared back unanimously. "Release Barabbas!"

Flabbergasted by the crowd's reaction, Barabbas grinned maliciously and nodded to them. "That's right, that's right," he snarled like a wild animal. "Release Barabbas!"

An irritated Pilate turned to the man guarding his outspoken prisoner and flashed him a sinister look, which invoked the guard to deliver a swift kidney punch to Barabbas, who doubled over in pain.

Turning back to the mob, Pilate shouted, "Then what do I do with Jesus, the Christ?"

For several heart-pounding moments, a deafening silence hung in the air, teeming with the imperceptible sound of a thousand stifled consciences. Then, all at once, the remorseless mob howled, "Crucify him!"

"You're no friend of Caesar if you release this man!" Alexander bellowed. "He says he's the son of God and a king! Would you rather have him as your king instead of Caesar?"

As enraged as the crowd that was vexing him, if not more so, Pilate lashed out uncontrollably, banging his fist on the railing. "What is wrong with you people? You're a spiteful nation of rebels, always antagonizing anyone who tries to do you a favor!"

"Who's ever done us a favor?" scoffed Annas.

"Your god for one!" Pilate snapped back. "First he rescued you from slavery in Egypt, then he led you through the Red Sea, as if it were dry land. He fed you with manna and quails in the wilderness. He brought you water out of a rock. It's said he even gave you a Law straight from Heaven."

"You've heard correctly, sir," cooed Caiaphas.

The governor glared back. "Still you provoked him! Why?"

Annas and Caiaphas exchanged a concerned look.

Pilate pressed on. "You demanded a molten calf. You worshiped it, sacrificed to it, as if *it* had delivered you from Egypt! So your god wanted to destroy you."

"But He chose not to destroy us, didn't He?" Annas countered. "He must have seen something in our nation that was worth saving."

"He didn't destroy you because Moses interceded on your behalf. That's why your god forgave you. Still you people got so mad at him and his brother Aaron, when they fled into the tabernacle, you wanted to kill them both. Apparently you do this to everyone who tries to help you!"

Turning from his balcony, the governor started to leave, but someone from the mob shrieked, "But we want Caesar as our king, not this Jesus!"

Summas then elbowed his way forward. "He's the reason Herod gave the order to kill the male infants of Bethlehem! It's time he account for this outrage with his own blood! If you don't execute this man, we'll have no choice but to take matters into our own hands, here and now!"

This alarmed Pilate, and the entire assembly grew restless and noisy again. The governor turned back toward the crowd and again raised his hands in an effort to silence them. "All right, people, calm down, calm down!" As the mob slowly quieted back down, Pilate turned to Jesus and implored, "Are you really a king, then?"

Caiaphas pointed an accusing finger. "He's no king. He's just an insignificant, little man, a usurper who wishes to replace our beloved Caesar."

"So, what's it going to be, Governor?" yelped Annas. "Will you actually risk your future to save a single man? One word from us, and this whole city could go up in flames, and Tiberius would have no one to blame but you!"

The seething crowd let loose with a discordant roar of approval, and for several agonizing moments Pilate glared back at them. He then motioned to one of his servants, who brought out a basin of water and set it down on the railing in front of him. Slowly and methodically, Pilate washed his hands in the sight of everyone there. "I tell you all, here and now," he bellowed above the din. "I am absolved from the blood of this innocent man! You work this out amongst yourselves!"

"Let his blood be on us and our children!" Summas shouted.

Pilate reluctantly turned to Jesus again. "Your own nation has charged you with making yourself a king. Therefore, I, Pontius Pilate, governor of Jerusalem, on behalf of Tiberius Caesar, emperor of Rome, do sentence you to be whipped according to the Law of former governors. Then, you will be bound and hung on a cross, along with two other criminals named Dimas and Gestas, until such time as you are dead."

WITHOUT A SINGLE word of protest from Jesus, He and the two thieves then proceeded to carry their crossbeams to Golgotha.

ARRIVING TO THE PLACE of execution, the prisoners were handed over to a trio of Roman soldiers who stripped Jesus of His seamless robe and wrapped a skimpy linen cloth around His waist. They placed a crown of thorns on His head and a reed in His hand. Then, Pilate personally wrote on a plaque that was placed atop the cross. Written in Hebrew, Latin and Greek, its message read: *This is the king of the Jews.*

With that, the soldiers nailed Jesus to the crossbeam, piercing His wrists. Lifting Him into place on the upright post, they finished the job by nailing his feet into place. Finally, the two thieves were lashed to their crossbeams and hoisted up so they could be crucified alongside Him, Dimas to His right, and Gestas to His left.

The mocking mob gathered as Jesus looked skyward. "Please, Father, forgive them," He murmured. "They don't really know what they're doing."

Near the foot of the cross, the three Roman soldiers each rolled a crude set of dice, then one of them happily grabbed Jesus' seamless robe and stuck it in his sash. That soldier was Longinus the centurion.

Meanwhile, the rest of the onlookers, accompanied by the priests and elders, stood by, gawking at Jesus as He hung there trying to catch His breath with each passing moment.

"He saved others, now let him save himself," Alexander barked, "if he can!"

"If he's really the son of God," yelled Summas, "let him come down from there this instant!"

"If you're really a king," said Longinus, "then command us to remove you from this cross, before it's too late." Then, taking a stick with cloth at the end, the centurion dipped it in vinegar, mixed with gall, and held it up to His mouth.

Gestas, the thief being crucified to the left of Jesus, turned to Him and sneered. "If you are the Christ, then deliver yourself, and us."

Dimas, the thief to His right, turned toward Gestas. "Doesn't a condemned man like you fear God even a little? We're at least receiving proper sentences for what we've done, but this Jesus, what crime has He ever committed?" And turning to Jesus, he implored, "Lord, please remember me when You enter Your kingdom."

With great difficulty, Jesus, His face mired in sweat and blood, replied, "Certainly, Dimas, today you will be with Me in Paradise."

AS THE SUN REACHED its zenith in the sky, an eerie darkness began to fall across the countryside with the onset of a total eclipse. The once mocking mob ceased its jeering as everyone stood staring up at the darkening sky, frozen with fear and dismay.

AROUND THREE O'CLOCK in the afternoon, with the darkness caused by the eclipse having fully enveloped the landscape by then, Jesus could be heard gasping on the cross. "My God, My God … Why … have You abandoned Me? Father … I now give You … My spirit." Then He died.

Suddenly a powerful earthquake struck the countryside, sending terrified spectators scrambling in every direction. The veil of the Temple was torn from top to bottom, and its foundations crumbled, causing the building to teeter to one side. All the cemeteries in the area were decimated. The ordinarily neat array of manicured tombstones was now a jumbled mess of jagged stones, tilted at every imaginable angle. Graves everywhere were ripped up, torn from the inside out, split open as though the ground had belched out its very interior.

Clearly shaken, Longinus gazed up at Him hanging on the cross. "This really was an innocent Man," he whispered. Then stepping forward, he raised his spear and plunged it into the right side of Jesus, directly between the fifth and sixth rib. Blood and water immediately gushed from the wound.

A NOBLEMAN WENT TO see Pilate late that same evening. As the man patiently stood before him, the governor looked up with his weary, bloodshot eyes. "What do you want?"

"My name is Joseph of Arimathea."

"I know who you are. I asked you: What do you want?"

"I'm here to request your permission to bury the Nazarene's body."

"Don't tell me. You're one of his faithful disciples, too, but because you fear those bloodthirsty zealots who demanded his death, you're here under the cover of darkness."

Joseph hung his head in shame. "Yes, I suppose you're right. I stand before you guilty as charged."

Pilate continued with his glib tone. "Still, you felt someone should see to it that the man be given a decent burial, and that someone just happens to be you. Is that about it?"

Eyes still downcast, Joseph painfully nodded. "That's correct, Governor."

"Well, I admit, you're not the first person who's come to me lately asking for the same consideration. But before I do give you permission, give me one good reason why I should allow *you* access to the body? Were you particularly close to the man in life, or, now that he's dead, are you feeling remorseful for having done nothing to save him from such a despicable fate?"

"I'm asking you, sir," said Joseph, lifting his head in all earnestness, "because the Man was not only my dearest friend and esteemed Teacher, He was also my nephew."

Pilate's expression abruptly transformed from that of the cynical antagonist to one of sympathetic ally. "Then, please, accept my apology, and, by all means, see to it that the good man receives the sort of treatment in death that he deserved to receive in life."

AS JOSEPH AND Nicodemus led a solemn procession of men who were carrying the body of Jesus, they all openly wept. Joining them in their solemn task, several women came out of the shadows to assist them. Together, they took part in wrapping Him, according to Jewish custom, in linen cloths sprinkled with spices of myrrh and aloe.

JOSEPH, NICODEMUS and the other men then transported the linen-wrapped body of Jesus to a tomb, cut out of rock, where they lovingly laid Him to rest. For the longest time the group stayed with Him there, mourning, sobbing, unwilling to leave Him even in death. Finally, however, they reluctantly exited the tomb, and having done so, the men rolled a huge round stone into place, sealing the doorway with a tremendous thud.

Blood on Their Hands

"THEY DID WHAT?" barked Caiaphas, wide-eyed and furious.

"They got permission from Pilate to bury his body," Summas timidly replied.

"Then what did they do with it?" wondered Annas.

Summas rolled his eyes in disgust. "Can you believe it? They buried it in Joseph of Arimathea's brand-new tomb."

"The fools," groaned Caiaphas. "That man's body should have been cast into the pit of Gehenna, like the rest of his kind. When will these heretics ever learn?"

Then turning to Annas, Summas asked, "What should we do now, sir?"

"It's time these infidels answer for their crimes against God," growled Annas. "Find them, Summas, and bring them before our tribunal; them, and anyone else who showed sympathy to the Nazarene. It's time, once and for all, that these men get a taste of what we gave their beloved savior."

STILL OBVIOUSLY disturbed by what he had experienced, the Roman soldier who had stood at the foot of Jesus' cross went to see Pilate.

"Hello, Governor Pilate," said the soldier. "I know you're a busy man, so I'll be as brief as possible."

"Of course," Pilate replied. "What can I do for one of Caesar's great and glorious centurions?"

"I came here today because it's my understanding we have a mutual interest between us."

"Really? And what might that be?"

"It seems we've both had an encounter with the Man called Jesus."

"Jesus," Pilate muttered under his breath. "You, too? That's why you're here?"

The soldier nodded blankly.

"By the gods, does this man plan to haunt me even from beyond the grave?"

"It does appear so, doesn't it?"

"What's your name, centurion?"

"My name is Longinus, and I was one of three soldiers directly responsible for the crucifixion of Jesus of Nazareth." Agonized, he held both hands out. "These hands, sir, are the hands of a soldier, hands that gloried in the sting of battle, the shedding of blood, the revelry of victory." Longinus paused and stared down at his hands, as though he were horrified that they were connected to the rest of his body.

Realizing he was unable to continue, the governor prodded. "And now?"

"Now, they're nothing but a horror to me."

"But why?" asked an incredulous Pilate.

"Because now they're the hands of the man who spilled the blood of the Savior of the World." Snapping out of his spell, Longinus looked up at Pilate, looking him straight in the eye. "Tell me, Governor, when you washed your hands of His blood, did it work? Did it really absolve you from your crime after all?"

Pilate stared back for the longest time before shaking his head. "No, sadly, it did not."

Longinus then turned and headed for the door. "Goodbye, sir, and may God have mercy on our souls." Almost to the door, he stopped and turned back toward the governor. "Oh, I almost forgot." Reaching into his sash, he pulled out a bundle of cloth and tossed it to the floor. "I want you to have this. I don't ever want to see it again."

Pilate gawked at the pile of cloth. "What is it?"

Longinus turned and headed through the doorway. "Just something I won in a little game of chance."

With a curious look in his eyes, Pilate walked over to the pile of cloth and picked it up. Confused with what he was looking at, he unfurled the cloth, which turned out to be a man's linen undergarment. It was the seamless robe of Jesus.

ONCE AGAIN PILATE was staring down the same group of black-robed Jewish leaders.

"So, did any of you see the miracle of the solar eclipse the other day?" asked the governor, agitated and tense.

They all smugly nodded at Pilate.

"Of course we did, Governor," Caiaphas calmly replied.

"And you all felt the earthquake?" asked the governor.

Again they nodded knowingly.

"But I'd hardly call what happened a miracle," the high priest quickly added. "Would you, Annas?"

The chief priest shrugged innocently. "Certainly not."

"Well," Pilate continued, "do any of you have a better explanation for the things that happened when Jesus died? A solar eclipse *and* an earthquake? Both occurring on the exact day of his death? That's quite a coincidence, if you ask me."

"But, Governor, be reasonable," Annas said with a feigned chuckle. "The things you're so alarmed about were natural, ordinary occurrences. There was nothing miraculous about them in the least."

"Natural?" blurted Pilate. "Ordinary? You can't be serious."

"On the contrary, sir," interjected Datam with a similarly innocent shrug of his shoulders, "we've never been more serious in our lives. The eclipse of the Sun took place according to its usual custom, and as for the earthquake, it just so happens that because of the celestial imbalance that occurs during an eclipse, earthquakes are actually quite common."

"By the gods," Pilate sighed wearily, throwing his hands up in sheer frustration. "You people are unbelievable. Why do I even bother?"

THEN CAME THE DAY when Joseph of Arimathea arrived at the Temple at Jerusalem.

"How dare you enter this synagogue?" Summas croaked, pointing an accusatory finger. "You were a collaborator with the Nazarene!"

"Why are you so angry with me?" asked Joseph. "All I did was ask Pilate for the Man's body. I wrapped Him in clean linen, put Him in my own tomb, placed a stone at the entrance. What harm is there in any of that?"

"You had no business doing any of it in the first place," snapped Datam.

"No, you're wrong. I had every right. Have you forgotten, the Man was my nephew? I owed it to my family to see that He had a decent burial. I did what any one of you would've done in my position. You should all be ashamed of yourselves. You did everything you could to destroy a perfectly innocent Man, and to top it off, you even prayed for the guilt of His blood upon your own heads."

"How dare you accuse us of something like that!" screeched Levi.

"We never said any such thing!" Datam yelped.

"Throw him in prison, I say!" howled Summas. "At least until the Sabbath is over. Then we can deal with the likes of him, once and for all!"

Annas nodded in agreement and stepped up to Joseph. "Better make your confession now, Joseph, while you still can. For the time being, it's unlawful to harm you. That is, at least until the first day of the week comes."

"And because you're unworthy of a decent burial," Caiaphas sputtered, "we'll just be giving your corpse to the birds and beasts!"

Joseph turned to address the assembly. "You know, talk like that reminds me of Goliath bragging to David, but you priests and doctors of the Law know full well what God says by the prophet: 'Revenge is Mine, and I'll repay you with the same evil you threatened Me with.'"

"Watch yourself, Joseph," sneered Caiaphas. "You don't want to end up like your poor nephew, do you?"

"That does it, Caiaphas," snapped the otherwise implacable Joseph. "I've had it with you. I'm through being afraid of you and your threats. You may think you've gotten away with murdering Jesus, and you may think you'll get away with doing the same thing to me, but one thing's for sure: No matter what you've done or what you're planning to do, your treachery will come back to haunt all of you!"

Putting his arm around his son-in-law, Annas led the high priest several feet away from Joseph. "On second thought, Caiaphas, maybe we should rethink this. I say, we turn this matter over to Governor Pilate. Maybe he could arrange to have Joseph taken care of for us. That way we'd avoid any further involvement in this whole mess."

Joseph stared back in disbelief. "What are you people thinking? Pilate is no ally of yours. Even *he* washed his hands when you insisted that he cooperate with your plan. He flatly stated: 'I'm absolved from the blood of this innocent Man.'"

This immediately evoked an irritated scowl from Annas, who dropped his arm from around Caiaphas as both men turned back toward Joseph.

"Enough of your insolent backtalk, heretic!" Caiaphas barked. "The innocent man, as you call him, got exactly what he deserved; nothing more, nothing less."

"Yes, and then you all agreed together," Joseph countered. "'Let His blood be on us and our children!' So, as you wish, I hope you all perish forever!"

With that, the whole group flew into an incredible rage.

"This man should not be allowed to speak to us this way any longer!" screamed Datam.

"Away with him!" grunted Caiaphas.

MANHANDLED BY A PAIR of temple guards and thrown into a room without windows, Joseph fell to the ground in a dusty heap. The iron door slammed shut, and a wax seal was placed on the lock.

"SO IT'S BEEN DECIDED," Annas announced to all the priests, Levites and doctors of the Law gathered before him. "We won't consort with the foreigner Pilate anymore. Instead, we take matters into our own hands this time. Agreed?"

"Agreed," they all said with one voice.

"We'll reconvene after the Sabbath," continued Annas, "at which time we'll decide this man's fate, as we see fit."

"Then, it will be unanimously decided," Caiaphas added, "how this infidel, Joseph of Arimathea, should be killed."

"So it shall be upon any man who opposes the will of the righteous," sneered Summas, "he'll go down into the pit of death, and there he'll rise no more."

"And the people said," Annas intoned.

"Amen," replied the group.

Earthquakes and Open Graves

AS THE LIGHT OF THE full Moon broke out from behind a cloudbank, it shined an eerie streak across the decimated cemetery adjacent to the Temple at Jerusalem, which now lay in complete ruins. Like the temple courtyard, the cemetery was littered with debris, with row after row of open graves surrounded by scattered piles of dirt and rock, along with its smattering of disheveled gravestones, jutting up at every angle.

Just then a tremendous flash of sunlight wiped away the darkness of night, followed by the abrupt appearance in the sky of a vast array of angelic beings, streaking about in every direction. "Glorify God above everything else!" one of the angels shouted. "Peace has finally come to mankind! You who are chained in the depths of Hades, come out!"

The ground visibly shook at the sound of that voice, and then suddenly a mound of dirt pushed up from out of one of the open graves, then some more dirt came up from another grave, and then some more. At which point many of the saints, who had been dead for so long, began to rise from these open graves, and wandering aimlessly, silently, alive in the flesh once again, they fanned out across the strangely lit landscape in no particular direction at all.

WHEN ALL OF the Jewish authorities reconvened several days later, the Assembly Hall was buzzing with the incessant droning of dozens of frenetic conversations.

"Quiet down, gentlemen, please," Annas exclaimed, waving his hands about at the head of the group. "I realize there are many questions you all wish to address today, but first we must attend to this business concerning the heretic Joseph of Arimathea."

Caiaphas then motioned to a temple guard, who hastily left the room. Slowly but surely the group came to order as everyone there gradually disengaged with their private conversations and solemnly turned to give the chief priest their undivided attention.

Hurrying to Joseph's prison chamber, the guard saw the seal on the lock was still intact, but upon opening the door, he gasped when he found that Joseph was not inside. Running as fast as he could back to the Assembly Hall, the anxious temple guard was nearly out of breath. "Sir, the seal … on the prison door was intact … but…" As he struggled to get the words out, the guard began wheezing for air and doubled over.

"But what?" Caiaphas demanded.

Standing upright, the temple guard grimaced. "But Joseph is missing."

"What?" Annas roared. "Impossible!"

Shocked by this unexpected turn of events, the whole room resumed its cacophony of alarm and dismay, and again Annas frantically waved his hands about. "Hold on, everyone, hold on! If you'll all kindly restrain yourselves, I assure you, we will get to the bottom of this. Now, please, quiet down!"

Again, in response to his plea, the room slowly simmered down to a quiet chatter.

"Now, guard," Annas continued. "Are you absolutely certain that no one tampered with the seal on the door?"

"Not a scratch, sir."

"Well, if the seal was still intact, then how could anyone have gotten out?" wondered Caiaphas. "It makes no sense."

"We'll just see about this," grunted Annas.

But before they had time to take a step, two Roman soldiers strode into the Assembly Hall, the effect of which elicited instantaneous silence from the entire group.

Annas eyed them suspiciously. "What is the meaning of this intrusion?"

One soldier stepped forward. "Look, we just needed to talk to you people about something very important. You have nothing to fear from us, I assure you. This is not an imperial matter; it's strictly personal."

Caiaphas moved in next. "How dare you invade this sacred place with your profane presence."

The soldier put up his hand as an intended sign of conciliation. "Please, sir, we mean no disrespect, but we have a genuine mystery on our hands, and we thought someone like you could explain it, that's all."

"Who are you people, anyway?" asked Annas.

"I am Petronius, and this is Marcus. My friend and I were among the soldiers who were assigned to guard the Nazarene's body as it lay in the tomb."

"How do you expect us to help the likes of you?" groaned Caiaphas.

Then the other soldier stepped forward. "See, Petronius, I told you this was a bad idea. Let's just go."

"No, Marcus," Petronius countered. "I want a straight answer from somebody, and I want it now."

"Very well, then," relented Annas. "Tell us why you've come here."

"I want to know if you can explain something for us."

"Explain something," chided Caiaphas with an equal mixture of impatience and contempt. "Explain what?"

"Explain to me what happened to us while we were on duty at the Nazarene's tomb," insisted Petronius. "Why was there an earthquake? Why did the night sky light up like it was daytime? Why did an angel roll the stone door away and sit on it?"

"An angel?" scoffed Caiaphas. "That's preposterous! You were probably drunk, as usual."

But Annas raised his hand to quiet his son-in-law. "Hold on, Caiaphas, hold on," he said, apparently intrigued. "Now, what did this angel look like?"

"You want to know what he looked like?" Marcus interjected, clearly still distraught from his experience. "All right, I'll tell you. He looked like he was made of lightning, but his clothes were made of snow. Care to explain that?"

"I'm telling you," snapped Caiaphas, "these men are either drunkards or lunatics."

Marcus turned to Petronius, shaking his head in disgust. "See, I told you this was how they'd react. I say we just leave. Find somebody else who'll listen to our story."

"No, wait!" Annas blurted. "Don't go. I want to know more. Tell me: What happened when the angel appeared? What did you do?"

"We didn't *do* anything," replied Petronius, thoroughly frustrated. "How could we? We were scared to death. We just collapsed."

"But then something happened after that?" pressed Annas.

"Yes," Marcus insisted, "that's what we've been trying to tell you."

"Then," Petronius continued, "the angel began speaking to the women at His tomb. 'Don't be frightened,' he told them. 'I know you're looking for

Jesus. They crucified Him, but He rose again exactly as He explained to you beforehand. Just look inside the tomb and see for yourselves.'"

Caiaphas rolled his eyes in disgust. "Oh, please. How long do you expect us to entertain such nonsense?"

"Was that all the angel said?" ventured Annas.

"Then he told the women to go and tell His disciples He'd risen from the dead," said Marcus. "And that very soon He'd be meeting them in Galilee, just as He'd told them."

Annas and Caiaphas exchanged a disturbed look, as did everyone else in the room.

"Please, follow us, if you don't mind," Annas said to the soldiers.

Then Annas and Caiaphas led the two Roman soldiers from the Assembly Hall and into another room, closing the door behind them. Now there were just the four of them standing there, two black-robed priests squaring off with two uniformed centurions.

"So, tell us," insisted Annas, "who were these women speaking to the angel?"

"And *why* didn't you seize them when you had the chance?" blurted Caiaphas.

"We don't know who the women were," Petronius replied. "And how do you expect us to grab someone while we're flat on our faces? We just told you. We all collapsed, we were so scared."

"As the Lord lives," yelped Caiaphas, "we don't believe a word of what you're telling us. We think you two stole the body of Jesus, and concocted this insane story to divert attention from this fact."

Petronius shook his head in disbelief. "But what would we gain by doing that? What possible motive would we have in stealing His body?"

"How should we know what goes through the mind of pagans like yourselves," said Caiaphas. "Blackmail, I suppose. If word ever got out that the body of Jesus was missing, then it might lend credence to this absurd movement of theirs."

"Undoubtedly!" Annas added emphatically. "A rumor like that could quickly fan the flames of insurrection. You know how volatile these heretics are, what with their silly superstitions. It's not at all hard to believe you might steal the body and blackmail us in exchange for its return."

"Blackmail," scoffed Marcus. "That's crazy. We didn't come here to blackmail you. We don't want your money; we want answers."

"Then I'm afraid you've come to the wrong place," Caiaphas replied, as contemptuous as ever.

"That figures," Marcus grumbled. "What did I tell you, Petronius? You can't reason with these people. When they saw Jesus performing His miracles with their own eyes, they still didn't believe in Him. You didn't really expect them to believe our story, did you?"

"You know, you people were right when you said, 'The Lord lives,'" quipped Petronius. "The Lord really does live! Because we just heard how you imprisoned the man who buried Jesus, but when you opened his cell, he was missing, too!"

"Never mind that!" snapped Caiaphas. "That doesn't concern you."

"Oh," exclaimed Petronius, "but it does concern us."

"How?" asked Annas.

"Well, you expect us to deliver Jesus' body to you, don't you?" said Petronius.

"In fact you'll be made to do so," snickered Caiaphas. "Or else you'll suffer the consequences."

"Consequences?" echoed Marcus. "What consequences?"

"If you don't produce his body in due time," Caiaphas continued, "then we'll have no choice but to see to it that the Roman authorities have you arrested for treason."

"What?" groaned a stunned Petronius. "Why would the authorities consider the theft of a body grounds for treason?"

Caiaphas pressed on, like a ravenous wolf closing in on its defenseless prey. "Because that theft would be in direct connection with a civil uprising that seeks to undermine Roman authority."

"That, or dereliction of duty," Annas interjected, "considering that if you didn't steal the body yourselves, then you at least aided and abetted the disciples who did. Either way, your only recourse is to produce his body … or else."

"Fine," Petronius replied. "But first you have to produce Joseph, whom *you* were guarding. Then we'll be glad to produce Jesus for you."

"Oh, we'll produce Joseph, all right," insisted Caiaphas. "You just make sure you produce Jesus! Besides, Joseph is probably in his own city of Arimathea right now."

"Well, if Joseph is in Arimathea," said Marcus, "then Jesus is already in Galilee. I'm sure I heard the angel tell the women He'd meet them there."

Annas and Caiaphas exchanged another concerned look.

"Would you gentlemen please excuse us for a moment?" asked Annas.

The soldiers dutifully nodded and stepped out into the hallway, where the two men stared at one another for several moments before Marcus finally broke the silence. "Well, this couldn't be going any worse. What a complete waste of time this turned out to be."

"I'm sorry I dragged you into this mess, Marcus," replied Petronius, shaking his head in exasperation. "What was I thinking? As if this bunch would've cooperated with us."

Spying both directions down the hallway, Marcus continued quietly, "I say we get out of here while the getting's good. I've had it with these pious hypocrites. There's no telling what they'll threaten us with next in the name of their precious god."

Back inside the room, Annas handed Caiaphas a leather bag and sighed heavily, "I don't see that we have any other recourse at this point. This whole thing is getting out of hand, I tell you. If any of this becomes public knowledge, then everybody might start believing in this Jesus, and we'll never hear the end of it as long as we live." Dreadfully concerned, Annas headed for the door. "See to it these soldiers understand how they're to save their own skins. Instruct them well, Caiaphas; we're all counting on you."

"Of course, Father; I'll take care of everything."

Almost to the door, Annas turned back. "I told you to never call me that."

"Yes, sir."

Annas then left the room and encountered the two soldiers in the hallway. "The high priest will see you again," he said, nodding politely. "Good day, gentlemen."

Doing their best to conceal their growing contempt, the soldiers nodded back and reluctantly went back in to see Caiaphas.

"Now, unless you men want us to report you to your superiors," Caiaphas continued, "you'd better start cooperating with us. Agreed?"

Petronius and Marcus looked at one another for several intense moments, then returned their attention to Caiaphas and nodded.

"It seems we don't have much choice in the matter," Petronius replied.

"Good," said Caiaphas with a smugly satisfied smile, and then he handed Petronius the leather bag. "Then take this to seal our deal."

Looking inside, Petronius was dumbfounded. "There's a lot of money in here. What if we're unable to return the body for you after all? Then what?"

"Look, between you and me," said the high priest, lowering his voice as if he were worried someone might overhear him, "I don't really care if you did or didn't steal the body. That isn't important."

"Really?" Marcus asked, momentarily taken aback.

"No, of course not. Who cares if Roman soldiers stole the body of Jesus? What good is that to me? But, if you help us convince everyone that his *disciples* stole the body, then that would provide a far more viable solution to our problem. You follow my meaning?"

Both men tacitly nodded.

"Good. Then off with the both of you; time to get to work."

"But what if Pilate gets wind of this?" asked Petronius. "What if he finds out we made a deal with you?"

Caiaphas shrugged unconcerned. "So what? If Pilate hears about it, then there'll be a reward in it for him as well."

NOT FIFTY FEET DOWN the road, Marcus stopped dead in his tracks and stared pathetically at the bag in his hand. "So tell me, Petronius; we're not really going to cooperate with that bunch of hypocrites just because we took a lot of money from them, are we?"

Petronius turned and stepped up to his comrade. "Of course not, Marcus."

"I knew it," Marcus said with a sardonic grin.

"We're going to do it because we want to save our sorry necks," grumbled Petronius, who then spun around and started off again, leaving Marcus just standing there as the grin on his face slowly turned to a frown.

DARKNESS NEARLY enveloped a cemetery dimly illuminated by the light of a Moon that was shrouded in clouds. It was a faint light that cascaded across the stone-littered landscape, creating pockets of visibility, interrupted here and there by a haphazard shadow, darting past a disheveled tombstone.

"Filthy, good-for-nothing vandals," a gravedigger muttered as he and a fellow worker were busy shoveling dirt back into an open grave. "Don't they have anything better to do than cause trouble for working stiffs like us?"

"Ah, quit your complaining, will you," said the other man. "We get paid the same whether we dig graves up or fill them back in. Makes no difference to me."

Pausing in his work, the first man stared back at his partner as though he were about to respond, but suddenly he was distracted by another one of those indiscriminate shadows. "Hey, what was that?" Dropping his shovel, the man peered into the streaky blackness.

"What?" asked the second man.

Wiping the sweat from his brow, the first man called into the night. "You there! What are you up to? This is private property, you hear me?"

Leaving the gravesite, the man ventured toward the moving shadows, followed by his associate. One shadow became two, and then two became four.

"Hey, what do you people think you're doing here at this hour?" the first man shouted. "Get out of here, right now!"

"Why should we leave this place?" asked a sad voice from out of the darkness.

"What's that?" blurted the first man, who turned in the direction of the voice with his curious eyes squinting in the moonlight. "Who's there? Who said that?"

Then from a different part of the cemetery, another voice called out. "I did."

"Wh—*Who's* that?" stammered the second man, nervously whirling about in the direction of the new voice. "What are you doing here?"

"This is our home," said still another voice. "We belong here."

"Don't be ridiculous!" the first man growled.

A peculiar sound of scratching began to invade the intermittent darkness, and the two men craned their necks in an effort to discern its source.

"What is that noise?" continued the first man.

"It sounds like chicken scratching," replied the second.

"Chickens? You idiot. This is a cemetery, not a chicken farm. Whatever it is, though," said the first man, who started toward the sound, leaving the second man standing there, "I aim to find out."

"Why not wait till morning to find out? Why do we have to do it now?"

"Help me," a plaintive voice said from beyond the pale of visibility. "Won't somebody please help me?"

As the first man disappeared into the relative darkness, the second man looked nervously about and muttered, "Help you? Who's going to help us?" And not wanting to be left behind, he darted after his friend. "Hey, wait for me."

The sound of chicken scratching then became the familiar sound of dirt being piled upon dirt, and when the first man made his way past several mangled tombstones, he stopped and stared aghast at the ground. "What in the world are you doing?"

Catching up with his friend, the second man stood alongside him, and he, too, gawked at what he saw. "Is that what I think it is?"

In utter disbelief, the two gravediggers stood in the pale moonlight, watching as a sad, little man, lying in an open grave, was desperately trying to cover himself with dirt. With the lower half of his body already covered, he pulled more and more handfuls over himself. Noticing the two men staring down at him, he looked up and murmured, "You there, kind sirs, won't you please help me?"

"Help you?" wondered the first man, who flashed his friend a disturbed look, then returned to address the man in the grave. "Help you do what?"

"Why, help me bury myself again, of course."

A Rumor in the Land

ONE HOT AND HAZY afternoon, a priest, a Levite and a schoolteacher were walking together through the dusty streets of Jerusalem.

"How much longer to the Temple, Phinees?" asked the schoolteacher, nearly out of breath.

"It won't be long now, Ada," the priest replied.

"If I'd known it was going to be such an arduous journey," said Ada, who stopped to wipe the sweat from his brow, "I might have reconsidered coming all the way from Galilee by foot."

Phinees stopped with his two companions. "I'm sorry you have such delicate sensibilities, Professor, but you knew what you were getting yourself into when you agreed to come along. Besides, what better way to investigate the rumors we've been hearing about the Nazarene?"

"Naturally, you would be the one to say something like that," Ada replied, "what with so many of your temples in ruins after the earthquake. So why didn't you put your back into restoring your own house first before dragging us out here like this?"

"You know very well why, Ada," said Phinees, suddenly perturbed, "because of what we've seen with our own eyes. Somebody has to say something—*do something.* Or are you having second thoughts about why we came?"

"It's not that I'm having second thoughts," insisted Ada, who turned to his fellow traveler, the Levite, for moral support. "Please, Ageus, make him understand. I'm simply not used to such deprivation. A month ago, I was in a classroom teaching a bunch of kids about Jewish history. Now here I am traipsing about the countryside in search of stories about body snatchers and the living dead. Needless to say, I'm just a bit out of my comfort zone."

"And not a moment too soon, if you ask me," blurted Phinees.

"Don't be so hard on him, Phinees," Ageus interjected. "Ada is right. None of us are used to this sort of thing. We're scholars, for Heaven's sake, men of learning, not adventurers. I just hope this ordeal is worth all the effort."

"Of course it's worth it," snapped Phinees. "Look, this is no time to lose our nerve. Not when there's so much at stake."

"I couldn't agree with you more, my friend," Ageus continued. "But I don't think it would help matters if we were to turn on each other in the process of pursuing such a noble cause. After all, *we* are not the enemy."

Suddenly reconsidering, Phinees thought better of it. "Your point is well taken, Ageus," he said with a decidedly apologetic tone. "I'm sorry, Ada; you're right. This journey *is* more than we're accustomed to. Forgive me, won't you?"

"Of course, Phinees," replied Ada. "I forgive you."

"Good," Ageus said, "because I can't wait to get to the bottom of all this. Considering everything we've seen, I think we can all agree that the disciples didn't steal His body."

"Of course not, no," scoffed Ada. "Not after what we've seen."

"Fine," Phinees continued, "then I suggest we proceed to the Temple. I'm sure the high priest will be very interested in hearing our version of the story."

AS SOON AS THE TRIO arrived to the Temple at Jerusalem, they began looking around.

Before too long, Summas, the priest, intercepted the men in the entry hall. "Pardon me, gentlemen," he began suspiciously. "Can I help you with something?"

Phinees stepped forward to speak for the group. "Yes, of course, sir. Please forgive the intrusion."

"Not at all. I see you're also a priest of the Most High. Welcome, I am Summas."

"And I am Phinees of Galilee." Then he motioned to his fellow travelers. "And these men are also from Galilee: Ageus, a Levite, and Ada, a school-teacher."

Summas nodded, and they, in turn, nodded back. "Welcome, gentlemen. I don't wish to appear rude, but could you tell me why you've come here all the way from Galilee, unannounced like this?"

"We're here to discuss the rumors concerning Jesus of Nazareth," said Phinees.

Summas blanched. "Rumors? What rumors?"

"The ones about His disciples supposedly stealing His body."

"What about them?" wondered Summas, shrugging his shoulders. "His disciples stole the body. What more is there to say?"

"Well, there's quite a lot more to say, actually," Phinees insisted. "That's just it. That's why we came all this way."

Summas seemed both confused and dismayed as he scanned the resolute faces of the three men standing before him. "You mean to say you've come all this way to talk about the body being stolen? Is that what you're telling me?"

"No, no, no," said Phinees, emphatically shaking his head. "His disciples *couldn't* have stolen His body. That's what we're trying to tell you."

"And how could you possibly know something like that?"

Looking both directions, Phinees cautiously leaned forward. "Because we've all recently seen Jesus with our own eyes, that's how," he whispered.

"What?" asked a smitten Summas. "Y—y—*you can't* be serious." His eyes darted to the other two men who both nodded affirmatively.

"It's true," insisted Ageus. "We really have seen Him."

"In the flesh, sir," Ada added, "looking as healthy as any of us standing right here."

"Now, please," continued Phinees, "can we just talk to the high priest about all this?"

Summas glared at the men for several moments. "Wait here," was all he said, and whirling about, he started down a corridor.

PHINEES, AGEUS AND Ada stood expectantly before Caiaphas, along with Annas and the rest of their black-robed colleagues.

"You what?" asked an incredulous Annas.

"We saw Jesus of Nazareth, alive and well, in Galilee," Phinees said. "You remember? The Man you crucified? He was talking to His disciples on the Mount of Olives."

"Impossible," groaned Caiaphas. "What do you take us for? A bunch of naïve schoolchildren?"

"The man you're talking about has been dead and buried for almost two months now," snapped Datam. "Haven't you heard? His disciples stole the body!"

"But that's where you're wrong, sir," Ageus interjected. "We saw Him for ourselves, gathered with His disciples, as though nothing had changed at all. He ate with them, drank with them, told them to pick up right where He left off. 'Go out into the whole world and preach the gospel to everyone,' He said. 'Baptize them in the name of the Father, the Son and the Holy Spirit, and whoever has faith in your teachings will be saved.'"

"Then, sometime after that," added Ada, "we saw Him ascend to Heaven."

Cut to the quick, the entire assembly roared in protest.

"Blasphemers!" squealed Datam. "Heretics!"

Raising his hands, Annas stood tall to quell the outburst. "Silence, everyone, silence," he said as the assembly slowly simmered down. "Give glory to the God of Israel, gentlemen, and make your confession before Him. I'm warning you three, you'd better start telling the real truth before it's too late."

"By the God of Abraham, Isaac and Jacob," said Phinees. "We *have* told you the truth. In fact, if we *didn't* stand by our testimony, we'd be guilty of sin."

Stepping forward, Caiaphas held up *The Book of the Law*. "You will stop declaring these things you're saying about Jesus! Return to your synagogues and never say another word about this to anyone. Do you hear me?"

"But we can't," said Phinees with a lamentable sigh.

"You can't, or you won't?" Caiaphas growled.

"We can't," insisted Phinees. "Our synagogues were destroyed in the recent series of earthquakes. You know that as well as we do."

"I say, flog them for blasphemy," Summas barked, "and send them away in the dust of their own infamy!"

"Is that really what you men want?" said Caiaphas, glaring coldly at the trio.

"Of course not," Ada sputtered. "But you can't punish us for speaking the truth."

"Oh, but they can, Ada," replied Phinees. "Don't you see? It's what they do to men who are willing to stand up to their tyranny of lies."

"Enough already!" cried Annas. "You men come with us so we can discuss this matter in private."

ANNAS AND CAIAPHAS were squaring off again with their adversaries in
the inner chamber; just them and the three visitors from Galilee.

"Now, gentlemen, before things spiral completely out of control," cooed
Annas, "let's be reasonable. We're not barbarians like our Roman usurpers.
We're pious men, one and all, am I right?"

Together, the three men nodded.

"Good, then above all," Annas continued, in his most conciliatory tone
of voice, "men like us should seek the greater good of our people. Agreed?"

Again the trio nodded affirmatively.

"Of course," said Annas as he motioned to Caiaphas, who stepped away
and picked up a leather bag. "Then why don't we try to put this nonsense
behind us. What's done is done. Yes, mistakes have been made, but laying
blame on our own kind won't do us or our congregations any good."

Caiaphas returned and handed the bag to his father-in-law.

Annas continued with a smile. "What we need is to heal the wounds of
our people who've been oppressed by the boot of Rome, because in the end,
Caesar is our enemy, not some deluded soul who thought he could save us
from foreign occupation. Am I right?"

Confused by his smooth talk, the trio exchanged nervous looks amongst
themselves.

"What are you saying?" wondered Ada. "You're not going to flog us?"

"Of course we don't want to have you flogged," Annas replied. "But
neither can we run the risk of you three needlessly inflaming another insurrection in our fair city. Certainly you can understand that, can't you?"

"So what do you propose to do with us?" asked Ageus, obviously suspicious.

"I propose you drop this matter entirely and return to your homes in
the spirit of peace," Annas replied and then handed the bag to Ada. "No
questions asked."

Looking inside, Ada was clearly surprised. "*Money*? And so much of it.
But why?"

"To keep us quiet, that's why," Phinees said with a steely tone.

"What?" blurted Annas. "Heavens, no! It's for your rebuilding efforts,
with a little extra for traveling expenses, for your journey home. Naturally,
it behooves us as fellow Jews to see to it that our satellite synagogues are
restored as quickly as possible. Am I right?"

The trio again exchanged furtive glances.

"Well, I have to admit, he does make a good point," said Ageus, however reluctantly.

"Then it's settled," Annas continued. "You'll return to Galilee. You'll start the process of healing your communities in such dire need of repair, and we'll never need to discuss another word about who did what to whom. Agreed?"

Ada and Ageus then looked to Phinees for his response. After much consideration, he finally relented with an amicable nod. "Fine," said Phinees, "if that's the way it has to be. We'll take the money; but only because the people of Galilee are in such need of it."

"Naturally," insisted Annas, who flashed a subtle smile at his son-in-law. "And just to show you men there are no hard feelings, we'll even have escorts sent along with you to insure your safe passage out of Jerusalem."

CARRYING THEIR HEFTY bag of money, the reluctant trio made their way toward the city limits, escorted by a pair of temple guards, and as the three men continued their journey, they did not say a word to each other.

BEYOND THE OUTSKIRTS of Jerusalem, Ada exhaled a sigh of relief. "Wow, that was close. Thank God we got out of there in one piece."

Phinees glared at him with an angry scowl. "Thank God? What makes you so sure it was God Who rescued us from those men?"

Ada, stung by his question, shrugged innocently. "I'm sorry I brought it up. Just an expression, I guess. I didn't mean anything by it. What I meant was—"

"Don't worry about it, Ada," interjected Ageus. "Phinees isn't mad at you; he's angry with himself. I am, too, if the truth be told."

"Well, it's a little late for that, don't you think?" snapped Phinees. "Frankly, I don't know how I'll ever look my congregation in the eye again. I had my chance to stand up for the truth, and I failed. I failed my calling, and I failed God. I'll never be the same again, *ever*."

"But think of all the good that can be done with the money," Ada asked plaintively. "Doesn't that make up for any of it?"

"Have you lost your mind?" blurted Phinees. "Is that why you think I agreed to take the money?"

"Naturally," Ada replied. "Why else take it?"

"Because in the eyes of pious men like Annas and Caiaphas, heretics like us are deserving of far more than a good flogging."

Confused and frustrated, Ada turned to Ageus with a woeful look in his eyes. "I don't understand. What's Phinees talking about?"

"He's saying that, according to our Law, flogging is merely a prelude for anyone accused of blasphemy. After that, if the heretic refuses to recant his testimony, there's only one course of action left for the high priest."

"And do you have any idea what that might be, Ada?" asked Phinees.

The schoolteacher shook his head. "Of course not, Phinees. You know I'm just a history professor; you two are the theologians."

"Then tell him, Ageus. Tell the good professor what was in store for us if we didn't take the money and scurry away like rats leaving a sinking ship."

Sadly, slowly, Ageus continued. "Our Law states that the blasphemer who refuses to recant is to be stoned until dead."

"B—*but*, I…" Ada stammered, trying his best to offer up some sort of reply, but seeing the look on both his companions' faces, he hesitated.

Thoroughly disgusted with himself, Phinees whirled around and marched away, leaving the two men standing there.

"Don't worry about him, Ada. He just needs some time alone to straighten things out in his head; in his soul, for that matter. We all do."

"I just wish there was something I could do to make up for it all," Ada mumbled pathetically.

"Who knows, Professor, maybe someday you'll get that chance," Ageus said with a subtle shrug and a knowing smile. "But until that day … keep praying to God that He helps you recognize that opportunity when it comes." Then, he turned and started after Phinees, leaving a disheartened Ada standing there just shaking his head.

NO LONGER TRAVELING side by side as they once had been, the three friends were now walking in single file; each one several yards behind the other. Eventually, they encountered a beggar standing along the roadside. Phinees walked by him first.

"Please, kind sir," said the beggar, with outstretched hands, "you look like a man who might have pity on a poor, wayward soul like me. May I bother you for a handout? Anything to help feed an empty belly; mine and my family's, I mean."

For a moment, it appeared that as Phinees walked past the man he had not even heard him. Still, Ageus, followed by Ada, continued on, headed right for the beggar, but then Phinees stopped in his tracks and turned around. With an odd look in his eye, he smiled strangely at his two companions, who were fast approaching him.

"Alms, you say?" asked Phinees.

The beggar's eyes lit up expectantly. "Why, yes, sir, that's right. Even the smallest sum would be most appreciated."

"Then today is your lucky day, my good man," Phinees said as he flashed a grin at his friends, who held their collective breaths. With eyes as big as saucers, they watched as Phinees then handed the moneybag to the beggar.

With utter gratitude, the man looked at Phinees. "I and my family thank you, sir. God bless you for your generosity."

"No, my friend, it's you who is to be thanked today." Satisfied with himself, Phinees turned and walked away, leaving the beggar quite perplexed.

"Me?" the man asked. "Why me? What did I ever do for you?"

By then, Ageus had made his way to where the beggar stood, bag in hand. With a sardonic smile, he patted him on the back as he walked by and said, "Today, my good man, you've helped redeem the souls of three wretched sinners. How do you like that?"

Thoroughly confused and a little intrigued, the beggar opened the bag to see what was inside. He gaped at its contents and sank to his knees, weeping at his good fortune, and still without so much as a word between them, the trio continued on their journey home.

A Sword to Pierce the Heart

ONCE AGAIN ANNAS and Caiaphas called the Jewish leaders together for a private session, and many of them had the most lamentable expressions on their faces.

"Can you believe something like this has happened in Jerusalem?" Cyrus moaned.

"Could there be any truth to what these Galileans are saying?" asked Nepthalim.

"Of course not," Annas assured them. "Just a lot of wishful thinking. That's all there is to it; believe me."

"But the Roman soldiers," pressed Alexander. "What about their sworn testimony? Certainly they aren't looking forward to the resurrection of the dead, are they?"

Annas shrugged his shoulders. "But why should we even believe what a couple of Roman soldiers told us? Just because they *said* an angel rolled the stone away?"

Caiaphas nodded in agreement. "No one pays any attention to foreigners. And besides, how do we even know they were actually the soldiers who guarded his tomb? After all, they did accept an awful lot of money from us."

"That's right," Annas added, "and we know they're already telling everyone the story exactly as we instructed them."

"So what more do you need, gentlemen?" asked Caiaphas with a confident wave of his hand. "Relax. Go home to your families. I assure you all: Nothing more will come from any of this. Trust me."

Finally convinced, the group exhaled a collective sigh of relief.

BACK IN THE TEMPLE, Nicodemus was again addressing the grim-faced assembly of black-robed authorities. "Greetings, men of Israel, I'm sure by now you've all heard the latest news. Three of the most upstanding men you could ever hope to meet have sworn by the Law of God that they recently saw Jesus speaking with His disciples on the Mount of Olives, and then saw Him ascend to Heaven."

"Nothing but hearsay, if you ask me," Summas muttered.

"But why do you say that?" asked Nicodemus. "None of this should seem unusual to anyone here. Doesn't the Scripture already teach us that Elijah, the prophet, was taken up to Heaven?"

"That was different," grunted Summas.

Growing impatient, Caiaphas asked, "And what does Elijah have to do with any of this, anyway?"

"Well, if you recall," Nicodemus continued, "when the sons of the prophets asked Elisha where Elijah had gone, he told them he'd been taken up to Heaven, but those sons replied: 'Maybe the Spirit of God carried Elijah into one of the mountains of Israel.' And they insisted that Elisha search with them for Elijah; but they never did find him, did they?"

"I'm afraid I still fail to see where you're going with all this," said Annas.

"What I'm saying is: Maybe you should send some of your own men to look for Jesus. What if the Spirit of God carried Him away like Elijah? Maybe you'll find Him wandering around in the mountains of Israel somewhere. Did you ever think of that?"

SO A GROUP OF MEN proceeded to do exactly that. They searched for Jesus throughout the hills of Judea, but even after a great deal of time and effort was spent searching the countryside, they never did find Him, either.

"WE LOOKED EVERYWHERE, sir, but we didn't find Jesus," one searcher told Annas and Caiaphas. "Funny, though, we did find Joseph in his hometown of Arimathea. Imagine that."

"Excuse me?" Annas mumbled. "What did you say?"

"I said, we did find Joseph, though."

"The man who escaped from our prison?" asked a dumbfounded Caiaphas. "You found *that* Joseph?"

"One in the same, sir, yes."

WHEN THE JEWISH leaders came together again, Annas and Caiaphas were looking rather disheartened, as was the rest of the group.

"Gentlemen, it would hardly be an understatement to say this is a most unfortunate turn of events," began Annas. "If Joseph starts telling people about the way we treated him, things could get really ugly for us."

"Why not just apprehend him and bring him before the tribunal again?" asked Summas.

"On what charge?" Annas replied.

But Summas shrugged his shoulders. "I don't know."

"No, my friends," continued Annas, half to himself, half to those who were there in the room. "I'm afraid the precarious nature of our position demands that things be handled in a much more diplomatic manner this time around."

ANNAS PRIVATELY dictated a letter to his scribe. "Hello, dear Joseph: We hope all is well with you and your family, and as shocking as it may be to you, we are writing this letter to inform you that we have had a change of heart concerning our position. After all, considering the extraordinary nature of your escape from prison, what else could we do? What we did was malicious, unwarranted and, most regretfully, done without thinking things through. Obviously the Lord Himself delivered you from our evil designs, and obviously we were wrong about you in every conceivable way. We now realize we have offended both God and you, and were hoping you might grant us a visit so we can personally make amends for the way we treated you. Take care of yourself, Joseph. You're a man respected by everyone. Most sincerely, Annas, chief priest of the Temple at Jerusalem."

GATHERING SEVEN of Joseph's friends, Caiaphas then gave each of them a copy of the same letter. "The next time any of you sees Joseph of Arimathea," he told the men, "I want you to salute him in friendship and give him your letter."

WHILE VISITING Arimathea, one of Joseph's friends saw him walking home. Running up to him, the man hugged Joseph and handed him his copy of the letter. Joseph quickly read it.

"Bless God," Joseph muttered. "It's a miracle."

"Why?" asked his friend. "What does it say?"

"I can hardly believe my eyes," said Joseph as he lowered the letter and gazed back at his friend in sheer disbelief. "The authorities in Jerusalem want me to make an appearance before their tribunal so they can officially make amends for how they treated me."

"You're right," his friend said with a smirk. "That is a miracle."

AS JOSEPH APPROACHED Jerusalem, a small group of black-robed Jewish authorities approached him.

"Hello, Joseph," exclaimed Summas, "it's so good to see you again. Everyone is very excited you've come back to us today!"

"We're so sorry for how we acted before," Datam said. "Will you ever forgive us?"

"Of course, Datam, I forgive you," replied Joseph. "God bless you, Summas, it's good to see you, too!"

"BY THE GOD OF ISRAEL," Annas said to Joseph, who was again standing before the austere group of Jewish authorities, "do you solemnly swear to tell the truth, the whole truth and nothing but the truth, so help you God?"

"I do, yes, of course," insisted Joseph. "You all know that."

"Good," said Caiaphas, "because we've been very anxious to get to the bottom of this mystery, Joseph. Are you ready to answer our questions to the best of your ability?"

"Certainly. I'd be glad to. What would you like to know?"

"Well, naturally," Annas continued, "we'd like to know how you got out of the prison cell we put you in. Did you bribe the guards?"

"No, of course not."

"Then how on Earth did you escape?" wondered Annas. "Until now, we considered that cell to be impenetrable."

Caiaphas continued. "So tell us, Joseph. How'd you do it?"

"And remember," added Annas, "God is your witness."

"Oh, you locked me up good and tight, all right, but sometime in the night while I was praying, Jesus appeared in the room, bright as the Sun, and I fell to my knees, terrified."

"You poor, deluded fool," Caiaphas muttered. "Here we go again."

"Hold on, Caiaphas," urged Annas. "Let the man speak. What happened next, Joseph?"

"Well, then Jesus took me by the hand and pulled me to my feet."

Caiaphas pressed on, sarcastic as ever. "You mean the Jesus who appeared to you as bright as the Sun?"

"Yes, that's the One."

"All right, then, Joseph," Annas said condescendingly, as if he were speaking to a confused child. "So this luminous Jesus pulled you to your feet. Then what?"

"Well, then, a dew sprinkled over my entire body, so Jesus wiped my face. He kissed my cheek and said, 'Don't be frightened, Joseph. It's just Me.' So I looked at Him, and said, 'Elijah? Is that you?' But He answered: 'No, I'm not Elijah. I'm Jesus of Nazareth. You buried My body, remember?' Then, in the twinkling of an eye, He took me to the tomb where I'd placed Him. He showed me the linen clothes I'd buried Him in, and finally, I realized it was Jesus."

"Uh, excuse me," Caiaphas interjected impatiently, "this is all very fascinating, but what do the delusional ravings of a madman have to do with our investigation? We just want to know: How did you get out of that prison?"

"Look, I'm sorry I can't do a better job of explaining any of this, Caiaphas," shrugged Joseph. "Really I am. But all I know is: One moment, I was sitting in prison, awaiting my doom, and the next, Jesus was with me in my cell. He reached out His hand, and just like that, we were in His tomb. Then, before I even had time to think about what had just happened, we were in my hometown of Arimathea."

"Just like that, eh?" snorted Caiaphas. "You took his hand, and *poof,* you were here and then you were there, and then suddenly you were home again. Is that about it?"

"Yes, that's about it. Again I do apologize if I can't tell you anything more than that."

"Is that all?" Annas continued, maintaining his conciliatory tone. "Did he at least leave you with some sort of message?"

Joseph thought about it for several moments, trying to push the memory back into view. "Yes, now that you mention it, I believe so. He did tell me something important."

"What?" asked Annas.

"He said, 'Everything is going to be all right, Joseph. He Who comes in the name of the Lord is blessed, and now it's time for Me to go visit My disciples in Galilee.'"

The priests, Levites and doctors of the Law were all so astonished that several of them fell face-down on the ground like dead men.

"What is going on?" Datam groaned. "How could something like this be happening in Jerusalem? After all, this Jesus had ordinary parents like all the rest of us, didn't he?"

Then a Levite stepped forward. "Oh, yes, he's as human as any of us, all right. I personally knew many of His relatives. They were all very devout people, always bringing sacrifices and burnt offerings to the Temple at Jerusalem."

"Thank you, Mattathias, for coming forward," said Annas. "Is there anything else you can add? I mean besides the fact that this man's family used to visit the Temple here."

"Please, sir," Caiaphas interjected painfully. "Haven't we already gone over this before? What good could possibly come from any further investigation into this matter?"

"Wait just a moment," insisted Annas. "I understand your reluctance, Caiaphas, but in this case I must insist on hearing more from Mattathias. Now, do continue, if you please, Mattathias. You said you were personally acquainted with the Nazarene's family. Can you tell us about any firsthand experiences you might have had with them?"

Mattathias nodded thoughtfully and began, "Well, sir, I can, yes. Let me see: Well now, as I recall, on one occasion, I do remember the time His mother Mary brought Jesus here, when He was still a baby. Yes, that's right. She brought Him here to be blessed by Simeon, the high priest at the time. That was when I overheard Simeon saying, 'Lord, Now You can let me die because I've finally seen the salvation You've prepared for everyone, the Glory of Your people, Israel, and a Light to the Gentiles.'"

"You don't say?" Annas mused.

"Yes, sir, that's what he said all right. Then, a little later, I heard Simeon saying to Mary: 'Let me tell you about this son of yours, Mary. He's been appointed for the rise and fall of the multitude, and He'll be a sign that many will speak against.'"

"I see," murmured Annas, who flashed a furtive glance at the disgruntled Caiaphas. "Is that all?"

"Oh, and something about a sword."

"A sword?" Caiaphas asked. "What about a sword?"

"I don't know for sure," replied Mattathias, struggling to retrieve the elusive memory from the shadows of his mind. "But I do seem to remember overhearing Simeon saying something; yes, I remember now. He was warning Mary."

"Warning Mary?" asked Annas. "What would he warn Mary about?"

"Yes, as I recall, he warned her that not only would a sword pierce her heart but that the same sword would also reveal the intentions of many other people in the process. Yes, that was it!" Mattathias stared back at his interrogators with the most peculiar look on his face. "Do you have any idea what that could have meant?"

Annas and Caiaphas exchanged an anxious look.

"How should we know," shrugged Caiaphas. "Sounds like the ravings of a lunatic, if you ask me."

The Mysteries of the Resurrection

STRUTTING BACK AND forth like a proud peacock, Annas was again addressing the entire assembly of austere Jewish authorities. "Well, gentlemen, once more we are reconvened in an attempt to deal with the events that continue to plague our city. So I ask every one of you here today: How do we, as a body of pious men, plan to respond to the outrageous allegations of men like Joseph of Arimathea, men like the three Galileans, who all insist they've seen the Nazarene alive and well, even after his supposed demise, not to mention the sworn testimony of the Galileans who say they saw Him ascend into Heaven? Who among us cares to offer his wisdom as to how we can handle these disturbing reports? Anyone?"

One man hesitantly stood to his feet. "Not that I would ever presume to advise this learned group, sir, but I would like to mention one thing in passing."

"Naturally, Cyrus, if you'd be so kind."

"Well, as we're already well aware of: Our Law states that everything should be confirmed by the testimony of two or three witnesses. So, taking this admonition into consideration, what do we know so far? Since our earliest days as children we've all heard the stories of men like Enoch and Elijah, men who have pleased the Lord and were transported to Heaven as a result."

"That's right, Cyrus, yes," added Datam. "And now, there's this man Jesus. Every day, more and more people keep coming forward to testify that they saw him ascend to Heaven as well."

"But that was then, and this is now," Summas insisted. "Certainly you can't expect us to believe there's any similarity between this Nazarene and two of the greatest heroes in our history."

"But why not?" asked a confident voice that filtered in from the wings of the crowd.

The entire group turned toward the voice, just as Joseph of Arimathea strode into the room. "Why not, gentlemen? Certainly a Man Who's performed the kind of miracles that Jesus of Nazareth has performed deserves to be held in the same regard as an Enoch or an Elijah, if not more so."

"Not you again," Caiaphas grumbled. "Who let you in? I demand that this man be removed from our solemn proceedings, immediately."

"Oh, Caiaphas," said Joseph with a condescending shake of his head, "how will you ever discover the real truth of this matter, if you're always trying to extinguish any opposing view to your preconceived notions? What are you so afraid of?"

"I am afraid of nothing; least of all you."

With an amicable nod, Joseph then turned to the group, just brimming with anticipation. "See, everyone? I'm nothing to be afraid of. Then I'll proceed, if you gentlemen don't mind."

To a man, everyone in the audience nodded, much to the chagrin of the high priest.

"So, as Cyrus has just astutely pointed out, there's nothing inconsistent about the reports concerning the risen Christ and previous accounts we've all read about in the Word of God. Just because the stories you're being told about Jesus are hard to believe, doesn't mean they should be disregarded simply because they don't conform to your expectations, does it? Of course not. Because I'm here today to tell you, no, I'm here to *insist*, with all sincerity, that these reports are absolutely true!"

"But it's a hoax, I tell you!" blasted Caiaphas.

"A hoax?" Joseph replied with an exasperated toss of his head. "You still think this whole thing is just a hoax? Even after all the testimony of your own people to the contrary?"

"Come now, Joseph, be reasonable," cooed Annas, "You can't really expect us to believe what you people are telling us. Enoch and Elijah, yes. These men were well known among our people to be great and holy men, but this Jesus was a common criminal. Certainly you don't expect us to believe that God would receive this scoundrel into Heaven, do you?"

"Very good, sir," exclaimed Summas. "Well said!"

"Look, everyone," Joseph continued, "I realize that what I'm telling you sounds too amazing to believe. I don't blame you, really I don't."

"Good," said Caiaphas, "then you admit you have no real proof to offer in your defense. Will you be so kind, then, as to stop promoting such heretical nonsense?"

"Oh, but I do have real proof, sir; I do."

"Preposterous," Caiaphas snorted, obstinately crossing his arms. "You're bluffing."

Joseph shook his head with a mild chuckle and a knowing look. "Bluffing, am I?"

"Of course, you're bluffing," groaned Annas. "If you had any real proof that these stories were anything more than hysterical delusions, you would've already offered it to us as evidence; pure and simple."

"Well, then, prepare to confront your worst nightmare, gentlemen," Joseph said, quite undeterred, "because not only did Jesus rise from the dead, but there are others who've also risen from their graves."

"Wh—*What*?" blanched Caiaphas, as did most everyone else in the room who mirrored the same sentiment. "That's the most ridiculous thing I've ever heard!"

"But I'm telling you all, here and now," insisted Joseph, who implored the assembly that buzzed with excitement, sensing that not all of them were as antagonistic to his cause as was their leadership, "these risen ones have been seen by numerous eyewitnesses throughout Judea."

"You mean *dead people*, besides this Jesus, have actually risen from their graves?" ventured Datam. "But how is that possible?"

"That, I'm afraid, Datam, I cannot say for sure. All that I am certain of is this is what I was told. Others have, in fact, risen."

"Who?" gasped Summas. "Certainly no one we would know."

"Well, now that you mention it, yes, there are some you might know. Everyone here remembers Simeon the high priest for the Temple at Jerusalem."

"Of course, we all knew Simeon," said Annas. "He had two sons, two fine, upstanding sons, actually. Both tragically died untimely deaths, though, within months of each other, as I recall. Absolutely tragic. Many of us here went to their funerals."

"That's right," Joseph continued. "And now, if we go to their graves, you'll find that the two sons of Simeon have actually risen from the dead."

"You must be joking!" blurted Datam, staring back in disbelief. "I knew the sons of Simeon myself. Charinus and Lenthius were good friends of mine. You mean to tell me that people have actually seen them alive, *recently*?"

Joseph nodded. "They have, yes."

"W—*well*, what are they doing?"

"Not much, actually. Some people have reported seeing them praying in silence, but for whatever reason they refuse to talk to anyone. They just carry on, mute as dumb men."

Datam was clearly intrigued by it all. "Like they still haven't figured out what they are yet; dead or alive."

Joseph nodded thoughtfully. "Something like that, yes, I guess so."

Caiaphas, as usual, rolled his eyes and shook his head. "Oh, please. Would you people listen to yourselves?"

Annas, on the other hand, frowned painfully. "How is any of this possible?"

A stunned Caiaphas flashed a look of disappointment in his father-in-law's direction.

"How should I know?" Joseph shrugged his shoulders. "I'm just telling you what I was told. Now it's up to us to go to Arimathea to investigate the mystery for ourselves. Does anyone care to go with me?"

"I'll go," said Datam. "I'd like to find out what's happening."

"Me, too," Summas chimed in.

But Caiaphas defiantly shook his head. "This is absurd, everyone. The mysteries of the resurrection are simply beyond any man's ability to comprehend. What makes you think you're any different?"

"Oh, I don't know, Caiaphas," Joseph replied with a serene smile. "Maybe it really comes down to faith after all. So the real question now seems to be: Who else has the faith to go with us?"

A People in Darkness

SO JOSEPH, NICODEMUS, Annas, Caiaphas, Summas, Datam and Gamaliel all went to Arimathea, and just as had been reported, they found that the gravesites of Simeon's two sons were no longer intact. Staring wide-eyed into the open graves, everyone exhibited a wide variety of deeply felt emotions, ranging from complete shock to absolute wonder.

"It's true!" exclaimed Nicodemus. "Their graves *are* empty! They really have risen from the dead!"

"Don't be too sure of yourself, Nicodemus," Caiaphas insisted with a disgruntled scowl. "I still say this is merely a hoax."

"A hoax?" wondered Datam. "Who would do such a thing?"

"Who knows," scoffed Annas, "probably gravediggers with nothing better to do. I certainly wouldn't put it past them. They probably concocted this whole thing as a prank to exploit impressionable minds that have nothing else to believe in."

"But look at the arrangement of the dirt around these graves," Joseph said, thoughtfully exploring an idea that seemed to be evolving as he spoke. "It doesn't look to me as though gravediggers were responsible for any of this."

"Whatever are you going on about now?" asked Caiaphas, staring down at the open graves, barely able to focus his mind, still unclear about what he was seeing.

"I mean, it doesn't look like this dirt was dug out from above," continued Joseph with a steely determination. "It looks to me like this dirt was pushed up from below."

"Look, see there," said Nicodemus, eagerly pointing his finger. "He's right. Notice how those footprints all lead *away* from these grave-sites. If this were the work of a fraud, then there'd be at least one or two sets of footprints facing toward them as a result of their having evacuated the graves."

"What's more," Joseph continued, "the footprints leading from these graves were clearly not made by anyone wearing shoes." Then turning to Annas and Caiaphas, he asked them point-blank, "Tell me, gentlemen, since when have you ever known gravediggers to do their job barefooted?"

The two men exchanged a disconcerted look, unable or unwilling to offer a response.

Datam stared incredulously at the grave-sites, along with their respective sets of footprints, and then turned to the group. "My God, I don't believe I'm actually saying this, but I think maybe they're right."

Everyone turned and stepped several feet away, wide-eyed at the implications of what they were seeing and saying; everyone, that is, but Caiaphas, who remained as obstinate as ever. "Now I've heard everything," he grumbled under his breath.

Even Annas appeared somewhat smitten. "So if the two sons of Simeon came out of these graves, as you're suggesting, then where'd they go?" He sighed heavily, clearly divided within himself as he weighed the potential meaning of the evidence they were confronting.

"That's a good question," replied Nicodemus. "I suppose we'll just have to look around for them. I'm sure they haven't gotten too far, though."

SCOURING THE COUNTRYSIDE in search of the sons of Simeon, they eventually came across two young men, huddled together, kneeling in prayer, in a nearby lemon grove.

"Is that them?" wondered Summas.

"Don't be absurd, Summas," snapped Caiaphas. "Of course it's not them. Have you lost your mind as well with all this insane speculation?"

"Well, there's always one sure-fire way to find out," said Joseph, who cautiously approached the men. Stepping up to the pair, he cleared his throat and spoke in a reverential voice. "Hello, Charinus, Lenthius? Please, excuse me. I'm sorry to disturb you, gentlemen, but in the name of the God of Israel, may I have a word with you both?"

Looking up at Joseph, the two men nodded blankly. The rest of the group slowly moved forward, and when they got a good look at them, they were positively stunned by what they saw.

"I—I—I don't believe it," stammered Datam, turning white as a ghost. "It *is* them. The two sons of Simeon."

"You mean the two *dead* sons of Simeon," Summas added, suddenly growing weak in the knees.

THE TWO SONS OF SIMEON dolefully accompanied Joseph, followed at some distance by the rest of the group, who shadowed them the entire return trip without so much as a single word between any of them.

ARRIVING BACK AT THE Temple, Joseph and his group then headed for the Assembly Hall. As they walked through the outer courtyard, everyone who saw them coming nervously stepped aside.

Once inside the hall, Nicodemus placed *The Book of the Law* in the hands of Charinus and Lenthius and adjured them, "By the God of Israel Who spoke to the Fathers by the Law and the prophets, if you believe Jesus raised you, then tell us what you've seen. How, exactly, did you rise from the dead?"

Charinus and Lenthius trembled, obviously disturbed.

"Lord Jesus and Father God," Charinus began. "You Who are the Resurrection and the Life. We're sworn by Your holy name."

"Please give us permission to describe the mysteries of Your cross," added Lenthius, "because until now You've forbidden us to speak about the secret things You did in Hades."

Everyone there exchanged a troubled look with the man standing next to him, and then their eyes darted back to the two sons of Simeon. After a long pause, the men reached out their hands.

"Give us some paper," Charinus said. "We'll write down everything we've witnessed since we died."

Summas quickly brought each of them a stack of paper and a writing utensil. Then the two sons sat down and began writing on separate pages.

"Just like the rest of our forefathers," continued Charinus, "when we died, we were placed in the depths of Hades, where we sat imprisoned in the shadow of death."

"Then after how long, no one knows for sure," Lenthius said, "a brilliant purple light appeared, filling the whole place with an incredible iridescence."

"LOOK," SHOUTED ADAM, the father of mankind, as he jumped to his feet, pointing like a giddy schoolboy. "It's the Author of Eternal Light Who promised to translate *us* to a world of perpetual light!"

Along with Charinus and Lenthius, a large gathering of spectators stood and turned to see the shimmering rays of purple light slice through the eerie darkness that shrouded their abysmal domain.

The prophet Isaiah stepped up next to the two brothers and proclaimed, "This is the Light of the Father and the Son of God!"

"It's beautiful, Isaiah!" exclaimed Charinus.

"I talked about this while I was still on Earth," Isaiah continued. "'In Galilee, beyond Jordan, in the land of Zebulun and Naphtali, a people in darkness saw a great Light.'"

"And it's coming our direction!" exclaimed Lenthius.

"This Light has risen to those of us in the grip of death," Isaiah said. "Now, He's finally coming to shine on us."

STILL, CHARINUS AND Lenthius wrote their letters as the rest of the group listened to them take turns recounting their experience.

"And as we all celebrated the approach of the Light," continued Lenthius, "our father Simeon, the high priest, entered our midst."

MARVELING AT THE purple light that moved closer and closer toward them, the group turned to see Simeon step up to them.

Charinus said with a smile, "Father, I'm so glad to see you. Can you tell us about this incredible light?"

"Certainly, son. The Glory of the Lord is approaching."

"What are you saying, Father?" Lenthius asked. "What's coming?"

"Not what, son—*Who*?"

"Who, then?" wondered Lenthius.

"The Lord Jesus Christ," he replied, awestruck at the thought. "While He was still just a baby, I held Him in my arms, and with the Holy Spirit's help, I recognized Who He was. I was so happy, I said, 'Lord, Now You can let me die because I've finally seen the salvation You've prepared for everyone, the Glory of Your people, Israel, and a Light to the Gentiles.'"

Then, someone looking like a hermit stepped forward, and quite puzzled, the group turned toward him.

"Who are you?" asked Isaiah.

"I am the voice of one crying in the wilderness."

"John?" said Charinus, squinting his eyes. "John the Baptist? Is it really you?"

"Yes, Charinus, it's me."

"The prophet of the Most High," Lenthius added, speaking in hushed, reverential tones. "You're also here because of this light we see coming toward us?"

"Yes, Lenthius. While I was still in the flesh, I went ahead of the Lord, bringing the knowledge of salvation to all men, and when I saw Jesus approaching me, I said, 'Look, the Lamb of God: Here's the One Who takes away the sins of the whole world.'"

"Tell us, John, is that what's happening now?" asked Charinus. "Is this the meaning of the light approaching us?"

"It is, Charinus, yes. After I baptized Him in the river Jordan, we saw the Holy Spirit descend on Him in the form of a dove. Remember?"

"Of course," said Charinus, as if waking from a deep sleep. "I do remember now."

"And that's when a voice from Heaven said, 'See: This is My Beloved Son. I'm so pleased with Him.' On Earth, I prepared the way for Jesus, and just as I did before, I'm here to let you know the Son of God is on His way. The Dayspring from On-High is coming to us, we who are imprisoned here in darkness and death."

Then Adam turned to his son Seth. "Son, did you hear what John just said? Jesus was baptized in the river Jordan." Adam shook his head in amazement. "Can you believe it?"

"I heard, Father," replied Seth. "Imagine that."

"Why, what about it?" Lenthius asked.

"Tell your sons, Seth," said Adam. "Tell the patriarchs and prophets all about the time I fell ill and sent you to ask God to anoint my head with oil."

Seth continued, "Once while I was praying to God at the gates of Paradise, Michael the archangel came to me and said, 'Hello, Seth, I've been appointed to preside over the human race.' So I said, 'Good; then you'll be able to help me, won't you?' But he told me the Lord had sent him to tell me to stop asking for the oil of mercy to relieve my father's pain."

"But why would he tell you that?" asked Simeon.

"Because he said God wasn't going to allow it until the Last Days; that is, not until after 5,500 years had transpired."

"Why?" asked Isaiah. "What was supposed to happen after 5,500 years?"

"That's when Christ would come to Earth to resurrect everyone."

"But that's not all; is it, son?" interjected Adam, who flashed a serene smile.

Seth shook his head. "No, Father."

"What?" cried Isaiah. "What aren't you telling us?"

"Tell them, Seth. Tell them the amazing part."

"Michael told me that when the Lord did come to Earth, He'd be baptized in the river Jordan."

Awestruck, the group sighed collectively.

"Imagine that," Seth said again.

"So very many centuries before it ever happened," Charinus intoned, "God made a promise to Adam and his descendants, and faithful as He is, the Lord made sure to keep that promise, at just the right time and in just the right place."

"So, as it turns out," continued Seth, "the oil of mercy I was praying for was not only granted to my father as a result of this baptism at Jordan, but it also opened the door for everyone who has faith in Him. That way the Lord can anoint them all with the oil of His mercy, and this oil will continue to future generations, bestowing eternal life on everyone born of water and the Holy Spirit."

"Simply amazing," Isaiah murmured.

"Was that all Michael told you?" asked Lenthius.

"No. He also told me that when the Son of God came to rescue mankind, He'd personally introduce my father back into Paradise.'"

"And here He comes now!" Adam cried as he flung his arms toward the dazzling light approaching them. "Just like He promised me!"

THE SONS OF SIMEON continued writing their story, much to the amazement of everyone in the Assembly Hall.

"Even as the saints were rejoicing at the approach of this tremendously bright light," said Lenthius, "it just so happened that there was another group who was just as startled at this appearing. This group, however, was not at all excited as they saw the coming of the light."

"Instead of rising up to greet this glorious new dawn," Charinus added, "this horrid gathering recoiled at its abrupt appearance. Immediately, their chief Satan, the prince of death, the father of lies, the scourge of the Universe, convened a war council with none other than Beelzebub, the prince of Hades, and together they planned how they might respond to this invasion of their damnable domain."

"PREPARE YOURSELF, Beelzebub!" Satan snarled at his grotesque prince of the dead. "You're about to receive Jesus of Nazareth himself, the very one who boasted *he* was the son of god."

"You don't say?" said Beelzebub, almost nonchalantly. "The son of god, coming here? To my infernal lair?"

"That's right," he replied, grinning maniacally. "Can you believe it?"

"Frankly, no, I can't. How did the old boy take it?"

"Oh, it was delicious, let me tell you. He turned out to be an ordinary man after all, afraid of dying, just like the rest of the little vermin he claimed to love so much."

"Really?"

"Yes, really. You should've seen it. He wept like a baby. *My heart is so agonized, I feel like I might die from grief.* It was pathetic!"

"So let me get this straight. This man you're bringing here; you say he's a powerful prince, yet he's terrified of death. Is that what you're saying?"

"Trust me. The man is a mere shadow of his former self. No more giving sight to people I made blind; no more healing those I made lame; no more curing the ones my minions utterly possessed! Nothing! Just pathetic tears and ignominious death. And this was the same man, mind you, that stole a dead man right out of your clutches!"

"Exactly; which is why I don't like what I'm hearing. We don't want someone like him coming down here!"

"Ah, you worry too much. Why are you so afraid to receive this Jesus of Nazareth, anyway? I told you: He's not the same man he used to be. When I stirred up the bitter ones among the Jews, he couldn't stop them. When I sharpened the thorns for his suffering, he couldn't prevent it. And when I prepared the cross to crucify him on, he was powerless before me, as I drove the iron nails into his wrists and feet!"

"Yes, yes, we already know all about that, but what you don't seem to realize is that a man capable of the things he did in life will be unstoppable here in the realm of the dead."

"Nonsense! I'm telling you: We have him right where we want him. Trust me."

"Trust you?" said Beelzebub, shaking his head in disgust. "You just don't get it, do you? Obviously when a man like Jesus of Nazareth tells you he's afraid of dying, he's only doing it to entrap you, and now that you've fallen for his devices we're both going to be sorry, *forever!*"

"But he's dead, isn't he? What can he do to us now? When he gets here, he'll be completely under our control!"

"Have you already forgotten? You said it yourself. He robs us of our dead, right?"

"Yeah. So what's your point?"

"Just look around you."

Satan obligingly turned every direction, looking out upon the endless rows of imprisoned human spirits, who were all beginning to notice the distant, purple haze that was punching an ever-widening hole through the eerie darkness. Then he turned back to his prince. "Okay, now what?"

"Well, tell me what you see," continued Beelzebub.

The devil shrugged his leathery shoulders and replied, "I see the dreary shades of countless human souls. Why, what do you see?"

"Oh, I see the souls of countless humans, all right, but apparently what you've conveniently overlooked is the fact that all these souls are being preserved and protected by their prayers to God. Otherwise, they'd be completely helpless before us."

"Yeah, so?"

"So? You fool. This Jesus of Nazareth seized the dead man Lazarus from me without the need of a single prayer! He did it entirely by his own authority!"

"So?"

"Stop saying that! What is so hard to understand? Obviously any man who can do the things he does must be almighty god!"

"Impossible. He's no god. He's just a man."

"But a man that powerful in his human nature, with the kind of authority he commands, must be the savior of mankind, don't you see?"

"So what do you think will happen when he comes down here?"

"Stop already. I don't even want to think about such a disaster, because if he ever did come here, I'm sure he wouldn't hesitate to rescue everyone from our grasp and lead them all away to eternal life."

Then from out of nowhere, a tremendous voice thundered. "Oh, princes, open these eternal gates of Hades so the King of Glory can enter!"

Beelzebub glared at the devil. "You see; what did I tell you?"

"What?" Satan sputtered. "I don't understand. What was that?"

"Are you deaf? Apparently the king of glory is coming."

"*Who*?"

"The king of glory, you imbecile, the king of glory!"

"What should we do now?" asked the devil, wide-eyed and bewildered.

"Well, if you're such a powerful warrior, then you'd better get ready to fight this king of glory! But what can you possibly do against Him?" Beelzebub then turned to his gruesome officers. "Hurry, you pathetic worms, secure the gates of cruelty! Make sure they're good and tight! And above all, fight courageously, you hear me? Or else we'll all be taken captive!"

From the Pit to the Pinnacle

CAIAPHAS LOUDLY cleared his throat. "Excuse me, gentlemen, but am I the only one here who doubts what these two men are telling us?"

The two sons of Simeon stopped writing and calmly looked up.

"Who are you, sir?" Lenthius asked without a trace of guile.

"Why, naturally, as you can see by the clothes I'm wearing, I am the high priest at Jerusalem. If you were really the sons of Simeon, you'd know that."

"You'll have to forgive my brother, sir," Charinus said. "But as you can imagine, the shock of being returned so abruptly to this life has been an unsettling occurrence, to say the least. Many things once familiar to us now seem somewhat unclear in light of what we've recently experienced."

Baffled by this, Caiaphas was not sure how to respond, and shot a plaintive look to the rest of the group.

"Please, Caiaphas," interjected Nicodemus, "give these men a chance to speak. Certainly you're not suggesting we dismiss the testimony of so many people concerning these risen ones just because you're uncomfortable with this startling, new report?"

"Of course not," he grunted back. "I'm merely suggesting that the outrageous nature of what we're being told is beyond the scope of any man to know. How can we possibly allow their story to be admitted as evidence? Clearly, these men are either delusional, or worse, they're making the whole thing up."

"Pardon me, sir," Lenthius continued, "but you say you're presently officiating as the high priest at Jerusalem, is that right?"

"That is correct, yes."

"What's your name?" asked Charinus.

"I am Caiaphas."

"Caiaphas, yes, Caiaphas," Lenthius murmured, mulling this name over in his mind, looking to his brother as he did. "Tell me, Charinus, could this be the same Caiaphas whom Father encountered while he was working as a teacher of rabbinical law?"

"It could be, maybe," replied Charinus, who then turned back to Caiaphas. "Tell me, sir, are you the same person who, as a boy, relished in bullying his fellow schoolmates?"

With an irritated frown, Caiaphas opened his mouth, as if he were about to reply.

But before he could Lenthius continued, "And were you the same mischievous lad who delighted in bringing worm-filled apples to his teachers?"

Again the high priest, with furrowed brow, thought about responding, barely opening his mouth.

Charinus pressed on. "And were you the same little scoundrel who was so fond of pulling the wings off of butterflies? Was that you, sir?"

Still Caiaphas stood there, his mouth slightly ajar, frozen with indecision, while the rest of the group awkwardly looked on.

"Enough already," Annas finally interceded. "There's no need for this. Please, can you two just get on with the task at hand?"

"We can, sir," Lenthius calmly replied.

"Then please do."

"As you wish," said Charinus, and so the two men turned their attention back to their pens and paper as if nothing unusual at all had just occurred.

"OH, YOU PRINCES of the underworld!" shouted the crackling, disembodied voice, "open up your eternal gates so the King of Glory can enter!"

Startled, Satan and Beelzebub recoiled, as did all the demons surrounding them.

"You heard him, you despicable legions of the dead," shouted John the Baptist, who, along with the whole company of saints, rushed forward to oppose Satan, Beelzebub and all their despicable officers. "Open up your gates so the King of Glory can enter, because now *you're* the ones who are about to be helpless and chained!"

Beelzebub snarled back. "How dare you speak to us like that! This is still our domain, you disgusting maggot!"

Again the deafening voice shattered the gloomy darkness. "Oh, princes, open these gates of brass so the King of Glory can enter!"

And again Satan, Beelzebub and their cadre of minions recoiled in abject horror.

Then the prophet David stepped forward. "Didn't I prophesy about this while I was still on Earth? 'Oh, that men would praise the Lord for the wonderful things He does, because He's broken down the gates of brass and shattered the bars of iron!'"

"That's right, David!" exclaimed Isaiah. "I predicted this, too, when I said, 'Dead men would rise from their graves someday and live again! Then everyone will celebrate because the dew of the Lord is going to bring them deliverance. Oh, death, where is your victory? Oh, death, where is your sting?'"

Again the great voice rang out like thunder. "Oh, princes, open up your gates so the King of Glory can enter!"

But Beelzebub called out as though he were ignorant. "But who is this king of glory?"

"I'll tell you!" David replied. "I understand what that voice is saying! The Lord is powerful in battle. *He's* the King of Glory! He's heard the prisoners groaning and will rescue those appointed to death!"

"So, Beelzebub," shouted Isaiah, "Prince of the Dead, open your gates right now so the King of Glory can enter!"

With a blinding flash of purple light, the Almighty Lord suddenly appeared in the form of a Man, lighting up all the places that had until then been shrouded in perpetual night.

"By His invincible power," Simeon said, as he stood tall among the ranks of the saints, "He's come to rescue those in the grip of sin and death, those bound by chains that could never be broken before but which have now been shattered."

And when they saw how bright this Light was and how abruptly Jesus Christ Himself had appeared in their midst, the grief-stricken legions of the damned let loose with a lamentable howl.

"Who are you?" moaned one of the demons. "Why isn't there even a hint of corruption in you? We're helpless in your presence."

"Of course, your incredible brightness is proof of your majesty," wailed a second. "But you probably don't even stop to notice such things, do you?"

"All-powerful yet compassionate, an average man yet a soldier of the highest rank," grumbled a third, "you command the very elements, even while in the form of a slave."

"First, you were dead," moaned the second. "Now you're down here with us, alive and well. No wonder the entire creation shuddered when you died. It seems you're immune even to death! Will you now disturb our legions, too?"

"How can you release captives bound so securely by sin?" shrieked the first. "How do you spread such a magnificent light over those who were made so blind? Where does this power come from?"

"Until now, the underworld has been completely subject to our control," spewed the second demon. "The prince of Hades has never had a dead man like you here before! How can you just enter our home like this?"

Jesus then gestured with His hand, and from out of nowhere, a brass chain spiraled up and over the bodies of both Satan and Beelzebub, a chain not comprised of brass links but of indestructible brass hands, squeezing and tugging in response to every movement, as its demonic prisoners attempted to break free.

Then turning to the saints, who all stood in anticipation of this long-awaited moment, Jesus offered another gesture. This time He reached out His hand, a hand that clearly bore the scar of the nail that had pierced His wrist, and in response, the hand of Adam reached out to grasp it. Slowly, these two began to ascend like a bubble caught up in a breeze, and as they did the other hand of Jesus waved the rest of the group upward. As if caught up in an invisible net, the entire gathering of saints began to rise with them.

The ensnared duo of Satan and Beelzebub helplessly watched the ascending saints being added to as, one by one, each new soul rose to join the group. Higher and higher, they all continued to ascend together into the misty vault of their conquered world. Unable to hold his tongue any longer, Beelzebub turned to Satan. "Y—y—*you prince of destruction!* You scorn of God's angels, hated by every decent creature! You've really gone and done it this time, haven't you?"

"Me?" Satan's reptilian eyes thinned with rage and recrimination. "Why me? I had no idea this was going to happen."

"You worthless jackass! What made you do something like this, anyway?"

The devil pathetically shook his wolfen head. "I don't know. I thought we were finally ridding ourselves of the little menace. Really, I did."

"Oh, I'm sure you thought that crucifying the king of glory was going to win us some great advantage, but you were completely ignorant of what you were really doing, you imbecile! Now just look at how this radiant Jesus has vanquished our horrid powers of darkness and death! Can you feel your world collapsing around you? Can you?"

Satan grimaced as though some unseen force had just struck him. "As a matter of fact, I *can*, yes. His sickening presence is everywhere now."

"So, Prince of Wickedness, Father of the Abandoned, tell me again: Why did you do something like this?"

Dumbfounded, Satan just shook his head, unable to offer a single thing in his defense, so Beelzebub spewed on. "You knew perfectly well our prisoners were without any hope of salvation or life. But now look! You, Keeper of the Infernal Regions, every advantage we ever gained when Adam forfeited Paradise has been lost."

"But I don't understand. I thought for sure that I'd killed him!"

"Oh, but you did, you did, you fool! But killing him wasn't the answer! Because the moment you crucified the king of glory, the moment you brought a perfectly innocent man down here to the region of the damned, that was the moment you forfeited our birthright to imprison every single person in the history of this world!"

Then Jesus abruptly reappeared in their midst, causing every hideous creature to recoil in His presence, and He pointed at the prince of Hades. "From now on, Beelzebub, you will have control over Satan, here in the room of Adam and all his faithful children."

With yet another gesture from Jesus, every miniature hand comprising the brass chains that were wrapped about Satan and Beelzebub released its grip, and in a shimmering cascade, they shattered into a thousand pieces and fell to the ground. Then, just as quickly as He had appeared in their midst, Jesus vanished.

IN THE BLINK OF AN EYE, the Lord reappeared among the gathering of saints and stretched out His hand. "Come to Me, My saints, everyone created in My image but condemned by the Forbidden Fruit, the devil and death. So live now because of the wood of My cross. Satan, the prince of this world, has been vanquished, and, along with him, death has been conquered." Jesus then placed His hand on Adam's head. "Peace is finally yours again, Adam, yours and all your faithful children who belong to Me."

Weeping tears of joy, Adam cast himself at the feet of Jesus. "Praise You, Lord. You lifted me up, and didn't allow my enemies to triumph over me. Oh, God, I cried to You, and You healed me. You brought my life up from the grave so I wouldn't remain in the Pit. Sing to the Lord, every one of His saints. Give thanks to Him, because His anger lasts only for a moment; but in His favor, there is life forevermore."

Everyone there bowed before Jesus, too, and spoke with one voice. "Redeemer of the World, You've come at last!"

David sang out. "You've actually accomplished everything You foretold through the Law and Your holy prophets!"

"By Your cross, You reached down and redeemed us," Isaiah exclaimed. "You delivered us from Hades and rescued us from the power of death!"

"Lord, just as You've placed signs of Your redemptive story in the Heavens," cried John the Baptist, "you've set up Your cross as the standard of Your salvation on Earth!"

"Now, Lord, set this emblem of Your victory here, too," Simeon said, "so death won't have dominion over mankind any longer!"

Jesus then made the sign of the cross over all the saints and, taking Adam with his right hand, continued His ascent while the rest of the group followed close behind. "Everyone, sing to the Lord," said the father of mankind, "because He's done such marvelous things! His right hand has brought us the victory!"

"The Lord has revealed His salvation," Isaiah proclaimed, "even explaining His righteousness to the heathen!"

"You went forth as the ransom of Your flock to rescue Your people!" shouted David.

"The Lord has enlightened us all!" cried Seth. "This is our God, and He will reign over us forever and ever!"

ARRIVING AT THE GATES of Paradise, Jesus handed Adam over to Michael the archangel, who then led the first man inside, followed closely by everyone else. The awestruck saints surveyed the sprawling landscape that spread out before them in every direction, a lush garden-land, overflowing with splendor and beauty. Much to their surprise, the group encountered two men who approached them as soon as they entered.

"Who are you two?" Isaiah asked. "You were never in Hades with us, yet you're already here in Paradise. How is that possible?"

The first man slowly began, "Yes, well, you see, that's because of all the people who have ever been born on Earth, the Scriptures record that only two men have ever temporarily 'cheated death.'"

"And you mean to tell us that you're those two men?" David asked.

"We are, yes," he replied. "I was the first person to attain this honor when I was transported to Heaven with the help of two of God's angels, Sariel and Raguel. I am Enoch, the scribe."

"Of course," exclaimed Abraham, who stepped forward to shake Enoch's hand. "I've heard about you my whole life. What an honor it is to finally meet you face to face." Turning to the group, he called out, "Boys, come here quick. I want you to meet someone."

Two men then walked up to Enoch and Abraham, who then said, "Isaac, Jacob, this is the man I told you all about, remember?"

Isaac reached out to shake Enoch's hand and replied sheepishly, "Of course, Father. How could I ever forget?"

Amused at this, the group laughed heartily.

Enoch nodded and said, "Nice to meet you, Isaac." And nodding to Jacob, who respectfully remained several feet back, he smiled graciously. "Young man."

Then Enoch turned to the second man next to him. "And what about you, sir?" he said with a playful grin. "Would you care to tell everyone your story?"

Clearing his throat, the man said, "Who, me? You want to know *my* story?"

Turning to the group, Enoch asked, "Well, everyone. What do you think? Are you interested?"

"Of course," came their collective reply.

"Well, like Enoch before me, I was also uniquely honored and transported to Heaven, when I was taken up in a fiery chariot. I am Elijah, the Tishbite."

"Elijah?" gasped Simeon. "Is it really you?"

"It is, sir," he replied.

Turning to his two sons, Simeon said, "Look, boys, it's Elijah. Can you believe it?"

Charinus and Lenthius smiled proudly at their father and nodded.

Then John the Baptist stepped forward. "We're honored to meet you both. Since the earliest days of our youth, many of us here have been regaled with the tales of your exploits. You've been quite an inspiration to us all." Moving up to Elijah, John reached out his hand. "And I'd like to mention that you, sir, were of particular inspiration to me. I thank you."

Shaking his hand, Elijah exchanged a smile and a nod of satisfaction with Enoch.

Moved to tears by this special moment, the whole group began to clap and sing praises to the Lord, and after a while, Simeon stepped back up and asked, "Please correct me if I'm wrong, gentlemen, but you did say you only cheated death *temporarily*. Is that right?"

"You heard correctly, yes," Enoch replied.

"What, exactly, does that mean?" wondered Simeon.

"It means that before our mission is fully complete," Elijah continued, "we, too, must be subjected to the same baptism of death that all of you here have undergone. As it is written: Everyone is appointed once to die."

"But how can that be?" asked Abraham. "If you're with us in Heaven, what could possibly happen to you in this place of incorruptibility?"

"What we're destined to undergo will not take place up here," Enoch exclaimed, "but must occur on the Earth below."

"Any moment now we'll be returning to Earth for the coming of the Anti-Christ," said Elijah, suddenly with fire in his eyes. "Armed with divine signs and miracles, we'll face him in the supreme test of our lives, a showdown of biblical proportions!"

Enoch defiantly shook his fist. "We'll engage the devil himself and his counterfeit offspring. We'll wage war with this Anti-Christ with every ounce of our courage, but in the end, we'll be slain in the streets of Jerusalem!"

"No!" shouted many of the saints there.

"God forbid!" Isaac intoned.

"Yes, I'm afraid so, everyone," insisted Elijah. But far from looking fearful at the expectation of such a fate, the prophet exuded a serene sense that likewise washed away any anxiety that the group was feeling for them. "But don't be sad for us. No, sir, because our death is by no means the end of our adventure; not by a long shot!"

"Tell us, please," insisted Jacob, wide-eyed with anticipation.

"It's just the beginning, actually," said Enoch, sporting his familiar grin, "because after three and a half days, our dead bodies will be filled with the same Holy Spirit that raised you all from your graves, and we, too, will rise in newness of life."

"And in plain sight of the whole world, Enoch and I will be taken up," said Elijah with an enthusiastic wave of his hand, "up into the clouds to be reunited with you all once again, to be with the Lord Almighty forever and ever!"

Everyone was astonished by their story, when suddenly another man came forward, a miserable looking figure, donning tattered clothes. Curious about his peculiar appearance, the saints turned to him.

"Who are you?" asked a confused Charinus, who turned to Enoch and Elijah. "I thought you told us you were the only ones who have never died."

Enoch nodded. "That's right; we are."

"Then what's he doing here?" asked Abraham. "He looks like some sort of criminal."

The strange-looking fellow stared back at everyone for several moments. "Yes, you're right about me. I *was* a thief, one who committed every sort of crime during my lifetime."

"Who are you, then?" Isaac asked. "And how'd you get here before any of us?"

"I, Dimas, of all people," continued the man, so emotional that he strained to get the words out, "observed the startling things that happened … at the crucifixion of the Lord Jesus Christ… Believing He was the Creator and the Almighty King, I asked Him: 'Lord … remember me when You enter Your kingdom.'"

"But how is that possible?" wondered Lenthius. "When did you ever have a chance to speak with the Christ? You weren't one of His disciples."

"I certainly was not, no… In life … I was a man completely unworthy to even sit in the same room with a Man so wonderful, so compassionate, so kind."

"Tell us, then," said Simeon with a gentle persistence. "When did you speak with the Savior?"

"I asked Him while we were both hanging … side by side … as we struggled with our last breaths … high upon a cross on that despicable hill called Golgotha."

An uneasy hush swept through the entire group.

"You?" asked Lenthius.

"Yes, me," said the man slowly, deliberately, as though he himself could not believe the truth of what he was saying. "I was the thief hanging at Jesus' right hand... And when I asked His forgiveness, He accepted my request, without hesitation … without a word of condemnation, saying … 'Certainly you will be with Me in Paradise today.'"

Everyone there was absolutely amazed.

"Thank God for His boundless grace," Abraham declared, "the Father of Eternal Goodness and Mercy."

Then Seth said, "You've shown such kindness to those who were rebels against You!"

"You've brought us all into the Mercy of Paradise, Lord," Isaac intoned, "and placed us amidst a land overflowing with Your marvelous provisions."

"You've restored us and brought us back into your garden-land," exclaimed Adam, who turned to Eve and reached out to squeeze her hand, "back into the very heart of the Almighty, a heart beating with eternal life, love and hope!"

And everyone there proclaimed with one voice, "Amen!"

The Truth be Told

STILL THE TWO SONS of Simeon were writing down the details of their amazing story.

"These are the sacred mysteries of God that we've both seen and heard," said Charinus. "We aren't allowed, however, to tell you anything more because Michael the archangel ordered us not to."

"So praise and honor the Lord," Lenthius added. "If you repent, He'll have mercy on you, and may Jesus Christ, the Savior of us all, bring you comfort and peace forevermore. Amen, amen and amen."

After they had finished writing their separate reports, Charinus and Lenthius put their pens down and turned to everyone who was still sitting there in eager anticipation of what they might say next, but without warning, the two sons of Simeon changed into incredibly white forms, and slowly faded from view.

As the befuddled group looked on, unsure of what to do next, Joseph and Nicodemus finally stood up and together, with a mutual look of astonishment, sucked in a deep breath.

"My God," gasped Nicodemus, "just when I thought I'd seen it all, something like this happens."

"You're telling me," Joseph replied with an exhilarated sigh. Then turn-

ing to Annas, Caiaphas and the others, he asked with unrestrained enthusiasm, "Now what do you have to say for yourselves? Are you convinced
now?"

Thunderstruck, the rest of the group jumped to their feet as they looked
to one another to see what each of their reactions might be to this startling
turn of events.

Caiaphas was the first to respond. "Well, I, for one, cannot say one way
or the other what just happened here."

"But, Caiaphas," blurted Nicodemus, "you saw it with your own eyes,
heard it with your own ears. What more do you need?"

Crossing his arms, Caiaphas continued with an obstinate scowl, "If I did
venture to guess, I'd say we've all been the unwitting victims of some sort of
satanic spell. This whole thing stinks to high Heaven!"

"A spell?" echoed Joseph in utter disbelief. "That's the best you can
come up with? I'm afraid the only thing satanic about this is the lengths to
which you people will stoop to blind yourselves to the truth." And turning
to the others, he implored, "What about the rest of you? Are you also so
willing to reject what you've just witnessed for yourselves?"

Summas, Datam and Gamaliel stood there, perplexed as ever, their eyes
darting back and forth from Annas and Caiaphas, and then back to each
other.

"Again I say," snapped Caiaphas, "what proof do you have that this
whole affair was anything more than the product of a spirit of delusion,
brought forth by the same demonic spirit that enabled the Nazarene to work
his cures? What proof, sir? Show it to me now, or else I'll have no choice but
to seek your immediate removal from the ranks of the Sanhedrin!"

"Removal?" groaned Nicodemus. "On what grounds?"

Caiaphas pressed on venomously. "On the grounds that you're both in
league with the devil himself, in your damnable efforts to delude and divide
this congregation of the faithful."

For several agonizing moments, Joseph and Nicodemus stood there,
stunned and speechless, as they looked to one another for a rebuttal to such
accusations and threats.

"Proof, you say?" Joseph murmured finally.

"Yes, proof," grunted Caiaphas. "As usual you haven't a shred of tangible evidence to support what you insist occurred here today. Nothing!"

Then, as if struck by a sudden inspiration, Joseph started to walk to the
table where the two stacks of paper had been left behind by Charinus and
Lenthius. "Proof," he quietly said again, half to himself, half to everyone
else in the room.

"Joseph?" said Nicodemus. "What do you have in mind?"

To the stack of papers, Joseph examined them carefully, and after several thoughtful moments, he said, "Come here, please, Nicodemus." Like a man on a mission, Joseph began to take a page from each stack and set them next to each other.

As Nicodemus stepped up to the desk, he, too, looked down at the pages as they were being laid out. "What is it, Joseph?"

The more pages that Joseph laid out, the more he seemed hypnotized by them.

Growing impatient, Caiaphas cleared his throat. "I demand that you tell us this instant; what do you think you're doing, Joseph?"

Stunned by some as-yet-undisclosed epiphany, Joseph looked up at Nicodemus with a twinkle in his eye. "I'm looking at the proof, Caiaphas, the *proof*."

The high priest's eyes thinned and his nostrils flared as he turned to Annas with his typically belligerent scowl.

"Nicodemus, look for yourself," Joseph blurted with an infectious enthusiasm. "Look at these pages when compared to one another. Do you notice anything unusual about them? Anything at all?"

"I think so, yes, but..." Nicodemus looked down at the pages and strained his eyes as much as he strained his mind. "But I just can't seem to put my finger on what it might be. What do you see, Joseph? Tell me."

"What is it, Joseph?" asked Gamaliel. "What are you thinking?"

He replied thoughtfully, "These two sets of documents bear an uncanny similarity, that's all."

"In what way?" wondered Annas.

Turning toward the group, Joseph spoke with an odd expression on his face, as though he were not looking at them but through them. "If I'm not mistaken, gentlemen, although these accounts have been written by two different hands, they have nevertheless been written in absolutely perfect agreement."

"What do you mean, *perfect agreement*?" Gamaliel asked. "You mean to say they agree in penmanship? Agree in grammar? Agree how?"

Looking back down at the pages, side by side, Joseph picked up two of them in his trembling hands and uttered what he himself knew should be impossible. "I mean, there's not a single letter more or less in either of them. I mean, they're mirror images of each other, exactly identical, down to the very last stroke of the pen."

"That's absurd," growled Caiaphas, who defiantly strode up to Joseph, almost knocking Nicodemus down in the process. "Step aside." And snatching the pages from Joseph's hands, the high priest placed one page on top of the other. "Have you lost your mind? Let me see those." Then he held them up in the sunlight that was streaming in through a sky light so he could see that the writing on each piece of paper was very nearly overlapping.

Curious, Annas stepped over to get a better look at what his son-in-law was doing. Looking over Caiaphas' shoulder, he watched as the high priest slowly slid the silhouette of the writing of the two pages, closer and closer, until what Joseph had been explaining finally became apparent to the naked eye. Much to the chagrin of both men, the writing on each page lined up perfectly with each other, word for word, letter for letter, stroke for stroke.

Upon seeing the incontrovertible evidence for himself, Caiaphas dropped the pages as though they were infected with the plague. "No, no, no," he gasped, and then turned to Annas. "This is sheer madness, I tell you."

"How can this be?" croaked a horrified Annas. "It *can't* be. It's not humanly possible."

PILATE WAS ON the march soon, accompanied by Joseph and Nicodemus, as he made his way past the outer wall of the Temple at Jerusalem, which still clearly bore the scars of the recent series of earthquakes, and up the steps that led to the ornate gate of the sanctuary.

GATHERED TOGETHER in a chapel room, the governor gazed out across the assembly of black-robed Jewish authorities, and then he began to address the group in austere tones. "Greetings, gentlemen. I'm here today to inform you all that, as one of my official duties as governor of Jerusalem, I've taken steps to create a written record of the events that have recently transpired in this city. Presently, this account, penned by none other than your esteemed colleague Nicodemus, sits among the public records stored in my Assembly Hall. Now, in conjunction with that effort, I'm here to offer you one last opportunity to add to this historical account, for your sakes, for the sake of your children, and for the sake of your children's children. Who among you, then, would like to be the first to add to this account?"

Everyone there looked to the man next to him to see what his response might be, and then returned his obstinate eyes back upon the governor. Clearly, none of them had any intention of offering up a single word.

"Anyone?" continued Pilate. "No one here has the guts to offer anything in his own defense. No? Not one of you has the slightest residue of a conscience to make amends for this stain on your nation? Is that what you're telling me?"

Then from out of the crowd strode that familiar pair, Annas and Caiaphas.

Pilate could not help but instantly convey a look that revealed both his frustration and disappointment. "No, no, no; not you two again. Haven't you *already* done enough on behalf of your people?"

Holding up his hand in reconciliation, Annas meekly replied, "Please, Governor, not so fast. I admit you have every reason to doubt our sincerity in this matter, but before you jump to conclusions, I want you to know something." And turning toward the assemblage, Annas bowed ever so slightly. "In fact, Caiaphas and I both want all of you to know that this is something we wish to add to this public debate in the sincere hope that it will help to mend the troubling circumstances to which the governor has so eloquently alluded."

Intrigued, Pilate nodded. "Really? Both of you are here for this purpose?"

With a conciliatory nod, Caiaphas replied, "We are, sir, yes. Above all, it is our hope that our nation begin to seal up this terrible wound that has plagued us, so that even our beloved Temple at Jerusalem has been made to bear the cracks of this bitter divisiveness."

The governor continued with a satisfied smirk, "Very well, then, after everything you've said and done to this point, I'd be very interested to hear what you have to say in light of the recent events I've been informed about."

"Certainly, Governor," Annas added with a gesture toward one of his temple guards, "and so you will hear it."

Within moments, the side doors of the chapel flung open, and four priests brought in a gigantic book, so huge and so heavily adorned with gold and precious jewels that it had to be equally supported by all four men in order to carry it.

"Gentlemen," Annas continued in his most reverential tone, "I offer you the testimony of our most sacred text, *The Seventy Books.*"

With tremendous effort, the four men maneuvered the huge book and carefully set it down on a brass pedestal. A priest then opened it, revealing its beautifully ornate pages.

"Now," Pilate said with a steely intensity, "I'm ordering you, by the God of your fathers who made this temple; tell me the truth today. You know everything written in this Holy Book of yours. So tell me: Have you discovered anything in your Scriptures about this Jesus Whom you crucified?"

"We have, sir," said Annas, nearly choking on his own words. "In fact, we actually discovered the very moment in history in which he was supposed to arrive."

"No." Taken aback, Pilate's jaw drooped ever so slightly. "How is that possible? Tell me, priest, tell me. I need to know the truth about all this, and I need to know it now."

"Very well, Governor, the truth is what you'll have," said Annas, who continued slowly, solemnly. "Soon after we crucified the man called Jesus we had a meeting in this very room. Of course we never even considered he might actually be the son of God. We naturally assumed he was performing his miracles through magical arts. But while we were deliberating about the true nature of his so-called 'miracles,' eyewitnesses from our own country kept coming to us and testifying that they'd seen him with his disciples even after his death. And as you already know, there was even a report involving two brothers who had also risen from the dead, who, in turn, provided an account describing in great detail what Jesus supposedly did while he was in the underworld, an account which happens to be in our possession to this day."

"As you can imagine," Caiaphas chimed in, clearly pained by what he was saying, "we were all quite shocked by these outrageous reports, so we decided that for the sake of our entire nation we had to get to the bottom of it, once and for all."

"Yes, I *can* imagine," said Pilate with a smirk. "So what did you do?"

"What else could we do?" Annas shrugged, stepped to the huge book, and placed his hand on it as though he were swearing by what he was about to say. "We began searching the pages of this sacred text for an answer, in the first of *The Seventy Books*, to be exact, where we found a passage in which Michael, the archangel, spoke to Seth, the third son of Adam. In it, Michael explained to Seth that the Christ, the most beloved Son of God, was to appear on Earth after 5,500 years. And so, because the God of Israel instructed Moses to build the Ark of the Covenant with dimensions of five and a half cubits, we surmised that the Christ would likewise come in an ark, or tabernacle, of a body after 5,500 years."

"So, you see, Governor," Caiaphas said glumly, "it does appear that our Scriptures have provided us with clues to his true identity all along."

Pilate then raised his hand to interject. "You mean to tell me you discovered all that from this book of yours?"

Annas and Caiaphas nodded solemnly.

"Is that all you found?" pressed the governor.

"Quite frankly, Governor, no, it's not," replied Annas, the words almost sticking in his throat, even as they sought to come out. "We now believe we've ascertained the identity of the Man that our people have waited for, prayed for, longed for, for 5,500 years."

"But how?" wondered Pilate. "How is that even possible?"

"How else?" Annas continued. "We traced the generations from Adam down to this one of Joseph and Mary, of course." Then Annas nodded to Caiaphas to continue.

"First, we found the story of Creation," said Caiaphas, who proceeded without a shred of emotion, as though he were reading an obituary of death as opposed to a genealogy of life, "where we determined that from the time that God created Adam up until the Great Flood, some two thousand, two hundred and twelve years had transpired. Then, from the Flood to the time of Abraham, there were nine hundred and twelve years; from Abraham to

Moses, four hundred and thirty years; from Moses to King David, five hundred and ten years; and from King David to the Babylonian captivity, there were five hundred years. Finally, from the end of the Babylonian captivity to the Incarnation of Jesus, five hundred more years passed; and, as it turns out, the sum of all those years really does amount to 5,500 years."

"So it appears this Jesus Whom we so mercilessly crucified," Annas said dryly, mournfully, "really is the true King of Israel, the Son of God, and the Almighty Lord. He is Jesus the Christ." And hanging his head, he whispered. "Amen."

It is Finished

SENATOR RUFUS was still reading the record aloud to the assembly while Pontius Pilate stood humbly before Tiberius Caesar. "So ends the account of the acts of the Savior, Jesus Christ, according to this history by Nicodemus, describing what happened after the Lord's crucifixion while Joseph and Caiaphas were leaders amongst the Jewish nation."

The words seared into the mind of Caesar, who could no longer suppress his fury. Enraged, he sprang to his feet and, before Rufus even had time to close the book, pointed his accusing finger. "Return this man to his cell until I can decide how to deal with him!"

A pair of Roman soldiers jumped into action and moved forward to seize the prisoner.

"No, wait," Pilate groaned. "I'm innocent, I tell you. Why are you doing this to me?"

"Silence!" snapped Caesar. "Take him away!"

Each guard grabbed hold of one of Pilate's arms, and together they started to march him out of the room.

"As God is my witness," Pilate exclaimed as he was being pulled through the door, "I'm innocent of this Man's blood."

"Enough, enough, enough!" screeched Tiberius, covering his ears. Then, as the door slammed shut, Caesar looked around at his senators and centurions, who were all taken aback at his temper tantrum. The emperor slowly lowered his hands and wiped himself with a perfunctory swipe, as if to rid himself of any taint of Pilate's guilt. Obviously embarrassed, he shook himself and glared back at his puzzled audience. "Now, summon my scribe," he said with a renewed sense of composure, "I wish to declare my verdict before the entire council and all my centurions."

IN NO TIME AT ALL, the scribe arrived and Tiberius began to dictate his decree. "Greetings from Tiberius Caesar, emperor of Rome, to Licianus, chief of the eastern sector: I've just been informed of the audacity of the Jews at Jerusalem. Recently, they acted cruelly and illegally by compelling

Pontius Pilate to crucify a certain god called Jesus, and this despicable crime of theirs darkened the world, very nearly ruining it! So I want you to order your troops to Judea at once! Proclaim their bondage by this decree. Strike them, enslave them, scatter them in every direction. By driving their nation from Palestine as soon as possible, we'll demonstrate to everyone who witnesses this act that they're all full of evil!"

ARRIVING AT LICIANUS' military outpost, Volusianus handed the emperor's decree to the Roman general, who promptly read it. With a steely glint in his eye, he turned to one of his field commanders. "Well, Proteus, are you ready to prove your loyalty to the Empire again?"

Jumping to attention, Proteus dutifully saluted his chief. "Of course, General Licianus, as always."

"Good. Then gather your troops. We've been chosen for a great and glorious mission, by no less than Tiberius Caesar himself."

"Say the word, sir. I, and my men, are ready to do your bidding. Who do we attack? Where and when?"

"We're to attack the Jewish rebels in their own country of Judea as soon as we've sufficiently mobilized our forces. How long would you say before we're ready?"

"To attack a backwater bunch like that, sir," Proteus grinned, "no more than twenty-four hours."

"Excellent," said Licianus, imagining the power of his army and the swath of destruction they were about to unleash. "May the gods have mercy on the innocent, and may they strike terror in the hearts of the guilty."

JUST AS LICIANUS' field commander had promised, his fearsome army was on the march the very next day. With astonishing speed, they spearheaded the people of Judea with all their might, hacking their way through the population with sword and spear, scattering the horrified inhabitants in every direction. Everyone who had been able to evade the edge of their hardened blades was quickly rounded up and forced into slavery, while the rest of the population lucky enough to escape death or bondage were chased into the countryside, where they were scattered among the outlying nations. A pillar of smoke and ash spiraled up from Jerusalem that could be seen and smelled for nearly a hundred miles.

TIBERIUS CAESAR sat brooding on his gilded throne as Volusianus entered the room and handed him a letter.

"For you, Great Caesar," Volusianus said. "Word from your distinguished chief in the East, General Licianus."

"I see." Tiberius read the letter while Volusianus turned and dutifully walked away. Finishing the correspondence, Caesar looked up with a hollow sense of satisfaction and simply let go of the letter. It fluttered to the floor as the emperor's lips barely parted. "It is finished."

PERCHED MENACINGLY on his throne in the Capitol building, Tiberius was flanked by his Senate and surrounded by his neatly clad centurions. Caesar merely gestured and a captain of the guards hastily approached him.

"Sire," the captain said, bowing dutifully, "I am honored to be at your command."

Tiberius nodded perfunctorily. "Very well, Albius. I take it you've been instructed in what's expected of you today?"

"Yes, My Lord, I have."

"Good, because should I require it, I'll need your blade to be one that is both swift and remorseless."

"As you wish, Great Caesar. I will not fail you."

"Good, then take your place," said Tiberius, motioning to Albius, who took several paces back and withdrew his sword from its sheath. Holding it at his side, the captain stood at attention as rigid as a statue. Caesar then proclaimed in stentorian tones, "Just as he laid hold of that innocent Man called the Christ, Pontius Pilate has fallen into my hands, and nothing will deliver him now."

Tiberius nodded to one of his guards standing at attention by the door. Nodding back, the guard swung the door open, and in walked a shackled Pilate, escorted by two soldiers, one on each arm. While he was being led to his place, Pilate prayed in silence. 'Lord, please don't destroy me with those corrupt Jews who were all so intent on provoking a riot against me, because You know I'd never have hurt You had I known it was You. But You understand I only did it in ignorance, so don't be too hard on me because of my crimes.'

The two guards slowly marched Pilate to where Albius stood at attention, and stepped away to take their respective places. Pilate then caught a glimpse of his wife, who stood in the wings, weeping quietly for her husband. He lovingly nodded at her, and she acknowledged him with a serenely sad smile.

'And please, Lord, have pity on Your servant Procla,' he continued to pray. 'You taught her to prophesy that You had to be nailed to the cross, and now she stands with me in my hour of disgrace. Don't punish her for my sins, but forgive us both with the portion of Your just ones.'

Suddenly a voice rang out from Heaven, causing everyone in the room to flinch. "All the generations of the Gentiles will call you blessed because everything that the prophets said about Me was fulfilled under you. Then you'll appear as My witness at My Second Coming, when I judge the Twelve Tribes of Israel and those who refuse to acknowledge My name."

With that, there came a simple gesture from Tiberius, and jumping into action his captain Albius took one step forward and, with a single, powerful stroke, cut off the head of Pontius Pilate. From out of nowhere, an angel appeared and caught his body as it crumpled to the ground, and when Procla saw what the angel had done for her husband, she was so overwhelmed with joy that she ran to his slumped, lifeless body and died, too, while tearfully clutching his hand.

Farewell to Achuzan

ENOCH CLOSED THE book and looked up at the group of family and friends gathered around him. No longer the overflowing mass of people it was before, the crowd had thinned out since he had begun his last story. Undaunted, however, the patriarch carried on. "So, everyone, what did you think of the story of God fulfilling His promise to rescue Adam and his faithful children after five and a half days?"

An astonished Methuselah shook his head. "Amazing, Father, simply amazing. I was particularly intrigued by the fact that you said you were going to battle some evil person in the Last Days. You called him—what was it again? The Anti-Christ?"

"Yes, that's right, son. My, oh, my. That will be something someday, won't it?"

"So, the mystery of the One," Lamech slowly began, as though he were thinking out loud, "is each person's faith. What seems insignificant to us actually turns out to be the very thing that God desires most—the faith of the one, hoping, loving, trusting. That kind of person can change the world, can't they, Grandfather?"

"Very good, Lamech. I don't think I could have said it better myself."

"Your books, son, I just…" stammered Jared, "I just can't get over them. I mean, the incredible detail you provide; such pathos and joy, such tragedy and hope. I'm very interested in reading these books for myself."

"Me, too, Grandpa," Lamech chimed in.

"Can I read them, too, Papa Enoch?" chirped little Eli.

A smile swept irresistibly across Enoch's face. "Of course you can, Eli. Everyone can read them, anytime they want, from now on. They're God's gift to you all!"

The crowd cheered tumultuously for a while, then Jubal stepped forward, flanked by his two brothers, Hiram and Tubal. They were clapping, too, but they did not look at all as if they were caught up in the festive spirit sweeping through the crowd.

"How touching," Jubal intoned, notably sarcastic. "The benevolent patriarch bestowing such wisdom from On-High. Makes a guy just want to worship you, doesn't it?"

The crowd noticed Enoch's expression abruptly change from that of jubilance to one of disappointment. Everyone but Jubal stopped clapping.

"Not you again?" groaned Eli's mother.

"What's wrong, my dear?" Jubal replied, as cold as ice. "Afraid we might ruin your pathetic celebration?"

"How dare you continue to stir up controversy like this, Jubal," snapped Jared. "This is a sacred gathering, and you know it. What's your problem this time?"

"Well, I guess you could say I'm here to let you all in on a little secret of my own. Now granted, it's not the secret of the wind or the stars or the snow, but it is a stunning revelation just the same." Then, grinning maliciously, he paused for effect.

"Just get to the point, will you?" insisted Methuselah.

Jubal turned first to his brother on his left, then to his right.

"Then by all means: Show them, my brothers."

Together, they each withdrew one of Enoch's books from beneath their cloaks. Holding them both up, they offered everyone a chance to get a good look at them.

Jubal pressed on with sadistic glee. "Do any of you recognize these?"

Enoch gasped. "Of course. Those are some of the sacred books I've already read to you from. How did you get hold of them before you were supposed to? It wasn't time yet for anyone to read them."

"Tell us, Jubal," insisted Jared, "how did you get your hands on these books? I know for a fact they've been guarded day and night since Enoch gave them to me for safekeeping."

"Never mind that now, Father," Enoch interjected. "I'm afraid you have no idea who you're dealing with." Enoch sat there with his book firmly planted in his lap, poised like a shield over his heart.

Jubal flashed another malicious grin. "Yes, well, you see, that's something else I wanted to talk to you about, Papa Enoch. After all, there really isn't an awful lot that you mere mortals can keep safe from me. Now is there?"

"Not really, no." Enoch nodded stoically. "I just can't believe it took me so long to figure out who you really were."

Methuselah turned with a confused look on his face. "What's going on, Pop? What are you saying?"

"Well, son, it seems as though the mystery of the One is being challenged by none other than the Evil One himself."

Eli's mother shook her head in despair. "Can't somebody please speak in a language that regular folks like me can understand?"

A guttural burst of Jubal's laughter crackled through the calmness of the crowd, leaving it chilled to the bone. "That figures," he snarled. "Always have to have it spelled out for you, huh? Because if it ain't on the page, then god knows we have no idea how to think on our own." Jubal then stepped over and opened the book in Hiram's hands. "So take a good look for yourselves, people, and tell me what you see." Rifling through it, he revealed that every page was blank. "Nothing, that's what!" And opening

Tubal's book, he showed that it, too, was blank. "Well, what do you know?" he sneered with a satisfied smirk. "There's nothing to read in any of these books after all, folks. I guess you've all been duped!"

An audible gasp rolled through the group of onlookers like a tidal wave.

Then, as if he were stalking a defenseless prey, Jubal took a menacing step toward the crowd and growled, "You all wanted to read for yourselves just what your beloved patriarch has been telling you? Didn't you? Well, here you go! Look! See! And, yes, your eyes have truly been opened for the first time ... to the charlatan who calls himself *our prophet!*"

The crowd suddenly grew restless and stood to their feet as one.

"Good God, son," exclaimed Jared. "What's the meaning of this? Can you explain why the pages of your books are blank? Is this some kind of a hoax, or what?"

"What do you think, Father? Do you think I'm a fraud now? A charlatan?"

"Of course not," Jared said without hesitation.

"Good. And what about you, Methuselah? Or you, Lamech? Do you think I've just been making up the stories that I say the Lord has given me?"

"Certainly not, Father," insisted Methuselah. "Just because Jubal shows us books that happen to look like yours doesn't mean you're lying to us."

Thoroughly frustrated, Jubal yelped, "What is wrong with you people? Can't you see? Clearly this man has duped you all!"

"I don't think you'd lie to us, Grandfather," Lamech said. "I trust *you*, not him."

"That's right," Eli's mother chimed in. "Maybe there's some other explanation for the blank pages in the books. Who knows?"

Slowly, Jubal's look of frustration turned to a scowl as he watched the faces in the crowd soften, one by one.

"You see?" chided Enoch. "What good is all your poison in the face of the One, you despicable creature? Your doubt and misery are powerless here."

Jubal and his two brothers started to groan lamentably.

The patriarch pressed on. "Your entire plan was based on a lie concocted in your own filthy minds. Now you're discovering the real truth of your predicament. Your evil cannot comprehend the purity of faith, so you choke on it."

With that, the trio of brothers began to writhe in pain, and the crowd took a collective step back, stunned and confused.

Methuselah asked, "Father, would you please tell us what's happening here?"

Enoch aimed a menacing finger at the trio. "Now, Satan, I want you and your two henchmen to leave this sacred place, this second! Do you understand me?"

The trio pathetically nodded their heads, like helpless doves caught in a net.

Lamech gawked. "*Satan*? Are you serious? Here?"

"Get out of here right now, Devil! Go!" Enoch pointed off into the horizon, and suddenly all three brothers transformed into none other than Satan and two of his grotesque demons. Grumbling, cursing, spewing, they flew away to the absolute astonishment of everyone there.

"But how, son?" Jared asked. "How did you know?"

"Because I've written about everyone's life in a book. Don't you remember?"

"Yes, of course, now I see," said Methuselah, still trying to grasp what had just happened. "At least I think I do."

"According to *The Book of Life*," Enoch continued, "the three brothers, Jubal, Hiram and Tubal were all tragically killed in a landslide while out on a hunting expedition. Killed that is, more than a month ago, never to be seen or heard from again."

"What? Oh, my word!" exclaimed Eli's mother. "You really have been sent by the God of Heaven and Earth. But, Grandfather, how long have you known about the real brothers being dead?"

"Quite a while now, actually."

"But why didn't you tell anyone when you found out?" Lamech asked. "Why'd you wait so long?"

"Yeah, Papa Enoch. How come?" wondered little Eli.

For several intense moments, Enoch gazed into the eyes of everyone there, eyes all filled with the same dire question, all yearning to know why he had not revealed the truth of his startling discovery sooner. "The answer to that question, dear family, is very much like the answer to your questions concerning the mystery of the One. Just as it is the duty of every man, woman and child to learn the truth for themselves about the Righteous One, each and every one of us must also stand alone in our quest to discern the truth about the Evil One. Does that make sense, everyone?"

"Of course, Father," Methuselah said with a knowing smile. "That makes all the sense in the world. Thank you for that."

Methuselah's wife then turned to Lamech's wife and said, "You know, I knew there was something about that Jubal that wasn't quite right. You could see it in his eyes."

Lamech's wife eagerly nodded back. "Oh, you are so right. I know what you're saying; I felt the same way, too. I just couldn't figure out what it was, though."

"Thank the Lord above for Father Enoch!" someone shouted from the midst of the people. "Not only is he a man uniquely blessed of God, but he's a blessing to all of us, too!"

A tremendous wave of excitement swept through the whole crowd like wildfire.

"Now listen, everyone," Enoch went on to say. "I appreciate your enthusiasm, really I do; but I'm afraid my days are numbered. Time is running out for me. I only have two more weeks before I have to leave."

"Leave?" groaned Eli's mother. "But you can't leave us now, Grandpa."

"But I have to, my dear. In fact, the angels who will be escorting me are standing by right now, ready to take me as soon as the Lord calls me to go. So they just stand there, biding their time, waiting eagerly to carry out God's instructions."

"Please don't go, Papa Enoch," Eli moaned. "We love you. What are we going to do without you?"

"Oh, Eli, are you trying to break my heart? Please be happy for me, won't you?"

Eli nodded obediently. "All right; for you."

"That's my boy. Just think: Soon, I'll be going back up to Heaven, to the uppermost Jerusalem and to my eternal inheritance."

"Oh, Pop, I wish I could go with you," said Methuselah, fighting hard to hold back his tears. "I'll miss you when you leave."

"And I'll miss you, too, my boy. I'll miss all of you! That is, until we're all reunited together again; which is why I want everyone to do whatever pleases the Lord."

"Certainly, Father, you know we will," Methuselah replied. "Just make sure you bless us before you go, won't you?"

"Of course, Methuselah, I'd be glad to do what you've asked."

"Is there anything I can help you with, son?" asked Jared.

"Yes, Father, I want you to help me get everyone together for one last meeting."

"Should I invite everyone?"

"Everyone."

"And Grandfather?" Lamech suddenly perked up.

"Yes, Lamech; what is it?"

"There's still one last thing you haven't explained to us."

"And what might that be, my boy?"

"When Jubal, I mean, the Evil One, opened the books you read to us before, all the pages in them were blank. I mean, they *were* blank, right?"

With a strange wrinkle to his brow, Enoch eyed his grandson for several moments. "Now that you mention it, I guess they were blank, weren't they?"

Obviously confused by his response, Lamech flashed a plaintive look at his father.

"Of course they were blank, Pop," Methuselah chimed in. "We all saw them with our own eyes. What Lamech is asking, I think, is more at: *Why* were they blank? Am I right, son? Is that what you're getting at?"

Lamech nodded, grateful that his father had stepped in. "Exactly. That's exactly what I wanted to know, yes."

"Why, that's very simple to explain," replied Enoch. "So simple, I'm surprised you even had to ask the question, actually. Doesn't anyone here know the answer to Lamech's question? Anyone at all?"

But after a long and awkward silence, no one seemed to have the slightest idea as to how to respond. Suddenly embarrassed, Methuselah cleared his throat and continued. "I'm sorry to disappoint you, Father, but I don't think any of us can say for sure. If I did offer some sort of an answer, though, would it be safe to say it has something to do with the mystery of the One?"

Enoch's eyes lit up immediately. "You see, son; I knew you wouldn't disappoint me. You're right, yes; it does, as a matter of fact."

"Like you told us before," Methuselah continued, spurred on by his father's infectious enthusiasm, "the mystery of the One cuts both ways, for good *and* for evil."

"That's right," Enoch beamed, like a proud teacher. "Go on."

"To the devil, the words in these books are incomprehensible, words of faith, words of hope, words of love. And because they're meaningless to him, they don't exist. So when he opened the books and looked inside, the pages were as blank as his soul."

"Very good, son; and the rest of you?" Enoch pressed further. "Can you tell us why everyone here saw the pages as though they were blank?"

"Yes, Father, I think so. In fact, that's the greatest tragedy of all, because—"

"Because," said Lamech, breaking in suddenly, his eyes flashing as brightly as those of his grandfather. "Because when Satan held up those books and all he saw were blank pages, we were foolish enough, in that moment, to look at the world through his eyes, so we saw the pages as being blank, too."

"Bravo, my children, bravo," Enoch exclaimed proudly. "It seems that my work here is complete at last."

SO TWO THOUSAND MEN and their families traveled to Achuzan, where Enoch and his family were gathering one last time. Everyone came together as a group, and, one by one, they each came and bowed before the beloved patriarch.

"Dear Enoch," said one man, "you're so blessed of the Lord, the Eternal Ruler. Won't you please bless us, too, so that we may be glorified today?"

Another fellow bowed. "After all, you'll be glorified forever before the Lord, since He's chosen you rather than anyone else. He designated you writer of all His creation, visible and invisible."

"God bless you, my dear family and friends," Enoch replied. "And now, just as anyone asks the Lord for something, I want you to know that He asks you to pray to Him on behalf of all living things, because in God's world, there are many creatures that He cares for. That's why in the great time to come there are countless mansions prepared by God, for humans and for angels, good houses for the good, and bad houses for the bad. Blessed are those who enter one of the good houses, because in the house of evil there is neither rest nor peace, and anyone going to one of those evil houses is never seen from ever again.

"But never forget, everyone, from the greatest to the least of you! The Lord did not create human beings in vain when He fashioned them in His own likeness. He knew exactly what He was doing when He created eyes to see and ears to hear, a heart to reflect, and an intellect to deliberate with. And because the Lord already knew what mankind was going to do, He created the phenomenon of time; and time, He divided into years, months, days and hours, precisely measuring them out so that everyone might reflect on their time in this life. That way people might consider the frailty of their lives, from birth to death, and maybe they'd reflect on their sins, whether their deeds were good or evil; because no work is ever hidden from the Lord. Then they'd understand the impact of what they had accomplished with their lives."

As Enoch continued, a peculiar darkness began to envelop the landscape, slowly but surely shrouding everyone in its inky blackness. Still Enoch's voice penetrated through the darkness. "And when the Lord's creation eventually comes to an end, everyone will proceed to Judgment Day, and then, time itself will be abolished. Imagine that: No more years or months, no more hours or minutes. From that moment forward, time will no longer be a consideration; time will simply cease to have any meaning whatsoever. There'll simply be an eon, and all the righteous who escape the Lord's judgment will be gathered into that great eon, and for the righteous, the great eon will begin, and they'll live eternally. Finally, there'll be no more sickness or humiliation or anxiety or violence. There won't be any more night or darkness. There'll only be a tremendous light, and they'll have an indestructible wall and an incorruptible Paradise, for all corruptible things will have passed away *forever*."

Suddenly Sariel and Raguel appeared at Enoch's side. The patriarch looked up at both of their glowing faces and smiled warmly. Reaching out, he placed a hand on each of their cloaks. The angels then extended their wings, sending out rays of light in every direction, which created quite a spectacle for everyone who was sitting in the otherwise impenetrable darkness.

A man pointed through the murkiness and toward the shimmering streaks of light emanating from Enoch's angelic escorts. "Look! Enoch has become an angel!"

Everyone stopped and turned to look, straining their eyes toward the flashes of brightness that eerily surrounded Enoch, as the angelic wings began to gently lift him up.

"No, no, no," his wife replied. "Enoch hasn't *become* an angel. God just gave him temporary wings so he could fly to Heaven without the help of angels... At least I think so."

Perplexed by this peculiar interplay of darkness and light, the people gaped at the dazzling figures rising upward, higher and higher. Still Enoch's voice rang out as everyone rose to their feet and began to wander about through intermittent pockets of visibility.

"So walk patiently, my children," Enoch continued, "and always rely on God's promises, loving one another until it's time for you to leave this age of misery so you can all become inheritors of eternity. And blessed are the just who escape Judgment Day, because they will shine seven times brighter than the Sun."

Finally, the shimmering dot disappeared from view, like the morning star being swallowed up by dawn's early light; except in this case, this twinkle disappeared into a desperately black void instead of warm blue sky. Once again everyone found themselves completely in the dark, so they all went right back to stumbling around, bumping into one another as they did.

THE VEIL OF DARKNESS that had gripped the landscape gradually began to unleash its oppressive grip, and as the light began to return, one man commented, "Well, I know I saw it with my own two eyes, but I'm still not quite sure what it was I saw."

"How in Heaven's name did Enoch go up like that?" asked his wife as her eyes tried to adjust to the return of the light.

"Don't ask me," the man insisted. "I just told you, I haven't the slightest idea."

"And what do you think happened to all the books that Enoch wrote?"

"There you go again about those books. How many times do I have to tell you? What good are books that don't have any writing in them?"

"So I'm sorry I even mentioned it. Why do I even bother?" said the woman as she walked away, leaving her husband just standing there.

AIMLESSLY WANDERING about, Methuselah stumbled over a ridge, when suddenly a disembodied voice registered quietly in his ear. "Open your eyes, Methuselah, and what do you see?" Looking toward the distant horizon, he squinted against the sunlight. "Books?" he murmured. Holding up his hand to shield his eyes, he could see that there were hundreds of books, lying strewn about an open field. "Everybody, over here! Look! It's the books we've all been searching for!"

The first person who came running was Lamech. Dropping to his knees, he opened one of the books and found that every page had words on it, front and back, and cover to cover. Lamech picked up another one and opened it, too. "And they're all full of writing, just like Grandfather promised."

Everyone else followed, eagerly gathering up the books as they went, and in the end, they counted three hundred and sixty-six of them in all.

ENOCH'S SONS SOON erected a monument on the very spot where the patriarch had been taken up to Heaven. Etched into this stone pillar was a simple inscription. It read: *In honor of Enoch, the man beyond time who graced us with his tales of forever, provided courtesy of the Invisible God.*

Post Script to Time

ENOCH REVERENTLY stepped forward and bowed before the molten Face of God.

"Hello, Enoch," said the Lord. "Welcome back."

"Thank you, Lord. It's good to be back."

For several intense moments, Enoch just looked up into those smoldering eyes as though he were about to say something.

"What is it, Enoch? Is there something I can do for you?"

Enoch smiled sheepishly, slightly embarrassed. "Yes, Lord, there is. Something has been troubling me. I'm sorry to have to even bring it up, actually; but I just can't help wondering."

"Of course, Enoch, I understand. Ask Me."

"Could you please tell me about the fate of mankind? I'm so curious. Did they ever accept the message I delivered to them in the books?"

The glowing eyes stared back at the patriarch for what seemed like an eternity. "What's wrong, Enoch? Don't you remember? The answer you seek is already contained in the stories you wrote yourself?"

Enoch was quite perplexed at this. "Yes, that is odd, isn't it?" He squinted as though that might help him jog his memory. "Come to think of it: You're right. I do remember, almost. More like a dream I had, though, that I can't get entirely straight now that I'm awake. At least I think I'm awake. Why can't I remember things the way I used to?"

"Because while you were still living on Earth, you were only concerned with earthly affairs, understanding things in strictly human terms, but now that I've chosen you for heavenly purposes, you're here with Me. Naturally, you'll never see things in ordinary ways again."

Enoch nodded thoughtfully. "I think I see Your point, yes. Nothing will ever be the same again."

"Are you disappointed?" asked the Lord.

"Oh, no, of course not. I'm just trying to figure some things out. Still trying to get adjusted, I guess."

"I understand."

"So tell me, if You'll be so kind as to refresh my memory: How does mankind respond to the message I left for them? Did they believe what I had to say? Or was I simply written off as a lunatic?"

"Well, Enoch, let Me put it to you this way: I'll describe two mysteries for you. First, many rebels will violate the word of truth. They'll speak incredible things and pronounce many falsehoods. Tremendous civilizations will be created, and many books will be composed in their own words."

447

"Books? More books?" said Enoch. "What about the ones You had me write? Won't anyone pay attention to *them?*"

"Of course," came the Lord's response. "Someday."

"Someday? What do You mean, someday?"

"Your books, Enoch, will be lost to mankind for a very long time."

"Lost? But why?"

"They're lost because only a handful of people ever appreciate them; people like Jared, Methuselah and Lamech, along with their immediate families. So after generations of neglect, they'll simply be lost to much of the world, and for a time it will be as if they'd never been written at all."

Enoch frowned at the mere thought. "But You say things will be different someday? You did say that, didn't You?"

"Yes. Someday people will begin to write all My words properly in their own languages without altering or diminishing them. They'll perform the task correctly, and then they'll possess everything I've said about them from the very beginning."

Relieved, Enoch beamed a tremendous smile. "That's wonderful, Lord. Please tell me more, if You would."

"Then I'll describe the other mystery I spoke about. This one, however, concerns the faithful and the wise, who will be given books of joy, integrity and remarkable wisdom, and having received the gift of those books, they'll believe in what they have to say."

"You mean books like the ones I wrote?" interrupted Enoch, unable to hold back his enthusiasm.

"Yes, Enoch, yes, books just like yours. And they'll rejoice in them, and all the faithful ones will acquire the knowledge of every righteous path through them and be rewarded, and someday, they'll call out to the people of Earth and make them listen to their wisdom."

"Then my efforts didn't go to waste after all," sighed Enoch.

"No, of course not."

Pausing for several moments, Enoch gazed longingly up at that incredible molten face. "So, Lord, I was wondering."

"Of course, Enoch. What is it?"

"I just thought that maybe…"

"Yes, Enoch?"

"You know … I was hoping You might have another story to tell me."

"Another story?" mused the Lord. "Certainly, Enoch. What did you have in mind?"

"Well, Lord, I was wondering. Can You please tell me more about this One You continue to speak about?"

"Ah, yes, of course," replied the Face thoughtfully, "and so the mystery of the One continues still."

BOOK THREE

Heroes must die so that they can be reborn... In some way, in every story, heroes face death or something like it... They magically survive this death and are ... reborn to reap the consequences of having cheated death.

Christopher Vogler, *The Writer's Journey*

A Hero for the Ages

The Imageness of God

IN AN AGE DOMINATED by higher criticism and scientific snobbery, the veracity of *The Bible* is often called into question, usually by casting suspicion upon the historical narratives or the miraculous events contained in it. Consequently, cynicism and skepticism rule the day as the necessary price of intelligent inquiry, while faith and hope are set aside as the pathetic contrivances of wishful thinking. Throughout the pages of this work, however, we have sought to refute many of the reasons for such short-sighted conclusions. We have noted the limited frame of reference that humans have regarding the Divine, which constitutes a dimension of reality that is virtually impenetrable to creatures like us who are imprisoned by a fallen nature. Therefore, because of this limited perceptual condition, God has deigned to articulate His truth to mankind in terms of dramatic significance that transcends the foibles of human language. In addition, we have seen how, due to the symbolic nature of "storytelling," the biblical message—in its conveyance of typological truth—is capable of both revealing and concealing knowledge.

So, when the scholar, fueled by higher criticism, demands a greater awareness of the historical process, which is said to dilute the integrity of textual information as it is transmitted from generation to generation, one need simply remind them that God is not nearly as frustrated as they are by such matters. He has already considered the problem and has preemptively designed the dramas of Scripture in such a way that they convey His truth regardless of such difficulties. More intriguing still is that one of the very objections offered by these same scholars is ironically a major proof of its divine authorship. According to critics, *The Bible* is said to have been corrupted as a result of being translated so many times. Yet the fact that the separate books still maintain such a clear-cut continuity from beginning to end is actually one of its most potent elements in demonstrating that mere mortals could not have been the only agency involved in its creation.

And when the scientist, gripped by intellectual snobbery, demands that *The Bible* be expunged of every trace of the miraculous, which is said to confound a realistic approach to the historical nature of the texts, once again, one need simply remind them that God has already figured out how to steer past that objection as well. Such scientific views appear all the more ironic when one considers that these same scientists, while denying the possibility of miracles when they are depicted in Scripture, still insist on believing in the miraculous when they pontificate about such things as the origins of matter or mankind. Never mind that no one was around to witness the Big Bang or has yet to observe the mutation of a gene. As long as one conveys such possibilities with the zeal of the medieval monk who was convinced that the Earth was the center of the Universe, then no one will ever dare to compare such leaps of faith with those that might be required in believing the so-called "poetic nonsense" of *Genesis*.

All this is to underscore another aspect of our prior discussions: One of the reasons that God has apparently chosen to convey the biblical message via dramatic symbolism is because we are creatures with brains that are uniquely tuned to such modes of communication. In other words, it seems that, even in our fallen state of consciousness, our brains are hardwired to interpret data in a symbolic, metaphoric—dare I say—mythic dimension. So that regardless of the immeasurable gulf that exists between God and us there yet remains something in us that is tuned to the frequency of the Divine. That is to say, even though we live in a world where we are imprisoned by our five senses, we still possess some residual aspect of a God-like sensibility, simply by virtue of the fact that we have been created in the image of God.

The psalmist spoke of such incongruities when he wrote, "Deep calls unto deep."[37] Though his tears had been "food" for him day and night, he still remembered that God was there. He placed his hope in the Lord, though everyone around him bombarded him with the same nagging question: "Where is your God? Where is your God? Where is your God?"[38] So how could he maintain a faith like that in the midst of so much misery and doubt? The answer was that the psalmist was able to stay connected to God, in spite of everything weighing in on him, because, as he put it, "deep calls unto deep, in the roar of Your waterfalls, all of Your waves have swept over me."[39] In other words, though everything and everyone sought to break his connection to God, there was something deep within his very being that mysteriously nullified the distance between his earthly existence and the Lord above. There was some ineffable quality—an "internal image," if you will—that somehow maintained a direct link between his mortal being and that of the divine nature, which can be none other than the *"imageness"* of God, to make up a word.

What is more, this connection between God and mankind existed prior to the Advent of the Spirit as it was recorded in *The Book of Acts*, prior to the time that was predicted by John the Baptist, who declared that "soon there will be One Who is going to baptize the world with the Holy Spirit and

---

37 *Psalm* 42:7
38 Ibid. 42:3
39 Ibid. 42:7

fire."[40] This ineffable connection, then, is not one that resides only in those who claim to be Christians but in all human beings. With this, I have finally come to the point I have been leading to in this chapter.

Whether or not one believes in God or *The Bible*, all human beings cling to a curious desire to believe in otherworldly possibilities. The believer has faith in his God of Scripture, while the atheist believes in his Big Bang of science. In both cases, however, the same mechanism is at work. Something inside each of us is calling out to some corresponding mystery embedded in the Universe in which we live. We sense it implicitly, and because of this peculiar sensation, we all set out in pursuit of whatever might substantiate this haunting sense of "knowing something" that is beyond our mortal selves.

The Secret Desire

HAVING SAID ALL that, I would like to take some time to demonstrate how this principle of "knowing" is presently at work in the lives of everyone around us, whether in those who believe in *The Bible* or in those who reject it. Furthermore, I will do so by way of another of the ideas already outlined in this work, namely, that the God of Scripture speaks to mankind via the dramatic narratives of *The Bible* because we are creatures that are uniquely tuned to such modes of communication. Therefore, if we as human beings have been created this way, then regardless of our specific belief systems we should find that we all reveal a similar reaction to this thing we call "storytelling." In this, I suppose, anthropologists and psychologists might describe it another way. Human beings, they might postulate, prior to the development of verbal skills, were predisposed to respond to symbolic modes of information, whether in the form of allegory, metaphor, or myth. As such, it is simply a fact of life that we humans, as a species, respond—though, quite arguably, in ways both endearing and disturbing.

The most obvious example of this phenomenon can be seen in the universal response to the mythmaking process that began in the earliest days of movie-making at the turn of the twentieth century, particularly as it was found in a place called Hollywood. Reaching its zenith in the golden era of the 1930s, the "dream factory," as it was dubbed, has ever since—in response to changes in public taste—adeptly alternated between fact and fiction, between drama and melodrama, between the heroic and the anti-heroic. Although it is by no means the only source for motion pictures throughout the world, Hollywood is still widely considered to be the primary cauldron of filmic mythmaking, even as it has endured such worldwide changes as world war and the global religious and economic strife of the twentieth century and beyond.

---

40 *Matthew* 3:11

In many ways, the enduring popularity of movies constitutes one of the most peculiar conundrums known to modern man. It is truly ironic when one considers the fact that this most modern of art forms should inflame so effortlessly the most ancient of ideologies. In a world that prides itself in rationalism and enlightenment, the typical moviegoer rarely objects to the sort of sentimentality and nostalgia that constitutes the primary output of this infamous dream factory, with its preponderance for such "superstitious nonsense" as destiny and redemption, resurrection and immortality, eternal love and self-sacrifice. Just imagine what the movies would be like if there were no monsters or saviors, no aliens or angels, no overlords or freedom-fighters to inhabit the screen. And what if there was no Heaven or God to gaze upon, no Hell or devil to avert our eyes from?

Even while audiences grow weary of worn-out clichés, the demand for more realistic depictions of the world has never quenched the more compelling urge—the secret desire in everyone—to be transported to alternate worlds of existence, where the movie experience becomes for them nothing less than a religious experience. Just consider the box office receipts for the top grossing films of all time, and one will notice a consistent pattern—no doubt exacerbated by Hollywood's reluctance to stray from anything that fails to generate boatloads of cash. In the context of our discussion, however, it is even more telling when one examines this list against the backdrop of the narratives found in *The Bible*.

The Power of One

WITHOUT EXHAUSTING the endless possibilities, a cursory comparison would certainly have to begin with the most mythic of all such motifs—that of the power of "one man." Undoubtedly, the most pervasive story element found in Scripture is that of one man who rises from the muddled masses, one man who alone possesses the skill, the courage, and the sense of destiny to save the day. The roll call of such iconic heroes fills the pages of both Holy Writ and Hollywood. For every Noah, Moses, or David offered in *The Bible*, there is a James Bond, Luke Skywalker, or Harry Potter among the pantheon of movie gods. When former President Ronald Reagan was asked about what film had most affected him, he cited *Mr. Smith Goes to Washington*.

> When Jimmy Stewart walked the halls of the Capitol building, I walked with him. When he stood in awe of that great man at the Lincoln Memorial, I bowed my head, too. When he stood in the Senate chamber and refused to knuckle under to the vested interests, I began to realize, through the power of the motion picture, one man can make a difference.[41]

---

41 *The Hollywood Reporter Book of Box Office Hits*, Susan Sackett, p. 21

In describing what Frank Capra, the director of the film, had done through his hero, film critic Neal Gabler wrote, "He created a powerful myth for the nation."[42] This myth, however, was not created out of thin air. It was, in fact, firmly rooted in those narratives found originally in *The Bible*. "Capra had propounded," Gabler went on to say, "a theology of comedy—a secularized displacement of Christ's tale, in which the common-man hero, blessed with goodness and sense, overcomes obstacles, temptations, and even betrayals to redeem his own life and triumph."[43]

Clearly, without such heroic figures for audiences to root for, movie producers would be sorely lacking the single most important ingredient that keeps people coming back again and again to see the same kinds of movies. Notwithstanding the fact that such things rarely happen in real life, as long as there is some sort of anchor, that is to say, an explicitly *human* anchor, to support such mythical motifs, then all the better. And what better "myth" is there to be found than in the pages of the most published book of all time; as famed American film director Cecil B. DeMille once observed: "Give me two pages from *The Bible*, and I'll give you a motion picture." Of course, Mr. De-Mille—who directed such films as *The King of Kings*, *The Sign of the Cross*, and *Samson and Delilah*—could never have anticipated the way in which future filmmakers would take the familiar heroes of old and, through a classic bit of Hollywood "rewriting," transform them into heroes for a new generation.

Batman, Spider-Man, Iron Man, X-Men, Superman, Men in Black, and *James Bond*: Besides representing seven of the all-time highest grossing film franchises in history, what do all these characters have in common? And more importantly, in view of what we are seeking to demonstrate in this work: What do these characters have in common with the narratives that are showcased in the most ancient form of dramatic narrative known to humanity? In a nutshell: They all portray a troubled world that is powerless to resist the overwhelming forces imposed upon it by various personifications of evil—both natural and supernatural. Next, enter into that world some special "one," who has been separated, equipped, and trained to perform a task that no one else is capable of. Then, through the selfless action of this someone—this one man, this one woman, this, dare I say, lone messianic figure—is the archenemy of mankind defeated and the scales of justice set right. Otherwise, without the personal intervention of this hero of biblical proportions, the world would surely remain trapped forever in the clutches of darkness and despair.

Add to the previous list of the super heroic and the not so super heroic: *Marvel's Avengers, The Lord of the Rings, Harry Potter, Star Wars, Transformers, Mission: Impossible, Indiana Jones, Star Trek, The Matrix,* and *The Chronicles*

---

42 *An Empire of Their Own: How the Jews Invented Hollywood*, Neal Gabler, p. 173
43 Ibid. p. 173

of Narnia. Together, the aforementioned franchises represent seventeen of the top twenty-five movie franchises of all time. Together, they have, as of the year 2016, amassed worldwide box office revenues to the tune of some 51 billion dollars.[44] The only thing I find more staggering than the untold wealth that such films have procured for their producers is the fact that these seventeen film franchises should so specifically correlate with themes and characterizations that were first described in *The Bible.* Could it really be just a coincidence that audiences the world over would respond with unabashed enthusiasm towards such "impossibly miraculous" storylines? Or, instead, is it simply a product of the kind of wishful thinking that is so common to all human cultures? Certainly, the anthropologists would say so. Or maybe it is just a function of some deep-seated human repression, where we as adults are simply expressing our childhood fantasies when we root for the good guys to triumph over the forces of evil? Of course this is what the psychologists would insist.

But before anyone jumps to such obvious oversimplifications, I believe we would do well to consider the possibility that there might actually be something else at work here. Maybe the answer lies not so much in the fact that audiences are indulging in child-like modes of wishful thinking, but rather that they are simply behaving in accordance with who and what they truly are? That is to say — whether one accepts the message of Scripture or not — we are all human beings who, for a lack of a better description, are much like tuning forks that inwardly respond to frequencies that exist outside ourselves. Anthropologists might call it "correspondence," while psychologists might call it "resonance." Biblical scholars, on the other hand, will insist that it is simply a case of "deep calling unto deep."

Return of the Hero

FURTHER PROOF OF this connection between Hollywood and Holy Writ is that not only is the lone messianic figure found at the core of all these film franchises, but the most prevalent *motif* among them is also the central theme of *The Bible,* which is, the resurrection of the dead. Hollywood filmmakers have repeatedly drawn from the all-too-familiar dramatic well of the vanquished hero who has died — apparently or in reality — while in the effort of saving the day, only to be miraculously restored to life in the end. Christopher Vogler, in his insightful book *The Writer's Journey,* put it this way:

> Heroes must die so that they can be reborn. The dramatic movement that audiences enjoy more than any other is death and rebirth.

---

44 *List of Highest-Grossing Franchises and Film Series,* Wikipedia

In some way, in every story, heroes face death or something like it—their greatest fears, the failure of an enterprise, the end of a relationship, the death of an old personality. Most of the time, they magically survive this death and are literally, and symbolically, reborn to reap the consequences of having cheated death.

Steven Spielberg's *E.T.* dies before our eyes but is reborn through alien magic and a boy's love. In *Excalibur*, Sir Lancelot, remorseful over having killed a gallant knight prays him back to life. Clint Eastwood's character in *Unforgiven* is beaten senseless by a sadistic sheriff and hovers at the edge of death, thinking he's seeing angels. *Sherlock Holmes*, apparently killed with Professor Moriarty in the plunge over Reichenbach Falls, defies death and returns, transformed and ready for more adventures. Patrick Swayze's character, murdered in *Ghost*, learns how to cross back through the veil to protect his wife and finally express his true love for her.[45]

This ubiquitous storyline involving death and resurrection is never more evident than in many of the most popular film franchises of all time. In fact, more than any other dramatic device, the lives of our most beloved characters have been shaped and forever changed by it. When one thinks of James Bond, Luke Skywalker, Superman, Mister Spock, Neo, Harry Potter, Batman, and Professor Xavier, one cannot help but think of them in terms of the age-old theme of the return of the hero. Case in point: Consider the following scenarios.

In *From Russia with Love*, James Bond is immediately involved in a cat and mouse game with a sinister SPECTRE agent known as Grant. Shrouded in the darkest of night, the two men maneuver adeptly through an outdoor arena filled with hedgerows, fountains, and Romanesque statues. Stalking his prey, Bond fires off a shot, barely missing his opponent. Then, quite unexpectedly, Grant turns the tables on our hero and strangles him to death. It is at this point that the darkened arena is lit up to reveal that we have actually been witnessing a training exercise. With a flick of the wrist, an unknown figure removes a mask from the face of the dead man that we had been led to believe is James Bond but instead turns out to be someone else, a mere pawn in a twisted game of death.

In *Goldfinger*, it is not the hero who is "resurrected" but the hero's helpers. In this case, the troops that guard the gold at Fort Knox are put out of commission by the nefarious villain by which the film derives its name. In one fell swoop, sixteen thousand soldiers are killed by a deadly nerve gas, which is dropped onto them via airplanes manned by Pussy Galore and her

45 *The Writer's Journey: Mythic Structure for Storytellers and Screenwriters*, Christopher Vogler, pp. 181-82

flying team of *femme fatales*. But once Goldfinger and his men move in for the heist, the troops all "miraculously" rise to their feet and quickly mobilize to eliminate the threat. As it turns out, Goldfinger's trusted pilot, Pussy — having been turned by the ever seductive James Bond — has switched the contents of the gas-emitting canisters; and the troops have only been faking their deaths in order to lure the enemy into a false sense of security.

In *You Only Live Twice*, James Bond is on assignment in Hong Kong, where he is double-crossed by a beautiful Chinese agent and killed in a hail of machine gun bullets. He is then buried at sea with all honors, commensurate with his rank as a commander of Her Majesty's Royal Navy. His co-cooned body is deposited into the sea with the eulogy: "For the trumpet shall sound and the dead shall be raised incorruptible… We therefore commit his body to the deep … looking for the resurrection, when the seas shall give up their dead." But no sooner has Bond's cocoon slipped into the depths than a pair of deep-sea divers intercept and whisk it away to the safety of a nearby submarine, where it is unwrapped, extricating Bond who has been breathing via SCUBA gear the entire time. Far from being an unsuspecting victim, then, Bond has actually been part of an elaborately staged hoax so that he will be even more effective in his job of infiltrating the enemy's camp because he is believed to be dead.

In *Skyfall*, James Bond is similarly killed in an opening sequence, only to return again with a vengeance, but unlike the "death" of the hero in *You Only Live Twice*, the one in *Skyfall* was not planned. Instead, Bond is accidentally shot, and as a result of his injuries, his skills are severely diminished, due in large part to his gunshot wounds and the wear-and-tear he has endured after many long years in the field as the vaunted Agent 007. Consequently, Bond is forced to muster every ounce of inner strength to free himself from the stigma that his near-death experience has thrust upon him, and only after an arduous journey does he reemerge in the end, reborn, ready to resume his rightful mantle as James Bond.

In *Star Wars IV: A New Hope*, Luke Skywalker is trapped with his companions in a gigantic trash compactor at the heart of the Death Star, when suddenly the huge tentacle of an unseen monster pulls him down into the murky ooze. Horrified, Han Solo, Princess Leia, and Chewbacca watch in helpless desperation as Luke's tell-tale bubbles cease to trickle to the surface. Then, just when they have given up hope, Luke breaks upward through the slimy surface and is reunited with his friends. Later, when Luke's mentor, Obi Wan Kenobi, is killed in a laser duel with Darth Vader, his body vanishes, and Luke, at that point, believes it will be the last time he will ever see his old friend again. But in Luke's greatest hour of need, Obi Wan returns — albeit in spirit form — to guide him with the most important advice of his life: "Trust the force, Luke."

In *Superman: The Movie*, Lois Lane's car careens into a ravine caused by an earthquake that was triggered by a nuclear missile reprogrammed to fulfill the twisted purposes of Lex Luthor. Trapped in her sinking vehicle during the ensuing landslide, Lois is slowly buried alive beneath the cascading rubble. Unfortunately for her, Clark Kent—a.k.a. Superman—is forced into the opposite direction to stop a second missile because he has promised to prevent it from killing the mother of the woman who mercifully released him from the crippling chain of Kryptonite that Luthor placed around his neck. So by the time Superman thwarts this missile, he fails to arrive before he can prevent Lois' death. In a fit of superhuman rage, the Man of Steel then takes to the sky and begins streaking around the globe, causing it to spin in reverse, thereby turning back time to the events prior to Lois' death. Upon returning to her now undamaged car, Superman finds that Lois is alive and well, and no one on Earth has any idea what he has done in restoring her life.

In *Star Trek II: The Wrath of Khan*, the crippled Enterprise, its warp drive damaged in a previous battle, is threatened with annihilation as it drifts in orbit around a dead planet that is about to be "regenerated" by the *Genesis* Device. As it turns out, this device—designed to terraform barren worlds into habitable ones suitable for colonization by the Federation—will also destroy any prior life forms in favor of its "new matrix." So, in a selfless effort to rescue the Enterprise and its crew, Mister Spock enters the ship's engine room, where he successfully restores the ship's warp drive. In the process, however, Spock exposes himself to radiation and dies while James Kirk, captain of the Enterprise, can only look on helplessly from the other side of the glass partition.

In the next film, *Star Trek III: The Search for Spock*, the lifeless body of Mister Spock has been jettisoned to the surface of the regenerated planet, but before long, scientists involved with the *Genesis* Device discover signs of an unexpected life form on the planet. Upon arrival to the planet's surface, they discover that Spock has, as a result of the regenerative effects of the device, been resurrected into the form of a child. At first, Spock is a blank slate, apparently mindless, with no apparent recollection of who he is or was. He then undergoes a series of metamorphic changes. As the planet they are on matures at an accelerated pace, so also Spock ages with astonishing rapidity. Soon, Spock has reached full maturity in body, but his mind, his soul, is still apparently absent. Eventually, Captain Kirk and the crew of the Enterprise are able to return Spock to Vulcan, where he is reunited with his soul, which he had at the end of the previous film secretly deposited in the mind of the ship's doctor, Leonard McCoy, prior to his entering the ship's engine room.

In *Star Trek: Generations*, a retired James Kirk is forced back into action when a mysterious ribbon of energy called the Nexus threatens the maiden

voyage of the Enterprise-B. In a valiant effort to free the ship, Kirk is apparently killed when this energy ribbon damages the section he was working
on. Many years later, we discover more about the Nexus, which has become
the singular obsession of the twisted Doctor Tolian Soran, who is hell-bent
on tapping into this ribbon of energy, even though he must destroy entire
planets in the process. In his attempt to stop Doctor Soran, Captain Jean-
Luc Picard unexpectedly finds himself inside the Nexus, which turns out be
more than mere energy. It is really an alternate Universe where, throughout
time and space, certain individuals have been known to become trapped.
While there, Picard learns why Soran is so determined to control the Nexus.
Apparently, one of its peculiar qualities is that for anyone inside the ribbon
it can generate their innermost desires, something Picard realizes he must
reject if he is to escape and return to the real world. Eventually, Picard learns
that Kirk is also one of those wayward travelers who has become "stuck"
in the Nexus, not yet understanding where he is or why he is there. After
some gentle but persistent persuasion, Picard convinces Kirk to reject his
comfortable place in the Nexus. They both return to the "land of the living,"
where the "resurrected" Kirk fights alongside Picard, and together they kill
Soran before he can destroy any more worlds in his attempts to gain control
of the Nexus.

In *Men in Black,* Agents K and J confront a gigantic, parasitic alien bug,
bent on destroying a rival species that is hiding out on planet Earth. In their
efforts to thwart this malevolent threat, Agent J watches helplessly as Agent
K first has his weapon eaten by the bug, and while in the process of taunting
the monster, K is gobbled up, too. Desperately, Agent J tries to restrain the
creature, to no avail. Then, just as it looks as if Agent J might be eaten like his
partner before him, the sound of Agent K's weapon is heard powering up
from within the bug's belly, followed by the creature exploding from within. After having been blown into a million gelatinous pieces, the creature's
disintegrated body catapults Agent K from its innards, alive and well.

In *Men in Black 3,* another nasty parasitic alien, this time a Boglodite
assassin by the name of Boris the Animal, escapes from a maximum security
prison on the Moon. A one-armed man—or should I say, creature—on a
mission, Boris is out for revenge. His target is the agent who is responsible
for his having lost his arm and being imprisoned. That person is none other
than Agent K. Boris' diabolical plan is to go back in time to kill Agent K
before he has the chance to do either. When Boris makes his "time jump"
to the past, the present world of the Men in Black transforms to a place in
which Agent K no longer exists. But strangely enough, Agent J is aware that
something is wrong with their world, while everyone else is convinced that
Agent K was killed some forty years earlier by Boris the Animal. Agent K,
however, is not the only victim of the Boglodite's scheme, because having

avoided being put out of commission by him, Boris is now able, in this "new present," to mount a full-scale Boglodite attack on Earth. Hoping to restore the world that he once knew, Agent J follows Agent K into the past, where he teams up with a younger version of K, and together they thwart both the younger and present-day versions of Boris, thus restoring Agent K to his proper place in the future, as well as preempting the Boglodite attack on planet Earth.

In *The Matrix*, mild-mannered Neo is living a boring, mundane life — software engineer by day, computer hacker by night; but he is searching for so much more. Before long, he meets a mysterious woman named Trinity, who challenges his acceptance of the status quo. Eventually, Neo is introduced to Morpheus, a man who, along with Trinity, attempts to draw him out of his comfort zone. Soon, Morpheus convinces Neo that the source of his frustration is due to the fact that he is actually an unwitting slave to a shadow world called the Matrix. As a captive of this world of illusion, Neo is offered a way out by Morpheus — a way of escape that plunges our hero into a stark new reality that is for him nothing less than a journey from one existence to another. Upon making this transition to his new life, Neo asks, "Am I dead?" Matter-of-factly, Morpheus responds, "Far from it." As a member of Morpheus' band of rebels, Neo finally learns the truth about the difference between the real world he now inhabits and the dream world that had until then held him captive. In time, Morpheus convinces Neo that he is the Chosen One who might lead mankind in an all-out rebellion to destroy the power of the Matrix and release humanity from its grip. Reluctant at first, Neo goes on to develop a variety of skills, both physical and mental, in order to fulfill the destiny that Morpheus and Trinity are convinced is his. In the final confrontation between Morpheus' team and agents of the Matrix, Neo is caught off guard and killed by the insidious Agent Smith, but refusing to accept that his death means the end of Neo, Trinity unflinchingly breathes life back into him with a kiss. Imbued with an entirely new sense of purpose and determination, Neo rises to his feet and, with a power previously unattained, disposes of Agent Smith, thereby ending the threat and turning the tide in the battle against the Matrix.

In *Harry Potter and the Chamber of Secrets*, Harry encounters Professor Albus Dumbledore's pet Phoenix, Hawkes. Right before Harry's eyes, Hawkes abruptly catches fire and disintegrates into a pile of dust. As Professor Dumbledore explains to Harry: "They burst into flames when it's time to die, then they're reborn from the ashes." To Harry's astonishment, just as Dumbledore has explained, a newborn chick wiggles out from the pile of ashes. Later, in his attempt to rescue one of his friends, Harry is confronted in a life-or-death struggle with a huge serpent called a Basilisk. When it attacks Harry, Hawkes comes to Potter's aid by clawing the creature's eyes out. Still, the monster can smell Harry as it relentlessly chases the young wizard. Eventually, Harry gets the better of the Basilisk, thrusting a sword through the creature's mouth, but in the process of killing the monster Harry is mortally wounded by one of its venomous fangs. As Harry languishes in the throes of death, Hawkes flies to his friend's side. Touched by Harry's infirmity, Hawkes begins to weep. One by one, the tears of the Phoenix drip into his wounds, and in an extraordinary turn of events, the young wizard is completely healed through the power of those tears.

In *The Dark Knight Rises*, a masked madman called Bane threatens to destroy Gotham City with a nuclear bomb that has been created by converting a reactor core, originally built for good by none other than Bruce Wayne— a.k.a. Batman. With no way to prevent its detonation, Batman lifts the bomb with the help of the Bat, an aircraft developed and built by Lucius Fox, a man who runs Wayne Enterprises on his behalf. All of Gotham City watches with great anticipation as the Bat streaks far away, out across the bay, where the bomb finally detonates well beyond the city limits. Assumed to have been killed in the blast, the much-misunderstood Batman is posthumously feted as a hero who has singlehandedly saved Gotham. With Bruce Wayne also presumed dead, his estate is divided up among the city's orphans and his faithful butler Alfred. Eventually, however, Fox discovers, to his amazement, that the Bat's autopilot, which had previously been malfunctioning, is now fully restored, and in one final scene, Alfred, while on holiday abroad, is quite relieved to find Bruce Wayne, alive and well, sitting in an outdoor café with his new companion Selina Kyle—a.k.a. Catwoman.

In *X2: X-Men United*, Jean Grey uses her awesome telekinetic power to save her comrades from a massive flood caused by a breach in the dam at Alkali Lake. In the process, however, she is engulfed in the powerful undertow and heroically sacrifices her own life while rescuing the others.

In the following film, *X-Men: The Last Stand*, the memory of Jean haunts her boyfriend Scott Summers, who stands mourning for her on the banks of Alkali Lake. Overcome by grief, Scott—a.k.a. Cyclops—unleashes his own mutant power into the center of the lake. A laser blast from his eyes energizes the waters before him, and from the murky depths, there emerges a figure engulfed in a blinding canopy of light. From out of this shimmering halo, Jean Grey emerges, inexplicably returned from her watery grave. Sadly, though, there is a downside to this apparently blissful reunion. It seems as though the "resurrected" Jean is not entirely the same person that she once was. In time, we find that, according to X-Men Professor Charles Xavier, Jean's personality contains a dark, hidden aspect he calls the Phoenix, a side that he has sought to control for many years, hoping to quell a virtually limitless aspect of her telekinetic power. In the end, however, this dark side consumes Jean, and in an uncontrollable fit of rage, she kills Charles Xavier, vaporizing his body in front of several horrified X-Men. But as one might expect in the peculiar Universe of superheroes, this does not spell the end for Professor Xavier, either. Before *The Last Stand* concludes, the professor's post-mortem presence is already revealing itself to a nurse as she attends to a comatose patient who unexpectedly speaks to her in a voice that she cannot help but recognize. To which the befuddled nurse whispers back, "Charles?"

A subsequent film, *X-Men Origins: Wolverine,* has Logan—a.k.a. Wolverine—making his way through an airplane terminal. There, he is stunned to see Professor Xavier nonchalantly roll up to him in his mechanized wheelchair, looking as fit as ever. "How is this possible?" mumbles a disbelieving Wolverine. To which Xavier glibly replies, "As I told you a long time ago, you're not the only one with gifts."

Tales of Me and You

SO TELL ME: ARE YOU convinced yet? Or should I continue? I could go on and on with a great many more examples, but suffice it to say, in these numerous scenarios, one is presented with sufficient evidence for the overwhelming correspondence between the narratives of *The Bible* and those of the most popular films of all time. In the end, my purpose in all of this laborious film exegesis remains constant. In a world that prides itself on rationality, logic, and objectivity—call it what you will—there is clearly an equal yet opposite dimension to its innermost belief system. As it turns out, the flipside to these so-called "normal" modes of thought cannot be explained away simply because so many generations of mankind have distorted, abused, and exploited the potential of such otherworldly realities. In other words, just because fanatics, zealots, and extremists are assumed to be the only kinds of people crazy enough to cling to such outrageous notions as the resurrection of the dead, do not fool yourselves with such rigidly shallow interpretations. The verdict has been handed down, and it has been done by way of the almighty dollar. In this most unexpected way, the "secret desire" of the average, everyday moviegoer has revealed the truth about what they really believe to be the meaning and purpose of their world. Moreover, they have done so to the resounding tune of—I repeat—51 billion dollars (and counting), proving once and for all that "audiences are not simply indulging in child-like modes of wishful thinking, but they are," contrary to all critical and scientific ways of thinking, "behaving in accordance with who and what they truly are."

This is why, I believe, *The Tales* found in this present volume can no longer be casually dismissed simply because they seem to contradict one's assumptions about traditional history—either biblical or secular. After all, if humanity's response to the irresistible force of the cinema is taken into consideration, as I am convinced it should, then this belief in nothing less than the redemption and rebirth of the human soul is one that clearly cuts across every known strata of existence. And if this is the case, then no longer should the fantastic accounts of Enoch, Adam, Abraham, and Pilate be excluded on the fallacious grounds that they must have been left out of *The Bible* for good reason.

Simply put, if the Scriptures declare that Enoch walked and talked with God, then it should come as no surprise that as a result of this momentous encounter he might have something of great importance to communicate. And, if Enoch as the first narrator of human history stated that God personally entrusted him with the story of mankind's past, present, and future, then who are we to say that what he wrote was a fantasy or, worse, the product of a delusional mind? After all, nothing is more consistent in this peculiar Universe of ours than the old adage: "Truth is always stranger than fiction." So, when Enoch insisted that he was assigned the task of writing books with the express purpose of detailing the lives of all those who *have* lived, who *were* living, and who *were yet to* live, who—again I repeat—are we to question the apparent improbability of such a thing?

And if God spoke face to face with Enoch, then why could not the Word of God have done the same thing with Adam, Abraham, and Pilate? When Adam suffered the consequences of his futile efforts to regain entrance to the garden, who is to say that the Word of God did not restore him to life again and again so he could fulfill the years that had been decreed for him? When Abraham was wrestling with whether or not God could make him a father of many nations, who is to say that the Word did not convince him he could also become the father of a multitude of children whose destiny is an incorruptible city in Heaven? And in the fullness of time, when this Word became flesh and dwelled among men, who is to say that He did not reveal Himself to Pilate, the most infamous political boss the world has ever known, and in that shattering encounter transform even a man like him into a most unwitting ally?

Who is to say, really? After all, one only needs to answer a few simple, straightforward questions. Have not the tales of wonder that this man Enoch was supposedly entrusted with made their mark in spite of everything that the world might say to the contrary? Do not tales of redemption and rebirth permeate our global community, within and without? Can anyone really tell us where one storyline ends and where another begins? If not, then maybe it is simply time for the world to finally embrace these *Tales* and, like our father Abraham, cease and desist in questioning the possibility of such impossibilities. Why not drink them in, imbibe them, and become intoxicated by the spirit of them, because through them one might just see the world anew. And maybe, the next time someone looks in the mirror, they will find staring back at them one who has been forever changed because they, too, have encountered the tales of forever—tales of heroes and villains, tales of me and you.

THIS CONCLUDES *The Book of Tales: Stories That Confirm the 5,500-year Prophecy Given to Adam About the Coming of Christ*. To read further, please refer to the companion text, entitled *The Book of Days: In Search of the 5,500-year Prophecy Given to Adam About the Coming of Christ*.

For those of you who are so inclined, it would be greatly appreciated if you could post a positive review of this book on such websites as Amazon Books so that others might become aware of its valuable contents. Because this book was not published by a conglomerate-style publishing house, we rely more heavily on word-of-mouth to advertise its importance to others who, like yourself, are searching for books like this. Thank you for your support.

THE CREDITS

If this present work has anything to add in the way of enlightening the world, it is only because I have been afforded the tremendous honor to "stand upon the shoulders of giants."

W. Kent Smith, *The Book of Tales*

Selected Biographies

W ITHOUT THE groundbreaking work of an intrepid band of discoverers, translators, and scholars, this book would never have been possible. For that reason, the following group must be acknowledged for their achievements, without whose contributions this planet would be a much sadder and bleaker place. Therefore, if this present work has anything to add in the way of enriching, enlightening, or educating the world, it is only because I have been afforded the rare and tremendous honor to, for a moment in time, "stand upon the shoulders of giants."

The Discoverers

Johann Grynaeus (1540-1617) was a Swiss Protestant divine, professor of *The New Testament*, and collector of biblical manuscripts. For more than twenty-five years, Grynaeus exerted tremendous influence on both church and state affairs, acquiring quite a reputation as a skillful theologian of the school of Huldrych Zwingli. His many works include commentaries on various books of *The Old Testament* and *The New Testament* as well as an exhaustive collection of patristic literature entitled *Orthodoxographa* (1569), from which we get the present-day version of *The Gospel of Nicodemus*.

Giuseppe Assemani (1687-1768) was a Lebanese Orientalist and Vatican librarian. Serving as a scribe of Oriental manuscripts, Assemani was sent, in 1715, to Egypt and Syria in search of valuable parchments. Two years later, he returned with one hundred and fifty choice documents, which then became part of the Vatican Library. This success eventually induced Pope Clement XII to send him east again, some twenty years later, and this time Assemani returned with a collection that was even more ancient and more valuable than his first trip. It was among this cache of manuscripts that he discovered a work attributed to Ephrem the Syrian, entitled *The Cave of Treasures: The Book of the Succession of the Generations* (c. 350), which later scholars determined bore an uncanny similarity to *The First Book of Adam and Eve*.

James Bruce (1730-1794) was a Scottish explorer and travel writer. Having spent more than a dozen years in North Africa and Ethiopia, Bruce, among other things, traced the origins of the Blue Nile. An examination of Oriental manuscripts at an early age led him to the study of Arabic and Geez, and eventually would determine his future career. Apart from his travels up the Nile River, Bruce also brought back a collection of rare Ethiopian manuscripts, which, according to British historian Edward Ullendorff, "opened up new vistas for the study of Ethiopian languages and placed this branch of Oriental scholarship on a much more secure basis."[46] Among this collection of at least twenty-six manuscripts were the Ethiopic versions of *The First Book of Enoch*, *The Book of Jubilees*, and *The First Book* and *Second Book of Adam and Eve*.

E.A. Wallis Budge (1857-1934) was a British Egyptologist, Orientalist, philologist, and author. Working for the British Museum, Budge made numerous trips to Egypt and the Sudan, where he was able to procure a great many objects of antiquity, which in turn helped to build up the museum's collection of cuneiform tablets, manuscripts, and papyri. His various publications on Egyptology helped bring a knowledge of these discoveries to a much larger audience. In 1920 he was knighted for his services to Egyptology and the British Museum. Perhaps his best-known work, which also incorporated his skills as a translator, was *The Egyptian Book of the Dead* (1895), while one of his lesser-known, though no less significant, was his translation of *The Book of the Cave of Treasures* (1927).

The Translators

William Wake (1657-1737) was a British clergyman, dean at Exeter, bishop at Lincoln, and archbishop of Canterbury. According to biographer Joseph Hirst Lipton, Wake was said to be "a man of wide reading, immense industry, and liberal and tolerant spirit."[47] Of his numerous writings, his most important work was an anthology entitled *The Genuine Epistles of the Apostolic Fathers* (1693), which includes the first English translation of *The Gospel of Nicodemus*.

Richard Laurence (1760-1838) was a British Hebraist and Anglican churchman. He was made regius professor of Hebrew and canon of Christ Church at Oxford, in 1814, and archbishop of Cashel, Ireland, in 1822. According to biographer Gordon Goodwin, Laurence's "writings are a model of exactness and judicious moderation. His erudition is well illustrated by the three volumes in which he printed, with Latin and English translations, Ethiopic versions of apocryphal books of *The Bible*, which include *The First Book of Enoch* (1821) from the manuscript Scottish explorer James Bruce brought from Abyssinia and presented to the Bodleian Library."[48]

Moses Samuel (1795-1860) was a British author and translator of Hebrew works. According to *The Jewish Encyclopedia*, Samuel "acquired a consid-

46 *James Bruce*, Edward Ullendorff, p. 133
47 *Dictionary of National Biography*, Joseph Hirst Lipton, 1885-1900, Volume 58
48 *Dictionary of National Biography*, Gordon Goodwin, 1885-1900, Volume 32

erable reputation as a Hebrew scholar and an authority on rabbinical literature."[49] From an early age, Samuel had a talent for mathematics and languages, speaking twelve languages in all. He is best known for having been the originally anonymous translator of a 1625 Hebrew edition of *The Book of Jasher* (1838) into English, printed in Venice, after becoming convinced by the core of the work that it was the same book referenced in Scripture.

S.C. Malan (1812-1894) was a British biblical scholar and linguist of Oriental languages. Malan was greatly occupied with theological controversy, and published some of his most valuable work illustrative of the Christian East, especially translations from the Syriac, Coptic, Ethiopic, Armenian, and Georgian literatures. According to biographer Cecil Bendall, "In practical knowledge of Oriental languages, Malan had no equal in England, and probably none in the world."[50] Among his more than fifty publications was his English translation of the Ethiopic works of *The First Book* and *Second Book of Adam and Eve* (1882).

William Wright (1830-1889) was a British Orientalist and professor of Arabic at Cambridge. He early developed a fondness for Oriental languages, devoting his main efforts to Syriac, but also acquiring a knowledge of all the Semitic languages together with Sanskrit. Many of Wright's works on Syriac literature are still in print and of considerable scholarly value. As a result of his extensive scholarship, he produced such works as *Contributions to the Apocryphal Literature of The New Testament* (1865), from which we have the first English translation *The Letters of Herod and Pilate*.

B. Harris Cowper (1822-1904) was a British archeologist, historian, and translator. As an archeologist, Cowper is credited with having discovered Loughton Camp, an Iron Age hill fort in England, dating from around 500 B.C. As a translator, his work appears in *Apocryphal Gospels and Other Documents relating to the History of Christ* (1865), which gave us English versions of *The Epistles of Pilate to Tiberius Caesar*, *The Trial and Condemnation of Pilate*, and *The Death of Pilate, who Condemned Jesus*.

W.R. Morfill (1834-1909) was a British professor of Slavonic languages at Oxford. He also became curator of the Taylor Institution and was appointed a Fellow of the British Academy in 1903. Writing in his obituary, Sir James Murray said, "We lose in him a unique scholar, whose knowledge of the Slavonic languages was greater than that of any other Englishman, so far as I know." Besides Morfill's various books on Slavonic grammar, he provided,

---

49 *The Jewish Encyclopedia: Samson-Talmid Hakam*, Isidore Singer, Cyrus Adler (Editors), Funk and Wagnalls, 1860, p. 24

50 *Dictionary of National Biography*, Cecil Bendall, 1901 Supplement

at the behest of R.H. Charles, the English translation of *The Secrets of Enoch* (1896), sometimes designated *The Slavonic Enoch* or *The Second Book of Enoch*.

R.H. Charles (1855-1931) was an Irish biblical scholar and theologian. He gained a Doctor of Divinity and was professor of biblical Greek at Trinity College. Charles is known particularly for English translations of apocryphal and pseudepigraphal works, which includes both *The Book of Jubilees* (1895) and *The Testaments of the Twelve Patriarchs* (1908).

The Scholars

Theophilus of Antioch (c. 120-181) was a Syrian theologian, apologist, author, and chronologist. The seventh bishop of Antioch, Theophilus was a prolific writer whom Eusebius, Jerome, Lactantius, and others mention in reference to his numerous works against the prevailing heresies of the time, of which only his three-volume *Defense of Christianity* (c. 175) survives to this day. Cited as the founder of the science of biblical chronology, he calculated the period from Adam to Christ at about 5,500 years, using a dating system derived from *The Septuagint.*

Julius Africanus (c. 160-240) was a Libyan historian and traveler. He is important primarily because of his influence on Eusebius, all the later writers of biblical history among the Church Fathers, and the entire Greek school of Christian chronologists. He wrote a history of the world entitled *Chronographia* (c. 222) in which he calculated the period from Creation to Christ as 5,500 years. This reckoning of time led to numerous creation eras being used in the Greek Eastern Mediterranean that placed Creation within one decade of 5,500 B.C. Although his history is no longer extant, copious extracts from it can found in the works of Eusebius, Georgius Syncellus, Georgius Cedrenus, and others.

Hippolytus of Rome (c. 170-235) was a Greek theologian, apologist, and chronologist. Hippolytus' voluminous writings embrace the spheres of exegesis, homiletics, apologetics, polemics, and chronography. As an important figure in the development in Christian eschatology, his *Commentary on the Prophet Daniel* is the oldest extant treatise on Scripture. In it, Hippolytus stated that, based on an interpretation on Moses' construction of The Ark of the Covenant it could be determined that the Christ was predicted to arrive on the Earth 5,500 years after the Fall of Adam.

Ephrem the Syrian (c. 306-373) was a theologian, deacon, and hymn writer. His works are hailed by Christians throughout the world, and many denominations venerate him as a saint. Ephrem has been declared a Doctor of the Church by Roman Catholics and is especially beloved in the Syriac

Orthodox Church. His hymns, poems, sermons in verse, and prose biblical exegesis were works of practical theology for the edification of a church in troubled times. He is considered the most significant Church Father of the Syriac tradition.

Giambattista Vico (1668-1744) was an Italian historian, political philosopher, and apologist of classical antiquity. Recognized as one of the greatest Enlightenment thinkers, Vico famously criticized the development of modern rationalism. Best known for his *magnum opus* entitled *New Science* (1725), he is generally regarded as the father of social science, having inaugurated the modern school of the philosophy of history.

George Smith (1800-1868) was a British historian, theologian, and author. According to biographer William Prideaux Courtney: "All his life he was a diligent student, and he was famed throughout Cornwall for his powers in speaking and lecturing. In 1823 he became a local preacher among the Wesleyan Methodists, and for many years before his death was one of the leading laypersons in that society."[51] A member of the Royal Asiatic Society, the Society of Antiquaries of London, and the Royal Society of Literature, he wrote, among other titles, *An Attempt to Ascertain the True Chronology of the Book of Genesis* (1842) and *The Patriarchal Age* (1854).

Joseph A. Seiss (1823-1904) was an American theologian, Lutheran minister, and author. Among his more than one hundred published works, perhaps his best-known are *The Great Pyramid of Egypt: Miracle in Stone* (1877) and *The Gospel in the Stars* (1882). In addition to pyramidology, Seiss was a Christian dispensationalist, a nineteenth-century millennialist school of thought, which viewed history as a series of covenants with God and which became the basis for beliefs widely held by contemporary evangelical Christians.

E.W. Bullinger (1837-1913) was a British clergyman and theologian. Educated at King's College, London, he was a recognized scholar in the field of biblical languages, and in 1881 the archbishop of Canterbury Archibald Tate granted him an honorary Doctor of Divinity in recognition of his scholarship. As an outspoken theologian, Bullinger's views were often unique and sometimes controversial. Among his numerous publications the most noteworthy are *The Witness of the Stars* (1893) and *Number in Scripture: Its Supernatural Design and Spiritual Significance* (1921).

Louis Ginzberg (1873-1953) was a Lithuanian professor of Judaism, a Talmudist, and a leading figure in conservative Judaism. As a result of his

---

51 *Dictionary of National Biography*, William Prideaux Courtney, 1885-1900, Volume 53

impressive scholarship in Jewish studies, Ginzberg was one of sixty scholars honored with a doctorate by Harvard University. The author of a number of scholarly works, he is probably best known for his four volume *The Legends of the Jews* (1913), which is an original synthesis of classical rabbinical, apocryphal, pseudepigraphal, and early Christian literature.

Edgar J. Goodspeed (1871-1962) was an American theologian and scholar of Greek and *The New Testament*. For many years, Goodspeed taught at the University of Chicago, and is best remembered for his various modern translations of *The Bible,* such *The Apocrypha: An American Translation* (1938), all of which stressed an emphasis on updating the archaic language of the original texts into the present-day vernacular English.

Cyrus H. Gordon (1908-2001), was an American biblical scholar and professor of ancient Near East culture and languages. Best known for his key role in the decipherment of Ugaritic, an ancient Semitic language of fourteenth-century B.C., Gordon's contribution has been called "the greatest literary discovery from antiquity since the deciphering of hieroglyphics and cuneiform."[52] With his textbooks in hand, later scholars have since been able to penetrate the meaning of numerous biblical Hebrew texts and discover striking parallels between the culture of ancient Israel and its neighbors. Prior to Gordon's pioneering work of synthesizing biblical and ancient Near East studies, most scholarship assumed that early civilizations such as Israel and Greece existed as entirely segregated entities, but that basic assumption completely changed with Gordon's publication of *The Common Background of Greek and Hebrew Civilizations* (1965), which boldly challenged the prevailing theories of the day.

---

52 *The Ancient Near East*, Cyrus H. Gordon, p. 99

Source Material

THE FOLLOWING titles represent a list of the various sources from which this present work is derived. They include written sources as well as audio and visual ones; while written sources range from the apocryphal to the scholarly and the Internet, audio visual sources range from art to film.

Apocryphal

The First Book of Adam and Eve, also called *The Conflict of Adam and Eve with Satan*, and *The Second Book of Adam and Eve*, translated by S.C. Malan, 1882

The Book of Enoch, also called *The First Book of Enoch*, translated by Richard Laurence, 1821

The Secrets of Enoch, also called *The Slavonic Enoch* or *The Second Book of Enoch*, translated by W.R. Morfill, 1896

The Book of Jasher, also called *The Book of the Upright*, translated by Moses Samuel, 1838

The Book of Jubilees and *The Testaments of the Twelve Patriarchs*, translated by R.H. Charles, 1895 and 1908, respectively

The Gospel of Nicodemus, formerly called *The Acts of Pontius Pilate*, translated by William Wake, 1693

The Letters of Herod and Pilate, translated by William Wright, 1865

The Epistles of Pilate to Tiberius Caesar, *The Trial and Condemnation of Pilate*, and *The Death of Pilate, who Condemned Jesus*, translated by B. Harris Cowper, 1867

Art

Descent into Limbo, Andrea Mantegna, 1492

Scholarly

New Science, Giambattista Vico, 1725

The Common Background of Greek and Hebrew Civilizations, Cyrus H. Gordon; W.W. Norton and Company, Inc., 1965

Edgar Johnson Goodspeed: Articulate Scholar, James I. Cook; Scholars Press, 1981

The Apocrypha: An American Translation, Edgar J. Goodspeed; The University of Chicago, 1938

The Criswell Study Bible, W.A. Criswell (Editor); Criswell Center for Biblical Studies, 1979

The Apocrypha and Pseudepigrapha of The Old Testament, Volume 2, R.H. Charles; Clarendon Press, 1913

A Dissertation on Sacred Chronology, Nathan Rouse; Longman, Brown, Green and Longmans, 1856

Dictionary of the Middle Ages, Volume 1: Aachen to Augustinism, Stephen A. Barney (Contributor), Joseph R. Strayer (Editor); Charles Scribner's Sons, 1982

The Epistle to Can Grande, Dante Alighieri, 1319

Icons of the Middle Ages: Rulers, Writers, Rebels, and Saints: Volume 1, Elizabeth K. Haller (Contributor), Lister M. Matheson (Editor); Greenwood Publishing, 2012

Spiritual Gems: The Mystical Koran Commentary, Jafar al-Sadiq; Louisville: Fons Vitae, 2011

The Legends of the Jews, Volume 2, From Joseph to the Exodus, Louis Ginzberg; The Jewish Publication Society of America, 1913

The Witness of the Stars, E.W. Bullinger; Kregel Publications, 1893

Profiles of the Future, Arthur C. Clarke; Bantam Books, Inc., 1961

Screening Out the Past: The Birth of Mass Culture and the Motion Picture Industry, Lary May; The University of Chicago Press Books, 1983

Seventy Years at the Movies: From Silent Films to Today's Screen Hits, David Robinson (Consulting Editor); Crescent Books, 1988

The Many Faces of Christ: The Thousand-Year Story of the Survival and Influence of the Lost Gospels, Philip Jenkins; Basic Books, 2015

The Making of the English New Testament, Edgar J. Goodspeed; The University of Chicago Press, 1925

Romantic Quest and Modern Query: A History of the Modern Theater, Tom F. Driver; Delacorte Press, 1970

The Ancient Near East, Cyrus H. Gordon; W.W. Norton and Company, Inc., 1965

About the Author

S INCE 1976, W. KENT SMITH has been an avid student of all things Bible, when he began at the tender age of sixteen to read every book on the subject in his father's private collection. By age nineteen, having digested the works of William Barclay, Werner Keller, and C.S. Lewis, Kent embarked upon a lifelong effort that provided the foundation for everything that followed—a biblical timeline that chronicles the history of God's dealing with mankind. As a result of this endeavor, Kent came to the realization that the traditional view of biblical history was fraught with contradictions and inconsistencies, and so required a radically original approach to reconcile such discrepancies.

Then, sometime during the mid-1980s, he was introduced to a body of ancient wisdom literature that unexpectedly steered him in a new direction that provided him with the missing pieces of a puzzle that is nothing less than the epic tale of God's control throughout the long ages of history. This wisdom literature—parabiblical literature, to be more precise—is known as *pseudepigraphal* literature, often called apocryphal literature. As it turned out, this fresh literary infusion opened up a brand-new chapter of biblical history for Kent, and more importantly, provided him with the framework for this very work, *The Book of Tales: Stories That Confirm the 5,500-year Prophecy Given to Adam About the Coming of Christ*.

Kent lives in West Covina, California, an eastern suburb of Los Angeles. He can be contacted at wkent@loststorieschannel.com or lodestarcinema@ msn.com.

www.ingramcontent.com/pod-product-compliance
Lightning Source LLC
Chambersburg PA
CBHW061545120626
46550CB00004B/1377